The OIL KINGS

How the U.S., Iran, and Saudi Arabia
Changed the Balance of Power
in the Middle East

ANDREW
SCOTT COOPER

SIMON & SCHUSTER

NEW YORK   LONDON   TORONTO   SYDNEY   NEW DELHI

Simon & Schuster
1230 Avenue of the Americas
New York, NY 10020

First Simon & Schuster hardcover edition August 2011

SIMON & SCHUSTER and colophon are registered trademarks
of Simon & Schuster, Inc.

For information about special discounts for bulk purchases,
please contact Simon & Schuster Special Sales at
1-866-506-1949 or business@simonandschuster.com.

The Simon & Schuster Speakers Bureau can bring authors
to your live event. For more information or to book an event,
contact the Simon & Schuster Speakers Bureau at
1-866-248-3049 or visit our website at www.simonspeakers.com.

Designed by Ruth Lee-Mui

Manufactured in the United States of America

1   3   5   7   9   10   8   6   4   2

Library of Congress Cataloging-in-Publication Data

Cooper, Andrew Scott.
The oil kings : how the U.S., Iran, and Saudi Arabia changed the balance
of power in the Middle East / Andrew Scott Cooper.
p.   cm.
Includes bibliographical references and index.
1. United States—Foreign relations—Iran.   2. Iran—Foreign relations—United
States.   3. United States—Foreign relations—Saudi Arabia.   4. Saudi Arabia—
Foreign relations—United States.   5. Iran—Politics and government—1941–1979.
6. Petroleum industry and trade—Iran—History—20th century.   7. Petroleum
industry and trade—Saudi Arabia—History—20th century.   I. Title.
E183.8.I55C66   2011
327.73055—dc22   011008319
ISBN 978-1-4391-5517-2
ISBN 978-1-4391-5713-8 (ebook)

To My Family

CONTENTS

The OIL KINGS

INTRODUCTION

"Why should I plant a tree whose bitter root
Will only serve to nourish poisoned fruit?"

—Abolqasem Ferdowsi, *The Persian Book of Kings*

On November 25, 2006, U.S. vice president Dick Cheney flew to Riyadh for talks with King Abdullah of Saudi Arabia, the elderly autocrat whose desert kingdom is home to one fifth of the world's proven oil reserves and is the largest producer within OPEC, the Organization of Petroleum Exporting Countries, the oil producers' cartel. The king was evidently in need of reassurance from his American allies. Earlier in the month the U.S. war effort in Iraq had been dealt a setback after voters in midterm elections routed Republican incumbents and turned control of the Congress over to Democrats. Almost immediately, President George W. Bush accepted the resignation of Cheney's partner in power Secretary of Defense Donald Rumsfeld, and offered "to find common ground" with critics of his administration's handling of the war. For the first time in six and a half years the talk in Washington was not of victory in Iraq but of an orderly withdrawal of coalition forces. The Saudis expressed concern that their neighbor and historic rival Iran would take advantage of the U.S. departure to assert its regional ambitions. Saudi Arabia's ambassador to Washington, Prince Turki al-Faisal, bluntly reminded the White House that "since America came into Iraq uninvited, it should not leave Iraq uninvited."

The price of oil also came up in the vice president's meeting with Saudi officials. Over the summer of 2006 world energy markets had tightened, driving prices to record levels. Soaring fuel prices threatened America's prosperity and the economies of its trading partners. Oil as high as $78 a barrel also posed a challenge to U.S. foreign policy in the Middle East, where oil producers reaped windfall profits. The Bush White House was especially concerned about what the government of Iran would do with its new billions. "Iran's profits from oil rose last year to more than $45 billion from $15 billion, surging at a rate not seen since 1974, when the country's oil revenues tripled," reported *The New York Times*. The surge in Iranian oil profits was accompanied by a marked upswing in regional tensions and violence that included a ferocious month-long war fought in Lebanon between Israel and Hezbollah, the Shi'a group whose leaders received political cover and financial and military backing from Tehran. The prospect of President Mahmoud Ahmadinejad using his country's oil revenues to speed up Iran's nuclear program, strengthen the Iranian military, and arm Hezbollah in Lebanon, the radical Hamas Islamic group based in Gaza, and pro-Iranian Shi'a militias in Iraq, was anathema to officials in Washington and Riyadh. The Saudi royal family had seen this before. Back in the 1970s Shah Mohammad Reza Pahlavi of Iran had been the driving force behind high oil prices that he hoped would transform Iran into an economic and military powerhouse. Only the 1979 Islamic Revolution had put paid to the Shah's ambitions to dominate the Persian Gulf, West Asia, and the Indian Ocean.

Although President Ahmadinejad would have never dared admit it, there were striking parallels between his effort to project Iranian petropower under the guise of pan-Islamism, and the Shah's earlier drive to revive Iran's long dormant Persian aspirations. Their strategic visions overlapped in ways that suggested some striking continuities. Both leaders saw Iran as the regional hegemon. They identified oil revenues and nuclear power as the keys to attaining international stature and domestic self-reliance. They relished provoking the same Western powers that at one time had treated Iran like a colonial vassal. Perhaps their most obvious shared trait was a King Midas complex. Like the Shah, Ahmadinejad was a big spender who believed that high oil prices freed him from the need to practice fiscal restraint. "Critics said that his plans for generous spending to create jobs and increase salaries were politically motivated and fiscally unsound," noted one observer. "His budget relied on high oil profits likely to invite inflation." The Iranian central bank proposed a $40 billion fiscal stimulus that included subsidies for families and newlyweds.

Ahmadinejad's spendthrift ways presented King Abdullah of Saudi Arabia with a golden opportunity. With petroleum responsible for 80 percent of income from exports, Iran's economy was perilously exposed to an unexpected price fluctuation in the oil markets. Tehran confidently expected consumer demand for oil to stay high, guaranteeing equally high prices. But what would happen to Iran's budget assumptions if oil prices suddenly plunged? Oil-producing countries base their spending plans and financial estimates on oil prices *not* falling below a certain threshold. If prices *do* suddenly plunge below that level—and if producers have not left themselves with enough of a financial cushion to absorb the blow from lost export receipts—the potential exists for a fiscal meltdown. Billions of dollars in anticipated revenue would disappear. Tehran would be forced to economize and decide whether to spend money on guns or butter—whether to lavish aid on Hezbollah and Hamas or to prop up the complex system of food, fuel, housing, and transportation subsidies that keeps Iran's middle class in check. Removing the subsidies would increase the potential for protests and clashes between security forces and opposition groups.

Only one country had the means and the motive to engineer a price correction on that scale. With its giant petroleum reserves and untapped production capacity, Saudi Arabia could flood the market by pumping enough surplus crude into the system to break the pricing structure and drive prices back down. The Saudi royal family has always understood that petropower is about more than creating wealth, developing its economy, and preserving power. Oil is also the Saudis' primary weapon of national self-defense and the key to their security and survival. Flooding the market is economic warfare on a grand scale, the oil industry's equivalent of dropping the bomb on a rival. A flooded market and lower prices would inevitably result in billions of dollars in lost revenues to the Saudis. However, the threat from Iran was seen as outweighing that loss, and by late 2006 King Abdullah was prepared to tap Saudi oil reserves.

"A member of the Saudi royal family with knowledge of the discussions between Mr. Cheney and King Abdullah said the king had presented Mr. Cheney with a plan to raise oil production to force down the price, in hopes of causing economic turmoil for Iran without becoming directly involved in a confrontation," reported *The New York Times*. Flooding the market would "force [Iran] to slow the flow of funds to Hezbollah in Lebanon and to Shiite militias in Iraq without getting directly involved in a confrontation." The Saudis may also have had in mind a second motive. From past experience they knew that if oil prices stayed too high for too long, the

United States would be forced to reduce its consumption of foreign oil and take steps to encourage energy conservation and diversification. Less reliance on Saudi oil would translate into a reduction in Saudi strategic leverage over U.S. policy toward Israel and the Middle East.

On November 29, 2006, four days after Cheney's return to Washington, *The Washington Post* published an essay by Nawaf Obaid, a prominent security adviser to the Saudi government and adjunct fellow at Washington's Center for Strategic and International Studies. Obaid's article warned that one of the consequences of a sudden U.S. withdrawal from Iraq would be "massive Saudi intervention to stop Iranian-backed Shiite militias from butchering Iraqi Sunnis." Obaid reminded his readers that "as the economic powerhouse of the Middle East, the birthplace of Islam and the de facto leader of the world's Sunni community (which comprises 85 percent of Muslims), Saudi Arabia has both the means and religious responsibility to intervene." Buried in Obaid's article was a chilling threat that officials back in Tehran could not have failed to miss:

> Finally, Abdullah may decide to strangle Iranian funding of the militias through oil policy. If Saudi Arabia boosted production and cut the price of oil in half, the kingdom could still finance its current spending. But it would be devastating to Iran, which is facing economic difficulties even with today's high prices. The result would be to limit Tehran's ability to continue funneling hundreds of millions each year to Shiite militias in Iraq and elsewhere.

Obaid's article drew my attention because for several months I had already been studying the impact of an earlier little known and less understood intervention by the Saudis in the oil market. In 1977, one year before the outbreak of revolutionary unrest in Iran, oil markets had been paralyzed by a bitter split among members of OPEC over how much to charge consumers. The Shah of Iran had proposed a 15 percent price hike for the coming year. King Khalid of Saudi Arabia had resisted the Shah's entreaties and argued that no price increase was warranted at a time when Western economies were mired in recession. The Shah won the day and persuaded the rest of OPEC to join him in adopting a double-digit price increase for 1977. The Saudi response was swift and ruthless. Riyadh announced it would take drastic steps to ensure that Iran's new price regime never took effect. It would do this by exceeding its production quota, pumping surplus oil onto the market, and undercutting the higher price offered by its competitors. Overnight, Iran lost billions of dollars in anticipated oil revenue. The Shah's government, reeling from the blow, was forced to take out a bridge loan from foreign banks. It made deep cuts to domestic spending in an attempt to balance the books and implemented an austerity plan that threw tens of thousands of young Iranian men out of work and into the streets. The economic chaos that ensued helped turn Iranian public opinion against the royal family.

Thirty years later, all the indications were that Saudi Arabia was prepared to replicate its earlier feat. There is still much that we don't know about U.S.-Saudi efforts to destabilize Iran's economy during President Bush's last two years in office. What we do know is that the Saudi government publicly reacted to the uproar over Nawaf Obaid's article by formally severing its ties with the consultant. Diplomatic observers in Washington understood that this was part of a much bigger game. "[Obaid] is widely expected to return to the government in some capacity," noted one expert. "The Saudi government disavowed Mr. Obaid's column, and Prince Turki canceled his contract," reported *The New York Times*. "But Arab diplomats said Tuesday that Mr. Obaid's column reflected the view of the Saudi government, which has made clear its opposition to an American pullout from Iraq." Then, one week later, Saudi Arabia's ambassador to Washington, Prince Turki, lost *his* job and was abruptly summoned home.

What was going on here? What message was King Abdullah trying to send Tehran and Washington? The best way to understand Saudi policy and what happened next is to follow the price of oil over the next two years. Saudi Arabia's budget for 2007 was reportedly based on oil prices not falling below $42 a barrel and production of 9 million barrels a day. By the summer of 2007, despite efforts to restrain their momentum, prices had returned to their earlier peak from a year before of $78. Publicly at least, OPEC members pledged not to allow oil to surpass $80 a barrel. Yet by the end of November 2007 the price of a barrel of oil had rocketed to $98. In January 2008, President Bush personally appealed to King Abdullah to practice price restraint—the U.S. economy was beginning to show signs of buckling under the strain of high oil prices, mortgage foreclosures, credit defaults, and shaky banks.

The Saudis, eager to reel in Ahmadinejad, opened the spigots and exceeded their OPEC production quota by 250,000 barrels a day. It turned out not to be enough. The Saudis cranked up their production yet again, this time from 9.2 million barrels a day to 9.7 million barrels. The price of a barrel of oil broke the $100 ceiling in April, $118 in May, and finally topped out at $147.27 in July. Prices then fell sharply as Saudi oil flooded the system even as the U.S. economy sharply contracted. By September, when oil had retreated in price to $107 a barrel, it was the turn of President Ahmadinejad to display anxiety. The Iranians had wrongly assumed that the price of oil would not fall below $90 a barrel. They appealed to the Saudis to hold the line on prices. King Abdullah responded by keeping the spigots open and collapsing OPEC's pricing structure. By December, the price of oil had retreated to $43 a barrel. Satisfied, the Saudis reduced output to 8.5 million barrels a day. When prices plunged to $33 in January 2009, the Saudis cut production still further, this time to 8 million barrels. The Iranian regime entered a crucial presidential election year having sustained a devastating reversal of economic fortune. The fraudulent outcome of its midyear election was accompanied by economic contraction and the worst political unrest since the fall of the Shah three decades earlier.

In the meantime I had located documents that revealed that President Gerald Ford and top White House officials had been closely involved in the first Saudi effort to flood the market in 1977. The documents raised the puzzling question of why the United States would back a covert effort to manipulate oil markets knowing it would damage Iran's economy and hurt its close ally the Shah. Presidents Richard Nixon and Ford each hosted the Shah at the White House, praised him as a statesman and friend, and furnished him with advanced weapons systems, thousands of military advisers, and even offered to sell Iran nuclear reactors. The documents raised the prospect of a secret crisis in relations at the highest levels, and that previously unknown tensions had led to a high-stakes showdown over oil prices and the long-term future of the OPEC cartel. As I wrote in the October 2008 *Middle East Journal*:

> While much scholarly focus has been on the internal political, cultural, economic and social origins of the revolution, the role of state finances—and oil revenues in particular—has received far less attention. The Iranian revolution shared similarities with two other great revolutions: France in 1789 and Russia in 1917. All three upheavals were preceded by fiscal crises. In Iran's case the dramatic revenue fluctuations of 1977 were acknowledged and duly noted at the time by Tehran-based foreign correspondents. But the underlying rationale for Saudi Arabia's decision to torpedo the December 1976 OPEC oil price increase, and particularly the Ford administration's role in that fateful decision, has not been explained until now.

My search for understanding uncovered a hidden history of U.S.-Iran-Saudi oil diplomacy from 1969 to 1977, the backstory of the crucial eight-year period when the United States went from being the world's number one oil producer to the biggest importer of petroleum, and when Saudi Arabia's House of Saud replaced Iran's Pahlavi king as Washington's indispensable ally in the Persian Gulf. Here, finally, is the inside story of how two American presidents, Richard Nixon and Gerald Ford, dealt with Iran and Saudi Arabia as they grappled with the challenges of America's growing dependence on foreign sources of energy, how Nixon's handling of U.S.-Iran relations in particular during the energy crisis of the early 1970s set the scene for a potentially catastrophic financial crisis in the waning days of Ford's administration, and why Ford eventually felt he had no choice but to throw his support behind a remarkable plan to break the power of OPEC with the help of the Saudis.

My book makes clear that the U.S.-Saudi oil coup directed against the Shah's leadership of OPEC was *not* a conspiracy intended to topple him from Iran's Peacock Throne. Revolutions are highly complex phenomena that cannot be simplified in conspiratorial terms or explained simply by one or two trigger causes. Yet there is no denying that the U.S. decision to break OPEC caused significant problems for the Shah, and at the worst possible time. It dealt a severe psychological blow to him by undermining his stature as OPEC's leader and creating a perception of political weakness at home and abroad. It signaled a loss of control by the Shah over Iran's primary source of state revenue. And it shook the foundations of Iran's troubled economy just as domestic unrest against the Shah was beginning to crest. U.S.-Saudi collusion to break OPEC from the inside and deliver it into Saudi hands turned out to be a disaster for U.S. interests. Although not wholly to blame for the economic chaos that engulfed Iran on the eve of the revolution, the U.S.-Saudi oil coup against OPEC intensified and accelerated the process of collapse in Iran.

The Oil Kings is a multilayered narrative written through the prism of U.S. oil policy. The book can be interpreted in different ways: as a parable on the corrupting influence of oil on America's national security policy; as a lesson in the limits of American power in the wake of the retreat from Vietnam, the Watergate scandal, and the energy crisis of the 1970s; as a contest of personalities such as Nixon, the Shah, Sheikh Ahmed Zaki al-Yamani of Saudi Arabia, Secretary of State Henry Kissinger, Secretary of Treasury William E. Simon, and defense secretaries James Schlesinger and Donald

Rumsfeld; as an autopsy on empire, in this case Iran's Pahlavi dynasty, and how the fortunes of the Persian crown rose and fell with the oil market; as the triumph of nationalism in settling scores between old rivals Iran and Saudi Arabia; and as a cautionary tale of what happened between friends of long standing and to old alliances when the geopolitics of the Cold War collided with the reality of the oil market and the global economy, whose rough outline was only just beginning to take shape in the mid-1970s. It is a narrative that internationalizes U.S.-Iran relations and Iran's revolution by placing bilateral and internal events in a strategic and geopolitical context outside the boundaries of the Persian Gulf. I found it impossible to address tensions between the United States and Iran over oil prices without also taking into consideration events in faraway Great Britain, France, Portugal, Italy, Spain, and Canada. How these events affected bilateral relations between Washington and Tehran will no doubt be debated for a long time to come by scholars in the field.

The narrative includes stories told for the first time, that, for example, illustrate the extraordinary degree of Iranian involvement—not to mention outright manipulation—in U.S. politics and foreign policy in the 1970s, and the extent to which the tentacles of the oil states of the Middle East reached right into the Oval Office to influence presidential decision making to an astonishing degree on domestic and foreign policy. We now know that the U.S. response to the 1971 India-Pakistan War, the 1972 U.S. presidential election, the Arab-Israeli War of 1973, the 1973–74 Arab oil embargo, the 1974–75 oil shock, the 1975 Middle East peace shuttle, and the 1976 U.S. presidential election all had an Iranian component. This book provides answers to long-standing questions about U.S.-Iran military contingency planning, the Ibex spy project, Iran's nascent nuclear program, and the mysterious dealings of Colonel Richard Hallock. It settles debates over the nature of the secret deals worked out between President Nixon and the Shah regarding oil prices and arms sales, the extent to which White House officials were aware of the terrorist threat to U.S. nationals in Iran, awareness of the rising opposition to the Shah from his own people, and whether anyone in the White House had any prior knowledge of the Shah's secret treatments for the cancer that eventually took his life.

Secretary of State Henry Kissinger once famously described the Shah of Iran as "that rarest of leaders, an unconditional ally, and one whose understanding of the world enhanced our own." For thirty years, we have had to take Kissinger's word for it. In the 1970s he concluded an array of highly secret deals with the Shah worth billions of dollars involving the transfer of men, money, and machinery on a scale that even today is almost unimaginable. Where exactly *did* all that national treasure go? How was it expended? In three volumes of memoirs totaling 3,955 pages and including 193 photographs of the former secretary of state with every world leader, foreign minister, and ambassador of note *except* the Shah of Iran in the 1970s, one wonders why Kissinger was photographed with a flock of geese in China but not pictured in the company of the man he claimed to so admire?

His books tell us nothing of substance about the intimate workings of his remarkable relationship with Shah Mohammad Reza Pahlavi. As an example, Kissinger devotes only three sentences to a secret bilateral oil deal that is a major focus of the second half of my book. British author William Shawcross once observed that "readers who seek understanding of the [U.S.-Iran] debacle will not find it in Kissinger's memoirs any more than in Nixon's before him. Indeed, the way in which the two men treat Iran shows how terribly inadequate autobiographies can be as points of reference, let alone accounts of history. . . . This skimpy treatment can be explained only by a desire to conceal." Kissinger was not alone. As Shawcross notes, Nixon made only two brief references to the Shah in his autobiography, precisely two more than his successor, Gerald Ford, in his autobiography. Richard Helms, the man who represented their interests as U.S. ambassador in Tehran, wrote a memoir that is a masterpiece of dissembling and obfuscation. I wondered: if the Shah was worth defending, why was he not worth talking about?

My book utilizes the declassified meeting notes of General Brent Scowcroft, Kissinger's deputy and eventual successor to the post of national security adviser. Scowcroft attended every meeting of importance in the White House that pertained to oil, Iran, and Saudi Arabia during the period from late 1973 to the end of January 1977. I also drew on the declassified transcripts of Kissinger's White House telephone conversations; the translated diaries of the Shah's senior adviser, Imperial Court Minister Amir Asadollah Alam; the diaries of former chairman of the U.S. Federal Reserve Arthur Burns; thousands of pages of declassified cables, policy briefs, and memoranda from the State Department, the Defense Department, the CIA, the National Security Council, and the Federal Energy Administration; Nixon's and Ford's personal correspondence with foreign heads of state including the Iranian and Saudi monarchs; approximately sixty bound volumes containing more than one thousand newspaper and magazine articles and primary and secondary source materials; oral history interviews; and interviews I conducted with the few surviving officials on either side who had some knowledge of the diplomacy of the time and were willing to talk about it: General Scowcroft, former Secretary of Defense James Schlesinger, former head of the Federal Energy Administration Frank Zarb, former Iranian foreign minister and ambassador Ardeshir Zahedi, and retired American diplomats. As it turned out, even they had been kept in the dark about the full extent of many of the deals revealed in these pages.

A feature of the Kissinger-Shah relationship was its emphasis on oral agreements and the absence of a paper trail. Kissinger compartmentalized their dealings, cut his colleagues out of his back channels to the palace, and was not averse to engaging in elaborate deceptions to throw them off his trail. Frank Zarb did not know that Kissinger sabotaged his negotiating stance during oil talks with the Iranian government. It was only in the course of our interview that former Secretary of Defense Schlesinger learned the rationale behind a $500 million U.S. arms deal to Iran that he had vigorously opposed but nonetheless was required to implement. During my investigation I did not turn up a single document that spelled out in specific detail the terms of each of the secret deals brokered between Kissinger and the Shah. There might be references here and there, sometimes spoken, sometimes written, but never in one place and often mentioned over a period of months, if not years.

Throughout the book I have tried to place the reader in the position of government officials in the United States, Europe, and the Middle East as they struggled to deal with the dangerous new world unleashed by the 1970s revolution in oil pricing. They faced a series of painful policy choices. In the wake of the pullout from Vietnam, the Watergate affair, and the energy crisis, the United States confronted a resurgent Soviet Union, oil shortages, and economic recession. Oval Office transcripts confirm that U.S. officials, including Nixon, Ford, and Kissinger, were convinced that the West was in crisis and that the fraught political and economic conditions of the 1930s were reasserting themselves. The decisions they made were based on the lessons of history from that earlier frightening period. This mind-set—that catastrophe was just around the corner—culminated in what I like to think of as the story of the greatest financial crisis never told, when in 1976 Treasury Secretary Bill Simon, Chairman of the Council of Economic Advisers Alan Greenspan, and Chairman of the Federal Reserve Arthur Burns warned President Ford that banks on Wall Street were at risk of collapse if OPEC raised the price of oil. The U.S. economy teetered on the edge of a double-dip recession as governments in Europe slid toward insolvency. It is a scenario that may sound familiar today.

To paraphrase the great historian Barbara Tuchman, America's tortured relations with the oil producers of the Persian Gulf have to date been one long march of folly. As we enter the second decade of the twenty-first century, more and more it is a march that is beginning to feel forced. The United States now imports almost two thirds of its oil from overseas and has gone to war twice in less than fifteen years to secure its Persian Gulf oil lifeline. "I am saddened that it is politically inconvenient to acknowledge what everyone knows: the war in Iraq is about oil," Alan Greenspan wrote with admirable frankness in his memoir. He continued:

> Thus, projections of world oil supply and demand that do not note the highly precarious environment of the Middle East are avoiding the eight-hundred-pound gorilla that could bring world economic growth to a halt. I do not pretend to know how or whether the turmoil in the Middle East will be resolved. I do know that the future of the Middle East is a most important consideration in any long-term energy forecast. . . . Until industrial economies disengage themselves from, as President George W. Bush put it, "our addiction to oil," the stability of the industrial economies and hence the global economy will remain at risk.

The American economy's chronic addiction to cheap oil is obvious. Less well known is the story of *when* that addiction began and *why* the United States became so reliant in particular on Saudi Arabia for its continued goodwill and cooperation. The same is true of America's toxic relationship with Iran. The two countries have been at each other's throats for so long now that it seems hard to believe they were ever allies—let alone partners in a secret contingency plan to invade Saudi Arabia and seize its oil wealth. Until these tensions are resolved, and until both countries come to terms with their complicated shared history, it seems inevitable that the tree of American-Iranian relations will bear poisoned fruit for many years to come.

The proud man at the center of the events in this book still looms large in our collective conscience. More than thirty years have passed since Shah Mohammad Reza Pahlavi of Iran left the world stage as a stateless refugee. The story of his triumphant rise and equally spectacular fall is a cautionary tale for other statesmen seeking to emulate his achievements. The question is often asked: Where did it all go wrong for the Shah? There is no single turning point in his fortune, though a good place to start may be in the spring of 1969, when the Iranian king traveled to Washington to attend the funeral of former U.S. president Dwight Eisenhower. It was a trip that did not at the time appear to hold any great significance, either for the Shah or for his host, Richard Nixon, who had been president for just two months. Only now can we see that the Shah's trip was an important early signpost on the road leading to revolution.

A.S.C.
Piraeus, Greece, 2010

A NOTE ON THE USE OF IRANIAN IMPERIAL TITLES

The Shah of Iran was both king and emperor of Iran. During the reign of the Pahlavi dynasty Iran was formally recognized in the international realm as the "Empire of Iran." The formal title of Iran's Shahanshah, or King of Kings, was "Mohammad Reza Shah Pahlavi," which is translated as "Mohammad Reza, the Pahlavi king." In his diaries, Imperial Court Minister Asadollah Alam simply referred to the Shah as "HIM" or "His Imperial Majesty." It was the same with the Shahbanou, a title that translates as the "Shah's Lady." Farah Pahlavi was both queen and empress, the later title granted after the couple's joint coronation in 1967. Asadollah Alam referred to her in his diaries as "HMQ" or "Her Majesty the Queen," and the Shah usually referred to his wife as "the Queen." In domestic and foreign media Farah's titles, like her husband's, tended to be interchangeable.

Part One

GLADIATOR
1969–1974

"If someone wraps a lion cub in silk,
A little whelp, who's not yet tasted milk,
It keeps its nature still, and, once it's grown,
Fights off an elephant's attack alone."
—Abolqasem Ferdowsi, *The Persian Book of Kings*

Chapter One

A KIND OF SUPER MAN

"Your Majesty, you're like the radiant sun
Bestowing light and life on everyone:
May greed and anger never touch your reign
And may your enemies live wracked with pain.
Monarch with whom no monarch can compete,
All other kings are dust beneath your feet,
Neither the sun nor moon has ever known
A king like you to occupy the throne."
—Abolqasem Ferdowsi, *The Persian Book of Kings*

"I like him, I like him and I like the country. And some of those other
bastards out there I don't like, right?"
—President Richard Nixon, 1971

FIRST AMONG EQUALS

They came to bury Caesar. In the spring of 1969 the funeral of Dwight
David Eisenhower, the great wartime commander, Europe's liberator from
Nazi occupation, and America's two-term president, proved an irresistible
draw to a generation of world leaders who owed their freedoms, fortunes,
and in some cases their lives to the soldier-politician from Kansas. On
March 30, millions of television viewers in the United States watched as a
stately procession of crowned heads and dignitaries including King Bau-
douin I of Belgium, King Constantine II of Greece, Grand Duke Jean of
Luxembourg, Lord Louis Mountbatten of Great Britain, and President
Ferdinand Marcos of the Philippines gathered in the Capitol Rotunda
in Washington to pay their respects. Two faces in the pantheon of greats

stood out. Onlookers were touched to see a stooped seventy-eight-year-old President Charles de Gaulle of France shuffle forward to salute his wartime comrade's bier. The other statesman familiar to Americans was the Shah of Iran, the fabulously wealthy emperor whose lavish titles were matched only by his three brilliant marriages. Standing erect in elevator shoes, still trim at age forty-nine, his hawkish features resolute, His Imperial Majesty Mohammad Reza Shah Pahlavi, King of Kings, Light of the Aryans, and Shadow of God, radiated the majesty of the fabled Peacock Throne and shouldered the weight of 2,500 years of Persian monarchy. Wearing a ribbon-slashed military tunic topped off with enough gold braid and orders of state to ornament a Christmas tree, the Shah looked for all the world as though he had just stepped out of a Habsburg drawing room at the Congress of Vienna.

Mohammad Reza Shah's decision to attend Eisenhower's funeral was not driven by sentiment toward the man who intervened to save Iran's Peacock Throne in 1953. "I pointed out that it will provide an ideal opportunity to meet the new American administration and he agreed," wrote Asadollah Alam, the Shah's closest adviser and minister of the imperial court. Alam kept a series of secret diaries in which he recorded daily life at the Pahlavi court. Richard Nixon had been sworn in as America's thirty-seventh president less than ten weeks earlier and the Iranian king was anxious to reaffirm their long-standing acquaintance.

If the Shah's Ruritanian splendor seemed misplaced in the year of Woodstock, the Apollo moon landing, and the Manson Family murders, the empire of oil he had reigned over for twenty-eight years made him the man of the moment in the Nixon White House. "The Shah is clearly the most important person in Iran," the State Department advised President Nixon in 1969. "By Iranian tradition any Shah is a kind of super man whose position and prerogatives have even mystical significance. This Shah adds to this tradition the weight of his enormous political sagacity, his intelligence and cunning, his ability to get things done as an executive." At Eisenhower's funeral the Shah was treated as first among equals. His scheduled private meeting with the president ran over by a half hour. During the funeral ceremonies in the National Cathedral the Shah was seated prominently in the front row beside Nixon's elder daughter, pretty blond Tricia. Tricia's sister, Julie, had recently married David Eisenhower, Ike's grandson, and received from the Shah a stunning blue and maroon Persian rug as a wedding gift. At a glittering dinner the Nixons hosted for their foreign guests it was the

Shah and de Gaulle who "stole the show," observed Alam. "None of the others got a look in."

ONE BIG GASOLINE BOMB

Mohammad Reza Shah Pahlavi was a hard man to say no to in the spring of 1969. Everything had turned in his and Iran's favor in recent years. The United States was mired in a punishing land war in Vietnam, one that had bitterly divided the American home front and exposed the perils of trying to enforce a Pax Americana on the unruly outer edges of empire. Nixon had promised to end the war and draw down the American presence in East Asia. The problem for Washington was that Great Britain had made a similar pledge to pull out of the Persian Gulf by the end of 1971, leaving the Asian continent's western flank vulnerable to seizure or subversion from radicals and mischief makers aligned with the Soviet Union. The cash-strapped British were ending more than a century of gunboat diplomacy in an area that held two thirds of the world's known petroleum reserves. Oil from the Persian Gulf accounted for one third of the petroleum used by the free world and 89 percent of the oil used by the U.S. military in Southeast Asia. The region's booming oil industry generated $1.5 billion in revenue for the United States economy and employed twelve thousand American expatriates. The pitiful reality was that the U.S. naval presence in the Persian Gulf consisted of a seaplane tender and two destroyers "assigned an area from Malaysia to South Africa."

The Persian Gulf's topography made it uniquely vulnerable to sabotage. The Gulf was located at the crossroads between the Middle East and Southwest Asia, a jagged gash of water separating Shi'a Iran in the north from its Sunni neighbors to the south. Oman, perched at the mouth of the Gulf, was torn by a rebellion fanned by leftist South Yemen. The pro-Soviet regime in power in Iraq was embroiled in fratricidal purges while it sharpened the knives against Kuwait next door. Saudi Arabia's ruling Saud dynasty trembled and tottered even as postage-stamp-size sheikhdoms clung to its coastline like fingertips clutching at a robe. Afghanistan and Pakistan were sinking under the waves like grand old liners taking in water at the heads. Oil was the prize. Fifty-five percent of NATO Europe's oil and a staggering 90 percent of Japan's petroleum supplies came from the Persian Gulf. If the Gulf was blockaded the lights would go out from Tokyo to Rome. Every day tankers laden with 25 million barrels of oil left ports in Iran, Iraq, Kuwait, and Saudi Arabia headed for the Arabian Sea and the Indian Ocean, bound for Rotterdam, Cape Town, and Singapore. Before reaching open water they had to pass through a tight choke point called the Strait of Hormuz, a razor-thin artery only twenty-one miles wide at its narrowest point that could be "interrupted by a few mines thrown over the side of a fishing dhow or by guerrilla attacks on the endless parade of tankers." Every thirty minutes a tanker passed through on its way to market. President Nixon and the Shah of Iran had talked about the fact that the whole of West Asia needed shoring up before it collapsed and took the free world's oil lifeline down with it. The greatest fear of Western military planners was that Soviet paratroopers would swoop in and seize the Strait of Hormuz during a regional crisis. "The Gulf is one big gasoline bomb," warned an oil industry expert. "It could blow up anytime, especially now that the British are leaving."

President Nixon and his most influential foreign policy aide, National Security Adviser Henry Kissinger, were anxious to secure Persian Gulf oil fields and shipping lanes once the British sailed for home. In July 1969 Nixon traveled to South Vietnam to rally the troops. During a stopover on the island of Guam he described his vision for how Washington could reduce its physical presence in Asia and avoid future land wars without compromising its national security. His remarks were later burnished for posterity as the "Nixon Doctrine" and they became Nixon's contribution to the formulation of American foreign policy during the Cold War.

Vietnam had exposed the limitations of American power. Under the Nixon Doctrine the United States would simultaneously draw down in Asia even as it ramped up its support for proxies willing to guard freedom's forts from Tehran to Sydney. The United States would provide these allies with the weapons and the training they needed to do the job on its behalf. "The U.S. is no longer in a position to do anything really helpful," explained a White House official. "That would be 'imperial.' We'll just have to rely on the people who live there and maybe it will go all right." When it came to defending the mountainous approaches to Central and West Asia, patrolling the warm waters of the Persian Gulf, and propping up the gateway to the Arabian Sea and the Indian Ocean, the only likely candidate for the role of American centurion was the Shah of Iran. Richard Nixon and Henry Kissinger were "dealing with the Vietnam drawdown and the reactions of the American people to Vietnam, and it drove the administration to look outside for gladiators," recalled James Schlesinger, the future secretary of defense who inherited the complexities and contradictions of their Iran policy. "We were going to make the Shah the Guardian of the Gulf. Well, if we were going to make the Shah the Guardian of the Gulf, we've got to give him what he needs—which comes down to giving him what he wants."

The decision to delegate authority and power to the Shah in West Asia seemed logical and practical at the time. The Shah believed that Iran's future lay with the non-Communist West. He intended to replicate Japan's success in pulling off an economic miracle in the aftermath of the Second World War. "His goal was to make Iran a modern major power before he died; that was what made him move," recalled Armin Meyer, who served as President Lyndon Johnson's ambassador to Iran in the late 1960s. "He openly talked of Iran becoming the 'Japan of West Asia.'" By 1969 the Shah was widely regarded outside Iran as a force for stability, a champion of progressive reform, and the bold leader who broke the power of Iran's feudal landowning aristocracy and conservative religious establishment to give women the vote and land to the peasantry. He appointed Western-educated technocrats to run Iran's government and economy even as he concentrated real power in his own hands.

The Shah admired the West for its technological advances and prosperity while distrusting its motives where Iran's oil was concerned. In 1941 Great Britain and the Soviet Union had invaded and occupied Iran to prevent the country's oil fields and rail links from falling into German hands. The Allies forced the Shah's father, Reza Shah, to abdicate in his son's favor and live in exile. For the remainder of the war young Mohammad Reza Shah reigned but did not rule. The monarchy's prospects were bleak. The end of war in 1945 did not bring peace to Iran. The Shah barely survived threats to his life and throne from right-wing religious fanatics and left-wing political extremists. Relations with Iran's northern neighbor the Soviet Union, with whom it shared a 1,250-mile border, were especially problematic. Moscow initially resisted evacuating its troops from Iran and tried to split the country by stirring up secessionist sentiment in the north. For the rest of his life the Shah remained deeply distrustful of Russia and its intentions toward Iran, whose vast oil reserves placed it on the front lines in the new Cold War.

The next great crisis involved Iran's former colonial overlord Great Britain. The British government had pulled out its troops but clung to the lucrative monopoly it had exercised over Persian oil reserves since the turn of the century. Iranians of all political stripes cheered when in 1951 Prime Minister Mohammad Mossadegh defied British threats and nationalized Iran's oil industry. Mossadegh was a charismatic leader whose nationalist instincts later raised the hackles of Prime Minister Winston Churchill and President Eisenhower. The political alliance that Mossadegh forged with Iran's Communist Tudeh Party hinted at a creeping Soviet takeover of Persian oil fields. Churchill warned Ike that the West could not allow an unstable Iran to fall into Stalin's hands. He advocated the overthrow of the Mossadegh government. President Eisenhower opposed direct military intervention and settled on a plan of covert action. In August 1953 the White House approved Operation Ajax, a joint conspiracy carried out by Iranian royalists with the support of the U.S. and British intelligence services. The lead American in the field was the Central Intelligence Agency's Kermit "Kim" Roosevelt, grandson of President Theodore Roosevelt. Within the CIA, Roosevelt reported up the ranks to the agency's chief of operations in the Directorate of Plans, a man named Richard Helms, who would play a crucial role in Iran in future years. "I just know that he would have been generally under my jurisdiction," was how Helms later modestly described their association. "I think it was agreed that Roosevelt would lead the field operation and that the British and American officers would work under him on this." As the coup unfolded Helms followed events by the flow of cables that arrived from Tehran.

The coup plotters succeeded almost in spite of themselves. At one point the Shah lost his nerve and fled Iran with his second wife, Queen Soraya, in a small plane. Yet the conspirators carried the day after intense street fighting erupted in Tehran. Mossadegh was overthrown and arrested and the Shah returned to Iran in triumph. Predictably enough, Operation Ajax left a mixed legacy. Many ordinary Iranians assumed the United States had replaced Great Britain as the foreign power now pulling the strings, controlling their king and Iran's oil riches. The Shah never quite succeeded in removing the taint of illegitimacy or puppetry. Pahlavi loyalists were unhappy too, bitterly complaining with some justification that the CIA later rewrote history by exaggerating its part while downplaying the Iranian contribution. Richard Helms would only admit that the CIA played a "rather important" role in bringing the coup about because "otherwise things would never come to a boil. I don't mean to, and I'm not interested in making generalizations, but organizing groups of people is not big in Persian life." Helms's view was that the CIA had acted as facilitator, cheerleader, and rainmaker for a powerful coalition of anti-Mossadegh groups whose elements included influential religious leaders, politicians, merchants, and generals. Helms insisted that he had not been "intimately involved in the planning."

The success of Operation Ajax led to American overconfidence in Iran. U.S. officials miscalculated when they concluded that the Shah understood that he "owed" the United States and that he would instinctively toe Washington's line rather than look after his own national interests. Only later did it become apparent that the Shah didn't see it that way at all. "The CIA felt they had sort of a proprietary interest in Iran, because they had helped get the Shah back," explained Douglas MacArthur II, who served as President Nixon's first ambassador to Iran from 1969 to 1972. The spy agency's own confusion about the legacy of Ajax was reflected in the two code names it assigned the Shah, almost certainly without his knowledge. Was the Shah "Ralph" and our guy in Tehran? Or was he "No. 1" and the imperious Shahanshah to whom U.S. officials deferred for the next quarter century? The agency never could decide.

For the first fifteen years after the coup U.S. officials kept a close eye on Iran. Presidents Eisenhower, John F. Kennedy, and Johnson worried about the Shah's propensity for diverting money toward the military rather than developing the country's economy and infrastructure. They feared another social explosion unless poor Iranians saw their lives improve. Liberals were particularly skeptical of the Shah and of Iran's future. At a closed-door session of the Senate Committee on Foreign Relations in June 1961 Senator Frank Church frankly shared his low opinion of the Shah. "I just think it is going to be a miracle if we save the Shah of Iran," he said. "All I know about history says he is not long for this world, nor his system. And when he goes down, boom, we go with him." Church's colleague Hubert Humphrey voiced similar pessimism about the Pahlavis when he said, "they are dead. They just don't know it. I don't care what revolution it is. Somebody is going to get those fellows. They are out. It is just a matter of time."

One of the main reasons for their concern was that during the Shah's reign military expenditures never accounted for less than 23 percent and often up to one third of the national budget. The Johnson administration in particular was determined to hold the line on the Shah's tendency to overspend on armaments. In the mid-1960s Washington erected a fiscal firewall to ensure that the Shah's appetite for military equipment did not drain too much capital from Iran's civilian economy. The firewall was named after General Hamilton Twitchell, who headed up the U.S. military mission to Iran. "The basis of the Twitchell Doctrine was that the Shah's military procurement program should be completely coordinated with the training program, and only equipment come in that Iranians could operate and maintain," said Ambassador Meyer, noting that at the time "there was a strong feeling in Washington that the Shah should not spend money on military equipment." Controlling the flow of arms to Tehran "maintained our relationship," he said. "Our whole relationship with the Shah, I think, depended on the military side of things. If we had left it to the Shah, during my days, the sky would have been the limit. He wanted everything. . . . I was always trying to talk him out of equipment."

Keeping arms sales in check also helped Washington retain influence in Iran. Supplying the Shah with too many weapons might strengthen him to the point where he could pull away and pursue an independent foreign policy. "The Iranians were forced to go through an annual economic review," recalled Meyer. "It was a rather humiliating thing for them to do, before they could buy—*buy*—fifty million dollars worth of military equipment." The Shah, who always kept a wary eye on his northern border, was "a little annoyed" at having to do it but "he realized he had to do it to get the equipment. He wanted to stay with us, although he needled us by buying a few Russian trucks and things of that kind during that period."

Even if a future president diluted or scrapped the Twitchell Doctrine, a secondary dike existed to block a potential flood of defense expenditures by the Shah. Following Operation Ajax the Eisenhower administration established a consortium of Western oil companies to manage the most lucrative 100,000 square miles of Iran's oil fields. During the negotiations Ike sent Vice President Richard Nixon to Tehran to impress upon the reluctant Iranians the fact that economic aid would not resume until the foreign oil industry was allowed back in. British Petroleum eventually took a 40 percent stake in the new consortium and Royal Dutch Shell 14 percent. A second 40 percent stake went to Standard Oil (Esso), Socony Mobil Oil, Standard Oil (California), Gulf Oil, and Texas Oil Company (Texaco), the remainder parceled out to an agglomeration of U.S.-owned companies. As a face-saving gesture to the Shah the companies declared that "the oil assets belonged, in principle, to Iran." Yet the members of the consortium split their profits fifty-fifty with the Iranian state and it was they and not the Shah who set crude oil prices and determined whether oil production would increase or decrease.

That Iran did not have full control over its own purse strings posed a problem for the Shah. The Pahlavi dynasty, Iranian economist Jahangir Amuzegar once observed, rested on "oily legs." Oil was the Shah's greatest source of strength and also his Achilles' heel. Petroleum revenues gave the Pahlavi state its lustrous sheen of prosperity, not to mention its veneer of legitimacy. The Pahlavi elite understood that "oil revenues are the foundation on which the present system maintains its stability." The thinking was that a rising tide of oil wealth would lift all boats, guarantee social stability, buy off and co-opt potential critics of the regime, and help avoid a repetition of the dangerous social and political unrest of recent times. By 1970, when oil revenues topped the billion-dollar mark for the first time, Iran's prime minister boasted that "public revenues will permit us to expand the ordinary budget by 23% and the development budget by 30%." Yet doubts persisted about the wisdom of relying so heavily on one stream of revenue to maintain political equilibrium and social harmony. What would happen if the tide of petroleum ran out or if, God forbid, oil revenues flatlined? The foundations of the Pahlavi state could be knocked out from under it. "His Majesty must see to it that oil revenues perpetually increase," wrote Marvin Zonis. "Fortunately for his style of rule, he has been successful."

To a great extent the dynasty's survival depended on the Shah simultaneously increasing oil production *and* charging consumers in the West more for their oil. The oil companies were interested in profits and not politics. They resisted the Shah's entreaties to increase output. The stage was set for round after round and year after year of punishing clashes between the Shah and the oil companies. The Shah gave hell to oil executives and Western ambassadors. One day in 1970 Britain's ambassador telephoned the palace to offer the Shah advice on oil policy. The Shah was incensed. "The British advise me," he exclaimed. "If they have the fucking audacity to advise me ever again, I shall fuck them so rigid that they'll think twice before crossing my path in the future."

The Shah's frustration was understandable. One of the ironies of the post-coup oil arrangement was that the American oil majors had been reluctant to set up shop in Iran after Mossadegh was deposed. They viewed Iran as an unstable and risky investment. That they had gone in at all was due to the prodding of the Eisenhower administration, which wanted to deepen the American strategic interest in Iran. The companies were much more invested in the lower Gulf states of Saudi Arabia and Kuwait, where production costs were lower and profit margins higher. The petroleum they produced, "Arabian light," was often referred to as "light and sweet" because its low sulfur content makes it easier to convert to gasoline. Iran's mostly heavier grade fuel oil drew a lower price on the world market. Esso's 7 percent stake in Iran's oil consortium paled in comparison to its 30 percent share in Saudi Arabia's national oil-producing company. Gulf Oil owned 50 percent of Kuwait's national oil company but held only a 7 percent share in Iran's consortium. Iran's return to the market in 1954 meant the companies were forced to cut back production elsewhere in the Gulf to avoid glutting the market with cheap oil. Even then they secretly agreed to suppress production in Iran to hold up prices elsewhere. They did so in the knowledge that "any drop in production or sale of oil mean less revenue to Iran."

There was natural tension between Iran and neighboring Saudi Arabia over oil production and pricing. The Shah wanted the smaller and weaker Gulf states to reduce their output so Iran could raise the revenues deemed necessary to defend the Gulf. He resented having to "bail out King Faisal's defense budget, effectively making him our pensioner; the same King Faisal who complains about the undue concessions made to Iran the moment the oil companies begin to review quota allocations." There were religious and cultural tensions, too, between the Persian Iranians, who spoke Farsi, and the Arabic-speaking Saudis. King Faisal's old ways repulsed the Shah, who modeled his court along European lines. In 1971 he hosted a luncheon for the Saudi king at which he had endured the old man's "absurd pronouncements" including the Saudi's belief "that every Jew has a sworn duty to dunk his bread in the blood of a Moslem at least once a year."

The Shah was at heart a Persian nationalist who shared the ambitions and imperial instincts of Cyrus the Great. The empire of his predecessors had at one time extended across the Gulf to include what was now Saudi Arabia's Eastern Province, where the desert kingdom's super-sized petroleum fields were located. There was perhaps more than a trace of wishful thinking to the Shah's oft-stated belief that Saudi Arabia was "ripe for subversive activities" and that King Faisal was headed for "serious trouble." The House of Saud's future—or lack thereof as he saw it—fueled the Shah's ambitions and constituted a major selling point in his campaign to convince the Nixon administration that only "a militarily strong Iran could safeguard the vital interests of the West in the Persian Gulf without the western powers having to intervene."

A complicating factor in this awkward balancing act was the tacit acceptance by President Nixon and his national security adviser, Henry Kissinger, that the Shah could only assume the burden of defending their interests if Iran's revenue stream expanded to generate the money to buy new advanced weapons systems, which in turn meant engineering modest increases in the price of oil and at regular intervals. What really worried Nixon and Kissinger was not the prospect of higher but *lower* oil prices. "It is not likely that the monarchies of Iran, Kuwait, Abu Dhabi, and Saudi Arabia would survive if petroleum prices fell," argued one scholar whose views were shared by the White House. High oil prices were the necessary price of stability in the Middle East because conservative monarchies like Iran and Saudi Arabia were "least likely to force a confrontation over American support for Israel." A greater share of oil revenues allowed pro-U.S. oil potentates to develop their economies while buying the weapons they needed to defend themselves and the free world's oil supply.

The combination of General Twitchell's firewall and the oil consortium gave Washington crucial leverage over the Shah, built the foundations for Iranian prosperity, and provided profits for the American oil industry. In 1969 Iran was hailed as a development success story as its economy reached the point of "take-off" when investment becomes self-renewing. Cheerful American diplomats in Tehran kept a chart on hand that showed Iran's industrial production climbing at a 45 degree angle and "getting steeper all the time." "The growth of the gross national product now going on is comparable only to that of Japan in the immediate postwar period, and is, with the exception of Libya, the fastest in the world—an average of 9.5 percent per year over the past five years and 11.3 percent over the last three of those years," gushed *The New York Times*. "That's about twice as fast as the United States," the paper of record reminded its readers. It was a comparison that delighted the Shah.

THE PRESIDENT HAS A STRONG FEELING ABOUT THE SHAH

Eisenhower's death gave President Nixon and the Shah their first opportunity in two years to talk in private. They had met several times in the 1950s when Nixon served as Eisenhower's vice president. During Nixon's years in the political wilderness in the 1960s they stayed in touch through Ardeshir Zahedi, son of General Fazlollah Zahedi, who commanded Iranian army units during the 1953 coup and led Iran's post-coup military government. After the Shah forced Fazlollah Zahedi to step down from the premiership, the general retired to Switzerland. He left his son behind in Iran to continue the family tradition of service to the Persian crown. Ardeshir's own personal proximity to the throne was cemented in 1957 with his marriage to Princess Shahnaz, the Shah's daughter with his first wife, Princess Fawzia of Egypt. An indication of the trust the Shah placed in his son-in-law came in 1959 when he asked him to lead the search for a third wife. The Shah's happy second marriage to Queen Soraya had ended in divorce because of Soraya's failure to provide her husband with a son and heir. The Shah was anxious to continue the hereditary line and secure a stable succession. "It was Zahedi and Shahnaz who found a tall young Iranian girl, then studying architecture in Paris, whom they introduced to the shah," wrote an Iranian historian. "Her name was Farah. It was in Zahedi's home that the original meeting between the shah and his future queen took place." The Shah's marriage to Farah Diba took place the same year. Zahedi was rewarded for his loyalty with diplomatic postings in the 1960s as ambassador to Washington and London. By the time he was appointed Iran's foreign minister in 1967 his marriage to Princess Shahnaz had ended in divorce.

Ardeshir Zahedi's personal style as Iranian chief diplomat was distinctly *un*diplomatic. The new minister spoke freely, even to the Shah. He made no secret of his nationalist inclinations or his sympathies for the Arab cause, scolded Iran's Western allies in public, and frequently threatened to resign if he did not get his way. The Shah indulged Zahedi as he might a hot-tempered, impetuous younger brother, even kicking him under the table at a diplomatic conference for an indiscreet remark. On one occasion, when the Shah was deep in conversation with Henry Kissinger, Zahedi arrived and hailed the American with a greeting that could most charitably be described as irreverent. The Shah muttered under his breath in Farsi, "Don't create a problem, Ardeshir!"

Over the years, Ardeshir Zahedi compiled a formidable Rolodex of famous names ranging from Hollywood celebrities to heads of corporations and presidents, kings, queens, and prime ministers. As ambassador and foreign minister, Zahedi was especially attentive to the great men who ruled American public life during the Cold War and especially Republican politicians like Richard Nixon, Nelson Rockefeller, Barry Goldwater, and Ronald Reagan. He was a Nixon favorite, whom he once described with great feeling as "a great man." After losing the California governor's race in 1962 Nixon had walked away from politics and public life. Zahedi reached out to him and the two stayed in touch. One evening in early 1967, Zahedi joined Nixon and William Rogers, Eisenhower's attorney general, for dinner at the "21" Club in Manhattan. Zahedi realized during the conversation that Nixon was planning a political comeback and meant to make a second run for the presidency. He returned to his suite at the Waldorf Towers and telephoned the Shah, who was on his annual ski vacation in St. Moritz.

In April, Nixon would be passing through Iran on his way home from a private fact-finding tour of the Near and Far East. Why not invite him to the palace for tea and a chat? The Shah, who closely followed American politics, knew that Nixon's star had long since waned in Washington. He drolly asked his foreign minister how much he had had to drink at dinner that night. But Zahedi put his foot down. "And I got kind of mad and sent letters to the court and foreign ministry and to the Shah," he remembered. "Everyone was against the Nixon visit to Tehran. I invited him. At that time the court minister [Asadollah Alam] and the prime minister [Amir Abbas Hoveyda] were against me." They warned the Shah not to do or say anything that might antagonize President Lyndon Johnson, the Democrat who was gearing up for reelection in 1968. The Shah finally agreed to receive Nixon but only so long as the visit was billed as a courtesy call and not a formal discussion. In any event, Nixon's 1967 visit to Tehran turned out to be much more than that.

The Shah would later refer fondly to his "long hours" of talks with Nixon at Niavaran Palace. What began as a friendly chat over tea in the late afternoon of April 22, 1967, turned into something much more substantial. The Shah and Nixon discovered they shared views on a range of foreign policy issues affecting their countries. After two hours, at 7:00 P.M. Zahedi drove Nixon back to his house, where they conversed again until four in the morning. "We talked about security, the Persian Gulf, the oil, about Soviet intrigues, about the British sometimes double-crossing us," said Zahedi. "I briefed the Shah the next day. This was an off-the-record talk." No notes were taken and U.S. ambassador Armin Meyer agreed to sit it out. "Nixon appreciated that and made Meyer ambassador to Japan after the election," said Zahedi.

Nixon's 1967 visit to Tehran and his talks with the Shah and Zahedi were a turning point for Nixon personally, for the future course of U.S. foreign policy, and for U.S.-Iran relations. Armin Meyer agreed that the Iranians left a deep impression on Nixon, who was looking for new ways to engage the United States in Asia. "In my judgement, the Nixon Doctrine germinated when Nixon visited Iran in 1967," Meyer later confirmed. Nixon and the Shah agreed that it would be better for "our allies [to] take care of their own problems. Give them the equipment to do it. Why should American boys fight in Iran?" Nixon also left Iran more convinced than ever that right-wing authoritarian regimes like the Shah's royal dictatorship should not be pressured to adopt Western concepts of democracy and human rights. Three months after he returned from Tehran, Nixon delivered a speech to the exclusive men's club at the Bohemian Grove outside San Francisco. There he outlined a theme that later became the foreign policy benchmark of his presidency. After mentioning Iran as an economic success story, Nixon reminded his listeners that despite Iran's lack of representative democracy "their system has worked for them. It is time for us to recognize that much as we like our own political system, American style democracy is not necessarily the best form of government for people in Asia, Africa and Latin America with entirely different backgrounds."

Nixon never forgot the Shah's hospitality or Foreign Minister Zahedi's friendship. Later on in the White House he reminded his staff that when he was out of office only the Shah of Iran and President de Gaulle of France had opened their doors to him and treated him with the measure of courtesy and respect he felt he deserved. The first time he welcomed Zahedi to the White House as president it was with a rare hug and the greeting, "You've been a good friend." The Nixon-Pahlavi relationship was based on a shared interest in grand strategy and geopolitics and a mutual fascination with power and its many uses. Nixon and the Shah were not friends in the traditional sense. Nixon had few if any true friends, and the reserved Shah, though he respected Nixon's talents and loyalty, would have never deigned to accept the son of a gas station attendant and grocer from Whittier, California, as his social equal. They were essentially two lonely and insecure men who found relief in the isolation their high positions afforded. "If I take a liking to someone, I need only the smallest shred of doubt to make me break it off," the Shah once said. "Friendship involves the exchange of confidence between two people, but a king can take no one into his confidence. I even observe certain distances with members of my family. I had to tell my mother, who is a very dictatorial woman, that it would be better if she didn't ask me for favors, for I might have to refuse her."

Richard Helms worked closely with both leaders over the years. He described speculation of a friendship between them as

> one of those myths. . . . And I can promise you that in the case of Richard Nixon even in the United States of America he had no close friends or associates. And the Shah had no close friends or associates either. That kind of person doesn't go in for that. Therefore, they were no "bosom buddies." They simply saw an identity of interest. They were both good geopoliticians. They were pragmatic. And they made arrangements of mutual interest.

Even so, the Nixons and the Pahlavis enjoyed warm relations. Visitors to the Nixons' homes in California and New York during their years in private life couldn't help but notice the framed photograph of the Shah strategically placed behind Nixon's desk or the Persian rugs. Nixon's White House quarters boasted such treasures as a fourth-century Sassanian necklace, a 22 karat gold tray, two gold watches, a solid gold presentation box, and a clock with the words "Generation of Peace" inscribed inside.

The president's sympathy and admiration for the Shah were obvious enough to make his advisers nervous about what Nixon might agree to do for Iran now that he was in the White House. "The President has a strong feeling about the Shah," was how Henry Kissinger warily told a colleague. Nixon was well known for making decisions off the cuff based on a few jottings on a lined legal pad and maybe a cocktail or two after dinner. When it came to the Shah, Nixon went with his gut, and that was not necessarily a good thing.

While he was in Washington for Eisenhower's funeral the Shah met with the president's national security team. Two incidents stood out in his conversations with them. In talks with Secretary of State William Rogers on April 1, the day Ike's body was taken across country to its final resting place in Abilene, Kansas, the Shah questioned American motives and specifically the wisdom of trusting an ally with a history of eating its young. He was referring to the American experience in Vietnam, where a half million GIs were mired in a seemingly intractable military stalemate. The Shah charged that the catalyst for the disaster had been the murder of South Vietnam's president Ngo Dinh Diem during an American-sponsored coup d'état in 1963. Diem, protested the Shah, had been "a strong leader [who] was making some progress in combatting corruption" when he was overthrown. This bald accusation of American regicide against a client who bore more than a passing resemblance to the Shah was telling. Rogers politely challenged the Shah's assertion that the United States had disposed of Ngo Dinh Diem but agreed that "the US should not interfere in the internal affairs of other countries."

Later in the evening the Shah met with Kissinger at the Iranian embassy on Massachusetts Avenue. The Shah was joined by Iran's ambassador to the United States, Hushang Ansary. During a discussion of Soviet ambitions in the Middle East the Shah made the case for one-man rule. He told Kissinger that Stalin's foreign policy had at least offered a measure of stability and assurance to the West in comparison to the "more venturesome" foreign policy followed by his Politburo heirs, who had adopted a consensual approach to policy making. Kissinger, a German-born Jew who had escaped Nazi Germany as a teenager and who lost many relatives in the Holocaust, said he "agreed generally" with the Shah's point about the merits of dictatorial government although there were "some exceptions such as Hitler where one-man rule proved highly dangerous." But the Shah demurred and insisted that "where one man ruled, he is normally more cautious."

Mohammad Reza Shah's reference to Ngo Dinh Diem hinted at his basic distrust of the Americans. By trumpeting the virtues of one-man rule, the Shah was making it plain that the days of Eisenhower, Kennedy, and Johnson were over—from now on he, and not the American president, would call the shots in Iran. If there was going to be a relationship, it would have to be between equals. The Shah also dangled a carrot. He offered Kissinger a secret deal to sell the United States one million barrels of oil a day over the next ten years at the discounted price of $1.00 for each barrel. He sensibly proposed that the United States put the oil away in case of a future emergency like a cutoff in the oil supply. But the timing was not right. In March 1959 the Eisenhower administration had imposed mandatory quotas on the amount of foreign petroleum that could be imported into the United States. The quotas were meant to protect the domestic American oil industry from foreign competition and to ensure that the United States never became too dependent on a single supplier of foreign oil. The Shah's offer to sell such a vast amount of oil at a reduced price showed that he was eager to increase America's economic reliance on Iranian crude.

On April 3, 1969, hours after the Shah's departure from Washington for Tehran, the National Security Council Group for the Near East and South Asia met to consider the issue of arms sales to Iran. It recognized that the Shah was stretching his legs and testing the new administration. This was to be expected. On the one hand, officials recommended a $100 million extension in military credits to Iran and the sale of two additional squadrons of F-4 fighter planes. But they noted that "although Iran's economic progress has been rapid, certain warning signs have developed" with a "decline in foreign exchange reserves, a growing debt service ratio, a substantial and rapid increase in budget outlay for military purposes, and a fairly static situation in agricultural output." The group agreed that "the key question is whether the increase in Iran's income from oil will keep pace with the shah's demands and Iran's expenditures." They also agreed that the annual U.S.-Iran review of Iran's economy "should continue to be a key part of our consideration of Iran's military purchases from the United States."

Secretary of State Rogers reinforced this cautionary approach in a memo he sent to the National Security Council and which Kissinger in turn forwarded to Nixon for review. In the first two years of Nixon's presidency it was Rogers and not Kissinger who determined the parameters of administration policy toward Iran. "The general issue since this [arms sales] program began has been its effect on Iran's economy," read the memo. "So far it has proved financially manageable, but Iran's future soundness is still fragile, depending as it does on the continued flow of oil revenues at a high level." President Nixon had been informed—and not for the last time—that Iran was hard-pressed to pay for even current levels of defense expenditures. Rogers cautioned that the only way for the pace of expenditures to keep up would be if Iran's oil revenues increased, and they did not want that to happen.

The Shah had also been warned. A few weeks earlier Court Minister Alam informed him that Iran's treasury was almost empty. Expenses on giant investment projects such as a gas pipeline that swallowed $650 million against an initial estimate of $350 million. "Briefed HIM on recent developments and raised a few points which upset him," wrote Alam in his diary. "I told him that the country is disturbed by the sudden doubling of water prices, that the asphalt in the streets is falling apart, that corruption by the Customs men is on the increase, that bank credits are being squeezed and that various businesses are heading towards bankruptcy. Finally I warned him of the financial crisis in the universities." The Shah, who did not like to hear bad news, lost his temper and snapped, "What can we do when there's no money coming in?"

THE GIANT POKER GAME

On the crisp fall evening of October 21, 1969, President and Mrs. Nixon walked out onto the Front Portico of the White House to welcome the emperor of Iran back to Washington. Just six months after President Eisenhower's funeral observances, the Shah had returned for a state visit. Pat Nixon used the occasion to kick off the fall social season in the nation's capital. The Shah was traveling alone. The official reason given for Queen Farah's absence was that she was expecting the couple's fourth child. This was only partly true. Her visit to the Kennedy White House seven years earlier remained "a traumatic event in my memory." Anti-Shah protesters—young Iranians studying abroad—had hounded the couple at every turn, protesting against the perceived influence of the CIA in Iran and in support of democracy and human rights: "They were everywhere, sometimes within a few yards of us, to the point where my husband had to strain his voice when he needed to speak. We heard them shouting from morning till night, even below our windows in the hotel." The queen, who chain-smoked and suffered from anxiety, had been badly shaken. She was appalled by the laxity of American security arrangements. "A few years later I refused to accompany my husband on an official visit there," she said. She indignantly told him, "If I go there only to be insulted again, I would be of much more use here in Tehran."

Among the 105 guests enjoying the sumptuous festivities were Kermit Roosevelt, Donald Rumsfeld of the Office of Economic Opportunity, National Security Adviser Henry Kissinger, Ambassador to Iran Douglas Mac-Arthur II, and Herbert Brownell, the attorney general under Eisenhower. The guests listened as the president and the Shah lavished praise on each other. Nixon went first. He expressed "love and affection and admiration" for Iran and declared that when he first visited Iran in 1953 the Shah "made a very deep impression on me and on my wife at that time." He quoted the Persian philosopher poet Omar Khayyám, who "referred eloquently to the ability of a leader, a great leader, to heed the roll of distant drums. His Majesty has that ability." And he lauded Iran as "one of the strongest, the proudest among all the nations in the world." In response, the Shah said he was "overwhelmed by the warmth of your sentiments which could only come from a true friend, someone who is sharing your problems and someone who is understanding of your problems. . . . I personally will always remember the long hours we spent together in 1967."

The Shah's state visit came in the midst of his latest fight with the oil consortium. The year before, Iran's government had announced a five-year $11 billion economic development plan to be financed mainly from oil revenues. If Iran was going to meet the plan's spending targets, the oil companies would have to boost their output by 20 percent a year for each of the next five years. This they refused to do. What ensued was "a giant poker game," though a more appropriate analogy might be a game of chicken. The Shah had approved a five-year budget knowing that his government lacked the income to meet its objectives. The fiscal commitments he approved could be paid for only with anticipated or *future* oil revenues. The Shah would have to hike oil prices to generate the revenue. He had no scruples when it came to the oil industry. Alam's diary suggests that the Shah bankrolled Kurdish guerrillas in neighboring Iraq to blow up oil pipelines in order to cut Baghdad's revenue stream and stampede foreign petroleum investment to Iran. In foreign affairs as in domestic politics, the Shah's brinkmanship was driven by a self-perpetuating money chase.

In the weeks preceding the Iranian state visit, briefing papers flew back and forth across the Potomac warning that the Shah wanted to end the Twitchell Doctrine. White House aides frankly worried that President

Nixon would be out-negotiated in his private talks with the Shah. Unlike Nixon, who couldn't be bothered reading his own daily intelligence briefs from the CIA and who loathed hearing from those "impossible fags" at the State Department, the Shah was a voracious reader and meticulous student of strategy and military affairs who always seemed to know more than anyone else in the room. He had a history of correcting the Pentagon's top brass when they talked about weapons systems that were still on the drawing board. Nixon squirmed to avoid personal confrontations and had a propensity for buckling under pressure.

On October 6, 1969, Embassy Tehran let the White House know that the Shah was looking for ways to jack up Iran's oil production as a means of raising fast money: "The Shah is in dead earnest in his quest for additional oil revenues, and Iran's current tight foreign exchange situation has added urgency to problem." The Shah expected President Nixon to intervene in his favor with the oil consortium and "nudge oil companies to take his regional responsibilities as well as commercial considerations into account in their negotiations and that we will be sympathetic regarding any barter deals for military equipment that he may be able to work out within current import quota system." And if that didn't work, he was peddling a new variant of his proposal earlier in the year for the administration to agree to buy discounted Iranian oil in violation of the 1959 oil import quota law.

The Shah had been sold on the idea by Herbert Brownell, who now represented a company called Planet Oil and Minerals. In his former capacity as President Eisenhower's attorney general, Brownell was more than familiar with existing U.S. law as it related to foreign oil imports. His plan called for the administration to give Planet Oil license to import 200,000 barrels of oil a day from Iran. Planet would buy the oil for distribution in the United States "and Iran would use the proceeds only for Iranian purchases in the US." A barrel of oil that would normally cost the United States $1.80 would be marked down by a dollar to just 80 cents. The Shah proposed that the United States use this oil to create a strategic reserve in the event of an emergency such as an oil embargo. The Brownell deal, like the million-barrel-a-day scheme, was shelved. Nixon was cautioned by his staff that "there have been some scandals involving oil allocation decisions in the recent past. The press had not fully exploited those scandals, but I'm sure would put the worst possible interpretation on any decisions by this Administration that might be of substantial benefit to one of Mr. Brownell's clients."

The presence of Kim Roosevelt and Herb Brownell at the state banquet was a reminder of the Shah's close ties with former members of the Eisenhower administration, of whom Richard Nixon was the most prominent. When it came to Iran, Washington's dividing lines between power, money, and access were often blurred. Since helping pull off the 1953 coup, Roosevelt had become an international arms broker working for the defense contractor Northrop. His two biggest clients were Mohammad Reza Shah of Iran and King Faisal of Saudi Arabia. The Shah flew to New York before heading down to Washington, and his schedule for October 18 shows that he met with Roosevelt and Tom Jones, Northrop's president, in the morning.

In advance of the president's meetings with the Shah, the State Department's Bureau of Intelligence and Research warned that giving in to the Shah's demands would inevitably lead to a decline in American influence over the Shah because "growing Iranian independence could result in less reliance on US support and less attention to American advice, especially on regional matters. . . . The Shah is convinced that Iran must play the dominant role in the Persian Gulf and he is determined that radical Arab or Soviet influence should be prevented, or at least kept to an innocuous level." The State Department believed that the Shah was exaggerating security threats to Iran in order to extract from the White House permission to raise oil prices and buy more arms. It had required a "major US effort" in recent years to make sure that the Shah's arms purchases from the United States do "not become a severe strain on Iran's economic development." But, according to the State Department, the Shah appears "determined to follow this course" even though "sharply rising military expenditures cannot but cause problems for Iran internally by hindering its development plans and externally by perhaps alarming and alienating its weaker Arab neighbors."

The Department of Defense did not stay quiet either. Secretary of Defense Melvin Laird, a former congressman and canny political operator, advised against sending U.S. Air Force technicians or "blue suiters" to Iran to maintain the Shah's fleet of new F-4 fighter planes. He wanted civilian contractors sent instead to avoid "deepening the involvement of US military personnel in Iran." During a recent clash between Iranian and Iraqi forces over border boundaries on the Shatt al-Arab waterway the Shah had requested that uniformed American personnel be deployed to a forward base in western Iran to provide backup. The Pentagon had been alarmed by the brazen nature of this request and concluded that the Shah was goading Iraqi leaders even at the risk of triggering a war. Laird declared himself "concerned about the implications of that sort of involvement" for United States ground forces, arguing that it had echoes of the sort of creeping escalation that lured America into Vietnam. The Shah's request for military support, if it became public, would hurt U.S.-Iran relations and arouse "serious Congressional opposition." He reminded the White House that the whole point of the Nixon Doctrine was to arm and train America's allies to defend themselves. When informed that American military personnel would not be allowed to move into western Iran, the Shah did not try to hide his disappointment—or his sense of entitlement: "What is the use of friendship if it is not good when [the] chips are down?"

Kissinger's aides worried that Nixon would give away the store when he was alone with the Shah. "Although we have suggested that the President try to steer clear of details of the Shah's military and oil proposals, the Shah has a way of pressing hard for answers," read one memo. "If the going gets heavy, the President may ask you on the spot what can be done or ask you to talk to Secretary Laird." But the president had also scheduled several twenty- to twenty-five-minute tête-à-têtes in which no one else would be present to offer help. Kissinger reminded Nixon that the Shah "is a persistent bargainer and he will read any generally sympathetic answer as assent. Precise and frank talk about how far the US can and cannot go is important in avoiding later miscommunications." Even telling the Shah that "we will consider" his requests was likely to be read by the king as "a promise to consider favorably. To avoid unpleasant misunderstandings, it is best where possible to say exactly how we will handle his requests, explaining where necessary why it is not possible to give a final answer immediately."

The Nixons welcomed their guest on to the grounds of the White House at 10:30 A.M. on Tuesday, October 21, 1969. The two leaders retreated to the Oval Office for a private meeting that lasted an hour and forty minutes. After meeting with Nixon, the Shah declared the president to have an "excellent understanding of Iran, its problems and its achievements." He told the White House staff that Nixon had promised to boost Iran's income from oil by either granting Iran its own special oil quota or by placing pressure on the oil consortium to increase production of oil in Iran. No mention was made of trying to close Iran's financial hole. Nixon had apparently agreed to do everything that his aides had advised him not to do.

The Shah pledged to spend every penny he earned from the additional oil revenues on American military and intelligence equipment. He confidently informed administration officials that if Iran was to defend itself and Western interests in the Persian Gulf, its armed forces would have to acquire "an overkill capability so that should anyone be tempted to attack Iran they would think twice or three times." What the Shah was proposing amounted to a massive new undertaking that would cost hundreds of millions, perhaps even billions, of dollars in new arms purchases. In private, Nixon's national security aides expressed concern. It was one thing to fly the flag for the West in the Persian Gulf, another entirely to outfit Iran's military to the point where it could face down Iraq and India, crush regional rebellions, and pacify not only the Persian Gulf but a vast swath of the Middle East and the Indian Ocean. Rearmament on the scale proposed by the Shah had the potential to bankrupt Iran. It would certainly divert precious capital, technology, and trained personnel from popular domestic programs intended to buttress the shaky pillars of the Shah's Pahlavi dynasty.

The real bombshell landed after Mohammad Reza Shah's farewell meeting with Nixon at 10:45 A.M. on Thursday, October 23. The Iranian cheerfully exited the Oval Office to inform a startled Ambassador MacArthur that he and the president had talked about "the problem of strengthening and equipping Iran's armed forces." The Shah was "under the impression that there were no problems of any kind, and that he could now obtain virtually anything that he wanted in the way of military equipment." The ambassador knew that no American ally—not Great Britain, not West Germany, not Israel—enjoyed blank check privileges. The Pentagon would never stand for it. MacArthur suggested there had been a misunderstanding: "So I said to him, If you have that impression, there's no point going back to Tehran and having any misunderstandings. I think you ought to clarify with the President, since you got the impression from your private talk with the President." When he returned to Tehran, MacArthur made a point of raising the issue with the Shah. Did he and Nixon get things straightened out? "He said no; he hadn't wanted to bring it up; the atmosphere had been so good; everything was going so well that he hadn't wanted to get back, at his last little meeting with the President just before he was leaving to return to Tehran, he hadn't wanted to get down into the details and so forth."

The White House staff spent the next few months trying to fathom the extent of Nixon's verbal commitments. On October 23, Kissinger telephoned Laird to tell him that the president "didn't completely promise, but he indicated" that he was in favor of a request from the Shah to increase the number of training slots open to Iranian air force pilots in the United

States. The Shah also wanted the Air Force to send over more blue suiters to work with his pilots in Iran, something the Defense Department had expressly opposed. When an exasperated Laird replied that the United States had its own shortage of technicians, Kissinger told him that Nixon was anxious to show that the Shah "got something out of his meetings here."

MacArthur was rattled when the Shah told him that Nixon had given him his personal guarantee that "a way will be found to permit Iran to increase its oil exports to the United States and that [the Iranians] are counting heavily on alleged Presidential assurances to the Shah, given during his October state visit." This was a real problem because Nixon's own cabinet task force reviewing oil import quotas was about to come out publicly *against* granting special exemptions to individual countries such as Iran. "Predictably, the Shah will be sharply disappointed if these recommendations become US policy," the State Department chided Kissinger. An aide to Secretary of State Rogers made a tartly worded request for additional information from the White House: "As there is no written record of the President's conversations with the Shah we find it difficult to assess the Shah's present expectations. We would appreciate it if you could shed light on this critical point."

Nixon was thus forced to backtrack on the promises he made to the Shah on Iranian oil production output and U.S. imports of Persian crude. He plaintively wrote: "There are, as you know, limits on what we as a government can do, and I cannot report any breakthroughs at this point." Meanwhile, the Shah's badgering of MacArthur sent the envoy into a panic. If Washington did not extend more military credits to Iran "we should have no—repeat no—doubt that result will be major crisis and end of special relationship Shah feels for us." The panicky communication was typical: the sky was always about to fall in Tehran. MacArthur reminded his colleagues in Washington that the "special relationship" with the Shah had resulted in "special privileges and facilities for us," a reference to CIA listening posts built along Iran's northern border with the Soviet Union.

The top brass at the Pentagon refused to budge. "The Shah continues to play hard on the same themes with us," was how Kissinger relayed the views of General Earle Wheeler, chairman of the Joint Chiefs of Staff, to Nixon. "He seems in fact to be testing the limits of our capacity to help him." Wheeler opposed the sale of four additional squadrons of F-4s to Iran because the Iranians "would have trouble digesting all of the equipment they have in mind" to purchase. They lacked the pilots to fly the planes and the specially trained personnel to maintain them. The Shah also wanted thirty-six additional C-130 transportation planes. He had told Wheeler that he needed to be able to move his troops around "threatened areas." Wheeler suspected the Shah was building a contingency plan to move large amounts of troops into Saudi Arabia "should the need arise." He knocked down MacArthur's canard that if the United States refused to sell arms to Iran the Shah would turn elsewhere, perhaps buying French or even Soviet weapons. The Iranian armed forces were too integrated into the American defense structure, France was an unreliable supplier of military spare parts, and the Shah would never allow Soviet trainers or personnel in Iran. Wheeler suggested that the Shah was a hypocrite for pressing the oil consortium to boost Iranian oil production when Iran had recently lashed the government of Kuwait for doing the exact same thing.

In October 1970 Secretary Laird bluntly informed his colleague Rogers over at State that the Shah's request for another four squadrons of F-4s crossed the line. The Shah had more than enough planes to defend Iran. His purchases would only prompt neighboring Iraq to turn closer to the Soviet Union and accelerate a regional arms race that could destabilize the entire Persian Gulf. It would place severe strains on Iran's economy and manpower. "There is little question that the Shah will be unhappy over our unwillingness to sell him all that he wants," warned Laird. "Nonetheless, I consider the course he follows to be inimical to Iran's interests and our own, and I think the time has come to talk bluntly with him about arms stability in the Persian Gulf area, as well as the excessive monetary and personnel costs which these programs would entail." Laird's deputy secretary, David Packard, implicitly rebuked MacArthur when he pointed out to the ambassador that the Shah did not appear to have a sound grasp of "the unique nature of Tehran's special relationship with the United States" as partner and ally. Yet even as Wheeler, Laird, and Rogers held the line, they were being undermined by the CIA and its director, Richard Helms, and by a sympathetic Henry Kissinger.

MR. HELMS INSISTS

During the Shah's 1969 state visit, "No. 1" had enjoyed a long breakfast with CIA director Richard Helms in the upstairs study of Blair House, the residence across the street from the White House where the Iranian monarch was quartered. Helms had met Mohammad Reza Shah for the first time in 1957 when he traveled to Tehran to negotiate the installation of a CIA radar station on Iranian soil to monitor Russian missile-testing ranges across the border in Soviet Kazakhstan. "He agreed that he would sponsor it, and what he decided to do was to make the installation an Iranian Air Force installation, have the Iranian flag fly over it, and then have the Americans do the work there under the guise of advisors and consultants to the Iranian Air Force," Helms recalled. A second base was established in the 1960s. The CIA regarded the posts as essential in its efforts to give the United States an edge in missile superiority and to verify Soviet compliance with arms accords. Helms had an indirect personal connection to the Shah through his younger brother, Pearsall, who had been in school with Crown Prince Mohammad Reza Pahlavi at Le Rosey in Switzerland in the 1930s. Every time the Shah came to Washington he received Dick Helms. In addition to briefing the Shah on intelligence matters, the director thanked the Shah for permitting construction of additional CIA facilities along Iran's Persian Gulf coast. According to Helms's notes from the 1969 meeting, "The Shah nodded his head, expressed his interest in the project, then went on to say that as long as we are not interested in having USA shining in neon lights on our installations, he is prepared to have us locate in Iran almost any kind of technical collection we desire."

This was music to Helms's ears. Documents show that it was Helms who repeatedly and decisively intervened on the Shah's side in the debate over arms sales. Like Wheeler, Laird, and Rogers, Helms frankly dismissed the strategic logic behind the Shah's military buildup. He confessed that the king's arguments were easily rejected "on grounds of cost, lack of urgency, limited capability, undesirable precedent and other arguments." But to Helms that was all beside the point when a much bigger prize existed in the form of the CIA spy bases. Iran hosted intelligence facilities "vital to our national security." With Afghanistan barely a functioning state and no longer politically feasible as an alternative center for espionage against the Soviet Union, "there is no place to which we could transfer these activities were Iran denied us. . . . The [facilities] are entirely dependent on the continued willingness of the Shah to permit them to operate and to transmit promptly the information they collect."

Echoing Helms's sentiment in a memo dated April 16, 1970, Kissinger praised Iran to Nixon as an "island of stability." He concurred with Helms that "there seems little reason not to give the Shah whatever he wants." This recommendation came even after he noted that the main argument against extending military credits to Iran had been to keep Iran's debt burden "within safe limits." It was an undeniable fact that the Shah had gone on a spending binge. Iran's debt service costs "are already high," observed

Kissinger. But it was equally "difficult, of course, to say what is too high; what can be said is that the level is high enough to be cause for concern in Iran as well as here about raising it much higher. . . . The problem arises as he pushes the limits of his resources and ours. He is understandably a man in a hurry who will press all resources available to their limits." Kissinger also recited Helms's opinion that "there is room to question whether the direct military threat to Iran from the Persian Gulf is as great as the Shah fears."

One month later, at 3:00 P.M. on May 14, President Nixon welcomed to the White House foreign ministers in town for a meeting of the Central Treaty Organization, CENTO, the alliance of anti-communist "northern tier" countries: Iran, Pakistan, Turkey, and Great Britain. At the end of the formal discussions he beckoned Ardeshir Zahedi into a small room off the Oval Office. He wanted the foreign minister to pass on a message to the Shah. Nixon's subsequent remarks suggested he was fed up with the bureaucratic wrangling over arms sales. He wanted to do something for the Shah and short-circuit Laird and Wheeler. After discussing Iran's cash flow problems, and the Shah's desire to generate higher oil revenues, Nixon made a remarkable and decisive intervention. "Tell the Shah you can push [us] as much as you want [on oil prices]," he told Foreign Minister Zahedi. "As long as you make this money for the good of the Iranian people and the progress of Iran [then] I will back you." This was the news the Shah had been longing to hear, that he could raise oil prices at will and finally bring pressure to bear against Western oil companies and oil consumers. Better still, he could do so secure in the knowledge that he had the backing of the White House. The president was letting him know that he would support in private what he might be obliged to oppose in public. It is an extraordinary fact that Nixon's back channel on an issue of such critical importance to the American and world economy was apparently made without benefit of any sort of cost assessment or risk analysis. It evidently did not occur to Nixon that he had placed in the hands of the Iranian leader the power to redistribute national wealth from the industrialized West to the oil kings of the Middle East. That the American way of life was built on a fragile foundation of affordable energy seemed to have eluded him.

Nixon's aides were oblivious to his intervention and continued to debate the merits of lifting restrictions on arms sales to Iran. During one briefing in Washington Ambassador MacArthur assured skeptical colleagues from the departments of State and Defense that "he was not suggesting that we give Iran a blank check to buy whatever it wished from the United States, but [he] wished to stress that in his view it might be preferable for us to cede to a sale." The ambassador's view was that the more arms the administration sold to Iran the more dependent Iran would be on the United States as an arms supplier. "Are we not in a better position to limit the arms race more effectively through our influence over the Shah than by his exercising his freedom to purchase what he wants from other suppliers?" he told the gathering. He was apparently unaware of General Wheeler's contention that no other country had the ability to replace the United States as Iran's most important arms supplier. When asked if he "was not concerned with the impact of Iran's military purchases on the [Iranian economy] over the next five years," MacArthur said he was not. Iran's credit was indeed tight, he noted, which was why he supported a mix of credit *and* cash sales.

In September 1970 Helms again struck hard against the Defense Department when he lobbied Kissinger to kill off a study begun to assess the military threat facing Iran. Helms correctly saw this as nothing but a stalling tactic by the Pentagon brass. He told Kissinger it was just the sort of thing to irritate the Shah and put at risk the CIA investment in Iran. He reminded Kissinger that the future of U.S. electronics eavesdropping along the Soviet Union's southern border "rests very directly on the Shah's support." Failure by the administration to cooperate with the Shah would lead to "increased pressure on oil interests, and possibly termination of US special facilities [i.e., spy bases] and military overflight rights."

Remarkably, Helms was pleading a case that his own analysts opposed in private. It was another sign of the dysfunction that epitomized American national security policy toward Iran. A study of data collected from the American military mission in Tehran found that the Iranians were buying "exotic equipment which they are not prepared to use and, in many instances, cannot afford to purchase." An even more remarkable study from 1971 linked weapons purchases with future financial collapse. "We don't know just how keenly the Shah appreciates the limits of financial elasticity," wrote the CIA's Office of National Estimates. It was an eerie and remarkably prescient analysis of the shock that awaited Iran. Although Iranian oil revenues had risen in recent years and contributed to a general sense of prosperity, they couldn't keep pace with the Shah's spending and "presently planned total expenditures are far larger than projected revenues." The Shah was digging himself—and his country—into a pit of debt. "At some point in the next several years, Iran will have to make painful choices as between military hardware and development priorities. Decisions would not require scaling down the military expenditures so much as restraining its growth. On past form, the Shah will only ease off on military expenditures after several prophets of doom have sounded Iran's economic death-knell, but before disaster has actually set in."

Behind the public cover of state banquets, eloquent toasts, and joint military exercises, what had once been a convenient patron-client relationship was beginning to resemble a straitjacket for two. It became even tighter when at the end of 1970 the issue of military credits was resolved in favor of Iran making cash sales for its purchases of U.S. arms. Then in November, President Nixon decided that henceforth U.S. strategic policy in the Persian Gulf would rest on a strong Iran supported by Saudi Arabia in a clearly subservient and secondary role. This became known as the "Twin Pillars" policy.

HE RUNS A DAMN TIGHT SHOP, RIGHT?

At 3:56 on the afternoon of April 8, 1971, President Nixon welcomed Ambassador MacArthur back to the White House. They were joined by General Alexander Haig, Kissinger's deputy. Photographs were taken, small talk was exchanged, and the ambassador had just settled in when the president got straight to the point. With less than six months to go before the British evacuated the Gulf, Nixon was hearing from the Pentagon that Iran still wasn't up to the job of taking over regional defense responsibilities. He said he was "stronger than a horseradish" for the Shah. But he needed to know: "Are they capable of it?" Melvin Laird and the generals were telling him, "Well, the Shah just hasn't got the stuff, is that right Al? Isn't that what we find? They don't think—they just don't think he's got the stroke to do it."

"There is a feeling, yes sir," Haig answered. "That he can't do it all the way."

"If he could do it, it'd be wonderful because he's our friend, right?" said Nixon.

"Yes sir," replied MacArthur. "Absolutely."

"He runs a damn tight shop, right?" inquired the president.

"He does," said MacArthur. "Your influence on him is extraordinary. He said to me—I've got a very good relationship with him, he said, he talks quite frankly, he said, 'You know, I admire your President. He understands the international world and this part of the world much better than either of his predecessors [Presidents Kennedy and Johnson].' He said, 'They really didn't understand the Middle East at all, with all its complexities.'"

Sixty-two-year-old MacArthur was the nephew and namesake of World War II and Korean War commander General Douglas MacArthur. Before taking up his post as ambassador to Tehran in September 1969, MacArthur had served as America's top diplomat in Japan, Belgium, and Austria. MacArthur's staff worried about his tendency to wilt in the Shah's presence. One former colleague recalled that the ambassador was "scared stiff" of the Shah. MacArthur's flattery and obsequious behavior was duly noted by Iranian courtiers. Douglas MacArthur had once even gone so far as to help cover up an attempt on his own life lest it cause the Shah embarrassment.

On the evening of November 30, 1970, the ambassador's Cadillac was ambushed by gunmen firing at point-blank range only a few hundred meters from the gates of the American embassy. "These boys opened fire, but we brushed the car aside," MacArthur later recalled. "They shot the windows out of the car. One of them had an axe, obviously to attack the window if I tried to lock myself in. They threw the axe. It hit me in the arm." The cover-up began almost immediately. "I am particularly anxious that this matter be treated publicly in way which will not repeat nor embarrass GOI [Government of Iran]," he cabled the State Department. "Accordingly, Court Minister Alam (after consultations with Shah and Prime Minister Hoveyda) and I have agreed that we will volunteer no statement about incident but if we are queried response will be that while returning to residence from a dinner last evening our car was sideswiped by a hit-and-run driver who was proceeding at a high rate of speed and that car suffered broken window and some other damage but nobody hurt. We can not speculate on whether accident was deliberate or part of hit-and-run driver or simply result of very bad driving for which Iran is known." The cover story concocted by the Shah, Alam, and MacArthur beggared belief. The embassy's guards had seen the Cadillac hurtling through the gates the night before with everyone inside in a state of panic, its windows shot out, and its windshield shattered. Mechanics at the embassy motor pool had found a bullet lodged in a rear door frame. An axe had struck the ambassador in the arm. What did people *think* had happened?

Four months later in the White House, Nixon asked MacArthur if perhaps the Shah might not be "thinking too big," in effect taking on more than Iran could handle. MacArthur didn't disagree. "Well, he may be thinking a bit big," he agreed. "But I can't say that—what we're trying to do is get him to program. To get him—you know, instead of just sort of saying, 'I need this, I need that, I need the other thing.' Because if you say, 'you don't need this thing,' it's through the roof."

"Sure," grunted Nixon. Hell, he had gone through the roof himself from time to time.

MacArthur said that to avoid upsetting the Shah he had not talked with him about the costs that would be associated with Iran's military buildup or "the infrastructure that's needed to support them. And then very important, the personnel that you have and will need to marry them and cost the whole thing. And that this serves the basis for identifying priorities and developing a five-year plan." What the ambassador said he *was* doing instead was working with U.S. government officials to secure a new line of credit for the Shah to make all the purchases he felt he needed to get the job done.

Nixon loved what MacArthur was telling him. Getting the job done was what counted. Screw the red tape and the experts. "Whenever they send anything in here that I can sign, I do," he said. "He should know that." The president said he had had to overrule the State Department a couple of times "on the damn things," but the fact remained that when it came to the Shah and Iran, "I like him, I like him and I like his country. And some of those other bastards out there I don't like, right?"

"Right," repeated MacArthur. He reminded the president that Iran was America's only natural ally between Japan and Europe. "And, Mr. President, between Japan, NATO, and Europe, it's the only building block we've got that is strong, that is sound, that is aggressive, and that above all regards us as just about its firmest friend. Elsewhere we're trying to shore up weaknesses and it's a problem." The ambassador was haunted by a remark made by Joseph Luns, the Dutch foreign minister and future NATO secretary general. MacArthur once asked Luns what he thought would happen if European nations were faced with the choice between a cutoff of their Persian Gulf oil supplies and caving in to blackmail from oil producers. Luns offered a grim prognosis: "I fear that Western Europe would have no choice but to reach some form of an accommodation, because the alternative would be a total collapse of its economy and its national life."

When Richard Nixon looked out at the world from the White House in April 1971 he had little to cheer about—with the possible exception of Iran. Elsewhere in Asia, "the Philippines is a can of worms," and "Burma's always in a mess. Always will be. And you know the Burmese, they just chew that weed. That black tea." Pakistan was going to hell. Iran somehow comfortably straddled different worlds. "But the point is, that by God if we can go with them, and we can have them strong, and they're in the center of it, and a friend of the United States, I couldn't agree more—that's something. 'Cause it just happens that, who else do we have except for Europe? The Southern Mediterranean, it's all gone," he mused. "Morocco, Christ, they can't last," neither can "all the little miserable countries around—Jordan and Lebanon and the rest. They're like—they go down like ten pins, just like that."

Unlike every other Muslim country in the Middle East, Iran maintained unofficial but close relations with Israel and didn't punish the United States for supporting the Jewish state. The Shah was "awfully good on that subject," affirmed Nixon. The Shah saw Iran and Israel as natural allies in the region, outsiders in an Arab sea, two bastions of tolerance, moderation, and anti-Communism with overlapping strategic interests. "Both our countries, Israel on one side, and Iran on the other, are confronted by a radical Arab nationalism and expansionism," explained an Iranian official to the Associated Press in 1969. Israel's unofficial representative in Tehran—no one liked to use the word "ambassador"—worked out of the Israeli trade mission, an unmarked and heavily secured compound located at 5 Takht-e Jamshid Avenue, near the American embassy. The Shah took great pride in protecting Iran's religious and ethnic minorities, particularly the sixty thousand Iranian Jews who had chosen to stay on after Israel was established in 1948. Their community, one of the most ancient Jewish entities, had ties with the Persians going back to biblical times.

By 1970, about $40 million worth of Iranian oil was exported to Israel every year. The Shah made the somewhat specious claim that the sale of oil to Israel was a business arrangement worked out with the oil consortium that had nothing to do with his government. Yet Tehran's newest supermarket sold Israeli food and publications, and Hebrew-language literature was openly sold in bookstores and at newsstands. In a country that loved cinema—Tehran boasted eighty movie houses—Israeli nationals ran three of the four biggest film distribution companies. Israel's state airline, El Al, flew two regularly scheduled flights each week between Tel Aviv and Tehran, flying over Turkey to avoid Arab airspace. Israeli engineers and advisers, meanwhile, were helping their Iranian counterparts dig deep water wells in Qazvin north of Tehran and irrigate farmland on the southern slopes of the Elburz Mountains. Iran's Jewish community and Israel were on the front lines of the Shah's crusade to modernize Iran and eliminate clerical influence.

The Shah's conciliatory approach to Israel defied the wishes of many of his own people, particularly young university students enamored with Nasserism and the Palestinian struggle for an independent homeland. Israel's lightning victory over Iran's Muslim brethren in the 1967 Six Day War had led to street protests, an upsurge in support for the Palestinian cause, and a tendency to lump Americans with the Israelis as a common foe. The decision by the Shah's government to raise bus fares and alter bus routes in February 1970 had led to street clashes between hundreds of students and riot police in Tehran. The U.S. embassy cabled Washington that the protests quickly took on nationalist and anti-American, anti-Israeli, and anti-government overtones even as MacArthur hastened to assure Washington that the sentiments expressed by the demonstrators were "insignificant." Two months later, more than thirty thousand soccer fans chanted anti-Israeli slogans and took to the streets when their local team defeated the visiting Israeli team.

The Shah's support for Israel was matched by his commitment to defend Saudi Arabia and the massive oil reserves of the lower Persian Gulf. If the Saudis and their oil fields got into trouble with domestic radicals, the Shah had offered to go in and sort them out. In his meeting with Nixon, MacArthur told the president that the problem with Saudi Arabia's King Faisal was that he had started too late in the game to reform his feudal monarchy; things would have been different "if he had started back when the Shah had made his great social revolution, and sir, it is a complete revolution."

MacArthur was referring to the Shah's 1963 White Revolution, an ambitious package of progressive social and economic reforms meant to reassure the Kennedy administration that the Pahlavi crown was on the side of progress. Iran's forests and waterways were nationalized. The royal estates and the king's vast private landholdings were broken up in favor of peasant ownership. Women were granted voting and political rights. Health corps, literacy corps, and reconstruction and development corps were created. Workers' profit sharing was introduced. The Shah was successful in co-opting many of the crown's critics on the left. But the anticlerical nature of the reforms enraged Iran's Shi'a religious establishment. Religious leaders, the mullahs, were especially offended by the emancipation of women, and they understood that the breakup of their estates would weaken their hold over the peasantry and make them financially dependent on handouts from the Pahlavi state. They damned the White Revolution as unconstitutional and un-Islamic and denounced a law to grant U.S. military personnel immunity from prosecution if they committed criminal acts on Iranian soil.

The Shah struck back, comparing the mullahs to "a numb and dispirited snake and lice who float in their own dirt," and he threatened that "the fist of justice, like thunder, will be struck at their head in whatever cloth they are, perhaps to terminate their filthy and shameful life."

On June 3, 1963, a charismatic cleric by the name of Ruhollah Khomeini denounced the Shah in words remarkable for their slanderous tone and bitter invective. "O Mr. Shah, dear Mr. Shah," he adjured, "abandon these improper acts. I don't want people to offer thanks should your masters decide that you must leave. I don't want you to become your father." Khomeini's detention at the hands of SAVAK, the state security police, triggered violent clashes in cities across Iran that briefly threatened the monarchy. The prime minister during the showdown between church and state was Asadollah Alam, and it was Alam who issued the order for troops to open fire on the demonstrators, restoring order at the cost of about one hundred lives. The question of what to do with Khomeini vexed the palace. The head of SAVAK during the crisis was General Hassan Pakravan, one of the few influential figures at court with clean hands. During his tenure as security chief torture was banned and the government kept open a dialogue with the opposition. Queen Farah described him as "a man of great culture, intelligence, and humanity." The Shah was won over by Pakravan's advice that the best way to keep peace at home was to exile Khomeini rather than have him executed for treason. Khomeini was sent first to Turkey and then to Iraq, where both governments kept a close eye on him. With Khomeini out of the way, the Shah felt sure he had seen off the threat from Iran's religious right with a few rounds of grapeshot. Now he could get back to the real work of modernizing Iran and fulfilling his imperial destiny. That was certainly how the White House viewed events. U.S. officials were confident that the Shah had passed his great crisis and was now home free.

"Basically there is great stability [in Iran]," Ambassador MacArthur assured President Nixon, disregarding the recent attempt on his life. The Shah had "totally disarmed the Communists—the Tudeh Party." Responding to a question about student unrest in Iran, he replied that "about ten percent are activists." Nixon earned a round of guffaws from MacArthur and Haig when he cracked, "Well that's less than we have."

"It's about fifty percent of ours," Haig added.

"They want a greater voice in the thing," MacArthur conceded. "But the Shah is wise enough to know that when you take a people that are from feudalism, and you drag them out of the womb of feudalism like a midwife driving a child out of the mother's womb, you let loose great elemental forces. And this is what he's done. Now he runs a fairly tight shop, but to channel these energies and forces."

"He always tries to keep one foot ahead of them, huh?" Nixon noted with admiration.

"He does. He said to me the other day before the oil talks, he said—he was talking about how they need more revenue—he said, 'Mr. Ambassador,' he said, 'I need more hospitals. I need more health services in my villages. I need more workers' housing. I need more schools for my people.' He said, 'I must do these things.'"

"Hmm." The president was clearly impressed.

"He's got a profound, he's developed a profound social conscience."

"I just wish there were a few more leaders around the world with his foresight," Nixon mused. "And his ability, his ability to run, let's face it, a virtual dictatorship in a benign way. Because, look, when you talk about having a democracy of our type in that part of the world, good God, it wouldn't work. Would it?" Democracy wasn't working in Africa where the people "are just out of trees." At least Iran had "some degree of civilization in its history." Democracy was a luxury that very few nations could afford. "And it's got to be that way. They aren't ready. You know this. You've got to remember it took the British a hell of a long time of blood, strife, chopping off the heads of kings and the rest before they finally got their system."

Chapter Two

GUARDIAN OF THE GULF

"Iran will get all available sophisticated weapons short of the atomic bomb."

—The Shah, 1972

"Now is time to cash in credit with Iranians."

—Henry Kissinger, 1972

THE SHAH'S REVENGE

Shell blasts and the crackle of rifle fire punctuated the first light of dawn over the Persian Gulf on November 30, 1971, the moment when Iranian commandos stormed three small islands strategically located at the mouth of the Strait of Hormuz. Three Iranian troops and four local police officers were killed in a brief firefight before the Pahlavi standard was raised in victory. Iran's lightning strike brought to an end lengthy and ultimately inconclusive negotiations between Tehran, London, and local Arab sheikhs over division of the islands, Britain's last imperial spoils in the region. The Shah had agreed not to challenge the decision by Bahrain, a former Iranian territory, to declare its independence but he wasn't about to surrender his claim to the islands and saw them as fair compensation. Foreign Minister Ardeshir Zahedi had dismissed the territorial claim lodged by one sheikh with the memorable rejoinder, "I will wipe my ass with this paper and then flush it down the toilet." With Iran's annexation of Abu Musa, Greater Tunb, and Lesser Tunb, Mohammad Reza Shah Pahlavi was now confirmed in his self-designated role as "Guardian of the Gulf" in an act of daring that subsumed whatever remaining doubts Richard Nixon might have had about Iran's military prowess or the Shah's ability to defend

America's energy lifeline. But Iran's Arab neighbors recoiled at the idea of ceding even an inch of Arab land to their Persian neighbor. Iraq broke off diplomatic relations with Tehran and expelled sixty thousand Iranian nationals, driving them over the border in wintry conditions. Libya's Colonel Muammar al-Qaddafi blamed British diplomacy for the fiasco. He used the seizure of the islands to nationalize British Petroleum (BP) assets in his country and to withdraw "close to $1 billion of Libyan deposits in British banks." Iran and Iraq exchanged insults and rushed troops into position to defend northern mountain passes and the rich oil lands to the south. While Queen Farah toured refugee camps, her husband traveled to a border town, where he proceeded to taunt Iraqi leaders. "We will not use our fist," he declared. "They are dying of envy at our progress and the things we have accomplished in Iran."

The fireworks in the Gulf brought to an end another year of triumph for Iran and its increasingly confident ruler. The Shah's latest high-wire showdown with the oil consortium, begun the previous November when he squeezed an additional 5 percent profit share out of its operations, had ended in February 1971 when under the terms of the Tehran Agreement foreign oil companies operating in the Persian Gulf agreed to raise the price of a barrel of oil by 35 cents to $2.15 and settled on a complex formula to stagger additional price increases over the next five years. Demand for Middle East petroleum was rising worldwide. The era of cheap oil was drawing to a close. During the negotiations Ambassador MacArthur had gone to the palace to appeal for restraint. What he got instead was an imperial rejoinder from the Shah: "Am I hearing the big voice of a superpower?" For the Shah, who oversaw the negotiations between the oil companies and their host states, the new oil deal marked a triumph and a turning point. As one foreign observer noted, "Finally Iran was able to rely on oil as a principal source of revenue. Between 1970 and 1972 production increased from an average of 3.82 million barrels per day to 5.02 million barrels per day and revenues from $1.12 billion to $2.39 billion." Iran swelled with national pride. The Shah boasted to Alam that the days when the Americans or anyone else could overthrow an Iranian leader were over. There would never be another 1953.

The Shah again took center stage when in October 1971 the royal family celebrated 2,500 years of Iranian monarchy in a lavish celebration at Persepolis. The Shah put great store in the ritual symbolism of state visits and the sort of grand pageantry that he hoped would further strengthen his standing with the Iranian people and identify the Pahlavi dynasty with its glorious predecessors. Millions of dollars and years of planning had gone into making this the coming out party of the century. As far as the Shah was concerned, Iran had now arrived on the world stage as a country of stature. To coincide with the public events the Iranian government built roads, tourist facilities, public health clinics, and 3,200 new schools. In cities around the world, exhibitions were held bringing Persian culture and music for the first time to a global audience. But there was sniping from the foreign media over the wisdom of building a Marie Antoinette–style tent village in Persepolis catered by Maxim's of Paris at a time when Tehran still had open sewers.

Ardeshir Zahedi had resigned as foreign minister over the summer after a bitter clash with Prime Minister Hoveyda. Now ensconced in his late father's villa in Switzerland, Zahedi wrote a strongly worded letter to the Shah protesting the extravagance and SAVAK's detention of hundreds of young people suspected of being leftist sympathizers. The Shah ignored Zahedi's criticism. If he betrayed any disappointment it was with Richard Nixon, who sent Vice President Spiro Agnew to represent the White House at the imperial gala. From the perspective of the Pahlavi court, Agnew was a nonentity, a "plebeian looking gentleman. Not well liked, with small eyes and the face of a not particularly intelligent sheep." Agnew in turn had not enjoyed the Carnival Cruise atmosphere and resented being relegated in the pecking order behind eight kings and queens, thirteen presidents, two sultans, Prince Rainier and Princess Grace of Monaco, and Emperor Haile Selassie and his pet chihuahua—so much so that he retired to his chandeliered tent in the desert to sulk and play chess with his Secret Service detail. He refused to acknowledge the nine American reporters traveling with him and snatched film from a photographer who tried to take his picture. To top it off, Agnew came down with a nasty case of what Iranians called "the Shah's revenge," prompting round-the-clock attention from camp nurses.

The White House failed to make the connection between the Shah's oil brinkmanship and Iran's worsening fiscal problems. During the first two years of the Nixon presidency Iran had "acquired nearly $750 million in American arms, roughly the amount it had received during the period 1955–1969." That was in addition to purchases from countries such as Great Britain, West Germany, and France. Defense expenditures were already acting as a drag on Iran's civilian economy. A pattern had emerged of overspending followed by a need to catch up. In March 1971 the CIA reported that at the end of 1970 Iran's holdings of gold and foreign exchange "had fallen to a six-year low (about $210 million), or less than two months' imports." The spy agency concluded that Iran's "rapid economic and military expansion has led to considerable deficit financing and balance-of-payments problems. The revenue increases generated by the February oil settlement afford Tehran an opportunity to push economic development further or to pay off burdensome short and long-term debt. It seems likely that the Shah will choose expansion and will spend to the limit of Iran's resources." Barely ten days after settling with the oil companies the Shah proposed a budget for FY 1971–72 "that not only will consume all the increased oil revenues but will also require substantial deficit financing. The new budget will include a $1.3 billion deficit, or one-fifth of the expenditures, which will be covered by drawdowns on foreign loans or about $800 million and domestic borrowing of approximately $500 million. Both forms of borrowing will exacerbate an already difficult financial situation." The CIA ended its analysis on a cautionary note: "By expanding its domestic borrowing, the government is using up credit normally available for private investment. Thus Iran will continue to walk a narrow financial tightrope." At the end of 1971, Iran's military absorbed more than 10 percent of GNP. Imported arms had caused $380 million in debt, "four-fifths to various western states, the rest to the USSR." The CIA reported that Iran would shortly "not have enough money to pay for the investment required by an ambitious development plan while servicing its foreign debt, and providing the consumer goods that make for political tranquility."

ARE YOU SURE THE BACK CHANNEL IS SAFE?

On December 2, 1971, three days after Iran seized the Gulf islands in a clear breach of international law, Secretary of State William Rogers reminded President Nixon that "the Shah of Iran is counting upon you to keep the commitment you made in 1969, and reaffirmed in 1971, to visit Iran during your present term in office." The Shah was a "proud and sensitive man" and likely to take grave offense if Tehran was not added to the White House travel itinerary in 1972. The Shah felt increasingly "apprehensive of Soviet Union long-range designs upon Iran and the Persian Gulf. He feels encircled by the Soviet penetration of the Middle East and the Indian subcontinent." Rogers warned the president that a meeting with the Shah was necessary to avert "serious trouble" with Tehran. His Imperial Majesty was feeling slighted.

A few hours later the Shah's neighbor and ally Pakistan launched an ill-advised attack against its old foe India. Relations between the two antagonists had been strained since Pakistan president Yahya Khan's merciless crackdown against opposition leaders in his country's far-flung eastern province, which clung to India's eastern frontier on the other side of the subcontinent. The Pakistani army had gone on a rampage in East Pakistan, slaughtering at least half a million people and triggering a mass exodus of 10 million refugees into India. Prime Minister Indira Gandhi made it clear that she would not stand idly by while her country was swamped by millions of refugees. Khan was a favorite of the Nixon White House and the president refused Gandhi's appeal to intervene. Pakistan, like Iran, was one of the so-called Northern Tier anti-Communist states that blocked the Soviet Union from the Mediterranean and Persian Gulf. Mrs. Gandhi had recently committed the ultimate sin in Nixon's eyes by concluding a treaty of friendship with the Soviets. He intended to bring "the bitch," as he called the prime minister, to heel. It was Nixon's belief that Mrs. Gandhi had deceived him when he hosted her at the White House only a few weeks before the war broke out. "I was treating her as a leader rather than a woman and all that," he complained to Kissinger. This was how she repaid him: "Dammit, you know she's smarter than she is." Nixon wanted to send her a strong message and "let the Russians know that they aren't going to screw around down there." Kissinger egged on the president, as he was wont to do, denigrating the people of India as "Russian stooges." To exact revenge on Mrs. Gandhi, Nixon and Kissinger decided to rouse their Persian gladiator from his lair.

On December 4, 1971, as fighting raged across the Indian subcontinent, Kissinger asked Iran's ambassador to Washington to relay an oral message from the president to the Shah, "Because we are sympathetic to anything you can do to give help [to Pakistan]." Under U.S. law the administration was constrained from sending military supplies to either side in the conflict. Nixon and Kissinger decided to skirt the law by asking the Shah to rush shipments of his own U.S.-made arms to Pakistan with the promise to reimburse and compensate Iran at a later date. Kissinger phoned Nixon at the White House residence to let him know that "another thing we have done is to send a back channel to the Shah from you saying that, trying to find out whether he wanted to give some support to Pakistan and saying if he did we would look to see whether we could find a way of letting, of replacing his . . ."

Nixon cut him off: "Are you sure the back channel is safe?"

"Yes."

"I wouldn't do it through MacArthur," cautioned Nixon, who wanted to prevent his own secretary of state from discovering their ploy. Besides which, Douglas MacArthur had earned a reputation as the house hysteric.

"No, no, that's why I didn't do it that way and we didn't put it as a message," Kissinger assured him. "We put it as talking points so it can be disallowed."

Nixon was delighted: "Good, well we'll have some fun with this yet. God, you know it would really be poetic justice here is if some way the Paks could really give the Indians a bloody nose for a couple of days."

Six days later, on Friday, December 10, a high-powered White House team consisting of Kissinger, Deputy National Security Adviser General Alexander Haig, U.S. ambassador to the United Nations George H. W. Bush, and Kissinger's aide Winston Lord met in New York City with China's ambassador to the United Nations. Washington and Beijing were coordinating their diplomatic efforts to isolate India and prevent the dismemberment of Pakistan. Communist China harbored long-standing grievances of its own against India and enjoyed warm relations with President Yahya Khan's military regime. They too wanted to give the Indians a bloody nose. Kissinger briefed Ambassador Huang Hua on the situation on the ground. The Pakistani army in West Pakistan had only two weeks of fuel left. "We think that the immediate objective must be to prevent an attack on the West Pakistan army by India. We are afraid that if nothing is done to stop it, East Pakistan will become a Bhutan and West Pakistan will become a Nepal. And India with Soviet help would be free to turn its energies elsewhere." The United States had informed Soviet leader Leonid Brezhnev that an Indian assault on West Pakistan "could lead to a U.S.-Soviet confrontation" because Pakistan is a "friendly country, toward which we have obligations." A U.S. naval flotilla including an aircraft carrier, six destroyers, a tanker, and a helicopter carrier was steaming toward the Bay of Bengal from the western Pacific to reinforce the presidential will.

Discussion moved on to the role the Shah and other regional allies could play in helping Khan stave off defeat. "This is terribly complex," Kissinger told Ambassador Huang. He explained that the United States was barred by law from supplying equipment to Pakistan, and also from permitting its friends to send their American arms and equipment to help the Pakistanis. The White House had quietly informed the leaders of Iran, Jordan, Saudi Arabia, and Turkey that "if they decide that their national security requires shipment of American arms to Pakistan, we are obliged to protest, but we will understand. We will not protest with great intensity. And we will make up to them in next year's budget whatever difficulties they have. . . . Ammunition and other equipment is going from Iran." Kissinger added, "This is very confidential obviously, and we are not eager for it to be known. At least not until Congress gets out of town tomorrow."

The effort to resupply Pakistan through Iran was not a success—India defeated Pakistan and the country's eastern provinces broke away to form the independent nation of Bangladesh. But the operation set the tone for future secret collaborations with Tehran. The idea took root in the White House that Iran could serve as an American aircraft carrier in Asia, a sort of giant regional arms dump and landing pad from which U.S. firepower could be quietly and quickly inserted and extracted at will. Asking the Shah to do favors for them meant that Nixon and Kissinger could bypass U.S. domestic law, avoid scrutiny from the media and the Congress, and avoid explaining their actions to the American public. It also meant that each time they asked the Shah to help them out of a tight spot, they owed him something in return. The danger was that if an operation of this sort ever came to light, it would likely prompt Congress to probe deeper into relations between the White House and Tehran. Kissinger had assured Nixon and no doubt the Shah that his back channel to Niavaran Palace was secure. Was he right?

That depended on whom you asked among the small army of intelligence and military officials listening in. Secretary of Defense Melvin Laird used his contacts at the CIA and the National Security Agency, an electronics eavesdropping facility, to monitor Kissinger's back-channel communications to foreign leaders. Laird also had the U.S. Army Signal Corps tap Kissinger's overseas phone calls. "Henry was very Machiavellian, but I knew how to beat him at his own game," Laird remembered with a dollop of pride. Laird was determined to defend his department's interests and not be shut out of the national security loop. "He worked his technique marvelously," recalled James Schlesinger, who succeeded him at Defense. "Not always scrupulously. But marvelously." The Joint Chiefs went one step further, planting a spy in Kissinger's office to keep tabs on him. For more than a year Navy Yeoman Charles Radford rifled Kissinger's briefcase, combed through burn bags and office files, and obtained transcripts of Kissinger's telephone conversations, which the national security adviser secretly recorded with the aid of dead keys installed on phones in his office. Radford handed his stash to his liaison, Admiral Robert Welander, who in turn made the documents available to Admiral Thomas Moorer, chairman of the Joint Chiefs. The Radford spy ring, exposed in the winter of 1971 but kept under wraps for many years, confirmed that foreign leaders who established back-channel communications with the Nixon White House did so at considerable risk. The danger always existed that other ears were listening in. By coincidence, young Radford was a social friend of Washington's most prominent Mormon personality, *Washington Post* columnist Jack Anderson, the most famous—and feared—muckraker in the country. He was also a man with visceral dislike of the Shah of Iran.

At New Year's 1972, Iran's prime minister, Amir Abbas Hoveyda, reminded Ambassador MacArthur—"with considerable feeling tinged with bitterness"—that the president had still not made good on his earlier promises to visit Tehran. The next day MacArthur accompanied Senator Stuart Symington to Niavaran Palace to talk with the king. When Symington cordially expressed the hope that the Shah would visit the United States soon, the monarch drew himself up and "replied stonily that he had visited us a great many times and he thought it was 'perhaps time for someone from over there to visit Iran.'" MacArthur fired off a panicky cable to Washington warning that although he was about to step down as ambassador, and so "will not have to try to pick up the pieces," U.S.-Iran relations hung in the balance.

MacArthur needn't have worried. Kissinger seconded the recommendation from Rogers that Nixon visit Iran in 1972. India had just snapped Pakistan in two like a twig: "While I had my doubts previously I now believe that with the momentous developments in South Asia and the potential in the Mid-East, a visit to Iran is a serious proposition."

TWENTY-FOUR HOURS IN TEHRAN

President and Mrs. Nixon deplaned from *The Spirit of '76* in brilliant sunshine at 4:04 P.M., local Tehran time, on Tuesday, May 30, 1972. A cool breeze rippled down from snowcapped mountains that hugged the metropolis like a wall of soft meringue. The Nixons were greeted at Mehrabad International Airport by the Shah and Shahbanou. During their fifteen-mile drive from the airport to Nixon's guest quarters at Saadabad Palace, the Shah and the president stood in the open roof of their automobile to "absorb and return the affection" of an estimated 250,000 people. Here were people who liked Americans. "Tens of thousands of ordinary citizens turned out to smile, wave and cheer," reported *The New York Times*. One correspondent wrote that it was without a doubt "the most jubilant overseas welcome Mr. Nixon has received since he toured Europe in 1970."

The turnout was deceptive. A great deal of planning had gone into making sure the streets were packed to create the appearance of spontaneity and enthusiasm. On his way to the airport Court Minister Alam noticed "that the streets were not nearly so well-lined with people as we'd planned. I'd apportioned school children to one part of the route but my orders had not been implemented; likewise the political and corporate representatives had been placed too far out of the city, along the road to the airport. I cannot describe my fury at this." Five thousand people were quickly bused inside the city limits to act as crowd fillers. Alam also noticed that during the welcome ceremony, the wind blew the cap off the head of the flag bearer, and he took this as a bad omen.

The Shah had asked his court minister to draw up an itinerary that called for a private meeting with Nixon. Now that he could raise oil prices at will, the Shah had the Twitchell Doctrine squarely in his sights. With the defeat of Pakistan six months earlier, all that remained of his neighbor to the east was a traumatized rump state scratching at Iran's back door for handouts of guns and butter. The real game changer, as far as Nixon and Kissinger were concerned, came on April 9, 1972, when Iraq followed Egypt and India in signing a treaty of friendship with the Soviet Union. The Shah had repeatedly warned them that Iran was being encircled by the Communists from all sides. Now the Soviets seemed on the verge of establishing a naval presence in the Persian Gulf. The Shah fretted that Nixon's policy of détente had emboldened the Soviets to probe south toward the warm waters of the Gulf. He wanted assurances from Nixon that the United States would not cut any side deals with the Soviets that compromised Iran's sovereignty.

The U.S. embassy in Tehran and the CIA had in the meantime begun tracking a sudden upsurge in terrorist activity in Iran. On February 8, 1971, a band of idealistic young anti-regime zealots attacked a gendarmerie post at Siakal near the Caspian Sea. If the brazen, amateurish nature of the assault suggested that in Iran long-suppressed discontents were beginning to stir, the regime's ham-handed response indicated that it was poorly equipped to wage a dirty war against its own people. The International Commission of Jurists later determined that two of the thirteen men convicted and executed for the Siakal incident "could not possibly have taken part in the attack as they were in prison at the time." The guerrillas stepped up their efforts to embarrass the Shah. General Ziaddin Farsiou, the chief of Iran's military courts and the man responsible for prosecuting the dissidents, was gunned down on his own doorstep. The Shah's nephew barely escaped an attempted kidnapping. In January 1972, bombers struck American landmarks in Tehran, including the U.S. embassy commissary where American nationals did their grocery shopping, the headquarters of the Peace Corps, and a cultural center. The next month one person was killed and five injured when bombs ripped through a pro-government political rally. The embassy reported that "criticism and dissatisfaction with the United States is growing, especially among students, and there are no indications this trend will be reversed in the near future." The CIA concurred: "The past year or so has seen a number of manifestations of discontent." There were "soft spots, real and potential in the Iranian situation." The universities were in turmoil. Guerrilla fighters had infiltrated Tehran and fought gun battles with the security forces. The Shah was isolated and there was "a regrettable lack of communication upward to him from his ministers. . . . Even foreign ambassadors cringe before the Shah's responses to official presentations which displease him."

Sycophancy at court stifled discussion and analysis. "The manner in which the Shah projects his royal will adds to the discontent, and more incidents are likely in the future." The Shah's tendency to overspend on weapons was bound to have political consequences: "Financial difficulties arising from overspending could hurt the development program which diverts much Iranian energy away from political affairs. . . . Iran's fundamental vulnerability lies in the unique concentration of power in the hands of the Shah." Ominously, the CIA warned that without the Shah at the helm the Pahlavi state might fall in on itself: "His demise will usher in change, perhaps involving tumult and chaos."

The West Wing was aware of the growing unrest. On the eve of their departure for Tehran, Kissinger had informed Nixon that the Shah's reforms were "producing increasing internal dislocations and pressures against a background of changes in the areas around Iran." He reminded the president that the Shah himself had "voiced concern" that Iran's "stability and progress are too exclusively dependent on [his] firm personal leadership and that institutions and leaders are not evolving that could make an orderly transition if he were to pass from the scene."

In advance of the summit the Shah presented the administration with a wish list of five big-ticket items. He wanted to buy 1) laser-guided bombs, 2) three squadrons of F-15 fighter planes and "a few F-14 with Phoenix missiles," 3) Maverick missiles to fit out his F-4 squadrons, 4) two additional squadrons of F-4Es and F-5Es, and he wanted to obtain the services of several hundred blue suiters, the uniformed American military personnel who maintained and operated U.S. weapons systems.

Understanding the flow of paperwork that followed the Iranian requests is key to comprehending the scope and scale of the disaster that ensued. The Defense Department recommended "in principle" to the sale of laser-guided bombs. But it advised holding off on the F-14s and F-15s. These sophisticated fighter aircraft had not even rolled off the assembly line. The Shah was once again getting ahead of himself. By the time the planes were produced under contract, conditions in the Middle East could well have changed to the point where a sale would be "counterproductive to US Government interests . . . we anticipate favorable action on the sale but the matter must be held in abeyance until the programs become more stable and predictable." Defense approved the future sale of Maverick missiles, which were still in the test phase, and additional squadrons of F-4Es and F-5Es. But the department cautioned that sending blue suiters should be handled on a case-by-case basis. The United States faced its own shortage of technicians and Secretary Laird was hesitant to station any more uniformed personnel in Iran.

In response, Kissinger drafted a memorandum that disregarded the advice he had received. We know that Nixon read it because his copy was stamped "THE PRESIDENT HAS SEEN . . ." Kissinger recommended that Nixon turn down the request for laser-guided bombs because "they represent our most advanced technology and are in heavy demand in Southeast Asia." Regarding the F-14/F-15 sale, "We anticipate selling them to Iran, but we want to be sure we have a good product before we commit ourselves." The United States would sell the Shah two additional squadrons each of F-4Es and F-5Es. But Kissinger made no mention of Maverick missiles or the Shah's request for several hundred American military blue suiters. The most charitable explanation for Kissinger's memo is that it was prepared in haste. He had forgotten his own golden rule when dealing with the Shah: "Precise and frank talk about how far the U.S. can and cannot go is important in avoiding later miscommunications."

Within ten minutes of their arrival at Saadabad Palace in the late afternoon of May 30, the president, the Shah, and Kissinger retreated for the first of two private two-hour discussions in which no other American or Iranian officials were present. Their first session involved an exchange of views on détente, the oil supply, and instability in West Asia. The Shah said he hoped Nixon would make American blue suiters available to help Iran's military become "self-reliant" and that the administration would supply him with "the most modern weapons" because "Iran, like Israel, must be able to stand alone." The leaders discussed Soviet support for Iraq and the potential for the region's large Kurdish population, which overlapped the borders of Iran, Iraq, and Turkey, to be used as pawns by the Iraqis to stir up trouble vis-à-vis Iran. The leaders agreed that a way had to be found to funnel more U.S. arms to Pakistan before their ally was "jumped" again by Mrs. Gandhi.

That evening, after the state banquet, Prime Minister Hoveyda took Kissinger out clubbing. At one point a Persian belly dancer sat in Kissinger's lap for several minutes. Iranian security officers failed to prevent photographers from recording the encounter. Kissinger laughed off the incident. Nadina Parsa was "a delightful girl" who is "very interested in foreign policy. I spent time explaining how you convert SS-7 missiles to Y-class submarines." Court Minister Alam was still at work in his office when he spotted Kissinger skulking back to his guesthouse at 3:00 A.M.

While Kissinger was out enjoying Tehran's nightlife, President Nixon and the Shah were having a quiet tête-à-tête back at the palace. The president's official daily schedule made no mention of their midnight rendezvous. But the Shah had instructed Alam to make time for him and Nixon to meet alone and his wishes were corroborated by a single sentence buried in Kissinger's preparatory memo to Nixon: "In connection with the schedule, it is worth noting that the Shah plans a substantive talk after his dinner with you." As usual, the Shah had done his homework. The state banquet didn't conclude until midnight. The president would be tired after a long day of travel. Drinks had been served at dinner. Nixon had a "fondness for martinis" and a famously low tolerance for alcohol. Nixon's close aide John Ehrlichman confirmed that "the only time [the president] drank a lot was in the evening with friends. . . . It didn't take a whole lot of gin to get him sloshed." The president's imbibing unsettled his staff and especially Kissinger. On the occasions when Nixon phoned Kissinger's office after hours, the national security adviser would give the signal for his horrified staff to pick up their phones and listen in while the president slurred "obscenities" down the line. Kissinger took to calling Nixon "my drunken friend," "that drunken lunatic" with "the meatball mind" who at any moment could "blow up the world." The Shah, on the other hand, rarely touched the stuff and maintained a reptilian focus. All the ingredients were in place for another serious miscommunication or presidential lapse in judgment on par with the Shah's 1969 White House visit.

The presidential party was still hungover from the night before when the first bombs went off, striking a Pepsi-Cola plant, the British cultural center, the offices of an Italian oil company, and, at 5:45 A.M., the offices of the United States Information Service in Tehran. They blew out windows but caused no injuries. A much louder boom was heard at 6:30, shattering the dawn calm and attracting the attention of Alam, who was already back at his desk in the palace. Suspecting a bomb, the court minister telephoned General Ja'farqoli Sadri, the chief of national police, for an explanation. Sadri told him: "Oh, it's nothing very serious, a car's brakes failed descending the hill. It hit a lamp-post and the petrol tank went up in flames, so what?" In fact, explosives had blown up a car being driven by United States Air Force Brigadier General Harold Prince. Prince escaped with lacerations and two broken legs, but a mother and child walking beside the vehicle were killed. Yet another big blast two hours later signaled that a major terrorist offensive was underway in the capital. Barely forty-five minutes before President Nixon was due to lay a wreath at 9:30 at the sandstone and marble tomb of the Shah's father, Reza Shah, and while American television camera crews were already moving into position to record the event, a loud roar shook the area behind them, bringing down a wall in a cloud of dust and brick. A faulty timer had prevented a major disaster.

The tomb was a potent symbol of the Pahlavi dynasty's modernist and anticlerical credentials. Reza Shah, the late father of Mohammad Reza Shah, had seized power in 1921 as the illiterate, ambitious, and strong-willed Reza Khan, the head of Persia's Russian-trained Cossack Brigade. In 1926 he was crowned Shah and adopted "Pahlavi" as his dynastic name. Reza Shah epitomized the 1920s ideal of the strongman on horseback determined to restore his country's national pride. Over the next two decades he instituted a series of draconian reforms that alternately exhilarated, traumatized, and disoriented Iranian society. His use of the whip hand was in keeping with the style of Peter the Great, the Russian czar who frog-marched his people out of the bogs of Slavdom in the 1700s. Persia was renamed Iran. The Arabic lunar calendar was scrapped and replaced with the Persian solar calendar. Women were liberated from the veil and all Iranians were ordered to wear Western dress. Iran's Shi'a clerics were stripped of their role in public life and children's education. The army was called out to pacify Iran's tribal lands. A national taxation system was established, a modern judiciary founded, and state finances overhauled. Reza Shah personally oversaw construction of the Trans-Iranian Railway, which united the country. Light industry was developed, factories built, and a network of irrigation channels dug. But the old shah went out as he came in, at the hands of Iran's colonial overlords Great Britain and Russia. After the war, his son, Mohammad Reza Shah, brought his father's body back from exile in South Africa and reburied him in the mausoleum that bore his name. The tomb remained a bitter reminder of Pahlavi power over the ayatollahs.

The president was already in his car ready to drive to the mausoleum when news of the blast reached Saadabad Palace. The Secret Service activated its emergency procedures and ordered Nixon to stay in the vehicle until they had a clearer sense of what was going on. Alam lambasted the incompetence of SAVAK, which enjoys "every advantage, yet they couldn't so much as guard a sack of potatoes let alone a national monument." He was further incensed to learn that First Lady Pat Nixon's motorcade had sped off in the opposite direction to the wrong engagement, leaving the queen cooling her heels at Niavaran Palace. The two first ladies had been scheduled to leave together to visit a children's library and crèche. Alam urged the Shah not to let terrorists disrupt the president's schedule lest the regime be embarrassed before the eyes of the world. He dashed to Saadabad Palace to find Nixon still sitting in his car after an hour. He could see that Nixon was nervous and hastened to reassure him that he was in no danger. Nixon agreed and the motorcade sped off.

The president's car left the palace surrounded by two dozen jeeps loaded with soldiers and a special motorcycle guard. The wreath laying went off peacefully. White House press secretary Ron Ziegler denied that "any of the reported incidents today were aimed at the well-being of the President or any members of his party." He was immediately contradicted by the State Department back in Washington. Spokesman John King admitted that the bombings were the latest in a "series of attacks in Iran over the last 18 months," and he repudiated Ziegler's denial of anti-American sentiment in Iran: "I'm going to withdraw the statement that there is no connection [with the United States]. Pretend that it never took place."

Back at the palace the leaders held a final round of talks that lasted from 10:30 A.M. to noon. Nixon was wound up. What had been billed as a sentimental trip for the Nixons, who first visited Iran in 1953, and a triumph for the Pahlavis, who saw the presidential visit as the American equivalent of a papal blessing, was ending in confusion and bloodshed. To make matters worse, news came through of a brutal attack carried out a few hours earlier by the pro-Palestinian Japanese Red Army against tourists disembarking at Lod Airport in Israel. The Lod terminus resembled a slaughterhouse with more than one hundred casualties, including seventeen massacred Puerto Rican pilgrims. Kissinger's meeting notes show that the Shah began the conversation "with a discussion of terrorism and the pressures on him from the left wing." Iraq's Soviet-backed regime was mostly behind the trouble, he insisted. The issue of Saudi Arabia's future came up. The Saud dynasty "was backward; there was no inclination to reform." The Shah said he was convinced "the Saudis would not be spared by the Egyptians once the Israeli problem was settled. They had a superiority problem but they were lousy fighters." Turning to the Middle East peace process, "Israel, the shah affirmed, was Iran's natural ally." Nixon was sympathetic and anxious to reassure the Shah that America would stand by him. According to Kissinger's notes, as the meeting drew to a close Nixon grandly announced that he had decided to "furnish Iran with laser bombs and F-14s and F-15s." Nixon appealed to the Shah to understand American policy. "Protect me," he said. "Don't look at detente as something that weakens you but as a way for the United States to gain influence." The Nixon Doctrine "was a way for the US to build a new long-term policy on support of allies."

Richard Nixon's sour mood hung over the final event of the trip, an intimate luncheon for twenty-one American and Iranian dignitaries hosted by the president and his wife in their guest quarters at Saadabad Palace. The terrorist attacks apparently triggered bad memories for Nixon of his old struggles against the left. To his guests at the luncheon, the president denounced American antiwar student protesters back home, saying they were working against the national interest and that "he'd like to see the culprits executed." Mrs. Nixon wondered why terrible events like the Lod massacre never seemed to happen in Communist countries. Court Minister Asadollah Alam assured her that freedom carried with it risks and that only under Communism would culprits be put to death without a trial. Alam's logic ran a fine line. Only a week earlier five young Iranians accused of subversive activities had been summarily executed after being convicted by a kangaroo court run by a secret military tribunal. Iran's dreaded secret police, SAVAK, censored all newspaper, magazine, radio, and television content; screened applicants for government jobs; approved the issuance of passports; engaged in espionage and counterespionage activities at home and abroad; and used systematic torture to extract false confessions from detainees.

Nixon stood to make his final remarks of the trip. According to Alam, Nixon declared that "the Kremlin may be a palace but an eight-day stay there was absolute purgatory. Only now, in the Shah's private residence, could he learn to breathe freely again. Indeed he considered it to be very much a home from home." The president found Iran to be very much to his taste. Watching the spectacle from his seat next to the first lady, Alam recalled his surprise at hearing a foreign head of state speak so bluntly. The Shah then rose to express similarly warm sentiments.

The Nixons and Pahlavis left for the airport by convoy. As their stately procession passed the halls of Tehran University, students ran out and hurled rocks from an embankment overlooking the highway. The lead vehicles, including the Nixons', sped off. But others, including Alam, weren't so lucky and their vehicles were pelted with debris. There was to be no dignified exit from Iran for Richard Nixon. *The Spirit of '76* lifted off from Tehran's Mehrabad Airport at 2:06 P.M. on Wednesday, May 31, bound for Warsaw. The American delegation didn't leave empty-handed. The Shah had instructed Court Minister Alam to "ensure that Nixon and his entourage, especially Kissinger, are presented with gifts truly worthy of the occasion." The next day, Alam found the Shah in a cheerful mood: President Nixon "seems to have agreed to every request that was put to him," wrote Alam in his diary. This was not an exaggeration: according to a Defense Dept. document at some point during the trip President Nixon "agreed to sell U.S. nuclear power plants and fuels to Iran."

ALL WEAPONS SHORT OF THE ATOMIC BOMB

Four days later, on June 5, 1972, Major General Ellis Williamson, Hamilton Twitchell's successor as the head of the American military mission in Iran, was summoned to Niavaran Palace. He found the Shah in an ebullient mood. It was from a foreign head of state, and not from his own government, that General Williamson learned the sensational news: "Iran will get all available sophisticated weapons short of the atomic bomb." Williamson was also told that the Shah had been promised enough blue suiters for "Iran to advance its armed forces as rapidly as possible." In his talks with the Shah, Nixon had secretly agreed to match the level of American military technicians in Iran with the number of Soviet technicians helping out the Egyptians—which meant the Shah expected the Pentagon to supply Iran with as many as twenty thousand personnel! Nixon's visit had given the Shah "complete satisfaction" and provided "a great psychological boost to this part of the world." Relations between Iran and the United States "were the best they have ever been."

The next shock for General Williamson came when the Iranian air force presented him with plans that called for U.S. military personnel to occupy "operational positions in Iranian units." The U.S. embassy in Tehran asked the White House to clarify its position. Had the president promised the

Shah that American GIs would "operate some combat elements of the Iranian forces"? It assumed there had been a misunderstanding. The Iranian plans were outlandish. The congressional implications were obvious and so too was the risk that the United States would be drawn into a regional conflict. The whole idea violated the spirit of the Nixon Doctrine. America's new ambassador to Iran, Joseph Farland, asked Kissinger for guidance on the matter. He and Kissinger were well acquainted. As ambassador to Pakistan, Farland had helped facilitate Kissinger's secret diplomatic initiatives to Communist China. Farland was a former agent in the Federal Bureau of Investigation and had worked closely with the CIA and Richard Helms during previous assignments abroad. Kissinger's reply hinted at the enormity of the deals cooked up by Nixon and the Shah. He conceded to Farland that "this is one of those cases where the commitment made was a broad one without specific reference to the kind of details we must now address." Yet while it was the case that United States military personnel would not take on operational roles with the Iranian armed forces, "it was very important that this not be handled in such a way as to dissipate the advantage gained from the President's very forthcoming response."

It was in this confused atmosphere that Kissinger on June 15, 1972, informed the secretaries of State and Defense that Nixon "was willing in principle" to sell F-14 and F-15 aircraft and laser-guided bombs to Iran, and that the administration was assigning "an increased number of uniformed military technicians from the US services." Kissinger neglected to mention the commitment to peg the level of American blue suiters in Iran with the number of Soviet technicians in Egypt. Still, the memo landed on Defense Secretary Laird's desk like a round of shrapnel. "WOW!" someone scrawled in the margin.

Events were moving rapidly on another front too. In early July, Nixon sent John Connally, the former governor of Texas and his preferred successor in the White House, to meet privately with the Shah in Tehran. Connally was also playing a crucial role in helping to manage and raise money for Nixon's reelection campaign. He told the Shah that the president had instructed the CIA to start funneling weapons to Kurdish guerrillas fighting the government of Iraq. The president was fulfilling one of the secret deals the two leaders had cut in Tehran six weeks earlier. The Kurdish mission was regarded as so sensitive that members of the 40 Committee, the administration's high-level panel of experts who authorized covert operations, were presented with a single piece of paper that contained a one-paragraph description of the venture, which they were asked to initial. Their opinions were not solicited. The Shah had lobbied Nixon for several years to arm the Kurds. Ambassador MacArthur and the CIA had previously expressed reservations about the wisdom of "encouraging separatist aspirations" in Iraq. Such an adventure, they cautioned, might provoke the Soviets to meddle in the region. "Furthermore, the road is open-ended and if we begin and then decide to withdraw there might be misinterpretations of our reasons which could adversely affect our relations with [our ally]." When a senior CIA official—most likely Director Helms—was asked by the 40 Committee why the agency's "negative views were not presented more forcefully," he replied that "the Committee must realize that CIA was told to prepare a paper on 'how' the project could be done, not 'whether' the project could be done."

From Tehran on July 12, Farland back-channeled Kissinger to complain that General Williamson "has hesitated to push US armament sales since there is definitely a point of view in certain echelons USG [United States Government] to effect that we should do that which is possible to prevent Iran, in our studied wisdom, from over-buying." In Farland's opinion, "as long as Iran can financially afford guns and butter there is no reason for us to lose the market, particularly when viewed over the red ink on our balance of payments ledger." The Shah's recent decision to order from Great Britain eight hundred tanks at a cost of $250 million was the result of Williamson's reckless caution. Farland asked that Williamson be "counseled accordingly."

The Shah also kept up the pressure on the White House. He wanted to know when Nixon would follow through on his private commitment to lift restrictions on all U.S. arms sales to Iran. "And what about Kissinger?" the Shah reminded Alam. "He told [Prime Minister Hoveyda] that Nixon would have given me every weapon in America if only I'd asked for it."

The National Security Council official who dealt with Iran was Harold Saunders. He proposed a straightforward solution to the squabble between Farland and Williamson. The administration, advised Saunders, "should leave decisions on what to buy to the Government of Iran and confine ourselves to assuring that the Iranian Government has good technical advice from our people on the capabilities of the equipment involved." Saunders had transferred to the NSC from the CIA in the early 1960s. He had accompanied Kissinger to Tehran and was sensitive to the linkages between economic development and arms purchases. "The decision to let the Shah buy what the Shah wanted or the decision not to have the [economic] review, all of that was virtually four years behind, three years behind us in any case," he later recalled. "I see the so-called 'Blank Check Talk' as simply a ratification of a posture that had long since crystalized." There was truth in this. The speed with which Kissinger took Saunders's recommendation and adopted it as broad-stroke administration policy suggests that he too saw unrestricted arms sales to Iran as the logical next step and not as a radical departure from existing policy. It certainly reflected Nixon's feelings on the matter. But Kissinger went a step further when he instructed Farland in a July 15 cable "to encourage purchase of U.S. equipment." He was placing his own diplomats in the role of peddling weapons.

The floodgates had opened. Two days later, Ambassador Farland met with Court Minister Alam and approved the sale of weapons and items the Shah had previously requested, including new Lockheed 10-12s, F-15s, and F-111s. The last two types of aircraft were still in the design stages. The White House also agreed to let Iran's national airline begin flights to Los Angeles, the home of many Iranian expatriates and critics of the Pahlavi regime.

Nixon's policy on arms sales to Iran was formally enshrined on July 25, 1972, when Kissinger sent a crisply worded presidential directive to secretaries Laird and Rogers, confirming the sale of F-14 and F-15 aircraft, laser-guided bombs, and sending blue suiters to Iran. To ram home his point, Kissinger told both secretaries that from now on, "in general, decisions on the acquisition of military equipment should be left primarily to the government of Iran," and that it was now up to the Shah and not them to decide whether or not he wanted to buy "certain equipment." Kissinger left them an inch of wiggle room when he inserted the words "in general" and "primarily" in his original directive. But there was no doubt in anyone's mind about what had just happened: the Twitchell Doctrine had been euthanized. The White House directive "pretty much gives us carte blanche to whistle up business with defense contractors," exulted a State Department official. Another diplomat left a copy of the edict in his office safe in a front drawer so he could refer to it and use it as a policy guide.

Iran's economic indicators were no longer factors to be taken into account by the United States when selling arms to Iran. The Shah knew what was best for his country's national interest and the administration would get out of the way. The air of unreality surrounding administration policy was confirmed that same month when Egypt's president Anwar al-Sadat publicly expelled all twenty thousand Soviet technicians from Egypt and ripped up the Moscow-Cairo friendship treaty. Sadat's bold move should have nullified the logic behind the Shah's insistence that levels of American personnel in Iran be pegged to those of the Soviets in Egypt. But they poured in regardless.

WE MUST WAIT FOR NIXON TO MAKE THE NEXT MOVE

The last week of July 1972 was one of frenetic deal making—and considerable intrigue—in Washington and Tehran. On Wednesday, July 26, the same day Embassy Tehran learned of the Shah's blank check to buy arms, White House aide John Ehrlichman was reassuring the president's personal lawyer, Herbert Kalmbach, of the legality of raising hush money. Five weeks earlier, in the early morning hours of June 17, five men had been arrested for breaking into the offices of the Democratic National Committee in the Watergate complex in Washington. Police discovered that the men, who had been trying to wiretap the offices of the DNC, were affiliated with President Nixon's reelection campaign. While they hunted for clues to the motives of the burglars, Nixon and his aides were engaged in an effort to shut down the investigation lest it reveal their complicity in this and other acts of political espionage and corruption. Ehrlichman told Kalmbach that hundreds of thousands of dollars was urgently needed to pay the defendants' legal fees and "other expenses." He warned that if the press learned about the solicitations and suitcases full of cash, "They'd have our heads in their laps."

On Thursday, July 27, Court Minister Asadollah Alam was in Birjand Province with Ambassador Joseph Farland on the second day of a three-day tour of military facilities. During a six-hour aerial inspection, the subject of the upcoming American presidential election arose. He recorded in his diary what happened next: "Turning to the practicalities of the election, the ambassador put a request to me that even fifty years from now I could never divulge for fear it would irreparably damage relations between our two countries. While I dare not set down his request in black and white, I can say that it demonstrates the extent to which Nixon is willing to rely on His Imperial Majesty." Alam promised to relay Nixon's request to the Shah.

Back in Washington on Friday, July 28—and while Alam and Farland were still in Birjand—Governor Nelson Rockefeller of New York placed a telephone call to Kissinger at 2:58 P.M. Rockefeller and Kissinger enjoyed a particularly close relationship. "Rocky" as he was popularly known, was the most high-profile of the heirs to the Rockefeller Standard Oil fortune and a perennial candidate for the presidency. He enjoyed warm relations with the Pahlavi family and regarded Kissinger as his personal protégé, someone he could call on to get things done.

Rockefeller explained to Kissinger that an important local defense contractor, Grumman Corporation, would go bankrupt unless it won a big new contract to manufacture the proposed new F-14 jet fighter, a long-range aircraft suitable for use on aircraft carriers. Long Island–based Grumman had just lost the contract to build the space shuttle. Without an injection of new cash it might not survive. Rockefeller knew that the Shah had expressed an interest in purchasing "some F-14s" from the United States but that he was mainly interested in purchasing three squadrons of F-15s. The Shah didn't have any aircraft carriers, so the F-14 made no logical sense as a priority purchase for the Iranian imperial air force, but no matter. Rockefeller wanted Kissinger to ask the Shah to order enough F-14s to make the aircraft commercially viable for mass production. Then he wanted the Shah to select Grumman as Iran's contractor of choice. Rockefeller was essentially asking the national security adviser to rig a defense contract. He explained that Defense Secretary Laird wanted to kill the plane but Admiral Elmo Zumwalt of the Joint Chiefs was in favor of the F-14 and was working slyly behind Laird's back to get it. The Shah's intervention could be crucial to swinging the fight Zumwalt's way.

Rockefeller also explained that saving Grumman was essential to carrying New York state for the Nixon-Agnew ticket in November and propping up his state's faltering economy: "Well Henry this could save both politically and financially our whole Long Island–New York area and it would be . . . save the, the company." When Kissinger replied that he too favored the deal, Rockefeller was ebullient: "Oh God, if this comes through now it would be the hottest, greatest thing and would save the company from bankruptcy and also save the F-14 which otherwise I'm afraid can be lost."

The next day was Saturday, July 29. At 1:45 P.M. Kissinger phoned Rockefeller to give him the good news: "I've looked into that situation and we have told Defense that they should go ahead and talk to the Iranians, of course it depends on the Iranians whether they want to buy it, but we have taken away the road block." Kissinger was being disingenuous. The notion that the Shah might not be receptive to an offer to buy more F-14s—even if he didn't need them—was absurd. It was like offering a nightcap to an alcoholic. Kissinger and Rockefeller were playing to the Shah's worst instincts and most self-destructive impulses, endangering the Iranian economy to further Rockefeller's political ends. "[The Shah] had no control over his own appetites for modern technology," former Secretary of Defense James Schlesinger later ruefully observed. "He had no capacity to resist those sales."

Kissinger told Rockefeller that he would "back-channel our ambassador," which meant asking Joseph Farland to have a quiet word on the side with Alam. As the Shah's most trusted aide at court, Alam was the Shah's preferred intermediary with American ambassadors. It was most convenient that Farland was with Alam in Birjand at that very moment.

Also on July 29, Alam flew to Nowshar to brief the Shah. The entry in his diary records that he made the trip to relay Nixon's response and that the Shah, when he heard it, gave his approval on the spot. The back channels continued until at least August 14. Then the trail goes cold.

What are we to make of the summer's tumble of events? Farland and Alam discussed Nixon's election campaign in the same seventy-two-hour period that Kissinger back-channeled Tehran offering the F-14 contract—a deal that as Rockefeller noted had important political overtones. Rockefeller had told Kissinger that an order from Tehran to buy $500 million worth of aircraft would save the nation's fifth largest defense contractor from bankruptcy, help the economy of Long Island, a Republican bastion, and bolster the Republican effort to carry New York in the November election. Grumman had also been approached in 1972 by the Nixon campaign to cough up a million dollars to help the president win reelection. Based on the evidence at hand, the most plausible explanation for Alam's mysterious diary entries relates to the joint effort to fix the F-14 contract to everyone's advantage. It is more than likely that either Kissinger or Farland hyped the deal's political significance, perhaps implying that without it the president's reelection effort could be in jeopardy when, in fact, Nixon was virtually guaranteed a landslide win over his Democratic opponent. His Imperial Majesty eventually placed orders for eighty F-14 fighters from Grumman totaling $2 billion. It should be remembered that Iran's oil revenues for the fiscal year 1972–73 came to $2.8 billion. The strain the orders placed on Iran's economy was incalculable.

Yet one cannot ignore the possibility that Farland approached Alam to ask a favor of a different sort, perhaps in addition to the F-14 deal. For years rumors have swirled that the Shah's oil money was in some way implicated in the Watergate affair and Nixon's 1972 presidential election campaign. While Farland and Alam were on their trip to Birjand, Ehrlichman and Herbert Kalmbach were talking about the need to quickly come up with hush money to keep the Watergate defendants quiet. The Watergate break-in had been financed by money rerouted from a secret $10 million Nixon presidential campaign fund and laundered through a bank in Mexico City. The money trail south of the border was dubbed Nixon's "Mexican laundry." Bank records for Watergate burglar Bernard Barker, a former employee of the CIA and a lead planner in the botched 1961 Bay of Pigs invasion of Cuba, contained four cashier's checks worth $89,000 drawn from the Banco Internacional in Mexico City. Within days of the Watergate break-in the White House aggressively moved to shut down the FBI investigation of the Mexican money trail. White House aides H. R. "Bob" Haldeman and Ehrlichman called CIA director Helms to the White House and told him that it was the president's "wish" that the CIA stop the FBI's spadework in Mexico City, but didn't say why. They wanted Helms to lie and concoct a cover story suggesting that the bureau's probe would endanger one of his agency's undercover operations.

Columnist Jack Anderson was close to Watergate burglar Frank Sturgis, even to the point of vouching for him in court when the self-proclaimed "soldier of fortune" was arrested and arraigned following the break-in. In the months that followed, Anderson began receiving tip-offs that Iranian money was somehow connected to Nixon's Mexican slush fund. Two disgruntled former high-ranking Iranian government officials told Anderson that "the Shah had routed hundreds of thousands of dollars to the Nixon campaign." He started digging. Swiss banking sources confirmed to Anderson that "the Shah had transferred more than $1 million from his personal, numbered accounts in the Schweizerische Bank Gesellschaft to the Banco de Longres y Mexico in Mexico City." This made sense because it was known that the Nixon campaign discouraged donations of less than a million dollars. Senate investigators probed too, but the Iranian angle was never a priority for them and, like Anderson, despite their best efforts they were not able to come up with a document implicating the Shah in Nixon's dirty pool. But suspicions lingered that the full truth about the Shah's possible involvement in Watergate had yet to emerge. "It's all very mysterious," one investigator told Anderson.

Later, in 1974, Anderson gleefully recalled that he and United Features, the wire service that syndicated his column, came under intense pressure from Iranian diplomats and from William Rogers, Nixon's former secretary of state, whose law firm now represented the Shah, to back off the story entirely. "Our inquiries, including overseas calls to Teheran, Geneva, Bonn, Mexico City and other faraway places, have got the Iranians in a dither," wrote Anderson. "Suddenly, we found Iranian officials were expecting our calls before we made them." Anderson enjoyed such adventures. At one point in 1972 CIA director Helms assigned sixteen of his men to spy on the journalist and his team of investigative reporters, even inviting Anderson to lunch to ask him to back off one particular line of inquiry. The CIA's surveillance operation, Operation Mudhen, ended only when Anderson turned the tables on the agents and dispatched his nine young children armed with cameras to snap their pictures.

Iran's foreign minister in 1972 was Abbas Ali Khalatbary, its ambassador to Washington Amir Aslan Afshar. Neither man was part of the Shah's inner circle. Ardeshir Zahedi was insistent that the Shah's money never influenced an American presidential election while he served as either ambassador or foreign minister. Yet Zahedi's absence from the political scene in 1972 coincided with the most intense deal making between Nixon and the Shah. If payments were made, Zahedi would likely have been kept in the dark. Alam's diary records that he and Ambassador Farland served as the back channel on matters related to Nixon's reelection. When Anderson's allegations surfaced two years later, Zahedi was back in Washington for his second term as Iranian ambassador. He asked Rogers to sue the columnist but dropped the matter when Rogers replied that the Shah would have to appear as a witness for the prosecution. Anderson mistakenly believed that the irate phone calls from Iranian embassy officials and from Rogers's office at the time were evidence of the Shah's guilt; in fact, the calls were the result of Zahedi's effort to clear his name.

We will most likely never know the truth of the matter. In any event, there was no question about motive. The Watergate break-in showed that when it came to politicking, Richard Nixon had no scruples. "The President's preoccupation with the election frightens me," chairman of the Federal Reserve Arthur Burns wrote in his journal. "Is there anything that he would not do to further his reelection? I am losing faith in him, and my heart is sick and sad." If Nixon did need to hustle up some fast cash in the last week of July 1972, no questions asked, he had the perfect money mule in Ambassador Farland. Farland had already proven his value and discretion by handling Nixon and Kissinger's sensitive back-channel communications during the opening to China. Farland's record in Tehran highlighted the extent to which he dealt directly with Kissinger, the man to whom he owed his prestigious appointment. A telephone transcript from February 1972 records Kissinger's sense of obligation: "We have to find Farland something. He helped us on China and had a rough time of it and we promised to get him out of there." Farland was the perfect appointee to Tehran during an election year. Years later a former colleague approached him and asked him what he had discussed with Asadollah Alam during their trip to Birjand. He teasingly replied, "My lips are sealed."

NOW IS TIME TO CASH IN CREDIT

Nixon and Kissinger were confident that they had built up substantial credit with their partner in Tehran. They had given the Shah the go-ahead to raise oil prices. They had lifted restrictions on arms sales and agreed to provide the Shah with his wish list of laser-guided bombs, missiles, fighter jets, airliners, blue suiters, and CIA support for the insurgency in Iraq. The F-14 contract was his for the taking. They had even thrown in the lucrative commuter air corridor servicing Tehran with Los Angeles, where many Iranian expatriates and exiles lived. Yet Nixon and Kissinger had again underestimated the Shah.

On October 20, 1972, seventeen days before the presidential election, Nixon and Kissinger decided to cash in their chips. Ambassador Farland received a notice from the White House via the State Department instructing him to seek an immediate audience with the Shah. He was told to "indicate you are [acting] on instructions from President." The cable explained that President Nixon wanted the Shah's help on a matter of the "highest urgency" involving Kissinger's secret diplomatic effort to bring the war in Vietnam to an end before Election Day. A day earlier Kissinger had presented America's ally in the war, President Nguyen Van Thieu of South Vietnam, with a fait accompli. Kissinger had secretly negotiated a peace settlement with North Vietnam behind Thieu's back. It called for Communist guerrillas to remain in the South after U.S. troops had gone home. "I wanted to punch Kissinger in the mouth," Thieu recalled of the moment when the terms of the deal were explained to him. Kissinger had just wheeled the equivalent of the Trojan Horse into downtown Saigon. When Kissinger's own staff raised doubts about the morality of the deal, he bellowed at them, "You don't understand. I want to meet their terms. I want to end this war before the election. It can be done, and it will be done."

To make the terms of the settlement more palatable to President Thieu, the White House hurriedly launched a worldwide undercover operation to airlift $2 billion worth of military supplies to bolster South Vietnam's defenses before a peace treaty freezing troop and armament levels took effect. The Shah was quietly approached to participate in Operation Enhance Plus with the promise that his donated equipment would be replaced with more advanced weaponry and machinery. The Shah's role in the enterprise was deemed critical. Kissinger's back channel called on the king to relinquish his "entire Iranian air force (90 aircraft) of F-5As." It was an extraordinary request. The aircraft were to be immediately disassembled and delivered to South Vietnam. Kissinger said he recognized the "unprecedented nature [of] this request, which is done only for reasons of unparalleled importance." He insisted that he needed an answer from the palace within twenty-four hours. To Ambassador Farland, the White House dispensed with the usual diplomatic language and bluntly couched its request in terms that left no possible room for misinterpretation: "Now is time to cash in credit we have built up with Iranians. We cannot guarantee that Vietnam settlement will be assured by this move, but without it prospects for peace are substantially dimmer."

The Shah, sensing that he had the upper hand, decided to play hardball. He insisted that he too wanted to help bring about peace in Southeast Asia. But he was prepared to turn over to Nixon only two squadrons of F-5A aircraft, a total of thirty-two planes. He explained to Farland that taking too many jet fighters out of service would constrain the Iranian air force's new training program. As compensation he demanded "accelerated delivery of military equipment" such as new F-5A and F-4A aircraft, the "rapid approval and assignment" of technicians to Iran, and a commitment by the United States to increase the number of training slots open to Iranian pilots.

According to Kissinger's biographer Walter Isaacson, who interviewed the former president, Nixon preferred to keep the peace process on the back burner until the election was out of the way. But Operation Enhance Plus was in full swing and Kissinger kept pushing things along. On October 25, to Nixon's surprise and fury, Kissinger leaked to a *New York Times* reporter the news that he had negotiated the terms of a cease-fire in Southeast Asia. The next day Kissinger stood before a bank of television cameras and dramatically declared: "We believe that peace is at hand. We believe that an agreement is in sight." News of the peace deal electrified the country, rallied the stock market, and sent Nixon's poll numbers soaring. The American electorate reacted as though a deal had finally been reached when in fact it had not. President Thieu, weeping in his palace, continued to hold out for a better deal and squeezed Washington for more concessions.

On October 30, just a week before the election, Farland was told to go back to the palace to ask for an additional sixteen aircraft. The ambassador's meeting with the Shah took place at 3:00 P.M. the next day. The Shah repeated his initial concerns about disrupting his air force training program and then added that handing over more planes would compromise the defense of Iranian airspace and leave the country vulnerable to an Iraqi preemptive strike. Farland took this as a hint that he needed to sweeten the pot. When he exited the Shah's study he left behind a piece of paper listing the goodies the U.S. was prepared to deliver, including a promise that "Iran's military support needs will be given most expeditious handling." The ambassador cabled Washington that "we will have to offer [the Shah] something more attractive" to win his cooperation.... Believe we should make every effort to reciprocate Shah's generous offer with equally generous credit for transferring aircraft and special measure to deliver replacement aircraft as early as possible."

Three dozen aircraft had already been shipped to Saigon, and the delivery of the final shipment of F-5As from Iran was still being negotiated in the first week of November when the Defense Department inadvertently went public and disclosed details of Operation Enhance Plus. The Shah was incensed—or so said Ambassador Farland in a dispatch to the State Department. No doubt the Shah was furious that his confidence had been violated. But it was also true that Court Minister Alam never missed an opportunity to put the wind up the ambassador's back. He and the Shah used the leak as an opportunity to extract even more concessions from Nixon. But Farland was convinced of the Shah's distress and fired off an emotional cable declaring that the "atmosphere and spirit of goodwill and cooperation generated by [the] Shah's forthcoming response to our request" had been "badly shattered." The Shah's confidence had been violated by this "incredible goof."

Kissinger's peace ploy helped catapult Nixon to his smashing reelection victory on November 7, 1972. In the meantime, South Vietnam suddenly acquired the world's fourth largest air force. With the election out of the way, Under Secretary of State Alexis Johnson gave his ambassador in Tehran the back of his hand. He dismissed as bogus the Shah's argument that taking sixteen additional planes out of service would have compromised Iran's air defenses against Iraq: the Pentagon had already studied the matter before placing the request. Johnson pointedly reminded his ambassador that Iraq was hardly likely to attack Iran when its own Kurdish minority was in open rebellion thanks to the CIA. Other factors constraining a possible Iraqi attack included infighting between Iraqi strongman Saddam Hussein and his rivals, financial problems brought on by falling oil revenues, and a dispute between Iraq and Syria. Johnson assured Farland that the United States would appease the Shah by speeding up the delivery of new F-5Es and F-4Es and providing more training slots for Iranian pilots. In addition, the ambassador was given permission to tell the Shah that the administration would sell Maverick missiles to Iran in the spring of 1974 even though it adversely impacted the U.S. Air Force and NATO. The Shah would also be given discounts on "several sales previously consummated" to the amount of $16,564,000.

Ambassador Farland let the Shah know that after Nixon was sworn to a second term, he would "do everything that we require," although he would have to be careful not to antagonize the Senate Foreign Relations Committee, whose chairman, Senator J. William Fulbright, had taken a keen interest in energy policy and Middle East affairs.

Chapter Three

MARITAL VOWS

"We welcome you here as not only an old friend, as a progressive leader of your own people, but as a world statesman of the first rank,"

—President Richard Nixon, 1973

"Nixon has the audacity to tell me to do nothing in the interests of my country until he dictates where that interest lies. . . . I say to hell with special relations."

—The Shah, 1973

IT'S NOT SOMETHING I HAVE THE SLIGHTEST COMPETENCE IN

In the summer of 1972, a few weeks after Nixon's meeting with the Shah in Tehran, the Saudis made it clear they wanted to renegotiate the terms of the oil production monopoly enjoyed by Aramco, the Arabian American Oil Company—Saudi Arabia's version of Iran's oil consortium—as an alternative to nationalizing its operations outright. King Faisal wanted the oil companies to agree to joint ownership and to commit to surrendering control of their concession within ten years. The Saudis and Aramco's American partner companies began discussing the terms of a new contract. The outcome of the negotiations was bound to have important implications for America's long-term energy needs and national security. A strategic energy alliance between the United States and Saudi Arabia was already taking shape.

American oil imports from Saudi Arabia totaled $13.5 million in 1970, rose sixfold in 1971 to $76.8 million, and surpassed $79 million in the first six months of 1972. By the fall of 1973 Saudi Arabia would be "the swing producer for the entire world," wrote oil industry analyst Daniel Yergin, accounting for 21 percent of global oil production and making it the largest exporter of crude in the world. Like the Shah of Iran, King Faisal of Saudi Arabia looked to Washington for military aid and assurances of support against unfriendly regimes in Libya, Egypt, and Iraq.

Administration officials took note that Faisal rejected the use of oil as a potential tool for political blackmail and favored only modest increases in the price of oil. "Oil isn't a weapon," the king insisted. "It is an economic force with which we can buy weapons which can be used in battle." Saudi minister of petroleum and mineral resources Zaki Yamani explained his government's view on oil prices this way: "My main worry was that if we increased the price of oil too much we would merely reduce demand for it in the future. I have always felt price increases should come in small doses. After all, the economic stability and the political stability of the west is very important to us. . . . Sudden and sharp increases disturb the economy of a country. Gradual increases can be absorbed. It's very dangerous for everyone involved when price increases come as a shock."

The Saudis were entering the negotiations with Aramco from a position of strength. Demand for oil was surging, prices were ticking upward, and energy markets had never been tighter. The oil companies appealed to the White House for assistance, confident in the knowledge that the administration understood the implications if they were steamrolled. Their trust in the president and his men turned out to be misplaced. In 1972 every facet of White House domestic and foreign policy was subordinated to the greater goal of securing a landslide election victory in November. The Nixon administration lacked even the barest semblance of a national energy policy—or a foreign economic policy for that matter. "Fuel policy emanates from everywhere, from the Bureau of Mines, from the Atomic Energy Commission, from the Environmental Protection Agency—from 64 government agencies in all," reported *Newsweek*. None of the men around the president had a sound grasp of petroleum economics or the implications of America's growing dependency on Middle East oil. Chairman of the Federal Reserve Arthur Burns described a meeting at the White House attended by Kissinger, Connally, and George Shultz, Nixon's director of the Office of Management and Budget. "Here we were," Burns confided in his diary: "Kissinger, a brilliant political analyst, but admittedly ignorant of economics; Connally, a thoroughly confused politician . . . Shultz, a no less confused amateur economist; I, the only one there with any knowledge of the subject, but even I not a real expert on some aspects of the intricate international problem! What a way to reach decisions! No one from the State Department there, no technical experts to aid us!"

Nixon was convinced that his national security adviser lacked the expertise to grapple with oil policy and energy security. When the president hired Peter Peterson as his special assistant for international economics he warned him that economics was "a field Kissinger knew nothing about," and the two advisers repeatedly clashed over policy. "Peterson, that's just a minor economic consideration," Kissinger lectured his colleague on one occasion, to which Peterson replied, "Henry, for you that's a redundancy because you see every economic consideration as minor." Kissinger had made it clear he expected to be rewarded with the post of secretary of state in Nixon's second term. Nixon was wary. "I did not really want to make Henry secretary of state," he later conceded. "I felt what we needed at State was someone with economic expertise. I thought that Henry had absolutely no competitors when it came to geopolitics, but economics is not his area of expertise."

In addition to acting as a courier between the White House and Niavaran Palace on the Kurdish insurgency in Iraq, former Texas governor John Connally was Nixon's point man on the Saudi negotiations with Aramco. In the second of three volumes of memoir, *Years of Upheaval*, Kissinger denied any direct involvement in the showdown between the Saudi government and the oil companies. "I had not been involved in the negotiation but at the request of the companies I had a long talk" with a Saudi government envoy, he later wrote. Kissinger was being too modest by far. Transcripts of Kissinger's telephone conversations reveal that he and Connally were deeply involved in a negotiated settlement that not only cost U.S. oil companies their strategic toehold in the Saudi oil industry but also hundreds of millions of dollars in financial compensation. Their meddling led to a blunder of epic proportions.

On August 2, 1972, Connally phoned Kissinger to describe a conversation he had just had with an envoy sent by King Faisal. Saudi deputy oil minister Prince Saud al-Faisal had arrived in town looking for guidance from the White House on the negotiations with Aramco. "I suggested to Saud that they just hold everything in abeyance until after the election," Connally told Kissinger. "I said, Now frankly, things have reached the point where we don't want the American oil companies negotiating foreign policy for us and I said you and I are deeply engaged in foreign policy." He said he had told Prince Saud that the United States has been derelict in not establishing over the years a more specific oil policy and an energy policy, but this President wants to do it and we're going to do it. But we can't do it in the next two weeks [the Saudis had set a deadline for action] and we don't want you all to take any action that would set you on a course that would make a confrontation with us inevitable because we're going to be a great [oil] consuming nation. We're the largest consuming nation in the world. You're going to be the largest producing nation in the world. You are now. Now frankly we don't want you to set a course that makes it absolutely impossible for us to work and coordinate policy with you.

Aramco was initially prepared to offer the Saudis a 20 percent participation deal. The Saudis wanted a full quarter share with the promise of an eventual takeover. Oil executives lobbied the White House in search of political cover. They came up short. After tacitly accepting they would have to acquiesce to Saudi demands for participation, the companies refused any settlement deal that did not include a generous compensation package. Oil executives warned Kissinger that the Saudis were trying to lowball them but balked at his offer to mediate.

Kissinger wanted to control the negotiations. He regarded the oil companies as irritants. On August 5, he made no effort to hide his irritation during a phone call with the chairman of Standard Oil of New Jersey, Ken Jamieson.

"I've sort of lost track of what it is you really want," Kissinger said.

Jamieson reminded Kissinger that the oil companies had to be paid fairly by the Saudis for their losses and also guaranteed continued access to Saudi crude production: "What we want is really adequate compensation and then also some security on the supply side of petroleum."

"But once we've said that you won't tell us what you have in mind," said Kissinger.

"You mean as far as compensation?"

"I personally couldn't care less because it's not something I have the slightest competence in," Kissinger said dismissively. If he couldn't control the process, Kissinger preferred to wash his hands of it entirely. In a phone call to Connally, he groused that the oil companies "were using us to set something up, and then they were going for the home run. The stupid bastards. They could have given me a figure $100 million higher than what they were going to settle for."

What Kissinger and Connally failed to grasp was that the Saudis had timed the talks precisely because they knew the White House would be distracted with the president's reelection campaign. Denied political cover by the Nixon administration, Aramco quickly folded. The Saudis secured their 25 percent participation deal with the promise of 51 percent majority control in 1982. King Faisal had won a stunning victory. The Saudi king's negotiating strategy differed from the Shah's, but when it came to outright nationalization and higher oil prices, the two monarchs had similar goals. One played the tortoise, the other the hare. Either way, sooner or later Western consumers would pay much higher prices at the pump.

Years later Kissinger severely criticized the way Jamieson and his colleagues handled the negotiations with the Saudis. By bowing to the Saudi terms "the companies would become instruments of nations whose interests did not necessarily parallel our own." Kissinger's telephone transcripts tell a different story. He confided to Connally that he had indeed given Prince Saud the green light to proceed against the oil companies, at the same time reminding him that it was not in the Saudis' interest to push the United States too far because "if they get into a confrontation with us, they will have to lean to states whose interest has to be to undermine them." Kissinger frankly admitted to Connally that "it was not in our interests to impose a settlement on [the Saudis] that made them come out worse than other states. Because we are interested in their stability." This was Kissinger's way of letting King Faisal know that the Nixon administration understood his need to raise oil revenues to build up the Saudi military and that he need not fear retribution by imposing tough conditions on the companies.

THE MAN WHO KNEW TOO MUCH

After Nixon won reelection in November 1972, he ordered his cabinet officers and all presidential appointees to resign. The president intended to smash the power of the Washington establishment and bend its agencies and bureaucracies to his will. CIA director Richard Helms ignored the presidential directive, citing the precedent that directors of the CIA and FBI should remain at their posts "during a change of administration"—a provocative stance given that no such change had occurred. Helms's act of defiance was an intolerable affront to a president determined to lay down the law. Nixon struck on November 20. He summoned the director to Camp David, the presidential retreat. "The President rose from a small sofa, we shook hands, and I took a chair," Helms recalled. "As usual, [Bob] Haldeman assumed his place at the President's left." After making several "disjointed, rambling observations," Nixon told Helms that he thought "new blood" was required at CIA. It was time to "make some personnel changes."

Richard Helms had just been fired as director of Central Intelligence. Nixon had never hidden his contempt for the CIA or its director, the patrician golden boy of the same clubby establishment that had never accepted Nixon's political legitimacy. He intended to gut the CIA and break its autonomy. "Helms has got to go," Nixon railed several weeks before the election. "Get rid of the clowns—cut personnel by 40 percent. Its info is worthless." Nixon's low opinion of the agency went back to his heartbreaking loss in the 1960 election to John F. Kennedy. He still blamed former spy chief Allen Dulles for throwing the election Kennedy's way by leaking intelligence data claiming that the Soviets had pulled ahead of the United States in missile production. Nixon had never produced the evidence to support his allegations but his hatred of the agency was certain. The contempt was mutual.

"The explanations for [Nixon's] attitudes, which in some cases seemed to blind his judgment, is best left to board-certified medical specialists," Helms later memorably observed. Helms had been a good foot soldier in Nixon's war against the left at home and abroad. He had compromised his agency's integrity and sanctioned lawbreaking when he unleashed the CIA against domestic antiwar protesters. He was not averse to lying to the public and his own employees when he denied ordering surveillance of American citizens. To this day his knowledge of the Watergate break-in and cover-up has never been satisfactorily explained. "Nixon and Helms have so much on each other, neither of them can breathe," Senator Howard Baker said.

Once Nixon finished his little speech Helms pointed out that under agency regulations he was already obliged to step down on his sixtieth birthday in four months' time. He asked if he could stay on until then. By Nixon's reaction Helms could tell that the president was "surprised at the Agency policy and at what I had assumed to be the indisputable fact of my age." Nixon had just fired a man who was about to retire and collect his pension. The blunder was compounded when Helms had to correct the president's intimation that he was a political appointee and not a career intelligence professional with thirty years' experience serving his country. At this point Nixon, a man who by his own estimation was not "a good butcher," lost the nerve to finish the job. Backtracking, he agreed Helms could stay on until March. He also decided that he needed to get Helms out of the country for a while. The director's wife, Cynthia, later described the scene: "Suddenly, as if it were a totally new idea—Dick felt it had never crossed the President's mind before—Nixon said, 'Would you like to be an ambassador?' Dick told him he would have to think about it. "If you were going to become an ambassador, where would you want to go?" asked Nixon, warming to the idea. The president had an idea: "What about Moscow?" Helms was "floored by the prospect of wintering in the Moscow embassy." The idea of sending the CIA director to represent Washington's interests in the Soviet Union showed just how little thought the president had given to the proposal: "I'm not sure how the Russians might interpret my being sent across the lines as an ambassador."

"That's a good point," admitted the president. "But what about some other country?"

"Tehran might be a more plausible choice," Helms answered. "But I'm not sure but [that] it's time to leave government and to try something new."

"Iran sounds good," said Nixon, who wanted the issue settled. "I've got something in mind for Joe Farland."

Nixon's decision to offer Helms a diplomatic posting abroad may have been a way of making amends for the crude manner of his dismissal, but it was also a smart tactical move. Helms was the quintessential company man who knew too much. The Watergate scandal continued to simmer. The president knew that his request back in June to have Helms turn off the FBI probe into his Mexican laundry had implicated both men in a criminal cover-up. It was better to keep Helms on his side and out of sight rather than turn him loose with the secrets he knew.

Helms told his wife that evening that he chose Tehran over a European post because "Iran is in an area where the influences of both East and West come to bear. With the West's increasing need for oil and the Shah's plans for modernization, I think it would be challenging to be there at this extraordinary time." Iran was the most obvious post for a man of his background and interests, dating back to Operation Ajax. Under the Shah's leadership Iran was assuming a crucial role in stabilizing West Asia and securing America's oil lifeline through the Persian Gulf. There were the CIA listening posts and the Kurdish operation to consider. From his perch in Tehran, Helms would have a frontline seat at the coming struggle for mastery of Middle Eastern oil. Besides which, the Shah was one of the few heads of state who would tolerate hosting America's top spy as its diplomatic representative. "Dick and I talked for long hours" before finally deciding to go, Cynthia Helms recalled. Nixon also needed convincing, it turned out. Days passed before Haldeman phoned Helms to pass on the president's blessing: "He feels more positively about it and he really wants you to go."

Henry Kissinger knew nothing about any of this. Nixon was still furious with Kissinger for prematurely declaring "peace is at hand" in Vietnam the month before. With the peace talks stalled yet again Nixon blamed Kissinger for weakening his ability to get a better deal for the South Vietnamese. He refused to take his calls or invite him to Camp David. Haldeman and Ehrlichman gossiped that Kissinger was out of control, that he blamed the president for the collapse of the negotiations, and that he had had a breakdown. "He's been under care," Haldeman informed Nixon. "And he's been doing some strange things." It was in this bloodied atmosphere that Kissinger first learned of a mysterious meeting at Camp David's Aspen Lodge. Perhaps fearing that *he* had been the subject of discussion, and frantic to find out what was going on, Kissinger confronted Helms at a meeting of the National Security Council. "I was silent for a moment because I thought he surely knew, and I did not want to violate Nixon's request that I keep my dismissal to myself," Helms recalled, not knowing that Kissinger had been deliberately kept in the dark. "Henry bristled a bit and snapped, 'If you won't tell me, I'll call Haldeman.'"

Armed with the bare facts, Kissinger phoned Haldeman anyway. Their conversation on the evening of November 28, 1972, began innocently enough with Haldeman complaining that Nixon's nominee to take over the post of United States ambassador to NATO in Brussels was demanding an array of perks and privileges including cabinet rank, a limousine in Brussels, a second car in Washington, and the use of a private plane. Haldeman thought these demands were "a little psycho" and evidence perhaps that the nominee was "power mad or something." The conversation turned to Vietnam. Kissinger searched for the right opening to make it look as though Helms had casually offered up the news of his dismissal and reassignment to Tehran: "One other thing which is not major—is there anybody with whom I am working who's been offered something—let me tell you what I have in mind—I ran into Dick Helms today at a meeting and afterwards he said I looked forward to cooperating closely with you. And he's been offered the ambassadorship in Iran—and I thought that it meant that he was staying on—"

"No, no," said Haldeman. "He has accepted Iran—I've got to go through that whole cycle with you because we have to work out the whole—what you do . . ."

"I think it is a very good appointment, incidentally, so it's not a reflection on that count—it just makes me look—"

"I understand—he called me this morning and gave me that and I should have let you know, but I was going to cover it with you when I got down there." Haldeman wanted Kissinger to believe that he had only just heard the news himself and that it had been Nixon's idea to send Helms to Tehran. Based on past experience, Haldeman may have worried that if Kissinger ever learned the full truth about the unpleasant scene at Aspen Lodge, subscribers to *The Washington Post* would read about it the next morning over their breakfast cereal. Their conversation ended with Kissinger agreeing to join Nixon in Florida the following Saturday. Donald Rumsfeld's appointment as the new U.S. ambassador to NATO was announced the next week.

The Shah was happy to have Helms in Tehran. But Alam had his doubts. Iran's Farsi- and English-language newspapers splashed the news of the appointment across their front pages. The ever perceptive Alam made sure they played down Helms's intelligence background. American diplomats cabled Washington to report that "we understand word has gone out to local press not repeat not allude to Ambassador Helms' past connections with CIA." When Alam phoned the U.S. embassy on December 9 to offer his commiserations to Joseph Farland, the ambassador "was literally in tears of grief." Two weeks later Farland was still pathetically trying to receive official word of his fate. Just before Christmas he placed a phone call to Kissinger imploring him "for 15 minutes of your time today. I want to talk to you about this change in my plans, this Helms thing."

In the meantime, Kissinger and Helms had spoken again. On December 15, Kissinger tried to console the director, assuring him that "you're the best intelligence professional I know. . . . You know you stayed three years longer than the intentions."

"Yes, I think that's right," Helms answered. "My soul is at peace."

Kissinger said he had had a talk with Nixon the previous day "about your role in your new job, and also I want to talk with you about some things we are thinking of doing. And I wondered if you could come over to see me at your convenience today?" They agreed to meet in Kissinger's office at 3:00 P.M. The wheels were turning again. But Nixon felt the need to twist the knife one last time. Richard Helms was at work on February 2, 1973, with six weeks to go before his official retirement when a call came through to inform him that James Schlesinger had just been sworn in as his replacement. Helms barely had time to clean off his desk, pack his boxes, and say farewell to his staff.

Helms was an accidental ambassador. There is a tendency to ascribe dark motives to random acts and deep meaning to illogical decisions. Many have theorized that the Helms appointment was evidence of a malign intent on the part of the Nixon administration to influence internal Iranian politics. Helms's biographer Thomas Powers noted that there was no taping system at Camp David. Haldeman, Nixon, and Helms are dead. All three men were eventually disgraced and implicated in crimes that involved cover-ups and lies. Helms was a convicted perjurer. But would he have allowed his wife, Cynthia, to publish her memoir knowing that it contained lies, and all the while knowing that one of Nixon's smoking-gun tapes might one day surface to expose her as a liar too? Hardly. Nor could he be accused of trying to cover up for Richard Nixon—the two men loathed each other. Additional evidence exists to corroborate Helms's version of the Camp David meeting. Alam's diary and the Kissinger telephone transcripts confirm that the appointment was unplanned and came as a surprise. It should also be kept in mind that Nixon, Kissinger, and Helms did not believe Iranian politics needed to be influenced—the status quo suited their purposes perfectly. The Helms appointment highlights the reality that the truth really is as banal as it appears to be.

POPEYE IS RUNNING OUT OF CHEAP SPINACH

On a moonlit winter night in late January 1973 the oil tanker *Overseas Aleutian* began unloading its precious cargo at a depot on New York's East River. The fuel was pumped into trucks lined up along the pier, ready to be transported the next morning to homes and businesses throughout the metropolis. New York City, in the grip of unusually frigid winter weather, was running low on supplies of natural gas, propane, and heating fuel. Texaco, the company that serviced New York's three regional airports, had already exhausted its supply of aviation fuel. Passenger jets flying to the West Coast could get only as far as Pittsburgh before they had to refuel. Shortages were even worse in the West and Midwest. Natural gas supplies were cut off to many factories, schools, churches, and office buildings in Iowa, Illinois, Ohio, Indiana, Nebraska, and Colorado. The Denver school system shut down because there was no fuel to heat classrooms. Officials at Stapleton International Airport relied on body heat to keep the airport terminal warm. In the Ohio township of Bellefontaine an eternal flame dedicated to war veterans was snuffed out to conserve enough gas to heat two average-size homes a year. In Sioux City, where fifty-five buildings were forced to close their doors and where the city fathers scavenged for fuel, the Edwards and Brown Coal Co. sent a crew to pump a three-year-old supply of oil from the basement of a funeral home. The South was not spared either. There were blackouts in Miami. The University of Texas postponed resumption of classes for 38,000 students. Mississippi's chicken broiler industry was crippled when gas supplies were requisitioned to heat hospitals and private homes. Job losses related to the crisis totaled forty thousand in the Jackson area alone. In Tennessee, barges were requisitioned to rush fuel to the Memphis Naval Air Station and City of Memphis Hospital.

What at first appeared to be a series of local curiosities quickly escalated into a national emergency in December 1972 and January and February 1973. "If anyone still needs evidence that this country's jerrybuilt system for supply and distribution of fuels has collapsed, look around," observed *The New York Times* in an editorial. The federal government drew up guidelines to implement fuel rationing. "We've had a happy era of low costs, low risks and high benefits," conceded Pete Peterson, the outgoing secretary of commerce. "But Popeye is running out of cheap spinach."

The severity of the first wave of what came to be known as the "energy crisis" was highlighted by the point of origin of the *Overseas Aleutian*. After disgorging 250,000 tons of U.S. wheat at the Black Sea port of Odessa in the Soviet Union, the tanker had filled up an equal amount of heating oil for the return journey to the East Coast. Even as Richard Nixon sold Mohammad Reza Shah unrestricted quantities of military equipment to keep Persian Gulf oil safe from malign Soviet influence, his administration accepted emergency shipments of Soviet fuel oil to keep the lights on at home. In return, the White House agreed to put bread on Russian tables by dumping surplus stockpiles of American wheat stored in government-subsidized granaries. The fuel-for-wheat exchange over the winter of 1972–73 symbolized the moral ambiguity of détente: the same two superpowers that pitted their regional proxies Iran and Iraq against each other in the Gulf were prepared to shore up each other with a barter exchange of fuel and food.

As Richard Nixon was sworn into office for a second term, American guns finally fell silent in Southeast Asia. That same month a powerful convergence of economics and geopolitics ushered in an era of energy crisis and insecurity that the United States was remarkably ill-equipped to meet. Regulations dating back to the Great Depression still kept gas prices artificially low and discouraged both exploration and conservation. The electrical power grid had already collapsed once during the Great Northeast Blackout of November 1965 but nothing had been done to fix it. Indeed, the Johnson administration had produced an internal report a year later that concluded that "the nation's total energy resources seem adequate to satisfy expected requirements through the remainder of the century at costs near present levels." The United States was still the world's biggest producer of oil in 1970. But that year American oil production peaked at 11.3 million barrels per day ending a happy era of low inflation, full employment, and rising living standards. To fill the growing chasm between consumer demand and energy supplies the Nixon administration loosened the import quotas of the Eisenhower era, then discarded them entirely in April. Foreign crude imports rocketed commensurately from 2.2 million barrels of oil per day in 1967 to 6.2 million barrels per day in 1973. The figures were even more striking when viewed in percentage terms, rising from 19 percent of domestic consumption in 1967 to 35 percent six years later. By 1980, U.S. oil imports were set to smash through the 45–60 percent barrier.

Within a remarkably short period the United States became vulnerable to the vagaries of the world oil market. The bulk of America's petroleum imports still came from Venezuela, but 70 percent of the world's proven oil reserves were located in the Middle East and especially the Persian Gulf. The world's center of economic gravity was shifting toward the Gulf monarchies of Iran, Saudi Arabia, United Arab Emirates, and Kuwait. By September 1973 the United States imported 28 million barrels of oil, 26 percent of its total imports, from Arab states—a statistic that represented a stomach-churning 35 percent increase over the same period the year before. "Like it or not, during the next decade the United States will have to import a lot of Arab oil—or face a national economic catastrophe," warned the *Chicago Tribune*. But the entry of the American leviathan into the global energy marketplace brought with it a slew of other complications. America's thirst for cheap oil quickly soaked up any excess capacity, tightening the market to the point where prices began spiraling in an upward direction for consuming nations everywhere. As oil industry analyst Daniel Yergin explained, in 1970 there were about "3 million barrels per day of excess capacity in the world outside the United States, most of it concentrated in the Middle East." But by 1973, "the surplus production capacity that could be considered actually 'available' added up to only 500,000 barrels per day. That was just one percent of world production."

The United States was now competing against its own allies in Europe and Japan for access to the same shrinking pool of oil and gas. What had historically been a buyer's market had now turned in favor of sellers. In 1973 the Middle East oil market, already vulnerable to an interruption in supply caused by an "event" such as a war, embargo, acts of terrorism, severe weather conditions, or outright political manipulation, had reached the precipice.

The Shah had watched with interest Aramco's abject surrender and the Nixon administration's decision to look the other way. A game of leap-frog began. The Shah naturally demanded more favorable terms from the Western oil companies that operated most of Iran's petroleum industry. He wanted Iran's domestic oil production company, the National Iranian Oil Company, to assume control over Iran's oil production in its entirety, reducing the fifteen-member foreign oil consortium to the essentially passive role of customers buying Iranian oil. But the Shah's timing was off. The White House had finally focused on the need to develop a national energy policy. In a toughly worded letter dated January 19, 1973, Nixon urged his old ally to rethink his takeover bid, issuing his appeal "in light of our long friendship and our mutual concern for stability in your area of the world. My concern is that the most recent proposals of Your Majesty's government could seriously affect the entire area and the whole course of our mutual relationship." Nixon asked that action be postponed until he had completed peace negotiations in Southeast Asia and given the issue the full attention it deserved. Taking "a unilateral step which doesn't meet the legitimate interests of both sides could have serious consequences for the objectives we are pursuing together."

The Shah was incensed. He had helped Nixon win re-election and for what? To be treated like a puppet? Alam counseled restraint, but the Shah bitterly denounced Nixon for issuing instructions and meddling in Iran's national affairs . . . "I say to hell with special relations," he said. "We shall accept no further advice from friend or foe."

The Shah made his break the same week Nixon was sworn in to his second term. On January 23, speaking to five thousand workers and farmers gathered to mark the tenth anniversary of the White Revolution, the Iranian leader announced that the foreign oil companies responsible for producing 92 percent of Iran's oil production would not have their contracts renewed when they expired in 1979. Instead, he would offer them two immediate choices. They could continue operating as they had under the terms of the 1954 accord, in which case they would be required to double their production output from 4 million barrels to 8 million barrels per day and not sell it at a price lower than that paid elsewhere. The consortium instead settled for the Shah's second and preferred option: they agreed to yield their operational role in Iranian oil production to the National Iranian Oil Company in exchange for a twenty-year preferred access contract to sell Iranian crude oil on the world market.

The Shah's decision to seize control of the oil consortium's operations had as much to do with fiscal pressures as national pride. Iran's government was readying a new five-year $32.5 billion economic development plan due to come into effect on March 21. It aimed to increase the country's economic growth rate by a startling 11.4 percent each year for five years. Once again the Shah had approved economic goals his treasury couldn't possibly meet without a massive injection of new oil revenues. Yet by giving the oil majors preferred access to buy Iranian oil the Shah had added another element of uncertainty to Iran's economic equation. The companies were not *required* to buy Iranian oil. A change in market conditions might cause them to slash their purchase orders. And that in turn might mean that the Shah, who meant to double his country's petroleum output, could be left with millions of barrels of unsold oil.

In fact, Nixon's letter to the Shah urging restraint had been a bluff. In the wake of the Vietnam War the United States seemed to have lost the will and the ability to back up threats with force. Yet the question remained: just how far could the Shah push his ally without crossing a line? The Nixon Doctrine gave the Shah more leeway to maneuver but it also increased the possibility that he would overreach either at home or abroad. He already had a track record of provoking his neighbor Iraq. Asadollah Alam's diary suggests the Shah never fully trusted Nixon and Kissinger. They had allowed their ally and his neighbor Pakistan to be dismembered by Mrs. Gandhi. They had forced President Thieu of South Vietnam to sign a peace settlement that resembled a suicide note. The Shah even saw Nixon's hand in Morocco, where King Hassan had barely survived several spectacular coup plots. President Diem's bloody end was never far from his thoughts: "But if it's the Americans who are to blame, why is it that they have refrained from curbing my independence?"

A gladiator had to look after himself. In the same twelve-month period that the Shah took control of Iran's oil industry and Nixon agreed to lift all restrictions on conventional weapons sales to Tehran, Iranian arms orders exploded from $500 million in 1972 to $2.5 billion within a year. The Shah was on the way to making himself both indispensable *and* untouchable.

It said something about the exigencies of fate that the next time Ambassador-designate Richard Helms saw President Nixon, at 11:16 A.M. on Wednesday, February 14, he was now the man of the hour. History had pivoted. From the vantage point of the new year the Helms appointment looked like an act of cunning strategic foresight on the president's part. The Saudi move against Aramco, the fuel shortages over the winter months, the Shah's attack on the oil consortium, the tightening world oil market, and higher prices for crude oil had all contributed to a growing sense of panic in the West. Who better than the former director of intelligence to help the administration develop a plan to secure the free world's oil lifeline? Alone with the president and his note taker, General Brent Scowcroft, Helms briefed Nixon on his departure plans. Helms said he had conferred with John Connally and the British government on issues concerning trade, oil, and regional security in the Persian Gulf. The Shah was in St. Moritz until March 15. Helms would present his credentials before the Shah left town again to spend the Iranian New Year at Kish.

Nixon's instructions to his envoy showed just how focused he now was on the Middle East and America's petroleum lifeline. "I want you not just to think of your CIA background," he told Helms. "It is important, but apply yourself to the oil problem generally. The question is whether the US can protect its interests adequately without government to government agreements." Nixon repeated his admonition: "Immerse yourself in the oil problem." What Nixon had in mind was for Helms to perform duties far beyond the scope of an ambassador. He wanted Helms to act as his plenipotentiary for the Persian Gulf and West Asia, including Pakistan. Helms was to help Mohammad Reza Shah Pahlavi fashion a strategic architecture that would place Tehran at the center of a new regional order. Helms later recalled that he was ordered to act as Nixon's eyes and ears in the region: "As a matter of fact, when I went out to Tehran I was told orally by President Nixon that he wanted me to also keep an eye on the whole Persian Gulf area. . . . The President wanted regular reports about what I thought about the political and military situation throughout the Gulf."

At 11:40 the president asked Scowcroft to leave the room so he could talk with Helms in private. No record exists of their twelve-minute discussion. But Helms and Nixon may have touched on an incident that had rattled Helms seven days earlier during his ambassadorial confirmation hearing on Capitol Hill. In an unusual move, senators had called a closed-door hearing, sworn him to an oath, and cross-examined him about his knowledge of the Watergate cover-up, CIA surveillance of American nationals at home, and reports circulating about the agency's alleged involvement in coup planning in Chile. Helms had been caught by surprise at the detail and intensity of their line of questioning. He had denied everything. And he had perjured himself.

Helms encountered Haldeman in the White House corridors. "What happened to our understanding that my exit would be postponed for a few weeks?" he asked. "Oh, I guess we forgot," said Haldeman. His face, said Helms, showed "the faint trace of a smile."

FIRST BLOOD

On May 21, Senator J. William Fulbright of Arkansas rose on the floor of the United States Senate to talk about the impact the energy crisis was having on American foreign policy. The chairman of the Senate Foreign Relations Committee was expected to deliver perfunctory remarks about an issue that had been pushed off the front pages by the latest revelations in the Watergate saga. The fact that the speech made even minor headlines during the Watergate summer was testament to its sensational content. With no quick fix in store, another cruel winter of fuel shortages approaching, and Arab oil producers threatening to cut off oil supplies to supporters of Israel, Senator Fulbright warned in the most dire terms that "our policymakers and policy-influencers may come to the conclusion that military action is required to secure the oil resources of the Middle East, to secure our exposed jugular." There was "no question" that the United States could take over the "oil-producing states of the Middle East" if it wanted to. They were "militarily insignificant" and their mere existence pointed to a power vacuum in the Persian Gulf. But why do it when others could do the job for us? "We might not even have to do it ourselves, with militarily potent surrogates available in the region," continued Fulbright, who then lobbed the verbal equivalent of a grenade onto the floor of the chamber. "The Shah of Iran is known to aspire to a 'protecting' role for the Gulf region," intoned Fulbright, "and there has been ominous talk" of Iran and Israel offering to "solve the energy problem for the United States by taking over Kuwait, there being no force in the desert between Israel and the Persian Gulf capable of resisting the Israeli Army." Fulbright warned Saudi Arabia in particular to take care: "The meat of the gazelle may be succulent indeed, but the wise gazelle does not boast of it to lions."

Fulbright's speech resonated because of its timing and specificity. Was he privy to classified information? Had someone tipped him off? Eight weeks earlier, on March 20, Iraqi troops had crossed over into Kuwait. They occupied an unarmed border post about fifteen miles inland and shelled a second post on the coast. It was a classic probing maneuver. Baghdad wanted to gauge Kuwait's ability to defend itself and test the reactions of its neighbors and allies. The Shah decided to call Saddam Hussein's bluff. Iraqi forces pulled back to their side of the border five weeks later. U.S. diplomats wasted no time in letting it be known that their gladiator had drawn his sword. At the end of that same week Israel's foreign minister, Abba Eban, paid a secret visit to Tehran to talk with the Shah.

Eban was in Washington on May 12 to brief Kissinger on his Tehran trip. "I found the Shah very relaxed" on the subject of the Persian Gulf, Eban reported, "and for two reasons: He was very satisfied with the United States for the first time. They are usually very querulous that he can't get enough; now he can. Secondly, on oil, he feels there is a United States interest now." Kissinger learned that the Shah "wants to be strong enough to resist any threat except the Soviet Union. He thinks the Soviets are shifting away from Egypt to the Persian Gulf because of less American resistance." The Shah's thinking had been greatly influenced by India's successful defeat of Pakistan in 1971. Treaties and defense pacts could easily be reneged on. "He feels that documents are not important," said Eban. "For instance, the India-Pakistan crisis showed this. But he is creating an American interest there which is more." The Shah envisioned a strategic posture that comprised a "triangle—Israel, Ethiopia, and Iran—which if buttressed by US support will be a stabilizing influence."

The Shah's perception was that Nixon had left his ally Yahya Khan to hang because there was no political price to be paid at home for doing so. The best way to avoid Khan's fate would be to deepen the American stake in Iran to the extent that an attack on Tehran would be viewed by Washington as akin to an attack on Chicago or New York. When the Shah talked about "creating an American interest in Iran" he meant a co-dependency in the areas of oil security, military cooperation, and commerce. He meant to increase the number of American citizens living in Iran. Washington might not be prepared to fight for Iranians but it would not hesitate to defend the lives of its own citizens. American men, women, and children would be the Shah's insurance policy—his double indemnity. He did not intend the American presence in Iran to be permanent or protracted. He recognized that this strategy was risky and rife with contradictions: even as the Shah sought to reduce his reliance on the United States in the long term he saw a need to temporarily deepen military and commercial ties until the Iranian military was strong enough to hold its own. The Americans "should be out of here in a few years," explained an Iranian government official. "That's the theory at least." The Shah had to hold out until around 1980, when Iran would be militarily self-sufficient.

Yet the Shah's gamble carried grave risks for Americans. The CIA, the State Department, and the Defense Department had bluntly warned the White House that the Shah overspent on arms, that anti-American sentiment in Iran was building, and that a financial crisis could help mobilize the Shah's enemies at home. But Nixon and Kissinger chose to disregard the advice of their government's trained professional analysts. By May 1973 there were approximately five hundred American soldiers, sailors, and Marines based in Iran with a further six hundred servicemen and their families due to arrive over the summer. They were the first wave of blue suiters and technicians promised by Nixon to help make the Shah's $2 billion worth of new defense contracts operational. "He wants the latest stuff and he thinks the United States has got the best," a U.S. embassy official in Tehran cheerfully told one visitor in the spring. The Shah would be getting "most everything short of atomic weapons. . . . Whether he needs it or not is his decision. His military knowledge is extraordinary and he knows what he wants." On one occasion the Shah instructed Alam to approach Helms with an urgent request for artillery and fighter planes. Ambassador Helms delivered a reply more suitable for an Iranian court minister: "If His Imperial Majesty commands it, I shall do my best to get Washington to approve."

Not even the murder of an American military officer in Tehran caused U.S. officials to reassess the logic behind their buildup. On the morning of June 2, Lieutenant Colonel Lewis Lee Hawkins, forty-two, a military adviser to the Iranian armed forces, was walking from his house to the car pool that took him to work each day. "As he passed a *kucheh*, a small alleyway, gunfire struck him in the back, spinning him around," recalled Cynthia Helms, who received a horrifying description of the crime back at the ambassador's residence. The Helmses had arrived in Tehran the first week of April to take up Richard's post as ambassador. "More bullets hit him in the chest, and he went down." Hawkins died where he lay in a pool of blood. His two assailants made off on motorcycles. The death of Colonel Hawkins was treated as a random event.

THE HUSH-HUSH PLAN

The Shah's four-day state visit to Washington in the last week of July came during a summer of high anxiety for Americans. With gas prices soaring and the Middle East churning, the pro-Western monarch of the most powerful petrostate in the world was welcomed with open arms. Nixon's decision a year earlier to lavish aid on the Shah seemed more than justified. "It was like coming home again," gushed *The New York Times* of the king's arrival, and it noted with approval a story currently making the rounds in Washington and Tehran. The Soviet ambassador had reportedly asked Iran's Prime Minister Hoveyda, "Aren't you annoyed that the Americans sent Richard Helms, the CIA chief, as Ambassador here?" Without missing a beat Hoveyda replied, "Well, at least the Americans sent their top spy." The paper reported that "in Washington, the anecdote is repeated to illustrate special attention, reserved only for the closest of allies, that the United States gives Iran. 'The Shah wants the best, and he gets the best,' a State Department official said here the other day." But to some Iranians, Helms's appointment was a source of humiliation. American scholar James Bill recalled the reaction of a prominent Iranian writer to Helms's presence in Tehran: "Why else has Helms been sent here? Why has the United States sent its head spy as ambassador to our country? Could not your country have had the decency to at least remain out of sight while you help the shah pull the strings?"

No one was more pleased to see Iran's Shah and Shahbanou walk across the South Lawn of the White House in the sweltering July heat than President Nixon. He welcomed the distraction they offered from his own mounting troubles. Onlookers noted that Nixon was still looking pale from his recent hospitalization for viral pneumonia. America's first family was enduring a hellish summer. The Watergate scandal had exploded. Televised congressional hearings had introduced the American people to Richard Nixon's dark side, the one that understood hush money and its uses, black bag jobs and break-ins, private investigators and wiretaps. "May God save America!" wrote Fed chief Arthur Burns in his diary as scandalous revelations poured forth on national television. Americans were informed that the Shah "evidently was the first foreign visitor since the spring of 1971 to meet the President in the Oval Office without the presence of listening devices." Battered by events and depressed by the forced resignations in the spring of his top aides John Ehrlichman and Bob Haldeman, Nixon showed signs of buckling under the strain when on the eve of the Pahlavi state visit he collapsed with pneumonia and was rushed to Bethesda Naval Hospital. Kissinger phoned Bethesda to update the president on the Shah's pending arrival. Kissinger seemed pleased to have Nixon safely tucked away while he made the rounds with visiting officials. When the president said he would check out on Friday and "probably come down to the office for one or two hours and then go to Camp David for Saturday and Sunday and be back in the office as usual on Monday," Kissinger suggested he linger awhile: "I would take it easy, Mr. President."

"We are only going to concern ourselves on the things that matter," replied Nixon, who had a tendency to refer to himself with the royal "we."

"The Shah will be coming in Tuesday and that really actually will be a very important meeting," Kissinger reminded him.

"Of course it will," agreed Nixon. He batted aside Kissinger's offer to "see [the Shah] on some details in order to spare you some time if you wanted me to." Nixon, perhaps suspicious of Kissinger's motives, said he wouldn't hear of it: "No, no. I want him to have the full treatment." He already had a job in mind for Kissinger.

For Nixon, giving his friend the Shah the "full treatment" extended to lining up a song-and-dance act for the King of Kings. And that meant asking his long-suffering national security adviser to call in a few favors. Nixon regarded Kissinger's fondness for all things Hollywood—and especially "all those beautiful broads" he met during trips to Los Angeles—as comparable to a moral vice. Yet Kissinger's show business contacts came in handy when the White House needed them. And so began the "Danny Kaye affair." The president asked his daughter Julie Eisenhower to phone Kissinger to see if he could persuade Kaye to perform for the Pahlavis at the White House state banquet. "Would you be willing to do that or do you not want to have to be asking him?" asked Eisenhower.

Kissinger said he didn't mind making the call "but I can tell you now he won't do it." Kaye had cut back his concert appearances in recent years and had already turned down one request from Kissinger to perform for the Nixons. Kissinger and Julie tiptoed around the elephant in the room: booking talent for the Nixons had become much harder in recent months—the first family was practically radioactive. Still, Julie was as insistent as she was polite: "The Shah would really like him very much."

A few minutes later the man whose stealth diplomacy had garnered him a *Time* magazine cover story as "Nixon's Secret Agent" mounted a different sort of charm offensive. He telephoned to try to convince the United Nations Children's Fund ambassador to hoof it up for the Pahlavis. Kissinger began with his trademark flattery. He wanted Kaye to know that he had been singing the actor's praises to the president and that the idea was his: "Danny, what I'm calling you about is the President—I've been raving so much about your various toasts—the President wondered whether you wanted to do something at a dinner he's giving for the Shah of Iran on July 24. I'm not urging it, I'm just transmitting the request."

"No, that I'm not going to do," Kaye declared. "No, I really don't want to do that."

Kissinger was taken aback by the actor's vehemence. "I just didn't want you to—I didn't want to exploit a personal relationship."

"No, no, as far as performing, that's out of the question, I don't want to do that," repeated the actor. He couldn't possibly get a band together in two weeks' time. His musical collaborator of twenty-five years had just died. "I can't put it together," he said.

When Kissinger pressed again, this time perhaps a little too hard—"Well, you didn't do badly at the [film director] John Ford dinner and if that wasn't formally performing—" Kaye got straight to the point.

"The Shah of Iran I am not too crazy about doing it for anyway because I couldn't get to see him when I was on the UNICEF mission in Tehran."

Danny Kaye's refusal to do a favor for the king who had snubbed him also reflected growing public awareness and dismay over Iran's scandalous record on human rights. But Kissinger had no way of knowing just how eager the Shah was to secure Danny Kaye's attendance at the banquet. Queen Farah was a fan of the star. In her memoir she expressed "great admiration" for him as an actor and as someone "who has done a great deal for UNICEF and has organized numerous soirees for the benefit of deprived children." The queen had carved out a role for herself in Iran as a patron of the arts and as the most prominent advocate for women's and children's rights.

But on the eve of her departure for Washington with her husband she had threatened to pack her bags and leave the palace for good. The Shah's infidelities were widely rumored in Tehran, a city whose whispering grapevine seemed at times to reach right into the royal boudoir. Moham-mad Reza Shah enjoyed the company of continental blondes including Lufthansa stewardesses, girls supplied by the legendary Madame Claude of Paris, and a bevy of young women brought to court by friends and "pimps" such as Amir-Hushang Davallu, a Qajar prince and who, in the words of the Shah's biographer, Gholam Reza Afkhami, was a "born courtier, clever and corrupt, a well-informed conversationalist, tasteful in dress and décor, a sycophant par excellence, and an opium addict." Philandering was some-thing that His Imperial Majesty had in common with his court minister, Asadollah Alam, who described their conquests in his diaries. The Shah's romances tended to be fleeting. "The encounters did not always conclude in sexual intercourse," wrote Afkhami. "Often a conversation, a dance, or a drink sufficed. But these occasions were soothing, and the shah enjoyed them. He called them *gardesh*, outings." Farah was nineteen years younger than her husband and aware of his infidelities. "Farah knew about her husband's adventures and was generally good-natured about them, but not always," concluded the biographer. "At times she would grumble and cry, and on rare occasions even threaten to harm herself. The worst crisis of this sort occurred in the summer of 1973."

Her name was Gilda. She was that most dangerous of paramours—a nineteen-year-old with dyed blond hair, big ambitions, and a vivid imagination. She decided that the Shah meant to exercise his rights as a Muslim husband and take a second wife and set about telling the news to as many people as she could. This was just the sort of farfetched rumor that Tehranis loved to repeat about their royal family. For instance, in 1960 the queen had made the decision to give birth to her first child in a public hospital amid the slums of south Tehran. She and her husband meant it as a gesture of solidarity with the common people of Tehran. But wild rumors soon began circulating that the newborn heir, Prince Reza Cyrus, was not the Shah's son at all, and that he was a deaf mute. "They have spread the rumor that the prince cannot speak, that his hands [are] like those of a duck, and that the queen's ears are so large that they had to cut them," observed Fatemeh Pakravan, the wife of the Shah's aide General Hassan Pakravan. "They said absolutely anything, anything—the most fantastic rumors."

Alam felt that the insidious gossip about Gilda had gone too far, impugning the queen's honor and slandering the throne, so he broached the topic with his old friend and master. He found the Shah surprisingly contrite, more than a little worried, but grateful for the offer of help.

When these rumors of a second marriage were brought to Farah's attention, her distress knew no bounds. One report claimed that she fled to Europe. Third-party mediation was called for and on the evening of Saturday, July 21, less than forty-eight hours before the scheduled departure for Washington, Farah's formidable mother, Farideh Diba, forced the issue with Alam and laid down the law. Without once mentioning the word "divorce," she left Alam in no doubt that her daughter was prepared to walk. Together, the Shah and Alam cooked up a scheme to marry off Gilda to a suitable husband, and the affair ended.

The Iranian party flew to Virginia. There they rested the night in Colonial Williamsburg, journeying the next morning to Washington, where they landed in a helicopter on the South Lawn to begin their formal four-day state visit. If the Pahlavis were under strain they didn't show it when they joined a waxen Dick and Pat Nixon on a "sun-drenched red-carpeted platform" in front of hundreds of tourists backed up against the White House railing. Everyone smiled and nodded and waved throughout the twenty-five-minute official welcoming ceremony amid a fanfare of trumpets, a military honor guard, and a handpicked crowd of enthusiasts and officials applauding and waving tiny Iranian and American flags. "We welcome you here as not only an old friend, as a progressive leader of your own people, but as a world statesman of the first rank," declared Nixon. The Shah in turn expressed appreciation for "the opportunity of talking to you and having wise advices that you can always give." Both couples tried to ignore the two hundred protesters across the street in Lafayette Park whose sound truck blared "CIA get out of Iran!" "Shah is a US puppet!" "US get out of Iran!"

The Shah had ostensibly come to Washington to secure pledges from the administration to sell him F-14 jet fighters from Grumman. This was of course a ruse. The deal had been fixed in secret a year before. But both governments had to go through the motions for appearances' sake, with the Shah expressing his interest, Nixon giving his approval, the Pentagon putting the contract out to tender, and Grumman placing the winning bid. The F-14 deal also obscured the real reason for the Shah's visit. Senator Fulbright had been more perceptive than perhaps even he knew.

After the welcoming ceremonies were over, Nixon and Kissinger escorted the Shah to the Oval Office for a two-hour tête-à-tête. Ardeshir Zahedi, who had since rejoined the Shah's government and been posted to Washington for a second term as Iranian ambassador, was blocked by Kissinger from sitting in on the session. The antipathy between the two could be traced back to Kissinger's contempt for Zahedi's friend Secretary of State William Rogers. Kissinger also wanted to make sure that as the sole note taker in the room he could control the official transcript of what the leaders discussed. The Shah later told Zahedi that Kissinger, having had a late night out on the town, had yawned his way through the meeting.

Six days earlier King Mohammad Zahir Shah of Afghanistan had been overthrown in a leftist coup. The Shah had been warning the administration for some time that the Soviet Union had set its sights on Afghanistan. "Even if it was not a Russian coup, they must have known about it," he told Nixon. He warned that Moscow planned to "push to the Indian Ocean. It is the same problem in Iraq." The Shah said he had told Soviet premier

Alexei Kosygin not to overstep the mark because "we can destroy Iraq in a few hours. If we have the power you can afford to be wise. We must have the deterrent power of the Air Force." The Shah also insisted to Nixon and Kissinger that Iran would not accept the partition or collapse of the Pakistani state that had emerged from the ruins of the 1971 secessionist war in the east.

One of the signatures of the late Pahlavi period was Iran's generally cordial relations with its neighbors and the nuclear powers. The Shah's balancing act extended to creating not only an American interest in his country but also a European interest. "I am having a pipeline built to Europe so that they feel our security is inseparable from European security," he explained. "The only viable oil-producing country for Europe is Iran. If I can link my country to Europe by a gas line, they have to pay attention to us. Thus Russia can't use détente with Europe and toughness with us; they must link détente with us to détente in Europe." Nixon and Kissinger did not blanch when the Shah said they should expect additional increases in the price of oil. Higher prices were seen as providing insurance for the Shah and enabling Iran to fulfill its security guarantees: "Oil policy is sufficiently crucial. We have asked for atomic stations even for Iran. The normal trend will be that oil will rise in price until shale or gasification of coal becomes profitable. We have produced stability in the oil negotiations. No other country can do this."

The Shah asked for help in building an Iranian navy. He said he had invited Hughes and Westinghouse to establish an electronics industry in Iran. He was also keen to start co-production in the defense industry. Nixon said he would help Iran attain nuclear power if the Shah wanted it. "It has been very helpful to get your survey of the situation," the president concluded. "Your analysis convinces me that it is indispensable that we have a policy of total cooperation. I want Dr. Kissinger to follow through on naval forces, [nuclear] breeder reactors, etc. I see the world and the part Iran plays pretty much as you do."

Nixon did not attend the second round of talks, which began in the Shah's reception room at Blair House at 5:00 P.M. and lasted for an hour and a half. Zahedi put his foot down and insisted he sit in with the Shah. It was in this meeting that the Iranians and Americans in the room—the Shah, Zahedi, Kissinger, and Helms—talked in detail about developing military contingency plans with respect to Kuwait, Saudi Arabia, and Pakistan. The Shah was deeply concerned about the intentions of the Soviet Union and its regional proxies Iraq and India. He said it was important that "we make it clear to the other side that we are not going to accept any monkey business, they will think twice before doing anything foolish. As I explained to the President . . . just the power of being able to knock out Soviet protégés will make them think twice."

"You mean Iraq?" Kissinger asked.

"All the countries who lean on them [the Soviets] for support," the Shah replied. "Our policy is not to insult them but to show them that adventures in our area will not work." Kissinger concurred, assuring the Shah, "We are trying to checkmate Soviet influence wherever it appears and to exhaust them in any adventures they may pursue. We want to create a frame of mind in the Politburo that is tired of costly adventures in the Middle East which do not produce results. We want to do this without confronting them. We want them simply to recognize that they pay a price for that kind of policy." Their joint project to support a Kurdish rebellion was just one facet of a strategy meant to drain Soviet proxy states like Iraq of their national treasure.

The Shah expressed indignation that Iran's conservative Arab neighbors refused to cooperate with Iran on matters of regional defense. Iraq's attempted takeover of Kuwait in the spring was still fresh in his mind. "Kuwait is so small that its early warning system will never be adequate to permit defense by fighters in time," explained the Shah. "Bombs can even be dropped from planes almost across the border. Kuwait must be protected by Jordan or Saudi Arabia."

It was at this point that Ambassador Zahedi raised the "additional idea" of developing a U.S.-Iran contingency plan to safeguard Gulf oil fields. This was an updated version of a plan first developed after the massacre of the Iraqi royal family in 1958 by leftist radicals in Baghdad. At that time the Shah had quietly agreed that if Iraq invaded neighboring Kuwait, American and British aircraft would be allowed to use Iranian airspace and airfields during an eviction operation. He now wanted to formalize and update emergency planning to take into account Iran's superior military strength. Although President Ahmad Hassan al-Bakr was the titular head of the Iraqi state, the Shah was keeping an eye on a rising young official named Saddam Hussein, whose radical credentials, reputation for brutality, and nationalist inclinations were already causing concern throughout the Gulf region. In the meeting at Blair House, Zahedi asked how the White House would react if Iran "were to help Kuwait" without receiving permission from the international community to do so: "For instance, would the US take a strong stand so that there would be no difficulties in the UN?" What the

Shah wanted to know was whether the United States would provide Iran with diplomatic cover to preemptively invade Kuwait in order to forestall an imminent Iraqi invasion of the sheikhdom.

Kissinger was intrigued by the Iranian proposal. He asked the Shah and Zahedi to outline their intentions. Discussion turned to the model for military intervention offered up by the Soviet Union when it invaded Czechoslovakia in 1968. The Shah feared that the Soviets would repeat the tactic in the Persian Gulf. The Shah then wondered aloud whether a contingency plan might have saved the recently deposed Afghan king: "If we had had an understanding, for instance, with the King of Afghanistan, he might have been flown secretly to some point in Afghanistan after the recent coup and appealed for help."

"Does Your Majesty have plans?" Kissinger inquired. "Or would the plans have to be developed?"

"The plans would have to be developed," replied the Shah.

"The diplomatic scenario will be very important," concurred Kissinger. "In a situation like this it may be desirable to move quickly."

"Yes," agreed the Shah. "We should take this up. [transcript redacted]. Kuwait would not be easy. If Iraq begins an invasion at breakfast time, they could take Kuwait by noon." Then the Shah observed, "At the same time, it is important to note that a coup in Saudi Arabia may have nothing to do with Soviet grand design. It could come about entirely from their own forces."

"As you develop your contingency plans for Saudi Arabia, it should be discussed with no one except Helms," warned Kissinger. "It can not be discussed in telegrams. That will mean Ambassador Zahedi will not be able to be informed by written communication."

"I agree," said the Shah. "We do the same for our communication with the Kurds. We have nothing but oral communication." The Shah wanted Nixon to pour even more weapons into Iraq's escalating ethnic conflict with the Iraqi Kurds, a request that Kissinger promised to look at sympathetically. But he had a concern. "Can we keep them from coming to terms?" he asked. He worried that Saddam might make Kurdish leaders an offer they couldn't refuse. The Shah advocated setting up a puppet Kurdish government-in-exile in Iraq's north. That way they could restrain the Kurds from signing a peace deal without their permission. He then directed the conversation back to Kuwait and Saudi Arabia. "Any contingency planning on Saudi Arabia must be most hush-hush," he insisted. "Saudi Arabia is different from Kuwait. I would not think this for myself. I think of it as useful more from the European viewpoint."

"We should agree under what circumstances any plan that is developed should be implemented," said Kissinger. "We would need to know what was being triggered. . . . After Your Majesty returns to Tehran, perhaps a plan could be developed." He turned to Helms: "Who should be involved here?"

"No one other than a couple of people in the White House," said Helms.

"Your Majesty can tell Ambassador Helms when you are ready," added Kissinger. "We can communicate either by sending someone out there or by someone come here. We probably should not even put this into our backchannel communication."

"That can be done easily," affirmed Helms.

"In the meantime, we should think about getting some Saudi like [Prince] Fahd or [Prince] Sultan to start an official cooperation with Iran," confirmed the Shah, who was thinking about the need for a cover plan to throw off Saudi suspicions. "Obviously we need to have a contingency plan. But as a complement, we should try to develop official cooperation with the Saudis. . . . I will talk to Helms about the contingency plan." He smiled and added, "I will not talk to the Senate Foreign Relations Committee about it tomorrow." Kissinger laughed at this and threw in a joke of his own relating to Watergate: "It might take the headlines away from our domestic concerns."

Military contingency plans are developed for every eventuality. But this one assumed that a contingency plan hatched in Iran and based on Iranian threat perceptions also reflected the American national interest. It did not. If activated, the plan would alter the balance of power in the Middle East and West Asia by making Iran the monopoly producer of Persian Gulf oil and gas, ensuring the West's complete reliance on the Shah's goodwill as its primary energy supplier. It was a plan that had the potential to ignite a religious-based war pitting Shi'a Iran against its Sunni Arab neighbors and potentially draw in the Soviet Union. The Shah was advocating regime change in Kuwait and Saudi Arabia under cover of declaring an unspecified regional "emergency" or "crisis," most likely one involving Iraq and its patron the Soviet Union. The problem was that the Shah was hardly an unbiased observer. Arab governments distrusted his ambitions and wondered how they fitted into his newly reconstituted Empire of Iran. Iran's unilateral seizure of the three islands in 1971 still rankled.

The new secretary of defense, James Schlesinger, later aptly summed up the 1973 state visit as "a renewal of vows, as it were—a renewal of marital vows" between Nixon and Kissinger on one side and the Shah: "The Shah, as you may know, since he was an absolute monarch, tended to spin out these theories in Tehran, and as he did so he was surrounded by a group of men who'd say, 'How wise you are, Your Majesty, how insightful!' And so he tended to be unchecked, as it were, in the development of his strategic views, some of which were soundly based, but some of which were pretty fanciful."

That evening the Nixons, the Pahlavis, and 115 guests were entertained after a sumptuous dinner by singer Tony Martin, whose first gold record was in 1938. He sang "Tea for Two" and somewhat inauspiciously crooned "There's No Tomorrow" for the two first couples. But the president was in good cheer, inexplicably sporting a suntan and displaying "unusual friendliness to reporters," even speaking to some. The modestly attired queen was outshone by socialite Cristina Ford, the wife of auto mogul Henry Ford II, who startled in "a strapless tube of sequins" topped off by "a necklace of crown-jewel proportions." Vice President Spiro Agnew tried to joke his way out of questions about Watergate by gamely telling reporters, "I can't understand what it's all about, can you?"

The next day the Shah held a news conference at Blair House. He repeatedly compared Iran to Britain, France, and West Germany "and rejected comparison with countries of the Middle East." Iran, he said, was the newest "big power." He announced that he "definitely" planned to buy F-14s but refused to say how many. He said he would also take a look at the F-15 produced by McDonnell Douglas—he described the planes as "sophisticated toys." Their Majesties arrived in Paris on Sunday, July 29. In the afternoon Court Minister Alam joined the Shah and his four children for a three-hour walk in the Bois de Boulogne. The Americans, he assured Alam, had given him everything he asked for.

Chapter Four

CONTINGENCIES

"It's America's inaction, or possibly America's impotence, that has landed us all in this mess."

—The Shah, 1973

"Can't we overthrow one of the sheikhs just to show that we can do it?"

—Henry Kissinger, 1973

WE'RE HERE TO GRAB THE OIL

In any normal August, Southern California's Mojave Desert would be a quiet refuge of triple-digit temperatures baking a barren landscape of sagebrush and sand. But August 1973 fit no one's definition of "normal." Against a sobering backdrop of scandal and political paralysis in Washington, the tightest oil market in history, and rumors of war in the Middle East, the largest desert warfare training exercises in the history of the U.S. Marine Corps began. For two weeks clouds of dust rose high above the Mojave as thousands of men and machines engaged in pitched battle. Surrounding hillsides echoed with the crackle of rifle shots and the dull thud of mortar rounds. Overhead, Phantom jets shrieked and HueyCobra gunships and Chinook helicopters kicked up curtains of dust and sand while offloading supplies and men.

There was little doubt what it was all for. "Officially, no parallels are drawn between Operation Alkali Canyon and the Middle East," noted one of the handful of civilians invited to observe the maneuvers at Twentynine Palms, the Marines' 932-square-mile desert warfare training facility in the Mojave. "Although most troops were lectured on Middle East desert politics and survival—and the 'aggressors' were clothed in khaki shirts and red collar insignia similar to those worn by the Libyan army, no one is supposed to talk about Arabs." As one reservist earnestly explained, "They told us not to say anything political. We can't even use Israel as a hypothetical example." Added one of his colleagues, "The Pentagon has a computer plan for the invasion of every civilized country in the world. The Middle East is the obvious powder keg, and we'd be fools if we didn't prepare."

Seven months after ending combat operations in the jungles of Southeast Asia, and four weeks after agreeing to draw up contingency plans with Iran to invade Kuwait and Saudi Arabia in an emergency, the Nixon administration was gearing up for war in the desert sands of the Middle East. The Alkali Canyon 73 exercises called for five thousand Marine Corps regulars and four thousand Marine reservists to split into two opposing sides. Eight hundred Marines from the fictional communist state of Yermos were ordered to invade peace-loving Argos to the south. Although "the entire war, all its battles and the eventual outcome, had been programmed in advance by computer," things went haywire from the get-go. Many of the reservists made it clear that with the war in Vietnam over, they just wanted to sign their discharge papers and go home. "I can give you my opinion of this entire operation in two words: F—— it," declared Private Willie Wilkins of Akron, Ohio.

The reservists seemed more interested in reaching for their bottles of Coppertone than their rifles. They retreated to their tents with crates of beer and got drunk. Confusion abounded. Men fainted in the heat. An exchange officer from the British Royal Marines, Captain Duncan Christie-Miller, sat out the "war" in his tent writing an article on skiing in Europe. "Our unit was supposed to be in a tank battle last night, but someone forgot to bring the tanks," groused Sergeant Bob Musmann from Pittsburgh. "Can you picture *Hogan's Heroes*, *F Troop* and *MASH* all together? We've got it." Lieutenant Colonel Richard Dennis lost his cool when he learned that his telegrapher had gone to chow without telling him, forcing a delay in calling up air strikes. "Goddamn!" screamed Dennis. "This is war! What's the matter? Doesn't anyone take this seriously?" One who did was Staff Sergeant Greg Anderson. Clambering aboard his tank to rally his troops, Anderson called them to arms with the irresistible cry, "Come on men! We're out here to get practice so we can grab the oil!"

LIBYA IS GOING TO KNOCK THEM OFF

The trigger man for mayhem that summer turned out to be not Iran's Mohammad Reza Shah Pahlavi but a man from the next generation, Colonel Muammar al-Qaddafi, the thirty-one-year-old ruler of Libya. Libya was a relative newcomer to the world oil market. Armand Hammer's Occidental Petroleum had struck it big in Libya in 1966 with gushers in the Sirte Basin, located a hundred miles inland from the Mediterranean. Libya's proximity to Europe's southern underbelly meant that within six years it was supplying the continent with 30 percent of its oil. Libyan petroleum was in high demand in the United States because it easily met the Nixon administration's tough new clean air standards.

Libya, three times the size of France but with a population of less than 2 million people, reinvested the profits from its daily exports of 2.3 million barrels of oil into a welfare state that boasted free education, health care, and housing. Qaddafi had staked out a reputation as the most mercurial and radical leader of the Arab world, espousing a hodgepodge of "isms": pan-Arabism, pan-Africanism, Islamic fundamentalism, anti-Zionism, socialism, anti-Americanism, and anti-Communism. He canceled military base agreements with the United States and expelled Libya's Italian community, threatening to empty Italian graveyards of their dead and ship the 21,000 corpses to Rome. He used Libya's fortune to acquire the biggest cash and gold reserves in the Arab world while lavishing aid on Egypt, Syria, and Yasser Arafat's Palestinian guerrillas. Qaddafi's most potent purchase to date was a $200 million order for a fleet of 114 French Mirage fighter-bombers. The aircraft threatened to tip the military balance of power in North Africa. Qaddafi's military pretensions and radical tendencies engendered enormous concern in Tel Aviv and Tehran. "This Qaddafi is a real nut," the Shah warned Kissinger. "He is making trouble."

Western oil companies operating in Libya presented Qaddafi with a soft target. In 1970 he forced Occidental Petroleum to raise the price of its oil by the then unheard of sum of 30 cents a barrel. The negotiations were conducted over rolls and a revolver—after the Libyan representative offered American oil executives coffee and rolls, he set his revolver on the table in front of them as a reminder of just how much the market in petroleum had changed in recent years. It was the first time the oil majors had broken ranks and surrendered to the demands of a host government. Kissinger explained in his memoirs that the White House assumed it was witnessing "commercial bargaining and not a revolutionary upheaval" in the oil market, and that "the dimensions of the problem were not immediately apparent. And because the symptoms, the price increases of the early 1970s, were extremely modest, no issue of domestic economic policy—not to speak of national security—seemed to be involved."

Kissinger's logic was specious to say the least. Although individual increases in the price of oil appeared at the time to be modest, their overall cumulative effect was striking enough—the price of oil jumped 72 percent between 1970 and September 1973. No one could miss the fact that oil prices were trending upward. Kissinger wrote that the U.S. government "did not as a general practice involve itself in commercial disputes" although his involvement in the Aramco negotiations and his frequent contacts with the oil companies suggested otherwise. Kissinger unfairly laid the blame for what he termed the Nixon administration's policy of "noninvolvement" in the oil market on William Rogers, Nixon's first secretary of state. "Our hands-off policy ordained the result: the companies yielded," Kissinger explained. He insisted that he on the other hand had been "increasingly alarmed by the escalating demands of the producers" in the spring of 1973. Yet Kissinger's declassified telephone transcripts tell a different story. They reveal missed opportunities, ignored warnings, and precious months lost to prepare the American economy for the wave that was about to break over its bow.

On May 15, 1973, Deputy Secretary of Defense William Clements telephoned Kissinger to ask for "a quick word because I know you don't like surprises, Henry." Clements had it on "good authority that the Libyans will likely this week starting today, perhaps tomorrow for sure supposedly, start nationalizing the American interest in Libya."

"So what?" was Kissinger's response.

Clements, a former oilman who enjoyed close ties with Middle East governments, asked that Libyan oil nationalization be "put on the agenda today" because of the "enormous pressure that's building up as an interface with that problem in Saudi Arabia. The two are related." King Faisal had in the past promised not to turn his kingdom's giant oil reserves into a weapon in the Arab-Israeli dispute. But the old king was losing ground to the siren call of Qaddafi and his radicals. In early May Faisal warned Aramco executives "with extreme urgency" that the Nixon administration should take notice of rising tensions in the Middle East. Clements said the White House needed to come up with a plan "because I don't think anyone is now addressing that problem or thinking in terms of how we will respond."

"To the nationalization," said Kissinger.

"Right. And the people are there and some of the other things that may happen." Defense was worried about the safety of American civilians working in Libya who were vulnerable to hostage taking or assassination.

"I agree," said Kissinger, who had still not grasped the extent of the problem. "You're not talking about the flights, you're talking about . . ."

"Oh hell, no, I'm talking about the takeover of 3 billion or more, 3 billion plus of our assets," answered Clements.

Kissinger agreed that something should be done. But two weeks later Deputy Secretary of State Kenneth Rush phoned with a warning of his own. "I had in all the heads of the companies doing business in Libya," he explained. "They are really—their backs are against the wall. What Libya is going to do is knock them off one by one and then leap-frog over to the Middle East, and the Shah has told me he does not want to raise the price of oil, but that if we [don't act], then he's got to do it at least back to Libya and back and forth. And all the heads of these companies say we've got to do something to show—to calm the emotional upsurge in the Middle East." Rush had just returned from Tehran, where he had held talks with the Shah. The Iranian leader was letting Kissinger know that if Qaddafi charged more for Libyan oil, then Iran would follow suit penny for penny, dollar for dollar. That would be like striking a match in a paper factory—it would ignite a bonfire of price gouging and profiteering among Gulf oil producers. By now, alarm bells should have been ringing at the NSC. But Kissinger instead brushed aside Rush's warning. Unlike his colleague, he knew that the Shah already had Nixon's permission to raise the price of oil. "But they are always wrong, Ken," he lectured his colleague and rival. "Every year they have another pet project to calm it, and they are never right."

A sound knowledge of global finance, commodity prices, and exchange rates would be as crucial to navigating the shoals of the new decade as moving flags and armies around the chessboard of great power rivalries. Nixon's decision in August to replace Rogers with Kissinger as secretary of state came with Nixon's recognition that his new secretary of state lacked essential expertise in oil and economics. Kissinger held on to the pivotal post of national security adviser. "Henry wanted State, felt he deserved it, and let me know that he would resign if he didn't get it," Nixon recalled. "With the Watergate problem, I didn't have any choices." The painful scenes that followed were reminiscent of Nixon's botched handling of Richard Helms's dismissal as CIA chief the previous November. When White House chief of staff Alexander Haig asked Secretary of State Rogers to do the right thing by the president and resign, the usually affable secretary of state exploded in a fury: "Tell the president to go fuck himself." Rogers expected a more honorable way out than to be presented with a pistol on a plate. Kissinger understood that "for Nixon my appointment was less an act of choice than a step taken against his will in the hope it would mitigate catastrophe."

Arthur Burns wrote in his diary that Kissinger had been in office only a matter of days when he asked for help "in reducing Treasury's role in international economic area, so that State's role may be enhanced." Burns wrote with horror of the way Kissinger used economics and international finance as tactical tools to settle scores and punish leaders who stood in his way. On one occasion he asked Burns to come up with ways in which the Fed could "cause economic trouble for the French? What can U.S. do, or the Fed alone, to cause economic trouble for the French?" Burns was shocked by Henry's suggestion that the administration should destabilize the economy of one of its most important allies and trading partners: "H. at times strikes me as a madman; a genius, yes; but he has a lust for power—a good pupil of Nixon's and Haldeman's, or perhaps one of their teachers? What outrageous thinking on his part!"

WE'RE PLAYING FOR REAL MARBLES NOW

Colonel Qaddafi struck on the evening of September 1, 1973. During festivities to mark the fourth anniversary of his coup the Libyan leader announced the expropriation of 51 percent of the assets of foreign oil companies operating in his country. As predicted, Qaddafi selected several companies, including Occidental, to test American resolve. When no resistance was forthcoming, he swept the board. Pressure now mounted on more moderate Persian Gulf oil producers to tear up their participation agreements, join Libya in hiking their oil prices by 30 percent, and refuse payment in dollars.

That same day news broke that during a recent unannounced visit to Saudi Arabia President Anwar Sadat of Egypt had won a pledge from King Faisal to "restrict oil production increases to the level of 10 per cent annually by the end of the year if American policy in the Middle East does not change." The problem for the United States was that it had been counting on Saudi Arabia to more than double production from its current output of 8.5 million barrels to 20 million barrels per day by 1980 to meet the growing chasm between domestic oil production and America's galloping rate of oil consumption. America could produce no more than 11 million barrels of oil per day even though it would shortly require 24 million for the economy to maintain current growth levels. Western economies including Japan were projected to see their oil consumption rise from 1.6 billion tons in 1970 to 2.8 billion tons by decade's end. Where would it all come from? Middle East oil producers had so far managed to keep pace with Western consumer demand by boosting their production rates by an annual 6.9 percent. Saudi Arabia's oil production had soared by 30 percent in the past year alone. But Faisal's threat to reduce rather than increase production threatened to drive Western economies to the wall. In a stroke it would wipe out surplus capacity in the market, pit consumers against each other in a mad scramble for scarce energy resources, and potentially destabilize financial systems worldwide by provoking a severe recession. The Saudi king had in effect placed his thumb on the windpipe of the American economy. "Faisal is no bluffer and we're playing for real marbles now," a worried White House official admitted to *Newsweek*. "We're talking about the flywheel of our economic system; if anything goes wrong with it, America stops."

TO THE BRINK

Despite explicit warnings provided to them by the leaders of Iran, Jordan, Saudi Arabia, and the Soviet Union that Egypt was rearming with the intention of attacking Israel, Nixon and Kissinger deferred to the confident assurances of Israeli government officials, who regarded such predictions as preposterous. One warm Saturday morning in mid-May, Henry Kissinger sat down with Israeli foreign minister Abba Eban in Washington. Eban rejected intelligence reports warning that Egypt and its ally Syria were preparing to hit Israel. They lacked the firepower and tactical expertise to pull off a surprise attack. President Sadat would not be so foolish as to gamble his house on a war he could not possibly win. "The result would be catastrophic for them, militarily, politically, domestically, and internationally," Eban assured Kissinger. "The humiliation at home; the Soviet Union would say we told you so." Nor was an Arab oil boycott of the West a realistic option. Besides, their friend the Shah would step in to break it by releasing additional crude into the system: "But a boycott wouldn't work, because Iran wouldn't go along."

Eban and Kissinger gossiped about Anwar Sadat's supposed lack of smarts. "Sadat is not bright, but he can think a few moves ahead," observed Eban. "He is not so volatile." "That is not my impression," replied Kissinger. "He shows no capacity for thinking moves ahead." Kissinger explained why the Nixon administration was sitting on its hands and refusing Faisal's entreaties to involve itself more in the Middle East. "As I have told your Ambassador, American passivity is due to a fortuitous combination of circumstances and cannot be counted on indefinitely. If you look at the constellation of leading officials, you cannot count on the continuation of the present. . . . So far, the Egyptian policy is so stupid there is no particular challenge." He told Eban that he was "reluctant to get us into a position where both sides can shoot at us without considering any scheme." The Israeli delegation returned home confident that Kissinger understood their concerns and shared their strategic assessment of the situation.

In August sixty-seven-year-old King Faisal received Aramco executives in Geneva. He made it clear that Saudi Arabia was under enormous pressure from its Arab brethren to turn its oil resources and revenues against Israel and its friends. Time was running out for the Nixon administration to reengage in the Middle East and nudge Israel toward dialogue. It wasn't until February 1974 that Americans learned the detailed nature of the king's warning. At a luncheon hosted in Washington by the Propeller Club, a merchant marine organization, guest speaker and Aramco vice president Michael Ameen Jr. described how King Faisal "told us in August, 1973, there would be another war within six months, and that he would have no alternative but to use oil as a weapon." The Saudi monarch even confided that Arab states were prepared to sustain fifty thousand casualties. "His warnings went unheeded," recalled Ameen. The White House never returned his calls, Ameen said. "We talked to the CIA, the Navy, the Army, the Marine Corps. They told us, 'Mike, you're out of your head—they don't want to get the hell kicked out of them.' They said, 'Don't worry about King Faisal—we're going to give them Phantoms.'"

King Faisal also took to the airwaves and granted rare interviews with American foreign correspondents to explain his concerns. He called for balance in U.S. foreign policy in the Middle East and explained that it was not necessarily in Saudi Arabia's interest to boost its oil production just to meet consumer demand in the West. "Logic requires that our oil production does not exceed the limits that can be absorbed by our economy," he said. Pumping billions of dollars in oil revenues back into an economy already registering the world's highest growth rate of 16 percent could be disastrous. Modernization had to proceed gradually and in stages. The king announced that Saudi oil production would not be increased until two conditions were met. First, he wanted the West to help industrialize and diversify the Saudi economy. Second, "a more suitable political atmosphere, hitherto disturbed by the Middle East crisis and Zionist expansionist policies, must be present."

The White House was thrown into confusion. On September 5 Henry Kissinger met with Secretary of Defense James Schlesinger for an eight o'clock breakfast meeting at the Pentagon. The two onetime academic rivals at Harvard would shortly have to deal with a cascade of crises in the Middle East against a backdrop of domestic political turmoil. Their immediate, if admittedly forlorn, objective was to "keep the Persian Gulf [oil production and pricing] issues away from the Arab-Israeli conflict."

"Let's talk contingency plans," said Schlesinger. "The Iranians could take Kuwait but not cross the Gulf."

"The Shah wants to know if the F-14 and F-15 mix," Kissinger replied. "[Israel's Yitzhak] Rabin said he wouldn't have the F-14."

Their brief but revealing exchange confirms that military contingencies, including plans involving Iran and Israel, were being reviewed by the White House in the first week of September. The timing of the discussion is significant because it came one month before war broke out in the Middle East and six weeks before Arab states embargoed oil sales to the United States. Historians have assumed that the use of force was seriously considered by the United States only *after* the oil embargo began to bite in November. We now know that the trigger events for intervention were not the outbreak of war or the imposition of the oil embargo—two events that Kissinger had already decided were implausible if not impossible—but Libyan oil nationalization and Saudi threats to reduce the flow. Traditionally, the use of force in international affairs is the policy option of last resort, to be activated only when diplomacy comes up short. But in the absence of diplomacy itself, military action becomes less a choice than a necessity. The end of summer brought with it the cruel realization that the United States had allowed itself to be marginalized in the Middle East. It had lost control of its oil lifeline even as it allowed billions of dollars' worth of assets to be expropriated.

Later in the day of September 5, President Nixon hinted at what was going on behind closed doors when he spoke to reporters. He insisted that he was committed to seeking a peace settlement in the Middle East. But he warned Arab oil states not to push him too far. "Oil without a market, as Mr. Mossadegh learned many, many years ago, doesn't do a country much good," said Nixon. Nixon liked to keep his adversaries on edge in the belief that he might use massive force against them—he called it his "madman" theory. That month Nixon and Kissinger were closely following events in Chile, where the CIA was involved in efforts to overthrow the elected government of President Salvador Allende, a Marxist who, like Colonel Qaddafi, had nationalized American corporate assets. It is likely that Allende's fate was weighing heavily on Nixon's mind when he invoked the specter of the deposed Mossadegh. But the president's decision to prise Mohammad Mossadegh from his crypt during a standoff with Middle Eastern governments—and at a time when Watergate investigators were probing his financial ties to the Shah—was a pointless provocation. For two decades American presidents had observed a discreet silence on the subject of the 1953 coup, not wishing to embarrass the Shah by resurrecting old accusations of puppetry.

Nixon had also unwittingly tipped the issue of U.S.-Iran relations and his deal making with the Shah into the shark tank of Watergate congressional investigations and media scrutiny. The result was predictable. "Because of our relationship with Nixon, they started hitting us," remembered Ambassador Zahedi. He was particularly worried about the tone of *The Washington Post*. "It was hardly market forces that threw Mr. Mossadegh out of office as premier of Iran in 1953," *Post* editors scolded Nixon in a particularly vociferous editorial that outed the Shah's CIA connections. "After a bitter dispute over his nationalization of British oil concessions, he fell in a coup ably and successfully supported by this country's Central Intelligence Agency." *Washington Post* columnists Rowland Evans and Robert Novak piled on the opprobrium, ridiculing Nixon's attempt to compare conditions in 1973 with those of twenty years before. His threat of retaliation against Arab governments was "dangerous poppycock . . . a hip-shooting challenge uttered without careful forethought." The president had "surprised his own aides" and "stunned the oil states of the Mideast, most particularly Saudi Arabia."

There was backlash in Arab capitals too. Nixon's threat coincided with a rash of news reports of the Marine exercises in the Mojave and an article in the French weekly *Nouvel Observateur* that described a joint American and British plan "to drop paratroopers in strategic oil and communications centers with the help of Iran and Israel." Invasion rumors swept the Middle East. A top-ranking Saudi official asked, "Do they think in Washington it is so easy to occupy oil fields with troops? Let them come and see." In Libya, Colonel Qaddafi warned that the "Nixon gang" wanted to take over his country. "The backlash is definitely there," a senior U.S. diplomat told *The Washington Post*. "More and more, Arab officials are convinced that justification for some kind of military operation against the oil countries is being built by the United States. This feedback is in itself becoming a factor in our relations with the Arabs—a negative factor."

The president's own advisers were appalled but for a different reason—it dawned on them that Nixon still believed Western consumers retained influence in the oil market. "My God, doesn't he realize that every single incremental barrel of oil today has to come from the Middle East," complained an adviser. Asked by a reporter why Nixon had decided to dredge up Mossadegh's name to threaten Arab governments, a White House official snapped back, "Because he was advised by a fool." The president, said the official, had since been "readvised."

Oil producers made their feelings clear when they announced plans to meet in Vienna on October 8 to raise oil prices and scrap the terms of the 1971 Tehran Agreement. The contracts they had previously signed with the oil companies "are no longer compatible with prevailing market conditions."

BUT WHICH COUNTRY ARE WE OCCUPYING?

The combined armies of Egypt and Syria attacked Israel on October 6, 1973, the high holy day of Yom Kippur. They punched through Israeli lines, pouring across the Suez Canal in the south and storming the Golan Heights in the north. Troops from Saudi Arabia, Iraq, Jordan, Kuwait, Morocco, and Tunisia rushed to join the fray. The fourth Arab-Israeli war was underway.

In Tehran, the Shah summoned his chief of staff and army commander to discuss Iran's options. The Shah was distressed that his warnings to Nixon and Kissinger about the prospects for war had been ignored. He wisely decided to keep Iran on the sidelines. He agreed to lend Iranian aircraft to the Arab states for strictly domestic use, refused Moscow's request that Soviet military aircraft be allowed to fly over Iranian airspace, and quietly assured the Israelis that Iran would keep selling them oil. But he instructed his court minister to convey his frustration to Ambassador Richard Helms: "Tell him he's under an obligation to find some sort of solution to this blasted war. It's America's inaction, or possibly America's impotence, that has landed us all in this mess."

Israeli leaders informed the Nixon administration that they could not hold two battlefronts for long. Faced with the prospect of Arab armies sweeping down from the Golan into Israeli towns and settlements, Prime

Minister Golda Meir activated Israel's nuclear deterrent and had a Mirage jet loaded with an atomic bomb readied for takeoff. The message was clear: Israel would not burn alone. Officials in Washington watched in shock as their strategic assumptions about Israeli military superiority crumbled. Early on the morning of October 10, Schlesinger phoned Kissinger to inform him that the Soviets were resupplying Arab forces and that King Faisal had committed Saudi troops. He made it clear that as far as the Pentagon was concerned all options concerning the Saudis were now on the table. Faisal had crossed the line and thrown in his lot with the radicals. "So I think that we are going to get into a position in which all of our interests in Saudi Arabia are at risk and it might be desirable to examine the fundamentals of our position—"

"Well, what are the fundamentals of our position as you see it?" asked Kissinger.

"Well, the fundamentals are that we may be faced with the choice that lies cruelly between support for Israel, loss of Saudi Arabia and if interests in the Middle East are at risk, the choice between occupation or watching them go down the drain."

"Occupation of whom?"

"That would remain to be seen—it can be partial."

"But which country are we occupying?"

"That's one of the things we'd like to talk about," said Schlesinger.

"Who's we?"

"Me."

"Okay, I have heard an urgent message which I've got to take up with the President and I'll be back to you later this morning and we'll get together this morning," said Kissinger, ending the conversation.

Kissinger's day of intense drama had just begun. His efforts to reach a cease-fire in the Middle East while discussing plans for U.S. military intervention came to a dramatic and historic pause at 2:05 P.M. when he received Vice President Spiro Agnew's formal letter of resignation. It was a procedure required under the terms of the Presidential Succession Act of 1792. Agnew had been under investigation for graft during his term as governor of Maryland. Under a plea bargain reached with prosecutors, the unhappy vice president agreed to resign in order to avoid a prison sentence. Within an hour private citizen Spiro Agnew stood in a Baltimore courtroom and "with barely trembling hands" pleaded no contest to charges of tax evasion. Two days later President Nixon nominated Gerald Ford, the sixty-year-old Republican minority leader in the House of Representatives, to replace him.

There was drama too in Vienna, where Persian Gulf oil producers renegotiating the terms of their contracts with Western oil companies abruptly quit the talks and threatened unilateral price increases. Abu Dhabi, Iran, Iraq, Kuwait, and Saudi Arabia were in no mood to compromise against the backdrop of war in the Middle East and crisis in Washington. They threatened to hike prices by 50 percent, well above those set by Libya and Algeria. Industry negotiators refused and warned them that such a big increase "would have exceptionally serious and wide-ranging implications, not only for the companies but for the world economy at large." Inflation would rise in the West and such a rapid transfer of wealth could destabilize the international financial system. Arab leaders decided to reconvene in Kuwait City in two weeks to discuss their options.

The Israelis meanwhile were bogged down, having lost a quarter of their air force and suffering hundreds of battlefield casualties. At 12:49 A.M. on Saturday, October 13, Kissinger and Schlesinger held a tense telephone conversation in which the secretary of state implored his colleague to get moving with an airlift of military equipment. Kissinger was panicked. Israeli commanders had told him they were running so low on ammunition and spare parts that a counteroffensive they had mounted against the Syrians in the Golan Heights was in danger of collapse. Kissinger knew that for a diplomatic deal to be brokered, the Israelis must be in a stronger military position. Schlesinger insisted that the Israelis had given him no indication they were in trouble. "Well they simply cannot be that short of ammo, Henry," he countered. "It is impossible that they didn't know what their supply was—and suddenly they run out of it."

Kissinger needed to keep Israeli guns in action for at least another twenty-four hours until a cease-fire resolution went before the Security Council. He confided to Schlesinger that Israeli generals were afraid to speak candidly about their dire predicament because "they don't trust the people in the room." Israeli army headquarters was in a shambles. "Look, they have obviously screwed up every offensive they've conducted and they are not about to take the responsibility themselves," he exclaimed. "I have no doubt whatever that they are blaming us for their failures."

"Are they short of ammo or aren't they?" demanded Schlesinger. The distinction was critical because, as the defense secretary knew, any decision by the United States to airlift military supplies to Israel would provoke retaliatory action from Arab oil producers and possibly lead to an oil embargo against the West.

"How the hell would I know," snapped Kissinger. The White House was operating in an information vacuum. Schlesinger worried that the Israelis were trying to, as he put it, "suck us in." Henry's behavior was also a concern. "As Israel began to fall apart, Henry began to fall apart," he remembered. Kissinger and Schlesinger both understood that the United States was in a dilemma, faced with a choice between losing Israel or losing Arab oil. The American position in the Middle East was untenable. Kissinger told Schlesinger that the Israeli officials he had spoken to were "so terrified now" of a renewed Egyptian drive into the Sinai. They could not hold both fronts for much longer.

"That's incredible planning on their part," answered an exasperated Schlesinger.

"Look, they fucked it up," fumed Kissinger.

"Hm huh. Okay, let me try to find out what the hell their status of supplies situation is. We had the impression they had 15 days of supply."

This was the fog of war. Kissinger was furious with the assurances the Israelis had given him over the past year. "Because you know what happened—as well as I do," he told Schlesinger. "These guys got the whole thing screwed up—every time. They are living in 1967. All day long yesterday they were telling me they were headed for Damascus and they were going to stop on the outskirts. . . . Now they obviously can't make it."

Kissinger and Schlesinger agreed to move military supplies through the Portuguese Azores. The next morning *The New York Times* reported that the administration had agreed to ship F-4 Phantom jet fighters to Israel to make up for its losses: "The step is being taken with unusually tight secrecy by the Administration, which is deeply concerned about the repercussions it could have on American relations with oil-producing Arab states as well as on Soviet actions in resupplying Egypt and Syria."

Nixon's national security team reconvened just after nine o'clock on Sunday morning, October 14. They were joined by the White House energy adviser, former governor John Love of Colorado, and special energy consultant Charles DiBonna. Their inclusion was a belated acknowledgment by Kissinger that the issues of the oil supply and the Middle East conflict might now converge. Kissinger asked his colleagues to come up with policy options in the event—still unlikely as he saw it—of interruptions to America's oil supply in response to the airlift. They should develop contingencies for a possible Arab oil embargo. He asked: "What do we do if the oil is cut off? What kinds of problems will we have?"

Israeli foreign minister Abba Eban had assured Kissinger back in May that in the event of an Arab oil embargo the Shah would step in and break it by ramping up Iran's oil output. But Eban had been wildly overoptimistic—it turned out that Iran had virtually no spare capacity. There was no way the Iranians could flood the market with enough oil to counter any Arab boycott. "How much could the Iranians increase?" asked Schlesinger. "Five-and-a-half to eight million?"

Love had some bad news for the White House: "Iran could perhaps get 200,000 barrels a day more but they have already kicked it up." Any hopes the administration had of breaking a future embargo with the Shah's help were dashed.

"If it happens it will happen next week," said Kissinger. "We are going to need a plan. It should consider a cutoff in the U.S. and a cutoff to Japan and Europe as well."

"To do so, we also have to consider consultations on the Hill, putting the President on TV, and the timing of what we do now," added Love. "We have to be ready."

"We don't want to push the button now and cause panic," Kissinger advised. "We need to have the program ready for the day when they do it."

Deputy Secretary of Defense William Clements described a cutoff of oil supplies from the Middle East as "a mega problem," one that could not be fixed by conservation at home, cutting the speed limit, or increasing domestic oil production. Schlesinger added, "On timing we must weigh the advantage of getting something out on the problem. If it is indicated this will happen, we will want to consider the deterrent impact." Defense was making it known that military contingency planning might have to come into play.

Kissinger was less sure: "So far no one has threatened us, but we have no program."

"We could announce something quickly," said Love.

"I wouldn't provoke it or threaten them," Kissinger replied. He explained that he had not heard any mention of a cut-off in his talks with Arab envoys: "All I have received are hysterical calls from oil companies. The Saudis have been better than any. We have good commercial relations. Some idiot says we shouldn't have said that but I don't want to challenge the Arabs to a test of their manhood."

"When we resupply to Israel, at that point we will have a problem," said Kenneth Rush of the State Department.

They looked at the impact of an embargo on the domestic economy. The crisis team was asking questions that should have been asked and could have been answered months earlier. "It will cause restrictions on the domestic economy," observed Clements.

Love concurred: "We would have to make some shifts and close down some factories."

The stunning fact was that even at this late hour in the crisis no one in the administration could offer specifics on how much spare fuel capacity was available to tap in the United States in the event of an emergency.

"In a short time there would be shortages in everything—perhaps a month," warned Love. But when someone suggested that the group consider worst-case scenarios, Kissinger refused, saying, "Let's not talk about consequences. We don't want to make it happen. We should be low key."

The following day, Saudi oil minister Zaki Yamani warned that if the administration undertook an aerial resupply operation of Israel, his government would retaliate by slashing its oil output by 10 percent immediately and then by 5 percent each succeeding month. Saudi production was running high at 8.5 million barrels per day, with 600,000 of those barrels bound for the United States. Reports were also circulating that Kuwait was considering a halt to petroleum exports to the United States.

At this critical juncture Richard Nixon roused himself and like his hero Teddy Roosevelt decided to charge up San Juan Hill one more time. On Tuesday, October 16, the president welcomed recipients of the National Medal of Honor to the White House. Nixon told his audience that he was prepared to use force in the Middle East and referred to "the policy we followed in 1958 when Lebanon was involved" and "the policy we followed in 1970 when Jordan was involved." In 1958, the Eisenhower administration had landed Marines in Lebanon to put down an insurrection. Twelve years later, Nixon had come close to dispatching airborne troops to Jordan to help King Hussein crush an uprising by the Palestine Liberation Organization. Nixon's threat to use force might have worked in another year, but Vietnam had damaged perceptions abroad of American resolve and Watergate had shattered the public trust in Nixon's leadership at home. Worse, the U.S. economy was not capable of absorbing a major blow like an oil embargo.

The next day, Arab oil ministers meeting in Kuwait agreed to monthly

5 percent cuts in production until Israel evacuated the territories it had seized in 1967. Separately, the six Persian Gulf oil-producing nations, including Iran, announced a double-digit percentage increase in the price of a barrel of light Arabian crude from $3.01 per barrel to $3.65, an increase of about 21 percent. The game of leap-frogging that Kenneth Rush had warned Kissinger about back in May had started. The next day Saudi Arabia sharply responded to the airlift of American weapons and supplies to Israel by slashing its oil output by 10 percent. Abu Dhabi announced that it would ban shipments to the United States altogether.

The mood darkened considerably on October 19 when Colonel Qaddafi imposed an oil embargo against the United States and raised the price of a barrel of Libyan crude from $4.90 to $8.92, which accelerated the sequence of price escalations for the rest of the oil producers. Libya's oil was a mainstay of the economy in New York City. The full impact of price increases and new taxes agreed to by Persian Gulf producers now became clear: the posted price of light Arabian crude had jumped by 70 percent to $5.11. "We are masters of our own commodity," declared Sheikh Yamani. "Stunned and confused" oil industry analysts warned of impending fuel shortages along the eastern seaboard. A private industry group in Washington warned with considerable understatement that "what the producing countries appear to have done is to have raised the price of running a factory, heating a home, and powering a car around the world by an unprecedented degree."

In Washington, meanwhile, a White House spokesman made the remarkably ill-advised statement that the United States would not take the Arab oil embargo seriously until "at least one million barrels of oil a day of supply had been cut off." King Faisal was glad to oblige. The next day he ended all shipments of oil to the United States. Saturday, October 20, was a historic day that began with a declaration of economic warfare by Saudi Arabia against the United States and ended with demands for the president's impeachment. American television viewers watched in disbelief as news anchormen broke into regular late night broadcasting to report that President Nixon had fired Watergate special prosecutor Archibald Cox, abolished the Watergate task force, and conducted a purge of his own Justice Department. Nixon accepted the resignation of Attorney General Elliot Richardson and sacked Richardson's deputy, William Ruckelshaus, for disloyalty when both men refused Nixon's order to fire Cox. (The number three Justice official Solicitor General Robert Bork fired Cox.) The calls for Nixon's resignation came on a day when the country still lacked a vice president—nominee Gerald Ford had only begun the process to win congressional confirmation—

and while the secretary of state was in Moscow conferring with Soviet leader Leonid Brezhnev on the war in the Middle East.

King Faisal's decision to cut off fuel supplies was bravely played down by a White House in the midst of chaos. Officially at least, the administration was "not surprised" by the Saudi action. Unofficially, the White House was stunned. The next day, Kuwait, Qatar, Bahrain, and Dubai announced that they were joining Saudi Arabia, Libya, Algeria, and Abu Dhabi in halting oil shipments to the United States. The embargo was complete.

DR. KISSINGER'S "FANTASTIC RISK"

Secretary of State Henry Kissinger arrived in Tel Aviv from Moscow on October 22, the same day that a Middle East cease-fire approved by the United Nations Security Council took effect. Flush with American fire-power from the airlift, and having trapped Egypt's Third Army on the east bank of the Suez Canal, Israeli leaders weren't ready to settle just yet. With Kissinger's tacit assent they fought on past the deadline to consolidate their last-minute territorial gains. It was an extraordinary gamble and one that caught the attention of Soviet leaders in Moscow already considering an appeal for help from President Sadat.

Kissinger was back in Washington on the evening of Wednesday, October 24, when Leonid Brezhnev challenged Nixon to join him in send-ing peacekeepers to the Middle East to enforce the cease-fire accords and separate the combatants. Brezhnev made it clear that he was prepared to land Russian troops in Egypt regardless of Nixon's decision. Moscow would not tolerate the destruction of Egypt's Third Army. To complicate matters, Brezhnev's ultimatum occurred on an evening when Nixon showed every sign of collapsing under the strain of Watergate. During a telephone call to Kissinger, the president was "as agitated and emotional as I had ever heard him." Nixon railed against "those bastards" in Congress who were kicking him around: "They are doing it because of their desire to kill the President. And they may succeed. I may physically die." The president intimated he was prepared to quit: "I would like them to run this country and see what they do."

By the time Nixon's rump national security team, the Washington Special Action Group (WSAG), gathered at the White House at 10:40 P.M., the president had passed out in his bed, emotionally spent and reportedly in a drunken stupor. Kissinger and White House chief of staff Alexander Haig concluded that Nixon was incapacitated and unable to participate in the crisis meeting to discuss the challenge from Moscow. Kissinger asked Haig if he should wake up the president, but Haig said no. A half hour later, Haig asked Kissinger if *he* had spoken to Nixon. "No, I haven't," replied Kissinger. "He would just start charging around. . . . I don't think we should bother the President." They agreed that the president was "too distraught to participate in the preliminary decision."

The scene that unfolded over the next several hours hovered between great drama and high farce. Kissinger and Haig did not brief their colleagues—the director of Central Intelligence, the chairman of the Joint Chiefs of Staff, or the secretary of defense—on the president's true condition. Instead, they engaged in an elaborate ruse. Kissinger ran the proceedings while Haig, "who was shuttling back and forth between the residence and the [Situation Room] where the meeting was taking place, reported that the president approved our recommendations," recalled Schlesinger. "Haig reported that the President was about and following events." The others were unaware that Nixon slept through one of the most dangerous nights of his presidency.

The crisis team was particularly concerned about intelligence reports suggesting that the Soviets were preparing to fly eight transport planes to Egypt and had "stood down their forces in East Germany, stood down their aircraft." That "conveyed to us the possibility that they were seriously contemplating moving in," said Schlesinger. There had been a substantial buildup of nuclear-armed Soviet naval vessels in the Mediterranean. Iran's northern border was also a potential flashpoint. "We had some concern about the northern Iranian border, although the Iranians had a lot more concern than we did." The Pentagon knew that it would not be easy for the Russians "to punch through [the Elburz Mountains] with ground forces." Of more immediate concern was their awareness that the Soviets had recently developed a highly effective rapid mobility force. Schlesinger recalled that the group worried that Soviet "air transport troops would swoop down into the Arab states including the oil fields." The wild card in their deliberations was Watergate. They wondered if Brezhnev, "hearing these calls about impeachment of the President in regard to the Watergate issue, might be concluding that the United States was paralyzed and could not act. And so our action that evening—which may have been more forceful and visible than necessity dictated—was driven in part by our concern that the Soviets might have concluded we were paralyzed and that we could not forcibly react."

A few minutes before midnight the seven officials in the Situation Room agreed to recommend that the president raise the readiness level of the United States military. The military's Defense Condition (DEFCON) alert system ascended numerically from DEFCON 5, the lowest level of readiness, to DEFCON 1, which was war. Nixon's aides decided to raise the alert to DEFCON 3, which, as explained by Kissinger, "increases readiness without the determination that war is likely; it is in practice the highest stage of readiness for essentially peacetime conditions." The secretary hoped that if the United States declared a worldwide nuclear alert and placed the military on standby, Brezhnev would withdraw his threat to send troops to the Middle East. They meant to call his bluff.

Haig left the Situation Room, ostensibly to present the president with their recommendation. When he returned, he told his colleagues that Nixon (who was still asleep) approved their decision. Kissinger turned to Admiral Thomas Moorer, the chairman of the Joint Chiefs, and asked him to implement the president's "directive." To reinforce the message to the Soviets, Nixon's aides placed the 82nd Airborne Division on alert, directed three carriers, the *Franklin Delano Roosevelt, Independence*, and *John F. Kennedy* "to move at full speed" toward the Eastern Mediterranean, ordered nuclear bombers readied for takeoff, and had U.S. submarines "sped to secret positions off the Soviet coast, prepared to launch." Kissinger later recalled that not everyone in the room agreed with the urgency of the threat. As he later recounted, he addressed the skeptics this way: "If we can't do what is right because we might get killed, then we should do what is right. We will have to contend with the charge in the domestic media that we provoked this. The real charge is that we provoked this by being soft."

The White House communicated its intent to Moscow. For a brief moment the world faced the prospect of a showdown between the nuclear superpowers. Brezhnev withdrew his threat. The next morning at eight when he received a personal briefing from Kissinger and Haig, Nixon was informed that he had declared a worldwide nuclear alert. He applauded their toughness. Basking in the presidential praise, Kissinger boasted to Haig, "You and I were the only ones for it. These other guys were wailing all over the place." In Tehran, the Shah was "dreadfully anxious" to hear of the alert but went ahead with a scheduled trip to watch a performance of *Carmen*. He was certain the Soviets would not have backed down without the speedy response from Washington.

Once the crisis had passed Henry Kissinger telephoned Israeli ambassador Simcha Dinitz demanding to know why Israeli intelligence officials were challenging the alert decision. He said that "on every television I heard yesterday that Israeli intelligence was of the view that there had been no threat of Soviet intervention."

"That I did not even hear," said Dinitz.

"I heard it from—you know it was Israeli intelligence officials were not aware of any unusual activity."

Dinitz described the reports as "ridiculous."

"Well, what I would like to stress to you, Mr. Ambassador, is this: If you could use whatever influence you have with the press here—I don't give a damn for ourselves because the historical record will support us. But we are not out of the woods yet and if the Russians look at this and see that when there is a crisis we then get flyspecked by the press, they may try again." This last point—that press coverage critical of the decision might tempt the Soviets to risk a second confrontation—stretched the limits of credulity. Kissinger had just invited Israel's embassy to help him manipulate domestic American public opinion to justify an action that had provoked a world-wide panic. "I mean, if you look at the Czechoslovak situation, they had a number of scares before they moved." He urged Dinitz to lobby senators, congressmen, and journalists in support of the alert.

"Because we took enormous risks," he continued, then implied the administration might have to apply pressure to Israel on a peace for land deal. "You may not like what we do in the U.N...."

"That's a different story . . ."

"But that is a question of tactics—on strategy we took a fantastic risk."

"Right, right," said Dinitz. "Absolutely. No, I am in complete agreement with you. And yesterday [redacted] was done and we will do more of it today."

The "fantastic risk" had been a bluff. Meanwhile, the same officials who had declared a worldwide nuclear alert to prevent Soviet troops from landing in Egypt were moving ahead with their own plan for military intervention in the Persian Gulf. With the cease-fire holding they could finally turn their attention to the crippling consequences of King Faisal's oil embargo.

THE SHAH IS RARING TO GO

Prior to the embargo the Saudis had supplied the U.S. Seventh Fleet in the Pacific with 120,000 barrels of oil per day. Those shipments had now ended. Also affected by the fuel cutoff was the U.S. Sixth Fleet in the Mediterranean. The Sixth Fleet relied on Arab oil supplied from Italian re-fineries. U.S. officials feared that once governments in Western Europe implemented fuel rationing, there would not be enough oil to keep the fleet at sea. The Mediterranean would then be exposed to a Soviet flotilla of ninety vessels that had just been outfitted with a battalion of marines trained and equipped for landing operations. A second blow for the U.S. strategic position came on October 20 when Bahrain announced that it was giving the U.S. Navy one year to close down its small naval station, America's last base in the Persian Gulf. Iraq meanwhile had granted a Soviet naval squadron docking privileges at a new port being built with Russian expertise at Umm Qasr. Schlesinger for one had had enough, telling Kissinger, "Well, we only have one facility and I am not sure we shouldn't move in and . . ." Kissinger finished his train of thought: "We are going to move on that thing."

Pressure was building within the ranks of the United States military to end what many officers regarded as a national disgrace. "The Naval War College was filled with Marine colonels walking around saying, we're going to put those Goddamned rag heads back on their camels," recalled a former senior official. There was outrage too because the Air Force and Navy, the two services most affected by the Saudi embargo, were heavily involved in building the kingdom's defensive systems. The Air Force was about to deliver the first shipment of Northrop F-5E jet fighters. The Saudis were also seeking permission from the United States to buy thirty Phantom F-4 aircraft. The services had been contracted to install an early warning radar defense system. Now, worried about the potential for an *American* invasion, Saudi officials had asked the contractors to speed up their work. Yet even as Saudi Arabia relied on American goodwill and treasure to defend it from regional predators, the kingdom's oil minister, Sheikh Yamani, wagged his finger at Americans and piously declared, "We are tracking down every last barrel of oil that reached the United States."

Officials at the Defense Department believed that a show of force was needed to restore at least the perception of American power in the Persian Gulf. Events had spiraled well beyond their control. Even the smallest thumbnail-size sheikhdoms felt free to act out in the era of Vietnam and Watergate. This posed a problem for U.S. policy makers. It greatly heightened the risk that a smaller state, say a Libya or an Iraq, might go too far with its provocations and cross an imaginary trip wire that invited massive retaliation from the outside. Lines of authority had to be clearly demarcated to restore order and reduce the possibility of a fatal error or reckless gamble that might trigger another war. All the players in the October crisis— the United States, the Soviet Union, Israel, and Arab governments—had mistaken each other's intentions and motives. They had committed a series of blunders that had ended in a nuclear showdown. Virtually unarmed oil states felt free to declare economic warfare against the United States. Then there was the Soviet Union. White House officials were convinced that Brezhnev would never have dared threaten to land Russian troops in the Middle East had he respected the U.S. military posture in the region. The United States had to find a way to reassert American power in the Middle East and at the same time smash the oil embargo. The White House could not accept a situation in which the United States was chased out of the Middle East, its armed forces ran out of gas, and allied economies throttled by the actions of a few lightly armed oil potentates.

The White House WSAG crisis group met over breakfast on Saturday, November 3, in the Map Room. The Saudis had sent troops to fight against Israel. They had imposed an oil embargo against the United States that had the potential to cripple the Air Force and Navy. Now they were threatening to tear up the terms of the 25 percent participation deal they had signed with Aramco a year earlier. "The Saudis are getting heady over the power of oil," said Schlesinger. "I am not sure they have a future aside from the West. They can't survive spitting fire and brimstone at the West."

"The Shah would play that game," replied Kissinger. "He is raring to go. The Saudis are having trouble surviving in this kind of world and they have to be more radical than the radicals."

Schlesinger believed he had found an ideal testing ground to restore at least the illusion of American power in the Middle East and cower the Saudis. Fifteen years earlier, before the discovery of oil in Abu Dhabi, the capital of the United Arab Emirates had been a fishing village. In 1973 its native population of thirty thousand enjoyed an annual per capita income of $100,000. Abu Dhabi was close to the mouth of the Persian Gulf and made for a convenient springboard from which the United States could launch future military strikes across a broad swath of the region. Abu Dhabi's twenty-seven-year-old oil minister had been the first to impose an oil embargo against the United States. "I was prepared to seize Abu Dhabi," Schlesinger recalled. He envisioned a clean surgical strike to land American troops in the heart of Arab oil country. "Something small. But nothing big. Militarily we could have seized one of the Arab states. And the plan did indeed scare them and anger them. No, it wasn't just bravado. It was clearly intended as a warning."

If it was a bluff, it was one with sharp teeth. Schlesinger anticipated an amphibious invasion using the Marines. They had spent August training in the Mojave for just this type of eventuality. "Abu Dhabi would give us what we want," he told Kissinger, CIA director William Colby, Moorer, and Scowcroft.

"The Shah is cynical enough to discuss this with us," said Kissinger, who liked the idea. He had a stopover planned in Tehran on his way to China the next week.

A date for military intervention was set for the last ten days of November. At that time several American destroyers would be in place at the entrance to the Persian Gulf to take part in previously scheduled CENTO naval exercises. It would be convenient to have military forces from the United States, Great Britain, Iran, and Turkey hovering just off the coast practicing such war drills as amphibious landings. The aircraft carrier USS *Hancock* with more than eighty attack aircraft was steaming toward the area. "We need a public line on the *Hancock* when it arrives," said Schlesinger.

"Routine. An exercise that we have been planning a long time," replied Kissinger. "I will discuss it with the Shah. If he wants in, I will let you know." He was about to leave in a few days for the Middle East and China and fretted that the Soviets still had not gotten the message from two weeks earlier. "The Russians may make a run at us while I am away," he said. "What can we do?"

"Turn Israel loose on the Third Army and tell Sadat if he lets the Soviets loose, it will be very bad," replied Schlesinger. They could also work with Turkey to close the Bosporus Straits, a key choke point through which the Soviets had been moving nuclear-armed warships.

A few hours later, on Sunday, November 4, the Shah received formal notification that a U.S. naval task force led by the carrier *Hancock* and accompanied by destroyers was moving toward a holding area off the coast of Oman. Helms asked the Shah if he would open Iranian airfields to American P2 spy planes and short-range flights to the *Hancock* for a period of twenty days. He also sought Iranian assurances of fuel deliveries to the task force. The Shah was willing to comply so long as the fuel was supplied indirectly through the Iranian navy.

Washington was now leaning heavily on the Shah, perhaps in ways Nixon and Kissinger had never intended. Iranian ports, airstrips, and fuel depots were opened to the U.S. military and supplies made available for American use during a major international crisis. At first glance the Nixon Doctrine appeared to have paid off with interest. Yet there were risks involved that neither Washington nor Tehran had properly thought through. For one thing, the deal was guaranteed to antagonize Iran's northern neighbor. Under the terms of a 1962 agreement signed with Moscow the

Shah had agreed to never "allow any foreign power to establish rocket-launching sites of any kind on Iranian territory." The Soviets were naturally anxious to prevent Iran from being used as a base for U.S. intervention on its southern border. The Shah's secret decision to supply the U.S. naval task force during the October crisis did not violate the terms of that treaty, but it did make him vulnerable to the accusation that the United States did not need to construct bases of any kind in Iran when it enjoyed free and unfettered access to Iranian facilities. There were also repercussions for the United States. Washington was in the humiliating position of having to ask an ally's permission before taking the measures it deemed necessary to defend its national interest. There had been a subtle but profound power shift within the relationship.

The Shah knew better than anyone just how eroded American power was in late 1973 and the extent to which the Nixon administration relied on his continued cooperation and goodwill. The political paralysis induced by Watergate and the growing mood of isolationism in the U.S. Congress made him question America's ability to defend the interests of its allies when it could barely defend its own. Over the summer King Hussein of Jordan let the CIA know that during a recent visit to Tehran the Shah had "opined that the Watergate affair was unfortunate for everyone since it appeared to have brought the U.S. Government to a standstill. There were many problems between the U.S. and its friends which need attention, the Shah continued, but these days they did not seem to be receiving it." His confidence in U.S. intelligence gathering had eroded to the point where he stopped receiving fortnightly reports from the CIA station chief in Tehran.

Kissinger arrived in Riyadh, Saudi Arabia, on November 8 for a three-hour discussion with King Faisal. Since the imposition of the embargo Saudi oil production had fallen from its daily average of 8.3 million barrels to 6.2 million barrels. The discussion took place in a tense atmosphere. Both men knew that just off the coast lurked enough naval firepower to reduce Faisal's kingdom to rubble. The *Hancock* was a reminder of who really wielded power in the relationship. Saudi Arabia was little more than a giant filling station whose primary goal was to service the needs of the industrialized democracies, as the United States saw it. Faisal intimated that he was ready to reach a deal to end the embargo. "You can make Israel withdraw immediately in the space of three weeks," Faisal implored Kissinger. The king pleaded, "Can't you help me? Can't you give me Jerusalem?" An unbending Kissinger told him, "That's the last. Our enemies would like to hang us up on a tough point like that one. Give us time and we will do it." The challenge now was for the White House to walk Faisal back from the edge with his honor and American integrity intact. Kissinger had the opening he believed he needed to pursue diplomacy.

On November 19, the same day the CENTO exercises kicked off in the Persian Gulf, the White House sent reassuring signals that the United States had decided "for the time being not to retaliate against Arab states." But lest anyone doubt American resolve, two days later Kissinger announced at a press conference that the administration would consider "countermeasures" if economic pressures continued "unreasonably and indefinitely." Washington would not tolerate a situation in which it was subjected to economic pressure while trying to negotiate a Middle East peace deal. It was the first time a U.S. official had publicly floated the idea of using force to smash the embargo. Sheikh Yamani issued a blistering response, threatening to slash Saudi oil production by 80 percent if the Western powers took countermeasures to break the embargo, and warning that military action would be suicidal for the developed world "because your whole economy will definitely collapse all of a sudden. There are some sensitive areas in the oil fields in Saudi Arabia which will be blown up."

The threat to blow up Saudi oil installations was no bluff. Throughout the region Arab governments were making contingency plans to defend their assets by rigging them with explosives. Anticipating a possible American invasion, Kuwait laid land mines around its oil wells and announced it could set them off "at a moment's notice." King Faisal also felt the need to publicly reiterate his hard-line demands for the withdrawal of Israeli forces to 1967 borders, recognition of Palestinian rights, and a restoration of "the Arab character of Jerusalem." But behind the scenes the king tepidly reached out to the White House. He was no Qaddafi and he had no stomach for taking on the American superpower. The White House also knew that Faisal credited Nixon with overthrowing the Libyan monarchy in 1969, a fact they used to their psychological advantage. "They think we knocked off [King] Idris," Schlesinger told Nixon's war council. In this instance at least, Nixon's "madman" theory worked as intended.

At 10:15 A.M. on November 28, 1973, Kissinger phoned Schlesinger to tell him that he had "a very interesting message from Saudi Arabia saying Faisal would like to ease the boycott and is looking for an early occasion which will provide him the way when the peace conference is agreed to—in the form of a presidential letter."

"Very good," said Schlesinger. This suited his purposes because he needed more time to assemble his amphibious task force. "That bears on the subject I was going to discuss which is that it will take six or seven weeks anyhow to accumulate the Marines in the Indian Ocean." The administration's carrot-and-stick approach meant that while Kissinger explored diplomatic options, his colleague over at Defense readied the Marines for action in case negotiations failed. The aircraft carrier *Hancock* would be their vehicle for the seizure of Abu Dhabi.

They believed they had the breakthrough they were looking for. On Thursday morning, November 29, WSAG, the president's crisis group, convened for two sessions in the Map Room. Kissinger briefed them on his talks with King Faisal, who, he reiterated, was in a real bind. The king "is a friend of the United States, but he is pressured by radicals. So he is leap-frogging the radicals so he isn't embarrassed by his U.S. relationship. . . . I get the impression that they are blinking."

"Yes, they are looking for ways to get us oil," observed CIA director Colby.

"They are turning up the screws on Aramco," noted Schlesinger. The Saudis had quietly told Aramco to start releasing more oil into the system. They were prepared to make secret deliveries of fuel to the U.S. Navy as a gesture of goodwill to avoid precipitating a clash with America. Five weeks after publicly imposing an oil embargo against the United States the Saudis were already breaking it in private to the U.S. military. The embargo had cracked. Faisal was now convinced that the administration was firmly engaged in the Middle East and that Nixon was committed to finding a negotiated settlement to the Arab-Israeli conflict. But most of all he feared for his life and his throne. Schlesinger's bluff had done the trick.

"They seem to be looking for a way out," Kissinger noted.

The crisis group agreed to relax the U.S. military posture in the Mediterranean. They decided to pull back the naval task force but keep it within easy reach of the Gulf. The *Hancock* was sent on a goodwill mission to Kenya and the destroyers steamed to Ethiopia, where they could be recalled at a moment's notice. But as they settled down to lunch Schlesinger made a shocking admission: "We have no fuel for the B-52s in Southeast Asia." Eighty-nine percent of the fuel used by U.S. forces in Southeast Asia originated in the Persian Gulf. American power projection was being compromised in the Persian Gulf, the Pacific, the Mediterranean, and now Southeast Asia. It was hardly any wonder that the Soviet bear was probing and nudging at the periphery, on the lookout for weaknesses in Western defenses. "We need to build a presence in the Middle East," he urged his colleagues.

The Pentagon needed a base from which it could secure the nation's fuel supply. Preferred locations faced the Indian Ocean and were in white-minority-ruled African states such as the city of Durban in South Africa and Lourenzo Marques (now Maputo) in Portuguese Mozambique. Ethiopia was a possibility. In West Asia, Prime Minister Zulfikar Ali Bhutto of Pakistan was eager to host the U.S. Navy and had offered to provide base facilities. It would take months, if not years, to negotiate leasing arrangements and build base facilities. Schlesinger proposed "putting 5–6,000 Marines into Bahrain," but Kissinger told him not to bother: "They will never agree." Kissinger's own feelings of frustration boiled over during a strategy meeting on November 29 with his colleagues when he exclaimed, "Can't we overthrow one of the sheikhs just to show that we can do it?"

ONE MAD FINAL FLING

Kissinger's helplessness was shared by millions of Americans as the first effects of the oil embargo were felt. "The energy crisis is like Watergate. We know something is wrong but we don't know quite what it is," said a Massachusetts school superintendent. Dramatic news reports spoke of the last fully laden oil tankers streaming toward the eastern seaboard, bucking their way "through the wind-blown Atlantic," headed for oil refineries along the East Coast. President Nixon went on national television to announce strict limits on weekend sales of gasoline, a blackout on all unnecessary outdoor lighting, and voluntary compliance with a new reduced highway speed limit. The administration announced plans to seek emergency powers over the fuel supply and to reduce private automobile use by 30 percent. The White House was assessing the impact of a 9.6 percent jump in the cost of living for the month of October, the first direct result of recent increases in the price of oil. It now estimated that the oil embargo meant an 18 percent reduction in the minimum amount of fuel required to keep America moving. Economists warned that a lengthy embargo might increase the unemployment rate to levels last seen during the Great Depression.

Western lights went out in November 1973. Half of the lights on the Golden Gate Bridge were extinguished and monuments on the Washington Mall were blacked out. Americans rallied around their president, temporarily setting aside their differences over Watergate to show off their newfound conservation credentials. Stirring stories were told of the lengths to which ordinary citizens were prepared to go to display their patriotism. There was Joe Conforte, "proprietor of a licensed house of prostitution" outside Reno known as the Mustang Ranch, who "turned the reception-room thermostats down from 75 degrees to 68 degrees and ordered his girls to wear pantsuits and gowns instead of bikinis." There was the plucky housewife in Belle Plaine, Minnesota, who "has found a way to retain heat in her concrete-block home; she wrapped it in transparent plastic, like a sandwich." A nursing home resident in her nineties offered some timeless advice to her fellow Americans: "Tell the people to turn off their electric blankets and cuddle. It's a lot more fun."

The oil embargo had immediate and fearful repercussions for a global economy still dependent on ocean-borne traffic. Around the world, freighters remained tied up in their last port of call because companies and governments began hoarding scarce fuel supplies. Reports of shortages of essential items led to housewife riots in Japan where a woman was crushed to death during a stampede for toilet paper in Osaka, and where a nation-wide run on sugar was supposedly traced back to gossip exchanged between two shoppers worried about power outages in the sugar-refining industry. Fishing boats were beached and farm machinery idled in Italy. West Germany announced a halt in the hiring of non-EEC guest workers. Sunday driving bans took effect in France, Holland, and Italy. Everywhere there were worries about rising inflation and unemployment as food costs soared and factories were shut down. The lights were dimmed in Piccadilly Circus and the wedding of Queen Elizabeth's daughter, Princess Anne, to Lieutenant Mark Phillips took place amid scenes resembling wartime austerity. "It's a mad final fling before the winter of our discontent," shrieked a London tabloid.

The U.S. economy rumbled with dislocations both anticipated and real. Wall Street suffered its worst back-to-back losses since the crash of 1929, with the stock market shedding 133 points in three weeks to end the month at an anemic 854. After wholesale prices of Cadillacs collapsed 25 percent, shares in Detroit automobile manufacturers swooned and General Motors announced it was closing sixteen assembly plants across North America. Citrus growers in California reported they were running low on the diesel fuel needed to save their crops from frost. The steel industry estimated that a 10 percent reduction in oil consumption would result in a 4-million-ton decline in production and twenty thousand job losses.

Americans knew that if they had one friend they could count on in times of trouble it was the Shah of Iran. Amid the panic the Shah issued a states-manlike plea to Arab oil producers to end their embargo. "Oil is like bread," he said. "You cannot cut it off during time of peace. Why do you want to look as if you want the world to starve." Arab governments weren't listen-ing. "In their hearts, the Arabs never forgave us for going it alone on the blockade," said Ardeshir Zahedi. They viewed Iran's refusal to participate in the oil embargo as a betrayal.

Chapter Five

OIL SHOCK

"If I was the President I would tell the Arabs to shove their oil."
—Henry Kissinger, 1974

"To hell with Kissinger. Pay him no attention."
—The Shah, 1974

THEY WILL HAVE TO PAY THE PRICE

Army Day marked the anniversary of the military campaign that ended the Soviet Union's occupation of Iran's northern republic of Azerbaijan in 1946. It was the highlight of the Pahlavi calendar and a reminder of the ruling dynasty's close ties to the armed forces. In 1973 Army Day fell on Wednesday, December 12. Fifteen miles outside Tehran, spectator viewing stands were filled with the cream of Pahlavi society and a host of bemedaled foreign dignitaries, generals, and ambassadors. The assembled guests drank tea, warmed themselves by kerosene heaters, exchanged the gossip of the day, and awaited the arrival of the Shahanshah. A tremor of anticipation rippled through the crowd when a lone figure in a khaki uniform was spotted advancing toward them on horseback trailed by members of the Imperial Guard who wore "silver breastplates and helmets, tricolor pennants fluttering from the tips of their lances." It was a sight that brought the crowd to its feet. A torrent of applause washed through the stands and a lusty cry arose from thousands of troops assembled on a plain opposite the reviewing stands ready to march for their king.

The skies overhead shook with a flyover of 150 Phantom jets, while on the frigid ground below row after row of British-made Chieftain tanks rumbled past the royal box. The Shah usually relished Army Day, an occasion that cemented his credentials as King-Emperor and Guardian of the Gulf. But today the monarch was distracted by some remarkable news. At the height of the worldwide panic over oil supplies the National Iranian Oil Company decided to gauge the mood of the market by holding two secret auctions of 80 million barrels of crude destined for export in the first half of 1974. The sale amount totaled less than 4 percent of Iran's estimated petroleum production for the coming year. In two weeks' time the Shah was set to host a new round of price talks for the six Persian Gulf states responsible for 43 percent of the petroleum consumed by the non-Communist industrialized world. The results of the auction would guide his hand during the negotiations. There was never any doubt that the Shah was also setting a spot price on panic. The auction came just five days after Arab states started pulling their money from American banks and two days after they unveiled a new plan to slash their daily output of oil by another 750,000 barrels starting January 1. Even so, Iranian government officials were "dumbfounded" and industry analysts "flabbergasted" when the foreign companies participating in the auction placed bids as high as $17.40 per barrel. Here was conclusive proof that the world oil market had blown out. At a stroke Iran's oil auction generated $1.5 billion in new government revenues. "There are a lot of people groping and grabbing for oil," said one oil expert. "The prices have gone quite insane. No one knows what's going to happen." Explained another, "The countries see how hungry the companies are, how desperate some of them are."

On December 21, the day before Gulf oil ministers were due to fly into Tehran, the Shah granted an interview to a *New York Times* correspondent. Iran's king appeared "wan and weary" as he sat on a sofa discoursing about his favorite topic: how oil receipts would catapult Iran into the ranks of the First World. "What I want for Iran is very simple, very clear, very ambitious and very possible. In 20 or 25 years I want it to be ahead of the greatest nations of the world. We will have 60 million people in 25 years. With that number of people, we can be the most advanced country and do better than any other country. Some people say that we will be one of the five most developed countries in the world." Iran's income from oil would pay for it all. He fired a shot across the bows of Western oil companies and consumers. "In the past," he said, the oil companies "did not attach too much importance to the problem. They took oil and profited. They closed all the coal pits. They didn't bother to find other sources of energy. They fixed low prices. Now they will have to pay the price."

THE SAFETY OF ALL YOUR LIVES
MAY DEPEND ON IT

Throughout the October War the Shah believed he had more than proven his credentials as an ally to the West. But he viewed oil prices as the one nonnegotiable issue in bilateral relations with the United States. Back in July, the Shah had warned Nixon and Kissinger that oil prices would rise "until shale or gasification of coal becomes profitable." Nixon had given him a blank check to raise oil prices three years earlier. The Americans did not ask him to explain what he meant or why the price of one commodity should be contingent on another. The Shah's views on oil pricing were never more clearly spelled out than in an interview that appeared in the December 1, 1973, issue of *The New Republic*. Italian journalist Oriana Fallaci was a provocateur who brilliantly manipulated the Shah during their stormy exchange, which had actually occurred before the outbreak of the Middle East war. When she asked whether the price of oil would keep rising, the Shah excitedly replied: "Of course it's going to rise. Certainly! And how! You can spread the bad news and add that it comes from someone who knows what he's talking about. I know everything there is to know about oil, everything. I'm a real specialist and it's as a specialist that I must tell you the price of oil must rise. There's no other solution."

The Shah prided himself on being an oil man of the new era. He was an early and avid proponent of peak oil, arguing that the world's major oil fields would run out of petroleum in the first decades of the twenty-first century. Iran was expected to maximize its oil production from 5.8 million barrels per day in 1973 to 9 million barrels per day in 1976–77. Iran's oil would then level off and enter several decades of decline. The Shah's modernization drive was intended to provide the Iranian economy with a soft landing once the wells ran dry. He evangelized on the topics of energy conservation and diversification. He drew a direct link between oil prices and how much the West charged Iran for its exports of food and petrochemicals. "You've increased the price of the wheat you sell us by 300 percent, and the same for sugar and cement," he lectured Fallaci. "You've sent petrochemical prices rocketing. You buy our crude oil and sell it back to us, refined as petrochemicals, at a hundred times the price you've paid us. You make us pay more, scandalously more, for everything, and it's only fair that, from now on, you should pay more for oil. Let's say . . . 10 times more." He predicted the day would come when mankind would dig for oil beneath the North Pole:

> In less than 100 years, this oil business will be finished. The need for oil increases daily, existing fields are becoming exhausted, and you'll soon have to seek some other source of energy. Atomic, solar or what not. You'll have to resort to several solutions, one won't be enough. For instance, you'll have to exploit the power of the ocean tides with turbines. Or else you'll have to dig deeper, seek oil 10,000 meters below the sea-bed or at the North Pole . . . I don't know. All I know is that the time has already arrived to take measures, not to waste oil as we always have. It's a crime to use it as we do nowadays.

The Shah was so unsentimental on the subject of energy pricing that he decided the U.S. war fleet off the coast of Oman should turn a profit for the Iranian treasury. Asadollah Alam was tasked with instructing Ambassador Helms that Tehran wanted payment in full for the fuel that kept the task force at sea. The Shah's crusade for higher prices also hid an inconvenient truth. In the words of the Shah's own budget planners Iran faced an "explosive deficit in the balance of payments." There was no doubt that by the end of 1973 spending on arms was draining capital and skilled manpower away from the civilian economy. Kissinger already knew that Iran's economy was beginning to groan under the strain of the Shah's military buildup. "Iranian purchases and orders of U.S. defense equipment and services since 1965 now total more than $3.7 billion," the State Department advised in an internal memo. "Of this amount, approximately $1.8 billion in orders were signed in FY 1973 alone." A disconnect had developed between U.S. and Iranian threat perceptions. "The Shah's view of his military needs is greater than ours. He is building a military base beyond the needs for internal security or to meet any reasonably acceptable threat, apparently in order to maximize his strengths and enable Iran to deal from a position of strength." The Shah was trying to do too much: "The Shah's as yet inexhaustible appetite for the latest sophisticated weaponry, at higher and higher annual costs for acquisition and maintenance, could impact on Iranian development spending. The rapid buildup is seriously straining manpower resources and risk equipment failures and sidelining."

If there was a silver lining for the United States it was this: Iran was unlikely to join an oil embargo against the West because it could not afford the loss to its revenue stream. The Shah would in fact be likely to exploit embargo conditions to maximize Iran's share of the market: "There is no likelihood that it will accumulate vast foreign exchange reserves beyond expenditures, or that it will voluntarily restrain production below projected levels. . . . Iran is not apt to curtail production because of the Arab-Israeli problems."

Major items on the Shah's shopping list for arms included 177 F-4 aircraft, 141 F-5E aircraft, 58 C-130 aircraft, 489 attack and utility helicopters, 2 U.S. surplus destroyers with Standard missiles, 302 self-propelled artillery pieces, 460 M-60 tanks, and 6 battalions of Hawk missiles. From the British he ordered 800 Chieftain tanks. The Shah added 14 Hovercraft to what was already the world's biggest Hovercraft fleet—one that could land "a battalion of troops on the [Saudi] side of the gulf in only two hours." Two new air and sea bases were projected to cost upward of $1 billion. Then there were the 8 destroyers, 4 frigates, 12 high-speed gunboats, and 2 repair ships. New KC-135 jet tankers meant that the range of the Shah's fleet of F-4 Phantoms was doubled to some 1,400 miles.

All these items were ordered *before* the outbreak of the fourth Arab-Israeli war in October 1973. The war convinced the Shah of two things. The first was that the oil market was about to spike. The second was that Iran needed to take urgent steps to prepare for a blitzkrieg invasion of the sort that had almost overwhelmed the Israelis. Moscow's new rapid mobility force influenced the Shah's calculations. His solution in December 1973 was straightforward enough—he would use the oil market to pay for his new arms, a fact later grimly conceded by U.S. officials in a classified study: "Although Iran's economic growth was averaging well over 10% annually in the period 1970–73, the Government of Iran then believed that armaments requirements for 1974–78 would be about $5 billion in excess of projected oil revenues for that period—and thus felt that in order to avoid burdensome external financing, a hike in the price of oil was in order." The report's devastating conclusion: the Shah intended to overspend on American weapons and military equipment by a whopping *$5 billion*—and he meant for American oil consumers to foot the bill.

In Pahlavi-era Iran government spending took the form of development plans. The $36 billion Fifth Plan drawn up by the state Plan and Budget Organization was budgeted to cover the period March 1973 to March 1978. Its projections were based on maintaining an annual economic growth rate of 11.4 percent. Senior officials at the PBO worried that the Fifth Plan was so ambitious as to be "perilously close to absorptive capacity." Their biggest fear was that another substantial injection of oil revenues into Iran's financial bloodstream might fuel inflation and overheat the economy. The one third of the state budget dedicated to the military functioned almost as a "black budget" because it was strictly controlled by the Shah and not subject to the oversight or review of his government's civilian technocrats.

The Fifth Plan had been in effect only a few months when the Shah and his generals raised fresh demands for new arms purchases. "The pressures for an increase in domestic spending were immense, with the Shah and his defense establishment in the forefront," recalled one Iranian official. The Shah also asked his planners to draft a long-range twenty-year forecast for economic development that "anticipated inflows of financial resources from the export of oil and gas." The Shah was giving his officials advance warning that a new windfall in oil profits was on its way. As the same official observed with technical correctness, the Shah's order "signaled that there was indeed an understanding within political circles as to the importance of recent events [the Middle East war and Arab oil embargo]."

Burgeoning oil revenues had swelled the ranks of the Iranian middle class. A growing economy absorbed their energies and channeled their ambitions into making money rather than demanding political reforms. But an economy experiencing dynamic growth was accompanied by shortages of consumer goods, skilled labor, and affordable housing in the cities. The Shah's wife and court minister brought these matters to his attention.

Senior court officials took their concerns to Kermit Roosevelt, the hero of Operation Ajax, when he made one of his frequent visits to Tehran in the early 1970s to lobby the Shah to buy more fighter aircraft. One former Iranian ambassador confided to Roosevelt "that he thought there was a growing gap between the government and the people of Iran. He said that the Shah's personal influence holds the government and the people of Iran together. He found inflation a serious problem and believed the credibility of the government was badly eroded." Roosevelt relayed the concerns of the former diplomat and others in a memorandum that he addressed to Kissinger's attention.

Two events occurred in the autumn of 1973 that reminded the Shah of his own mortality. In early October a terrorist plot to either kill or kidnap the Shah, Queen Farah, and Crown Prince Reza at an awards ceremony in Tehran honoring the movie industry was foiled. At around the same time—the exact date is unknown—the Shah noticed swelling around his abdomen. He made a self-diagnosis of a swollen spleen, probably the result of "some sort of blood disorder," but chose not to share the news with his wife or anyone else at court apart from Alam. In November the Shah summoned Prime Minister Hoveyda, the speaker of parliament, top court officials, and the commanders of the armed forces to Niavaran Palace. When Alam arrived at the secret conclave he was surprised to see the queen at her husband's side. The court minister was further startled to hear Mohammad Reza Shah deliver his political will and testament. Apparently alluding to the recent attempt on his life, the Shah began his remarks with a warning: "God alone determines the hour of our deaths, but we live in an age in which the instruments of death are wielded by terrorists and subversives. At any moment my life may be snatched from me." He announced that in the event of his premature death, "and until the Crown Prince attains legal age, authority is to lie with Her Majesty the Queen and the members of the Regency Council." He ordered the armed forces to obey his wife's commands if that day ever came: "Their orders may come from a woman or a man of tender years, but they are to be obeyed with no less respect. The safety of all your lives may depend on it."

No one said a word. The room, recalled Alam, fell into "absolute silence as His Imperial Majesty finished; everybody too electrified to utter a sound. I myself was so overwhelmed that I could think of nothing, save that I no longer wish to live a single moment once the Shah has gone. Pray God that I die before my beloved Shahanshah." The Shah was preparing his inner circle for a coming storm—but what? And from where?

I SHALL DEFEND OUR ACTION BEFORE THE ENTIRE WORLD

The Shah never hid from his Western allies his intention to force through one final increase in oil prices when OPEC ministers reconvened in Tehran on December 22, 1973. Iran's habitual big spender needed to raise the money to pay for $5 billion in new military equipment. He decided that market conditions might never be as favorable to the producers as they were now. The combined effects of the war and the embargo had led to panic buying and squeezed all excess capacity from the market. Prices were about to spike. The Shah knew that Nixon and Kissinger were anxious to appease him at a time when Iran was refueling the carrier *Hancock*, supplying Israel with oil, and ignoring the Arab oil embargo. The Shah also knew that Watergate had crippled Nixon's ability to back up any demands with the threat of force.

The Nixon administration's inept handling of foreign economic policy played a crucial role in the disastrous sequence of events that unfolded that December. On the 6th, Federal Reserve Bank chairman Arthur Burns attended a meeting at which President Nixon and his economics team discussed the crippling impact of the oil embargo. In his diary, Burns described Nixon at the meeting as a broken man. The president was "list-less; looked sad; his mind elsewhere; shook his head now and then, but he was clearly not interested." Nixon perked up only when Burns proposed a crash energy program that the Fed chief dubbed Project Independence and which he envisioned would be "on a scale comparable to [the] Manhattan Project and the Space program . . . that will free us from dependence on Arab blackmailing sheiks." Nixon loved it. He made clear, however, that he and not William E. Simon, the administrator of the Federal Energy Office and the White House official in charge of coordinating the administration's response to the oil crisis, should receive credit for announcing the new initiative. "President expressed concern about Simon," wrote Burns. "He indicated that he wanted to make major policy pronouncements himself." Burns also recorded that Treasury Secretary George Shultz, supported by others in the room, "urged a sharp increase in oil prices and reliance on market to equate demand & supply" to combat the effects of the oil em-bargo and reliance on oil from the Middle East. Nixon's economics team still underestimated the potential for another price jolt to inflict widespread damage on the economy. Burns did not think highly of Shultz, whom he caustically described as having "not the slightest understanding of inter-national economics or finance! What a pity that this quiet, persuasive, but woefully ignorant ideologist, has such influence with the President."

The incoherence of the Nixon administration sent mixed signals to oil producers and consumers alike, which resulted in another, deadlier mis-understanding. The Shah decided to test American resolve when he told Ambassador Helms that he planned to increase the price of oil to the point where it reflected the price of other sources of energy. Helms left their meeting assuming that the Shah meant to raise the price of a barrel of oil by the hefty sum of one or two dollars. In fact, the Shah meant to raise the price by *seven* dollars. How did this miscommunication happen? Despite his fluency in English, the Shah did not always express himself clearly on the subject of oil prices. Here is his reply to a journalist when he was later asked to justify the $7 a barrel price increase:

> So we charged experts to study what prices we should put on oil. Do you know that from oil you have today 70,000 derivatives? When we empty our wells, then you will be denied what I call this noble product. It will take you $8 to extract your shale or tar sands. So I said let us

start with the bottom price of $7; that is the government intake. Suddenly everybody started to cry foul.

If the words "that is the government intake" are removed it might appear as though the Shah wanted oil to go up in price from $5.11 to $7 per barrel. What he actually meant was that the Iranian government's "take" or profit per barrel would be $7 *in addition* to the posted price of $5.11. The distinction between the *dollar price* per barrel and the *profit margin* per barrel was lost in translation. Ambassador Helms similarly misunderstood the Shah's intention. The British ambassador later told Alam that he too had misunderstood the Shah's explanation of $7 income for every barrel of oil sold. This helps explain Kissinger's belated admission many years later "that he had assumed that the Shah might hike oil prices by a dollar or two a barrel to pay for his weapons."

In Paris on December 19, three days before the OPEC summit, France's foreign minister, Michel Jobert, told Kissinger that the French government "could not understand the American Government's attitude toward the Shah of Iran. It was clear, he said, that the Shah was going to push for another major oil price increase by exploiting the current embargo, induce shortage and yet the United States acted as if it considered the Shah to be a friendly country with the same interest . . . these artificial prices would be used as a pretext to justify higher overall OPEC prices." But Kissinger brushed aside Jobert's complaint. The French believed that Kissinger "underestimated the economics and overestimated the Middle East political problem in the terms of time sensitivity." Oil prices "were more immediately vital to the French." President Georges Pompidou wanted Nixon to know that he was prepared not only to join the United States in holding the line against further oil price increases—he also extended an offer "to join us in military intervention." James Akins, the American ambassador in Saudi Arabia, raised the alarm too. The Saudi government appealed to Washington through the ambassador to restrain the Shah and "use our influence for moderation with all the OPEC nations." Kissinger went through the motions of issuing a general appeal for restraint to the governments of Iran, Saudi Arabia, and Venezuela but otherwise made no effort to exert American leadership, perhaps because he suspected that Jobert and Saudi Arabia's Yamani were trying to drive a wedge between Washington and Tehran. What happened next seems to have genuinely taken him and everyone else in the United States government by surprise.

The Shah opened the December 22 Tehran oil producers' meeting from the fortified Ministry of Finance building in Tehran. He reminded the delegates that "we are establishing the prices ourselves" without interference from Western governments or oil companies. He urged them not to raise the price of oil to the point where it hurt the industrial nations whose capital was essential for their own development. But he also inveighed against wasting oil for use in "power generation, moving ships or heating homes. Oil must be reserved for use in more sophisticated industries such as petrochemicals." He recommended they adopt his own price formula which was "a price comparable to the price of coal oil derived from shale or other sources such as coal gasification or coal liquefaction." It was the same pricing formula he had mentioned to Nixon and Kissinger in July. The Shah ended his remarks by assuring the delegates that if they adopted his proposal he was "quite prepared to bear the consequences. I shall defend our action before the entire world, confident that my nation will support me."

The Shah won over the delegates and turned out to be as good as his word. The next day at a press conference in Niavaran Palace Iran's leader shocked the world when he announced that Persian Gulf oil producers had agreed to more than double the price of a barrel of oil from $5.11 to $11.65, thereby ensuring themselves a profit margin of almost $7 per barrel. "The industrial world will have to realize that the era of their terrific progress and even more terrific income and wealth based on cheap oil is finished," he declared.

> They will have to find new sources of energy, tighten their belts. If you want to live as well now you'll have to work for it. Even all the children of well-to-do parents who have plenty to eat, have cars, and run around as terrorists throwing bombs here and there—they will have to work too. We don't want to hurt the industrialized world. We will be one of them soon. What good will it do if the present industrialized world is crushed and terminated? What will replace it?

This last, massive hike in prices for the year meant that the price of oil had risen 470 percent in the space of twelve months and that the economic wealth of OPEC members had rocketed by the then astronomical sum of $112 billion—an amount that represented the largest single transfer of wealth in history. Iran quadrupled its oil revenues to $20.9 billion and total petroleum income over the next five years was projected to climb to $98 billion. Iran's gross national product was on target to expand an astonishing

50 percent a year. In fact, the empire of Iran had just been launched into the ranks of the wealthiest nations on earth.

The Shah had his $5 billion. For the rest of the world the Shah's oil coup was a disaster. In some countries national treasuries emptied practically overnight. America's bill for foreign oil imports soared from $3.9 billion to $24 billion in one year. "Among other things, this means that the woolen mills of Lancashire, the auto plants of Bavaria, and the electronic assembly lines of Japan will have to produce and sell four times as much as they did a year ago to meet the cost of the oil they use," reported *The New York Times*. France calculated that the combined effect of the fourfold increase in the price of oil in 1973 would lead to a rise in unemployment from 2 to 6 percent, a 10 percent increase in the cost of living, $2 billion in additional fuel costs, the erasure of its trade surplus, and the devaluation of the franc. Spain's $500 million trade surplus was turned into a $3.1 billion deficit.

"In pushing up prices beyond what is tolerable to western economies [the Shah] is aware of the strains he is imposing," concluded *The Economist*. "In apparently changing his colors he may now feel he is running with the tide of world history and that Iran must rely on its own strength to keep off the Russians." The magazine also noted the domestic pressures on the Shah and his unending quest to erase the taint of the 1953 coup. "Even after 20 years, the ghost of Mossadegh, the politician who laid claim to the mantle of Iranian nationalism and outbid the Arabs in challenging the West, still haunts the Shah."

When they realized the enormity of what had happened, the Nixon White House was thrown into a panic. "The oil increase to us is $10 billion," CIA director Colby told his colleagues on December 28. "Two can play at this," replied Admiral Moorer of the Joint Chiefs. "Maybe we should raise the price of our stuff to the Shah."

"We are," Defense Secretary Schlesinger assured him. From now on the Shah would foot the bill for all research and development costs associated with the weapons systems he bought from the Pentagon. "We had a policy in the Department of Defense in which the United States paid the research and development costs of developing new equipment," recalled Schlesinger. "We were engaging in sort of charitable activities in the sense that we were loading onto the Navy Department or the Air Force Department all of the charges for these equipments when some of the clear beneficiaries were overseas clients. And there was no need in the wake of the '73 oil prices run-up to engage in charitable activities." Iran's already high defense expenditures were about to go through the roof.

Arthur Burns attended a second White House meeting on January 8, 1974, to discuss the economic and financial aspects of the crisis. The participants realized they had been snookered by the Shah. "Kissinger had nothing to contribute about oil problem," Burns observed. "In fact, no one did—apart from the contribution I left in my memo on Abuses of Economic Power. Kissinger talked wildly—we should agree to nothing; we should not even talk to [the French?]. Not at all helpful."

Three years earlier Nixon had secretly given the Shah permission to push hard on oil prices. Even if he blasted the Shah in public, what would be the use? If the news leaked that he had approved the oil price hikes now wreaking havoc on the world economy, his presidency would be further imperiled. Privately, Nixon appealed to the Shah to reconsider. "The diplomatic response was to try to bring pressure to bear on the Shah not to raise the prices," recalled Helms. "This is what the State Department was trying to do." Helms presented Alam with a letter to give to the Shah expressing Nixon's alarm.

The Shah had left town for his ski vacation and Helms and Alam talked about what had happened. "As I recall, His Imperial Majesty granted you an audience," Alam said, "in which he would certainly have explained that oil prices can only be set in accordance with the price of alternative energy sources. I know for a fact that His Imperial Majesty made this point to the British ambassador." Helms admitted that this was true. "In that case, what's your objection? Our approach seems perfectly rational." According to Alam, Helms replied that "he had no objection and that he had sent a detailed report to Washington."

Helms then asked Alam if he could raise "a rather impertinent question." American diplomats had learned that the majority of the Arab oil ministers who attended the Tehran conference, and in particular Saudi Arabia's Sheikh Yamani, had opposed the price hike but had felt disinclined to challenge the Shah. Alam subsequently learned from the Shah that the Saudis had suggested a profit margin per barrel of $6. But Abu Dhabi, Kuwait, and Iraq had all pushed for a profit margin of $9. The Iranian view was that the Shah's pricing formula represented the middle ground and that it was unfair to characterize him as a price hawk. Alam explained the pricing formula to Helms, noting that "the U.S. ambassador has begun to realize the true implications of the Arab proposals, which has really put the wind up him."

In his letter to the Shah, Nixon urged his ally to reconsider the price increase because of the possible destabilizing impact it would have "on the world's economy and the catastrophic problems it could pose for the international monetary system. Not only will it result in raising the prices of manufactured products but it will have severe repressive effect on the economies of oil consumers which could cause a world-wide recession and which would eventually benefit no one, including the oil exporters." The Shah simply ignored Nixon's request. "I was involved in delivering these messages to the Shah, but he was having none of that," said Helms. The Shah's attitude was simple and uncompromising: "I've tried in the past to get oil price rises and the American and British companies wouldn't give them to me. Now I've got them and you're going to have to live with them." The Shah was deeply offended by the criticism leveled at him by his allies in the West. He dismissed Britain's ambassador Peter Ramsbotham as an "idiot" when the envoy begged for restraint and instructed Alam to give him a dressing down.

Nixon and his aides later came under severe criticism for allowing the Shah to get his way on oil prices. But did they have any choice? Decades later, Secretary of Defense James Schlesinger confirmed that U.S. officials feared crossing the Shah at a time when "relations between the United States and the Saudis in the case of the Nixon administration were somewhat tenuous. They became *extremely* tenuous because of the decision to provide Israel with aid sometime in October '73 which led to the oil embargo and which fed the Shah's economic ambitions. He was the one that was pushing the price up to $12 a barrel. The Shah was our ally." Schlesinger's naval task force relied on Iranian fuel supplies to keep the pressure on King Faisal to end the embargo.

> And as a result we were ambivalent about the Shah because we didn't want to fight him on energy prices. We didn't want to fight him on the point of energy prices [to the point where] we alienated him, right? On the other hand, it was plain that the run-up in prices was not in the interest of the United States or the Western world. That was the problem. At the same time we wanted him as our ally in the political conditions in the Middle East so we didn't want to go so far as to alienate him and lead him to be hostile to the United States.

The best explanation Henry Kissinger gave for what happened came in a secretly recorded telephone conversation with newspaper reporter Jack Anderson in 1975. The enterprising Anderson had somehow gotten his hands on a classified summary of Kissinger's December 1973 meeting with France's foreign minister Jobert. Kissinger at first claimed to have no recollection of the event. "I just—you know, I just can't remember that," he blustered. "I would have to check my records."

"Well, there is even a charge here that they offered to join us in military intervention," Anderson persisted.

"Oh, that is totally—that is totally—that, I know, is total nonsense."

"I will read it exactly the way it said: They raised the issue of joint U.S. military action—just raised the issue—references to this French proposal were made at the Embassy level and were reflected in the cable traffic. I don't have the cable traffic—what I have is a summary of it that comes from the State Department or from people in the State Department."

Kissinger's memory suddenly improved: "Well, look, Mr. Anderson, it is a very complicated issue, but this conversation, even if it would possibly turn out to be true, which I can't confirm—I'll have to look to see whether I can find a copy of this memo or an equivalent of it," he said. "Because you know, it does sound plausible to me." Kissinger proceeded to explain that the United States had been desperate for Iranian oil to keep flowing at full capacity during the embargo, telling Anderson that "at a time when we were facing an embargo for us to take on the Shah who was our only supplier of oil in that area was not the most intelligent thing to do . . . the geopolitics are not irrelevant and it's not irrelevant to have one country that won't join an embargo and that might be available in case of a Middle East conflict but that is not the only consideration." Kissinger added that in December 1973 there was a high risk of another war in the Middle East. The United States was under an oil embargo. "You have to look at our strategy in light of that period. . . . And not wanting to add Iran to the embargoing countries is not the worst—it is not a senseless judgment."

American impotence was separately reinforced when the Shah informed the administration that he would authorize an increase in Iranian oil production to alleviate fuel shortages in the West only if the United States supplied him with construction materials such as cement, steel I-beams, reinforcing rods, copper sheeting, and aluminum. On two fronts—oil pricing and production—the Shah was now playing a very hard game with the White House. The Iranian leader had the Nixon administration—and the economies of the Western industrialized world—over a barrel. The irony was this: in July 1973 Kissinger had been told that the Shah would be highly unlikely to join any oil embargo because Iran's economy could not afford the loss in revenue. The memo from the State Department concluded that the Shah's military buildup would "enable Iran to deal from a position of strength," though it did not say against whom. Kissinger either ignored or disregarded the analysis. Some in Washington now wondered whether the Shah's newfound petropower actually enabled him to deal with the United States from a position of strength. The Shah is "definitely using oil as a lever" a top U.S. official told *The Washington Post*. He added that it was "a touchy matter" in the White House.

YOU ARE GOING TO GIVE ME GAS OR I WILL KILL YOU

On February 9, President Richard Nixon met at the Western White House in San Clemente with Kissinger, Shultz, and William Simon, whom everyone now knew in shorthand as the White House "energy czar." They were coming out of another hair-raising month in which the United States had experienced the geopolitical equivalent of a power system failure. In Southeast Asia, Europe, the Mediterranean, the Persian Gulf, and throughout the Middle East the administration was on the defensive. The president had flown out to California on a commercial flight as a cost-saving measure. Nixon tried to lighten the mood when Kissinger pointed out that even a small country like Uganda had turned against them. "Look at Amin," he complained in reference to the murderous Ugandan dictator Idi Amin. "He used to be ours and the Kenyans bought him."

"The problem with Amin is not something he ate but someone he ate," Nixon cracked. "I'm sorry for the Africans, but it will take a long time." They had more critical issues to deal with than Amin or Uganda—like trying to prevent the collapse of law and order at home and save the industrialized world from bankruptcy.

Americans were experiencing oil shock. It began over the New Year's weekend when motorists in New York City fought one another with fists and knives outside gasoline stations and a man in Albany walked into a gas station with what looked like a hand grenade and left with all the gas he could carry. Service station attendants armed themselves as holdups and assaults proliferated across the country. "You are going to give me gas or I will kill you," one was told. Fully laden gasoline trucks were hijacked. Police reported a rash of suspicious automobile fires as car owners found ingenious ways of disposing of their gas guzzlers and claiming the insurance value on their cars. Motorists in Hawaii slept outside gas stations to hold their place in line. A strike by independent truck drivers angry over fuel prices and scarcity led to food shortages, which in turn triggered panic buying at supermarkets in the Midwest. Bitter clashes with strikebreakers resulted in three shooting deaths and many injuries, "and there have been scores of fist fights, slashed tires and smashed windshields." Truckers besieged the town of Streator (pop. 16,000) in Illinois and prevented trucks from entering the city limits. The town's biggest employer was forced to close its doors and frenzied residents mobbed stores to stock up on provisions. The governors of eight states called out the National Guard to patrol highway overpasses and truck stops and to escort convoys of trucks laden with food.

The Federal Energy Office monitored FBI reports of shootings and growing social unrest around the country. "The key during that period, the most intense motive was the survival of sectors of the country that were desperately short of oil, shutting down plants, shooting prices up, doing all sorts of bizarre things," recalled Frank Zarb, one of the officials charged with responding to the emergency. Zarb tried and failed to persuade House speaker Carl Albert to shut off the lights on the dome of the U.S. Capitol as a cost-saving measure. By early February gas lines in the nation's capital stretched for two miles. "I went into a line for an hour this morning to get some gasoline," Kissinger's deputy, Joseph Sisco, complained to his boss. "Getting gasoline is a small problem if you are not Secretary of State. The line was around the block twice, can you believe that? While sitting in the line I was thinking about you yesterday and thinking it would be nice to get this shortage over."

Kissinger shared Sisco's sense of frustration. "If I was the President," he joked with Brent Scowcroft, "I would tell the Arabs to shove their oil and tell the Congress we will have rationing rather than submit and you would get the embargo lifted in three days but I am not the President [under] this god-damn constitutional amendment." (Kissinger was referring to the Constitution's proscription against foreign-born citizens becoming president.) Not all the side effects of the fuel shortages were bad. After the national speed limit was lowered, traffic deaths fell 25 percent, pedestrian deaths by 30 percent, and the number of schoolchildren killed annually in automobile accidents dropped from ninety-eight to fifty-seven.

The pressure on the president and his administration to ease the energy crisis was intense. The man tasked with restoring order to the nation's fuel supplies, William Simon—universally known as Bill—was a forty-six-year-old former Wall Street bond trader, close friend of Nixon's former attorney general, John Mitchell, and protégé of George Shultz at Treasury. Simon was a Wall Street moneyman. Within nine months of starting work at the investment house Salomon Brothers in 1963 he became one of seventeen partners and was responsible for managing government and municipal bond trading. With his slicked-back hair, granite jawline, and signature square eyeglasses, Simon publicly exuded the confidence of the well-heeled establishment man. His subordinates knew him as a bully in the office, a man who "terrified" his staff and worked them like draft horses. One time he walked past a trainee whose desk was cluttered with papers. Simon saw the mess and barked, "Clean off your desk. It's a [expletive] pig sty." The trainee was so busy he still had not cleaned his desk when Simon returned from lunch. "And Simon leans over and, with the back of his arm, he just sweeps all the junk off that desk and onto the floor," recalled the trainee. "And then he says, 'See. See how easy it is to clean off a desk.'" Having Bill Simon as your boss made life "generally miserable."

Simon was a die-hard Nixon man who believed the country needed saving from the excesses of liberalism. During the 1968 presidential campaign he contributed $15,000 of the $100,000 donated to Nixon's campaign by Salomon partners. In December 1972 he was rewarded with the post as Shultz's deputy at Treasury. A year later Nixon chose him to run the Federal Energy Office and coordinate the allocations of fuel supplies across the country. Simon was unsettled when Nixon told him that his post would be like "Albert Speer's position as armaments overlord in the Third Reich." But he quickly emerged as the public face of the energy crisis, hailed by *Time* magazine in a cover story as "A Fitzgerald Hero in Washington," and "one of the freshest and most appealing faces in Washington." He relished the attention and the challenge. He worked till ten o'clock each night and his long-suffering wife, Carol, the mother of their seven children, admitted to a reporter that she and the kids hardly ever saw him—half an hour a day at most, including weekends. It was reported that on weekends he thought nothing of shocking his children out of their sleep by emptying buckets of cold water over them. Bill Simon loved his job and he hero-worshipped Nixon, using adjectives to describe the president that would have astonished Pat Nixon, such as, "fun, charming, enchanting and witty." The admiration was not mutual. Nixon and Kissinger generally held Simon in low regard and dismissed him as an intellectual lightweight. Nixon had scrawled over Simon's initial job application, "NO! East Coast Establishment! Other options?" After a January 23, 1974, cabinet meeting Nixon phoned Kissinger to gossip. "I thought that Simon was a wipe-out," he complained.

"A disaster," repeated Kissinger.

"I felt I had to say a few things, didn't you?"

"You saved him," said Kissinger.

"At the cabinet meeting—just running the Goddamn thing. They're all so weak. What they need is leadership. What was your feeling?"

"Exactly," chimed Kissinger. "As you said, they're weak. You certainly got it across to them."

Bill Simon and Henry Kissinger were bound to cross swords handling the domestic and foreign policy repercussions of the oil shock. Kissinger's great mistake was to underestimate Simon's capacity for ruthlessness and his love of a good scrap—played by Wall Street rules, of course, which meant no rules at all.

Kissinger was still having no luck in persuading King Faisal to lift the embargo. "He has himself locked in concrete," Kissinger told Nixon on February 5.

"He's really locked in concrete," Nixon agreed. "Until Syria has disengagement, there'll be no lifting the embargo."

"We are there on a roller-coaster," said Kissinger. "We have their solemn assurance in writing that they would lift the embargo. This is not our imagination."

Another leader frustrated with the Saudis was President Sadat of Egypt. Having emerged from the war with his stature enhanced throughout the Arab world, Sadat was ready to embark on his quest for a lasting peace with Israel. He distrusted the Soviets and wanted to improve ties with Washington. But he couldn't move until Faisal ended the embargo. The day after Nixon's talk with Kissinger, the Egyptian foreign minister in Cairo invited the U.S. and Saudi envoys to his office and, Kissinger told Al Haig, "in the presence of our ambassador called in the Saudis and gave them hell, and now they're pulling back."

On February 7, Nixon held a thirty-five-minute meeting with Saudi ambassador Ibrahim al-Sowayel in the White House Map Room. Nixon told the ambassador that he understood King Faisal was in a bind and unsure of how to proceed. Nixon knew that the king feared rousing the animosity of radical elements at home and abroad if he was seen to be dishonoring the Arab cause. Yet Faisal was also worried about the impact the embargo and the price increases were having on the economies of Saudi Arabia's trading partners. "I know your government wants to normalize the situation, but you feel you can't get out in front of the Algerians and the Syrians." Nixon came close to offering an apology for not working harder in his first term to help reduce tensions in the Middle East. He wanted Faisal to know that "I am determined now that the Middle East be settled." He told the ambassador, "I am the first President since Eisenhower who has no commitment to the Jewish community, and I will not be swayed." Nixon was not exaggerating when he said he would not bow to pressure from Israel or its supporters in the United States when working to reach a regional peace settlement. The war had still been raging when he had phoned Kissinger and told him that once the fighting had ended, "what ought to happen is that even though the Israelis will squeal like stuck pigs—we ought to tell [Soviet Ambassador Anatoly] Dobrynin—we ought to say that the Russians—that Brezhnev and Nixon will settle this damn thing. That ought to be done. You know that."

Nixon told Ambassador Sowayel that his efforts to reach a settlement "are being hampered and will be seriously jeopardized if the embargo is the issue. . . . It makes it terribly difficult to move as quickly as we want, with the embargo. I understand it, but with lines at the gas stations, and so on, I don't want our people to start blaming the Arabs."

WE ARE GOING ALL OUT NOW WITH THE SAUDIS

In an attempt to learn more about the Shah's thinking on a range of issues, over the Christmas holiday season American newspapers republished his interview from a month earlier with Italian journalist Oriana Fallaci. In an instant the Shah's carefully cultivated image as a friend to the West, a benevolent ruler, and a loving family man was shattered. His views on women ("You've never produced a Michelangelo or a Bach. You've never produced a great cook"), democracy ("I don't want any part of it, it's all yours, you can keep it, don't you see? Your wonderful democracy"), and dissent ("Those guilty of homicide, certainly. They are shot. But not because they're Communists, because they're terrorists") caused a sensation. Many Americans decided they had never really known the Shah at all, and what they knew of him now they didn't much like. "The sugar-coated image of the Shah of Iran (as regularly presented in the U.S. press) has suffered a telling blow, via the excellent interview you published," one woman wrote the editors of the *Los Angeles Times*. "I have recently returned from an extensive tour of Iran. The so-called White Revolution has been a dismal failure. Most villages have neither electricity nor running water; illiteracy stands at 72%. The slightest political dissent results in arrests and torture by the dreaded secret police. The slums of Tehran compare to those of Calcutta, while the wealthy live lives of incredible luxury." "His values are undignifying and based on sand," declared another angry reader. "May Allah protect the Empress Farah." "I could not believe how he disgustingly put down women," wrote a third.

Stung by the criticism, Mohammad Reza Shah went on the CBS News program *60 Minutes* to defend himself to interviewer Mike Wallace. The program, which aired on Sunday evening, February 24, only compounded the damage. The Shah appeared tense and ill at ease. Angered by a question about corruption in Iran he struck back, accusing U.S. oil companies of breaking the embargo and smuggling oil into the United States by rerouting tankers "two or three times" in mid-ocean. He spoke of oil "being sold for one destination and ending up somewhere else." He declared that the United States was in fact "not short of oil" at all and was importing more petroleum than ever before. The Shah's comments "created tremors in Washington," reported *The New York Times*, because they implied the Nixon administration was manipulating the embargo for domestic political reasons.

Bill Simon was summoned to Capitol Hill the next day to answer the Shah's charges before the House Ways and Means Committee. He arrived distinctly out of sorts. The abrupt summons had disrupted his busy schedule. Hurrying to make it to the Hill on time, he gashed his head on the edge of his car door. His request to receive medical attention and stitches was turned down by the committee chairman. With his head bandaged, Simon spent the next five hours "in considerable pain and discomfort, bleeding profusely as various congressmen screamed at me," as he put it. He faced them down and angrily threw the Shah's allegations back at them. He described the Shah's views on the embargo as not only "irresponsible and just plain ridiculous" but "insane." Later he bitterly recalled having to listen to Congressman Charles Vanik of Cleveland laud the Shah and implicitly question his own expertise in the field: "Are you telling me the Shah of Iran, the world's most renowned oil expert, doesn't know what he's talking about?"

"That's what I'm telling you," Simon retorted. He fared no better before a Senate subcommittee.

"I'll say this Mr. Simon," said Senator Henry "Scoop" Jackson. "We will have to dig a big bomb shelter for you by April if the lines are longer." Jackson's comment had a bite to it. Simon's rambling estate in northern Virginia was already under twenty-four-hour Secret Service protection because of death threats leveled at the energy czar by enraged Americans. When the Simon family attended a college football game, agents scoured the crowd for a stalker they knew to be sitting several rows behind.

"I remember the Secret Service being very present in our lives," said daughter Katie Simon. "I remember the Secret Service taking me to McDonald's one day before school."

Two days after his testimony on Capitol Hill "well-placed sources" contacted the offices of the Associated Press in Washington to say that Simon had "made a major mistake" by denouncing the Shah and had hurt his chances of succeeding George Shultz as secretary of the treasury. A second article appeared in *The Washington Post* warning the administration that Simon's comments had provoked "consternation and anger" in Iran. The Shah had been in contact with Ambassador Zahedi "several times." There was talk of recalling him from Washington. President Nixon took the extraordinary step of publicly and privately disassociating himself from Simon's remarks. He apologized to the Shah in a letter noteworthy for its contrition.

Simon now understood that the Shah had powerful supporters in the nation's capital, in the media, on Capitol Hill, and in the White House, although he knew nothing about Nixon's and Kissinger's secret history of dealings with the Iranian leader. For him the incident was a lesson in how raw power really worked in Washington. It was also the beginning of his remarkable, quixotic crusade to rid the corridors of power of Pahlavi influence in Washington. Simon was an idealist who believed that morality mattered in foreign policy. The Shah appalled him. "The Shah, in my opinion, was not only an uninformed, misinformed, irrational megalomaniac given to hallucinating, he was also duplicitous," he later said.

The Saudis, by contrast, were proving to be much more receptive to overtures from the White House. In early March, Nixon offered Faisal the equivalent of a grand bargain to end the embargo and start a new chapter in U.S.-Saudi relations. In return for resuming oil exports, boosting oil production, and holding firm on prices, the United States was prepared to fulfill the king's long-cherished goal of sealing a separate military and economic alliance with the United States. On March 7, Kissinger explained the proposed pact to Deputy Secretary of Defense Bill Clements: "We are going all out now on the Saudis. I worked it out with the King. We had to pick the right moment and we are going to send out a military mission and an economic mission. . . . It may take us another three or four weeks to get it worked out. We don't want to seem over anxious. The King liked the idea and we are now exploring it." He added that the Saudis "have learned a good lesson on the embargo. They may put it on again but never again with the other Arab states."

Kissinger phoned Nixon on Monday the 11th to tell him that "as you know, Mr. President, we had approached the Saudis on bilateralism and their response has been so enthusiastic, in fact so wildly enthusiastic that I can't help but believe this must affect their decision at the embargo."

"Yes. Well, that's the way we want to deal."

"Absolutely," agreed Kissinger. He explained that what the Saudi royal family "was getting out of it is a military relationship and a long-term economic relationship . . . And the commitment of the U.S. strategically to help them against their enemies in Iraq and South Yemen and so forth."

"And internally as well."

"Yes, that's right," said Kissinger. "That response has been amazing."

What Nixon and Kissinger were offering the Saudi leadership was a special, even unique, relationship. In return for resuming the flow of oil at an affordable price, the United States would help the Saudi rulers crush their political opponents at home and ideological foes abroad. U.S.-Saudi relations were about to undergo a profound seismic shift. No longer would the Shah be expected to defend Gulf oil from the radicals. The Americans would shield the Saudis until they could defend themselves. The United States was choosing to become directly and intimately involved in Saudi Arabia's internal governance, its foreign policy, and its economic development. Faisal had been right to hold out for a better deal. On that same day in Tehran, upon hearing reports that the Saudis were about to cut a deal with Nixon, the Shah told a guest not to worry. "Washington relies on Zaki Yamani," he declared. "But not even a hundred Yamanis could interrupt the flow of events."

The oil embargo was lifted at a meeting of OPEC in Vienna on March 18. The Saudis also announced an immediate boost in their oil production by one million barrels a day. When Iran proposed raising oil prices by a further 5 percent, Yamani declared that Saudi Arabia would sooner pull out of the cartel. The other delegations reacted angrily but were powerless to prevent the world's swing producer from using its reserves as leverage against them. A week later Saudi oil production was back at its pre-embargo level of 8.3 million barrels a day and Yamani announced that his government had decided to expand its production capacity to 11.2 million barrels a day by the end of 1975, an increase of 37 percent over its current rate.

The impact of the embargo and the monthly 5 percent production cutbacks became the focus of a great deal of subsequent debate. The embargo initially targeted the United States and the Netherlands for their strong support of Israel. West European states and Japan were eventually exempted from the embargo because they rushed to cut private deals with Middle East governments or issued public statements designed to mollify Arab concerns about the return of Israeli-occupied territories. Portugal, Rhodesia, and South Africa were also targeted by the cartel. Oil producers Iran, Nigeria, and Venezuela profited from the panic when they rushed to try to fill the gap in supply. Iraq's Saddam Hussein also increased his country's oil production by arguing that the embargo was actually an American-Saudi plot to weaken Europe and Japan to increase their dependency on the United States. Nonetheless, as industry analyst Daniel Yergin has pointed out, the loss of even 9 percent of the 55.8 million barrels of oil consumed each day by the free world was "made even more severe because of the rapid rate at which oil consumption had been growing—7.5 percent a year." With no spare capacity in the market, even the loss of a few million barrels was enough to dislocate supplies worldwide. Panic, hoarding, and clumsy government efforts to allocate fuel supplies also played their part in the crisis.

SOMEONE HAS TO TALK TO THE SHAH

In Washington and elsewhere, the Shah's policies were causing a great deal of concern. In the early evening of March 29, 1974, Kissinger hosted a top-level meeting of administration officials and oil executives to discuss the next moves on Middle East peace talks and the oil crisis. It was the latest in a series of briefings the secretary held with petroleum industry leaders to coordinate administration policy with their concerns. The presidents and chairmen of Texaco, Standard Oil of California, Exxon, Mobil, Amerada Hess, Atlantic Richfield, Continental Oil, and Gulf Oil were in attendance. An old Washington hand, John McCloy, was also there. The law firm he represented, Milbank, Tweed, Hadley & McCloy, handled negotiations between the oil companies and Arab governments. Kissinger began by assuring his guests that the written transcript of their conversation "isn't going to go anywhere, except into my own personal files. If it makes you nervous, we will stop. . . . You may not realize what an achievement it is in this building to keep notes from being made in 500 copies." Then he made a typically acerbic crack at the expense of Bill Simon, who was sitting in with them. "You know everybody, don't you? Do me a favor and say you don't recognize Simon." Laughter. "That's the only thing that will instill a measure of humility in the czar." More laughter.

After briefing the oil executives on the latest developments in the

Middle East peace talks, Kissinger learned that the recent doubling in the price of oil had been one increase too many: consumers in the West and elsewhere were cutting back their imports of foreign oil and implementing tough conservation measures. These measures were placing pressure on OPEC's pricing structure—and cutting into oil company profits. The industry was also in agreement that the high posted price of oil was driving up the rate of inflation amid panicked efforts by oil-consuming nations to enter into barter deals with oil producers. Consumers were anxious to recoup the cost of their fuel bills and secure long-term and guaranteed access to supplies of Middle East oil. Taiwan wanted an oil-for-refinery agreement with the Saudis. Poland had agreed to supply Libya with tankers and industrial equipment in return for oil shipments starting in 1980. Argentina was bartering grains and meat for oil from Libya. France was in talks with Iraq to conclude a twenty-year contract to supply it with 5.6 billion barrels of crude, and with the Saudis to swap weapons and industrial goods in return for three years of oil. Iraq had agreed to supply Japan with 320,000 barrels a day in a ten-year deal that would see Tokyo offer Baghdad a $1 billion credit to build a natural gas processing plant, a refinery, a petrochemical plant, a fertilizer plant, and an aluminum plant.

The barter deals were affecting the world economy by holding prices up everywhere else. Inflation had risen because of the explosion in fuel and commodity prices. "This reflects a sharp acceleration in the last three months, when, particularly under the initial impact of higher oil costs, the increase expressed at an annual rate was of the order of 16%," reported the Organisation for Economic Co-operation and Development. Between a quarter and one third of inflation was blamed on rising energy costs, which in turn "kicked up the prices of countless oil-based products, including fertilizers, petrochemicals and synthetic textiles." In 1974 the inflation rate in the United States climbed as high as 12 percent. Rates of inflation doubled in Western Europe with France and Belgium registering 16 percent, 18 percent in Great Britain, 25 percent in Italy, 32 percent in Iceland, and Greece at 33.4 percent. Japan reported a 24 percent rate of inflation. Inflation of 55 percent blew unchecked through Argentina. The oil shock also had a devastating toll in many corners of the Third World. Africa's combined $10 billion fuel bill all but erased the $11.4 billion it received in aid from the industrialized world. In Asia, rice harvests collapsed 40 percent in Sri Lanka because farmers had to pay 375 percent more for fertilizer. The social fabric of many countries was beginning to tear. The barter deals were only making matters worse, setting a floor price below which oil would not fall.

American oil company executives had another immediate concern: they worried they were being pushed out of the Persian Gulf oil market. Exxon's Ken Jamieson complained to Kissinger, Simon, and their aides that "more and more oil that was Aramco oil is being diverted to these other countries on government-to-government deals. So we are losing effectively oil that was under our control before." The oil producers "are attempting to use this device to establish a market price," agreed Gulf Oil's B. R. Dorsey.

Jamieson explained that "the price problem is more critical than the supply problem" and that "Our judgment is the one who has really been pushing the prices the worst is the Shah." He urged the White House to bring pressure to bear on the Iranian leader.

"He is also the hardest one to push," agreed Kissinger. "He is a tough cookie." He added, "Simon is our specialist in treating with the Shah."

"If the posted price went down, the barter deals would go down," explained William Tavoulareas, the president of Mobil Oil. "So would the price at which they sell. That would work." When Kissinger asked how prices could be forced down, Tavoulareas answered, "Someone has to talk to the Shah."

Kissinger assured the group that he planned to see the Shah "next time I go out there." What he did not tell them was that neither he nor Nixon retained any influence over Iranian oil policy or had any leverage to influence the Shah's behavior.

The Saudis, said Jamieson, favored a price reduction and an increase in their oil production to flood the market and break OPEC's pricing structure.

"Faisal has dead aim on the Shah in this deal, Henry—I guarantee you," Deputy Secretary of Defense William Clements warned Kissinger.

Simon was all for it: "[The Saudis] don't have to reduce the posted price—just raise the [level of their oil] production and let the market take care of it."

Chairman Robert Anderson of Atlantic Richfield emphasized that the oil market was softening and that the Shah had overreached. A recent price auction held by the Saudis had generated offers only as high as between $9.50 and $11.50 per barrel, significantly lower than the Shah's $17.40 from December. Kuwait had canceled its auction because it reported bids between only $8.50 and $10 per barrel. Oil liftings at Iran's Kharg Island were averaging less than 300,000 barrels a day. The market had started to settle down, an indication that if it were left undisturbed prices would start to drop. But instead they were being held up artificially by the Shah, who had already committed future oil income to pay for $5 billion in future U.S. weapons systems.

Jamieson and his colleagues urged the administration to enter into bilateral trade pacts with Saudi Arabia and Iran instead of barter deals. It was in the American national interest to increase the oil producers' economic dependency on the United States. Bilateral deals, explained Clements, "will sop up this available resource that they have over there, either in money or manpower or time to handle the arrangements and the deals. They can only take on so many of these things . . . if we started in some serious move, like through technology, industry, this sort of thing, just sop up whatever was available over there in that regard, it would help." Separate bilateral deals between the United States and Iran and Saudi Arabia would give Washington a bigger say in how both countries ran their economies and how much they charged for their oil. The United States could also soak up billions of dollars in petrodollars to stabilize its own financial situation and improve its trade balance with the Gulf states.

"I think the more inter-dependent the two countries become, the better chance you have of getting to be more reasonable on price," agreed Mobil's Tavoulareas.

Deputy Secretary of State Kenneth Rush made the perceptive observation that the barter deals and bilateral trade pacts worked out between the industrialized West and oil producers in the Persian Gulf "will involve a lot of [Americans] going in there." He assumed, wrongly as it turned out, that a flood of expatriates into the region "would draw us closer to them." No thought was given to the possibility that the influx might instead arouse anti-American sentiment.

I WANT THEM FINISHED IN MY LIFETIME

Nixon and Kissinger had encouraged the Shah's dream to transform Iran into a regional military powerhouse. A classified U.S. analysis noted:

> The desire of Iran's leadership to revive the splendors of the ancient Persian Empire and to become politically and economically co-equal with England and France before the end of this century is well known. Geographically, the USSR in the north, and a growing, competitive

Arab presence to the west precludes the expansion of an Iranian sphere
of influence. However, Iran can increasingly be expected to try to attain
a more important position to the east in Afghanistan and Pakistan, in
the Indian Ocean, and in international forums.

With a vast supply of petrodollars and U.S. weapons pouring in, there
seemed to be nothing to stop the empire of Iran and its Shahanshah from
dominating not only the Persian Gulf and the land bridges into Central
Asia but even extending Iranian influence down along Africa's east coast,
and driving deep into the Indian Ocean.

"Iran is not a volcano now," the Shah assured a visitor to the palace who
asked about the country's political stability. "The Iranian air force ought
to be strong enough to protect the whole area from the Persian Gulf to
the Sea of Japan. India is going to collapse. India and Pakistan will become
natural markets for Iranian industrial projects, but I shall have to protect
Pakistan against Indian aggression."

The imperial family retreated to Kish over the Persian New Year in
March. On April 8, the Shah broke from his vacation to fly to Bandar Abbas
with Asadollah Alam and Ambassador Helms. From there they boarded
the U.S. aircraft carrier *Kitty Hawk*, which had joined the naval task force
stationed off the coast of Oman. The task force mounted naval exercises for
the Shah's benefit.

The Shah of Iran basked in his new stature as one of the world's most
important statesmen. "In the 33rd year of an often uncertain reign, Mohammad Reza Pahlavi has brought Iran to a threshold of grandeur that is
at least analogous to what Cyrus the Great achieved for ancient Persia," declared *Time*, which in 1974 dubbed Iran's leader the "Emperor of Oil." "But
I have so many aspirations," the Shah confided to Alam. "To be first in the
Middle East is not enough. We must raise ourselves to the level of a great
world power. Such a goal is by no means unattainable."

On Tuesday, April 9, just six days after hearing the Shah utter those
words, Alam drove from his residence on Kish to the summer palace. Expecting the Shah to be in good spirits, he was troubled to be met outside
the royal quarters by General Karim Ayadi, the Shah's personal physician, who asked him to send for Professor Jean Bernard, a leading French
hematologist. The request, Ayadi insisted, was urgent. Dr. Jean Bernard,
who practiced at a leading cancer institute in Paris, was treating Alam for a
type of incurable blood cancer whose true dimensions had been concealed
from the patient. It was not unusual in Persian medical culture for doctors

to protect their patients from the trauma of learning news of incurable or terminal illnesses. Avoidance was intended as a mark of respect and a gesture of humanity. Alam knew he was ill but did not know that he was slowly dying. Alam was shaken by the news that something might be wrong with the Shah, although the monarch displayed no trace of emotion or distress. As they drove to the airport the Shah asked Alam about the progress of hotel construction on the island. "They must hurry up," he said, "I want them finished in my lifetime."

In fact, the Shah—like Alam—had cancer. The Shah's curious behavior on the island of Kish—his unruffled demeanor and calm fatalism during a medical emergency—suggests two possible scenarios. One is that he was genuinely unconcerned about his health and had no foreboding of a fatal illness. The second scenario, and the version later accepted by the queen, was that the Shah *already* knew about his cancer and that he had already had several weeks to absorb the initial shock of diagnosis by his physician. "I was told that Professor [Karl] Fellinger had informed the Shah in 1974 about his health problem," she remembered. "I think that the Shah knew when the first French doctors first visited Tehran to treat him."

The queen's account is confirmed by Dr. Fellinger. As was their custom, in early 1974 the Shah, Shahbanou, and their children traveled to Switzerland for a ski holiday. It was the Shah's habit to break away from his vacation to fly to neighboring Austria for his annual medical checkup. Dr. Fellinger was a world-renowned internist, the "Doctor of Kings" whose patient roster included the rulers of Saudi Arabia, Afghanistan, and Morocco, in addition to the Shah. It was in Vienna in Dr. Fellinger's consultation rooms that the Shah was first diagnosed with lymphoma, a form of blood cancer that was treatable but at the time incurable. Dr. Fellinger later recalled how the Shah's personal physician, General Ayadi, who accompanied the king to Vienna, emphasized to him the need for total secrecy. Some posit that Fellinger and Ayadi conspired to keep the Shah in the dark about his illness. While this possibility cannot be ruled out, the likeliest scenario is that the Shah did know and that he and Ayadi decided to keep it secret for as long as they could. The Shah's life was thoroughly compartmentalized and it made sense that he would treat his lymphoma as a state secret for fear of what might happen if his domestic opponents, Iran's ambitious neighbors, and the leaders of the great powers—including the Americans—learned that he was now marking time. The Shah immediately began covering his tracks, ending his association with Dr. Fellinger, and in 1975 switched to an internist in Switzerland. Medical visits to Austria were now out of the question. "Had he gone to a hospital in Vienna, the test results could not have been kept secret," recalled an aide.

What prompted the Shah to seek medical attention for the swelling in his abdomen, and why did he consult French specialists? It seems likely that by early April 1974 General Ayadi realized he needed help. Perhaps the swelling in the Shah's abdomen had increased, or perhaps the king felt unwell. At least one foreign newspaper reporter who interviewed the Shah around this time commented on his wan appearance. Ayadi's panicked decision to summon expert help on April 9 may also have been hastened by the death in Paris five days earlier of President Pompidou after a lengthy and secret battle with Waldenström's disease, a form of lymphoma. The Shah and Alam had been deeply impressed with Pompidou's quiet determination to stay in office despite his terminal diagnosis. Pompidou's condition was kept from the French people but quietly acknowledged in diplomatic circles. Secretary of Defense Schlesinger had alerted the National Security Council on September 5, 1973, when he brusquely announced, "Pompidou is dying." The Nixon administration began an intensive study of the French president's illness and how it might affect American-French relations. Visiting London on February 26, 1974, Kissinger confided to Britain's foreign secretary, Sir Alec Douglas-Home, that the White House "had an analysis made. Our people give him eighteen months to three years. He is deteriorating and increasingly susceptible to infection. He is taking massive doses of Cortisone which bring out the personality traits of stubbornness." Pompidou was dead in six weeks.

The Shah intended to follow Pompidou's honorable departure from the world scene. The French specialists summoned by Asadollah Alam flew out of Orly Airport in great secrecy and arrived in Tehran on May 1. Dr. Bernard and his young protégé, Dr. Georges Flandrin, were initially told that it was Alam who needed their services. The French doctors were instructed to bring their own medical equipment because once in Tehran they were to have no contact with local medical specialists. At Mehrabad Airport "two cars with flashing lights were waiting for us at the foot of the gangway, and we shook hands with some gentlemen we had never met but whose faces we would regularly see at our arrivals in Tehran," recalled Flandrin. The cars took them to Alam's house. It was there they learned "that we would be taking care of his 'boss's' health—that is the word he used with his best smile." Alam's own health problems turned out to be the perfect alibi. If anyone spotted the doctors entering or leaving the palace, their questions could be directed to the court minister. Flandrin and Bernard were driven to Niavaran and ushered into the king's study. Flandrin took note of Mohammad Reza Shah's soft voice, his fluency in French, and his athletic physique. The Shah lifted his shirt to show them how he self-diagnosed his swollen spleen. The French doctors went about their work knowing nothing about the Shah's consultation earlier in the year with Dr. Fellinger in Vienna. They believed they were making a diagnosis for the first time.

The doctors made an immediate diagnosis, the same as Fellinger's from earlier in the year, and left the Shah alone while they talked to General Ayadi and informed him of the Shah's lymphoma. Then it was their turn to be shocked. Ayadi told them that "as far as he was concerned, His Majesty had to be told that everything was fine!" The word "cancer" must not be mentioned in his presence. An intense conversation ensued. The doctors reminded Ayadi that although the Shah's overall health appeared good, the blood disease "would ultimately become malignant"—they had to tell him *something*. Bound by their instructions from Ayadi, Flandrin and Bernard "felt they could not act otherwise."

When they returned to Paris the doctors asked Ayadi to monitor their patient. "As is the rule in similar medical situations, we had decided to begin with supervision but no treatment," recalled Flandrin. They settled on a diagnosis that they hoped would satisfy General Ayadi's desire not to unduly alarm the king yet not compromise their own medical ethics: the Shah was told he had Waldenström's disease—the exact same disease that had just killed Pompidou. Any remaining doubts that the Shah might have had about the state of his health were surely settled when he learned this. It hardly seems plausible that the Shah did not understand the message. According to Dr. Flandrin, at this stage only five people knew about the Shah's health crisis: the Shah, Bernard and Flandrin, Ayadi and Alam. But if Alam ever learned of the Shah's diagnosis for lymphoma he never let on in his diaries.

One consequence of the Shah's diagnosis was that those who worked alongside him began noticing subtle changes in his leadership style. "We have to prepare the grounds for the crown prince," he said one day to a surprised confidant. Officials remembered the Shah hurrying their projects along. "The Shah is pushing," they complained. "We have the equipment but we don't have the people." The Shah also became less concerned with how his actions would be received in Washington. When Kissinger let it be known he would not be coming to Tehran in April 1974, the Shah was dismissive. "To hell with Kissinger," he told Alam. "Pay him no attention and tell Ardeshir Zahedi that he's to avoid offering any sort of invitation or giving any hint that we're expecting a visit."

In the spring of 1974 Iran's supreme leader and his closest aide had both contracted incurable cancers. Shakespeare could not have imagined a more exquisite tragedy of state: unbeknownst to each other, the empire's two most experienced helmsmen were mortally ill. It brought to mind another empire whose fate rested to a large extent on a secret illness—Russia's ill-fated Romanov dynasty and the deadly hemophilia suffered by Czarevitch Alexei, son and heir of Czar Nicholas II.

THE FIRST EMPIRE FALLS

In April 1974 an event occurred thousands of miles away from Iran in Europe, one that at the time appeared to have no connection whatsoever with the fate of the Shah and the House of Pahlavi. An army rebellion deposed the government of Premier Marcello Caetano in Portugal and declared an end to forty years of right-wing authoritarian rule. The centuries-old Portuguese empire had finally come crashing down. A close look reveals that oil prices had claimed their first head of state. The financial foundations of Portugal's tottering dictatorship had suddenly been blown apart by raging inflation and a simultaneous collapse in the country's overseas oil revenues.

Oil had been discovered in Portugal's colonial enclave of Cabinda in Angola in 1968. Cabinda oil was low in sulfur and thus especially attractive to the United States and Canada, which paid premium prices to satisfy strict new clean air regulations. Portugal resorted to buying cheaper and dirtier oil from the Middle East for domestic use. That arrangement abruptly fell apart when Lisbon agreed to Nixon's request during the October crisis to fly military supplies destined for Israel through the Portuguese Azores. Arab governments retaliated by stopping all fuel shipments to Portugal, in turn forcing Lisbon to curtail its own petroleum exports to North America. As a consequence the government relinquished hundreds of millions of dollars in sorely needed oil revenues. Even the doubling of oil prices didn't help stanch the financial hemorrhaging—Portugal's $400 million in income from petroleum was more than wiped out by the $650 million annual cost of defending its rebellious colonies in Africa. Inflation ignited by high energy costs elsewhere in Europe sapped the economy and demoralized Portuguese society.

"Discontent over unchecked inflation, about 20 percent last year, and one of the highest in Europe, has been general," observed *The New York Times*. "Few seemed to make any connection between the spectacular rise in living costs and the war [in the rebellious Portuguese colony of Mozambique], but inflation contributed to general dissatisfaction and the feeling that the Government should have been worrying more about conditions at home and less about the African colonies."

The ripple effect continued. Portugal's new ruling military junta took a hard turn to the political left, suddenly raising the specter of a radical socialist state in Western Europe. The Portuguese Azores, the islands viewed as crucial springboards for American aerial power in North Africa and the Mediterranean, had been lost to the Pentagon. With hopes of establishing a U.S. naval presence in Portuguese Mozambique also dashed, the Shah once again proved his value to Washington with his intention to build a $200 million military base at Bandar Abbas and a giant $600 million naval base at Chabahar, located at the mouth of the Persian Gulf. American and Iranian naval officials held talks to consider ways in which the United States could secure an "option" to operate out of Chabahar in the event of another regional emergency such as a coup in Saudi Arabia or a second oil embargo.

The Shah had no way of knowing that his own fate was tethered to the outcome of the chaotic scenes that would play out on the Iberian Peninsula over the next two and a half years.

Chapter Six

CRUEL SUMMER

"The financial markets are close to panic."
— Treasury Secretary William Simon, 1974

"I will have to meet and talk with the Shah."
— President Richard Nixon, 1974

A FINE ROMANCE

Saudi Arabia's oil alliance with the United States was sealed in the first week of June 1974 when Prince Fahd Ibn Abdul Aziz al-Saud, the most influential of King Faisal's brothers, led a contingent of officials to Washington to sign a series of economic and military accords. The official events culminated in a lavish banquet at which more than 1,400 guests wandered through the Saudi embassy grounds, mingling and straining to catch a glimpse of newlyweds Nancy Maginnes, a former aide to Nelson Rockefeller, and her husband, Secretary of State Henry Kissinger, the "queen bee at the center of the hive." According to one observer, the tables groaned beneath trays piled high with pastries, cakes, and creme-filled confections. "If you have money you can buy anything, probably. These strawberries— fertilized with oil, I imagine. High carbon."

Two joint commissions were established to handle economic and military relations arising from the new arrangement. The Economic Cooperation Commission was chaired by Bill Simon, sworn in almost a month earlier as the nation's sixty-third secretary of the treasury. The Security Cooperation Commission was chaired by Robert Ellsworth, director of International Security Affairs at the Pentagon and a former U.S. ambassador to NATO. Together Simon and Ellsworth used their formidable clout at Treasury and Defense to strengthen and deepen ties to Saudi Arabia, a country as big in size as the United States east of the Mississippi, but with only 5.7 million people living atop 132 billion barrels of crude oil reserves. Prince Fahd emphasized that improved relations were contingent on the United States making progress toward the establishment of a Palestinian state. American officials felt they had little choice in the matter. "America runs on oil, and you don't talk about oil very long before you mean Saudi Arabia," remarked *The Washington Post.* The Shah was much less enthusiastic about the idea of institutionalizing economic and military relations with Washington. Back channels to the White House, his preferred way of doing business, ensured privacy and a high level of manipulation. The joint commission would create a bureaucracy run by outsiders and require input from his ministers and the U.S. secretaries of treasury and defense. He smelled trouble. The Shah decided to keep Washington happy by signing the pact. But he made sure it became little more than a talk shop. Distrustful as ever, the Shah suspected the joint commission was an excuse for the Americans to gain influence over Iran's oil-based economy.

WE REALLY HAD A GRAND TIME

The Shah's worst fears would have been realized had he been witness to the raucous scenes played out at Bill and Carol Simon's sprawling seven-acre estate in McLean, Virginia. On Friday afternoon, June 7, the portly Prince Fahd "had been first in the swimming pool," followed by a tumble of male and female dignitaries, the women frolicking in specially made Arab dresses. Lunch was served to His Highness on the terrace and everyone ate from full plates. This was diplomacy, Treasury-style. Bill Simon telephoned Henry Kissinger at the State Department to say how sorry he was the secretary of state couldn't be there with them. The Saudis were having an "absolutely super" time, chortled Simon, "and they are going back with great enthusiasm." Simon's boyish enthusiasm for the art of the deal came through in comments that left Kissinger cold: "So everything is just perfect. They got so excited this morning at one point in the meeting that they are sending their chief petroleum economist over here this next week and he is going to stay as long as possible."

Simon's appointment to head up Treasury had been a typically messy affair. Nixon had already been turned down by David Rockefeller, Nelson's youngest brother, who ran Chase Manhattan Bank. According to Arthur Burns, whom White House chief of staff Alexander Haig confided in, Nixon believed Simon had "grave shortcomings—a publicity hound, not reflective enough," but that the job had already been "virtually promised to him." The president intended to keep Simon confined to Treasury, deny him a White House office, and strip him of any real responsibility. "What a mess!" Burns lamented. "Simon is clever but he shoots from the hip and may be (I don't really know) a political opportunist."

Kissinger was struggling to match Simon's enthusiasm for the Saudis. Things were moving too quickly on the oil pricing front for his liking. He still viewed the geopolitical relationship with the Shah as the essential building block of America's strategic architecture in the Middle East and West Asia. While he had developed something of a grudging respect for King Faisal, Kissinger loathed Zaki Yamani, Faisal's charming oil minister and a man who also enjoyed a high media profile. Kissinger shared the view of Iranian officials that the Saudis were cunning parvenus bent on increasing U.S. dependency on Saudi oil reserves while displacing the Shah as America's senior ally in the Persian Gulf. "Dependent on the West for military and diplomatic support yet fearful of the radical Arab regimes' capacity to threatened Saudi domestic stability, the Saudi royal family maneuvered with consummate prudence," Kissinger later wrote. "Carefully modulating conservative foreign and domestic policies with occasional radical rhetoric, it professed sympathy for America's concern with the price of oil. Yet whenever American importuning on the subject turned practical, we were shunted off, in the politest way possible, to some other address, usually Tehran." Kissinger dismissed Yamani as a showboat and a lightweight, telling him to his face that "one minister of his training and capacities would greatly buttress the existing Saudi institutions, but ten thousand like him would probably destroy them." When Yamani came back to Washington in late June, Kissinger stood him up, prompting Bill Simon to tell him that the minister "was, I think, a little hurt, as Arabs get." Kissinger shrugged off the incident.

Henry Kissinger was faced with the unhappy irony that one of the biggest foreign policy challenges Americans faced on his watch had important economic and financial components that were outside his realms of expertise. Developing a coordinated response to the oil shock would require help from the Treasury and its freewheeling cadre of ex–Wall Street executives, men like Bill Simon and Frank Zarb, the new energy czar and head of the renamed Federal Energy Administration, whose personal energy, ambition, and confidence frequently left Kissinger perplexed, frustrated—and enraged. Instead of engaging them, Kissinger resented their contributions and blocked their initiatives at every turn, usually behind their backs. What followed was a knock-down, drag-out fight that split the Nixon and, later, Ford administrations at the highest levels with Kissinger on one side defending the Shah, and Simon on the other arguing that the Shah was the real obstacle to resolving the energy crisis.

"[Bill Simon] and Henry had a complicated relationship," recalled Brent Scowcroft, Kissinger's deputy at the NSC. "And I think at least Bill Simon, and it probably went both ways, saw them as competing for power inside the White House." Kissinger worried that the treasury secretary, with no prior experience in diplomacy and geopolitics, was being manipulated by the Saudis. According to Scowcroft, Bill Simon was "mesmerized" by Yamani and had lost all sense of perspective. "And whatever Yamani was, and he was very skillful and clever, he was not a policy maker," said Scowcroft. "The two of them were always at loggerheads," concurred Frank Zarb of the Simon-Kissinger feud. "I think it was more of a competition between who interfaced with [OPEC] governments on the [oil] issue—between Treasury in general and State in general. And this may have fed the Simon-Kissinger debates." Nor was there any doubt that the men from Wall Street brought their own distinctive style of diplomacy to Washington and in the process caused Kissinger much heartburn. It was a clash of styles and temperament as much as one of policy. There was an uproar over a remark Zarb made in response to a question posed during a meeting of business leaders. When asked what he thought was the best way to deal with OPEC, Zarb answered with what he thought was a joke: "With a two-by-four!" Unfortunately for him a newspaper reporter was in the room to record the comment.

At the conclusion of the Friday afternoon pool party Yamani accepted an invitation from Simon to move into his house for the weekend. This may have been the occasion for Yamani to mention a curious incident that had occurred six months earlier during the Tehran OPEC meeting. In Yamani's telling of the story the Shah and the oil ministers were seated around a table when he asked them what they thought of his idea of charging $12 for a barrel of oil. Yamani worried that an increase to that amount would hurt the economies of Saudi Arabia's trading partners. He said he couldn't offer an opinion on the matter without first phoning King Faisal for instructions. Three times the minister dialed the number to the palace and three times the call would not go through. "It was at a very critical moment," remembered Yamani, who suspected that the phone lines had been sabotaged. Faced with the choice of opposing the Shah and splitting OPEC, or accepting the Shah's proposal and then trying "to bring prices down eventually," Yamani opted for the latter. But he returned home to find King Faisal deeply unhappy with his decision to follow the Shah's lead.

Yamani and Simon decided to play Kissinger and the Shah at their own game. They opened their own separate lines of communication. "We used to correspond quite regularly as far as confidential messages were concerned," Simon reminisced. "We used what we call 'back channel' messages. They didn't go through the State Department. It was more private that way."

THE SHAH HAS US

In the summer of 1974, with the Watergate investigation in high gear, Richard Nixon announced a grand tour of Middle East capitals in what turned out to be his final attempt at self-preservation. The Egyptians and the Israelis, the Syrians and the Saudis, were happy to receive the president. Only the Shah said no. On at least one occasion he had considered making a public show of support for the beleaguered president. His ambassador in Washington wisely talked him out of it. By the spring of 1974 Nixon had become a liability to the Shah, their association an embarrassment. The time had come to cut Richard Nixon loose. "By no means," the Shah told Alam when he was asked whether or not he wanted Nixon's itinerary to include a stopover in Tehran. "His present trip has nothing to do with us, though of course I'll be happy to receive him if he particularly wishes it. All in all the Americans have been behaving with admirable tact towards us and there really is little for us to discuss." Alam's personal opinion was that the Shah felt the need to distance himself from his ally: "HIM's reluctance to issue an invitation stems from Nixon's deteriorating position at home."

The Shah's singular act of disloyalty backfired when Nixon decided instead to spend three full days with King Faisal. Alam assumed Nixon was trying to divert attention from Watergate and that he was intent on rolling back oil prices. The Shah was first perplexed, then anxious at news of Nixon's stop in the Saudi capital. Nixon's political collapse shook the Iranian leader's confidence in his American ally. What would happen to the secret agreements worked out between them concerning oil prices and arms sales, the Kurds of Iraq, contingency planning in the Gulf, and ferrying military equipment around West Asia? The feverish whiff of conspiracy permeated the corridors of Niavaran Palace. Mohammad Reza Shah thought he knew who and what was behind Richard Nixon's losing fight to stay in office. "There's more than meets the eye to his present predicament," he lectured Alam, who asked whether his master was referring to sabotage by "the Jewish lobby." "Not the Jews," replied the Shah. "No, the whole thing is a conspiracy put together by the CIA, big business and a handful of influential men whose identities remain a closely guarded secret. It was they that arranged Kennedy's assassination. Now they have a score to settle with Nixon, though I don't know why." After a moment's pause he continued: "Maybe I'm just imagining things. But I sincerely hope I'm right about the conspirators. If all this is the result of mere chance it doesn't bode well for the future of the free world."

Nixon's presidency crumbled as the global economic crisis triggered by high oil prices entered a dangerous new phase, with the aftershocks now threatening to overwhelm financial systems and the banks. Officials at Treasury were growing more worried by the day. At 10:00 A.M. on July 9, Treasury Secretary Simon sat down with the president in the Oval Office to discuss his own forthcoming visit to Middle Eastern and European capitals. Nixon seemed overwhelmed by the scale and impact of the financial dislocations set in motion by the oil shock. His core constituents in small-town Middle America were hurting. "He is getting a lot of mail about little guys being hurt," Alexander Haig confided to Arthur Burns. Two weeks before Simon's meeting Burns had been privy to a bizarre scene in which Nixon "began by expressing his skepticism about economics and economists. He wanted, so he said, to explore ways of dealing with inflation; but he felt, he added, that old ways do not seem to work, and that something radical—like dictatorship—might be the answer. This, of course, he added is also no answer." It said something about Nixon's state of mind that he looked to Simon for reassurance. Simon told him that Treasury estimated that Arab oil revenues for the year would total $60 billion, two thirds of which would be spent or reinvested in the Arab world. King Faisal would hold $10 billion or half of the outstanding sum and Simon hoped to persuade the king to invest that money in U.S. government notes "that would pay the same as Treasury bills." Washington was anxious to recycle OPEC oil money to improve its own balance sheet and stabilize financial systems buckling under the strain of the massive fluctuations taking place in the markets and banking sector.

Nixon told Simon that during his own recent visit to Saudi Arabia he too had discussed the vexing issue of oil prices with the Saudis. Nixon agreed with Simon that the Iranians and not the Saudis were responsible for blocking efforts to reduce oil prices and that the current posted price was set for political reasons and not because of demand and supply. He did not tell Simon that he had personally triggered the crisis four years earlier when he gave the Shah the green light to increase oil prices as he saw fit. "With

Faisal, I have raised it privately, and you can, that the oil prices can't go on," he said. "This, of course, will have to be done privately. I doubt that you can do very much as long as the Shah holds up prices, but we want to explore whatever might be possible."

"Yamani recently spent the weekend with me," said Simon. "I told him that the high prices were strengthening their potential opposition—that the current high prices help others, but not the Saudis." Simon was referring to the Shah's military buildup, which was causing great concern to Saudi leaders.

"Sure. It gives us an incentive as well to develop alternatives," added Nixon. High oil prices would help wean the United States off its dependency on cheap Middle East oil. But for now prices had to be reined in. "Tell them our efforts for self-sufficiency do not mean we do not care about them. The important thing now is to get prices under some control."

"Is it possible to put pressure on the Shah?"

"You are not going there," said Nixon.

"No," said Simon, who had been all but declared persona non grata in Tehran. He wanted the Shah to think he was cutting a separate deal with the Saudis to reduce prices. He saw the trip as a way of exerting psychological pressure on the Iranian leader. "We thought we would let them sweat a bit while we were discussing goodies with the Arabs."

"He is our best friend," answered Nixon warily. "Any pressure would probably have to come from me."

Simon was dubious: "I wonder. He is the ringleader on oil prices, along with Venezuela. Without them, oil prices would be down." Within OPEC, Iran had formed a tacit alliance with Venezuela to make sure oil prices did not retreat to their original levels. Like the Shah, President Carlos Andrés Pérez of Venezuela had embarked on a multibillion-dollar drive to modernize his country and had already spent oil revenues that were anticipated but had not yet been generated.

Treasury was worried about the stability of financial networks and the banking system. The economies of the Arab states were too small and primitive to absorb or recycle the billions of petrodollars pouring in from industrialized and developing nations. "With all the states with money and nowhere to spend it, the banks and financial markets are in trouble. Oil prices have caused great instability in the international financial markets."

"How about the stock market?" asked Nixon.

"There is fear borrowing going on."

"Why?"

"They are afraid of future inconvertibility moves and interest hikes," said Simon. "The financial markets are close to panic. There are major corporations which are unable to borrow."

Treasury's forty-strong delegation stopped off in Nice before flying on to Egypt, where President Sadat was anxious to secure U.S. financial aid. While in the French Riviera Simon agreed to be interviewed by Willard Rappleye Jr., the editor of the trade publication *American Banker*. Rappleye's article, published after Simon's plane touched down in Cairo, kicked off a furor. Simon was quoted as explaining that Tehran was not included in his itinerary because "The Shah is a nut," and, "maximization of the oil price is in his best interest as he sees it." The Shah "wants to be a superpower," explained the treasury secretary. "He is putting all his oil profits into domestic investment, mostly military hardware." This was harmful to the long-term interests of America's friends in Saudi Arabia: "It is crazy from their point of view. The Saudis helping keep oil prices high is making Iran, their natural rival, strong." Headline writers back home had a field day. "Simon to Skirt 'Nut' Meeting," headlined the *Chicago Tribune*.

En route to his next stop, Riyadh, Simon received a cable from Kissinger: "I am besieged by queries about you calling the Shah 'a nut.'" Simon wired back that his comments had been "taken out of context." "Just exactly how do you call the 'King of Kings' a 'nut' out of context?" asked Kissinger. Simon subsequently explained that he "was using the vernacular in the same way anyone would describe himself as a nut about tennis or golf. I was using a slang expression to show that the Shah had very firm ideas about oil."

Niavaran Palace wasn't buying it. Regardless of his poor choice of words, Simon's willingness to stoke Saudi fears about Iran's military buildup gave the Shah a troubling insight into American tactics to roll back oil prices. In Tehran, a U.S. diplomat drove to the palace to hand-deliver a note from the treasury secretary explaining that his comments had been taken out of context.

Kissinger telephoned Ambassador Ardeshir Zahedi at 4:23 P.M. on July 15 to personally apologize for his colleague's behavior. With Zahedi, who had already written Nixon a letter of protest, Kissinger was not above resorting to groveling and flattery to smooth over the tensions aroused by Simon's impertinence. The fact that a transcript of their conversation required redaction shows the level of outrage at the palace: "Mr. Ambassador, I call you about once every three months about our errant Secretary of the Treasury. Will you convey to His Imperial Majesty our affection, regard, mortification and needless to say [redacted]. He denies having said it."

"Yes," said Zahedi. "Fortunately, I got it a few hours ago."

"Well, you convey to His Imperial Majesty that every member of the cabinet, with the exception of the Secretary of the Treasury, and particularly the Secretary of State and the President, hold him in the highest esteem and we will put a stop to this," he replied. Kissinger announced that he was personally taking over chairmanship of the joint U.S.-Iran bilateral commission. He reiterated that "we consider [His Imperial Majesty] one of the great leaders and we will convince our Secretary of the Treasury that this sort of [redacted] is out of the question. I am not sure he said it. He denies saying it but whatever he did say I apologize for."

The conversation must have been particularly galling for Kissinger, who relished every opportunity to denigrate Zahedi behind his back, even as he accepted the Iranian's lavish hospitality. A royal blue Persian rug was a wedding gift from Iran. "I can remember it being rolled out one day so people immediately around the ambassador could view it," remembered Delphine Blachowicz, Ambassador Zamani's secretary. By law U.S. government officials were required to turn over gifts from foreign governments; the blue rug never appeared on the list of items turned over to the State Department by Kissinger. "He's certain they turned everything in," was how William Hyland, a Kissinger aide, later sheepishly put it. "Mrs. Kissinger wasn't wildly happy about [the State Department] ruling requiring the handing in of gifts."

One man who was not on Zahedi's gift card list after July was Secretary Simon. Relations between the two men chilled to the point where Washington hostesses knew not to have them in the same house, let alone at the same table. There had been a scene at one of David Brinkley's famous dinners where insults were hurled in the presence of various society doyens. Thereafter the two men never appeared at the same event, formal or otherwise. It said something about Zahedi's popularity that his stock continued to rise while Simon, perhaps uniquely for a sitting cabinet officer, found himself dropped from formal events involving Iranian dignitaries.

The treasury secretary's attack on the Shah had been calculated. Simon was sending a message to the Saudi leadership that he understood their concerns and was ready to do business. He was in Riyadh on July 21 when his friend Yamani announced that an auction would be held in August of one million barrels of government-owned oil set for delivery during the last quarter of 1974 and the first quarter of the next year. This was the breakthrough Simon had been hoping for. Yamani hoped to break the Shah's lock on pricing and put pressure on the world oil market to drive prices down.

It was a strategy that amounted to a countercoup in the oil market. But it didn't quite work out that way. The governments of Iran and Venezuela informed Faisal that if the Saudi auction went ahead they would slash their own oil production to further tighten the market and squeeze prices even higher. Venezuela, Libya, and Kuwait had already reduced their production to bolster the $11.65 per barrel posted price. They sent emissaries to inform the king that they were prepared to drive prices up still higher. Faisal lost his nerve and retreated; the auction was canceled.

The collapse of the auction was a blow to Yamani personally and it marked a setback for Treasury's efforts to stabilize global financial institutions. Yamani told U.S. ambassador to Saudi Arabia James Akins, whom he knew to be a staunch supporter of closer U.S.-Saudi ties, that Kissinger was to blame because he "is speaking about lower oil prices but in secret doing everything possible to jack them up." Akins shared Yamani's assessment of how things stood: "The Saudis had urged us on numerous occasions to put pressure on the shah to cooperate with Saudi Arabia and reduce the oil prices. Yet we had refused to do this." Kissinger dismissed the auction as a ruse. "My belief was that the Saudis did not want to get prices down but wanted to place the onus for the price rise on the Shah," he confided to Jack Anderson five years later.

Bill Simon now had what he considered irrefutable proof that the Shah was blocking sincere efforts to reduce oil prices. Simon's 10:30 A.M. meeting with Nixon on Tuesday, July 30, to go over the results of his trip was pushed back to three o'clock because the president was still asleep. It had been a dramatic day of developments in the Watergate case. The House Judiciary Committee had drawn up articles of impeachment against the president and would shortly present them to the full House of Representatives for a vote. When Simon arrived at the White House he was told the president was in the Lincoln Sitting Room. Nixon had sequestered himself, listening to tape recordings of his Oval Office conversations. One of the tapes included the infamous June 23, 1972, "smoking gun" conversation in which he and Bob Haldeman had discussed having Richard Helms and the CIA block the FBI investigation into the Watergate break-in. Aware that the tapes implicated him in a criminal cover-up, Nixon nonetheless went ahead with his meeting with the treasury secretary. A transcript of their conversation betrays no sign of the enormous pressure Nixon was under. As usual with foreign policy, Nixon stayed focused and engaged. "It was as if he could pull down a screen and utterly separate his professional duties from his political problems," Simon later remarked.

The treasury secretary began by telling the president that the situation on oil prices was out of control. "The Arabs are acting like nouveaux riches," he said. During his trip to the West German capital of Bonn, Chancellor Helmut Schmidt had expressed concern that high oil prices were destabilizing the continent's political structures. "The oil prices are a problem everywhere. Faisal says he has gone as far as he can without our help. The Shah is threatening to cut production."

"He is our good friend, but he is playing a hard game on oil," Nixon conceded.

"Faisal asks our help with the Shah," said Simon. "There is an internal fight in Saudi Arabia between those who want price cuts and those who wish to keep production up. Faisal really wants our help with the Shah. In discussions with other Ministers I said Saudi Arabia has probably 150 years of production left, whereas Iran has only 15 years. Maybe Iran will build its industry and when the oil runs out, they can take you and get the oil back." In other words the treasury secretary had told Saudi leaders that the Shah might invade Saudi Arabia to seize its oil fields.

"We have to see what we can do," said Nixon. "I will have to meet and talk with the Shah." The president clenched his fountain pen between his teeth, yanked off the cap, and scribbled a note to himself on a scrap of paper. Simon understood this to mean that the president would contact the Shah. Nixon had finally come around.

"The Shah has us," Simon pressed on. "No one will confront him. The producer nations are locking in the consumers and keeping them away from us. Schmidt said, 'If the prices don't move down, I have to move against the companies and deal with the producers myself.' This issue will require strong action by the United States."

Nixon perked up: "Like what? This should be developed. We need discussion with you, Ken [Rush], Henry and Brent. Keep it small."

"It is a terrible problem. I was not thinking so much of energy as of balance of payments. I am worried about production cuts . . ."

"[Schmidt] is worried about the banks," Nixon mused.

Perhaps not understanding German sensitivity on the issue, Simon thought the chancellor was "overboard on that." But the West German leader had been badly shaken by the recent collapse of a West German bank, the first of four German banks to fail in the summer of 1974 and a further worrying sign of the extent to which European financial institutions were being battered by the aftershocks of the spike in oil prices. Bank collapses, rising levels of unemployment and inflation, plunging consumer demand, and a slump in the nation's export sector revived memories among older Germans of the financial distress that preceded the fall of the Weimar Republic and the rise of Nazi extremism in the early 1930s. Lengthening shadows were falling over Europe. The Portuguese empire had imploded and Lisbon was in the hands of leftist colonels. Britain, France, and Italy were in the grip of deepening recessions. Economists in Brussels predicted inflation of 20 percent in Britain and the number of unemployed to clear the one million hurdle by year's end. In Italy too, inflation was forecast to breach 20 percent a year. Italians had been panicked by a rash of mysterious terrorist bombings carried out by neofascist groups with loose affiliations to state institutions and the military. Nixon and Kissinger were convinced it was just the beginning of a repeat of the instability of the early 1930s. "In France there'll be a popular front within five years," Kissinger grimly told the president. "That will drag Italy the same way or there'll be a right-wing coup."

Nixon then shared his Manichaean anxieties with Simon, giving him a quick *tour d'horizon* of the world scene as he saw it. Simon was an eager listener. Relations with Britain's new Labour government were surprisingly good and Britain's [Chancellor Denis] "Healey is a strong good friend." The Italians were hopeless. "Italy has no government," Nixon sighed, adding that "the Latins are unstructured without a dictator. Right now the great nations of the West must be united politically—the lack of stability in the world sets everything loose." Nixon was keeping an eye on Europe's disintegrating southern tier nations of Greece, Italy, Spain and Portugal. He smelled trouble ahead. Churchill was right, he told Simon. He launched into a discourse on Gallipoli, Verdun, the 1918 Spring offensive against the Germans. The only organized force in Portugal today were the Communists. Spanish dictator Franco was dying and who knew what would succeed him? "If Spain goes, Italy goes. In Yugoslavia—when Tito goes, the Soviets will make their move. Greece and Turkey are so important because they are the rest of the southern tier."

Simon shared Nixon's concern with Italy in particular. The Italian economy was leaning at a dangerous tilt: "We will have to aid Italy before too long. I talked to [Federal Reserve Bank chairman] Arthur Burns about a [credit] swap line. He is opposed, but I'll get it. Even if the new fiscal measures take, they will have problems."

As he approached the depths of his second Watergate summer Richard Nixon's world was falling apart. His presidency was collapsing. Impeachment was not a question of "if" but "when." Henry Kissinger, his own secretary of state, now referred to Nixon behind his back as "the felon." As network television crews mounted a death watch at the gates of the White House, the president was consumed with paranoia. Everyone was lying to him. Old friends had turned their backs on him. He was drinking every other night now. Despite his daily agonies, Richard Nixon stayed focused on foreign policy and strategy. What happened next suggests that he was having second thoughts about his old friend the Shah. Bill Simon had indeed gotten through to him. To Kissinger's great consternation, a meeting of White House senior advisers was scheduled for the first week of August to thrash out the whole issue of oil pricing, the Saudi-Iran debate, and why the Shah was refusing to cooperate with the Saudis to seek a reduction in oil prices. Kissinger heard the news in a late afternoon phone call on August 1, from Deputy Secretary of State Robert Ingersoll. "[Treasury] would like to have a meeting with you and Simon next week," Ingersoll advised him. "We're checking your schedule to see if it's possible."

"I just don't trust his assessment of the situation," said Kissinger.

Ingersoll said that Treasury officials wanted to clear up the conflicting versions of stories about the Shah's role in torpedoing Yamani's oil auction.

"I don't see that the Saudis should run a risk to get oil prices down," protested Kissinger.

"We'll try to get a meeting on Tuesday with all of them. We're checking your schedule."

"Just because there's a vacancy on my schedule doesn't mean you can put something on it," snapped Kissinger. "You better check with me first."

"Okay."

THE RAMSAR EFFECT

The first three days of August 1974 would prove to be a turning point for American-Iranian relations and for the future of the Peacock Throne. By a quirk of fate, at the same time Kissinger and Simon were having their showdown over oil policy the Shah was making a crucial decision on what to do with Iran's new petrodollar fortune. Should the money be spent? Should it be invested? The previous autumn the Shah had instructed the government's Plan and Budget Organization to adjust its budget forecast in anticipation of a new windfall in oil profits. Since then Iran's income from petroleum had climbed from $2.8 billion for the year 1972–73 to $4.6 billion for the year 1973–74, a total revenue increase of 65 percent over a period of twelve months. The full impact of the boom would be felt in 1975 when revenues rocketed to $17.8 billion, a stunning leap of 287 percent in twelve months. The Shah had dreamed of the day when he could buy what he wanted when he wanted it. That day had finally arrived. "We have no real limit on money," boasted his chief economist. "None."

The danger was always from inflation. By the summer of 1974 the Iranian government was collecting $1 billion in oil receipts each month. "For at least a dozen years, the Shah has had the plans to rebuild his country," observed *The New York Times*. "Now, apparently, he has the money, and the problem of pumping it into the economy without causing disastrous inflation." The Shah was aware of the potential danger. If handled incorrectly the deluge of petrodollars could blow the economy out from under his feet. The Saudis faced a similar problem. For now they decided to park much of their oil wealth offshore to reduce the risk of inflation and dislocation at home, investing in real estate, foreign industry, and bank deposits that allowed for rapid withdrawal.

Iran's inflation rate was already in double digits in marked contrast to the previous year. The economy was heating up even without the infusion of most of the new petro-stimulus. Eyewitness accounts and hard statistics from the spring and early summer of 1974 indicate that a form of financial hysteria had taken hold in Iran where oil money was being ingested like so much cheap cocaine. "Inflation is running wild, anywhere from 15 to 22 percent," reported one observer. "Anyone who can is moonlighting. Tehran now has an extra set of traffic jams each day as workers rush from one job to another. Although duty on imported cars runs between 200 and 500 percent, dealers have a hard time supplying customers with enough Mercedes Benzes, Jaguars and Citroëns. Glittering boutiques and department stores along broad, tree-shaded Pahlavi Avenue are jammed with women anxious to have the latest Charles Jourdan and Yves St. Laurent creations." There were remarkable scenes of excess. In the city of Mashhad a blond woman drove through town in an open car handing out fistfuls of dollar bills estimated to be in the thousands to passersby she assumed were poor. While women in north Tehran mobbed furriers, the Shah's own palace guardsmen were unable to feed their families because of a bread shortage.

The Pahlavi cult of personality had reached its zenith. Every front-page of every newspaper published in Iran was required to carry a picture of members of the imperial family accompanied by their latest appearances and achievements. A new portrait of His Imperial Majesty appeared in public buildings and private businesses that showed the Shahanshah "standing on what appears to be the top of the world, waving, with clouds rolling by behind him." He resembled North Korea's Great Leader. Another portrait depicted the Shah and Shahbanou resembling movie stars Jeff Chandler and Sophia Loren. The whole country was high from the fumes of oil profits.

The Shah's personal management skills were abysmal. Distrustful of everyone around him, the Shah was a micromanager who refused to delegate to subordinates, kept his ministers on a tight leash, and made sure anyone who was too smart or too popular was removed from the center of power. Court Minister Alam recorded the bizarre scene on the same day in 1974 that the Shah's ally Emperor Haile Selassie of Ethiopia was deposed in a left-wing coup. His Imperial Majesty was preoccupied not so much with the geopolitical consequences of the coup and what it meant for Iran's security, as by the placement of new furniture ordered for one of his palaces. The Shah managed the armed forces the same way, to the point of approving the appointments and promotions of even the most lowly ranked junior officers. It was just this sort of rigid management style that led Henry Kissinger's good friend Hushang Ansary, Iran's minister of finance and economics, and a cunning businessman who piled up his own fortune while serving in the Shah's cabinet, to tell an interviewer with a straight face that Iran's economic problems were no big deal because, as he put it, "His Imperial Majesty has an extraordinary ability to make the right judgments."

One early and prominent American skeptic of the Shah's handling of the Iranian oil boom was David Rockefeller. The Rockefeller-Pahlavi connection was personal and financial. Mohammad Reza Shah's social ties to the Rockefellers were primarily through his relationship with Nelson. By contrast, the younger David addressed the Shah as "Your Imperial Majesty" and he in turn was addressed as "Mr. Rockefeller." "The primary topic in all our meetings was business," David Rockefeller recalled. The Rockefeller bank, Chase, enjoyed strong relations with Bank Melli, Iran's largest commercial bank, and Chase was the lead bank for the National Iranian Oil Company, which managed Iran's oil wealth. After oil prices rose fourfold in 1973 Iranian deposits in Chase "increased dramatically" and "our finance business boomed because we continued to finance a significant portion of Iran's oil exports. By the mid-1970s as much as $50 to $60 million a day passed through Chase, and Iranian deposits at one point in late 1978 exceeded $1 billion." It was Chase that the Shah turned to when he needed to raise international financing for Iran's big industrial projects. Rockefeller thought it ironic that "we were never successful in attracting the Shah himself as a customer; he preferred to keep most of his money in Switzerland."

In January 1974 David Rockefeller flew to St. Moritz to talk to the Shah about expanding Chase's business opportunities in Iran. Before the trip the Rockefeller family's still loyal former retainer Henry Kissinger "had told me that the Shah was an exceptionally able man with a strong grasp of international affairs." But during his two-hour audience with the Shah, Rockefeller developed doubts. He observed

> an arrogance that underlay his pronouncements on many of these issues; they lacked plausibility and betrayed an alarming isolation from political and economic reality. The Shah seemed to think that because he believed something, it was automatically a fact. The term *hubris* occurred to me as I sat listening to him outline his startling vision of an imperial Iran reclaiming the ancient domain of the Medes and the Persians. He seemed unconcerned about the havoc the high oil prices had already caused in the global economy, let alone what his extravagant proposals would generate.

When he traveled to Tehran a few days later, Rockefeller discussed his concerns with Ambassador Richard Helms. He found that Helms too thought the Shah was overreaching, that the Iranians were "really feeling their oats": "Oil wealth and their predominant military position in the Gulf, largely the result of assistance from the United States, had transformed Iran's strategic and economic position." According to Rockefeller's notes of their meeting, Helms observed that "their biggest problem is that [the Iranians] have the money, the materials, but not the trained manpower necessary to handle them. What is perhaps even more serious, the ministers are not sophisticated or experienced enough to cope with the added governmental complications which their sudden enormous wealth is bringing them." In retirement Helms conceded that "the embassy was certainly concerned" with the economic effect of the increase in Iran's oil income. "I think the Shah himself was aware of the implications of those decisions," he added.

From August 1 to August 3, the Shah, the Iranian government, and leading bureaucrats and experts retreated to the resort town of Ramsar on the Caspian Sea to approve a spending and investment plan to handle Iran's new oil wealth. Budget planners had laid out several scenarios in which they tried to predict the consequences of a big spending stimulus on inflation, infrastructure, employment, housing, and agriculture. Ramsar became synonymous with the deluge that followed.

The Shah opened the meeting by making it clear that the only opinion that counted was his. This was no joke. "I not only make the decisions, I do the thinking," he boasted to one foreign visitor at about this time. Two days later, on the 3rd, he brushed aside warnings of disaster if profits from the oil boom were pumped straight back into the economy. The Shah approved a plan to grow the Iranian economy at the stunning rate of 25.9 percent each year for the next five years. It was an exceptionally high figure even by the standards of an economy already growing at an official annual rate of 11.4 percent. Virtually overnight, government expenditures doubled from $35 billion to $69 billion. Government ministers reacted as though a starter's gun had gone off and raced to assemble spending projects. "My head is spinning with the whole series of incredible statistics," Alam wrote in his diary. "Two years ago the target outlay was $24 billion. Today it's more or less trebled to $68 billion."

The Shah had laid a trap for himself. He had not taken into account the possibility that the recession in the West might lead to a sharp fall in demand for Iran's oil or that OPEC members might fall out among themselves and try to undercut each other in the marketplace. The government's Plan and Budget Organization had already cautioned that oil and gas income "was subject to the vagaries of world supply and demand conditions and therefore highly erratic." Iran could not, "on the most optimistic assumptions, become the world's fifth industrial power in this century." Iran would remain an importer of food. There was an urgent need to invest in transport, ports, power, and the water supply to avoid infrastructure bottlenecks that could throttle economic growth. Iran should concentrate on building nuclear power plants to supplement hydroelectric power and develop heavy industries such as steel, petrochemicals, and machine tools. The Fifth Plan was based on estimates that wrongly assumed the oil market would remain tight, oil prices would keep rising, and demand for oil would stay high. *Financial Times* journalist Robert Graham concluded that the Shah's decision to go for broke was the natural result of his string of unbroken victories over the oil companies and the Nixon administration. His habit of overspending on arms and big development projects, and then hiking oil prices later to pay for them, had become a dangerous compulsion. "At the end of the Ramsar meeting, few realized they had just agreed to a 'hyper-boom,'" wrote Graham. "Even as the Shah pushed through this doubling of proposed expenditure, all the evidence pointed to dangerous overheating of the economy."

The Shah believed that he had to move quickly before Iran's oil fields went into decline. Two former economic planners in the Iranian government, Dr. Hossein Razavi and Dr. Firouz Vakil, have described their monarch's infatuation with Big Push economics. Advocates of Big Push were in favor of countries like Iran—economically undeveloped yet rich in commodities like oil and copper—plowing revenues back into their economies in the form of big development projects. Instead of investing their money overseas like the Saudis, the Iranians should build steel mills, petrochemical plants, highways, and textile factories—anything and everything that would create the foundations for a modern, diversified industrial economy. But Iran's Big Push could work only if its economy was big enough to absorb the financial stimulus. The cash infusion had to be ingested in stages, not swallowed at once. If these conditions were not met the results would be comparable to an overdose. Perhaps the Shah felt the need to move quickly on the economic front because of the uncertainty surrounding his health. He was a fatalist and sensed that time was not on his side.

As a result Iran, one of the world's oldest societies, was hurled into the future like a pebble flung from a slingshot. The Shah set out on an ill-conceived Persian-style Great Leap Forward that he hoped would bolster the monarchy, inoculate Iran from outside threats and pressures, and build a legacy for the ages.

For the Shah, thinking big meant that nothing was off-limits. The Shah unveiled a $3 billion plan to bulldoze Tehran's city center and replace it with a grand plaza bigger than Red Square in Moscow. The 2.5 mile border around the proposed Shah and Nation Square would include six hotels, forty thousand parking spaces, 55 million square feet of office space, housing for fifty thousand residents, and the new Pahlavi National Library. Upon completion, Iran's national library would comprise one of the great scholarly wonders of the world, boasting a staff of five thousand and more than 5 million books, a hotel for visiting scholars, and the most advanced cataloguing system in the world. Iran's Persian heritage would also receive a boost from a ten-year, multimillion-dollar project to rebuild the seven fluted columns of Xerxes in Persepolis. Oil money would meld Iran's past to its glorious future. The Shah had already placed orders for two supersonic Concorde airliners with the option to buy a third. He signed a $6 billion trade deal with France that included construction of a forty-mile subway system, the introduction of color television, construction of 200,000 housing units, and an automobile plant that would initially produce 100,000 Renaults. "I will sell you aspirins, I will sell you proteins," declared the king as Tehran's bakeries ran out of bread, "I won't sell you crude oil."

WE ARE HEADING TOWARDS DISASTER

At 10:00 A.M. on Saturday, August 3, the same day the Shah wrapped up the budget deliberations at Ramsar, senior Nixon administration officials gathered at the State Department for their long-awaited showdown over high oil prices. This meeting marked the first time in four and a half years that Henry Kissinger had been asked to explain, let alone justify, his unconditional support for Iran's Shah. It was a discussion that he did not want to have. Kissinger still adhered to the view that the conservative monarchies of the Persian Gulf were entitled to raise oil prices to generate the revenues that kept them in power and allowed them to buy the American firepower that defended Western political and economic interests throughout the Middle East. What Kissinger had failed to anticipate was that too high oil prices might also damage the U.S. economy and the economies of its NATO allies, even to the point of compromising the security of the free world.

Yet Kissinger may have anticipated something that his colleagues over at Treasury did not—the potential catastrophe that awaited the Shah if oil prices retreated. Kissinger knew that the monarchies of the Gulf, and Iran in particular, spent more money than they generated in oil profits and that their finances were as a result overextended and therefore dangerously vulnerable to sudden shifts in demand and supply. "Falling prices would quickly bring the revenues of all of the producing countries below their current levels of expenditure," wrote one scholar who sympathized with Kissinger's view. "With the government unable to meet expectations conditioned by past experience, conservative regimes would probably not survive, and more radical governments would also be threatened." Iran was not like Saudi Arabia, a country whose small population and vast foreign exchange reserves meant that it could safely absorb a big reduction in the price of oil and accommodate a substantial decline in its revenues. The Shah never saved and always spent. There was no financial cushion to act as a shock absorber for the Pahlavi monarchy if oil prices suddenly dipped. A sudden adjustment in income could lead to a fiscal crisis followed by social unrest and political instability. The Shah's "oily legs" would melt away. Kissinger's actions in defending the Shah and trying to fend off Treasury and the Saudis must be seen in this light. He was gradually beginning to appreciate that high oil prices were choking economic growth and causing instability in the industrialized world, but he was equally attuned to the fact that high oil prices were the key to propping up the Peacock Throne. He faced an excruciating dilemma: how to ease the oil shock for Western economies without breaking the Shah's regime?

The small group at the table included Kissinger, Treasury Secretary Bill Simon, chairman of the Federal Reserve Board Arthur Burns, Deputy Secretary of State Robert Ingersoll, and Assistant Deputy Secretary of State for Economic and Business Affairs Thomas Enders. Kissinger was by now thoroughly alarmed at what he perceived to be Simon's reckless meddling in foreign policy. Addressing his colleague on that August morning, he got straight to the point: "You are saying the oil situation is unmanageable."

"Yes," Simon declared authoritatively. "It will force a massive realignment—you can assess whether that is good or bad for us. Europe is becoming dependent on the Arabs for both oil and money."

"You must also know there is a real chance for another Arab-Israeli war," said Kissinger. "Are the Saudis really prepared to cooperate in getting lower prices, and how far?"

"If production doesn't get cut, oil prices would drop by 30 percent," Simon replied. "We would consider production cuts an unfriendly act, and for Iran, we could cut military supplies."

Kissinger wanted to know who would do the confronting—the U.S., or the U.S. and Europe and Japan? "The second question is what happens after the opening round?" he asked. "I think Iran would be supported by Algeria and many others. If the U.S. is alone this certainly would be the case." Kissinger described Algerian president Boumediène as "psycho on oil prices" and warned that if the U.S. challenged the pricing structure "Algeria would mount a campaign. They would carry the Syrians with them. In effect, the Saudis would be isolated and I don't think they could or would stand up to it." Kissinger reminded the group that their European allies had buckled under pressure from the Arab states and could not be relied on to stand with them in a showdown with the producers. If the United States cut off arms sales to Iran, "The Europeans could supply the Iranians with hardware." He turned to the question of the Saudis: "The Saudis may be preparing an ultimatum on Israel. They want to be our sole supplier so they can squeeze us when they want." Kissinger had just voiced his worst fear. He was looking ahead to a day when Saudi Arabia used its oil power as a choke hold over American foreign policy in the Middle East, specifically toward Israel. "My conclusion is that we have to move with enormous care—we can take on the producers at the right moment—to disassociate Israel from the oil problem. But it must be at a time when we can't be isolated and it can't be linked to oil. We first need to get the consumers together. Then we can do some confronting—but it will only work if we are willing to use force."

The problem, as Kissinger knew all too well, was that the United States in the summer of 1974 lacked the ability to confront OPEC with the use of force. Kissinger said he would once again tell the Saudis "that we will not stand for another oil embargo. If all this is correct, we need to get the Europeans together and share this with them. They first will be shocked, but I see no other way to go. I, though, am prepared to talk privately with the Shah."

"I think we have to work with the Saudis—telling them hard out what we need," replied Simon.

At this point Burns reminded the group of what was at stake: "We are heading towards disaster in the industrial world. Withholding arms from Iran won't help. Getting the consumers together would work. I think the Germans would go with us. We have a firm chance with the British. The French would drag their feet but might go along after all the others do. The Japanese, I don't know. Conservation should be pushed. The tax on gas has gone up everywhere but in this country. How about hanging a tax on exports to the producing countries by all of us—on the exports?"

The Fed chief was anxiously monitoring the buildup of monetary reserves in countries that had even less absorptive capacity than Iran, which at least had a population of 33 million and a burgeoning industrial base. The World Bank estimated that if current levels persisted five countries with a combined population of only 11.5 million—Saudi Arabia, Libya, Kuwait, Qatar, and Abu Dhabi—would accumulate total monetary reserves of $453 billion of the projected $650 billion of all reserves held by OPEC member countries in 1980. The bank warned that "the world banking system cannot possibly handle the recycling job that such a volume of foreign exchange holdings would require." Oil consumer nations had in the meantime plunged into the red to pay exorbitant fuel bills, taking out loans and seeking financial assistance through the World Bank, the International Monetary Fund, and private lenders like Wall Street banks to finance ballooning deficits. The lending binge left unresolved the question of whether the debtors would ever have the means to pay back their loans, particularly if oil prices continued to rise, placing greater strain on government budgets. Global financial networks and banking systems had never been subjected to such intense pressures over such a prolonged period of time.

If the United States was to avoid "huge foreign debts," wrote one scholar who studied the impact of petrodollars on financial networks, oil prices would have to be "substantially lowered by OPEC, or [unless] American oil imports are drastically curtailed, or domestic fuel and industrial production is continually expanded, the United States will have to endure the financial onus of an additional, ever-mounting multibillion dollar outlay each successive year. Such a course of policy would appear, politically, as well as economically, ruinous."

Simon and Burns were trying to get a handle on the financial crisis. Knowing nothing of Nixon's and Kissinger's secret dealings with the Shah, they may as well have been performing surgery blindfolded. The American economy was shedding jobs at the fastest rate since the Great Depression. The deficit was climbing. Inflation had roared to life. Consumers were cutting back on spending. The export sector had slumped because of falling demand for American goods overseas. Factories were closing down. A noxious economic phenomenon known as "stagflation"—high levels of unemployment and inflation—had taken root. If relief did not come soon, feared some economists, then a financial catastrophe on a par with the Great Crash of 1929 could not be ruled out.

Inflation was on Richard Nixon's mind three days later when he presided over a full meeting of the cabinet. His presidency had finally stoved in on itself. The explosive "smoking gun" tape recording had been released to a shocked public. Cabinet officers assembled in the expectation Nixon would announce his resignation. "I would like to discuss the most important issue confronting the nation, and confronting us internationally, too," he started. Steeling themselves for the next line, those in the room were bewildered by what he then said: "Inflation. Our economic situation could be the major issue in the world today." He then talked about the economic challenges facing the nation caused by skyrocketing oil prices. It took Vice President Gerald Ford to steer the meeting to the Watergate issue. He told Nixon that he could no longer publicly defend the president's handling of the scandal and he predicted impeachment by the House. Ford assured Nixon that come what may, "I expect to continue to support the administration's foreign policy and the fight against inflation."

Bill Simon, watching the surreal drama unfold, thought the president "seemed to hear nothing that the vice president had said, save the remark about inflation. 'I think your analysis is exactly correct,' said Nixon. Then the president turned to me. He started to question me about an upcoming economic summit. I was virtually speechless but answered the best I could." When the cabinet meeting wrapped up at 12:30 it was Simon whom Nixon asked to address the waiting throng of reporters outside the White House and who now mobbed him "as the rest of the cabinet scooted out a back exit." By focusing on Simon and ignoring the rest of his cabinet—including his vice president—the mortally wounded president was finally acknowledging Simon's loyalty and tacitly accepting that their talks about oil, the Shah, and economics had left an impression. It was Richard Nixon's final gesture of defiance to a political establishment that he believed had its priorities in the wrong order.

Thick, wet heat clung to Washington like a dead vine on the evening of Thursday, August 8. Simon was still at his desk when the call came through from Haig. "It's all over, Bill. You'd better get Carol down here right away." The president had decided to resign. Carol was staying at the family's summer home in East Hampton on Long Island. A second phone call came in from Ken Rush, Nixon's economic adviser: "Bill, what are you doing?" he asked. "Come on over and have a Scotch." Simon walked out into the night and headed for the White House, "where Ken and I proceeded to consume a bottle of Dewars. A half-hour before the President's address, we walked over to the Oval Office." As Richard Nixon ended his speech of resignation and the television cameras pulled away he "walked past Ken and me, tears streaming down his cheeks, his mouth set in a quivering frown, and when he was a few feet from us he abruptly turned right and headed into the residence."

Bill Simon was "frozen in my spot, overcome with grief and disbelief." He remembered King Faisal's words from just a few weeks earlier: "The American people are too wise to get rid of a great president because of something as insignificant as Watergate." Simon's window of opportunity to confront the Shah over oil prices had just slammed shut.

SIXTEEN MARINES

President Nixon's resignation speech was broadcast around the world and heard live in Tehran at 4:30 A.M. local time on August 9. Cynthia Helms, wrapped in a dressing gown, walked downstairs and carried a shortwave radio into the garden of the American embassy to get better reception. When the Voice of America signal proved too weak she tuned to a Swedish station to hear Richard Nixon become the first American president in history to resign from office. Her husband was so convinced that Nixon would stonewall that he refused to get out of bed. "It was a warm and starry night, and the lovely garden looked like a fairyland, brightened by the security lights," she remembered. Iranian armed guards were posted under the trees and around the perimeter of the embassy grounds. Nixon's voice carried over the lawn and back up to the house. The ambassador, suddenly curious, pushed up a bedroom window and called down asking for news. "For us, it was a dramatic and sobering moment," his wife said of the moment when Nixon quit. "We were filled with a sense of history, and, I must confess, relief."

The embassy grounds had been purchased in 1928 for the then princely sum of $60,000 from a local family anxious to settle a gambling debt. The property occupied a twenty-five-acre walled compound at the corner of Roosevelt Avenue and Takht-e Jamshid Avenue. Cynthia Helms likened the compound to a cool oasis of shrubbery, trees, and fountains, a refuge from the dust and noise on the streets outside. Visitors were escorted up a driveway shaded with tall pine and sycamore trees that ended in front of two big blue doors and pots of oleander. The ambassador's residence was a hybrid of contemporary American and Persian architecture. The upstairs living quarters included four large guest rooms and a private apartment with sitting room, bedroom, and bathroom with a large black marble bath. "We were charged a monthly rent for this apartment, but it was a haven of privacy," Cynthia later wrote. The small family dining room offered "a glorious view of the mountains."

By the fall of 1974 Embassy Tehran was one of the busiest and biggest American diplomatic posts in Asia and the hub of the fast-growing U.S. presence in Iran. Few embassy employees learned Farsi or developed a firm grasp of Iranian culture and customs. "In inquiring why this was so, I came to the conclusion that most officers and their families who lived once in Iran had no great compulsion to go back," recalled one former U.S. ambassador. "It is a rather forbidding country, and its culture is not congenial to foreigners." The majority of the local hires were not Shi'a Muslims but Armenian Christians, Assyrians, and Jews. Shi'a Muslims cited cultural reasons for avoiding foreign employment. This unfortunate but perhaps inevitable tendency to hire outsiders to work for outsiders only reinforced the isolation of American diplomats. The Iranians they did mix with tended to be members of minority groups with gripes against the majority Shi'a.

Embassy Tehran fulfilled a dual but vital function as a regional base of operations for the Central Intelligence Agency. Other embassies in the capital provided a similar function but none matched the scale of the American enterprise. Tehran during the years of the oil boom was to the world of espionage what Vienna had been in the early years of the Cold War, rife with intrigue. CIA staff worked alongside American diplomats and in some cases used diplomatic credentials as a cover for their work. Armin Meyer had been the ambassador when the decision was made to build a "warehouse" on the embassy grounds in the late 1960s. The warehouse was actually a basement that held nothing but electronic gear and served as an important listening post for the agency. "In the meantime we had all kinds of other monitoring devices on the compound," Meyer recalled. "We had invaluable devices at the Shah's game preserve" and "extensive facilities out north of Meshed, monitoring every blast that the Soviets ever emitted, every missile they ever shot, their intercommunications between their military units, and so on. It was fabulous, really. The Shah was working with us on that." These were the facilities monitoring the Soviet Union that were so prized by Helms and Kissinger and whose importance they argued far outweighed concerns about the Shah's spending on arms, oil prices, and Iran's record of torture, extrajudicial executions, and human rights abuses.

When Ambassador Helms arrived on post he took a close interest in making sure the embassy compound was secured. He personally inspected the locks on doors, vaulted areas, and emergency exits. Despite everyone's best efforts, security at Takht-e Jamshid Avenue remained porous and problematic. One incident in particular stood out. It was an evening when Cynthia Helms came downstairs a few minutes early to greet guests about to arrive for a dinner party. "I walked into the room to find my husband talking to a woman I didn't know." She leaned in to her husband and asked, "Who is our guest?"

He whispered back, "I thought she must be a friend of yours. She just walked in through the front door."

Husband and wife realized they were dealing with an intruder. "With growing horror I focused on her large handbag on the couch next to Dick," said Mrs. Helms. "Where were our guards? I couldn't see them anywhere." She maneuvered the woman, who was becoming visibly distraught, into the library while the ambassador tended to the guests. She lifted the intercom telephone to call for help from one of the sixteen Marines who guarded the compound. No one answered. Then she walked across the grounds to the security office to summon assistance. When someone finally did arrive he had to excuse himself to retrieve his sidearm and radio from downstairs.

The intruder turned out not to be a security threat but the troubled wife of an Iranian judge who had been friendly with the previous ambassador's wife. But the incident left the Helmses unnerved. Their guards had allowed someone onto the grounds who was not on their guest list. A policeman had even escorted the judge's wife to the front door, which was open for the party. The servants had not thought to challenge her. The Marine usually on duty inside the residence was not at his post. The Marine guard Mrs. Helms called for assistance was not carrying his sidearm. A potential assassin had casually walked into the ambassador's residence "and sat down beside my husband, probably the most guarded man in Iran besides the Shah." This incident and others that followed convinced the couple that "too much was expected of the marine guards at the age of eighteen or nineteen in handling the complexities of protecting our embassy and its occupants."

RAISE THE RED FLAG!

Factory closures, rampant inflation, long unemployment lines, food shortages, carless days, and populist revolts became signs of the times. Political structures began to shake loose. The Portuguese empire had disintegrated in the spring; over the summer of 1974 it was the turn of the Italian state to drift toward the abyss of financial ruin and collapse. The oil shock at times resembled a series of seemingly disconnected crises that threatened to converge and form one monstrous upheaval. At the end of the month West Germany's chancellor Schmidt held crisis talks with Italy's premier Mariano Rumor at Bellagio on Lake Como. The bottom was about to fall out of an Italian economy staggered by high fuel costs, galloping inflation of 18.7 percent and 800,000 unemployed. The German leader granted Italy a $2 billion loan. The credit was to last six months but could be renewed for three additional six-month periods. Italy agreed to pay interest of 8 percent and put up 515 tons of gold or one fifth of the state bank's bullion as collateral.

The West German rescue package signaled an ominous new turn in Europe's worsening financial crisis. With weak governments in Britain, France, and Italy, it was left to Helmut Schmidt to take the lead in shoring up the continent's banks and currencies. Over the next two and a half years the chancellor played the role of Europe's fireman-in-chief, rushing from one crisis to the next to douse the flames of each new flare-up with his bucket of deutsche marks and easy credit. His efforts were immensely complicated by a historic political realignment transforming Europe's sclerotic southern tier. Within eighteen months, dictatorships of the right collapsed in Portugal, Spain, and Greece. These convulsions created opportunities for democracy to flower from Lisbon to Athens. Yet the most immediate and obvious beneficiaries of unrest were the local Communist Party chapters that had led the resistance to dictatorial rule. In the summer of 1974 buildings in the Portuguese capital Lisbon flaunted the hammer and sickle, and Alvaro Cunhal, the Communist Party's secretary-general, held cabinet rank in a unity government. Inflation was running at between 30 and 40 percent, tourism receipts were down 30 percent, and the breakdown of basic public services coincided with a deadly cholera epidemic.

Greece was in crisis too. In Athens, the collapse of the military junta led to the formation of a United Left coalition of opposition parties dominated by Communists. Deeply angered by the brand-new Ford administration's handling of the conflict over Cyprus, the new Greek government withdrew its troops from NATO and anti-American protests rocked Greek cities. Financial analysts took note of the country's $2.8 billion trade deficit and the "perennial deficit in Greece's international payments account." Greek tourism revenues had been hard hit, first by a war with Turkey and second by the worldwide slump in the tourism industry as Americans and Europeans chose to save money by staying close to home. On September 6, five days after Italy received its bailout, the government of Greece received a loan of $100 million from a conglomerate of banks headed by Chase Manhattan and Goldman Sachs. Athens also made an appeal for a second cash injection of $800 million from West Germany and the Common Market. Foreign Minister George Mavros, touring European capitals that week, made the case for Greek membership in the Common Market. He got a chilly reception. "They want a new patron because they have always had a patron," a European diplomat coolly observed of Greece's decision to break with Washington. "They spit on the hand that used to feed them, so now they're looking for someone else." Other analysts fretted that Greece would become a financial albatross about the necks of the Common Market's parsimonious northern members. "Nobody really wants them," sniffed a Common Market official. "It would be another debtor country on our hands, and if we take them it would be hard to resist countries like Portugal and Spain."

The red tide was also running high in France and in Italy, where Communist Party leaders Georges Marchais and Enrico Berlinguer, respectively, were seen as attractive and unsullied leaders-in-waiting. Fueling the rise of Euro-Communism was inflation driven by high oil prices. The Great Inflation of 1974 discredited Europe's postwar political order and brought back memories of the hyperinflation that led to the collapse of Western democracies in the 1930s. Many European and American analysts frankly suspected the durability of the continent's postwar democratic institutions. Foremost among them was Henry Kissinger. To Kissinger and other pessimists the countries of Southern Europe were like dominoes ready to fall. Advocates of the domino theory feared that Portugal was on the verge of becoming the first Communist state in Western Europe. Western Europe could be splintered between an anti-Communist north and Socialist and Communist-ruled south. NATO would be paralyzed. Détente would collapse. Faced with the grim prospect of a Communist takeover of Southern Europe, Henry Kissinger, the student of great power politics, finally grasped the damage high oil prices were inflicting on the economies and political structures of the Western democracies. Following the overthrow of the Portuguese government by leftist army officers, Italy's fate weighed heavily on his mind.

In early September Kissinger expressed grave fears about Italy's future at a meeting with congressional leaders where he defended ongoing covert activity by the CIA in Italian politics. Kissinger was just as forceful in talks with Israel's prime minister Yitzhak Rabin. "The increasing cost of oil is prompting a significant number of Americans I met during my visit to consider the price of oil as the main reason for the collapse of the democratic regimes in Western Europe, which would make these countries ripe for Communist domination," Rabin told the Israeli newspaper *Maariv* after returning from a trip to Washington. "American personalities pointed out to me in many talks the serious danger of Communist domination in Italy, and perhaps in other European countries."

"You have to look upon him in this case as a historian," one of Kissinger's aides explained of his boss's concern about Europe. "He grew up in Nazi Germany and knows how economic depressions can lead to acceptance of authoritarian regimes, and he fears that this could happen in the West if something is not done to solve the problem."

Part Two

SHOWDOWN
1974–1977

"Bring up a little lion cub, and you
Will be rewarded when his teeth show through;
Forgetting all the kindness he's been shown
He'll maul his master when his claws have grown."

—Abolqasem Ferdowsi, *The Persian Book of Kings*

Chapter Seven

SCREAMING EAGLE

"I will tell the Shah. He is an admirer of mine."

—Henry Kissinger, 1974

"Pride comes before a fall, although in [Kissinger's] case it's more conceit than pride."

—The Shah, 1974

WE CAN'T TACKLE THE SHAH WITHOUT BREAKING HIM

Gerald Ford's first months in the White House were tumultuous. Richard Nixon's resignation was followed in short order by Ford's controversial decision to pardon him, First Lady Betty Ford's bout with breast cancer, Turkey's invasion of Cyprus, and the continuing economic fallout from the oil shock. Within hours of being sworn in to office the new president was advised that he had three months to bring inflation under control "or face possible social unrest" at home amid mounting job losses and soaring inflation. Ford's first address to a joint session of Congress echoed the urgency of those August days—and his predecessor's parting words—when he declared, "My first priority is to work with you to bring inflation under control. Inflation is our domestic public enemy No. 1."

Ford reappointed Henry Kissinger to his dual roles as secretary of state and national security adviser. Nixon had cautioned Ford about Kissinger's arrogance. "Henry is a genius, but you don't have to accept everything he recommends," he told his successor. "He can be invaluable, and he'll be loyal, but you can't let him have a totally free hand." In private, Nixon got straight to the point: "Ford has just got to realize that there are times when

Henry has to be kicked in the nuts. Because Henry starts to think he's president. But at other times you pet Henry and treat him like a child." Unlike Nixon, Ford tolerated Kissinger's churlish behavior and petulant threats to quit in the face of criticism. "I would take however long it required, which was sometimes minutes and often a whole hour, to reassure him and tell him how important he was to the country and ask him please to stay," Ford told Kissinger biographer Walter Isaacson. The new president lacked the confidence and sure touch in foreign policy that he displayed in domestic politics. Whereas Nixon had enjoyed a long-term working relationship with the Shah and relished their exchanges and deal making, in his first months in office Ford lacked the requisite knowledge to ask Kissinger and his other advisers the right questions about geopolitics, strategy, and foreign economic policy. Ford kept Bill Simon on at Treasury because he appreciated his fiscal conservatism. These two reappointments ensured the carryover into his own administration of the disagreement over whether the key to America's energy security and future oil needs ran through Iran or Saudi Arabia.

President Ford's first briefing on oil, OPEC, and the Shah came on Saturday morning, August 17. A transcript of their conversation shows Kissinger anxious to deflect blame for the oil shock away from the Shah and onto the Saudis and the rest of the OPEC cartel. He did not explain to the new president that he and Nixon had approved previous oil price increases to pay for the Shah's military buildup. Nor did Kissinger brief Ford on the spider's web of secret pacts reached between Nixon and the Shah that were among the new president's most troublesome inheritances. Kissinger wanted to make sure that Ford, a foreign policy novice, saw things *his* way. "On the energy situation, we have to find a way to break the cartel," explained Kissinger.

> We can't do it without cooperation with the other countries. It is intolerable that countries of 40 million can blackmail 800 million people in the industrialized world. Simon wants a confrontation with the Shah. He thinks the Saudis would reduce prices if the Shah would go along. I doubt the Saudis want to get out in front. Also the Saudis belong to the most feckless and gutless of the Arabs. They have maneuvered skillfully. I think they are trying to tell us—they said they would have an auction—it will never come off. They won't tell us they can live with lower prices but they won't fight for them. They would be jumped on by the radicals if they got in front. The Shah is a tough, mean guy. But

he is our real friend. He is the only one who would stand up to the Soviet Union. We need him for balance against India. We can't tackle him without breaking him. We can get to him by cutting military supplies, and the French would be delighted to replace them.

Kissinger did not mention that Iran's air force was by now so dependent on American training and spare parts that it would be grounded without them. French military equipment was no substitute for the U.S. hardware favored by the Shah.

"He didn't join the embargo," offered Ford.

"Right," said Kissinger. "Simon agrees now, though. The strategy of tackling the Shah won't work. We are now thinking of other ways." They discussed efforts to improve cooperation with other consumer nations: "We are organizing the consumers. Then we are organizing bilateral commissions to tie their economies as closely to ours as possible. So we have leverage and the Europeans can't just move in in a crisis. We want to tie up their capital. When the Shah sees us organizing the consumers—he will see, if we don't do it in a way appearing threatening to him. I should perhaps visit him in October, in connection with the Soviet trip, and talk about bilateral arrangements."

"Does he want higher prices?"

"Yes," said Kissinger. "He has limited supplies. He knows the profit is higher on petrochemicals and that the Saudis get more from the companies in everything. We won't be in a position to confront the producers before the middle of 1975. We have got to get rolling."

Kissinger had just made five extraordinary assertions. He accepted that the Shah was the key to lowering oil prices. He knew the Shah was planning additional price increases. He dismissed offers of help from the Saudis as not to be taken seriously. He conceded that the United States had surrendered its strategic leverage over its ally in Tehran. Most intriguing was Kissinger's oblique admission that the Pahlavi regime was brittle. Tackling the Shah over oil prices might "break him." This last remark of Kissinger's hinted at deeper concerns about the potential for instability inside Iran. Had U.S. officials already concluded that the Shah's regime was not as strong as it appeared to be? "Yes, and I think we all thought that," conceded Brent Scowcroft in an interview conducted thirty-six years later. In 1974 Scowcroft was Kissinger's deputy at the National Security Council. "That [the Shah] had destroyed some of his greatest enemies—that is, the power of the church and the power of some of the great landowners—but that he hadn't built a replacement support for his policies, so that in the end he was bereft when the revolution came. So we were very cautious in how much pressure we put on him."

Scowcroft, who admired the Shah, nonetheless "tended to be ambivalent" about the American-Iranian special relationship because "we had a number of goals with respect to Iran and some of them were conflictive." Iran was the pillar of America's Middle East policy, protector of the oil fields and shipping lanes, and guarantor of Israel's oil supply. Yet Iran was also responsible for propping up the high oil prices that threatened American prosperity and the stability of the Western alliance. Further complicating matters, the Shah made it clear to the White House that high oil prices were the price of political stability in Iran. "I think [the Shah] was a true and sincere ally," said Scowcroft. "He also had his domestic interests and, as you can see, pressures were growing on him too. And it's quite possible he thought he had to relieve those pressures economically to [save] his own regime." What leverage did White House officials think they still had to influence the Shah? As it turned out, not much. "Well, the leverage we had was that in the end the Shah was dependent on us, on U.S. support, and the difficulty was we didn't know exactly how he viewed that and whether he saw it the same way," conceded Scowcroft. "That explains part of the ambivalence. Some people like Bill Simon, for example, were very impatient with him and thought he was the cause of the oil price rise. . . . He tended to blame the Shah and we, basically Henry and I, and I think [President] Ford agreed with us, were not prepared to put the kind of pressure on the Shah that Simon wanted."

The administration was pursuing a self-paralyzing policy. Kissinger's close aide Winston Lord privately reminded his boss of the fix they now found themselves in: "To some extent, arguments over oil prices can be compartmentalized in our dealings with Iran. *Yet unless we press some of the levers we have, thereby incurring political costs on both sides, [the Shah] is unlikely to move on the oil price issue.*"

BEWARE THE EMPIRE OF OIL

Iran's ambassador Ardeshir Zahedi was ushered into the Oval Office at 12:35 P.M. on Wednesday, August 21, for an introductory meeting with the new president. Kissinger's behavior during the meeting was revealing. It was as though he and not Zahedi was the Pahlavi envoy to Washington. Zahedi's meeting with the president followed by a day Ford's nomination of the Shah's friend Nelson Rockefeller, a brother of David, the Shah's banker, to the vacant post of vice president. Tehran could not have been more satisfied with this turn of events. The Shah interpreted the appointment as a vindication of his prestige and power in Washington and as a decisive blow against Bill Simon and the Saudi lobby. Zahedi said he was "very pleased with the Rockefeller appointment. We have very close contacts with the Rockefellers. David is setting up a branch in Tehran. Our Minister of Finance and Minister of Economics—he wears two hats—is coming here to set up a joint commission. I am glad Secretary Kissinger is heading your side rather than Simon."

"They don't care about me—just so long as it is not Simon," joked Kissinger.

"I have been talking to our Ambassadors in Paris and London, and also His Majesty's feeling was excellent," said Zahedi. "[Nelson] knows Iran and [he has a] close relationship with Iran."

When Ford said he looked forward to meeting the Shah, Zahedi effused that, "The U.S. holds the highest place in his heart," and subtly referenced the 1953 coup. "It has always been so. The U.S. has helped when we needed it most, without strings. We remember those days. . . . So many forget all that the U.S. has done."

"The Shah has always been our best friend," Kissinger effused and cited the Shah's refusal to allow Soviet overflights during the October Arab-Israeli war.

It was Zahedi who raised the touchy subject of oil: "The oil problem—there is one. I want to do what I can." But he explained that Ken Jamieson, the chairman of Exxon, had recently been to Tehran and met with the Shah. The Shah was now arguing that the renegotiated terms of Saudi Arabia's participation deal with Aramco meant that "Saudi Arabia and others get $10" in profit for each barrel of oil that they produce, whereas Iran was only getting $7: "Some countries want to do away with the posted price." Kissinger added that Iranian complaints about the Saudis were justified: "The basic point is that these prices are complicated. The Shah's view is he gets 15 percent less on buy-back oil than the Saudis. Iran is tied to the price of oil, but Saudi Arabia can maneuver around and vary the participation."

"I will work on it and we want to help and we understand the problems," Zahedi assured the president.

"Please express to the Shah my deep appreciation for this attitude."

It was Saudi Arabia's turn next. Umar al-Saqqaf, Saudi Arabia's minister of state for foreign affairs, stopped by the Oval Office eight days later. After discussing the prospects for peace in the Middle East, Ford steered the conversation toward the oil supply and pricing: "We hope we don't have an embargo again. We understand the circumstances last time, but we hope there is no repeat. It would be very serious. And then about prices."

"I have said that oil is not a toy to play with," Saqqaf austerely replied. He insisted that another embargo was out of the question and was equally forthright on the question of pricing, explaining to Ford that, "On price, we were the last to accept it." Without naming the Shah, the ambassador reminded them of Yamani's scuttled auction, but his oblique reference to Iran was unmistakable when he warned: "There is an empire of oil. We must be very careful. The auction was stopped to avoid playing with oil."

"An auction could have counter-results," added Kissinger. He did not explain that the Shah had threatened to cut Iranian oil production to drive prices even higher if the auction went ahead: "If there is not a surplus, an auction would drive prices up."

Ford reminded the ambassador that the health of the American economy was inextricably linked to U.S. leadership in world affairs and the Middle East.

"I know and I see people taking advantage of it," replied the Saudi. "I know if it hurts you it hurts us. It is not a matter of billions; it is a matter of balances."

MR. FORD GOES TO WAR

Economic imbalance lay at the heart of the challenges facing President Gerald Ford in the autumn of 1974. The Dow Jones Industrial Average had slumped 35 percent and shed $300 billion in national wealth since reaching its high-water mark of 1,051 points on January 11, 1973. Economists were already raising the specter of a second Great Depression. In the first three years after the 1929 stock market crash share prices collapsed a staggering 86 percent. Analysts noted that during the six-year period from 1968 to 1974 shares had fallen an almost equally impressive 79 percent. "Investors have seemed frightened of an economy that seems out of control," reported *Time* magazine in the autumn of 1974. Housing starts fell 38 percent in the same period. Pan American airlines, battered by high fuel costs, appealed to the federal government for a taxpayer-funded bailout of $10 million a month. Cost cutting became a national pastime. Massachusetts General Hospital stopped changing bed linen every day.

The federal government estimated that in only eighteen months the number of Americans living below the poverty line rose by 5.6 percent, the number of children living in poverty increased by 8 percent to 10.2 million, and real income declined 4 percent over a twelve-month period. The American middle class was under real pressure. Here was the true cost of the Shah's oil shock. It came as no surprise that 46 percent of Americans told Gallup they "feared a depression similar to the classic one of the 1930s." In a year of constitutional crisis, financial meltdowns, and hard-luck stories, Americans flocked to the big screen to watch their favorite Hollywood stars be incinerated, suffocated, crushed, drowned, and maimed in celluloid disaster epics like *The Towering Inferno, Earthquake*, and *Airport 1975*. Gerald Ford's America wallowed in its impotency.

The picture overseas was, if anything, even worse. High oil prices exacerbated a global food crisis. Famines caused by drought conditions and "the soaring cost of oil and fertilizer" stalked sub-Saharan Africa and India. Unable to pay its fuel bills, India shut off irrigation pumps and "lost enough wheat to feed 50 million people for a year." Hunger led to an increase in child mortality in Tanzania. In Latin America, inflation roared out of control and at one point topped 207 percent annually in Chile. Falling consumer demand in the West for textiles led to factory closures in Singapore. In Western Europe, where the price of heating oil jumped 60 to 100 percent, thermostats were turned down. French president Válery Giscard d'Estaing switched off the heat altogether and worked beside an open fire. Electrical light displays were banned in Britain in the daytime and in France after 10 P.M. In Greece the floodlights around the Acropolis were turned off and at nightfall darkness enveloped democracy's birthplace like a mourning shroud. Few omens have been so loaded with significance.

South Vietnam was especially hard hit. Doing business in Saigon during the oil shock was likened by one American entrepreneur to "making love to a corpse," and President Thieu's government admitted its finances had been "overwhelmed" by surging fuel costs. Oil prices of $1.50 a gallon threatened to achieve what the Communists had so far failed to do: drive South Vietnam to collapse. There was a sour irony in the fact that oil was also seen, at least by President Thieu and the increasingly desperate U.S. embassy, as a panacea for South Vietnam's worsening economic fortunes. For years there had been rumors of vast oil deposits in the coastal waters off the Mekong Delta. In the spring of 1974 a consortium of four Western oil companies purchased exploration rights to the area and announced plans to start drilling by the end of the year. American officials crossed their fingers in the hope that oil would magically transform South Vietnam into the Kuwait of Southeast Asia. "Please God, just let them bring in one well," was the impolitic reaction of one American diplomat to the treasure hunt.

A new globalized economy was emerging, one that carried with it great promise but also enormous risk. "What happens in the economic realm in one part of the globe often induces quick repercussions in other places," wrote Thomas Mullaney in *The New York Times* in September 1974. "So it has often been with respect to the major current problems—rampaging inflation, soaring interest rates and the explosive rise in international oil prices. . . . Serious as they are, the world's economic ills might have been addressed effectively over a period of time without too much difficulty had there not occurred the dramatic change in Middle East oil policy almost one year ago." The world's oil bill for 1974 would be $100 billion. The United States alone faced an increase of $16 billion over the previous year.

"The quadrupling of the price of this key resource in such a short time has created widespread distortions and financial problems that are intensifying week by week," wrote Mullaney. "And the Western world has been almost powerless to deal with a most perilous situation. The public has not fully grasped the potential implications of the sudden change in petroleum economics, though certainly political leaders have sensed it. But coping with these dire new circumstances is another matter." Oil producers, wrote *New York Times* financial affairs columnist Leonard Silk, would not be so foolish as to doubt American resolve to bring them to heel. The United States in the aftermath of the oil shock was like "a screaming eagle. . . . But the crucial question is not where some of the oil producers, such as Saudi Arabia, will be frightened into making some modest appeasement gesture, but where there is enough force behind the new United States line to bring down the price of oil significantly—such as by one-third or more." OPEC members had crossed a line when they decided to prop up the market price by reducing their collective output, rather than allow prices to settle as Western consumption slackened. "It looks as though the battle in what could be a long energy war—the first in history—has now been joined," wrote Silk. "Its outcome, failing a quick backdown by OPEC, could be years in coming."

President Ford did not fire the first shot in the great oil war. But he did issue what amounted to a formal declaration of hostilities against oil producers in a landmark address to an international energy conference in Detroit on September 23, 1974. It turned out to be the most important foreign policy speech of his presidency. "The danger is clear," said the president. "It is severe." Ford explained that sovereign nations "cannot allow their policies to be dictated, or their fate decided, by artificial rigging and distortion of world commodity markets." Oil prices should move freely with the laws of the market and not because producers wanted to lock prices in at a particular level. Financial systems and political structures were under enormous strain. "Exorbitant prices can only distort the world economy, run the risk of world-wide depression, and threaten the breakdown of order and safety." He admitted it was not easy to avoid discussing the issue of oil without resorting to "doomsday language. . . . The whole structure of our society rests upon the expectation of abundant fuel at reasonable prices," an expectation that "has now been challenged." The president refused to rule out the use of force to stop the escalation in oil prices. "Throughout history, nations have gone to war over natural advantages such as water, or food or convenient passages on land and sea," he said, while conceding that "war brings unacceptable risks for all mankind." Ford's speech was described by *The Wall Street Journal* as "harsh and even threatening" with "a thinly veiled—and unspecific—threat of possible retaliation against any nation that seriously disrupts the U.S. economy by using oil as a political weapon."

Henry Kissinger and Bill Simon delivered equally hard-hitting speeches on the same day to drive home to producers the message that the president and his inner circle were speaking with one voice. "What has gone up by political decision can be reduced by political decision," Kissinger told the United Nations General Assembly. "Oil prices cannot go up indefinitely. Strains on the fabric and institutions of the world economy threaten to engulf us all in a general depression. . . . The world's financial institutions are staggering under the most massive and rapid movements of reserves in history. And profound questions have arisen about meeting man's most fundamental needs for energy and food." A senior U.S. official told reporters: "Yesterday's actions were a signal . . . that an important battle will be fought on this issue. Up to now we, and they, thought the problem would go away or that supply and demand would come into play."

While Kissinger kept a close eye on events in Lisbon and Rome, Bill Simon was anxiously monitoring the health of America's banks. Treasury's worst-case scenario was not a Communist takeover of Southern Europe but a banking collapse at home. Another big increase in oil prices might lead to "economic catastrophe" over the winter. Treasury warned of "a drastic business decline with depression-level unemployment—thanks to the traumatic impact on the West of wildly rising oil prices." Ten months earlier the Bank of England had been forced to step in and bail out two British banks drained by panicked investors rushing to reclaim their deposits. The crisis had left the City of London, *The Economist* reported at the time, "on the brink of a terrifying collapse of confidence in the banking system." More recently, the failure of banks in West Germany had startled financial analysts. In September 1974, the same month that Franklin National, the forty-seventh-largest U.S. bank, ran into trouble, representatives from ten Western governments met to agree on the terms under which they would bail out big international banks "in danger of succumbing to financial pressures." What if these were not isolated events but the first in a coming wave of bank failures? Simon, like Kissinger, worried about falling dominoes, specifically "skyrocketing escalation of energy costs [that] will generate critical bank failures in Western Europe, which will spread to American banks and American businesses bringing a flash-fire business decline with unemployment exceeding 10 percent."

The Ford administration's energy offensive provoked outrage in the Middle East. "America Warns the Arabs, Threatens Nuclear War over Petroleum," blared the headline in the Lebanese newspaper *Al Sharq*. "Ford Threatens to Seize Arab Oil by Force of Arms," declared a second paper. But Saudi Arabia's Sheikh Yamani didn't see it that way at all. "It is calling for cooperation rather than confrontation, and emphasized the danger of confrontation," he told reporters in Chicago. "I was amazed to see the media interpret it in a different way. I think the President's statement is a well-balanced statement because it pinpoints the problem. He was talking about a period of inter-cooperation."

Iran's emperor thought he smelled a bluff. Mohammad Reza Shah was in the Australian capital, Canberra, when a reporter at the National Press Club asked him to comment on President Ford's remarks from Detroit. The Shah's haughty reply was all too quickly flashed around the world by the wire services. "No one can dictate to us," he famously declared. "No one can wave a finger because we will wave a finger back." He again demanded parity between oil prices and a basket of twenty to thirty other commodity items: "If the world prices go down, we will go down with oil prices. But if they go up, why should we pay the bill?" He should have stopped there. He announced that Ford's speech was unacceptable to the Iranian people: "We will be ready to provide our energy resources against the Westinghouses and General Motors and General Electrics and all the other generals they have."

When he returned to Tehran the Shah and Court Minister Alam talked about his decision to publicly slap down an American president. It was something he never would have dared do while Nixon was in power. The Shah had respected and feared Nixon. "Ford is an utter booby," he declared. "He does nothing but repeat whatever cretinous nonsense he's fed by Simon." Alam replied that "Kissinger was the real power behind the throne," a remark that the Shah found agreeable. As Kissinger was the Shah's great admirer they felt they had nothing to worry about. Still, they should remain on their guard. "Pride comes before a fall," the Shah contemptuously said of Kissinger, "although in his case it's more conceit than pride." Just a few years earlier the Shah had bitterly complained to Ambassador Douglas MacArthur that President Nixon still had not taken him up on his offer to visit Tehran. Now he feigned indifference when he was told that Ardeshir Zahedi had approached the White House to suggest that Gerald Ford stop off in Tehran on his way to a summit meeting of Western leaders in Tokyo. He was much more preoccupied with planning the forthcoming visit of Britain's Queen Elizabeth the Queen Mother.

HE WAS OUR BABY, BUT NOW HE HAS GROWN UP

The Pahlavi tour of the Far East was a smashing success. A stopover in New Delhi was required. India was now a member of the atomic club and the Shah was eager to patch up relations with Indira Gandhi and enter into trade deals. He wanted to court Australia, a country he identified as a potential partner and emerging power in the Indian and Pacific oceans. The Persian caravan traveled through Singapore and Indonesia, and as far southeast as New Zealand, whose lamb and dairy products were expected to feed the growing ranks of the empire's burgeoning middle class. In the cities of Australasia the imperial couple were treated like rock stars. There was a concert at the Sydney Opera House, banquets, a day at the races, and in Melbourne a horse-drawn carriage ride through streets lined with cheering crowds. Farah was a particular draw. Her good works had earned her the informal title of Iran's "Working Empress," and her renowned beauty and effortlessly stylish wardrobe garnered a great deal of attention.

Behind the glamour of the state visits was a push by the Shah to project Iranian imperial power from Tehran to Wellington. Hemmed in to the north and west, Iran should pivot south and east in search of allies, influence, and markets, as the Shah saw it. He envisioned a new regional order comprised of Iran, Israel, Ethiopia, South Africa, India, Indonesia, Australia, and New Zealand. Buoyed by the crowds and headlines, the Shah correctly sensed a power vacuum in the Far East in the wake of the American draw-down in Southeast Asia. If it was leadership these people wanted, the heir to Cyrus the Great was happy to step in and give it to them. He had already called for a common market binding regional economies. In Canberra he proposed a "military understanding," a collective security pact that would keep the Indian Ocean free from U.S. and Soviet naval rivalry, enabling it to be jointly patrolled by the Iranian and Australian navies. The Shah spent time courting Prime Minister Gough Whitlam because the Australian had two commodities the Shah wanted: uranium and bauxite.

The Shah owed Iran's rise to regional power status to Richard Nixon, who provided him with the guns and money to pursue his ambitions. The Iranian also owed his atomic dreams to the Americans, who had helped save his throne. After the 1953 coup the Eisenhower administration provided Iran with a small nuclear reactor under the terms of its Atoms for Peace program. "It was primarily used for university research," said Dr. Akbar Etemad, the president of the Atomic Energy Organization of Iran from 1974 to 1978 and the man widely regarded as the father of Iran's nuclear program. "Then, in the early 1970s, the Shah came to the conclusion that Iran should develop its nuclear technology. We needed more power plants to generate electricity: the population was increasing and people were using more electricity than before." President Nixon had responded to these concerns in 1972 when he secretly agreed to sell the Shah nuclear power plants and fuels. When Iran's oil income quadrupled a year later, the Shah was finally free to pursue his ambition of acquiring the atom. The next year Iran and the United States entered into formal talks "with the precondition that [Washington] should have complete control over our nuclear fuel cycle," recalled Dr. Etemad. In 1974 the Shah announced his intention to buy eight nuclear power plants from the United States and five from France.

From the outset, Secretary of Defense James Schlesinger, whom Ford had also kept on, forcefully registered his concerns about Iran's nuclear program. Before taking over at Defense, and before his even briefer stint as CIA chief, Schlesinger had served as chairman of the Atomic Energy Commission. "I was resisting the efforts of American firms to sell reactors to Third World countries," he recalled, noting that it "irritated some of my fellow commissioners on the Atomic Energy Commission who thought it was our job to go out and sell." Schlesinger's view was simple: "Any sales that we make should be in the American interest and not in order to but-tress the balance of payments." Pentagon analysts suspected that the Shah's motives were not entirely peaceful. They questioned what would happen to Iran's nuclear program if he died or was removed from power. The Shah did nothing to ease their fears when in June 1974 he gave a provocative interview to a French journalist. Asked whether Iran would one day possess a nuclear weapon, the Shah boasted, "Certainly, and sooner than is believed."

"I always suspected that part of the Shah's plan was to build bombs," Dr. Etemad later admitted. A flurry of cables from Embassy Tehran sought to assure the White House and the Pentagon that the Shah had been misquoted. Ambassador Helms even peddled the Shah's disingenuous line that he had been unfairly quoted because his remarks were "off the cuff." It was a preposterous attempt by Helms to cover up a gaffe that revealed too much about the Shah's ultimate strategic ambitions.

The Pentagon stiffened its resolve to oppose sharing nuclear technology with Tehran. The Shah wanted to build a nuclear reprocessing plant in Iran. "At that time, reprocessing did not have significant commercial potential," reported the *Bulletin of the Atomic Scientists*, "but it did enable scientists to recover plutonium from nuclear fuel once it had been used in a power reactor, and that plutonium could be used to manufacture nuclear weapons."

"If Iran were to seek a weapons capability, it is noted that the annual plutonium production from the planned . . . Iranian nuclear power program will be equivalent to 600–700 warheads," warned an internal report prepared for the assistant secretary of defense. "Although Iran is currently stable, that stability is heavily dependent on the Shah's remaining in power. In a situation of instability, domestic dissidents or foreign terrorists might easily be able to seize any special nuclear materials stored in Iran for use in bombs. . . . An aggressive successor to the Shah might consider nuclear weapons the final item needed to establish Iran's complete military dominance of the region."

American intelligence and military officials watched with great interest the Shah's triumphs overseas. In the minds of some the Shah was becoming too powerful too quickly, while the Persian Gulf was descending into an unchecked arms bazaar. The Defense Department had been quiet for two years on the subject of unrestricted arms sales to Iran. That changed on September 25, 1974, when Schlesinger publicly disassociated himself and his department from arms sales to Iran and Saudi Arabia. "I should make it meticulously clear that the Department of Defense does not have its own policies with regard to the sale of arms," he told reporters at a press conference. "In general, military assistance rests under the purview of the Secretary of State. We are the administrators of the programs." Schlesinger was also taking a very hard look at the Shah. "By mid-1974, the shape and scope of the Shah's arms purchases were arousing concern in the Department of Defense," concluded a secret history of U.S.-Iran relations prepared six years later for President Jimmy Carter's National Security Council. "This concern was reflected in an internal memorandum of October 3, 1974, which stated, 'There are sufficient negative indicators in relations to the Shah's prospects to prompt the USG [United States Government] toward a somewhat more cautious and guarded relationship with the Shah.'"

The Shah's ambitions caused concern at the CIA. As one perplexed U.S. intelligence official remarked at about this time of the proud fifty-five-year-old King of Kings, whose throne the agency had helped to restore, "He *was* our baby, but now he has grown up." The spy agency conducted an analysis of Iran's economy in October 1974 that in hindsight reads like a distress flare. The CIA had always been skeptical of the Shah's financial acumen. Intelligence analysts now concluded that the world's fastest growing economy was having trouble digesting its billions of dollars in oil revenues. Iran's economy had taken off like a booster rocket but no one knew where it would land or how hard it would fall. "The latest surge in oil revenues has contributed to an acceleration in the rate of growth," reported the CIA. "The economy grew by 33% in 1973 and is expected to grow another 40% in 1974." These were astounding figures. "Oil revenues will continue to exceed the economy's absorptive capacity over the next few years." So much money was pouring into the domestic economy that the Iranian government couldn't spend it fast enough: "The Shah's ambitious development program and arms build-up are creating domestic economic problems." Inflation, skilled labor shortages, and urban unemployment were occurring.

Inflation was eroding the earnings of Iranians who were poorer and more religious-minded. "The cost of living in Iran—where more than 60 percent of the families have a subsistence level income under $15 a week—is jumping almost daily and is expected to rise soon to 20 percent above what it was last year," reported *The New York Times* in October 1974. "Prices for staple foods, textile goods and home appliances have been soaring, in some cases to 100 percent above last year's levels. A black market has developed to circumvent the Government's price controls." The government was trying to keep a lid on inflation with the help of expensive subsidies of basic household items. Despite its best efforts, "inflation still dissipates the income of many Iranians, leaving them little if anything to spare and far below the consumption levels of Western nations whose money is pouring into this country in petroleum."

The CIA did not take the logical next step, which should have been to study the impact an inflationary economy would have on political stability in Iran. CIA director William Colby might have paid closer attention to Iran had he any inklings about the Shah's health. Just before his departure for Australia, on September 9, 1974, the Shah had complained to Court Minister Alam about a rash on his face. His spleen was also enlarged again. The Shah had so far not responded to the French doctors' diagnosis of Waldenström's disease from last May. The Shah and Shahbanou opened the second Tehran International Exhibition on the evening of September 17. The next morning they were due to depart for New Delhi en route to the Far East. While the queen busied herself with some last-minute packing, the Shah's French doctors, Flandrin and Bernard, with a third colleague in tow, Professor Paul Milliez, were smuggled into the palace through a back entrance. "Medically, the patient was still in excellent shape, but his spleen had grown larger," noted Flandrin. The doctors aspirated samples from his bone marrow. Alam described it as "a very painful exercise but necessary if they're to make a proper laboratory analysis. [His Imperial Majesty] chatted with them while they went about their business, recommending that they take a look round our new heart hospital." Alam thought this unwise, pointing out that if they were seen in a local hospital it might give rise to rumors about the king's health. The doctors decided to begin treatment with small doses of chlorambucil, a drug prescribed to combat the Shah's lymphoma. They disguised the medication by placing the capsules in plastic containers that usually held vitamin pills.

The number of individuals who now knew that the Shah was being treated for blood cancer had likely risen to seven: the Shah; the three French doctors, Flandrin, Bernard, and Milliez; General Ayadi, the Shah's physician; presumably the high-powered and unnamed Iranian who was close to the Shah and whose home the French doctors stayed at during their visits; and Professor Abbas Safavian, primary physician to Asadollah Alam. If Alam suspected the truth he never let on.

IBEX, OR CHASING THE GOAT

In early 1974, flush with oil revenues, the Shah decided to build a new Iranian-controlled complex of radar installations that would allow him to listen in on all civilian and military communications in the Persian Gulf. It is unclear whether the Shah proposed the concept himself or if it was presented to him by Ambassador Helms. Either way, Helms took it upon himself to personally shepherd the $500 million project—code-named

Ibex after the horned alpine goat—through the planning and construction stages. According to one of the few published reports ever to mention the project, Ibex envisioned the construction of eleven ground monitoring posts connected to six airborne units and mobile ground units. In the initial stages fifteen CIA employees were sent to Iran undercover to act as an advisory team to the Iranian government. Four U.S. corporations, among them Rockwell International, entered into the bidding war to win the first-phase $50 million contract to design the project's specifications. In November 1974 the bidders were cautioned by the CIA not to pay Iranian middlemen to help their chances of winning the contract. At the time it was common practice for well-connected Iranian businessmen to help foreign defense contractors win business at court in return for lucrative sales commissions. It was their job to grease the wheels by greasing palms. Executives at Rockwell ignored the directive, which had been forwarded to the CIA by General Hassan Toufanian, the Shah's highly trusted chief weapons procurement officer. In January 1975 Rockwell hired Universal Aero Services Co. Ltd. to help state its case to the Shah. UASCO's mail address was a post office box registered in Bermuda and its agent was Abolfath Mahvi, a well-connected Iranian businessman. In return for Mahvi promising to provide "the necessary marketing services," Rockwell agreed to pay him a fee "ranging from 5 to 10 percent of sales." Mahvi stood to make millions of dollars if Rockwell won the contract to build Ibex.

On February 17, 1975, the Shah decided to award the contract to Rockwell. He was acting on the recommendation of the CIA advisory team that had screened the four contenders. The Shah was insistent that Ibex and the Rockwell contract remain top secret. He did not want to alert Iran's neighbors, particularly the Soviet Union, to the project. Nor did the Shah want the Iranian people to be reminded of his long-standing ties to the CIA. When he visited Andrews Air Force Base in May 1975 he inspected specially outfitted planes carrying radars, airborne warning and control systems that were referred to as AWACS. These aircraft, the airborne component of the Ibex project, had been built to pick up and send signals to the ground-based receiving stations.

Ibex ran into trouble when General Toufanian learned of Rockwell's decision to hire Mahvi as its middleman. Toufanian, no stranger to intrigue, insisted that the U.S. Defense Department place Mahvi on a blacklist, essentially banning him from future involvement with defense contractors operating in Iran. To quell the uproar, Rockwell notified Mahvi that his services were no longer required. There was just one problem: Rockwell had signed its contract with UASCO for five years. That left Rockwell liable for the grand sum of $4,526,758. A check in this amount was duly sent off to the Bermuda mail drop. Documents later surfaced confirming that payments to the mail drop were then forwarded to a Chase Manhattan bank account in Geneva. A *Washington Post* investigation later showed that the Ibex money trail led all over Washington, D.C., involving the CIA and various U.S. companies.

Quite apart from financial irregularities, the Ibex contract was remarkable for several other reasons. First, the Department of Defense was shut out of Ibex. The contract was quietly rushed through the State Department's Office of Munitions, an obscure office that Kissinger used to handle special projects he deemed essential and wanted to keep tabs on. Ibex was very much a Kissinger-Helms project. Second, the Ibex contract allowed for Rockwell to hire away former and current National Security Agency and Air Force Security staff. This unprecedented breach in security protocol sent shock waves through the American intelligence community. One former NSA employee declared himself "amazed" that the Ford administration would allow its own intelligence specialists to put their skills to work for a foreign government. "We can't say who the Shah's targets would be," one unidentified official told *New York Times* reporter Seymour Hersh. "We have to assume that among the people intercepted would be Americans—those working for the Mil [military advisory] Groups in Iran and elsewhere in the Persian Gulf." He pointed out that Ibex might one day be used to spy on Israel "and even used by the Iranian secret police, SAVAK, to help locate dissidents inside the country and for other internal security functions."

The Shah was distressed when *The New York Times* published a lengthy front-page exposé of the Ibex project on June 1, 1975. The article included enough unnamed sources, anonymous leaks, and inside information to suggest that it could have come only from top officials in either the CIA or at the Defense Department. Ibex was now public knowledge and not only to the thousands of Iranian students studying in the United States. Almost immediately, the official newspaper of the Soviet Communist Party, *Pravda*, swung into action. *Pravda* retaliated with its own front-page article reminding the Shah of the 1962 treaty forbidding construction of foreign rocket bases on Iranian soil. *Pravda* pointed out that in 1960 the Soviet Union had shot down a U-2 spy plane that flew out of an American spy base located in Peshawar, Pakistan, an action that led to the collapse of a summit between President Eisenhower and Nikita Khrushchev and chilled superpower relations through the Kennedy years. Ibex was not technically a foreign or a missile base but the Russians were deeply concerned that "it will be built by Americans and will require the long-term presence of American personnel." Ibex created a rift between Iran and its northern neighbor and provided extremist groups in Iran with one more charge of puppetry to level against the Shah.

A WALK IN THE HILLS OF THE ROSES

The American public was unaware of the policy disputes and spy intrigues that lay at the heart of American-Iranian relations. Its concern was holding on to jobs and homes as the recession caused by high oil prices worsened. Over the winter of 1974–75, America's unemployment rate climbed to 7.1 percent and there were more Americans out of work than at any time since 1940.

Two faces among the 6.5 million unemployed were Ron and Jill Stuber, young newlyweds from Brentwood, Long Island. Ron was a heavy-machine technician and Jill a dental assistant. The Stubers had planned to travel to Iran for their honeymoon. But when they read that the Iranian embassy in Washington was accepting job applications from Americans to help the government fill a shortage of skilled labor the Stubers decided to pack up and move to Iran for good. They weren't alone. By the spring of 1975 Ardeshir Zahedi's embassy on Massachusetts Avenue was taking more than one hundred applications each week from teachers, engineers, technicians, academics, lawyers, and accountants looking for work. "We are being flooded," chortled an Iranian consular official.

The Stubers joined the growing exodus of Americans moving to Iran, a country they believed offered them their best chance to live out the American Dream. An internal survey conducted by the Department of Defense in January 1975 revealed that seventeen thousand Americans were already living in Iran, triple the number from just four years earlier and predicted to increase 20 percent a year for at least the rest of the decade. Sixty-eight percent of the incoming arrivals were attached to the military mission. A further 5,200 were doctors, Peace Corps volunteers, teachers, lawyers, accountants, construction workers, contractors, and husbands and wives joining their Iranian spouses. Defense traced the upsurge to Nixon's 1972 visit and his decision "to provide advanced weapons systems and uniformed technical assistance personnel to Iran." American trainers and technicians— the blue suiters promised to the Shah—usually arrived in-country some eighteen to thirty months after an arms deal was concluded. Based on current trends, and with almost $6 billion in expenditure for U.S. armaments already signed for 1973 and 1974, a massive influx of American nationals eventually numbering fifty thousand was expected to be residing in Iran during the peak years of 1979–80.

Tehran was also the major hub for Pan Am flights connecting European capitals with major destinations in the Far East. Pan Am's vast operation extended to training Iranian pilots, and air and ground crews. Its presence exposed Iran to Western tourism on a mass scale for the first time. Then there was the chance to make some fast cash. "Our ambition is to make as much of America out here as we can," said the wife of a Bell helicopter pilot. "We owe it to our children."

If the thousands of Americans who descended on Iran in the mid-1970s knew nothing about Iranian history, culture, language, religion, or politics, that was all right too. Once they settled into the American colony in north Tehran these Americans entered a rarefied world of cocooned privilege unlike any they had ever known. For the first time in their lives they had servants, pools, tennis courts, and country club memberships. They worshipped at a Presbyterian church dating back to the nineteenth century. They sent their children to one of three exclusively American elementary and secondary schools, where parents had over the years successfully resisted the introduction of Farsi and Persian culture studies. The children were transported to school in sixty school buses. The American School fielded three football teams, and a cheerleading and drill team. Football games were played under lights on Friday night against the dramatic backdrop of the Elburz Mountains. American housewives shopped at the commissary attached to the embassy grounds, the largest of its kind anywhere in the world, and where the only Iranians admitted were members of the royal family. Everything Americans ate and consumed was airlifted or shipped in from home. They preferred to buy their Coca-Cola from the commissary even though it was sold on the streets outside at half the price.

American universities suffering the effects of the recession joined the money chase and rushed to enter into joint ventures with their Iranian counterparts. Georgetown University signed an $11 million contract with Ferdowsi University in Mashhad. George Washington University trained fifty-four Iranian army officers in computer science. Harvard accepted a $400,000 grant from the Iranian government to begin preliminary planning for a campus on the south shore of the Caspian Sea. New York's Columbia University accepted $361,000 to conduct a three-month study for a huge new $500 million international medical complex in Tehran. Columbia was also helping Iran plan a new school of social welfare. "There are tons of dollars there—it's like a gold mine," exulted one East Coast college administrator.

Washington encouraged the recycling of petrodollars and established joint ventures of its own. Kissinger believed that the best way, perhaps the only way, to retain some form of influence over the Shah and Iran now that the Twitchell firewall had been breached, was to integrate the Iranian and American economies to such an extent that one could not function without the other. Kissinger's "super economy" would swap petrodollars for weapons. But that was not how the Shah saw it. "We're spending so much money on U.S. military supplies that no U.S. government, let alone the arms manufacturers, could afford to deny us," said Alam. Economic ties led to misunderstandings on both sides about the ability of each to influence the policy of its partner.

Many of the government-to-government deals had obvious dual civilian-military purposes that held little immediate benefit to the Iranian people. The Federal Highway Administration sent out teams to survey Iranian highways. The Federal Communications Commission negotiated for a study of frequency allocation. The Federal Aviation Administration sent three hundred personnel to support a $270 million Iranian procurement package to coordinate Iran's civil aviation authority, navigation aids, and communications. In October 1974, Iran signed a $4.5 million agreement with NASA to build a satellite receiving station to monitor the NASA Earth Resources Technology Satellite. U.S. defense contractors rushed to enter into co-production projects and opened factories in Iran. There was a $1.5 billion contract with Bell Helicopter for two hundred of its 215s. Emerson Electric would build one thousand TOW missile launchers in Iran at a cost of $60 million. Contracts to make these items and many more, including rockets and lightweight fighters, inevitably meant that hundreds more Americans and their families would have to relocate to Iran. Co-production fitted into Kissinger's grand plan to turn Iran into a giant regional arms depot from which he could insert or extract men and machinery at will to impose regional order.

Iranian defense plants and military facilities were dispersed around the country as a precaution against invasion. That meant American defense contractors and their families were also required to move out of Tehran, often to remote parts of the country deeply imbued in conservative Shi'a Islam. "The major distributional change is occurring in [Isfahan] and Shiraz where two large American civilian defense contractor communities are growing," reported the Pentagon. "Bell Helicopter and Grumman Aircraft will locate about 4,000 American families there, probably by 1980. Thus, while the appearance of Americans outside Tehran was not unusual in the early 1970s, by the latter part of this decade U.S. citizens will be a significant part of the Iranian 'frontier areas.'" From the Shah's perspective, this was ideal—American men, women, and children based near the frontier areas were there to act as a trip wire or human shield to deter Soviet aggression and invite an automatic American response in the event of invasion. They were his insurance policy until Iran was strong enough to stand on its own around 1980. But neither the incoming Americans nor their Iranian hosts were ready for the cultural disorientation and confrontations that followed. "Many American families are poorly prepared for life in an alien culture," reported the United States Information Service even as it noted that Iranian universities were "producing a highly nationalistic and self-assertive younger generation, skeptical of the American cultural model."

Embassy Tehran's economics counselor was William Lehfeldt. He liked to take his family on road trips into the Iranian countryside. One time they made a trip outside Kashan, up into the mountains, "where they harvest the rose petals to make attara roses." The villages up in the hills had been converted from Zoroastrianism to Shi'a Islam by Reza Shah in the 1930s. The Lehfeldts were wandering through one of the rose villages when they were approached by some local children. The children "came up to us and started talking to us and reflected their teachings from the mullahs, which were that 'you Christian, you no good; me Muslim, me good,' in their medieval English. A medieval modicum of English." It was a jarring, if slight, incident on an otherwise peaceful spring day. "But the attitudes that they displayed were symptomatic, I think, of what came later," he reflected. Even here among children living in the remote hills of the roses above Kashan the Americans were unwelcome.

IT TAKES TWO HANDS TO CLAP

In the autumn of 1974 Secretary of State Henry Kissinger traveled to capitals in West Asia and the Middle East. Egypt, Syria, and Israel had still not concluded a deal to disengage their forces and enter into formal peace talks. The shattering events of late 1973—the October War, the oil embargo, and the oil shock—remained a constant source of open-ended conflict and grievance. During his talks with the leaders of Saudi Arabia, Pakistan, and

Israel, Kissinger was also made aware of growing unease in the region with Iran. Nixon had delegated to the Shah the powers of a gladiator and stabilizing presence. But transcripts of Kissinger's meetings with foreign leaders confirm that the Shah's neighbors were concerned with their neighbor's sudden wealth and vaulting ambitions, and increasingly saw him as a source of mischief and even instability in a tinderbox region.

Saudi Arabia. On October 13 Kissinger was in Riyadh, where the inscrutable King Faisal proved resistant to Kissinger's flattery and charm. The secretary of state assured the king that President Ford's Detroit speech had not been directed at the Arab people but at "all oil producers," an obvious reference to Iran. He asked the king for help on oil prices and phrased his appeal in ways that he hoped would resonate with Faisal's reflexive anti-Communism. "There is a big problem which, if it continues, will contribute to the spread of Communism everywhere in the world, and not only in the under-developed countries," Kissinger explained. "In Europe, if Italy goes Communist, France will follow and the political map of the world will change. This will be to the detriment of the Middle East. . . . We can solve our problems in the U.S. without a catastrophe but if Western Europe, India and Japan go Communist, or are taken over by other radicals, there will be no peace for anyone. Our concern is not profit or money but the entire world structure. This would bring Communism into power and the producers would end up with clients who are worthless and whose money had no value."

Faisal was not about to accept blame for the parlous state of Western Europe or the world economy. "Our policies are consistent with what you have said but other countries including some of your friends such as Iran and also Kuwait and Algeria are not cooperating," he lectured the secretary. "They can wield great influence. You should intensify your contacts with them and try to get them to understand the situation as you and we do."

"I will see the Shah in two weeks for this purpose," he assured Faisal. "Your Majesty is doing all he can and we realize that other leaders must support him if he is to be able to lower the prices."

Faisal insisted that Kissinger must make the Shah see reason. "While you are trying to convince others, we are trying our best," he said. "I sent my son to explain about policy to the Shah. I am also working with Algeria. But, I cannot do it alone." He then administered the final sting: "It takes two hands to clap. The U.S. must also do its best."

Pakistan. At the end of the month Kissinger was in Islamabad where Prime Minister Zulifikar Ali Bhutto was clinging to power. As Bhutto sadly explained to his American guests, he was also the foreign minister and defense minister these days "since one has to maintain tight control in order to avoid a coup." The Shah's recent rapprochement with India's Indira Gandhi had caught the State Department by surprise. Nixon's decision to arm the Shah in 1972 had been at least partly influenced by his conviction that Iran could shield Pakistan from its neighbor. Now the Shah's commitment to Pakistan's survival seemed less assured. Pakistan's economy was also reeling from high fuel prices. "Our balance of payments is terrible and we need fertilizer which has become extremely expensive," explained Bhutto. "The increased oil prices are having a disastrous effect."

Bhutto's complaint prompted Kissinger instead to launch into a vicious appraisal of King Faisal and Saudi Arabia. Away from Washington he could speak freely. "Faisal is trying to speed up the end of his own monarchy by bringing in foreign resources and exports and techniques, which will speed up radicalization at home, and at the same time weakening the countries abroad on whom he must depend for support," said Kissinger. "He is also making Saudi Arabia more attractive for its covetous neighbors. I am saying this to you, a friend of Faisal, just as I am. But when he tells me of the modernization he is encouraging, I think 'Oh you fool.'"

"I agree," Bhutto exclaimed. "The monarchy cannot last with $29 billion floating around!"

Kissinger let the Shah increase oil prices because he believed oil revenues would cushion the pro-American monarchies of the Persian Gulf from internal revolt and external invasion. But his cynical comment to Bhutto gave every appearance of being a tacit admission that he knew his policy had resulted in blowback and that Saudi Arabia's oil wealth now might actually *incite* domestic revolution and *provoke* foreign aggression—most likely from Iran. Nixon's two pillars of stability in the Gulf might in fact attack each other. But rather than take responsibility for a failed policy Kissinger instead blamed the victim when he assumed the pose of a finger-wagging bystander who has watched someone he plied with alcohol run a red light. He was anxious to sound out Bhutto on the Shah's push for regional hegemony and his future prospects: "What are your relations with Iran?"

"Very good," replied Bhutto. He had recently upset the Shah by referring to the Persian Gulf as the "Arabian Gulf" in deference to King Faisal, whose financial assistance helped keep the prime minister in power: "We have no problem with the name of the Indian Ocean. But if it comes to a crunch we will call it the Persian Gulf. Iran is our neighbor. Saudi Arabia is far away."

Kissinger praised the Shah as "a man with big conceptions," then made the following jarring statement: "The Shah must understand that his security will be in jeopardy if the high price of oil keeps up."

"I wish we had his money to buy some."

"You have 75 million persons," Kissinger said, trying to make Bhutto feel better. "You have a skilled people so do not despair. You are a martial people, but there is no evidence of the Persians fighting anyone for the past 1,000 years! Pakistan has great opportunities." It was typical of Kissinger to make one foreign chief feel better at another's expense, though his suggestion that the Iranians were the first to back away from a fight raised the question as to why he had approved the Shah's military buildup in the first place.

What did Kissinger mean when he told Bhutto that the Shah's security would be jeopardized "if the high price of oil keeps up"? Was he referring to a possible reduction in military cooperation? Perhaps the withdrawal of Nixon's blank check on oil prices and arms sales? Was the United States planning some sort of covert or military action to overthrow the Shah if he refused to cooperate on oil prices? While it was the case that some officials at the Pentagon and the CIA were raising questions about the Shah's judgment and loyalty, no evidence has emerged to suggest that replacing him or cutting off military aid was ever considered. The Shah was still seen in Washington as a strong and essential—if increasingly uncooperative and belligerent—ally by most of the political and military establishment. The security threat that Kissinger envisioned to the Shah was not external but internal, most likely in the form of a leftist coup or uprising ignited by economic hardship. Kissinger was not concerned about a threat to the Pahlavis from the Ayatollah Khomeini, who languished in exile in Iraq. He agreed with the Shah that Iran's Shi'a clergy was finished as a dynamic force in Iranian life. What most worried Kissinger was the threat from the left, the emergence of a second Mohammad Mossadegh who might take Iran out of the Western orbit. Kissinger's remarks to Bhutto suggest that he feared a repeat of the anti-Shah disturbances of 1953 and 1963, that he now accepted that high oil prices posed as much a threat to the stability of Iran as they did to, say, Italy—to oil producers as well as oil consumers—and that friendly authoritarian dictatorships as well as Western democracies were in equal peril from the ructions of the oil shock.

To Bhutto, Kissinger complained that the oil shock could have been avoided had the Nixon administration accepted the Shah's offer in 1969 to buy millions of barrels of Iranian oil at a special discount. The deal promoted by Herbert Brownell had been judged illegal under U.S. law because it violated the quota laws that applied to petroleum imports. Kissinger knew that the quotas no longer existed. "If we had made that deal we would not have trouble today," he told Bhutto. He was ready to deal again.

Iran: Kissinger was in Tehran on November 1 to preside over the first meeting of the U.S.-Iran Joint Commission to coordinate trade and industrial development, military and security, nuclear energy, agriculture, and science and technology. The Iranian side was led by Hushang Ansary, Iran's minister of economic affairs and finance and Kissinger's friend. Kissinger's relief at being back in Tehran, among people who saw the world the way he did, was obvious. He admitted to Ansary that there was an undercurrent of tension in U.S.-Iran relations:

> I come here when it isn't clear from the American press and even some American officials whether I'm here to negotiate a disengagement of our forces [laughter] or an armistice [laughter], or whether we're dealing with friends. But the press isn't making foreign policy. If we could control them, we could keep them from writing about me [laughter]. So the people who make foreign policy consider Iran a traditional friend, and our relationship has a significance far beyond our bilateral relationship. Therefore, I am not here to discuss this or that technical issue.

The "technical issue" Kissinger was referring to was the touchy subject of oil prices. He wasn't about to let Bill Simon or Treasury ruin his chess game in West Asia. To Ansary, Kissinger harked back to the golden days of their relationship when deals could be struck without having to go through the "experts" at Treasury, Justice, or Defense. Referring to the Shah's 1969 oil deal, the one he had earlier mentioned in his discussion with Bhutto, Kissinger announced he was ready to do business the old way: "I owe it to our Iranian friends to point out that I submitted this proposal to our experts [at the time] who said this was a sly Iranian trick to capture a bigger share of the limited oil market and squeeze the Arabs out. This sounds ridiculous today. Our Iranian friends were 100% right, and we were 100% wrong. So we should look ahead into the real future, and not just project a little bit forward like bureaucrats."

"Kissinger flew in this afternoon accompanied by his wife," observed Court Minister Alam. "He was received by HIM between six and eight thirty. At dinner he was placed to the right of HMQ with me on her left.

He was full of praise for HIM, saying how much he wished President Ford could emulate his example. . . . Afterwards he and HIM resumed their private discussions, breaking off at midnight." Nancy Kissinger and Empress Farah watched a film while their husbands, joined by Ambassador Helms, held their discussions.

Kissinger's behavior at the imperial table—belittling his own president in a foreign capital and in front of foreign heads of state—was not out of character. More unfortunate was the false impression his comments may have left with the Shah about Ford's qualities as a man and as a leader. Kissinger's remarks had the unfortunate effect of undercutting Ford's authority with an autocrat who only responded to and appreciated power. It also left the Shah with the false—and erroneous—impression that Ford was not a man of his word. As Alam's diary makes clear, it was about this time that the Shah, following Kissinger's lead, began denigrating Gerald Ford as a "hopeless old donkey" and ridiculing him as "that idiot Ford." He even repeated Lyndon Johnson's sour one-liner "that Ford was so thick he couldn't chew gum and walk straight at one and the same time."

In their talks, the Shah explained to the Americans that a fall in demand for Persian crudes meant that Iran had millions of barrels of unsold oil on its hands. As he had tried to do unsuccessfully in 1969, the Shah offered to secretly sell surplus petroleum to the United States at a discounted price. If Iran could be assured of an intact, albeit slightly diminished stream of oil income, the Shah could keep buying military equipment and pay for existing orders. Kissinger liked the idea. He wanted to break OPEC without harming Iran's economy. The Shah and Kissinger also saw the deal as a way to increase their strategic leverage over each other. "And one of the notions we had was that we could both break the cartel and help the Shah by buying excess oil from him at a lower price than OPEC charged but still help him with his economic policy," recalled Brent Scowcroft. The Ford administration had also decided to build an emergency strategic petroleum reserve as insurance against a second oil embargo. Officials hoped the Shah's stockpile of surplus oil could be used to build the reserve. Kissinger believed he could relieve the pressure on the American and Iranian economies and at the same time block the effort by Simon and Yamani to strengthen Saudi Arabia's toehold in the American domestic fuel market.

The Shah and Kissinger were in agreement. The deal they struck was that the Shah would support a price freeze at the next OPEC ministers meeting in Bali in May 1975. Kissinger had until the end of the summer to work out the details of their plan and get the president and the administration on board. The Shah made it clear that if a deal was not forthcoming by the end of next August, he would have no choice but to increase prices still further to cover his budget deficit. Iran's economy could not wait.

Before Kissinger left Tehran he held a press conference to announce that "the United States is now attempting to halt new increases in oil prices, rather than trying to negotiate lower prices." Kissinger prized stability above all else. Knowing that the Shah was immune to persuasion and to pressure, the best the secretary could do was to try to extract a commitment from the Iranian not to increase oil prices until the world economy had stabilized. Although no notes remain of what was said in their meeting—most likely none was made—Kissinger undoubtedly made it clear to the Shah that a deal on oil prices was in their mutual best interests. The Shah would have been equally insistent that he could not allow prices to retreat. Kissinger accepted that if the Shah would not or could not roll back oil prices he might at least agree to a price freeze on condition that the United States accept a level below which prices would not fall. This became known as the "floor price" and it dominated policy discussions in the White House over the winter of 1974–75. A floor price for oil would protect Iran's economy from a sudden loss in revenue if consumer demand in the West continued to decline. Not everyone in the Ford administration was happy with this new policy. They regarded it as one more triumph of convenience over morality and yet another victory for the Shah. The pricing structure that kept oil prices artificially propped up—that everyone knew resisted market forces and the laws of consumer demand and supply—was now to all intents and purposes a fait accompli. The Shah's own self-satisfactory comments at the end of Kissinger's trip were cabled to U.S. embassies and back to Washington where one analyst scrawled "B-S," "F. Bull!" in double underline and "Not any more!" in the margins.

Israel: Kissinger was in the prime minister's residence on November 7, 1974, for consultations with Prime Minister Yitzhak Rabin. Rabin and his ministers were anxious to hear more about the details of Kissinger's meeting with the Shah. "How do we stand on oil?" asked Defense Minister Shimon Peres. Israel's rate of inflation was running well over 30 percent. Kissinger explained that his strategy was to stabilize prices, then seek reductions while increasing the insecurity of the producers so they would not threaten an embargo.

Kissinger was convinced that the administration's top strategic priority must be to prevent a second oil embargo during the Middle East peace talks. The Shah, supplier of half of Israel's oil, must be kept on the United

States' side. Kissinger revealed details of his just concluded talks with the Shah in Tehran. He told Rabin and Peres that the Shah assured him that "he would refuel us in an Arab-Israeli war if we could keep it quiet." The Shah said "he would like us to improve our airlift capability in the Middle East, not only for Israel but for him. Because he doesn't think we have reliable bases anywhere. On which he is right. I will look into this." Then there was the Shah's cooperation with the Kurdish insurgency in Iraq. During his meeting with the prime minister, Kissinger pulled out an Israeli list of weapons they wanted the Shah to send to the Kurds. Rabin was embarrassed when Kissinger explained that when he pulled out a similar list with $24 million in military hardware, the Shah had pulled out the same Israeli list estimated at $108 million. Were the Israelis trying to pull a fast one over on the Shah?

"No, it was not given," Rabin said. "Why would we do that?"

"It cost us ten minutes in that conversation comparing the lists," Kissinger replied. "There was one item on his list that wasn't on mine, I agree. Let's not worry about it."

Rabin told Kissinger that the Kurdish leadership was disappointed in the Ford administration. It had expected more military aid for its fight against Saddam Hussein. Kissinger didn't disagree. "Everyone around the world is disappointed in the U.S. attitude," he admitted. He referred to Watergate and the resignations of Nixon and Agnew and the perception it had created of an America weakened by its own internal divisions and unable to project its will in international affairs.

> I am not talking about Israel. With all these pressure groups. The general impression of knocking off a President, then a Vice President, and almost knocking off the Vice President–designate. I am not blaming this on Israel or the Jews. This is becoming a security problem for the world. . . . The biggest security problem in the world is the domestic weakness of the United States. I can keep it going in the Middle East for a few more months because of the romantic cult of personality and the belief I can somehow do it.

CHRISTMAS EPIPHANY

From Kissinger's perspective a deal with Iran on oil prices was inseparable from the Shah's support for Israel and the Kurds, contingency planning in the Gulf, and preventing Iran from joining a future oil embargo against the West. A freeze on oil prices was the best deal he could get if he was to keep his other balls in the air. But the Shah continued to spring surprises on him. In early December the Lebanese weekly magazine *Hawadess* published an interview with the Shah in which he hinted "at a possible shift of Iranian policy toward closer alignment with moderate Arab governments on the Arab-Israeli conflict." According to *Washington Post* columnists Evans and Novak, a transcript of the interview "rushed to high officials [in Washington] via official cable from Beirut" indicated the Shah had delivered a threat to the Israelis: "Either Israel accepts the implementation of the United Nations resolutions or there is no alternative to war. Of course, it will be our war. We support the Arab view because the Arabs became a victim of foreign occupation."

Our war? The Shah had lately become enamored of President Anwar Sadat and had agreed to pay a state visit to Egypt in the new year. The Sadats and the Pahlavis subsequently became good friends and the Shah began to entertain the notion of an Iran-Egypt axis in the Middle East. The Shah made other comments in the interview that raised eyebrows back in Washington. He stressed that American military intervention in the Middle East to smash OPEC was "unthinkable as long as oil-producing countries maintained their cohesion." He criticized the Ford administration for failing to provide Egypt with more aid. Perhaps most intriguing was his prediction that "Iran needs only six or seven years to become a military power capable of defending the region." By 1980, implied the Shah, Iran would be off the leash for good and could stand up to any great power or aggressive neighbor.

The Shah's interview "is causing high-level consternation inside President Ford's national security apparatus," reported Evans and Novak.

> Until now the leader of the Middle East's most populous and powerful country had dealt with Israel on special, almost intimate terms. But the Shah's latest pronouncement last weekend warned that the special relationship was coming to an end. . . . While devoid of overtly nasty anti-Israel rhetoric, it raises serious alarms considering the multibillion-dollar American arms sales to Tehran and Washington's policy of depending on Iran for western defense of oil-rich Persian Gulf and northern approaches to the Soviet Union.

The Israelis were puzzled and then concerned by the Shah's wooing of the Arab world's most powerful leader, with whom they were still technically at war. On Monday evening, December 23, Kissinger met with Israeli ambassador Simcha Dinitz and Mordechai Shalev, a minister attached to the embassy. It was Dinitz who turned the discussion around to the Shah: "But there is another visit to Egypt—the Shah's. Do you know anything?"

"*The Christian Science Monitor* says he will offer arms," prompted Shalev.

"It is inconceivable that he would do it without consulting us," Kissinger confidently assured them. Dinitz agreed but sought direction on how to respond.

"No, let me handle it," Kissinger assured him. "I will tell the Shah. He is an admirer of mine."

The Kissinger-Dinitz conversation was troubling for several reasons. Neither the United States nor the Israeli governments, both of which enjoyed close ties with Tehran, knew the Shah's long-term strategic objectives nor had specific intelligence about Iran sending guns to Egypt. Over the past couple of months Henry Kissinger's excuses for justifying the Shah's oil and arms policies had been undermined by the Shah's own words and deeds. By now it should have been abundantly clear that the Shah was pulling away from Washington to pursue a foreign policy based on independent nationalism, as Ardeshir Zahedi had been advocating since the late 1960s. Years earlier the CIA had warned that as the Shah became more assertive the chances would increase that Iranian foreign policy goals would diverge from those of the United States. Whereas Saudi Arabia was making inroads in Washington, Iran was increasingly identified as a source of tension and instability. Kissinger's boast that the Shah was his admirer only added to the surreal nature of his exchange with Rabin.

Anxious to restore momentum to U.S.-Iran relations, in December Kissinger and Zahedi agreed that His Imperial Majesty should make a state visit to Washington in May 1975 as part of his tour of the Americas. Much would be riding on the success of the visit and the secret deal on oil prices that Kissinger and the Shah had worked out in Tehran the previous month. The Shah had agreed to a price freeze for one year. Kissinger had not yet told the president what he had agreed to do for the Shah in return.

Chapter Eight

POTOMAC SCHEHERAZADE

"You heard the Shah sold out the Kurds?"

—Prime Minister Yitzhak Rabin, 1975

"Tehran continues to be worrisome from the standpoint of security."

—Under Secretary of State Roy Atherton, 1975

LET'S TRY THE LOW-COST OPTION—WAR

By January 1975 a degree of competition, however slight, was returning to the world oil market. The days of $17 spot prices were over. By February spot prices of $9.50 and $10 had been recorded for Persian crudes. The steep falloff in demand from recession-hit Western consumers meant that oil producers risked pumping oil into a softening market. Most OPEC members accepted the new reality and reduced their output to avoid flooding the market with cheap oil. They reduced their overall output from 30 million to 26 million barrels per day. Not everyone went along with the majority view. The Saudis announced they favored a modest price reduction over less output. King Faisal had no interest in propping up the Shah's market price and would have let prices drift back if he could. The new uncertainty in the market, with changing patterns of demand and supply, left Iran's economy exposed. In August 1974 the Shah had approved Iran's $69 billion Fifth Plan on the basis of an assured tight market that guaranteed consistently high levels of price and production. His biggest gamble yet, $30 billion in spending commitments against only $21 billion in government income, meant Iran was now running a giant deficit. OPEC's existing price structure was a firewall that the Shah had no choice but to defend at all costs—or risk the implosion of his revenue base.

In the United States, the downward pressure in the oil market in early 1975 offered a glimmer of hope but little consolation to the Ford White House. Over the winter the American economy experienced its most severe contraction since the Great Depression. President Ford was prepared to consider the Shah's under-the-table offer to buy Iranian crude oil at a discount because he faced his own domestic financial and economic crisis. "A sense of emergency engulfs Washington, as a recessionary U.S. economy spirals down faster than almost anyone had expected," reported *The Christian Science Monitor* in the first week of January. When building construction ground to a halt, labor leaders warned that "other segments of the economy are collapsing." The Department of Commerce reported that "the nation's output of goods and services declined by an estimated 7½% in the last quarter of 1974, the biggest annual drop since World War II." New car sales for December plummeted 26 percent and Detroit automakers shed seventy thousand jobs on top of the 300,000 workers already laid off. "With few exceptions, it was the bleakest New Year's since the cold winters following World War II," reported *Newsweek*. "In towns from Brest to Baltimore, long lines of the out-of-work waited patiently to sign up for their unemployment benefits."

President Ford's chairman of the Council of Economic Advisers, Alan Greenspan, wrote a memo to Vice President Nelson Rockefeller urging the White House to engage in some straight talk with the American people. The oil shock had altered the national economy. The halcyon days of the 1960s, when "the base of our society and the base of our economy were secure," and when the average American family "rarely had national or international problems affect their daily lives," were gone for good. Until now, Greenspan told Rockefeller, "Most of the world's problems were perceived as quasi 'soap operas' narrated by Walter Cronkite. . . . Now the real world is beginning to press in on the average American and could very well devastate family life and standards of living if we do not confront our longer-term problems and protect the United States from the ever increasing dangers to which it is becoming exposed." America had to confront its addiction to oil. "The immediate problem is oil," Greenspan advised, "although I would list our national defense posture and fiscal erosion as equally critical. It is important for the American people to understand how the oil crisis emerged, what it is and what are its potential consequences worldwide if we do not come to grips with it."

The pressure on the White House to jolt the economy back to life before the president ran for election in 1976 was intense. A Louis Harris poll showed that 86 percent of Americans disapproved of Ford's handling the economy. "We are in trouble," Ford conceded to a nationwide television audience on January 13, 1975. "But we are not on the brink of another Great Depression." Early on in his administration, Ford had recalled Donald Rumsfeld from his post as ambassador to NATO in Brussels and assigned him the task of restoring order to a West Wing split between Ford loyalists and Nixon's holdover barons Kissinger, Schlesinger, and Simon. The new forty-two-year-old chief of staff hired as his deputy Richard "Dick" Cheney, thirty-four, an earnest conservative from Wyoming who had first worked for him in 1969. "They're like two peas in a pod," sniped one colleague, and their way of doing business was likened to a German panzer "blitzkrieg." "Mr. Rumsfeld has been accumulating power at a dizzying pace," observed *The New York Times*. "[Rumsfeld] has complete and total control over the White House," complained one Ford aide. "He has command over things big and little and decides who eats in the White House mess, who gets a White House car, and now has even decided that the carpenter shop should stop framing pictures for White House people." Rumsfeld never denied harboring presidential ambitions of his own and at times seemed to be practicing for the role. On one occasion reporters from the *Chicago Tribune* interviewed President Ford in the Oval Office and asked him "who his next Cabinet change might be." The president sat mute as a smiling Rumsfeld answered for both of them: "I never discuss Cabinet changes." Ford quickly changed the subject.

Bill Simon walked into Rumsfeld's rifle sight in late December 1974 when the president convened a two-day summit of his economics and energy advisers at Vail, Ford's favorite getaway. The first family was spending the Christmas holidays at the luxury ski resort. Ford was under mounting pressure from conservative Republicans, and especially from former California governor Ronald Reagan, not to add to the national deficit by spending his way out of the recession. Simon and Arthur Burns, the Fed chief, made the case against a big fiscal stimulus. They wanted to keep federal spending under control and prevent the deficit from going over $20 billion. Budget Director Roy Ash and Ford's political advisers took the opposing view. Driven by more practical concerns—such as the president's election—they were eager to kick-start the economy to prevent even higher job losses. Bill Simon also fiercely resisted the Kissinger-Shah proposal to establish a floor price of $8 for a barrel of oil. Kissinger's viewpoint was represented at Vail by Under Secretary of State Thomas Enders, a man not known for his humility, and he soon got into it with the treasury secretary.

"That proposal set off the angriest debate at Vail, so intense that the president had to admonish officials not to interrupt each other," with Simon "denouncing [the idea of a floor price] as a sop to oil companies and politically impossible." Kissinger knew he couldn't sell the idea without pitching it as beneficial for American workers and business interests. In his public statements and later to members of Congress, he avoided all mention of how the floor price would help Iran's economy. Instead, he informed them that the measure

> would protect American domestic production. We must protect domestic production by tariffs or a floor price or some other mechanism. . . . If the international price drops below the domestic price then our domestic producers will be badly hurt. If OPEC uses economic warfare, dropping the price that low, it would make us more dependent on them and wipe out our investment in alternative sources. Then they would raise the prices again and we would be more dependent on them than ever.

When details of the talks at Vail appeared in the press, Rumsfeld and Kissinger blamed Simon for leaking them and struck back hard. Reports circulated that President Ford was "irritated" with his Treasury secretary. Reporter Helen Thomas predicted that Bill Simon was "expected to leave the Cabinet soon." Columnist Joseph Kraft, who was close to Kissinger and a staunch admirer of the Shah, dismissed Simon as someone with the temperament and skills "of a Wall Street bond trader. . . . He has been the prisoner of a theology which sees market forces as totally benign and government as evil. In the interests of driving inflation from the market, he has repeatedly fought against government programs designed to ease recession. Time after time he has gone public in ways embarrassing to the administration." Kraft went so far as to publish a list of names "who would add distinction to the Cabinet and bring new competence to the Treasury."

With Bill Simon's future hanging in the balance, a great clamor arose from the conservative free market wing of the Republican Party against the president's deficit spending plan and in favor of keeping Simon on. Ronald Reagan, Arizona senator Barry Goldwater, and Senator James Buckley of New York rallied to provide Simon and the budget hawks with cover. Arthur Burns also intervened on his colleague's behalf. He told Ford that changing the guard at Treasury in the midst of the worst financial crisis since 1929 would be sheer "folly." With his right flank protected, Simon called Ford's bluff and in effect dared the president to fire him. "I am the chief economic spokesman for the President," he declared. "If I am on the way out I have not been told." Ford backed down, issuing a statement in which he said that Simon enjoyed his confidence and would stay at his post. This episode inoculated Simon against further attacks from his cabinet rivals. It also diminished Ford's stature and emboldened his GOP critics.

High oil prices had exposed deep cleavages within the Ford administration and ideological rifts within the conservative movement. Yet if there was one thing everyone agreed on, it was the need to break OPEC. How to do that became the subject of intense debate in the White House. High oil prices were "upsetting the established routine," recalled James Schlesinger. "And the failure of the United States to crack the whip meant that the whip hand on such matters was passing away from the United States." Ten days before the meeting in Vail, from December 14 to 15, 1974, the president's men had retreated to Camp David to take a second look at the idea of sending the Marines into the Persian Gulf. At one point the conference participants, having been informed that by 1985 oil producers would have monetary reserves of $1.2 trillion at their disposal, read a note attributed to Frank Zarb that said, "Let's try the low-cost option—war." Gallows humor or not, the sentiments expressed in Zarb's note reflected the belief among U.S. officials that time was running out to offer relief to financial markets, the banks, and flailing allies in Europe whose economies were tanking. In early January 1975 Kissinger made headlines around the world when he told *BusinessWeek* that although the use of force was "a very dangerous course," the United States was prepared to use all available means "to prevent strangulation of the industrialized world."

Pressure on the White House to move decisively on the military front came first and foremost from the outriders of the conservative movement, the neocons who advocated boots on the ground in the Middle East to secure America's oil lifeline and the outright seizure of Saudi oil fields. Most neoconservatives were disillusioned liberals turned right-wing policy mavens, though not all became Republicans. The most prominent neoconservative on Capitol Hill was Democratic senator Henry "Scoop" Jackson, a determined critic of Nixon and Kissinger's policy of détente with the Soviets and a passionate defender of arms sales to Israel. In January 1975 the neoconservative journal *Commentary* published a lengthy essay that considered the question of military intervention. The author proposed the outright seizure of the long strip of Persian Gulf coastline that extended from Kuwait down to Qatar and that held 40 percent of world oil reserves.

It supposedly would be a logistical cakewalk because of the area's lightly populated desert terrain, which ruled out the danger of a second Vietnam. If the Soviet Union tried to stop an American invasion of the Gulf by making a southward thrust from its proxy Iraq down into Kuwait, the author's solution was for the United States to take Kuwait for itself.

The neoconservatives were on a roll and their opinions were shared by others in Washington as the energy crisis worsened. In March 1975 the current affairs journal *Harper's* published "Seizing Arab Oil," a lengthy and provocative essay by an anonymous author with the Latin name "Miles Ignotus," translated as "Unknown Soldier." A long-running parlor game ensued as to who the real author or authors might be. In his essay, Miles Ignotus called for a ten-year military occupation of Saudi Arabia's oil-rich eastern provinces. He predicted an easy victory for American firepower in the Persian Gulf with virtually no chance of a protracted guerrilla insurgency, sabotage of oil installations, or terrorism. Saudi oil fields, pipelines, port facilities, and airstrips could be seized with a force of just forty thousand men. The author of "Seizing Arab Oil" noted that the only country in the region capable of resisting a U.S. drive into the Gulf was Iran. His suggestion: buy the Shah's silence by offering up Kuwait on a plate:

> Then there is Iran. Iran could in theory do a great deal to oppose intervention. . . . Why not then discreetly ask whether the Iranians might be willing to "protect" Kuwait—and, incidentally, appropriate their oil. This oil would offset Iranians' loss of revenue on their own output as prices decline. To be sure, if the Iranians move into Kuwait the Russians may be tempted to invade northern Iran, but this would be a high-risk operation for the Russians, since Iran is already a protected area of the other superpower, the U.S.

The idea that the United States might be prepared to trade Kuwait to Iran in return for an American occupation of Saudi Arabia sounded farfetched. Yet it brought to mind something James Schlesinger had said to Henry Kissinger in early September 1973: "The Iranians could take Kuwait but not cross the Gulf." The *Harper's* essay took on new meaning when it turned out to have been the collective effort of several officials in the Department of Defense office responsible for developing contingency plans. To this day it remains a brilliant example of leveraging the mainstream media to conduct psy ops, psychological warfare, against an opponent—in this case the timid Saudi royal family, which still hesitated to challenge

Iran's oil pricing policy. The essay worked. "It has deeply shocked the upper echelons of the Saudi Government and King Faisal's royal family," reported *The Christian Science Monitor.*

King Hussein of Jordan came to the White House in the spring of 1975 and relayed a message of concern from the Saudi royal family. The Saudi cabinet had met in special session to discuss the article. "Prince Fahd [of Saudi Arabia] asked me to convey one thought directly to you," King Hussein told Ford. "He is still deeply concerned about reactions in his country to any statements about possible U.S. intervention regarding the Saudi oil fields. There was an extensive and severe public reaction to this, and he asks if you can do everything possible to hold the publicizing of these statements down."

"I don't think there have been any statements recently since the one made some time ago," said the president, an apparent reference to Kissinger's "strangulation" threat from January. The president had not read the *Harper's* article or been briefed on it.

"Prince Fahd is very sensitive on this issue," Kissinger explained. "In March there was an article in *Harper's* magazine by someone labeled as a defense analyst from a think tank. The article was written under a pseudonym and presented arguments for taking over the oil fields. It caused a severe reaction in Saudi Arabia."

Critics on the left and right of American politics were beginning to grasp the connection between high oil prices and arms sales to Iran. The conservative American Enterprise Institute think tank published a major critique of U.S. arms policy toward Iran that concluded "excessive" arms sales were feeding the Shah's appetite for higher oil prices and hurting America's national security interests. Arms sales to Iran gave the Soviets an excuse "to respond by providing Iraq with more modern equipment." Washington insiders noted that the foreword to the report was written by former Secretary of Defense Melvin Laird, stout defender of the Twitchell Doctrine and a longtime skeptic of the Shah. The AEI report urged placing "well-defined limits on further sales to Iran" because "if more weapons are bought then oil is the most likely source of new revenues for both arms and domestic projects."

The wall of secrecy around Nixon's secret arms and oil deals with the Shah was beginning to unravel. In December 1974, Representative Clarence Long, Democrat of Maryland, wrote to President Ford asking if it was true that President Nixon had expanded arms sales to Iran "without national security studies of the possible consequences." A month later *The*

Washington Post reported that indeed it *was* true, that neither the Nixon nor the Ford administration "has carried out a major National Security Council study of where the Persian Gulf arms race might lead 10 years from now, as is usually done with crucial issues." One of Kissinger's aides offered the rather startling excuse that the secretary of state viewed the sale of military equipment as "basically tactical, immediate foreign tools," that he did not want to be tied down "to a hard policy that could come out of a study." The *Post* quoted an unnamed Pentagon official who conceded, "There is no policy limit on the dollar amounts of what the Shah can buy." A second expert was asked what would happen if the Shah used his weapons to "supersede, or erase, American influence" in the Persian Gulf and West Asia. His response was hardly reassuring: "Then we'd lose our gamble."

THE SHAH NEEDS THE MONEY

Kissinger initially designated George Shultz, Nixon's former treasury secretary, as his back channel with the Shah to discuss the terms of their bilateral oil deal. Shultz was now the president and director of Bechtel Corporation, an engineering firm that specialized in building nuclear power plants, dams, subway lines, and in the case of Saudi Arabia an entire industrial city. The Bechtel connection meant that private commercial motives were now entangled in the administration's handling of sensitive policy discussions with the Shah concerning oil prices and nuclear energy, and specifically nuclear enrichment. Kissinger viewed the Shah's nuclear ambitions, as he did oil prices and arms sales, in purely tactical terms. Shultz's Iran trip had the dual purpose of following up on the oil talks while selling the Shah on the idea of building a U.S.-based uranium enrichment facility. "Also, at our instigation, approaches have been made by the Bechtel Corporation to Iran to encourage the Shah's investment (on the order of $300 million) in a private uranium enrichment plant to be built in the United States," Kissinger was reminded by an aide in December 1974. The administration calculated that if the Shah went ahead and acquired half his nuclear power program from the United States, the equivalent of between six and eight nuclear power plants, the United States stood to earn $6.4 billion in revenues. On top of that staggering sum, if the Shah followed through on his commitment to cover the costs of 20 percent of a privately run U.S.-based enrichment plant, the U.S. government stood to reap an additional $1 billion in receipts.

A nuclear deal consummated between the United States and Iran would be the crowning achievement in Kissinger's ambitious plan to recycle Iranian petrodollars and integrate the two countries' economies. He knew that Iran, as a signatory to the Nuclear Non-Proliferation Treaty, was "obligated to place *all* its nuclear facilities under IAEA [International Atomic Energy Agency] safeguards and to refrain from acquiring peaceful nuclear explosives." Yet Kissinger was also explicitly warned by his advisers that pursuing a nuclear accord with Iran carried with it a potential for conflict later on. Failure to bridge differences between the two governments over the handling of nuclear fuels "could have serious, as well as long-term, adverse effects in our relations. . . . Should we not be able to resolve our differences the shah is likely to view our unwillingness to treat Iran as we have other NPT parties as a reflection on Iran's stability and the integrity of its commitments as well as an indication that the U.S. cannot be relied upon because of the uncertainties of our political process." Indeed, the Shah might conclude that he should look elsewhere for nuclear fuel suppliers who were "less cautious" than the United States.

Shultz was ushered into the Oval Office on February 7, 1975, to give President Ford, Kissinger, Brent Scowcroft, and Charles Robinson, the under secretary of state for economic affairs, a report on his talks with the Shah at the Pahlavis' ski chalet in Switzerland. "The Shah was very cordial and anxious to do what he could to be friendly," said Shultz. He had come away impressed with the Pahlavi king. "It was a beautiful setting in St. Moritz. We talked for an hour and a half. He is a broad-gauge, secure, and very impressive man." This conversation was Ford's first real exposure to the Shah as a man and as a leader. A transcript reveals he knew virtually nothing about him but was curious to learn more. "Where was he educated?" the president asked.

"In Switzerland," Kissinger interrupted. "He is very tough-minded."

Shultz explained that the Shah was offering to sell oil to the United States as part of a side deal. The two men had not discussed the number of barrels or price. But the Shah said Shultz wanted Ford to know that "the U.S. should regard Iran as her country in the Middle East. It is important to the United States that Iran develops—Iran is a western country. He places great value on the [U.S.-Iran] Joint Commission."

"I agree: he is profoundly a friend of the United States," Kissinger affirmed. "He is a cold-blooded realist. He needs the money and there is a level below which he won't cut the price." Kissinger explained that the administration was putting together a $10 billion program of investment with Iran that would be ready for the president's signature for when the

Shah came to Washington in May. He seconded Shultz's enthusiasm for the bilateral oil deal.

President Ford knew very little about the Shah. He asked his age, and queried Kissinger on how the Shah had come to the throne. Kissinger, who was vague himself, explained that "His father or grandfather, was a sergeant," and that "[the Shah] took over as a very young man and was kicked out by the leftist Mossadegh. Then Mossadegh was overthrown with CIA help, and the Shah was put back on the throne. He runs the country himself. He is a total autocrat, but a man with a global vision. He is convinced that we can't fight another Middle East war from our basic structures. So he is thinking of buying some 747 tankers to help us. He is a good friend of the United States except on oil pressures. He can't afford to cut his oil production because he needs the income. If we shifted some of our imports from Saudi Arabia to Iran, we could increase the pressure on Saudi Arabia."

"The price of oil is likely to erode," Shultz confidently predicted. "A buyers' market is returning. Bilateral deals are an indication of weakness."

From the outset there were questions about the legality of the United States buying oil under the table from a foreign government. "It was a tough issue because the U.S. government buying oil from another government and redistributing it to the private sector was an entirely different arrangement to the marketplace," recalled Frank Zarb, Simon's successor as chief administrator of the Federal Energy Administration. Red tape hadn't stopped Henry Kissinger before. But in Washington's brave new post-Watergate era the merest whiff of illegality would be enough to ignite a political and media firestorm. President Ford asked Zarb to evaluate the merits of the deal. Consider every angle. Don't rush into anything. Above all, it had to make sense from a financial point of view. "My take on all of that was that [President Ford] really wanted to determine whether it was feasible, whether the economics would work, whether we would get behind it and find a way to get this oil at a discount to OPEC, thereby putting some pressure on OPEC, probably creating a little strain between Iran and the rest of OPEC," Zarb recalled. "And if it looked like it was doable from an economics and logistical standpoint then pursue the legal questions. I did raise it with the president and I told the president there was no legal authority to do this and I was concerned with newspaper leaks."

Ford still enjoyed close ties with legislators on Capitol Hill and so he advised Zarb to quietly talk to Senator Henry Jackson and Representative John Dingell, the Democrats who oversaw his agency. This would ensure "we had air cover from those two guys as we were pursuing [the deal],"

Zarb recalled. "The last thing I wanted to do was to be sitting in Tehran and have this hitting the newspapers and have an uproar on the Hill. So the president authorized me to go tell them. And from that we got their protection. Not to do the deal but certainly pursue the numbers to see if it was doable." The irony for Kissinger was that one of Bill Simon's protégés would now be responsible for negotiating the terms of one of his secret deals with the Shah—a deal that held enormous significance for both men.

Over the next eighteen months Zarb held meetings with Hushang Ansary, the Shah's minister of finance, in a variety of settings, including London, Paris, and Tehran. Although he was not introduced to the Shah during this period, "I was in the same room with him at one point." Ansary, he remembered, "was a perfectly good negotiator. Very smart. He clearly had the ear of the Shah." But Kissinger was unhappy with his colleague's tough negotiating stance. Zarb never understood why the talks dragged on for month after month with no resolution in sight. "There was a great deal of stress over this transaction," he remembered.

In late February 1975 Kissinger traveled to Zurich to pursue the oil deal and other matters with the Shah. It was a meeting that garnered a great deal of media interest. Everyone wanted to know if Kissinger would leave with a commitment by the Shah to lower oil prices. The world economy hung in the balance. Both men relished the drama of the moment. The Shah interrupted his ski vacation at St. Moritz to fly in by helicopter. Onlookers described him as looking tanned from weeks of skiing in the Alps. Kissinger was thirty-seven minutes late to the hotel where they retreated behind a wall of security. "Swiss police patrolled the airport and the streets of the city," reported *The Washington Post*. "Police were stationed five feet apart along the roadway to the hotel."

At the end of their talks Kissinger and the Shah held a press conference at which the Iranian leader confirmed he would not join a future oil embargo and that Iran would keep selling oil to Israel. "We have never boycotted anybody," declared Iran's king. "Once the tankers are loaded it is of no importance; we don't know where it goes." Kissinger regarded the Shah's pledge to keep Israel supplied with oil as the most important outcome of their talks. He was still trying to broker a disengagement agreement between Israel and Egypt that would allow the Israelis to pull back from their October 1973 forward positions on the eastern side of the Suez Canal. The Israelis were reluctant to withdraw because it would mean handing back the oil wells they had captured at Abu Rudeis in the Sinai in 1967. Oil was a strategic resource and also an important source of revenue for a country faced with a balance of payments gap estimated at between $200 and $400 million. The Shah's pledge meant the Israelis could no longer argue that leaving Abu Rudeis would hurt them militarily. A financial aid package put together by the United States would meanwhile offset their budget troubles.

Quite aside from the trade pact, the oil deal, and guaranteeing oil sales to Israel, Kissinger and the Shah discussed another matter in Zurich whose sensitivity required the utmost discretion: the future of the Kurdish operation in Iraq. As with everything Kissinger did, the Kurds became part of a bigger package deal, a carefully balanced piece of strategic architecture that, depending on one's viewpoint, resembled either a beautifully constructed Alexander Calder sculpture or a precarious house of cards.

On Tuesday, March 4, Kissinger brought good news to the Oval Office. He said that he and the Shah had discussed the bilateral oil deal and also a trade pact that included American nuclear reactors to Iran worth $12.5 billion over five years. "The Iranian stuff is going well," he explained. The Shah had agreed to sell the United States 500,000–700,000 barrels of oil a day at a price below the OPEC price, though tied to military purchases. "The oil deal will bring pressure on the price structure, because the purchasers will have to find where else they can make a cut of that size," said Kissinger.

Kissinger was getting too far ahead of himself in claiming success for a deal that had yet to be legally signed off on and whose technicalities had not yet been negotiated. Negotiator Frank Zarb began to question the finer points of the deal: it was beginning to resemble a straight oil-for-arms swap.

THE KURDS ARE BETRAYED

At midday, on March 9, 1975, Henry Kissinger was riding in the back of an official car with Syria's foreign minister, Ab al-Halim Khaddam. Kissinger was on a tour of Middle East capitals. He had flown in from Saudi Arabia, where King Faisal had confided to him that he was "frightened of being assassinated." The radical Arab tide exemplified by Syria's Hafez al-Asad, Libya's Qaddafi, and Iraq's Saddam Hussein was lapping at Faisal's front door. Kissinger told Khaddam that he appreciated the lavish welcome laid on by his hosts, especially the roadside flags that lined the route into the capital. "Why are all the flags up?" he said. "I appreciate it. You didn't have to do it." The foreign minister set him straight: "It's a national day."

It was the beginning of a very rough afternoon for the American delegation. Kissinger had flown to Damascus in an effort to persuade President Asad of the merits of joining the leaders of Egypt and Israel in signing a treaty to end hostilities. Three days earlier, at a summit meeting in Algiers, the Shah and Saddam Hussein of Iraq had met for four and a half hours and agreed to settle their differences. The Shah had agreed to turn off the CIA-backed Kurdish insurgency. Saddam Hussein reciprocated by making territorial concessions to Iran on the river boundaries at the mouth of the Persian Gulf. The Iraqi had also agreed to allow Iranian Shi'a pilgrims to cross the border to visit holy sites at Karbala and Najaf.

The Shah's decision to turn off the Kurdish operation was motivated by the need to ease tensions on Iran's northern border with the Soviet Union, Baghdad's ally. During the Shah's recent trip to Moscow, the Soviet leader, Leonid Brezhnev, had berated him for stoking superpower rivalries in the Gulf and meddling in Iraq, and slammed his fist down on the table. He specifically mentioned Iranian support for the Kurds in Iraq and challenged the Shah's military buildup in the Persian Gulf. The Shah was apparently affected by Brezhnev's blunt-force diplomacy and concluded that the Kurdish operation had outlived its usefulness. He had also concluded that the Kurds were losing ground and that Iran could not risk being drawn into open warfare with an Arab neighbor. The costs associated with the Kurdish operation now outweighed any possible benefits. Ardeshir Zahedi had opposed the operation from the outset. The Shah, he remembered, did not mince words when he "very plainly" announced his intentions to Kissinger in Zurich. He did not want any misunderstandings over the matter. What did Kissinger say in response? "He didn't say anything," remembered Zahedi. "His face went completely white."

Over the past three years the role of the CIA in Iraq had mainly consisted of providing the Kurdish leadership with psychological support. The $16 million the agency spent on the operation was a good-faith gesture to the Shah and to Kurdish leader Mustafa Barzani. A postmortem conducted by the U.S. House Select Committee on Intelligence concluded that the Kurdish leadership had always distrusted the Shah and relied heavily on American assurances provided by Kissinger. The United States "acted in effect as a guarantor that the insurgent group would not be summarily dropped by [the Shah]." U.S. participation in the Kurdish operation was seen as yet more recompense for the Shah's willingness to host CIA bases on Iranian soil. Right at the outset the CIA and Kissinger understood that the Shah would most likely trade in the Kurds if the opportunity arose to settle Iran's perennial border dispute with Iraq. From a CIA memo of October 17, 1972: "[The Shah] has apparently used [another government's] Foreign Minister to pass word to [Saddam Hussein] that he would be willing to allow peace to prevail [in the area] if [Saddam Hussein] would publicly agree to abrogate [a previous treaty concerning their respective borders]." A CIA cable from March 22, 1974, captured the cynicism of the whole operation when it described the Kurdish nation as "a uniquely useful tool for weakening [Saddam Hussein's] potential for international adventurism." Mohammad Reza Shah meant to stoke the conflict but not to the point where it might inflame Kurdish communities on the Iranian side of the border. "Neither [the Shah] nor ourselves wish to see the matter resolved one way or another," said the CIA.

For three years the Kurds fought. They endured thousands of casualties and tremendous suffering but were heartened by Kissinger's promises of protection. The secretary of state insisted they continue the struggle even when Saddam offered a path to peace. Kurdish leader Mustafa Barzani frequently told the CIA that although he distrusted the Shah, when it came to the United States "he trusted no other major power" and asserted that if his cause were successful he was "ready to become the 51st state." Barzani went to great lengths to show his appreciation to Kissinger and even sent him "a gift of three rugs and later on the occasion of Dr. Kissinger's marriage, a gold and pearl necklace." Congressional investigators uncovered a memorandum to Brent Scowcroft dated May 20, 1974, which explained the need to keep Barzani's gifts to the Kissingers a secret: "As you are aware, the relationship between the United States Government and the [Kurds] remains extremely sensitive. Knowledge of its existence has been severely restricted; therefore, the fact that Dr. Kissinger has received this gift should be similarly restricted."

In Damascus, President Asad told Kissinger that the Shah's decision to abandon the Kurds was proof that Iran was distancing itself from Israel and moving closer to the Arab world. Asad now saw no need to sign any sort of diplomatic bargain with Israel. He picked up on the theme of American impotence in the wake of Vietnam and Watergate. "In the long run we believe Americans will have to give up their support for Israel," he predicted. "We are not going to wait that long! But it's the natural thing: America has her interests. Because for a great power to stand by a little aggressor is not in the interests of America. We can quote examples—countries that America has stood by but circumstances forced America to stand aside and say goodbye to: Cambodia, Formosa, Turkey." Like Vietnam and Cambodia, which the United States was also abandoning, Israel would one day find itself cut loose. Even the Shah was losing faith in American power and American promises. "Again, generally speaking, the Arabs see the long run is favorable for their interests. And there are possibilities, military and economic. For example, yesterday the eradication of the problem between Iran and Iraq. Regardless of differences between Iraq and us, I regard it as a strategic victory for the Arab world."

"I agree with you," Kissinger admitted in what must have been a moment of intense discomfort.

Kissinger's long day wasn't over yet and the worst was yet to come. He flew directly to Jerusalem and the prime minister's residence for a late working dinner with Prime Minister Yitzhak Rabin, Minister of Defense Shimon Peres, and other top Israeli officials. Kissinger told them about Asad's confident prediction that "history is on the side of the Arabs," that it was just a matter of time before the Americans walked away from Israel the way they had discarded Taiwan, Cambodia, Vietnam, Turkey, and Portugal.

Questions about loyalty and betrayal were clearly on Rabin's mind that night: "You heard the Shah sold out the Kurds?"

"I told Yigal [Allon, Israel's deputy prime minister]; I told Simcha [Dinitz, Israel's ambassador to Washington] two weeks ago," Kissinger said.

"Yes."

"I warned the Shah against it and he did it anyway," said an embarrassed Kissinger. The collapse of the operation showed just how little influence he had in Tehran. "That was part of [Asad's] review of the international situation. He said the trends were in his favor. . . . He was sort of implying that there would be war between the Arabs and the United States. He said he could afford to lose 50 million [people] and we weren't, so they had an advantage. I got tough with him. He mentioned the Iran-Iraq agreement which frees the Iraqi strategic reserve. He said there were difficulties between him and Iraq but they could be bridged easily for the sake of anti-Israel."

The Israelis had until now relied on the Kurdish operation to keep Iraqi forces pinned down on the country's eastern frontier with Iran. With that pressure now relieved Saddam was free to move his troops and tanks to the west within striking distance of Israel. Israeli perceptions of trust, a matter of vital importance to a small country surrounded by hostile states, had been rudely violated.

"There are three events recently that are psychological political facts," Rabin explained to Kissinger. "First, the fact that the Shah took such a decision to agree with the Iraqis to sell out the Kurds. Though that is not known to the public, it's known to us. It has to be taken into account."

"I agree," said Kissinger. Under the circumstances he could say nothing else.

"If half our oil comes from him, if someone on whom we rely takes a whole different outlook here . . ." The other two points were a recent Palestinian terrorist attack in Tel Aviv and the injection of Syrian troops into parts of Lebanon under the control of Yasser Arafat's PLO. "Those are three completely new points," said Rabin. As he saw it, the Shah's decision to turn off the covert operation without first consulting him meant that he could not accept the Shah's guarantees to keep Israel supplied with oil in any future Arab-Israeli conflict. To do so would not only be foolish—it could be suicidal. And if Israel could not accept the word of an ally it could hardly accept the word of Anwar Sadat, whom it had gone to war against. The Abu Rudeis oil fields were not going anywhere. The deal was off.

Kissinger conceded that the Shah had introduced a dangerous element of uncertainty and distrust into the peace process. "Let me be fair. Let me be as honest as I can," he pleaded. "I'll give you my judgment, but my judgment has to include the possibility of Sadat's changing course in the future. What the Shah did, he's capable of doing. . . . I was shaken too by the Iranian decision. Because we had participated in it too. The brutality of it."

In the hill country of Iraq the slaughter was already underway. The day after the Shah sealed their fate in Algiers, Saddam Hussein launched a surprise attack that overwhelmed the Kurdish resistance. On March 10 Mustafa Barzani issued a frantic appeal to the CIA for help: "There is confusion and dismay among our people and forces. Our people's fate in unprecedented danger. Complete destruction hanging over our head. No explanation for all this. We appeal you and USG [United States Government] intervene according to your promises and not letting down ally, to save [Barzani's] life and dignity of our families, to find honorable solution to our problem." The CIA station chief followed up with his own plea to headquarters for something to be done. "Is headquarters in touch with Kissinger's office on this; if USG does not handle this situation deftly in a way which will avoid giving [the Kurds] the impression that we are abandoning them they are likely to go public. [The Shah's] action has not only shattered their political hopes; it endangers thousands of lives." After asking for some sort of intervention the station chief concluded, "It would be the decent thing to do."

Barzani also wrote to Kissinger. The lights were going out all over Iraqi

Kurdistan. His people were being butchered. He still had no idea that Kissinger had known for two weeks about the Shah's intention to betray them yet had given no warning. Barzani plaintively wrote that "our hearts bleed to see an immediate by product of their agreement is the destruction of our defenseless people in an unprecedented manner as [Iran] closed its border and stopped help to us completely and while [Iraq] began the biggest offensive they have ever launched which is now being continued. Our movement and people are being destroyed in an unbelievable way with silence from everyone.... Mr. Secretary, we are anxiously awaiting your quick response and action and we are certain that the United States will not remain indifferent during these critical and trying times."

Barzani never heard from Kissinger. "No reply has been received from Secretary of State Henry Kissinger to the message from [Barzani]," the CIA station chief cabled the State Department on March 15. He described scenes of "acute anxiety" among Kurdish leaders who sought an extension of the cease-fire and "the peaceful passage of . . . refugees to asylum. . . . Hence if the USG intends to take steps to avert a massacre it must intercede with [the Shah] promptly." The Ford administration made no effort to rescue the Kurds or extend humanitarian aid to the 200,000 refugees who poured over the border into Iran. Even when the Shah forcibly repatriated forty thousand Kurdish women and children to Iraq, where they awaited almost certain incarceration, torture, and mass murder, "the United States Government refused to admit even one refugee into the United States by way of political asylum even though they qualified for such admittance" concluded a congressional probe. Asked later by congressional investigators to justify his inaction Kissinger delivered a cynical answer that said more about his methods than any memoir ever could: "Covert action should not be confused with missionary work."

The Algiers accord between Iran and Iraq had two other major consequences. Kuwait was left pitifully exposed to its neighbor's predations. On March 19, Kuwaiti ambassador Salem al-Sabah met privately with President Ford. Kissinger's absence may have encouraged him to speak with a greater degree of candor than usual. Iraq laid claim to Kuwaiti territory and its oil. The ambassador feared that Saddam Hussein was sharpening his knives with a view to heading south. "It's like the wolf and the lamb," the envoy told Ford. "They still have their eyes on us. With the Kurds problem solved, they may turn their eyes to the south . . . So it is a little distressing over the long run."

The Algiers accord also led to blowback for the Shah. As part of the agreement Saddam Hussein would permit Shi'a pilgrims from Iran to cross into Iraq to visit Shi'a holy places. If the Shah thought this gesture would bolster his standing at home among the clergy he was sadly mistaken. Many of the faithful sought out Ayatollah Khomeini, who was living in exile in Iraq. "People knew about Khomeini," said Ambassador Richard Helms. "This was particularly true after the Algiers Agreement of 1975, when Iranian pilgrims were again permitted to visit the holy shrines in Iraq at Karbala and Najaf. Some pilgrims brought tapes back from Khomeini, and one began to hear reports of their being played in the mosques and circulated clandestinely. So that as a political factor, people were aware of him."

THE IDES OF MARCH

In March 1975, from Lisbon to Saigon, American power was in retreat. The collapse of Kissinger's peace shuttle in the Middle East raised the prospects of another armed conflict and oil embargo. In Europe, Portugal went to the brink of civil war when opponents of the left-wing government mounted a coup attempt. Communist guerrilla fighters launched offensives against the U.S.-backed regimes in Cambodia, South Vietnam, and Laos. At the end of the month the world's attention swung back to Saudi Arabia. On the morning of March 25, King Faisal and Sheikh Zaki Yamani were welcoming a visiting delegation of Kuwaiti officials. A Saudi television crew filmed what happened next. As the king was greeting his guests with the traditional salutation, his American-educated nephew Prince Faisal ibn Musad Abdel Aziz rushed forward, pulled out a revolver, and fired three rounds, each bullet striking the seventy-year-old monarch in the head—one severed the king's jugular vein. Mortally wounded, King Faisal crumpled to the floor in a pool of blood while palace bodyguards lunged at the assassin, whose eyes were now trained on Yamani. The guards wrested the revolver from the young man's hand. King Faisal was quickly succeeded by his brother, Crown Prince Khalid, with Prince Fahd exerting real authority behind the scenes. The speed and ease with which the brothers assumed power reassured Washington and Tehran that this was a random act of violence and not a radical coup. Yet although young Prince Faisal had a troubled past he was not the "mentally deranged" killer portrayed by Saudi authorities. While living a bohemian existence in California and Colorado he had been arrested for conspiracy to sell LSD and become involved with an assortment of radical left-wing and anti-Zionist groups. The prince was haunted by the execution of his older brother, Khaled, whose embrace of fundamentalist Islam had led him years earlier to launch a terrorist attack against a television transmitter in Riyadh. When he returned to Saudi Arabia Prince Faisal embraced conservative Islam, shunned contact with members of the royal family, and proudly refused to accept the royal stipend offered to all male members of the royal house. His decision to assassinate the king was an act of vengeance against the throne and a bid for martyrdom. He got his wish. The young prince was beheaded in public and his head placed on a stake in Riyadh's town square before a large crowd.

"An extraordinary conjunction of forces shook the world last week," commented *Time*, "a historic seven days in March that saw the decline of old hopes and the rise of new dangers." It was a month that irretrievably damaged the mystique of Henry Kissinger's diplomacy. The romance of his personality wouldn't work now. He knew it too. "Our Middle East policy has been smashed," he bitterly lamented to Max Fisher, a prominent leader in the American Jewish community and back channel to Israeli leaders. Kissinger blamed Israel and American Jewish groups for sabotaging his shuttle mission, conveniently forgetting that the Shah's abandonment of the Kurds had destroyed Israeli faith in promises of oil and security. "I have to tell you as a friend—the failure of this negotiation is the worst disaster since the Yom Kippur War [October War], not because of what we will do but because of what will develop," he told Fisher. "We have lost control."

"American foreign policy has not since the early days of the cold war had at the edges so many actual or threatened losses, so many intractable and unresolved problems, and so much reason for anxiety about some of these problems as today," wrote Joseph Harsch in a lucid analysis published by *The Christian Science Monitor*. "For the President and his Secretary of State, the Ides of this March are certainly not propitious. To keep it all in perspective it must be remembered that except for the political deterioration in Portugal these troubles lie around the outer fringes of American interests and influence, not the center. But there are plenty of them. They have piled up in the short span of three weeks." Harsch blamed the Nixon Doctrine for what amounted to a systemic collapse of American power on the edge of empire:

> Essentially the Nixon Doctrine contemplated a fallback of American power from the mainland of Asia, and reliance everywhere on air and sea power rather than land power. But this process of going over from a forward to a defensive national strategy is extremely difficult to execute. It means distress around the fringes. The loss of one client makes

all others uneasy. On the frontiers, no one can be quite sure where the contraction is going to end. If Washington lets Cambodia and Vietnam go, who else might be abandoned?

It was a question that held obvious—and ominous—implications for Mohammad Reza Shah Pahlavi. American foreign policy was in crisis and Kissinger's realist approach was coming under sustained attack from the right by the likes of Senator Henry Jackson, and his brash young aides, Richard Perle, Elliott Abrams, and Paul Wolfowitz. The neoconservatives argued that the Shah's decision to abandon the Kurds dealt a blow to Israel's security. Jackson wrote to Kissinger on March 22 demanding that the Ford administration reopen its decision to sell nuclear reactors to Iran. The Shah's foreign policy, said Jackson, showed a lack of "reliability and continuity." For that reason Iran had forfeited the right to be treated as an unconditional ally worthy of American support: "Such transactions as the transfer of a sizable nuclear power production capability, with its plutonium byproduct, need to be assessed in light of disturbing evidence that . . . Iran is capable of policy shifts so precipitous as to border on the quixotic."

The tensions spilled over to infect relations between the Iranian and Israeli leaders. When Senator Jacob Javits telephoned Kissinger to ask whether it would be all right for him to bring the Israeli ambassador to Kissinger's forthcoming luncheon in honor of the Shah, the secretary thought not: "Well, I think not, frankly. The Israelis have antagonized him by accusing him about the Kurds."

U.S. relations with Iran were also indirectly affected by Ambassador Helms's mounting legal troubles back home. Congress had launched a sweeping investigation into allegations that the CIA had tried to sabotage democracy in Chile in the early 1970s. Investigators suspected that Helms had lied to senators during his February 1973 ambassadorial confirmation hearing when he denied knowledge of agency dirty tricks in Chile. The ambassador was recalled from Tehran thirteen times over eighteen months to give one hundred hours of testimony to Senate and House investigators. "In those days, if the weather and flight connections were perfect, the trip from Tehran to Washington, with a change of aircraft in London, averaged from seventeen to eighteen cramped, chairbound hours in the air," Helms recalled. The ambassador's legal problems and heavy travel schedule prevented him from focusing on his work in Iran. In April he broke down outside Vice President Rockefeller's office when he spotted a crowd of waiting reporters, including Daniel Schorr, the journalist who had first reported the CIA plots. "You sonofabitch!" Helms shouted before a crowd of startled onlookers. "You killer! You cocksucker! 'Killer Schorr'—that's what they ought to call you!"

On the eve of the Pahlavi state visit to Washington in May 1975 President Ford received an extensive briefing paper from his secretary of state outlining the history of U.S. Iran relations. It offered a rare window into Kissinger's knowledge of the Shah's intentions and what he knew about conditions inside Iran. The memo included a frank admission of U.S. arms policy toward Iran though with caveats that had not been included in the original policy adopted three years before. "After President Nixon visited Tehran in May 1972," wrote Kissinger, "we adopted a policy which provides, in effect, that we will accede to any of the Shah's requests for arms purchases from us (other than some sophisticated advanced technology, armaments, and with the very important exception, of course, of any nuclear weapons capability . . .)." Ford was advised that although the Shah was in firm control at home, "student/intellectual unrest and a persistent terrorist movement are causes for concern." One of the regime's weak spots was the state of the Iranian economy: "Iran does face inflationary problems and shortages of skilled manpower and communications."

Kissinger was much less concerned about Iran's internal situation than with the Shah's restlessness, his foreign policy adventurism, and his growing belief that American power was waning and that Washington's assurances of support for allies like Iran were now in doubt. "He is worried about our ability to continue to play a strong world role, to retain a dominant position over the USSR in the Middle East and Indian Ocean, and to maintain close cooperation with Iran in the political, military, and economic fields." America had abandoned its gladiators in Taiwan, Cambodia, Vietnam, and Turkey—the Shah feared that Iran might be next, that "Congress and America may be moving toward isolationism." Kissinger told Ford that the Shah was a difficult but important ally: "He may have some excessive ideas of his importance and some people consider him arrogant, but there is no gainsaying the sharply rising economic and military strength of which he disposes." Within a few short years the Shah "will have the key, if not the controlling, role among the regional powers in helping to assure stability in the Persian Gulf area."

The briefing paper described bilateral tensions over oil policy and arms sales and an ally who did not like being second-guessed. "Closer to home, the Shah is upset by Congressional and American public criticism of Iran's oil pricing policies; widespread criticism in the U.S. of our military supply to Iran, now our largest foreign buyer of weapons; and problems in completing some major proposed deals with private American corporations." Kissinger advised the president not to antagonize the Shah by raising the issue of high oil prices. "I see little point in your trying to argue with the Shah that prices were raised too fast and too much, inasmuch as he is utterly convinced of the correctness of what was done and easily takes umbrage at suggestions to the contrary." This was remarkable advice to give a president whose political fortunes had fallen into the trough of an oil-induced recession. More than anything, Kissinger's advice confirmed just how little he grasped the intense political and economic pressures bearing down on Gerald Ford in the spring of 1975.

WE TOLD HIM WE WOULD SUPPORT
A PARATROOP OPERATION

At 9:45 on Thursday morning, May 15, President Ford and Secretary Kissinger were in the Oval Office waiting for the Pahlavis to arrive. Both men were physically and mentally drained by the events of the previous night. America's disastrous military involvement in Southeast Asia had ended a few hours earlier in one final, bloody convulsion when U.S. Marines rescued American merchantmen seized by Khmer Rouge gunboats from the freighter *Mayaguez* off the coast of Cambodia. Communist regimes had already been declared in Cambodia, Laos, and South Vietnam. President Ford hailed the air, land, and sea operation to liberate the crew of the *Mayaguez* as a crucial first step to restoring American prestige in the world. In reality, the operation reinforced the limits of American power and resulted in a near-fiasco that cost as many lives as it rescued. The *Mayaguez* episode is remembered today as the botched precursor to a second, riskier rescue mission—the ill-fated attempt to liberate U.S. diplomats held hostage in Iran in 1980.

As they waited for the Shah, Kissinger's remarks revealed his anxiety. He wanted Ford to impress the Shah, to talk to him the way Nixon used to. "Tell him you used more force than necessary," he urged the president. "The Shah is a tough, unemotional, and able guy. He has a geopolitical view.

"On the oil deal, he will do it if we can do it secretly," he reminded Ford. "We haven't figured out how to do that. One way would be to pay in non-interest-bearing notes, if we could do it secretly. He would prefer a swap of military equipment for oil, with high prices for the equipment. But we haven't figured that out." Then there was the whole issue of high oil prices: "I would go over the energy thing. He will slap you down, but it would be good." Kissinger also used those few minutes to inform Ford about U.S.-Iranian contingency planning in the Gulf. Contingency planning had not appeared in Kissinger's briefing paper because it was a secret oral agreement. Now Kissinger told him about it. Ford had no time to ask questions let alone digest what he was hearing. "Ask him about the Middle East," said Kissinger. "He is worried about Saudi Arabia. We told him we would support a paratroop operation in Saudi Arabia in a crisis. You could say you are aware of this contingency planning."

The Fords welcomed the Pahlavis on to the South Lawn of the White House with a twenty-one-gun salute and an honor guard. Across the street several hundred masked demonstrators gathered in Lafayette Park to chant slogans calling the Shah a puppet and murderer. While Betty Ford had tea with Empress Farah, the men retreated to the Oval Office for the first of two ninety-five-minute introductory sessions. Once again Kissinger cited protocol as the reason to block Ardeshir Zahedi from sitting in, and the ambassador was forced to wait in the Cabinet Room with other officials.

Ford, the Shah, and Kissinger began by reviewing the *Mayaguez* incident and the Middle East peace process. Brent Scowcroft, took notes. The Shah began by providing them with his customary overview of strategy and geopolitics. But this time his observations about Middle East politics revealed a troubling disconnect from the region's realities. He blamed Israel for the failure of Kissinger's peace shuttle. He claimed that the Syrians "don't like our rapprochement with Iraq." He was defensive on the subject of the Kurds: "I had to make a quick agreement on the Kurds. I have to say this in the face of all the press reports that I had abandoned them. They weren't fighting—we were." He said he had acted on the advice of the Egyptian, Jordanian, and Algerian leaders, who saw the accord as a way to weaken Russian influence in Baghdad. He was even convinced that the accord actually strengthened Kuwait's security because Saddam Hussein was now more likely to pursue a regional treaty for the joint defense of the Gulf.

Following King Faisal's assassination, the Shah had flown to Saudi Arabia to take the measure of the new generation of Saudi leaders. President Ford raised the issue of the contingency plan: "Henry told me what he told you we would do if there were a Qaddafi-like development in Saudi Arabia. I reaffirm it."

The Shah was pleased. He told his hosts that Egypt should also participate in an invasion scenario, though in a limited capacity. He predicted trouble in the region if the landing party was entirely non-Arab.

Now it was apparently Kissinger's turn to be surprised. The Shah was seriously proposing a joint Iranian-Egyptian invasion and occupation of Saudi Arabia. Not only that—he had apparently already given the idea a great deal of thought. He wanted his friend Anwar Sadat to share in the spoils of occupation. Contingency planning was rapidly evolving into something far more ambitious and extensive than Nixon and Kissinger had ever intended. One of the primary motivations behind sending blue suiters to Iran and to engage in contingency planning had been to *balance* Egyptian aspirations in the region. "I would worry about an Egyptian army in Saudi Arabia," said a wary Kissinger. "Political support is good; maybe a few troops."

That night the Fords hosted a white-tie state dinner for the Pahlavis.

The first lady had asked Ann-Margret, the star of *Bye Bye Birdie*, *Carnal Knowledge*, and lately, *Tommy*, to provide the after-dinner entertainment with a medley of song-and-dance numbers from her acclaimed Las Vegas show. "We picked her because the Shah of Iran likes pretty women," the first lady told reporters, apparently missing the implied innuendo. "And so does my husband."

The atmosphere inside the White House was elegant and subdued, like Scheherazade on the Potomac. "The Air Force String Players walked among the tables playing romantic melodies while dessert was served," recalled Cynthia Helms. The crowd formed a bobbing sea of low bows and deep curtsies around the royal couple and strained to get a glimpse of Shahbanou Farah, whom Washington wags playfully dubbed the "Shahbunny." In attendance at the Pahlavi state dinner were fixtures of the Washington establishment, the captains and kings of American industry, ambassadors, Hollywood stars and Broadway legends—Kissingers, Rockefellers, Rumsfelds, the Fords of Detroit and the Bloomingdales of Palm Springs. Bob and Dolores Hope were there, so too were Fred Astaire, Pearl Bailey, Dionne Warwick, Douglas Fairbanks Jr., and Andy Warhol, a favorite of the queen. Everyone was there, it seemed, except Bill and Carol Simon.

The Shah was back in the Oval Office the next day, Friday, at 5:30 P.M., for a second session with Ford and Kissinger. Kissinger was late to the White House meeting. While he was out of the room, Ford gingerly raised the taboo subject of oil prices. Politically, he had little choice; an American president could hardly avoid raising the subject of oil, with the so-called

Emperor of Oil, in the White House. The Shah did not bite. "I know you have a great knowledge here and look at the world picture," Ford told his guest. "We have to recognize the rights of the producers and they must see our problems. Any suggestions you have would be appreciated."

"This is a very important subject, Mr. President," the Shah answered. "The U.S., as champion of the Free World, almost doesn't have the right to let itself be dependent on the outside. As a matter of fact I will take up with Dr. Kissinger a swap."

"He has told me," said Ford. "It sounds like a fantastic arrangement."

"Yes," said the Shah. "But the United States has to be independent. So the oil price has to be equal to other forms of energy. In the meantime, maybe a swap would work. It would not create petrodollars." The Shah had just told President Ford that he would not now be offering much if any price discount in return for the United States taking 500,000 and 700,000 barrels of oil a day off Iran's hands. The Shah wanted to swap oil for more arms. Kissinger walked in and the president updated him on what he and the Shah had just discussed.

The Shah had spent the day at Andrews Air Force Base inspecting planes carrying AWACS, airborne early warning and control systems. Each Boeing 707 cost $110 million and the Shah wanted to buy at least four or five of them. He also decided Iran's air force needed Fairchild A-10 attack bombers and more Grumman F-14 fighter jets. From there he helicoptered to the Pentagon for a talk with Secretary of Defense James Schlesinger. The Shah told Ford and Kissinger that he had raised with officials at the Pentagon "the matter of exorbitant price of spares, and leasing the C-5s."

Kissinger reminded the Shah, "We have to overcharge some way so you can send spares [on to third parties] and we replace them."

"On the grounds my technicians are using too many," the Shah concurred. "But your people must keep their mouths shut." Turkey was running so low on spares "they can't hold maneuvers. We need your people to keep quiet on the spare parts deal."

The second session drew to an end. Both leaders exchanged best wishes and pleasantries. "Thank you for inviting me here," said Mohammad Reza Shah. "I am grateful for establishing these personal contacts. We need you like the rest of the world needs you. Maybe we can be of some help." President Ford returned the compliment and thanked the Shah for gifts he had brought for himself and the first lady. "Henry has told me if I wanted to talk to someone who has an objective view of the world, it was you. I have confirmed that."

"I hope you win the election," replied the Shah and left the Oval Office.

The Shah held a farewell press conference at the Iranian embassy on Saturday afternoon, May 17. Tea and cookies were served. *The Washington Post*'s Sally Quinn thought the monarch looked very pleased with himself. "He posed for photographs, adjusted his cufflinks, swung his slightly elevated shoes, leaned casually back on the satin pillows of the sofa smoking occasional cigarettes, and brushed off tough questions with questions of his own," she recalled. It was quite a performance. The Shah was in the final stages of negotiating a $300 million deal in which Iran would lend Pan Am $245 million in return for board representation and a controlling stake in the airline's Intercontinental Hotel chain. Pan Am held a special place in the United States defense establishment. It was the largest U.S. flag contributor to the civil reserve fleet and the backup for the Air Force in case of a national emergency. Then the Shah dropped a bombshell. He announced that oil would have to go up in price again when OPEC met in September. "We have lost 30 to 35 percent of our purchasing power because of world inflation," he complained. The Shah didn't mention a percentage amount for this new increase in price. That came two weeks later when the governor of Iran's central bank, Mohammad Yeganeh, announced that the Shah would push for a 30–35 percent oil price increase as direct compensation to Iran for its loss in purchasing power. As he surely knew, the world economy had still not successfully absorbed the price shocks of 1973. Another increase in oil prices of that magnitude would be not only excessive but frankly dangerous. It was a remarkable snub to the president who had just hosted him so generously.

The official kowtowing was too much even for newspaper columnist Joseph Kraft, who admired Kissinger and the Shah. In a column entitled "America Bows Low as the Shah Pays a Visit," Kraft severely criticized Kissinger for avoiding all discussion of oil prices during the Shah's visit. He argued that it was time for the Ford administration to put its foot down. "[The Shah] has embarked Iran on a vast program of economic and military expansion that depends heavily on American products, American expertise and American money, which he will soon have to be borrowing again," wrote Kraft, who knew nothing about Kissinger's secret arms and oil deals. "But you would never have heard it by what happened here last week. The Shah was feted in a well-nigh shameless way by the President, the Vice President and the secretary of state." Kraft said he had personally asked the Shah during his stay whether President Ford had raised the subject of oil prices. "Only casually," the Shah had replied. Kraft then asked the Shah whether he believed the Ford administration was prepared to live with the present price. "Not only live with the price, but accept further increases," the Iranian leader retorted. "The message that the Shah received from the bowing-down of American officials is the message the whole world will get," Kraft scolded the White House. The Ford administration "has no foreign economic policy. Positions are taken as a result of haggling among the White House, the State Department and the Treasury. The result is an appearance of jitteriness that will continue as long as the President depends so heavily on a secretary of state whose basic feeling about economic problems is that they should go away."

Kraft's brutal dissection of Kissinger's handling of U.S.-Iran relations was more than a case of friendly fire. Kissinger was losing the confidence of his realist admirers in the press. He seems to have understood at some level that the Shah's threat to hike prices another 30–35 percent unless the Ford administration found a way to help him shift Iran's stockpile of unsold oil amounted to blackmail.

WE'RE GOING TO HAVE ANOTHER BAD SITUATION

Each morning a car with an Iranian driver collected the two Air Force colonels from outside their homes in northern Tehran. On May 21, 1975, Colonel Paul Shaffer bid his wife and two children goodbye and climbed into the waiting car with his colleague Lieutenant Colonel Jack Turner, whose wife was getting their three children ready for school. Shaffer, forty-five, from Dayton, Ohio, and Tucker, also forty-five, from Carbondale, Illinois, both worked for the United States military mission in Iran. Security for Americans living in Tehran had deteriorated to the point where senior U.S. military officers and diplomats were assigned chauffeurs and bodyguards. Junior employees were shuttled back and forth from work in armor-plated shuttle vans whose bulletproof windows were sealed shut. The death toll in the ongoing antigovernment insurgency waged by extremist Muslim and leftist groups against the Pahlavi state was running upward of two hundred. In the past few weeks two government officials had been assassinated in the capital and nine young detainees shot in Evin prison. On that third Wednesday in May the capital was bracing for the Shah's return from Washington. The colonels' driver made the decision to avoid heavy traffic by turning onto a side street, and it was here that the three men came to grief. "A car blocked the path of their vehicle while another rammed it from behind," an embassy statement recorded. "Three gunmen surged out, shouted at the Iranian driver of the car to lie down and opened fire at point-blank range. Then they drove off in a third car, leaving a propaganda leaflet behind with the two dead officers in the bloodstained car." The murders were followed by the bombing of the American cultural center in Mashhad.

The attack on the colonels' car was in revenge for the extrajudicial executions at Evin. It made for quite a homecoming for the Shah and was a reminder of rising anti-American sentiment throughout Iran. Ambassador Helms initiated a broad review of security for Americans living in the capital. "There was concern on my part," recalled Ambassador Helms. "I felt that the American presence was getting too large. It was 10,000 when I arrived. I think at one time it got as high as 40,000 or more all through Iran. I felt this was wrong and unnecessary. I attempted to take actions to alleviate it." Iran was overloaded with men and matériel pouring in from the now defunct war theater in Southeast Asia and also from Turkey, where a U.S. arms embargo was in effect. "As things were closed down in Turkey there was great pressure to use Iran as a physical location for various kinds of equipment," recalled Helms. "And particularly during the latter two years I was there, I tried to fight these off. I thought it was a great mistake to put more assets, military or otherwise, into that country. There was too much there already in my opinion." The ambassador's efforts to reduce the American imprint in Iran never gained traction. "I did away with the Peace Corps," he insisted, even though the Peace Corps was one of the very few American governmental agencies to have earned the respect of the Iranian population. Its small staff of ten Americans managed 142 volunteers working on a variety of language training, urban planning, and community development projects. The closure of the Peace Corps was a purely symbolic act at a time when fifty retired military personnel arrived in Iran each month to take up employment as defense contractors.

The city of Isfahan, where Grumman and Bell Helicopter employees were stationed, was ground zero for the backlash against Americans in Iran. Iranians were especially shocked by incidents in which American citizens defiled Shi'a mosques. On one occasion in 1975 three American women wearing tight shorts and halter tops "strolled into the ancient Friday Mosque where, laughing, gesturing, and talking in loud voices, they toured the holy place in their own good time." In their off-hours, Bell helicopter crews "passed the time by drinking, fighting and even racing motorcycles into a mosque." American teenagers were seen racing motorbikes through another house of worship. It was hard to imagine similar scenes being played out in Catholic churches in San Antonio or Baptist churches in Oklahoma City. Women wearing chadors were accosted by American men in the streets. American defense contractors recently relocated from Saigon "had their own way of life," recalled one U.S. diplomat—some put their bargirl wives into business as prostitutes. An Iranian taxi driver was shot in the head by an American in a dispute over the fare. Iranians were referred to in their own country by Americans as "sand-niggers," "ragheads," and "stinkies." Muslim radicals spread rumors through the bazaars of Tehran: "Americans are desecrating mosques, insulting Iranian women."

"That's where Nixon and Kissinger went wrong," said former U.S. ambassador Armin Meyer. Meyer was one of the old Iran hands appalled by the scenes he witnessed when he visited the country in the mid-1970s. "They allowed thousands and thousands of Americans to come," recalled Meyer. "Isfahan became a fleshpot. All these helicopter crews were down there, some bringing in their Vietnamese prostitutes. In my judgment, this cultural issue was very much a contributing factor to the blow up in Iran." At the Pentagon, James Schlesinger was receiving alarming reports of similar outrages. American behavior in Iran was, he remembered, "a disaster area. Here you had these Americans in these bases, sort of semi-colonies, but they were behaving like Americans, women running around in bikinis, you had this Iranian population and particularly outside Tehran that was immensely conservative and the American behavior was just offensive to their sensibilities."

American nationals living in Iran experienced their own traumas. The State Department set up a hot line to help Americans suffering social or psychological problems or to help them deal with rampant drug use among American teenagers. Some families complained with good reason that they had been given just seven days' notice before being transferred to Iran. The culture shock they experienced upon arrival was in its own way as intense as that felt by their Iranian hosts. By 1976 Grumman was offering its employees classes in Farsi, and other corporations held orientation classes to help their employees assimilate. They set up buddy programs for new arrivals. But it was a case of too little, too late. "Companies started sending workers to Iran too fast," said Betty Chapman, who ran the Iran Resource Center in Los Angeles, which tried to help employees adjust to their new surroundings. "They gave them no preparation." The helicopter pilots employed by Bell believed that they were being unfairly cast as villains. They bitterly accused Bell of luring them to Iran with false promises of quality housing, schools for their children, and health insurance. The trouble began when the pilots threatened to form a union. SAVAK informers began sitting in on their meetings. Ambassador Helms refused to meet with the pilots and made it clear to them that his sympathies were with the Iranians. One Bell executive told a pilot's wife that the company regarded men like her husband as "much the same as migrant workers."

The conclusions of Embassy Tehran's security review were presented to Secretary of State Kissinger and senior State Department officials at their daily 8:00 A.M. staff meeting on July 7, 1975. Earlier in the week gunmen had shot and killed the driver of a U.S. embassy car in downtown Tehran after mistaking him for a CIA agent. "Well, in addition to Beirut, Tehran continues to be worrisome from the standpoint of security," said Under Secretary of State Roy Atherton.

> We've had a report that the embassy has identified 65 possible members of the mission [at risk from assassination]—mostly officers. It looks like surveillance by people who could be connected with the guerrilla group there. And they recently killed two medical officers, and it's an almost impossible situation totally to deal with because of the large American community—the fact that they're scattered all over town—the fact that they have to travel in certain very crowded groups, going back and forth to the office. That's why [Defense has] been sending out teams; sending out more equipment, armored vehicles. The Iranians have given help to the limit. They can't put a bodyguard on every American. It's almost inevitable that we're going to have another bad situation there.

Kissinger listened in silence to Atherton's presentation, which ended with a few words on India. The secretary limited his feedback to a single word: "So?"

Chapter Nine

HENRY'S WARS

"Greenspan is terribly worried about an OPEC price increase."

—President Gerald Ford, 1975

"The Shah is seeing French doctors."

—Richard Helms, 1975

IN SOME COUNTRIES WE CAN
EXPECT SOCIAL UNREST

The leaders of the Western industrialized democracies could be forgiven for assuming that the worst of the oil shock was behind them. Only with the benefit of hindsight was it apparent that the summer of 1975 was the eye of the hurricane. One year earlier, Treasury Secretary Bill Simon had urged President Nixon to confront the Shah over the high oil prices that he believed might fatally weaken the banking system and lead to a financial collapse. The recent slump in consumer demand for oil had not changed Treasury's estimation of the danger. Officials knew that many countries were staying afloat financially only with the aid of huge loans taken out from international lending institutions and private banks. At some point in the near future those loans and the interest on them would be due for repayment. It was no longer clear that the debts were recoverable. West Germany's chancellor, Helmut Schmidt, understood the dangerous shoals that had to be navigated before the world economy reached safe harbor. Schmidt was also deeply concerned about the opportunities economic dislocation presented for political and social instability in Europe. At the end of May 1975 President Ford met with Schmidt in Brussels to compare notes. Ford was cautiously optimistic about the prospects of an economic recovery. He told Schmidt that "all our economists—even those who don't agree with us—agree that we have largely bottomed out. There are substantially more good signs than bad signs. . . . The unemployment statistics, new orders, and so on, are good."

Schmidt wasn't buying it: "But orders being placed in Germany are dropping badly."

"Housing and autos are not doing well," Ford conceded. The president had been persuaded by Simon, Arthur Burns, and Alan Greenspan to squeeze inflation from the economy and not to prime the economy with a big spending stimulus. Ford noted that inflation had fallen from 10 percent to 6.5 percent: "But I'm afraid if we stimulate too much, we'd get a return of inflation."

Schmidt worried that Ford's austerity package might dampen economic growth and kill the green shoots of recovery before they had a chance to bud. "Your statistics are persuasive," he said, "but this is the greatest depression since 1932. And in some countries we can expect social unrest. I am deeply worried. 1975 is very different from 1932, but the behavior of the governments—trying to ride it out—could be similar. We can't use the methods of recent years for a situation that none of us have lived through. The situation has led to an enormous drop in real wages—which is unprecedented. This is happening in a monetary system of floating rates, which compounds every problem. I really don't know why this is happening. Japan is looking to New York. Britain is in a shambles." Schmidt offered the president the use of his country's "enormous foreign currency reserves and considerable gold. All this is at the service of the United States." He then conceded that his own efforts to prop up the ailing Italian economy were not working: "We did do something with the Italians, and they are close to losing their gold."

Schmidt's mention of the dread year 1932 was significant. The economic catastrophe of the last great global slump had undermined the foundations of German democracy and permitted Adolf Hitler and the Nazis to ascend to power. Schmidt's Social Democratic government was grappling with the next generation of extremist violence coming from young German fanatics. A month earlier members of the murderous Baader-Meinhof Gang had stormed the West German embassy in Stockholm and executed two diplomats. West German cities were rocked by fire bombings, violent protests, and a wave of assassinations targeting prominent business and political figures. Like Nixon and Kissinger, Schmidt was deeply troubled by what he saw as the historical parallels between the conditions of the mid-1970s and the mid-1930s. He wondered if he might not be witnessing the rise of a new form of toxic populist politics feeding off economic misery and weak leadership.

Schmidt and Ford met again in the German capital, Bonn, in July. The chancellor predicted that the critical period for the West would be the winter of 1976–77, "because if the economic situation improves, oil demand will rise." That in turn would put upward pressure on oil prices. Schmidt stressed the relationship between high oil prices and political instability throughout the free world. "The political effects of the recession—really a depression—threaten political stability in several countries—in Italy, where the Christian Democrats may accept the Communists in government," he said. "France also, where there is always a potential for domestic upheaval. The British problem is not social unrest, but strikes and paralysis. Here also, the problem is not upheaval, but bad election results. I don't know about Japan." Schmidt made it clear that no greater challenge faced the West than high oil prices: "The economic problems are a greater threat to the West than the Soviet Union, the Middle East, or Southern Mediterranean problems. Giscard [d'Estaing, the president of France] and I both feel that the strongest country—the U.S.—must take the lead. It is a dramatic situation."

I SOMETIMES WONDER IF HE IS REALLY, NATURALLY A TOUGH GUY

Future shock had already arrived in Iran in the form of an upsurge in religious-based political unrest and growing signs of economic crisis. By the summer of 1975 the world oil market was in a slump. Production was down from 84.9 million barrels a day to 64.9 million barrels a day. In the first half of the year Iran's oil production slid 12 percent, to 5.4 million barrels a day from 6.2 million barrels. The dropoff in June was 17.7 percent. Saudi Arabia reported a fall in production from 8.1 million barrels a day to 6.6 million barrels a day. Production fell by 27 percent in Kuwait and 41 percent in Libya. The problem for the Shah was that Iran's large population, heavy industry, and big spending made it much more vulnerable than Kuwait and Libya to even modest fluctuations in output and income. The dire projections of the Shah's economic advisers about the dangers of allowing billions of petrodollars to wash through the economy were borne out when the torrent retreated, leaving in its wake a floodplain of debt, double-digit inflation, and shortages of consumer goods. The government's own economic planners later conceded that the 270 percent increase in government oil revenues in 1974–75 propelled Iran down an "economic path toward the generation of malcontent and eventual revolution.... By 1975 the economy was out of control, and Iran was losing as a nation on two counts." Those two counts were inflation and "losing real resources (barrels of exported oil) as the cost of development projects soared."

The implications of declining oil revenues for Iran's balance of payments was already a source of concern for U.S. diplomats in Tehran. Iran's economy was hobbled by transportation bottlenecks and shortages of skilled labor. As anticipated, the country's ports, roads, railways, and airports were overwhelmed by the gyrations set in motion by the oil boom. Tankers and freighters arriving at Iranian ports waited on average 250 days to be unloaded. Longshoremen struggled to clear a backlog of 800,000 tons of goods. By one estimate 10 percent of the machinery and other capital goods lying on the docks and in warehouses were ruined by corrosion. Perishable goods were thrown into the harbor. The government was forced to pay $2 billion in demurrage to compensate shipping companies for the delays. When containers were eventually unloaded at dockside there often weren't enough trucks to move them. Ports resembled container graveyards with acres of rusted machinery and abandoned produce. Works of art purchased for the queen's collection "eventually turned up in a warehouse near the Tehran bazaar in unbelievably filthy condition.... Two massive bronzes by Henry Moore were found in vast packing crates said to contain road-working equipment." The government rushed to buy four thousand trucks; when the trucks arrived there were no drivers.

"The highways are choked, cracking from increased truck traffic, and being improved only slowly," reported the U.S. embassy. "Rather than bringing in all of the 721,000 workers which the country is expected to be short of during the Fifth Plan period ... the economy to a great extent will improvise relying on poorly trained Iranians, but thousands of foreign workers will continue to arrive monthly. These already are badly straining available housing and other facilities, and the worst is yet to come."

"The government had to scour the country to find 2,000 carpenters, masons and other Iranians to work on two nuclear reactors West Germans are building in southern Iran," said one American observer. "Where will they get people for future projects? And no power grids exist to carry the electricity by the nuclear plants to towns and cities. These grids will involve investment equal to, or greater than, the nuclear plants themselves."

"During the summer of 1975 Dick and I realized that there was a financial crisis," recalled Cynthia Helms. "Businessmen were complaining that they were getting only partial payment on contracts, and I was receiving telephone calls from Americans who said they were not being paid at all. By the end of the year the situation was worse, with many projects delayed." The flood of foreigners and rural migrants into the capital meant that housing was in short supply. A female World Bank employee sought refuge at the American embassy after two nights sleeping in a broom closet at the Hilton.

By now the folly of allowing unlimited arms sales to Iran was glaringly obvious. Over the summer of 1975 Embassy Tehran conducted an evaluation of the impact of U.S. arms sales on Iran's civilian economy. Although the Iranian government did not publish statistics related to purchases of military equipment, the embassy's economics analyst pointed out that Iran's balance of payments numbers "suggest that nearly one-half or $10 billion spent on imports during the Iranian year ending on March 10 went for military imports. Our own military sales data suggest that about half of this money was spent on U.S. equipment. Accurate data are lacking because much of Iranian expenditure is buried elsewhere in the budget, but current estimates for this year put total Iranian military spending at more than $10 billion or perhaps one-third of total GOI [Government of Iran] outlay." The report concluded that "serious damage is probably being done to the civilian economy." Only the fact that other sectors of the economy had reached their absorptive capacity prevented an immediate financial crisis. There had already been an "incalculable loss" to the Iranian economy because trained personnel worked in the military instead of the private sector where their skills were desperately needed. The embassy analyst then offered his own thoughts on the causal relationship between a sound economy and political stability:

> It is almost impossible to believe that in the long run even as seem-
> ingly strong and stable a regime as that in power in Iran can get by
> with changing the country in only a few decades from a nearly illiter-
> ate, poor, and basically peasant society into a well educated, reasonably
> affluent, modern, and dynamic nation without at some point going
> through a period of serious political upheaval and perhaps even radical
> social change. Put in another way, the current Iranian leadership is ask-
> ing the people to accept modernization in almost every respect while
> maintaining an autocratic political system which still denies them most
> of the basic human freedoms taken for granted in most of the advanced

western societies which Iran is striving to emulate. What the outside observer, of course, hopes for in Iran is political evolution rather than revolution.

Ambassador Helms and Secretary Kissinger were reminded that "history provides discouraging precedents about the declining years of autocrats. I can recall no example of an absolute ruler willingly loosening the reins of power. The recent establishment of a one-party state removed even the facade of the existence of a loyal opposition to His Majesty's government." The passivity of the educated elite to the Shah's control meant that the chances for peaceful change in Iran were growing slimmer—"one cannot help but fear they are abdicating in favor of the radicals. . . . More assassinations and other acts of terrorism seem likely." There was little hope that the United States could influence events in Iran: "Should we choose to try to use any of our apparent leverage to influence Iranian policies, our first aim probably would be to try to force a more moderate Iranian position on the price of oil. But in this or any other area in which we might try to sway Iranian policies we are limited by our dedication to the free market mechanism."

The internal stability of the Pahlavi state came into question in the first week of June 1975 when seminary students in Qum rioted to mark the twelfth anniversary of the arrest and exile of Ayatollah Khomeini. The students jeered that Iran was "like a harlot running after the evil ways of the West." The Shah rushed security forces to Qum to restore order. A week after the rioting in Qum subsided, Abdul Majid Majidi, Iran's minister of state and the head of the Plan and Budget Organization, announced that the government was halting spending on secondary development projects and scaling back its $69 billion Fifth Plan. The government faced a staggering $10 billion shortfall in income for the year because of a 1.3 million barrel per day slump in petroleum exports. Iran's oil production facilities were producing at only 77 percent capacity, "not quite enough to cover Iran's foreign-exchange outlays in the period." Over the summer Iranian banks were forced to take out hundreds of millions of dollars in loans to cover the gaping hole in their balance sheets. "Our revenues have dwindled considerably," the Shah told his people.

The unrest in Qum in June 1975 was the most visible sign yet that pressure was beginning to build deep within the Pahlavi state. The Shah's decision three months earlier to declare a one-party state had closed the last door to peaceful dialogue between the regime and its critics. Political parties act as steam vents in a democracy. The Shah had for several years contemplated the idea of creating a single political structure that his advisers hoped would bring the monarchy closer to the people. As early as October 1972 a U.S. diplomat reported that "there are vague signs that the Shah may be toying with the idea of letting [the smaller of Iran's two political parties] wither away and opting for a one-party system."

Ambassador Richard Helms took the declaration of a one-party state on March 2, 1975, to mean that the Shah was circling the wagons. He did not think this latest gambit would work. "Press reports to the contrary, the Shah's announcement was received by most of the embassy's contacts with a wave of cynicism and confusion which has not yet fully subsided," he informed Kissinger in a cable that summer.

> The arbitrary nature of the announcement tended to reinforce the prevailing Iranian mood of skepticism and cynicism about virtually everything connected with politics. To ordinary Iranians we have talked with—shopkeepers, small merchants, and others—(as distinct from party activists whose personal interests were involved), the previous political parties were ineffective as a means of expression and so far they seem to anticipate a similar result from this party. . . . This [decision by the Shah] inhibits the process by which political institutions can learn to function without his guidance.

A few days after the riots in Qum, on June 10, Senator Edward Kennedy, who had just returned from a trip to Iran, stopped by the secretary's office at the end of the workday. Kissinger's conversation with Kennedy offered the first indication that he was beginning to take a second look at the Shah. To the president and his cabinet colleagues, Kissinger had waxed lyrical about the Shah's tough qualities and loyalty. Now he betrayed his own doubts about the Shah's judgment and character as a strong leader. "You knew the Shah before, didn't you," he asked Kennedy. "Were you impressed with him?"

"Yes, I've known him before and I must say having now looked into his background and how he came to power, I begin to understand some of his preoccupations and his desires to be seen as a tough person against the Soviets," replied Kennedy.

"I sometimes wonder if he is really, naturally a tough guy though," mused Kissinger in what for him was a rare moment of reflection about Washington's "tough cookie" in Tehran.

"Well, there is something uncharacteristic about it given his background," Kennedy agreed. "In his talks with us, he used some old figures on oil prices and other economic factors. The Minister of Oil . . . what's his name?"

"Amuzegar," interjected Robert Hunter, one of Kennedy's aides.

"Amuzegar is a very able guy, but they're using some figures which are different from those we have here, and I think they should really be worked out," said Kennedy. "One impression I came away with with both the Shah and the Saudis is their feeling of isolation. The Shah is certainly sympathetic to the West, but he's very thin-skinned. He was always talking about *The New York Times* and *The Washington Post.*"

"Unlike some people I know," Henry cracked. Everyone laughed.

Kennedy told Kissinger that the Iranian officials he spoke to felt "that they're being hard pressed by things like . . . the State/Treasury differences [on oil pricing]." The Shah felt he was getting mixed signals from the Ford White House. The State Department gave him the green light to raise oil prices, but when he followed through he was attacked by Bill Simon at Treasury. The Shah was looking for direction. This observation may have surprised Kissinger, who assumed that the Shah resented advice as unwarranted interference in Iran's affairs. Then there was the issue of the Shah's poor grasp of economics and his lack of understanding of the impact high oil prices had on the industrialized world. "But I think they missed seeing our serious economic problems here in this country," said Kennedy. "They are saying we are so large and so wealthy that nothing can be seriously wrong."

"That is correct," Kissinger conceded. "I think their image of the West is that it is stronger than it really is. They think they can raise the price of oil $4 a barrel without seeing that it may throw the entire West into a deep depression."

Kennedy urged Kissinger to talk to the Shah: "Agreement on figures on inflation and on the economic implications of such a thing would be important though."

The senator, like most people, assumed that Kissinger enjoyed a close relationship with the Shah and that they communicated frequently. This suited Kissinger's purposes and burnished his reputation as a statesman. But the secretary of state's telephone transcripts show that in 1975 he was already trying to reduce his public affiliation with the Shah, who had long since stopped listening to him or taking his advice. Kissinger was particularly anxious not to be seen as having anything to do with the sale of military equipment to Iran. That is presumably why the man who wrote out and signed off on the Shah's blank check on purchases of military equipment telephoned columnist Joseph Kraft to assure him ("just for your information") that,

> while I'm for these sales, I was not the chief energizing factor. I was more a benevolent tolerance. I wasn't pushing it particularly. . . . There is no "be nice" strategy [toward the Shah]. I am opposed to having a political and economic confrontation with Iran because I do not believe it will get oil prices down or because what it would take to get them down—the amount by which they would get down that way wouldn't be worth the political and economic cause. I'm strongly in favor of creating the objective conditions that will get them down and we are well under way on that.

PUT THE TANKERS RIGHT INTO GUANTÁNAMO BAY

A lot was now riding on the bilateral oil deal Kissinger had promised the Shah and that Frank Zarb was negotiating with Hushang Ansary. The ultimate decision whether to go ahead and buy the Shah's unsold stockpile of oil rested with the White House Economic Policy Board presided over by Treasury Secretary Simon. Together with Zarb, Simon now held a lock over White House foreign economic policy. Kissinger was too slow to grasp that he would not have the final say on the deal. It was not until June that he insisted the Economic Policy Board broaden its membership to include State Department representation. Kissinger had every reason to be worried about Simon's tactics and motives. Back in May the Shah's plane had barely taken off when the treasury secretary attacked as "false" the Shah's call for a new price increase, describing the logic behind it as "confused." He denounced the Iranian leader for using oil "for political blackmail. He doesn't see this as an economic question at all." There were to be no more favors or sweetheart deals with the Shah on oil prices. "Secretary Simon is not bashful about going after the Shah and regrets that the lord of the Persian Gulf isn't challenged more on economic statements," reported the *Chicago Tribune*. The treasury secretary "believes in the genius of the free market [and doesn't] buy the secretary of state's notion that economics should be used for military-diplomatic goals."

Bill Simon held four immediate advantages over Kissinger and the State

Department in deciding the future of the bilateral oil deal. The terms of the deal—pricing, volume, and duration—would be debated on his turf at the Economic Policy Board by economists and financiers like Alan Greenspan, White House economic adviser William Seidman, Arthur Burns, and Frank Zarb. It would be decided on its financial as opposed to its geopolitical merits. The second advantage was that Ford was already under pressure from conservative Republicans to reduce Kissinger's influence in foreign policy and not to do any more favors for oil producers. A third factor militating against a deal was the potential downside for the U.S. economy at a time when oil prices were under pressure. If the administration entered into a long-term deal to buy hundreds of millions of barrels of Iranian oil at a fixed price, it ran the risk of locking itself into terms less favorable than it might ultimately get on the open market. Fourth, Simon was not interested in signing off on *any* deal to help the Shah. He and Sheikh Yamani wanted to turn the OPEC producers cartel over to Saudi leadership, which meant breaking the Shah's hold over its pricing decisions. President Ford was trying to straddle the divide between the financial concerns of his economic team and his secretary of state's geopolitical priorities. It turned out to be a bridge too far. In the Oval Office on June 12, Ford told Kissinger that he favored the oil deal only if it prevented a further price increase. "Greenspan is terribly worried about an OPEC price increase," he said. "If this will stop that, I think he would favor it."

While the terms of the oil deal were being evaluated, a series of widely syndicated, anonymously sourced articles unfavorable to the Shah began appearing in Jack Anderson's *Washington Post* column. One item reminded readers that the Shah owed his throne to the CIA. Anderson also cited a senior French official who said his government "cannot understand why the U.S. government continues to pay tribute to the Shah, particularly in the aftermath of his recent Washington trip where he 'spit in your eye' with his announcement of a September (oil) price rise." The article also quoted from a confidential Senate analysis commissioned to study U.S. oil policy: "Kissinger's handling of the oil problem exhibited his tendency to treat adversaries kindly and our friends shabbily."

On June 23, the day after the column appeared, Kissinger hosted Frank Zarb, Alan Greenspan, and Charles Robinson for lunch in his private dining room. Zarb and Greenspan now expressed doubts about proceeding with the oil deal. The government had no purchasing authority to buy oil from a foreign government. Worse, the White House had headed off an attempt by the Democratic Congress to give it one. "We definitely do not want a government purchasing authority," explained Zarb. "This notion of a government agency handling this sort of matter is inconceivable and inconsistent with our idea of a free-enterprise system. The liberals have been pushing it in order to further their efforts to nationalize the oil industry. So, success in this venture we are discussing would play into liberals' hands."

Kissinger also balked at the notion of asking Congress to pass special legislation authorizing the purchase, though his reluctance had less to do with ethics than with secrecy. "We might not want Congress to take too close a look into it," he confessed, a clue that there was more to the deal than met the eye. Greenspan reminded his colleagues that Saudi Arabia was OPEC's swing producer. Only the Saudis had the massive oil reserves necessary to challenge and break the cartel's price structure. The Shah's offer of 700,000 barrels a day would not in itself do the job.

"Well, we all understand that the critical path would be getting it done without going to Congress," said Zarb.

Robinson reminded Zarb and Greenspan that for the State Department the deal was about much more than economics. "You've got to understand that we see certain political benefits that go far beyond the oil price concern," he said. "It gets into the whole question of American leadership." He suggested that the administration bypass Congress by asking the Department of Defense to "get [the oil] on the basis of military need." This would require the secretary of defense to authorize the purchase on the basis of national security.

"[The deal] must be in the next six weeks, otherwise, it's lost," Kissinger reminded them. What he didn't say was that the oil deal had become a matter of trust between himself and the Shah. The Shah needed to know that Kissinger could still deliver for him. Kissinger dismissed Greenspan's idea that lawyers should vet the deal before it went any further. "I'd rather have to go back to the Shah then and tell him that we have legal problems with it than go to him now with 5000 caveats," he explained. "Otherwise he'll say these guys are for the birds. It's the same problem we face in general. The Shah's worry is that the United States has had it. I'd rather tell him afterwards. He can say he's basically with us or he's not with us. We'll never get to bat if this story leaks. Let's just explain to the President that we still have to look at the technicalities. . . . I'm not sure I understand what Bill [Simon] is trying to do. We would make the Shah an irreconcilable enemy, if not a participant in another embargo."

While U.S. officials debated the merits and logistics of the deal the Shah was losing patience with Kissinger. He refused to meet with Robinson when Kissinger sent him to Tehran to propose a long-term contract guaranteeing "additional supplies of oil, offset against Iranian purchases of U.S. goods."

"These aren't exactly the most sincere people we're dealing with," the Shah told Court Minister Alam on June 26. "What asses these people are."

The Washington Post of June 27 brought fresh bad news for the Shah and Kissinger. Jack Anderson published portions of a leaked Treasury report disputing the Shah's claims that high oil prices did not affect the rate of inflation and that high prices were justified to pay for the higher prices of imported Western goods. "Behind the scenes," reported Anderson, "some administration officials are eager to challenge the shah, but the President has instructed them to keep their comments to themselves. In their private papers, however, they have demolished the shah's economic arguments." Later in the day Kissinger took a phone call from Simon in which the treasury secretary played the innocent, professing to be concerned about what Jack Anderson was up to. "Jack Anderson called me last week and he says, you know I'm going to be doing some articles on Iran, and then he starts to talk to me and he's talking all over the place, most especially over in the State Department and the CIA about everything he can conjure up," said Simon, who sounded less than convincing in the role of Henry's confidant. "He's written two articles already and who knows what he will come up with next." Kissinger did not rise to the bait though he undoubtedly took note of the fact that members of his own staff, in addition to officials at CIA, were now poisoning the well against the Shah.

Kissinger's opinion of his colleagues on the Economic Policy Board was about as low as the Shah's was of him. Transcripts show that he belittled Greenspan and Zarb behind their backs. "They are small timers," he assured Chuck Robinson before delivering the final insult two days later: "There isn't a brain between the two of them. I think I understand economics as well as they do." It was inconceivable to him that he would not get his way on the oil deal. His ego could not entertain the possibility of defeat. The transcripts also confirm that Kissinger's tutor in petroleum economics was none other than Mohammad Reza Shah. "The Shah is a tough cookie," Kissinger had lectured Zarb and Greenspan. "Do you know him? He knows more about oil prices than anyone." This made sense. Kissinger's every move on oil pricing and production since 1969, intentionally or not, seemed intended to benefit the Shah and Iran's economy in one way or another, often at the expense of the American economy. Kissinger had more faith in the Shah's economic prowess than did the Iranian leader's own Plan and Budget Organization. Kissinger's irritation was no doubt a reflection of what he knew and his colleagues still did not: that if the deal was *not* signed off on by the end of August, the Shah would follow through on his threat to raise oil prices at the next meeting of OPEC oil ministers in September. Time was running out for Kissinger to deliver on his end of the bargain.

Eager to raise the stakes, and determined to make the oil deal a geopolitical package with political benefits for the president, Kissinger dangled before Ford the prospect of diverting some of the Shah's surplus oil to Israel. This would speed up the chances of a successful conclusion to the stalled Middle East talks on disengagement. "They [the Israelis] want reimbursement for losing the [Abu Reis] oil fields and a guarantee of oil supply in case of an embargo," Kissinger told President Ford at Camp David on Saturday, July 5. The secretary of state announced that he had found the ideal solution to the standoff: "We could use the Iranian oil. We have a deal with Iran if you want it."

Anderson's third and most provocative column, "CIA Finds Shah Insecure," appeared on July 11. "The Central Intelligence Agency has compiled a disturbing psychological profile of the shah of Iran whom the United States is building up to be the guardian of its interests in the Persian Gulf," wrote Anderson. The CIA's resident psychologists had been hard at work applying various Freudian theories to make sense of the Shah's personality and behavior. They described the Shah as "an uncertain ally" and blamed his insecurities on (1) an overbearing father who used "to string up enemies by the heels and kick them in the teeth," (2) the long years the Shah ruled in name only, (3) the Shah's "fears of impotence" and the many years it took him "to produce a male heir to the Peacock Throne." The Shah was for good measure (4) a former playboy who "never got over his lack of royal lineage and the ignominy of being a puppet monarch.... Now this insecure man, showered with oil billions and bolstered by the United States, is determined to show the world, psychologists suggest." Anderson did not explain why, if the Shah was so weak and insecure, he had repeatedly outmaneuvered and out-negotiated American presidents, secretaries of state, secretaries of defense, ambassadors, and intelligence officials to secure for himself billions of dollars in armaments and billions more in oil revenues— or what that said about the men with whom he was dealing.

Anderson's column did not fall on deaf ears. Ambassador Helms was so enraged when he read it that he "would not allow the column to be circulated among the staff." He had already adopted a policy of preventing his officials from reading CIA analyses he deemed unfairly critical of the Shah. There can be few recorded instances in history in which an American ambassador, let alone a former head of Central Intelligence, decapitated his own intelligence-gathering facilities, but Helms pulled off this feat with his usual aplomb.

Kissinger went another round with Zarb and Greenspan on July 14. Zarb told the others that the administration could get congressional authority to stockpile the Shah's oil only if details of the deal were made public. Kissinger said to go ahead anyway: "I think you should just go ahead negotiating with what you can and say that we have got some legal problems."

He asked whether the Defense Department could buy the oil. When Zarb replied that under the law Defense could buy but not resell it, Kissinger erupted. He had had enough of all the wild talk about legal niceties. This was no way to run the foreign policy of a great power. Things had been done differently in Nixon's day. "As a historian, I say this country has had it," he snapped. "I spend two-thirds of my time explaining to other countries why this country cannot do what is clearly in its own interest."

Chuck Robinson brought up Jack Anderson's latest column: "The article in the *Post* wasn't very helpful: the psychological study of the Shah."

"No, it wasn't, even though it was very interesting," said Brent Scowcroft, who also attended the meeting. "But how it got out, I just don't understand."

"You and I are rapidly getting to the point that, should it be decided that this can't be done, every step is pulling us in deeper and deeper," Robinson warned Kissinger. The Shah was under the impression there were no problems with the oil deal. Yet the White House still lacked the legal authority to go ahead. Why go any further? Why push their luck?

"If you go to the Shah and say that you have legal problems, you will be making a great problem for him," Kissinger explained. "He knows oil and knows it better than any of us here. He could easily sell his oil to Europe without any reductions at all. We might as well go ahead and complete the deal, and see if we can then get authorization."

"But if it is not completed by October 1, then it will be almost impossible to complete it at all," said Robinson.

The absurdity of their predicament became glaringly obvious when Greenspan announced that he had come up with the perfect hiding place for the oil. It was a location that satisfied Kissinger's obsession with maintaining secrecy and Greenspan's concerns about keeping costs down: "Well, at least we've come up with a good idea for economical storage: tankers. We can fill up tankers and put them right into the Guantánamo Bay."

"If it has anything to do with breaking an embargo, the Cubans will love it," said Kissinger, who dismissed the idea as ludicrous.

"No, it's a serious idea," said Greenspan. "We have a lot of potential for floating storage. A lot of these tankers are not used anyway and it's relatively inexpensive."

"Look, I want to be a little more realistic than I usually am," said Frank Zarb, who was trying to square the circle. Gerald Ford had told him to play by the rules. "I don't see any way we could possibly complete the deal without Congressional hearings . . . the question then is, can you live with it? And can the Shah live with it?"

"If we cannot complete it, we have got real problems," Kissinger told them. "I don't understand why so many people are demanding that we be tough on Iran. Being tough on Iran is not the key to breaking the cartel."

The last of Jack Anderson's articles, "Iran May Be Spending Beyond Means," was published on July 31. The article's real value lay not so much in what it said about the Shah as in its perceptive revealing that senior White House officials were keeping a close eye on Iran's economy, which they knew to be in trouble. "American officials at the highest levels are worried that the Shah of Iran may be living beyond his means," wrote Anderson. "Signs of the Shah's financial embarrassment are everywhere. . . . For all its oil riches, Iran is deeply in debt. The Shah, according to American officials familiar with his finances, owes about $3 billion in bilateral and multilateral loans." Tossed in with the economic analysis was this juicy morsel:

> According to the latest confidential estimates, however, the Shah's oil reserves will last, at best, for another two decades. This will leave the unpredictable, ambitious, recklessly greedy Shah with little more than a down payment on his dream of glory. Rather than abandon his dream, they fear privately, he may march his American-made army into neighboring Saudi Arabia and Kuwait and annex their oil fields.

President Ford received Prime Minister Takeo Miki of Japan at the White House on August 6. Japan imported 73 percent of its oil from Iran and the Middle East. Miki stressed to Ford the importance of easing tensions in the Middle East and the strain placed on Japan's economy by high oil prices. "If there should be a fifth war in the Middle East, Japan's industry would no longer be viable," he remarked. "For that reason, a Middle East peace settlement is absolutely vital to Japan. Any renewal of hostilities in that area would have an immediate impact on Japan's access to oil." He reminded the White House that Japan's fuel bill was four times higher now than it had been a year earlier, "and we expect our oil bill this year to total 23 billion dollars." Japan's economy was "in severe financial straits this year." The government in Tokyo had built a sixty-eight-day stockpile of petroleum to guard against a second embargo. Its goal was to have a ninety-day stockpile in place by the end of 1976.

President Ford was still leaning in favor of a deal with the Shah on oil so long as it held clear-cut economic benefits for the American economy. The day after his meeting with Prime Minister Miki, Ford listened to Kissinger's complaint that "Zarb and Greenspan are dragging their feet on the Iranian oil. . . . I had a scenario ready and I have to get an answer to Ansary today. I have no doubt they will approve it, but they want to prove their manhood. I would like to tell Ansary and you can rescind it tomorrow if you want." Go ahead, Ford said, tell Ansary the deal was on. But still they couldn't make all the parts fit. The president was unwilling to assert his authority over Treasury. Ford, Kissinger, Zarb, Greenspan, and Scowcroft met again the next day, Friday, August 8, to discuss the impasse. Bill Simon, who was not in the room, was refusing to sign off on the deal.

Then Kissinger's attempt to link the oil deal to a Middle East peace settlement collapsed on August 15. Israel agreed to evacuate the Abu Rudeis oil fields in return for a written pledge from the White House to supply it with oil in the event that at some future date Iran, Israel's regular supplier, reneged on the Shah's pledge made in Zurich to keep the oil flowing.

Brent Scowcroft later recalled that the Economic Policy Board, set up to streamline and formulate U.S. foreign economic policy, "was paralyzed because of the hostility" between Kissinger and Simon. "Anything Henry proposed Simon objected to, anything Simon proposed Henry objected to," he said. "So it was a very complicated period economically. And that spilled over into oil policy."

The bickering within the Ford administration left the Shah hanging. He was, not surprisingly, exasperated and irritated by the delay. Court Minister Alam's diary includes the copy of a letter Mohammad Reza Shah sent to Kissinger dated August 24 in which the king said he was "very much disappointed that our talks on oil have not been successful and might even be inconclusive." Alam expressed to the Shah "my doubts as to how much we can rely on Kissinger's goodwill in fixing oil prices." The Shah agreed with Alam: "But still," he said, "we've got to go through the diplomatic niceties."

On August 28, the Shah received a Saudi delegation in Tehran to discuss the forthcoming OPEC summit. Hoping to prevent the Saudis from breaking ranks, the Iranian leader admitted to his guests that Nixon and Kissinger had approved in advance each of the previous oil price increases so that Iran could bankroll its military buildup. Kissinger had also lied to the late King Faisal when he promised to ask the Shah not to raise oil prices again, the Shah told the Saudis. The Saudi delegation was incensed.

When Sheikh Yamani returned home he confronted U.S. ambassador James Akins about the Shah's allegations. Akins had just learned from reading *The New York Times* that Kissinger intended to replace him as envoy for taking the Saudi side in the dispute over oil pricing. During the secretary's meeting with Senator Kennedy back in June, Kissinger had snidely asked, "How was our Pro-consul there? He's very bright, but he's becoming very lordly." Kennedy joked that his sisters had mistaken the American ambassador for "another sheik when he arrived."

After talking to Yamani the ambassador wrote a memo in which he described Saudi agitation and outright fury over the direction of U.S. policy in the Gulf. "Although the Saudis know the Iranian propensity to lie, they believe in this case that the Iranians are telling the truth," Akins wrote. Someone had leaked to the Saudis the military contingency plan that called on Iran to send paratroopers into Saudi Arabia. Yamani angrily accused the United States of preparing "the Shah of Iran for an armed invasion of Arabian oil fields . . . the conclusion the Saudis were reaching was that we had an agreement with Iran to let it take over the entire Arabian littoral of the Persian Gulf." Iran's military buildup "was quite clearly aimed at occupying the Arab states across the gulf, the emirates, Qatar, Bahrain, Kuwait and even Saudi Arabia itself." In the next Arab-Israeli war "Israel would be encouraged to occupy Tobuk in northern Saudi Arabia, and Iran would be told to occupy the Arabian littoral." Yamani even believed that the Algiers accord signed by the Shah and Saddam Hussein to settle border differences and end the Kurdish insurgency was part of a conspiracy "so Iran would have a freer hand in the lower Gulf." Yamani reportedly told Ambassador Akins: "If Iran should succeed in occupying part of the Arabian coast, it would find only smoking ruins, and the Western oil consumers would face catastrophe." He concluded by telling Akins that in his own view the Shah was "highly unstable mentally."

HAVE YOU SEEN THE LETTER
FROM THAT IDIOT, FORD?

The Shah moved on his threat to increase oil prices. The Saudis were now in the enviable position of being courted simultaneously by the Shah, who needed their support if any price increase was to stick, and the Americans, who were determined to stop OPEC from yet another hike in price. Ambassador Helms cabled Under Secretary of State Robinson to tell him that "from what we know and what you have heard personally of the shah's attitude on this question, frequently stated politically and therefore all the more difficult for him to retreat from, he feels there is ample justification for a price increase and is pressing hard for acceptance of his point of view." Helms included this crucial piece of intelligence: "Further, he is in something of a cash flow bind and therefore not able to do all he (or we) would like him to do." The Shah's bad habit of overspending had finally caught up with him. Helms knew it and so now did Kissinger. Even if the Shah wanted to help the Americans he was unable to do so; the result for Iran would be a financial crisis. The Shah backed himself even further into a corner several days later when he declared before the Iranian parliament that he sought a big increase in oil prices. For him to back down now would be seen at home as an act of weakness in the face of pressure from the Americans.

On September 2, a scene of abject humiliation was played out in King Khalid's compound at Taif. Kissinger had come to plead with Yamani not to support the Shah, who was now talking about a 15–20 percent price rise. Here was a moment for Yamani to relish. Kissinger tried to assure Yamani that he was not anti-Saudi. "I have read of some conversations in which you indicated that you believed that the U.S. was embarking on a policy of getting tough with Saudi Arabia," he said. "I just wanted to tell you personally that this is not our policy. . . . Let me assure you that you have nothing to be concerned about. There is absolutely no truth to this. It is certainly not our policy." He said that a price increase "will be used by our opponents in the U.S.—by those opponents of our policy toward the Arab World. They'll say we are not tough enough with the Arabs knowing full well that if we get tougher the Arabs will retaliate." This was an apparent allusion to Senator Jackson and the neoconservatives.

"Sometimes we are confused," Yamani haughtily replied, his remarks making it clear that he did not believe Kissinger. "When His Highness

Prince Fahd was in Tehran, the Shah told us that your view was that it was necessary to have a price increase."

"It is not conceivable that that could be portrayed as my view," said Kissinger, who presumably now understood that the Shah had betrayed his confidence. He explained to Yamani that an increase in oil prices "will lead to massive political problems for our efforts in the Middle East. It would also have enormous economic consequences which you know."

"We know your views," said Yamani. "We are not in the forefront of those who want a price increase. That is not our traditional position. But your views should be told to other OPEC countries who feel differently."

Kissinger promised to clear up any confusion about the American position. "When I return the President will send a message to the Shah so he can be under no misconception about our attitude on this," he said and returned to his original remarks: "I can assure you there is no tough line. It is pure newspaper idle speculation. There is no truth to it. I give you my personal assurances."

The next day, September 3, Yamani pressed home his advantage. He wrote a "strictly personal" letter to his friend Bill Simon urging the White House to exert maximum pressure on the Shah. "I would like you to know that there are those amongst us who think that the U.S. administration does not really object to an increase in oil prices," Yamani continued, an obvious reference to Kissinger. "There are those who think that you encourage it for obvious political reasons, and that any official position taken to the contrary is merely to cover up this fact." If the United States did not intervene with the Shah then Saudi Arabia would join the rest of OPEC and support a double-digit increase in oil prices. Simon was rattled enough to write a six-page memo to the president summarizing his conversation and laying out the case for confronting Iran.

Ford wrote the Shah on September 9. Court Minister Alam kept a copy of the letter in his diary. The president cautioned the Shah not to raise prices again because doing so "could raise serious questions among the American public regarding the close cooperation we seek and are actively developing with your country in several fields of our bilateral relationship. . . . I am asking you to weigh heavily the adverse effects—both psychological and real—which a price increase could have."

The Shah was incensed. "Have you seen the letter I received from that idiot, Ford?" he asked Alam. He was convinced that Bill Simon or "that devil Kissinger" was behind it. Yet the Shah was nonplussed. He had stood up to Nixon in 1973 when prices quadrupled and he felt sure he would get this latest raise, which after all was only 15 percent.

Both sides were now playing a very hard game. In his response, dated September 10, the Shah disputed the administration's arguments and said a price freeze was unfair to oil producers. "I also appreciate very much and greatly value the special relationship that exists between our two countries which, as you fully realize, Mr. President, is not only in favor of Iran but is mutually and equally beneficial to both sides," he wrote. "If, in defending our legitimate interests, we might raise serious questions among the American people, we would be very sorry to ascertain that the real facts have not been set before your public." This final remark was a calculated insult, a dressing-down from the King of Kings to an unelected president in office only thirteen months.

The bitterness lingered. On September 22, President Ford narrowly escaped assassination when a troubled woman fired at him outside the St. Francis Hotel in San Francisco. World leaders expressed relief that the president had not been hurt or killed. Mohammad Reza Shah also cabled his congratulations. He shared his private feelings with Alam. "But why on earth do people want to dispose of such an old donkey?" he asked, smiling.

Five days later, OPEC oil ministers meeting in Vienna announced a 10 percent increase in price to take effect on October 1. The price would remain frozen for nine months as a gesture to oil-consuming nations stuck with a new $10 billion addition to their fuel bills. The Iranian oil minister, Dr. Jamshid Amuzegar, declared himself "very happy" with the outcome of the discussions. Sheikh Yamani was downcast. He had hoped to prevent any new price increase from taking effect, and at one point demonstrated his pique by delaying the proceedings for twenty-one hours to fly to London to contact Crown Prince Fahd using more secure communications. Analysts noted that "the walkout was also calculated to demonstrate . . . the naked power of Saudi Arabia as the leading oil state. It was a signal to the United States that Saudi Arabia was playing hard, this time." The Saudis were gradually learning to assert themselves against the Shah. The latest price hike boosted Iranian government revenues by $2 billion, though not nearly enough to pay outstanding debts and cover expenditures. Court Minister Alam sagely noted in his diary that the outcome of the OPEC meeting in Vienna "can only be regarded by the Saudis, and for that matter by the USA, as a relative climb-down by us and our supporters."

President Richard Nixon with the Shah of Iran at the White House, April 1, 1969. Nixon admired the Shah, who was in Washington to attend the funeral of former president Dwight Eisenhower.

The Strait of Hormuz at the mouth of the Persian Gulf. Great Britain withdrew its military shield from the Gulf by the end of 1971, leaving the vital oil fields and shipping lanes vulnerable. The Shah offered to protect them in exchange for arms and higher oil prices.

Chairman of the Joint Chiefs of Staff Earle Wheeler (left) and Secretary of Defense Melvin Laird opposed Nixon's plan to grant the Shah a blank check in the Persian Gulf.

Above: King Faisal of Saudi Arabia visited the White House in 1971, the year when U.S. imports of oil from the desert kingdom increased sixfold. Unlike the Shah, King Faisal was sensitive to the price of oil, but also unlike the Shah, he strongly opposed U.S. support for Israel.

Above: Washington Post columnist and muckraker Jack Anderson hounded the Nixon and Ford administrations with revelations about secret oil and arms deals with the Shah. Administration officials Henry Kissinger and William Simon used Anderson to settle scores with the Shah and with each other. *Left:* The oil crisis of the mid-1970s began prior to the outbreak of the October 1973 Arab-Israeli war. Panic buying caused shortages of gasoline and home heating oil.

When the U.S. rushed aid to Israel during the 1973 war, Arab states led by Saudi Arabia imposed an oil embargo on the U.S. in retaliation.

On November 9, 1973, Secretary of State Henry Kissinger and King Faisal met to discuss the oil embargo. Kissinger and Defense Secretary James Schlesinger were discussing breaking the embargo by occupying Abu Dhabi. With the Shah's approval, a U.S. naval task force was steaming toward the Persian Gulf.

On November 13, 1974, Chairman of the Council of Economic Advisers Alan Greenspan (left), Chairman of the Federal Reserve Arthur Burns (center), and Treasury Secretary William Simon conferred after meeting with President Gerald Ford to discuss how to respond to the oil shock rattling the U.S. economy. "There isn't a brain between them," Kissinger scoffed. "I think I understand economics as well as they do."

President Ford conferring with West German Chancellor Helmut Schmidt. Schmidt alerted Ford to the danger of failing banks and political instability in Europe. The Chancellor wanted to confront the oil-producing states.

Henry Kissinger never hid his contempt for Saudi Oil Minister Sheikh Zaki Yamani. But in September 1975, Kissinger was forced to travel to Saudi Arabia to ask King Khalid for relief on oil prices. Yamani embarrassed Kissinger by revealing that the Shah had confided that all his price increases had been approved in advance by the White House.

Treasury Secretary Simon holding forth on *Air Force One* while Kissinger sits alongside. The rivalry between the two men ensured gridlock on oil policy within the Ford administration.

National Security Advisor Gen. Brent Scowcroft regarded the Shah as an American ally but expressed ambivalence about the way U.S.-Iran relations had been conducted under Kissinger. He approved the plan to try to break OPEC from within with the help of the Saudis.

King Juan Carlos and Queen Sofia of Spain at the White House. Spain's economy was crippled by high fuel costs, and the country faced a debt crisis as well as political violence on the left and military revolt on the right. In Italy the Communist Party was on the verge of forming a new government amid worsening economic conditions and political paralysis. Kissinger was deeply concerned about the various crises in Europe.

The Shah's refusal to provide price relief gave Simon the opening he had sought to improve U.S. relations with the Saudis. On July 9, 1976, President Ford received Saudi Ambassador Alireza (center) and Prince Abdullah, brother of King Khalid, to discuss oil prices, missile sales, and the Middle East peace process, among other topics

Kissinger's last visit to Iran as secretary of state failed to resolve disagreements between the United States and the Shah, as is evident from the faces of the two men at this press conference. There was concern over the Shah's health. Kissinger warned Ford, "If we get rid of the Shah, we will have a radical regime on our hands."

Above: On September 17, 1976, Saudi Foreign Minister Prince Saud bin Faisal al-Saud spoke with President Ford and senior officials at the White House. The Saudis wanted to see progress on arms sales and trade legislation before agreeing to the plan to try to break OPEC and oppose the Shah's proposed oil price increase. The president assured the prince of his support.

Left: President Ford and Betty Ford exchange a hug as election returns on November 2, 1976, showed Ford being defeated by Jimmy Carter. The recession, oil prices, and unemployment cost Ford his job.

A month after the election President Ford met with Iranian Ambassador Zahedi to issue a final appeal on oil prices. The meeting ended without an agreement. Zahedi reminded Ford that the Shah and Kissinger had struck a deal to delay price increases until after the election and Iran needed the revenue now.

Tear gas wafts across the lawn of the White House, stinging the eyes of the Shah, Empress Farah, Rosalynn Carter, and President Carter as United States Park Police tried to contain hundreds of pro- and anti-Shah demonstrators. The fuse of revolution had been lit.

THE SHAH LIED TO ME

In the summer and fall of 1975 diplomats in Tehran began picking up on rumors that the Shah was in poor health. The September 23, 1975, edition of *The New York Times* ran a brief item under the headline: "Aide Denies Shah of Iran Is Ill." The paper's correspondent informed readers that a spokesman for the Shah "in an interview yesterday denied persistent rumors in Tehran's diplomatic community that the reason the Shah some-times appears drawn, worn and thin is that he is suffering from a lingering and increasingly grave malady." The spokesman was undoubtedly Court Minister Asadollah Alam, an expert in cover-ups and subterfuge. "No man who is ailing could work under such pressure as he works under and travel around the world the way he does," he protested. He put the Shah's weight loss down to a twelve-hour workday and "overwork and fatigue." The Shah himself read the *Times*.

It was around this time—the exact date is uncertain—that Ambassador Helms surprised his senior embassy staff with a remarkable piece of news. "The Shah is seeing French doctors," he said. Helms also told them that the Shah had written his will. How was it possible that Helms knew the nationality of the Shah's doctors, let alone that he was receiving medical attention? Did he also know about the Shah's cancer diagnosis? And who provided him with the details of the November 1973 conclave at which the Shah had read out his last will and testament?

During his lifetime Richard Helms remained publicly tight-lipped on the subject of the Shah's cancer. The episode clearly troubled him. He understood that the failure of U.S. officials to diagnose the Shah's illness amounted to a catastrophic intelligence failure. After he left government service he ruminated with at least one former colleague, former National Security Adviser Brent Scowcroft. And in the mid-1980s he unburdened himself to a historian during an oral history interview. His remarks, pub-lished here for the first time, shed new light on one of the great riddles of the Iranian Revolution. They suggest the episode remained a great source of regret and embarrassment. "I know that he lied to me about it," said Helms of the Shah.

> If it wasn't a direct lie saying, "No, I do not have cancer, I do not have leukemia," or whatever it was, he certainly gave me the impression by devices such as, "Well I am reading in *Newsweek* that I'm supposed to have cancer. Have you ever seen anybody looking healthier than I

look right now?" Things of this sort. So as nearly as I've been able to establish . . . the only person to whom he confided this information was the Empress. Nobody else knew about it. And nobody else was told about it.

But in 1975 Empress Farah had still not been made aware of her husband's lymphoma. The one conclusion we can draw from Helms's admission is that if he knew about the presence of French doctors in Tehran then so too did Henry Kissinger. It is inconceivable that the ambassador withheld such a crucial and intriguing tidbit of information from the secretary of state. Should we then take it one step further and accept Helms's assurance that he took the Shah's lie at face value? The answer is a surprising yes. When French president Georges Pompidou was diagnosed with Waldenström's disease the National Security Council was alerted and a study undertaken to assess the impact of the French president's illness and medication on U.S. relations. President Nixon and his top officials made the necessary adjustments in their dealings with Paris. In the case of the Shah of Iran no policy adjustments were made, no contingency plans were drawn up, no legwork was asked of the intelligence community. The transfer of high-tech weaponry to Iran did not slacken. The negotiations to sell Iran nuclear power technology remained on track. No steps were taken to reduce the number of expatriate personnel. In short, the United States continued its march to folly in Iran. Richard Helms's failure to request CIA surveillance of the Shah's French doctors—prominent cancer specialists at a leading medical institute in Paris—was as much a failure of imagination as intelligence. No one, it seems, not even the man who knew too much, seemed to realize that the Shadow of God was indeed mortal.

JAMES SCHLESINGER AND THE ROAD NOT TAKEN

At 3:30 p.m. on September 2, the same day that Henry Kissinger was meeting Sheikh Yamani in Taif, Secretary of Defense James Schlesinger met in private with President Ford to discuss the vexing matter of U.S.-Iran military sales and defense relations. Earlier in the year Schlesinger had ordered a top-to-bottom review of the American defense posture in Iran, bilateral defense relations, and weapons sales. The results of that review confirmed his own instinct to scale back the American presence in Iran and reassess the entire basis of the relationship. He was worried about Iran's internal situation, corruption involving American military personnel, the safety of American civilians from terrorist attack, and the Shah's refusal to accept U.S. conditions regarding the handling of enriched uranium.

The White House was aware that the Shah's refusal to back down over oil prices hurt the chances of securing congressional approval for a U.S.-Iran nuclear accord. "We can anticipate very critical Congressional scrutiny of any agreement that we might negotiate with Iran based on Congressional concerns about nuclear exports as well as hostility towards the Shah's oil pricing policies," concluded a study undertaken by the National Security Council. As both secretary of state and national security adviser, Henry Kissinger enjoyed the unique position of accepting on the NSC's behalf proposals advanced by the State Department and then forwarding their recommendations to the president for his approval. Kissinger recognized that the United States was trying to achieve two "potentially conflicting goals" by trying to prevent the spread of nuclear technology and concluding a nuclear accord with Iran when "some are concerned over [Iran's] possible longer-term nuclear weapon ambitions should others proliferate." Iran needed enriched uranium to provide fuel for the network of nuclear reactors it proposed to build. But the same material could also be used to construct nuclear bombs. The Shah had made it clear he wanted Iran to acquire its own "fuel cycle capabilities (including an enrichment capability)." Other Non-Proliferation Treaty signatories were allowed to reprocess nuclear fuels so long as they did so in accordance with international standards and safeguards. The Shah rejected the proposal first advanced in February to invest in a joint U.S.-Iran Bechtel-constructed facility in the United States. If Iran was such a trusted ally, the Shah wanted to know, why should it not receive the same privileges as other American allies?

The Ford administration offered the Shah a new deal that represented a significant concession. The United States indicated that it would look more favorably on Iranian requests to reprocess and store plutonium on Iranian soil if the enrichment process was carried out in a "multinational plant that the United States would jointly manage and secure with Iran. Other friendly countries in the region, such as Pakistan and Turkey, which had expressed a desire to acquire nuclear power, would be invited to participate in the consortium. The administration hoped that a multinational approach under nominal Iranian leadership would take the sting out of American veto power and appeal to the Shah's personal sense of grandeur. The State Department saw it as a win-win solution for both governments. "Iran has no dearth of remote areas for long term storage of radioactive waste," U.S.

embassy deputy chief of mission Jack Miklos cabled Washington. "And the public is insufficiently educated in the dangers of radioactivity to rise against the idea." Iran was politically stable "as long as the Shah survives," said Miklos. The Shah, of course, was slowly dying, but Miklos had no way of knowing that.

Mohammad Reza Shah's hackles were raised. "The Iranians recognize and resent the regional reprocessing plant concept as a device to impose international control on this very sensitive stage in the nuclear fuel cycle," Ambassador Helms cabled Washington. "Iranian bruised honor aside, they believe the idea is ridiculous in the Middle East setting." Iran and its neighbors did not have the sort of "close functional relationships" required to overcome the "tremendously complex" problems involved in "joint management, distribution of costs, and actual physical arrangements for storage, transport, and processing of material." Helms offered his view that if the United States wanted to figure in Iran's nuclear future it would have to reach an accommodation with the Shah in the matter of enrichment. If such an accommodation was not possible, the administration should "cut our losses now rather than to prolong an issue which may fester and poison our relations more in the future."

Secretary of Defense Schlesinger and the Joint Chiefs of Staff urged the president to hold firm and not offer any further concessions to the Iranians. They worried that once again Kissinger and Helms were preparing to give away the store. "We recognize the importance of the U.S.-Iranian relationship both for energy and national security," Schlesinger informed Ford. "At the same time, due to the potential for instability and uncertain political situation in the Middle East, the proposed agreement for nuclear cooperation could have serious national security implications." The Pentagon's civilian and military leadership were united in their belief that the United States should "delay the operation of such nuclear fuel reprocessing facilities for as long as possible." The United States must never surrender its veto over "where any future reprocessing activity of U.S. fuel provided Iran could occur." Conditions must be attached so that if Iran evicted international inspectors from the multinational plant, the American presence on site would remain.

Schlesinger had never understood the logic behind the Shah's military buildup. Nixon's May 1972 deal to provide the Shah with all weaponry short of the nuclear bomb had never been explained to him. "I don't recall that I had any direct briefings," he said.

As one reflects on it, there were kind of hints at this and that, but there was no documentation. It became clear to me over the period ahead, that the relationship was very deep. But now I cannot recall any explanation of the degree of commitment, and indeed I have not to this day had it confirmed from the participants that those commitments were made that you can have anything you wanted. I did not, at that time, believe that such deep commitments had been made, although I understood that we were supposed, in general, to support the Shah—because I resisted certain arms sales, certain commitments by the United States which I did not think were in our interest, and sometimes were not in the Shah's interest, and on some of them I just got overruled.

He fretted about the influx of American technicians and their families. "I could not control it," he explained. "I could influence it to some extent and hoped to influence it to more extent, but that was driven by the Shah."

Schlesinger had been in office only three weeks when the Shah made his July 1973 state visit to Washington. "I urged the Shah, the first time I met him, to use his resources prudently rather than squandering them on a diverse set of military hardware," he recalled. He warned that Iran would have trouble absorbing such vast quantities of high-tech weaponry and finding the trained personnel to use them. The Shah disregarded his warning, perhaps because Nixon had secretly promised to supply Iran with as many as twenty thousand American technicians—as many as the Shah needed. Schlesinger never learned about this directive. He was also concerned in 1975 by reports of rampant corruption involving American defense contractors and uniformed military personnel. His trusted personal liaison to the Shah, retired army Colonel Richard Hallock, filed hair-raising reports to Washington alleging that the U.S. government's policy of foreign military sales pricing "is not correct or consistent and often not honest . . . the credibility problem is deeper than the absolute costs; and it is heightened by the fact that nearly every case questioned by the [government of Iran] shows that there were overcharges and abuses. The amount of money that Iran is spending with the U.S. together with the lack of leadership and discipline . . . has greatly increased the corruption in the FMS [foreign military sales] system in the Services." Hallock warned of "marriages of interest between the Services and major contractors for conducting business in Iran which is not authorized by either the Secretary of Defense or [the government of Iran]—projects born of deception and lies and greased by influence and payoff." Hallock described the leadership of the American military mission as "weak and child-like," actively sabotaging Schlesinger's efforts to root out the corruption that now extended to uniformed officers. The Air Force section within the U.S. mission "has not been cleaned up and is waiting like a bomb to go off."

An example of such corruption was the 1972 Grumman deal cooked up by Nelson Rockefeller and Kissinger. It had finally drawn the scrutiny of congressional investigators and led to embarrassment for the Pentagon. The probe uncovered evidence that Grumman had agreed to pay "commissions" to Iranian middlemen in the amount of $20 million over five years starting in 1972. "It was normal practice," claimed Grumman's president, John Bierwirth. Members of Congress demanded to know why Grumman was forking out millions in kickbacks at a time when the company was taking taxpayer dollars in the form of a loan extended by the Pentagon for it to stay in business—and whether this deal was connected to a second $200 million loan offered by Bank Melli of Iran, the bank that enjoyed close commercial ties with David Rockefeller's Chase Manhattan Bank. Schlesinger had been kept in the dark on the Grumman deal.

For Schlesinger, the news just kept getting worse. In June 1975 an audit prepared by Northrop Corporation's accounting firm revealed the company had shelled out $30 million in bribes to middlemen to secure defense contracts with Middle East rulers, including the Shah of Iran. This sum was part of a total $200 million in kickbacks or "commissions" paid by U.S. defense contractors to foreign governments or their agents since January 1973. Prominent among the "sales agents" was a man well known to the Shah and Richard Helms: Kermit Roosevelt. Northrop's audit confirmed that Roosevelt, the CIA's lead agent in the 1953 coup, leveraged his background in intelligence to secure for Northrop defense contracts "running close to a billion dollars." In one incident in 1965, Roosevelt flew to Iran to successfully persuade the Shah and his self-described "old personal friend," General Mohammad Khatam, the commander of Iran's air force, to buy F-5 fighter aircraft. "The Shah could not have been more cordial personally—he said that next time I visit I should bring my wife, and the two families should take a vacation together," Roosevelt wrote a Northrop official. "My friends in the CIA are also keeping an eye on things." In another memo dated from 1968, Northrop's president instructed Roosevelt to ask the Shah to lobby on Grumman's behalf in a meeting with the West German chancellor.

Schlesinger was unaware that one of the biggest corruption bombs was ticking under his own feet. Richard Hallock had weakened and decided to do some double-dipping of his own. Hallock had earned the moniker "the Grey Ghost" for his shadowy comings and goings in Tehran. Hallock's Pentagon file showed that his California-based consultancy firm, Intrec Corp., was paid $2,697,067 for the period of Hallock's employment by the Defense Department, which lasted from August 17, 1973, to January 6, 1976. In the spring of 1975 Hallock casually asked Schlesinger how he would feel if Intrec accepted separate contract work with the Iranian government. "I simply told him it was totally unacceptable," Schlesinger recalled. "So I assumed it had gone away." Schlesinger did not know that even as Hallock was consulting for the Defense Department, he was also quietly advising U.S. defense contractors on the side. Worse, he had *already* signed a contract to do business with the Shah—some nine months earlier.

Schlesinger was later told that Hallock's son had reportedly fallen ill and that the boy's father agreed to work for General Toufanian to recoup the cost of medical bills. That was the start of it. Intrec signed "a multi-million dollar contract with the Iranian government in July 1974 to advise it on research, planning, and training," wrote scholar Barry Rubin. "The programs [Hallock] advocated to the shah, however, were not necessarily those backed by the MAAG [Military Assistance Advisory Group] and the Defense Department." Hallock's status as Schlesinger's personal representative thus "put him in the enviable position of advising the shah on what to buy, advising the United States government on what to recommend to him, helping the arms supply companies close the deals, and overseeing the program under which all these transactions were being made." Hallock's game of double cross ended when General Toufanian paid him a handsome cash settlement to leave the country. Thirty-five years later, Hallock's double cross still stung Schlesinger, who found it incomprehensible and a personal betrayal of trust.

Hallock was not alone in cashing in on his connection to the Shah. For the second time, former Vice President Spiro Agnew passed through Tehran looking for business. Nixon's former envoy John Connally also came calling. Alam complained to Ambassador Helms that Connally's presence was particularly odious because he had been implicated in corruption scandals in the United States. Helms assured him that Connally "was acquitted of any wrong-doing and might even run as a Republican candidate in the next presidential election." Alam's response: "What a bizarre country America is!"

In the Oval Office on September 2, James Schlesinger presented his report to the president and offered a brief summary of what he considered to be its major findings. Brent Scowcroft sat in as note taker. "I have a paper on Iran and its problems," Schlesinger explained.

> It is not the best literary effort, but I'll sign it. Iran has an almost limit-less appetite and has so much on its plate they can't digest it. We have tried to slow them, but we have given in when the Shah really wanted it. Our problem is that we are building up our American population in Iran . . . which could be a problem. It could provoke anti-Americanism and terrorism. If the political situation turned sour it could leave us very vulnerable. I think we need a thorough review of our short-term and long-term policy toward Iran.

President Ford took the document. "I will look at it," he said. "Inciden-tally, Simon told me this morning that the Saudis, Kuwaitis and the Emir-ates all wanted to hold the line on the oil price and asked me to appeal to the Shah." Weeks later, on October 10, Ford told Schlesinger that he sup-ported Defense's call for a thorough review of where U.S.-Iran relations were headed. The findings contained in Schlesinger's report had apparently made an impression.

Since 1972 Iran had contracted to purchase $10 billion in U.S. weap-ons, equipment, support, and training through the tainted foreign military sales program. Eight billion of that amount had yet to be delivered to Iran, which raised "the specter of severe management problems downstream." Iran's armed forces construction program for 1973–78 was more than $5 billion and military construction was underway at more than three hundred locations around the country. "Frankly, the U.S. itself would find it extremely difficult to handle expansion programs of this size and speed; the Iranians cannot do it," concluded the secretary's analysis. "The military supply system is a shambles . . . the expansion is too great for them to cope with."

There were too many Americans living in Iran. Defense estimated that "the number of U.S. citizens in the eight Gulf countries is likely to increase by 135 percent by 1980, from about 63,000 to about 150,000, including 70,000 in Saudi Arabia and nearly 76,000 in Iran." This number far exceeded the State Department's projected estimate of fifty thousand Americans living in Iran by 1980. Iran had an "unhealthy reliance upon U.S. skilled manpower." The Pentagon was worried about terrorist strikes against Americans in Iran. The large number of skilled uniformed technicians moving to Iran was proving to be a drain on U.S. military resources and hurting American combat readiness.

Finally, Schlesinger's memo cautioned the president that "there are prospects that U.S.-Iranian relations will become difficult in the years ahead for a variety of reasons." These reasons included the Shah's position on oil pricing: "The issue of oil prices obviously is one in which U.S. interests and the Shah's perceptions of his interests could easily collide, and soon. The question of nuclear safeguards for the reactors he seeks is also likely to be troublesome." He urged a National Security Council review of U.S. defense and security interests in Iran. A complete review was needed "concerning the supply of arms and related goods and services to Iran. . . . It would appear important that we consider whether and to what extent the changes in our relationship with Iran are irreversible and what future policies we should follow—especially in the area of military sales and support, which is central to our relationship."

Historians looking for the road not taken by the United States on the eve of the outbreak of revolution in Iran will find no better place to look than here. The secretary of defense was worried about rising anti-American sentiment and American citizens being caught in the middle of intensifying political unrest. He viewed the future of the Shah's regime as uncertain. He saw disturbing parallels with the American experience in Vietnam. He worried that the Shah's expenditures on defense were overloading Iran's economy and society.

"Well, I had considerable concerns about it," he remembered. "And I expressed them repeatedly. They were not concerns that went to the intelligence data; they were concerns that reflected a general analysis of the kind of forces that were working in Iran." The Shah's rapid buildup of the Iranian armed forces was creating internal tensions and draining the civilian economy of precious resources. The military buildup deprived Iran's economy of its best talent.

> Those were general, that was a general thought. As it turned out, it was more accurate than ever I thought at the time. The other point that I should make is that—a simple historical point made by every historian since [Alexis] de Tocqueville—which is that the time of transformation of these societies that they become unstable. That as you root up people, move them from traditional settings and traditional occupations into new occupations—and particularly, if there is a growth of real income that might be interrupted—that the society is far more vulner-

able than when it is functioning as a traditional society. That's sort of a general observation: one was worried about that in a general way.

Schlesinger's recommendation that the NSC launch a review offered the president an off-ramp from the Nixon-Kissinger policy of appeasement of the Shah. It also gave Ford political cover. Schlesinger enjoyed the support of prominent conservatives and defense hawks like Ronald Reagan who were deeply unhappy over the direction of Ford's domestic and foreign policy. Ford could proceed with a review of U.S.-Iran relations secure in the knowledge that his right flank was covered. Iran was very much on Ford's mind. Zahedi informed the Shah that at a dinner on October 21, the president had sought him out and asked, "Please tell me candidly. What is wrong? Is there any trouble or misunderstanding between us?" What happened next was as much travesty as tragedy.

Almost immediately, the memo ran into two roadblocks. In his capacity as national security adviser, Henry Kissinger diverted the memo and sent it to the bottom of his in-box, where it languished for the next six months. The White House lost precious months in which to consider options and draw up contingencies. And the president's election campaign took priority over the review. The second roadblock came at 8:30 A.M. on Sunday, November 2, when Schlesinger was fired as secretary of defense, the most prominent victim of a political purge masterminded by White House chief of staff Donald Rumsfeld, who wanted the job at Defense for himself. Ford had been unhappy with Schlesinger for quite some time. Kissinger, Schlesinger's old rival, had poisoned the well by feeding Ford's suspicions that Schlesinger was leaking to the press to undermine Kissinger's arms negotiations with Moscow. In the Oval Office on October 2, Kissinger could not contain himself. "I hate to bring this up, but I must mention Schlesinger," he blurted out. "I think he is demented. . . . He is really devious."

"He should be here trying to get the Defense budget through, instead of traveling around," groused Ford.

"Your problem is executive authority," Kissinger prodded. "He should be supportive."

"I would like to fire him, frankly," said Ford. "But I think that would give us too many problems. If we can't fire him, we can pull the things away from him which he can use against us. Like cruise missiles."

"He is so devious. He rarely tells you or us the real or full truth."

The events of November 2, known to history as the "Halloween Massacre," had severe repercussions for U.S.-Iran relations. Rumsfeld's deputy, Dick Cheney, became the new White House chief of staff. CIA Director William Colby was sacked and replaced by George H. W. Bush. At Rumsfeld's urging, Ford also stripped Kissinger of his oversight of the National Security Council and appointed his deputy, Brent Scowcroft, in his place. Rumsfeld was also gunning for Nelson Rockefeller. Rockefeller, deeply unhappy in the role of vice president, jumped before he was pushed when he declared that he was taking himself off the ticket as Ford's running mate in 1976.

Almost immediately, Ford's decision to fire Schlesinger backfired. Lieutenant General Daniel Graham, chief of the Defense Intelligence Agency, which coordinated military intelligence, handed in his resignation in protest. Ronald Reagan declared himself "shocked." The two winners in the political drama were Treasury Secretary Bill Simon, who emerged unscathed, and Rumsfeld, who now began to stalk Kissinger. At a single stroke, the Shah's two most powerful protectors in Washington, Henry Kissinger and Nelson Rockefeller, had been marginalized. Bill Simon telephoned Kissinger to sympathize. They both knew what was coming. Having disposed of Schlesinger, Colby, and Rockefeller, Rumsfeld was coming after Kissinger.

"The guy that cut me up inside this building isn't going to cut me up any less in Defense," Kissinger said.

"It is going to be worse, Henry," said Simon.

"Huh?"

"It is going to be worse."

"That's right."

"And I . . ."

"And I know you and he are going to form a team."

"That would be a team!" Simon exclaimed. "That'll be a team!"

Kissinger could only laugh. Despite their differences on oil policy, he enjoyed Simon's charm. The same could not be said for the new team over at Defense. On December 22 Kissinger telephoned Robert Ellsworth, Simon's counterpart as the chairman of the U.S.-Saudi Security Cooperation Commission. Gerald Ford had just appointed Ellsworth to the post of deputy secretary of defense under Rumsfeld. At year's end, the U.S.-Iran bilateral oil deal had landed on the desk of one of the Shah's most severe critics and a strong proponent of closer military relations with Saudi Arabia. "We have been talking about this for nine months with Iran," said Kissinger. "Time is running out. We have to make a proposal or say we are not going to do it. I just wondered what your objections were. Since I am told you are the one holding it now."

Ellsworth explained that he had two problems. "We do not operate in the world crude market," he explained. "We deal with refined products." Maybe Frank Zarb could do something about it.

"It has been my experience that when Defense wants to do it, you can hire somebody to do it," Kissinger shot back.

Ellsworth told Kissinger that his advisers in the Pentagon were not lying when they told him that nothing further could be done. Moreover, he explained that the deal offered no real economic benefit to the United States: "The whole crude market is full—they are not really offering very much in order to get rid of the 500,000 barrels a day." The only way it could be done, he said, was as a straight oil-for-arms deal. In the meantime, Iran's economy continued to bleed.

Chapter Ten

THE SPIRIT OF '76

"I genuinely fear that this may be the first vague rumbling of impending revolution."

—Asadollah Alam, 1976

"The dilemma we are in is that rumors are spreading that we are in collusion."

—Prince Abdullah, 1976

IRAN IS ON THE VERGE OF MOVING AWAY FROM US

At the dawn of the American Bicentennial year U.S.-Iran relations were at their lowest ebb since the early 1960s. The obvious tensions over oil pricing remained unresolved. Arms sales were mired in scandals involving cost overruns, price fixing, and kickbacks. The collapse of the Kurdish resistance tarnished the Shah's standing among conservatives and liberals. There were questions too about Iran's commitment to the security of Israel. Kissinger's inability to deliver on the bilateral oil deal only added to the growing sense of mutual distrust in both capitals. The latest flare-up was over nuclear cooperation. The White House learned that during a recent trip to India Dr. Ahmad Etemad, the chairman of Iran's Atomic Energy Organization, had told his hosts that Iran was committed to developing nuclear power for economic reasons that included the detonation of "peaceful nuclear explosions" to dig canals and move mountains. Etemad also insisted that Iran would not allow foreign governments to dictate the terms of its handling of nuclear fuel. His stance appeared to rule out the American preference for a multinational enrichment facility.

Three months earlier Iran had entered into a secret pact with South Africa to buy enough uranium to power up to a hundred nuclear power plants at an estimated cost of between $700 million and $1 billion. Under the terms of the deal Iran would help to finance the construction in South Africa of a big new uranium enrichment facility. The South Africans would supply Iran with ore from its occupied territory of Namibia. The Ford administration had agreed to sell Iran eight nuclear power plants but opposed granting Iran the right to reprocess uranium in Iranian-built and managed facilities. The Shah's South Africa deal directly challenged U.S. domination of the international uranium trade. This was his way of evading his ally's restrictions. "This story has been denied publicly, but in confidence an [Iranian] official has confirmed that there is a secret agreement to purchase uranium from South Africa," Embassy Tehran alerted Washington. "It is evidently being kept under wraps at the insistence of South Africa." In a separate communication, Ambassador Helms informed Secretary of State Kissinger that Iran was "seeking foreign—including American—expertise to help prospect for uranium within Iran, and is reportedly entering into joint ventures for uranium exploration in central Africa."

On January 12, a tetchy Henry Kissinger faced a revolt from his senior staff on the two key issues of nuclear cooperation and unrestricted arms sales. Deputy Secretary of State Robert Ingersoll asked if Kissinger had had a chance to "look at this nuclear position with Iran."

"No one has given it to me yet," Kissinger groused. "What if they gave it to me? In a way, it is not comprehensible."

"Well, we need to give them some guidance—"

"Well, we better get it into our heads that Iran is on the verge of moving away from us. And since we always apply our morality to our friends—"

"This isn't morality," Ingersoll calmly replied. "This is a suggestion that we go to see the Shah by top-level State Department—"

"Tell him what he has already known," said Kissinger. "He will not accept it, I'm sure. I haven't read it. Am I wrong?"

"No. It's really to find out—"

"It's a lecture on nuclear proliferation and its contribution to it," interrupted Kissinger. He ridiculed Ingersoll's suggestion that Washington send an envoy to Tehran to clarify whether Dr. Etemad's views were shared by the Shah. "Well, Helms can find that out," he retorted. "That's easily found out. To send a top-level guy to Iran to ask him where he stands in relation to his bureaucracy is an insult."

"It isn't just that. It's to point out the problem of proliferation and—"

"Oh, come on!" snapped Kissinger. "He knows the problems of prolifer-ation. This is one of these—we're going to wind up with a combination of things—pushing the Shah in a direction where five years from now we'll be on our knees begging him to do a tenth of the things he now does volun-tarily at a heavy price. That's going to be the end result of all this brilliant, profound, moral—"

Remarkably, Ingersoll and his colleagues kept at it. Under Secretary of State Joseph Sisco joined the fray. The exchange was polite, the message clear: it was time for a course correction in relations with Iran.

"There's a concrete proposal in the paper," said Sisco. "I think you ought to look at it." Sisco wasn't done. The Shah was threatening to cut back on his defense expenditures unless the U.S. members of the oil consortium agreed to buy more oil from the National Iranian Oil Company to sell on the world market. Under the terms of the 1973 accord they signed with the Shah the companies yielded their operational role to the Iranian company in exchange for a twenty-year preferred access contract to sell Iranian crude oil on the world market. But they weren't required to buy the oil and now, with market demand in a slump, they had no incentive to do so. As usual, the Shah wanted it both ways. He would not allow the National Iranian Oil Company to cut back any further on production. Yet he refused to haggle with the companies over price. The result was a standoff that left the Shah with still more millions of barrels of unsold oil on his hands. He threatened another big price increase when OPEC met in Bali in May unless the com-panies fell into line. Kissinger's aides thought the time had come to call the Shah on his bluff. They accepted that U.S. arms sales were gnawing at the foundations of the Iranian economy and saw in the Shah's threat to reduce defense spending an opportunity to force fiscal restraint on Tehran.

"Mr. Secretary," said Joseph Sisco, "on the related question that you mentioned, how concerned are you on this move of his to cut back? I don't personally believe that it's all bad."

"I'm sure that Senator Kennedy will love it."

"But the Shah was basically, in my judgment, overcommitted in terms of what he's trying to do—particularly on the military side—over the last year or two," said Sisco. "I think he's terribly overcommitted. And if he comes to his own judgment to cut back, I'm wondering if that's so bad."

"The great specialty—first of all—of this Department is to tell other people how to run their affairs, not having solved our own," Kissinger rebuked Sisco. "I have proceeded on the premise that we should let other countries determine their own priorities. Secondly, why is he cutting back?

If he came to the conclusion that he should cut back on general grounds, we would certainly not urge him to over-defense himself. Thirdly, he generally feels that our role in the world is declining, and he has to reassess. Those are his principal reasons, and because some other deals he wanted to make with us are falling through. So for a combination of a number of reasons, he's cutting back; and that's not at all helpful. It can't be helpful to American foreign policy. Of many American friends in the world, there's no one who can point to something forthcoming we've done for them."

"Well, that's a general problem," Sisco concurred.

Two days later, Kissinger and his senior deputies reconvened.

Sisco suggested to Roy Atherton that they prepare a briefing memo for Kissinger that would examine not only the vexing question of oil liftings but also the array of problems taking a toll on American-Iranian relations.

Still the problems kept piling up. On January 19, Defense Secretary Rumsfeld hosted General Toufanian, the Shah's head of weapons procurement, in a private dining room at the Pentagon. They quickly got into a dispute over who was responsible for the swirling military contract scandals that included the sale of Grumman F-14 fighter jets. Rumsfeld took umbrage at Toufanian's tone of voice. It was the Iranians, he insisted, who were at fault and not the Americans. Toufanian gave Rumsfeld a tongue-lashing, calling him "uninformed . . . not his own man." The general wanted to know: "How can Iran be responsible for Grumman and Litton cost overruns as reported by your own U.S. press?" They were stealing from Iran.

"Yeah, but the price of your oil has tripled," Air Force General Howard Fish tartly replied.

The lunch broke up in rancor.

Back in Tehran, Toufanian wrote a scathing assessment of Rumsfeld for the Shah. He described the forty-two-year-old secretary of defense as "political, forceful, shallow, immature, inexperienced in the defense matters of his job." The Shah severed relations with Eric von Marbod, the Pentagon representative in Iran, and ordered no further contact with his staff.

Relations between the Department of Defense and Iran descended into a deep chill. "It's raw, it's awfully raw, more than anyone dares show," said one American official. "From the way we've behaved, they've lost all trust in us." Washington insiders speculated that Treasury Secretary Simon might have a new ally in his crusade against the Shah. "Attempting to bully Rumsfeld, one of Washington's most cold-blooded infighters, was a colossal tactical error," wrote Evans and Novak. "What remains to be seen is whether Rumsfeld might join Treasury Secretary William Simon in renewing an old policy dispute inside the Ford administration. Simon still wants confrontation against the international oil cartel (OPEC) in general and Iran in particular to break world oil prices. Until now, President Ford has rejected Simon's advice and accepted Secretary of State Henry Kissinger's policy of aiding OPEC members—including heavy arms aid for Iran."

The furor left Ambassador Richard Helms despondent. "Nothing good would happen in the U.S. government until the end of the election," he reportedly told one colleague who kept a note of their meeting. "He had never seen such a weak government and so many people out of control in the Pentagon."

Also out of control was Iran's economy. On Thursday, January 22, Court Minister Alam received a briefing from Abdul Majid Majidi, the head of the Plan and Budget Organization, which left him shocked and depressed at the dire state of the government's finances. "I genuinely fear that this may be the first vague rumbling of impending revolution." Alam had always understood the causal link between economic prosperity and the survival of the Pahlavi dynasty. The regime's "oily legs" were trembling. "He told me that we're in deficit on this year's budget by as much as $4 billion and that the government is conniving at the most senseless extravagance. . . . The losses we've incurred in buying wheat, sugar and other foodstuffs are beyond belief."

BREAKFAST AT THE RITZ-CARLTON

The Shah suspected the White House "was stalling" on the secret oil deal being negotiated between Hushang Ansary and Frank Zarb. He knew that the refusal of Western oil companies to increase their Iranian liftings left his economy doubly exposed to the vagaries of the market. "The bastards have thrown down a serious challenge to us," he said of the oil companies. "So much for their protestations of goodwill." Alam was shocked to learn that Iran's oil production had plunged by 1.7 million barrels per day, a decline equal to a $6 billion shortfall in government income for the coming year. Alam suspected Kissinger was playing a double game behind their backs.

In early January, Kissinger and Helms flew to London for a private meeting with Finance Minister Ansary. Iran's fiscal crisis threatened to have profound flow-on effects for American national security objectives and the array of covert military actions being undertaken in the developing world with the help of Washington's Persian gladiator. The Shah had recently declined the U.S. request to funnel aid to anti-Communist guerrilla fighters in Angola. A flurry of meetings ensued between American and Iranian envoys in London. On Saturday, January 24, Kissinger's aide Joseph Sisco held follow-up talks with Ansary and cabled a summary back to the State Department. He reported to Kissinger that the Iranian had expressed frustration that the terms of the bilateral oil deal had still not been concluded in Washington. He told Sisco that he believed he had reached an "understanding" with Kissinger and Helms at their meeting in London earlier in the month "although one key element (i.e., discount) remained to be worked out." Ansary offered to meet with Kissinger again, this time in New York or the Bahamas, where he would be recuperating from a hospital stay, so they could complete a draft agreement for the Shah's approval. On the same day in Tehran, Alam met with Ambassador Helms to talk about oil production and pricing. Helms said he understood the difficulties facing Iran's economy and "promised to do what he can on our behalf."

A week later, on January 30, Ansary telephoned Kissinger to remind him of the sense of urgency on the Iranian side. Kissinger recorded the conversation. "You know our last meeting in London—we got over so many problems," said Ansary. "I am sorry things have not moved as fast as anticipated because I don't know what the problems are on your side but I have the strong feeling that you and I should get together." Kissinger said they would meet again soon: "I understand you are going to see [Charles] Robinson next week. After you talk to him, you and I should get together."

Kissinger was caught in a bind. He had a habit of telling his interlocutors what he thought they needed to hear so that he could get what he wanted from them. At one time Kissinger would have had no trouble delivering on his end of the oil deal for the Shah. But this was 1976, not 1972, and the political landscape in Washington had changed since Nixon's departure. Kissinger, however, had not changed with the times. Nixon had given him carte blanche to manage U.S. foreign policy. Gerald Ford was much more focused on teamwork, the economy, and managing the fallout from the oil shock. Foreign economic policy was the strong suit of men like Simon, Zarb, and Greenspan. By January 1976 Kissinger knew that he could not deliver everything he had promised the Shah. Yet he worried that if the Shah knew this, he might find other uses for Iran's oil wealth and its 436,000-strong armed forces. This was not an irrational fear on Kissinger's part. The Shah was determined to hold American feet to the fire. He wanted no more excuses. "If you try to take an unfriendly attitude toward my country, we can hurt you as badly if not more so than you can hurt us," he told *U.S. News & World Report* in early 1976. "Not just through oil—we can create trouble for you in the region. If you force us to change our friendly attitude, the repercussions will be immeasurable. . . . A false sense of security will destroy you."

A turning point came on February 11 when Kissinger signed a presidential memo that reflected the views of his aides Sisco and Atherton. "The Shah of Iran has, during the last six to eight months, come to realize that, in spite of a dramatic increase in Iran's income from oil since 1973, his expected revenues will not meet the costs of his ambitious civilian and military development programs," Kissinger told Ford. In the fourth quarter of 1975 Iran's exports of heavy crude oil had plummeted by 1.5 million barrels per day. The Shah had approached the administration to help him plug the gaping hole in his finances. "In the last few weeks the Shah has made a series of direct and indirect approaches to us seeking assistance of this Government in putting pressure on American oil companies to increase their purchases of Iranian oil," read the memo. "He has suggested that, if Iran's oil income does not rise to meet his development spending plans, he will have to revise his foreign policy to fit the country's more modest financial capabilities." Kissinger explained that Western consumer demand for Iran's heavy crude oil had collapsed. That made it "impossible for us to be of any substantial assistance in increasing Iran's oil income." Further, Kissinger made it clear that the United States could offer no relief in the sensitive matter of cost overruns for the Shah's imports of American military equipment.

Kissinger's memo was his first acknowledgment of the damage to Iran's economy and society wrought by arms sales. "We note, incidentally, that a decision by the Shah to slow the pace of his defense development program would have the positive aspect of permitting Iran's strained manpower and infrastructure to catch up with equipment procurements," he wrote. Kissinger had in effect thrown in his lot with those who argued that the Shah's profligate spending had gone too far and that it was now in the American interest to see that the Shah had fewer resources (that is, less income from oil) to devote to the military purchases overloading Iran's economy. Kissinger urged that "a damage-limiting effort is in order to reassure the Shah that our inability to be of assistance has not diminished our interest in maintaining and expanding our special relationship with Iran." He proposed that the president send the Shah a letter providing the necessary assurances. Kissinger's memo was sent first to the desk of National Security Adviser Brent Scowcroft.

What Kissinger did next defied the laws of logic. He flew back to London for a breakfast meeting with Hushang Ansary at the Ritz-Carlton. Kissinger might have been expected to brief Ansary on the change in U.S. policy and the administration's belief that Iran's economy warranted a cooling-off period and fewer weapons purchases. This he did not do. Like the Shah's doctors, aides, and family members, Kissinger did not believe the Shah capable of hearing the truth, let alone dealing with its consequences. So he engaged in a deception, one that would have far-reaching consequences for both the United States and Iran. Kissinger's private meeting with Ansary was kept low-key to avoid alerting the press. That we know their tête-à-tête happened at all is due to a remarkable cable summary of the talks prepared by Charles Robinson, who accompanied his boss to the Ritz-Carlton.

According to Robinson's memo, Iran's finance minister explained to Kissinger the scale of the financial crisis unfolding in Iran. The country's income from oil had flatlined. Western oil companies were buying only 3.3 million barrels of Iranian oil per day. Ansary admitted that this was "to some extent" the fault of the Shah, who stubbornly refused to reduce the price of Iran's crude exports to adapt purchases of Persian crude oil to the new market reality. The Iranian government hoped to "push" the oil companies' liftings back up to 4.9 million barrels per day. Together, Ansary and Kissinger agreed that the bilateral oil deal, now dragging into its second year of negotiations, offered the Shah a financial lifeline and a way out of the trap he had set for himself and now could not get out of. Robinson's document suggests that Kissinger was playing for time. He explained to an apparently surprised Ansary that the deal had not in fact been approved by President Ford. And he lied when he claimed he had just learned that the deal required congressional authorization before it could proceed. The Iranians, he added, should lower their asking price for the oil they sought to offload.

Kissinger informed Ansary, also apparently for the first time, that the deal was violently opposed within the White House by Simon, Rumsfeld, Zarb, and Bob Ellsworth. Ansary agreed with Kissinger that "we would not push this program for the moment, recognizing the need to get Rumsfeld, Ellsworth and Zarb on board before proceeding with an aggressive effort to conclude this arrangement." In the meantime, to help the Shah meet his defense needs and pay his suppliers, Kissinger agreed that officials from the State Department would quietly meet with representatives of leading U.S. defense contractors to encourage them to pursue arms-for-oil swaps with

Iran, Kissinger and Ansary also decided that confidence-building measures were required to get U.S.-Iran relations back on track. Kissinger promised to set up a meeting between Ansary and President Ford to discuss "the importance of continued U.S. support for Iran's expanding military capability." Ansary's meeting with the president would be followed up with "a small dinner affair with Rumsfeld, Ellsworth and Zarb in an effort to [increase their] sense of participation in our relationships with Iran."

Incredibly, Kissinger then assured Ansary that he still supported Iran's current high levels of spending on defense. It was a stance totally at odds with what he had just recommended to President Ford four days earlier in his memo of February 11. "You supported Ansary's view that Iranian oil exports should be maintained at a high level to provide funds necessary for purchase of U.S. military equipment," Robinson reminded Kissinger. Nor was that all. At the conclusion of the meeting the note takers left the two men alone at Ansary's request so they could discuss "personal matters."

The nature of those "personal matters" was hinted at several weeks later during one of Kissinger's recorded telephone conversations. "Are things moving satisfactorily on the personal front?" Ansary asked.

"I think so," replied Kissinger.

"Are you getting the businessmen together?"

"Yes," said Kissinger. He left it at that and moved on to other matters. We still don't know what Ansary's private business proposition involved, why the American secretary of state's help was needed in "getting the businessmen together," or how such dealings may have affected U.S. foreign policy toward Iran.

It is never an easy matter to interpret the motives of a master tactician like Henry Kissinger. What we do know is that over the winter of 1975–76 President's Ford's foreign policy team had been alerted to Iran's deteriorating fiscal situation. The Shah had quietly reached out to them for help. The U.S. foreign policy team knew that U.S. arms sales were draining Iran's civilian economy of precious capital and skilled manpower. Nixon's 1972 blank check on arms sales to Iran had created its own inevitable, destructive dynamic. But how to stop it? How to break the cycle? The Shah made it clear that any decision to reimpose restrictions on arms sales would be seen in Tehran as a loss of confidence by the Americans in their ally.

"Now the question was what did [Iran] need, what did it want, and that was kind of complicated to figure out," remembered Brent Scowcroft. "I think we were concerned because weapon prices were going up and that was taking more money out of the Iranian budget which the Shah didn't have, and that was a concern to us. But how to deal with that?" The problem the administration faced on arms sales was that "if you tell the Shah we're not going to give [him] enough arms that looks to him like we're decreasing our support for him to try and put pressure on him."

Iran's military buildup had gone far beyond what Kissinger or Nixon ever intended. Worse, the Shah did not know when to stop. "He was trying to do too much, too soon, always," said Scowcroft. Kissinger's memo to Ford proposed a course of action that ensured Iran would generate *lower* oil revenues so that the Shah had *less* money to spend on arms. Yet to Ansary, Kissinger pledged his commitment to help the Shah generate *higher* oil revenues to maintain *high* spending on arms. As a result of Kissinger's assurance, the Shah apparently felt no need to adjust spending patterns or rein in fiscal profligacy at home. He kept placing orders for more military equipment because he expected another bailout in the form of a future hike in oil prices. Why did Kissinger tell Ford one thing and Ansary something completely different? "Well, these [things] aren't always carefully coordinated, as you can see, because we're playing against ourselves," Scowcroft ruefully observed.

HIS MAJESTY IN A LITIGIOUS MOOD

Henry Kissinger took to handling the tiresome Shah in the same way he had handled Nixon on his worst days, responding to any unpleasantness by ladling out dollops of flattery with the regularity and enthusiasm of Mr. Bumble feeding the workhouse boys. It was a task made infinitely more difficult and unpleasant for him by Jack Anderson, the journalist who continued to hound the Shah at every turn. Ambassador Ardeshir Zahedi phoned Kissinger to warn him that the Shah was threatening to sue Anderson over remarks he had made on a morning television news show. Anderson had repeated his earlier claim that the CIA had produced a psychological profile of the Shah that concluded the Iranian leader was "mentally ill." Kissinger claimed not to know anything about the profile but promised to follow the matter up with CIA director George Bush. Kissinger and Zahedi were eventually successful in persuading the Shah not to proceed with a lawsuit that would result in public embarrassment for both governments.

Kissinger was convinced he knew who was behind the sabotage. "What was it Simon said last year?" he asked Zahedi. "What was the word he used?"

"I don't dare repeat it," said Zahedi.

"You have to give the Shah my affectionate greetings. He is one of the few world leaders for whom I have substantive regard. If he had a country of 200 million we would all be better off. Come to think of it, if he had a country of 200 million he might conquer the world."

"You don't want me to tell him that?"

"You can tell him that. You don't think he would mind?"

"No, I think he would like it."

"Tell him I said it with affection."

MR. FORD ASKS A FAVOR OF THE SHAH

The dangerous games continued. President Ford's political advisers, apparently knowing nothing of Kissinger's assurances to Ansary, decided that if the Shah wanted the United States to take Iran's surplus oil off his hands then he should reciprocate with a freeze on oil prices, at least until the end of the year when the election was out of the way. Oil ministers from OPEC were due to meet in Bali at the end of May to consider another price increase. There had always been the risk that Gerald Ford would repeat Richard Nixon's mistake of turning to the Shah to cut a deal and help his chances to win election. The White House wanted to strengthen consumer confidence in the run-up to November. The risk to Ford was obvious—if the Shah agreed to the trade, the two leaders would then be indebted to each other. This naturally suited the purposes of the Shah. Cutting deals with the Shah was a temptation for American presidents because their Tehran back channels allowed for speed and flexibility. More than anything, Gerald Ford wanted to win the presidency on his own terms. He detested his Republican rival, former California governor Ronald Reagan, the darling of their party's conservative wing, a politician who shared Simon's free market orthodoxy. On March 30, Ford was in the Oval Office with Kissinger when he asked, "How did you make out with Ansary and the oil deal?"

Kissinger described where things stood.

"I think we should ask the Iranians to hold the line on prices this summer," said Ford. It was not so much a request as an order to his secretary of state. Ford wanted an extension of the OPEC price freeze: "That would mean much more to us than a discount on 200,000 barrels a day."

"I think we can get them to do that," said Kissinger, who may have been surprised at Ford's assertion of authority. Until now Kissinger had enjoyed a free hand in U.S.-Iran relations and running his back channels to Tehran.

The president wanted to make one other thing absolutely clear. He had heard that Nixon was planning a trip to Iran to see his old friend the Shah. Under no circumstances, Ford told Kissinger, should that trip proceed. The president couldn't have been more explicit: "I have heard maybe Nixon is going to Iran. He cannot do that." Scowcroft recalled the incident this way: "I think it was probably because negotiations here were pretty tense and delicate and God only knows what Nixon might have said or done. Because he felt very close to the Shah." Nixon maintained their connection through Ardeshir Zahedi, who kept up his friendship with the former president. The ambassador would helicopter to Nixon's oceanside retreat at San Clemente during weekend getaways to the Palm Springs home of Walter and Lee Annenberg, who were also close friends of the Reagans.

Kissinger said he would take care of the problem. "Let me talk to the Iranians. I think this is the best way to turn it off." He then telephoned Ansary and told him the bilateral oil deal was back on: "I have talked to the President and we are going to push it now. We have to find out—we don't want to get into the position Zarb proposed to you, but we want something we can live with."

Zarb, coincidentally, was required to come up with a plan by December 15, 1976, to buy one billion barrels of petroleum on the world market for the planned U.S. strategic reserve. Of that total, 150 million barrels had to be accumulated within three years of Congress approving the president's energy plan. "It is important that we move as quickly as possible, to accumulate strategic reserves as a buffer against a potential embargo," NSC official Robert Hormats reminded Scowcroft on March 12, "and as a deterrent to less wealthy oil exporters who might be reluctant to participate in an embargo knowing that the U.S. can sustain itself for a relatively long period without imports." This latter point was an obvious reference to Iran. The United States was preparing for a showdown with OPEC.

Kissinger's transcripts confirm that Zarb was negotiating at cross-purposes to the secretary of state. Zarb's hard-line terms were a seven-year agreement with Iran to sell 300 million barrels of oil to the United States for its strategic reserve. He stuck to his threshold of a $3 discount per barrel. When Ansary complained that Zarb's negotiating terms were unacceptable to the Shah ("Zarb's proposals would put him in a spot"), Kissinger agreed they were "ridiculous" and told him not to worry—he would take care of it. This pleased Ansary, who replied that "it would be a good thing to get Zarb to see the light."

A SUDDEN ICY WIND

Nineteen seventy-six marked the fiftieth anniversary of the founding of the Pahlavi dynasty in Iran. A round of royal celebrations and provincial tours was planned at the beginning of the Iranian new year beginning in late March. Alam's diary shows that Mohammad Reza Shah was also keeping an eye on the American presidential contest. The Shah wanted to learn more about the leading Democrat, former governor of Georgia Jimmy Carter, a supporter of human rights and a vocal critic of the international arms trade. He worried that if Carter were elected he would demand liberal political reforms in Iran as John F. Kennedy had done in the early 1960s. Alam forwarded to the Shah a cartoon from an American publication depicting both Ford and Carter in an unflattering light. Alam said "the artist had grasped Ford's native stupidity." The Shah was amused. Nonetheless, Alam warned him, "Carter may turn out to be an even greater ass than Ford."

The terrorist threat in Iran was intensifying by the month. January began on a low note with the announcement that an Iranian army tribunal had sentenced to death ten terrorists for the murders of Colonel Lewis Hawkins in 1973 and Colonels Paul Shaffer and Jack Turner two years later. The Shah was impressed yet bewildered by the level of fanaticism displayed by his young opponents.

On Sunday, March 21, the imperial family gathered in the rain before the tomb of Reza Shah to mark their jubilee. The dour public mood was as overcast as the gray skies. A rumor had taken hold that the jubilee would bring bad luck to the crown. "Particularly on that day I felt something had changed between the people and the monarchy; I could feel it in my bones, like a sudden icy wind," recalled Queen Farah. "There seemed to me an intangible shadow over the harmony and confidence between us." Six months earlier the queen had hosted an international symposium in Persepolis to consider the impact and future of Iran's economic changes and social reforms. In her opening remarks she acknowledged that the people of Iran were "traumatized by the conflicting winds of tradition and change." Others at the assembly warned of the "alarming" buildup of pressure within the political system, and of a ruling elite that was "vulnerable to popular disaffection." In the summer of 1976 the queen took her concerns public when she described as "dangerous" the exodus of rural migrants into cities where they faced social isolation, unemployment, and destitution.

The Shah was surrounded by enablers and sycophants. On the eve of the

Pahlavi jubilee celebrations the royal couple hosted a dinner party. When the queen made a gesture to stop her husband's dog "from poking his nose into people's plates," the Shah asked what she thought she was doing. "Flatterers everywhere!" she snapped. "I refuse to follow their example. Even this dog is fawned upon just because he's yours. I alone refuse to stoop to such nonsense." The queen noticed something else—swelling on her husband's upper lip. She still knew nothing about his lymphoma but later remembered that it was around this time the Shah began immersing her and their oldest son, Crown Prince Reza, in the art of statecraft. He was in a race against the clock to train his heirs and lay the groundwork for a peaceful transfer of power. Still, he did not think the time right to confide in his wife. "Several times a week Reza and I were taken to confer with the prime minister, then with each of the ministers involved in current affairs," she recalled. "We also received the chiefs of the armed forces, representatives of different institutions, and particularly those of the parliament. I found it a difficult and delicate situation, for I didn't imagine for one second that I would have to succeed him one day, and yet I obviously had to take this 'training' seriously and question him as if he were going to die."

To mark the Pahlavi jubilee President Ford wrote a letter of congratulations and sent Vice President Rockefeller to Iran. The Shah was deflated. He noticed how the dynasty's jubilee had been welcomed with greater enthusiasm by eastern bloc countries than by Iran's allies in the West. The Pahlavis received Rockefeller at their winter palace on the island of Kish. Cynthia Helms watched the Shah's stricken reaction when the vice president publicly lauded him as the heir to Alexander the Great, seemingly unaware that Alexander was the man who invaded Persia and "destroyed Persepolis and stole Persian wealth." In the car on the way to the airport, Rockefeller, still bitter from the events of last November, told Alam that he resented "the slowness of decision-making in the USA, a great contrast to the way things are done here." He seemed to think the lash would do the American people some good: "You should lend us His Imperial Majesty for a couple of years. He'd soon teach us how to govern America."

Iranian society, meanwhile, was coming unhinged. During a state visit to Tehran, President Anwar Sadat of Egypt and his wife, Jehan, were the guests of honor at a dinner hosted by an Iranian government official. "The steps leading up to the very large house were made of crystal. Crystal! Never had I seen that before—nor have I seen it since," remembered Jehan Sadat. "Nothing was ordinary. Chocolate mousse was offered as one of the desserts in swans made of spun sugar and presented against a backdrop of a huge aquarium filled with tropical fish. Fountains splashed, the guests strolled between the food tables and the dining tent on a bridge over a small pond, and we ate off place settings of gold." To Sadat she whispered: "There will be a revolution. I can feel it. The rich here are too rich and the poor too poor without enough of a middle class to provide stability. The Shah must do something quickly to calm the people, give more of his land away, perhaps drop the title of emperor and call himself president. . . . I am going to tell this to the Shah." Her husband forbade her to do any such thing. "You must not stick your nose into other people's business," he cautioned her. "The Shah will listen to you out of politeness and then he will not change anything. So what's the use?"

European jet-setters flocked to Tehran's nightlife and kept the discotheques and hotels full. Yet Iranian society was coming to the boil. Many young Iranians, traumatized by the disorienting, chaotic effects of Western modernization, found solace in the mosques or simply retreated behind the veil. Alam visited Pahlavi University in Shiraz where, he told the Shah, he had been "rather alarmed to see so many of the girls wearing the veil." Students continued to protest against the Shah's policies. Alam urged the Shah not to put too much pressure on the university presidents because they have "enough trouble as it is and are literally battling for survival . . . they are genuinely afraid of assassination by the terrorists."

Few events in late imperial Iran were as revealing as the "Charles Jourdan Incident," a scandal that became a byword for the regime's air of fin de siècle exhaustion and decadence. Parviz Sabeti was a high-ranking SAVAK official. One day his wife went shopping in Tehran's chic Charles Jourdan ladies shoe store, only to discover when she reached the cashier's desk that her purse was missing from her bag. According to the version of the story that circulated at court, Mrs. Sabeti raised such a loud fuss that her bodyguards barred anyone from entering or leaving the store. "Close the doors," they announced. "We are going to search the people." Also in the store that day were two members of a family of high social standing, a middle-aged woman who was helping her daughter prepare for her wedding day.

"We have finished our business," said the aggrieved older woman. "We have not stolen anything. We are respectable people. We are going to go out."

"No," said the guard, "you cannot go out." The guard physically blocked her from leaving. The daughter's fiancé was waiting for the women outside in his car. He saw the commotion through the glass doors and ran to their assistance. Mrs. Sabeti's bodyguard reacted to the sudden movement by pulling out a gun and opening fire. The young man was shot to death in front of his fiancée and future mother-in-law. The store erupted in pandemonium. The story of the wedding tragedy quickly spread around town. Even the most cynical Tehranis were amazed that a son of privilege could be executed in broad daylight merely for defending the honor of female relatives.

The tragedy split Pahlavi society at the highest levels. When Mrs. Sabeti offered to attend the funeral of the young man, his family reportedly sent her this message: "Come if you want. But if you come, you must know you will be torn to pieces."

Perceptive diplomats and intelligence analysts living in Tehran sensed that something was happening though they could not as yet put their finger on what it might be. The capital was seething. In 1976 at least eighty-nine people in Tehran were killed in shootouts between the security forces and the underground or were executed by the regime for plotting terrorist actions.

On Saturday night, May 15, four policemen and eleven terrorists were killed in shootouts in three locations in Tehran. Six of the terrorists died within the city limits and five in Tehran's northern outskirts. Police seized machine guns, handguns, and explosives for bombs and booby traps. The following Tuesday a second firefight left seven male and three female terrorist fighters dead. Four innocent passersby were killed in the heavy barrage of crossfire between security forces and the young extremists. Rumors circulated that the crackdown and the killings were the work of a team of trackers operating on the margins of the Shah's security apparatus. Ambassador Helms raised the issue of the violence and unrest directly with Alam. Alam told Helms that "the entire movement is obviously inspired from abroad." Helms didn't buy it. He told Alam that "we cannot rule out public dissatisfaction here in Iran."

The bloodshed coincided with the Saturday night departure of Air Iran's inaugural 747 flight between New York and Tehran. In the tradition of the decade's great celluloid disaster epics the inaugural eleven-hour flight was packed with 150 celebrities from Hollywood and Washington. "Startrek to Iran, with Glitter," gushed *The Washington Post* of the junket billed as Iran's Bicentennial gift to the United States. Elizabeth Taylor led the way. The actress had spent the preceding week in Washington romancing Ardeshir Zahedi. Others on board included actress Cloris Leachman ("by all accounts the most refreshing and vivacious celebrity on the trip"), singer Connie Stevens, and oldies crooner Tony Martin, who had entertained the Pahlavis at the Nixon White House in 1973. Upon their arrival the Americans were greeted at Niavaran Palace by Queen Farah and treated to a reception. At the central bank they were given a guided tour of the vault containing the crown jewels. A belly dance performance brought a smile to the face of Ambassador Helms. The party hit the road, moving on to Isfahan, Shiraz, and finally Persepolis, where Ms. Taylor, evidently in need of rest, announced she was going to spend a few days in the Shah's tent city. It had indeed been a long week. "They were wined, dined and entertained in a splendor that rivaled the excesses of Xerxes," crowed Jack Anderson, who as usual couldn't resist an opportunity to rain on the Shah's parade. "None was invited, of course, to see Iran's seamier side. But behind all the glitter, the Shah rules by torture and terror, which are the antithesis of the U.S. principles he pretends to honor."

Over the summer of 1976 all of Iran was fixated on a murder mystery: who killed Ayatollah Abolhassan Shamsabadi in Isfahan? The revered cleric's funeral drew crowds estimated at 100,000 and stoked widespread indignation against the Shah. A rumor took hold that SAVAK had disposed of the respected religious leader in a clumsy effort to silence one of the Shah's leading religious critics. Iranians were also deeply offended, not to say left disoriented, by the Shah's unilateral decision to mark his jubilee by abolishing the country's Islamic calendar and instituting a new imperial calendar. "Few regimes have been foolhardy enough as to scrap their own religious calendar," wrote Iranian historian Ervand Abrahamian. The new Pahlavi calendar "allocated 2,500 years for the presumed length of the Iranian monarchy and another 35 years for Mohammad Reza Shah. Thus Iran jumped overnight from the Muslim year 1355 to the imperial year 2535." Mass confusion ensued. The Shah also announced intrusive new measures designed to increase state control over Shi'a religious institutions, publications, and teachings.

I DO NOT BELIEVE EUROPE LOOKS GOOD RIGHT NOW

The final and most dangerous phase of the oil shock for Western democracies was about to begin. For the past two years U.S. officials at State and Treasury had closely watched as two separate sets of dominoes, one geopolitical and the other financial, trembled under the impact of skyrocketing oil prices. The great danger was that governments in Europe, unable to pay their debts, would falter and trigger a wave of defaults. The defaults would wash through the canyons of Wall Street toppling banks that had taken on too much debt at the height of the recession. Europe's bleeding southern gut had been stitched together with transfusions of emergency bank loans, intensive diplomacy, and, in the case of Italy, outright bribery in the form of $6 million in cash from the CIA to prop up Rome's ruling Christian Democrats. The stitches came undone when revelations of these payments in January 1976 caused a national scandal that led to the fall of Italy's thirty-seventh postwar government and the collapse of the lira.

Italians sensed that this political crisis would not be like the others. Many middle-class and wealthy Italians began spiriting money out of the country. In one month Italy's caretaker government spent more than $500 million—half its foreign currency reserves—to defend the lira. It closed the foreign exchange market, applied for a $500 million loan from the International Monetary Fund, and appealed to the United States Federal Reserve to activate the terms of an accord under which Washington would make emergency funds available to prevent outright collapse. By the spring of 1976 Enrico Berlinguer's Communist Party governed all major cities north of Rome. There were Communist or Communist-Socialist administrations in five of Italy's twenty regions and in forty-two of its ninety-four provinces. Local Communist governments ruled 48 percent of the Italian population. "It has reached the point where the Christian Democrats cannot agree to govern with the Communists but cannot agree to govern without them either," a diplomat told *The New York Times*. "I find it hard to accept that all Western European countries are now watching like frightened rabbits while Italy goes Communist, doing nothing," Kissinger confided to Sir Anthony Crosland, Britain's foreign secretary, in the officers mess at the Royal Air Force Base at Waddington on April 24. "I can't think nothing can be done."

Further west, the Iberian Peninsula was in ferment. Following the death of Spain's Francisco Franco in November 1975 the dictator's successor, King Juan Carlos, had decided to break with more than three decades of Fascist rule and steer Spain toward Europe and liberal democracy. The king's chances of success were not high. Spain's economy was ravaged by high fuel costs and double-digit levels of unemployment and inflation that stoked political unrest in the form of strikes, protests, and extremist violence. "We think that the political situation has improved but that there is a serious economic problem that will have to be dealt with," Foreign Minister Jose Maria Areilza confided to Kissinger during a trip to Madrid. Spanish democracy would rise or fall with the economy. "We want to improve the economic situation and gradually move towards Europe but this we can only do when the reforms have taken hold." The king faced the very real danger of a coup from the far right and political violence from the far left. The loyalty of the Spanish army was in question. Areilza said it was "a question of order and discipline. . . . The most dangerous thing for an army is to be defeated and bored. We have some 200,000 conscripts but we only have enough money to have any kind of maneuver once each month."

Neighboring Portugal was preparing for its first free parliamentary and presidential elections. Washington's preferred candidate for the post of prime minister was Socialist Party leader Mario Soares. Soares was a respected pragmatist quietly working behind the scenes with leaders of the Catholic Church to block the Communists from making electoral gains. "We are now entering a period of progressive democratic nationalization," Soares told Kissinger. "Unless the economic situation produces an explosion with unexpected social agitation; the Communists would use that to attack us." Kissinger told Soares that while he still opposed allowing Communists into government on principle, he had erred in "analyzing your situation in an Italian framework." He agreed that the Portuguese Communists lacked real leadership and had overreached, though he felt this was something Enrico Berlinguer was not likely to do in Italy. "The tactical adjustments you have to make I cannot comment on," he told Soares. "But I must tell you that what you have done surprised me. I must admit this. I don't often make mistakes of judgement." Soares warned Kissinger that Euro-Communism was cresting across Western Europe. His own view was that "the overall situation in Italy is more dangerous than that in France." Mario Soares went on to form Portugal's first democratic government in April.

Euro-Communism was at high tide across the continent. The sense of crisis deepened in early June when Enrico Berlinguer flew to Paris to appear before a roaring crowd of forty thousand with Georges Marchais, leader of the French Communist Party. On the eve of the Italian parliamentary elections on June 21, widely seen in the United States as a crucial showdown between the ruling Christian Democrats and Berlinguer's Communist Party, a Gallup poll showed that 22 percent of Americans supported military intervention in Italy if Berlinguer came to power, 49 percent believed the United States should impose economic sanctions and use political pressure, and a further 13 percent advocated American withdrawal from NATO. In the event, the election ended in a virtual dead heat. The Christian Democrats won a victory in the popular vote but the Communists captured forty-nine new seats in the lower house Chamber of Deputies.

The Communists also picked up twenty-three seats in the Senate, leaving Berlinguer's 116 seats within striking distance of the Christian Democrats' 135. There was a dramatic rise in support for Italy's neofascist far right. But Kissinger's sole focus as usual was on the role the Communists would play in the next coalition government. "The essential problem which we confronted in the spring has not been fundamentally changed by the Italian election," he announced. Kissinger put the Italian political establishment on notice not to cut any side deals that might give Berlinguer political legitimacy. Western leaders gathered in Puerto Rico to announce they were placing tight strings on the availability of any new financing to bail out Italy's listing economy. Italy had already drawn its full quota of funding from the International Monetary Fund. "Bill Simon is going to treat Italy the way he treated New York," said one U.S. official, referring to Simon's unwillingness to provide loans to New York City during a financial crisis the previous year.

There was a sense that events in Italy were rushing to a climax. On July 1, West Germany's defense minister Georg Leber called on Kissinger at the State Department. "Italy needs a democratic alternative or [Berlinguer] will win out," he said.

"We agree with you on the [Communist Party] danger in Italy," said Kissinger. "They cannot participate in government. If they get in, it will influence elections in France, Spain and Portugal."

Two days later, Berlinguer won a major psychological victory when Italy's other political parties elected a Communist to the powerful post of president, or speaker, of the Chamber of Deputies. Kissinger swung into action. His telephone logs record that on July 10 he telephoned Henry Cabot Lodge, President Ford's envoy to the Vatican, to carry out a special assignment for the White House. Lodge had gained notoriety in South Vietnam in 1963 for advocating the coup that led to the ouster and assassination of President Ngo Dinh Diem. Lodge was widely regarded as an old-guard stalwart of the Washington establishment. Kissinger advised Lodge that "we need somebody to go to Italy and talk to some of the leaders there about our view on communist participation in government, and to do it as a sort of private emissary. We were wondering if you would be willing to do that."

Lodge accepted the assignment.

The Italians took the hint. On July 13, President Giovanni Leone asked the outgoing Christian Democratic minister of the budget, Giulio Andreotti, to form Italy's new government. U.S. officials breathed a sigh of relief.

YAMANI HOLDS THE LINE IN BALI

OPEC ministers met in Bali at the end of May and failed to agree on a new oil price. The current posted price of $11.51 per barrel remained frozen while members of the cartel agreed to try again at their December 15 meeting in Doha, the capital of Qatar. Bali was the scene of a bitter standoff between Saudi Arabia and Iran. The Iranians supported a 15 percent price rise, something that Sheikh Yamani made clear was unacceptable. In Washington, President Ford welcomed the stalemate and the news that oil prices would remain frozen through the summer. "In today's interdependent world, a stable and growing world economy is in every country's interest and the United States looks toward further improvements in the relationships between oil producing and consuming countries," he said. Ford had asked Kissinger to ask the Shah to hold the line on oil prices through the summer. In his diary on June 8, Court Minister Alam wrote that the Shah had recently sent a back channel through Helms agreeing not to approve an increase in oil prices at Bali, "in order to save President Ford embarrassment in the midst of his re-election campaign." Ford wrote a letter of reply to the Shah thanking him for the price freeze but making no mention of his presidential campaign.

BONFIRE IN BEIRUT

While American officials focused their attention on Southern Europe a new crisis exploded in the Eastern Mediterranean. On June 1, Syrian armored divisions invaded Lebanon to end the civil war that threatened to draw in its neighbors and engulf the region in a wider conflict. The U.S. and Israeli governments shared President Hafez Asad's fear that a victory by Palestinian and Muslim guerrilla fighters over Lebanon's Christian community would lead to the creation of a radical state aligned with Saddam Hussein's leftist regime in Iraq. While Syrian troops massed on the outskirts of Beirut waiting for the order to relieve a besieged, desperate city where armed gangs roamed with impunity and whose residents were running low on supplies of water, food, and fuel, gunmen ambushed a car driving U.S. ambassador Francis Melloy to a meeting with Lebanon's president. The bodies of the ambassador, his economics counselor, and their chauffeur were later found in a seaside garbage dump. Melloy had been shot in the head and chest.

President Ford ordered the evacuation of all 1,400 American nationals from Beirut and U.S. naval warships steamed toward the Lebanese coast. There were scenes of panic at Beirut airport when incoming shells ripped through an airliner sitting on the tarmac ready to fly out foreign nationals, killing the pilot and injuring crew members. Hundreds of Americans and other foreign nationals made a dash for the Syrian border in a land convoy. Secretary Kissinger ordered the embassy staff to get out immediately because "the PLO might be so desperate that they would be delighted to kill a few hundred Americans." Into the breach stepped King Khalid and Crown Prince Fahd of Saudi Arabia. The Saudis used their influence among the warring factions in Lebanon to help guarantee security for Americans who left Beirut by road. They were more than willing to prove their goodwill to the White House. With all his nationals accounted for, President Ford cabled King Khalid to thank him for "the effective assistance which you and your Government rendered us in our successful efforts to bring a substantial number of Americans and other citizens out of Beirut to safety. We were gratified that with this assistance the difficulties we encountered when we were preparing our road convoy were ultimately removed. This is the kind of cooperation which, I am sure, will continue to characterize our relations as we work together to bring the Mideast to a just and lasting peace."

THE SHAH'S CLOSE CALL

On Saturday, June 26, Mohammad Reza Shah played host to the president of India, who was known to have a heart condition. The Shah ordered that the route of the processional drive through the streets of Tehran from the airport be shortened to take into account his guest's declining health. The Shah's own health was less than ideal that month. In June he complained of stomach pains, a skin rash, and headaches.

The Shah's decision to alter the route at the last moment may have saved the lives of both heads of state. The Iranian hosts were at the airport waiting for the Indian delegation to deplane when Alam learned that a female terrorist had struck the original route back to the palace. Seeing that she had missed her chance, she tossed a grenade at two police officers who opened fire, killing her. The next day Alam advised the Shah to end the tradition of driving state guests through city streets; it was too dangerous.

He suggested in the future driving straight back to the palace and either avoiding the ceremonial procession or helicoptering from the city outskirts. Alam pointed out that but for the Shah's "change of plan, a stroke of inspiration," the day could have ended in disaster. "Not inspiration, merely common sense," the Shah replied. "Though perhaps the Almighty does have some sort of desire to protect me. No doubt so I may fulfill my mission to the people of Iran."

Tehran simmered. In the early morning hours of June 29, Iranian security forces quietly entered the basement of a building near Mehrabad airport. After months of surveillance they discovered that inside the building was Hamid Ashraf, the most wanted man in Iran, an iconic figure in the underground and a hero to many young Iranians. Ashraf was the oldest surviving member of the group of revolutionaries who carried out the original 1971 attack on the gendarmerie station at Siakal. Ashraf had taunted the Shah for years and carried out a string of headline-grabbing acts of sabotage. According to one scholar the security forces ringed the neighborhood seven times to make sure their quarry did not get out alive. Gunfire erupted as the commandos were trying to evacuate a couple and their child trapped in the building. With Ashraf were nine of the most senior members of the resistance leadership. They had gathered in an emergency session and been caught by surprise. In the ensuing firefight snipers in helicopters picked them off as they clambered up onto the roof to try to escape. The death of Ashraf and his nine comrades was a significant propaganda victory for the regime.

BICENTENNIAL SURPRISE

On July 2, the Ford White House received jarring news in the form of a report on the number of jobless Americans. A month earlier, the chairman of the President's Council of Economic Advisers, Alan Greenspan, had gone before Congress and confidently predicted that the United States was well on track to economic recovery: the worst of the oil shock was behind it. He forecast strong job growth and a drop in unemployment below 7 percent, a fall in annual inflation to between 5 and 6 percent, and an expansion in the gross national product by about 7 percent annually in real terms. He said the Ford administration did not need to provide fiscal stimulus to boost economic growth. America had cleared the hurdle of recession. Instead, Greenspan cautioned members of Congress that increased government spending might increase inflation. Ten days later the White House confidently brushed aside figures that showed the steepest fall in consumer retail spending in fourteen months. "Variations in the pace of economic activity during an expansion aren't unusual," said one economist at the Treasury. "The consumer can't be exuberant every month."

Yet the bad news kept coming, this time with the June jobs report. Instead of a decrease in the number of unemployed, the jobless rate climbed from 7.3 to 7.5 percent. "Temporary pauses of this kind aren't uncommon during periods of cyclical expansion," said Federal Reserve chairman Arthur Burns, who tried to reassure Americans they were not headed back into recession. Credit would remain tight because he and Greenspan wanted "to reassure the business community and financial community that we intend to stick to a course of monetary policy that will support further growth of output and unemployment, while avoiding excesses that would aggravate inflationary pressures." The danger for President Ford was that the economy was teetering on the brink of a double-dip recession in the middle of his presidential campaign with Jimmy Carter.

America's Bicentennial summer reached its fever pitch with a state banquet at the White House where Queen Elizabeth II was serenaded by pop duo singing sensation the Captain & Tennille warbling "Muskrat Love," a ballad about exactly what the title suggests. Critics deemed the song "unsuitable entertainment" for British royalty but Her Majesty "seemed to enjoy it thoroughly," said first lady Betty Ford.

Even now the country could not escape the shadow of Vietnam. In New York City on July 4, 225 tall ships sailed up the Hudson River to take the salute from President Ford on the carrier *Forrestal*. Kissinger was furious with a snafu involving the diplomatic corps. "The Pentagon is incredible and the Secretary of the Navy must be the dumbest alive," he unloaded to his staff. "For the review of ships on the Bicentennial he decided that the Navy had lost too many helicopters in Vietnam so the diplomatic corps would have to use barges to get to the *Forrestal* for the review." The result was that the ambassadors were stranded on the carrier without refreshments for hours and most watched the Bicentennial fireworks from a bus stuck in a traffic jam: "They were infuriated at such treatment." In Tehran, where the American School was the focal point of celebrations, the expatriate colony raised a toast as a giant American flag lit up a mountainside overlooking the metropolis.

The next morning's *New York Times* reported that yet another aftershock caused by high oil prices was headed toward American shores. The massive transfers of petrodollars that had followed the quadrupling of oil prices in 1973 had mostly been handled by American banks. The flexibility they had shown to international lenders and debtors had so far helped avoid the worst-case scenarios outlined by Ford, Kissinger, and Simon in their doomsday speeches from September 1974. But this had led to another potentially bigger threat to the world economy. "So great was the activity that American banks have been thrust into the role of the major suppliers of money to the world," reported the *New York Times*. "This development is causing some mixed reactions abroad and concern in the United States." Spain was about to receive a $1 billion loan from a syndicate of private lending institutions. Wall Street was eager to establish a presence in a country whose banking sector had until now been closed to foreign competition. Peru and Argentina were cited as just two of the dozens of countries lining up to take loans out from U.S. banks. Underwritings of this sort were "proceeding outside the control of monetary authorities." The danger for Wall Street was that American banks might be dangerously overexposed and left at risk from a single default somewhere along the line. "Concern has been expressed in Congress that American banks may be exposed to risks of withdrawals—and possible blackmail—by the large petrodollar depositors from the oil countries. Risks of insolvencies by major debtors are another cause for anxiety." Some 40 percent of Bank of America's earnings now came from its international business activities. The Morgan Guaranty Trust Company acknowledged that half of its outstanding loans were now made through overseas branches. Citibank and Chase Manhattan were also now heavily invested in lending to governments staggered by high fuel bills.

Wall Street banks had already been put on notice by H. Johannes Witteveen, the managing director of the International Monetary Fund. Earlier in the year Witteveen sounded the alarm when he declared that banks had to accept "some share of responsibility" if mounting debt burdens became hazardous for developing countries. He reminded them that "credits were sometimes granted in a market climate that wasn't very conducive to the maintenance of adequate [credit-worthiness] standards." Developing countries able to borrow money on an "all-too-easy" basis, warned Witteveen, were now struggling to meet their debt repayment schedules. Witteveen asked at what point "the mounting debt burden becomes hazardous." Total international lending to governments by private commercial banks had reached $250 billion at the end of 1975, a substantial increase from the $150 billion recorded in December 1973. U.S. banks and their foreign branches accounted for 40 percent of those totals.

Others took up the cry. In early June the Bank of International Settlements in Switzerland announced that the debt load taken on by many countries had reached "disturbingly high levels." The following week Allen Lambert, president of the International Monetary Conference, drew headlines when he warned that many countries hit by the fourfold increase in oil costs had taken out unwieldy loans and "the ability of these countries" to repay them "will be a dilemma which all of us must face." Peru, Indonesia, and Argentina were already trying to renegotiate their existing debt load. Panama, Zaire, Ghana, and countries in Southeast Asia were expected to join the queue. The real problem would come when these countries, especially the least developed states, which had taken out between $15 billion and $17 billion in private bank loans in 1975 alone, faced a hike in fuel costs. Another big increase in the price of oil might tip one or more countries to default on their debt repayments. The president of Morgan Guaranty Trust lectured his colleagues that "in a greedy drive for profits, American banks in the early 1970s had made bad loans in real estate investments and for other questionable purposes."

Only now was Wall Street beginning to take stock of its post-1973 lending binge. "How can presumably sophisticated bankers, who weigh every nickel of a $20,000 home mortgage loan, get so tangled up in bad or weak-quality loans running into the billions?" asked *Washington Post* columnist Hobart Rowen. The real issue, as he saw it, was their unwillingness to conduct effective risk assessment of those they extended loans to. "Banks simply must do a better job to assure their survival," he wrote. "To be sure, they are private institutions, but their solvency and stability have public ramifications." The warning signs "should be taken seriously by those bankers who still regard news media discussion of banking problems as an assault on the free enterprise system."

There were many weak links in the debt load chain. In the first six months of 1976 the IMF lent more money to member countries than in any previous year in the fund's history. By June 30, the total outstanding drawings, or loans, was counted at $15 billion. The biggest user of the fund was Great Britain, which had requested and received two separate drawings, one for $1 billion, and a second for $700 million. The British economy, which for the past several years had been treated with the fiscal equivalent of Band-Aids, was about to hemorrhage. On the evening of July 20, 1976, Chancellor of the Exchequer Denis Healey gravely informed backbench members of the governing Labour Party that if the government did not implement drastic cost cutting to reduce the deficit, the country faced the "possible collapse of the economy."

THE DANCE BEGINS

The threads of the final crisis of Gerald Ford's presidency were coming together and in the midst of his campaign for election. Officials in the White House were focusing on the December 15 OPEC ministers meeting in Doha, Qatar. Bill Simon's moment had arrived: it was time to bring the Saudis in from the cold. King Khalid's support for an oil price freeze and Saudi assistance in the evacuation of foreign nationals from Beirut had impressed administration officials as acts of statesmanship and proof that the kingdom was ready to take its place on the world stage. Oil prices, financial stability on Wall Street, political stability in Europe, the civil war in Lebanon, and the Middle East peace process were all elements of a grand bargain about to be struck by the American and Saudi leaders. They had to move quickly.

At 10:30 A.M. on Friday, July 9, 1976, Ford, Kissinger, and Scowcroft received Prince Abdullah bin Abd al-Aziz-Saud, Saudi Arabia's second deputy prime minister and commander of the Saudi National Guard; Sheikh Tuwayjiri, deputy commander of the National Guard for Finance and Administrations; and Saudi ambassador Ali Alireza. President Ford wasted no time in getting down to business. "We are grateful for the strong position that your government took on oil policies," he told his guests. "We think it is the right thing to do in terms of economic recovery and it's in the long term interests of both producers and consumers. As I am sure you know, we are doing our utmost to be helpful to the political settlement in Lebanon and we want to move as rapidly as possible to a settlement in the Middle East as a whole."

"This is a true fact, expressed brilliantly yesterday by the Secretary of State," Prince Abdullah complimented the president. "The dilemma we are in is that rumors are spreading that we are in collusion. As you are aware, these rumors are spread by enemies of us both—the Communists." Abdullah proceeded to lecture his hosts, politely but nonetheless firmly, of the risk the Saudi royal family was taking in associating so closely with the Americans "because we as your friends have been embarrassed on many occasions. For example, with Pakistan, Vietnam and Angola. We were told by people to look at the way you abandon your friends. The fact is we have been embarrassed by those accusations of the Arab people. It is known that the United States stands by its friends no matter what the situation is. But this talk is exploited by the Communists. This is my point."

Ford assured Abdullah that "after the election we will take action in accordance with the aims and principles we have in mind."

"That is what we expected," said Abdullah. The prince parted with a comment about power and its uses that had preoccupied American officials since Watergate, the October War, and the oil embargo: "The rule of government is prestige—if prestige disappears, the government is lost."

On July 31, the Ford administration announced that it had decided to sell thousands of new-generation "smart" missiles and bombs to Saudi Arabia. The sale included 2,500 Maverick air-to-surface missiles, 1,000 laser-guided bombs and 1,800 TOW missiles. This sale was in addition to a separate one involving 2,000 Sidewinder interceptor missiles and 16 Hawk ground-to-air missile launchers. Over the past two years the United States had sold the Saudis $6 billion in military equipment, second only to the amount purchased by Iran. U.S. officials stressed that "the continuing build-up of Iran's armed forces was not a factor in the Saudi request."

Chapter Eleven

ROYAL FLUSH

"Many countries have in fact virtually reached the end of their ability
to borrow."

—President Gerald Ford, 1976

"Nothing could provoke more reaction in us than this threatening
tone from certain circles and their paternalistic attitude."

—The Shah, 1976

WE WILL HAVE A RADICAL
REGIME ON OUR HANDS

Henry Kissinger made his final trip to Iran as secretary of state in August
1976. Three days before Kissinger flew to Tehran with wife, Nancy, and
David, his son by his first marriage, Senator Hubert Humphrey's subcommittee on Foreign Assistance, of the Committee on Foreign Relations,
released a damning report on U.S. arms sales to Iran. It described them as
"out of control" and concluded that the Iranian military was now so dependent on U.S. technical support that Iran could not go to war "without U.S.
support on a day-to-day basis." The report warned that tens of thousands
of Americans living in Iran were potential hostages if relations between
Washington and Tehran ever broke down. President Ford's challenger for
the presidency, Jimmy Carter, attacked as "cynical and dangerous" the Ford
administration's policy of "almost unrestricted arms sales" to Iran. Kissinger's anger was directed not at the Democrats but at his fellow Republicans
whom he knew had influenced the report's findings. "It couldn't be a worse
time," he complained to Ford. "Treasury and Defense are going after the
Shah. Simon is going around saying the Shah is dangerous and shouldn't

have exotic weapons. And [Robert] Ellsworth and Defense are viciously anti-Iran." He wanted Ford to clean house after the November election: "You can't do anything before November, but between Treasury and [Defense] they are on a vicious campaign."

"I will talk to Don [Rumsfeld] because I think Iran is very important to us," Ford responded.

"We are playing with fire," Kissinger warned Ford. "We have thrown away Turkey and now Iran. . . . Anyway, it will be rough in Iran. But if we get rid of the Shah, we will have a radical regime on our hands." Kissinger fretted that the anonymous slashing attacks from within the administration ran the risk of demoralizing the Shah and emboldening his domestic foes. It was beginning to look as though the United States was abandoning its ally.

Kissinger vented again in Tehran on August 7 when he hosted a gathering of America's Middle East ambassadors inside the U.S. embassy compound on Takht-e Jamshid Avenue. "I am really mad at all this criticism," the secretary told his envoys. "When has [the Shah] done anything that we disapprove of?" In the seven and a half years he had been in Washington the Iranian leader had never let him down. "Whenever we have needed his help he has been willing to apply positive pressure to help, to send special messages or emissaries," said Kissinger. "Look at the time when we wanted some pressure applied to Iraq and he responded right away."

"And when we wanted those 36 aircraft for Vietnam, the Shah sent them immediately," Ambassador to Jordan Thomas Pickering reminded his colleagues.

The Humphrey report, said Kissinger, "illustrates the problem we have at home." He blamed the Israeli government and the sympathetic coalition of strange bedfellows it had assembled in Washington from among the ranks of the neocons and liberals. The Israelis were prepared to hurt the Shah to achieve their broader objective of choking off arms sales to Arab governments in the Middle East. The Israelis, explained Kissinger, were "lobbying to change the entire course of our policy to coincide with their own policy rather than our interests. Look at the parallelogram of forces and you can see. Even on Iran, 50 percent of our trouble is the Israeli lobby. They want a carom shot off of Iran onto arms sales for Saudi Arabia and Kuwait. Since we are doing so much for Israel and it is so strong, it is hard to kill arms sales to the Saudis who are much weaker. So the best approach is to attack through Iran and kill the idea of all arms sales to the Gulf, thus blocking the Saudis and Kuwaitis." The secretary believed the real threat to the Shah came from the neocons: "This is despite the close relationship between Iran and Israel. Look at *Commentary* magazine and you can tell me what is happening. There is a Joe McCarthy–like cold war line so that if we wanted to get Israel to give up two kilometers on the Golan it would be made to appear that we were selling out to the Soviets as part of a vast worldwide plot against Israel and the free world."

Kissinger wanted to reassure the Shah that he retained Washington's full backing. He urged Iranian officials to shrug off the criticism contained in the Humphrey report and downplayed it as election year politics. To Court Minister Alam, Kissinger lavished praise on the Shah, knowing the compliments would be relayed to his master. His Imperial Majesty was "the most diligent statesman in the entire world," and he spewed bitter invective against the Saudi royal family, disparaging them as "a stupid, narrow-minded bunch interested in nothing but money.... As things stand they seem to live in a world of make-believe." Kissinger should have cautioned the Shah that the Iranian embassy was being outgunned by an intensive Saudi lobbying effort on Capitol Hill conducted with stealth precision.

The Shah hosted the American delegation at his palace on the Caspian Sea. He had arranged a sightseeing trip for them to a caviar-processing factory at the port of Bandar Pahlavi. He no doubt wanted to remind his guests that there was more to Iranian industry and commerce than oil production. Kissinger viewed the excursion as a waste of his time and embarrassed U.S. embassy personnel by making his feelings publicly known. At the factory he shamelessly mugged for the American press pool, making it clear he would rather be *anywhere* but here. "The secretary appeared bored with the whole thing, his eyes somewhat glazed as an official explained the process," reported the Associated Press. "At times he had to suppress laughter when he noticed reporters grinning at his reception." Kissinger's showmanship came to an abrupt end when a sturgeon was sliced open in front of him and its innards exposed. The combination of 110 degree heat and gutted intestines proved too much and a blanching Kissinger "looked away, paled and seemed extremely uncomfortable."

During the formal talks the Shah took a hard line. He made it clear to Kissinger that he expected the United States to continue selling him all the military equipment he deemed necessary to defend the Persian Gulf oil fields and shipping lanes. For a start, he wanted to buy the next generation of American fighter aircraft, including three hundred F-16s and two hundred F-18s. Iran did not have the money to buy the planes, the technicians to maintain them, or the pilots to fly them, but no matter. Every weapons purchase and transaction had become a test of Kissinger's willingness to follow through on his and Nixon's unwritten secret commitments. The Shah repeated the threat he had lodged back in March that the United States should not reimpose restrictions on arms sales to Iran. He would not tolerate a return to the days of the Twitchell Doctrine. "Can the United States or the non-Communist world afford to lose Iran," he asked reporters at a press conference with a tense-looking Kissinger at his side. "What will happen if one day Iran will be in danger of collapsing? Do you have any choice?"

Before his departure the secretary announced that the United States had agreed to sell another $10 billion in military equipment to Iran. A diplomat at the scene reported that Kissinger came up with the total dollar amount practically as an afterthought. For Kissinger, the important thing was to provide the Shah with the necessary reassurance. That Iran lacked the money to buy the equipment and could not possibly use any of it was irrelevant to Kissinger, whole sole motive now was to distract the Shah with tanks and guns. The trip had done nothing to advance the cause of American-Iranian relations. As Kissinger was leaving Tehran he casually remarked to the newsmen traveling with him that, "on historical precedent, a rate of economic advance like Iran's was bound to lead to revolution." Recalling the incident in his memoir, Kissinger played it down as "idle musing, for I added immediately that apparently the momentum of a very rapid growth could overcome the political perils of industrialization."

When he returned to the White House Kissinger renewed his call for President Ford to sack Rumsfeld and Simon. "In Iran, I don't think we realize what our domestic politics do to these people," he bitterly complained to the president. "This Humphrey report was a disaster. We have no better friend than the Shah. He is absolutely supportive."

"What is Humphrey doing?"

"He now feels badly," said Kissinger. "But he has [Bob] Ellsworth's former staff assistant who did the study and Bob is anti-Iranian. Then the Jews want to stop arms to the Middle East and there is an anti–arms sale binge on the Hill."

Frank Zarb followed Kissinger to Tehran in August. Once again he came up short. Ansary followed Kissinger's advice and still refused to settle for Zarb's request for a $3 discount on each of the 300 million barrels the Shah wanted to off-load. The Iranians had their own reasons for holding out for better terms. Back in the spring the modest improvement in economic growth in the West had led to bigger factory orders and an increase in demand for heavy fuel oil. The Iranians were confident that when full economic recovery took hold, demand for their oil would rise, the market would tighten, and they could charge even higher prices for their exports of heavy crude. The negotiations deadlocked and Zarb returned to inform the president that the Iranians were still not prepared to offer enough of a discount to help the U.S. economy. Ford told his staff that the negotiations were over. Kissinger predictably blamed Zarb for the fiasco and called him a "nit-picking Talmudic scholar" for driving too hard a bargain and refusing to accept the Shah's terms.

Ford's patience with the Iranians and, it seems, with Kissinger's coddling of the Shah, had finally run out. Even Ford's hard-fought nomination victory over Ronald Reagan in Kansas City's Kemper Arena late in the evening of August 19, 1976, had been clouded by reports of Iranian intrigue, this time involving Ambassador Ardeshir Zahedi. Zahedi had grown close to Reagan through Mr. and Mrs. Walter Annenberg, so close indeed that the Reagans warmly regarded him as an honorary member of their famous "kitchen cabinet" of political advisers. The previous Christmas the Fords had extended an invitation to Zahedi to visit them in Vail. Zahedi had turned them down, citing as an excuse a prior engagement with the Reagans. The timing was unfortunate because Reagan had just announced his intention to run against Ford and claim the mantle of the 1976 Republican Party presidential nomination for himself.

Zahedi flew to Kansas City in August to attend the GOP convention after spending a weekend golfing with Annenberg. It was not unusual for foreign diplomats to attend national political conventions as impartial observers. The difference this time was that the Iranian ambassador stayed in the Reagans' hotel and was with the couple and their supporters in their suite on the night of the dramatic delegate count when Reagan lost to Ford by a narrow margin. Zahedi recalled that he was there as a friend and not as a political supporter. Yet there was no doubt where his own sympathies lay. "Ford was a nice, wonderful person, but he was weak and he was dominated by Henry," he said. At some point during the long, drawn-out night, amidst all the excitement, Zahedi's enthusiasm got the better of him. "With [Walter] Annenberg, I was trying to bring these two men together," he said of his participation in the fraught mediation efforts between the Reagan and Ford camps over what role if any the Californian would play in the upcoming national presidential campaign against the Democrats. "I was trying to tell the Republicans that they should make up between themselves. If Reagan and Ford could come in to the picture [together, the

GOP would emerge unified]." Zahedi's intervention hurt him when furious White House officials saw him in the company of the same cabal of wealthy Californians who had just tried to roll a sitting president. They may have concluded that the Shah, through his ambassador, was trying to influence the outcome of a Republican Party presidential contest. "This is why Ford was maybe a little upset," said Zahedi when he recalled the air of tension that surrounded his relations with the Ford administration during the tense end-of-year confrontation over oil prices: "They were not happy with me because of this Ford business."

Ardeshir Zahedi had underestimated the personal antipathy between Reagan and Ford, the depth of the ideological chasm dividing the Republican Party, and the bitterness that lingered long after GOP delegates left Kansas City. Ford never forgave Reagan for his primary challenge, which in his view constituted an act of unforgivable treachery against a fellow Republican. Returning to Washington to receive an update on foreign policy matters from his secretary of state, the president let loose in the privacy of the Oval Office. "Now that we have gotten rid of that son-of-a-bitch Reagan, we can just do what is right," he brusquely told Kissinger.

THE THREE ENGINEERS

From every side, the American-Iranian alliance so carefully constructed years earlier by Richard Nixon and Mohammad Reza Shah Pahlavi was unraveling. The next blow to the relationship drew headlines around the world for its shocking brutality.

In Tehran on August 28, at the height of the morning rush hour, a red Volkswagen veered sharply in front of a car with an Iranian driver and three American passengers, forcing it to a halt. A minibus then rammed the car from the rear and several men brandishing guns jumped over a wall adjoining the roadway. One of the gunmen told the driver to lie down. When the driver raised his head he was sharply reminded to get down. The first assassin then shot the passenger in the front seat, William Cottrell, who fell out onto the street. Cottrell moved a hand and was finished off with a bullet to the face. Cornered in the backseat, Robert Krongard and Donald Smith were shot in the head at point-blank range. The attackers sprayed the men with automatic weapons fire and the car's interior exploded in a fury of blood and lead. The assassins left behind a note claiming responsibility for the previous killings of the three American colonels. This was no random attack. Cottrell had been shadowed for two weeks by a team of between six and eight terrorists who had good reason for tracking him down. Cottrell was employed by Rockwell Corporation to manage construction of the first phase of the top secret Ibex electronic surveillance program. The two other victims were Rockwell technicians who had hitched a ride to work with Cottrell after missing their morning shuttle bus. Someone had betrayed Cottrell's identity to the underground. There had apparently been a second major security breach. "One of the pistols was stolen from the United States Military Assistance Advisory Group (MAAG), and another one was believed, from the cartridge cases, to be a Browning," Ambassador Helms confided to a colleague. The assassins, he made clear, had inside help. "There were about 43 rounds of expended ammunition on the ground. . . . The job was professional with the same modus operandi as in the past."

The cover-up began almost immediately. The Shah had been tipped off by Israel's Mossad that the Islamic guerrilla underground would try to exploit the findings contained in the Humphrey report and find ways to drive an even bigger wedge between Washington and Tehran. The Shah instructed his court minister to pin the blame "for this atrocity" on the Communists in an obvious attempt to win back sympathy in Washington. Helms was told that Russians were behind the attack. He knew better but accepted the Shah's line that Moscow was to blame. This was reminiscent of how his predecessor, Ambassador Douglas MacArthur II, had dealt with the 1970 attack against his car in Tehran.

Until now the lives of American civilians in Iran had been spared by the urban terrorists. In the days that followed the attack, foreign expatriates "stayed close to home and kept their children away from the public playgrounds and sports fields that they normally frequent," and 170 frightened Americans, mostly representatives of companies doing business in Tehran, packed the U.S. embassy auditorium for a security briefing. Everyone's nerves were on edge. Businessmen representing defense contractors began registering at hotels under false names. The embassy's twenty Chevrolets and limousines were outfitted with sealed side windows resistant to single bullet shots, though not machine gun fire, and metal plates were installed behind the backseats. Cynthia Helms recalled that she "sometimes had nightmares. I awoke one night when Dick was in Washington to what I thought was the sound of a shot. Convinced that I was about to be kidnapped, I leapt out of bed, grabbed my nightie, and rushed to the door."

She accompanied her husband to the Fourth International Trade Fair in Tehran surrounded by sixteen American and Iranian plainclothesmen and tailed by two backup cars.

Before the Rockwell murders the estimate of the number of Americans living in Iran was assumed to be anywhere from between 24,000 to 31,000, though no complete census had been undertaken. The State Department was operating on the mistaken assumption that, based on current growth patterns, fifty thousand Americans would most likely be living in Iran by 1980. Ambassador Helms now asked his staff to check those numbers. He was under pressure to back up the official estimates appearing in press accounts back home. Embassy staff contacted U.S. companies based in Iran and asked them to fill out a questionnaire asking questions about the number of employees and family members. They were taken aback when the questionnaires revealed that between 45,000 and fifty thousand Americans might already be living in Iran. In truth, no one really knew. Sales of military equipment were not the only aspect of U.S.-Iran relations that had spun out of control.

Democratic vice presidential nominee Walter Mondale cited the deaths of the Rockwell employees as the inevitable outcome of "scandalous" arms sales undertaken by two Republican administrations. "Richard Nixon gave a blank check to Iran for the purchase of the most sophisticated arms in the US arsenal," he told a crowd in San Francisco. "Unfortunately, it's a check that President Ford has fully endorsed."

IF I COULD SPEAK FOR A MOMENT ABOUT OIL PRICES

On August 30, half a world away from the anxieties of Tehran, Alan Greenspan reported to the president and his cabinet that the economic recovery of the spring had slowed down. "The pattern is spurt and pause, spurt and pause," explained Greenspan. "We are in one of those pause periods." In his memoir, *The Age of Turbulence*, Greenspan wrote that the economy's growth rate of less than 2 percent was not unusual given the depth of the 1974–75 recession. "From an economist's standpoint, this was not a cause for concern," he wrote. "Because a modern economy involves so many moving parts, it rarely accelerates or decelerates smoothly, and in this case all the major indicators—inflation, unemployment, and so on—looked fine." But the major indicators weren't fine. New figures showed the nation's rate of unemployment increased for the third month in a row, to 7.9 percent. The

White House was forced to retract Greenspan's earlier confident prediction that unemployment would fall to 6 percent by Election Day. Confirmation of the economic slowdown couldn't have come at a worse time for President Ford.

The origins of what pundits instantly dubbed the "Greenspan Pause" were not in dispute. For reasons that no one could adequately explain, billions of dollars set aside for federal stimulus programs remained unspent. "Economists and analysts noted that during the first three quarters of 1976 the Federal Government spent $15 billion less than it was supposed to," reported Leonard Silk in *The New York Times*. The dollar amount "translates into a shortfall of $20 billion at an annual rate. Talk about balancing your checkbook!" Arthur M. Okun, a former chairman of the Council of Economic Advisers, described the oversight as "the biggest budgetary gaffe since the buildup of the Vietnam war in 1966, when military spending was underestimated by some $10 billion—with inflationary results." Another prominent economist lamented that the federal budget was "in a state of chaos." The administration's shortfall in stimulus spending, which now threatened to tip the U.S. economy back into recession, added urgency to White House anxiety on oil prices: "If the oil-producing countries impose another price increase, it not only will affect the American economy directly by draining purchasing power, it also will weaken other industrial economies, further eroding demands for U.S. exports and, therefore, slow U.S. production."

Uncertainty in the United States quickly spread across the Atlantic to the anemic economies of Great Britain and France. Prime Minister James Callaghan's Labour government was faced with the toxic combination of a sharp fall in the value of the pound, 13.8 percent inflation, and 1.5 million people out of work—the highest number of unemployed since the end of the war. Trade unions vowed to fight Callaghan's pledge to cut spending. "Things are going to get worse before they get better," said an official with Britain's Confederation of Industry, adding that if the economy did not pick up soon the country would be "effectively bust as a viable industrial nation." Across the Channel in Paris, where inflation was at 12 percent, Prime Minister Raymond Barre imposed a three-month wage and price freeze and a ceiling of $11 billion on oil imports for the next year. Barre blamed high energy costs for France's worsening trade balance.

The White House stepped up its campaign to win support from Saudi Arabia for an oil price freeze at Doha. The deal to sell thousands of new-generation smart missiles to the Saudis was part of that effort. But it ran aground when liberal and conservative members of Congress protested the sale of sophisticated weapons systems to a country still technically at war with Israel. They were reluctant to be seen doing favors for the world's richest oil producer during an election campaign. For good measure, lawmakers expressed support for legislation that if signed into law would punish any American company that complied with the Arab trade boycott of Israel. Gerald Ford appealed to Republican opponents of the deal not to antagonize the Saudis and to keep their support for Israel in its proper perspective. "The Saudis have been very helpful in keeping oil prices under control," he reminded Senators Jacob Javits and Clifford Case in the Oval Office. "I don't think we can kick them in the teeth on this in light of their importance."

On September 7, U.S. Ambassador William Porter traveled to Taif in Saudi Arabia to deliver a letter from President Ford assuring King Khalid that Washington remained committed to the missile deal. Crown Prince Fahd accepted the letter on the king's behalf and assured Ambassador Porter that His Majesty "will certainly not approve a price rise this year. He is against any increase in the price of oil. If other OPEC members continue to apply pressure we will agree to talk to them next year, but there is nothing planned for then as far as the Saudis are concerned." Fahd made it clear that discussions on the matter must be kept quiet. "At that point he asked for [United States government] assistance with Iranians and Venezuelans," Porter cabled Washington. "Anything we could do to make them understand dangers of raising prices would be helpful all around especially for Saudi Arabia. I said I would send the message."

On September 16, Ford had a new letter to send to King Khalid. National Security Council officials Robert Hormats and Robert Oakley explained in a memo to the president that

> the main objective of the letter is to attempt to lock the Saudis into the position taken by Fahd, in Khalid's name, opposing any decision this year to increase oil prices. If we can hold the Saudis to this, it will at least mean no price rise at the December OPEC meeting, buying us several months more of status quo. It could produce a freeze of longer duration, but this is more problematical. As an encouragement to Fahd and Khalid, the letter indicates that the U.S. will follow their advice and make known to other OPEC countries (especially Iran and Venezuela) our opposition to a price increase.

At 11:00 A.M. on Friday, September 17, President Ford, National Security Adviser Scowcroft, Assistant Secretary of State Charles Robinson, and Ambassador Porter met with Saudi Arabia's foreign minister Prince Saud bin Faisal al-Saud, Ambassador Ali Abdullah Alireza, and Hassan Shawwaf, the chef de cabinet, to discuss oil prices and arms sales. The Saudis were offended by the recent controversies over the missiles and the trade boycott. They felt they were being singled out for punishment. "There are many aspects of the U.S.-Saudi relationship which we would hope to discuss," said Prince Saud. "We are not a warlike country, but the threats in the area compel us to improve our forces," he explained. "The constant questioning of our efforts by the United States leads to grave questions on the part of the Saudi people. We don't see why they should be looked on with suspicion. Our efforts are not just in arms, but for schools, hospitals, barracks, etc. What we are asking for is less even than your military experts say is needed."

The president said he was in total agreement with the prince's sentiments. He promised to fight for Saudi interests in the Congress and he gave an assurance that his administration was applying pressure to Israel to accept Syria's occupation of Lebanon. "Let me say we agree completely that you have no aggressive designs and we fully support your defense efforts," he assured his guests.

> The reluctance is not on the part of my Administration. Our cutbacks have been pragmatically designed to get Congressional approval. This is a difficult time for us. I would hope that in January we could move ahead in a better climate here. Last year we spoke of progress in the Middle East. Tragically the Lebanese conflict has intervened. We appreciate the Saudi support in the area. We are doing what we can to support Lebanon and the moderate forces and keep Israel restrained. . . . I understand and fully support your needs.

Ford wanted to move on the pressing issue of oil prices. "If I could speak for a moment about oil prices," he began.

> I greatly appreciate His Majesty's comments about a price increase. Last year when you were here, we were at the bottom of a recession. We are moving out now, but it is fragile. The OPEC action last summer under your leadership was very far-sighted, but any increase this

December or for '77 would be extremely damaging, not only for the United States, but even more so for our industrial colleagues who are in a much more fragile situation. We plan to discuss this matter with you but also with Iran and Venezuela." It would be disastrous to push the world economy back to the recession of last year. So we hope His Majesty's views will prevail.

"His Majesty is just as determined as last summer not to have an increase," said Prince Saud. "But it will be difficult, and it will depend heavily on what you can do with Iran and Venezuela. His Majesty has said at least he will refuse more than a modest increase, and will categorically refuse anything beyond 5 percent. If we can get support from Iran and Venezuela, we can hold to no increase, but without that, it will be extremely difficult." President Perez of Venezuela continued to support the Shah's hawkish stance on oil producers on behalf of non-Arab producers.

"I appreciate that and we will work on them to the best of our ability."

"Our ability in this regard depends strongly on the overall state of U.S.-Saudi relations, not only in military supplies but in other things," Prince Saud reminded the president. "We need a measure of reciprocity to justify and strengthen our ability and to keep our public opinion and the Arab public opinion mollified."

"None of these acts is needed and I will do my best to defeat it," the president observed of the boycott legislation. "Part of this is an education process, and my Administration will do its best to explain the situation to the American people."

The National Security Council convened to discuss oil prices at 3:00 P.M. on September 23. The stock market had just crawled past the 1,000-point mark to reach 1014.79—"the highest record in almost four years." Ford's national security team assumed that the majority of OPEC members, starting with Iran, favored a price increase at Doha of between 10 and 20 percent. The president's men faced a delicate balancing act. The country was headed into the final stretch of a presidential election campaign. Speculation about a possible banking crisis had not yet spilled over into the mainstream press. Their efforts to apply pressure to the oil producers had to be kept quiet to avoid triggering public panic and a contagion of fear that might lead to the very crisis of confidence in the banks they wanted to avoid. The NSC decided to focus its efforts on three countries: Saudi Arabia, Iran, and Venezuela. Officials urged President Ford to write letters to the three leaders appealing to them for price restraint. Frank Zarb was assigned the task of applying pressure to the Venezuelans. It was important to drive a wedge between the Shah and Perez. Kissinger was asked to meet again with Prince Saud, who was in New York for the opening of the United Nations General Assembly. Around the world, American diplomats were instructed to mount an intensive but low-key effort to persuade oil producers and consumers alike that a price increase posed a serious threat to the world economy and to their security. No one wanted to panic the markets.

Administration officials already knew their leverage over Iran and Saudi Arabia was limited. The Shah held a persuasive bargaining chip in the CIA bases in northern Iran. White House hands were also tied when it came to Saudi Arabia. Officials considered issuing a threat to withdraw the U.S. Army Corps of Engineers, which was building the kingdom's military facilities and offering trade and investment incentives. None of the other measures considered was deemed practical, desirable, or even legal. The use of force was not considered. In short, the administration lacked leverage over the Saudis *except* in the area of arms sales—and the missile deal and military equipment were being dangled as incentives to get them on board anyway. It was for this reason that American oil companies rushed to top up their storage tanks. By the end of October stocks of crude oil were at their highest level since April 1939, a record 293 million barrels. The oil companies weren't taking any chances. They anticipated that the long awaited showdown was coming between the United States and OPEC and they wanted to be ready for it.

WE SHALL BRING THE COUNTRY THROUGH!

Bill Simon charged into battle. In the first week of October 1976 the treasury secretary joined finance ministers, bankers, and more than three thousand advisers and guests in Manila for the annual meeting of the IMF and its sister organization the World Bank. The big men of American banking were in attendance, among them the chief executives and chairmen of Bank of America, Chemical Bank, Citicorp, Morgan Guaranty Trust, and Morgan Stanley. Everyone was now focused on the "debt bomb" and the prospect of another big hike in oil prices. Britain's borrowings had reached $45 billion and the government was about to ask international lenders for another emergency infusion. Brazil, Mexico, and Italy owed more than $20 billion each; France, Finland, and Indonesia had foreign debts near $10 billion each. "No one really knows just how large the mountain of debt is," wrote one analyst. "But what is important is not the aggregate figure, which runs into hundreds of billions of dollars, but the ability of particular nations to meet their payments." The wild card in the risk factor was the prospect of another big hike in fuel costs. "If OPEC puts the price up substantially—say by 10 percent or more—would this aggravate the payments problem of all oil-importing countries and push some closer to the brink of default? Can the United States and others dissuade OPEC from a stiff increase?"

H. Johannes Witteveen, the head of the IMF, repeated his call from earlier in the year for rich and poor nations to stop borrowing to cover their balance of payments deficits. Speaking to the delegates in Manila, Witteveen warned that bad lending practices had begun "to affect the credit worthiness of some borrowers and to create the possibility of economic and financial problems." Witteveen's dour prognosis was followed on Tuesday, October 5, by an even harsher assessment provided by Treasury Secretary Simon, who urged a cap on lending by the World Bank and reminded delegates that they "are approaching the limits of their ability to take on more debt." Simon issued a stark warning of the dangers of another increase in oil prices, and drew a line in the sand. "If the oil-producing nations take, as is now rumored, the dangerous step of again raising the price of oil, it would seriously aggravate an already troublesome economic and financial situation."

Britain turned out to be the weakest link. Amid boisterous scenes in the House of Commons on October 12, Prime Minister Callaghan tried to calm public fears and offer reassurance to nervous investors about the state of his country's sickly finances. "We shall not waver!" he cried. "We shall bring the country through!" The IMF made it clear that it would not even consider Britain's request for further aid of $3.9 billion if Downing Street did not agree in advance to tough cuts in public spending. The loan was Britain's fourth overseas bailout in twelve months. Callaghan's own backbenchers opposed fiscal austerity and there was no guarantee the government would get its way. Insolvency beckoned and with it the specter of national bankruptcy. Chancellor of the Exchequer Denis Healey defended the loan and warned Britons that failure to act would result in an "economic policy so savage that I think it would produce riots in the streets. It would mean an immediate and very heavy fall in living standards and unemployment, maybe 3 million." Healey also knew that Britain was obliged to somehow meet the first payment on a separate $5.93 billion international standby credit due to fall on December 9. There was wild talk of the overthrow of the government. "Nobody wants to talk about it, but the possibility of a breakdown in law and order, or an extremist revolt in Great Britain, gives the United States and other NATO governments the chills," reported *The Washington Post*.

The threat of contagion was real too in Italy, Portugal, and Spain, where the economic slowdown suddenly threatened to unseat the reformist governments of Giulio Andreotti, Mario Soares, and Adolfo Suárez. "Of course, the economic situation is serious," Italian foreign minister Arnaldo Forlani confided to Kissinger. "The problem as I see it in Italy is this," replied Kissinger. "We favor reforms if we have to and if you have to but we don't want you to take a stringent policy of deflation to the point that it helps the Communists. We will push you for reforms. We will push you but you will have to tell us what is not politically tolerable for you. Don't let our technical people push you around to a point beyond what is politically tolerable for you."

In early November Prime Minister Soares of Portugal appealed to Washington to release an emergency $300 million loan to prevent the wipeout of its foreign exchange reserves. Tens of thousands of Portuguese settlers were pouring back into the mother country after fleeing the fallen empire's newly independent and war-torn African colonies. Inflation was running to 30 percent and nearly 20 percent of the population was un-employed. Strikes, terrorist bombings, food lines, and the emergence of a black market economy confirmed the image of Portugal as a stricken, sinking ship. Political observers agreed that the future of the Soares gov-ernment and perhaps democracy in Portugal would be determined by the outcome of local and regional elections set for December 12 when the radi-cal left and right would surge in strength.

Spain was not only broke but in the dark. Madrid experienced blackout conditions when the government decided to trim its $4.3 billion oil bill by turning out the lights in the capital after 8:00 P.M. and ending television transmissions at 11:30. The national speed limit was reduced to 62 miles per hour. "The energy crisis has turned the country's economy topsy-turvy," reported one visitor to the Spanish capital in October 1976. "Spain's once glittering, throbbing capital will now have to throb without the glitter." Political observers in Spain forecast a "hot autumn" ahead as labor unions and Franco loyalists flexed their political muscles in the weeks leading up to a nationwide referendum seen as crucial to the king's plan to hold free parliamentary elections in early 1977. The date set for the referendum was December 15. Wall Street had a big stake in the outcome of the vote. One third of Spain's outstanding foreign debt of $12 billion was owed to

American banks, which had rushed to establish a presence in the country earlier in the year. "The growing foreign debt is linked heavily to Spain's petroleum imports," noted *The New York Times*. An oil price rise of 10 or 15 percent "would push the current account deficit toward $4 billion," up from its current figure of $3.5 billion.

Wall Street's debt bomb and the turmoil spreading through Europe looked set to converge in the space of a few hair-trigger days in mid-December. Britain's scheduled debt repayment fell on the 9th; Portugal's elections on the 12th; Spain's referendum on the 15th; oil ministers from OPEC were also due to meet on the 15th. Over the next six weeks the future of the Ford presidency, worldwide financial networks, Wall Street banks, NATO allies in Europe, millions of jobs, and America's economic recovery could well be decided by the actions of a few governments in the Middle East. What would be the impact of the uncertainty surrounding these events on the presidential election in the first week of November?

HIS MAJESTY AND I HELD A RAPID-FIRE DEBATE

Around Washington, patience was running out with the Shah. "How much pressure has there been from the United States to keep this oil rise down," a British journalist asked the Shah. "Oh . . . A lot," he admitted. But he refused to back down and rejected evidence of a possible economic disaster in the West if prices went up. "I cannot accept this as a crisis," he said in reference to a question about West Germany's unemployment rate. "It is a strange situation. There are three million guest workers in England and West Germany. For this very reason I shall have none of your talk about unemployment." He advised the Germans to come to Iran, where he would put them to work. Western criticism of Iran's oil policy was based on "pure jealousy." He said he was confident that the United States, West Germany, and Japan would have no trouble absorbing a 15 percent rise in oil prices but agreed it would be difficult for Italy, France, and Britain. "If you just decided to work a little more, just decided to have a little more discipline, and modernized your industry, you could become the strongest country in Europe," he lectured a British visitor to the palace in the autumn of 1976. He felt confident that he would get his way.

At Kissinger's request the Shah had agreed to delay the Bali price increase until Doha, after the outcome of the presidential election. Despite Washington's protestations, the Shah still fully expected a quid pro quo from the American side. Besides, Kissinger had assured him that the administration still supported Iran's high levels of spending on defense and would see to it that he generated the oil revenues to pay for them. The Shah never took seriously Saudi opposition to an end-of-year price rise. Over the years the Saudis had protested loudly in favor of price restraint but never summoned the courage to actually stand up to the rest of the cartel and exert their swing power.

The Shah's hard line on oil prices, at least in public, obscured a behind-the-scenes debate among his military and civilian advisers about the wisdom of seeking a 15 percent increase. Iran's top generals argued that a price rise was more than justified to recoup the exorbitant cost of imported U.S. military equipment. General Hassan Toufanian was still smarting from his clash earlier in the year with Donald Rumsfeld over allegations of corruption and price gouging by the U.S. Defense Department and American defense contractors. An American visitor to Toufanian's office received a lesson in the economics of military procurement when the general pulled out from his desk drawer a cardboard box "filled with small aircraft parts and produced some odds and ends." Toufanian held up one small gadget, the door handle to a helicopter, and said, "This costs us one barrel of oil." He explained that it cost Iran the equivalent of ten thousand barrels of oil each year to pay for just one of the thousands of American blue suiters and mechanics brought in to help the Iranians maintain their arsenal of military hardware. Americans who described themselves as "logistics representatives," but who in reality were storekeepers, billed the Iranian government for annual salaries of $115,000. This kind of "imported inflation," Toufanian complained, had so far added $2 billion to Iran's defense expenditures. He argued that raising the price of oil by 15 percent to recover these costs was more than justified.

But the Shah's civilian advisers were not so sure. Officials at the National Iranian Oil Company were worried that another big price hike might suppress consumer demand for oil at a time when Iran's petroleum revenues remained in a slump. They recommended a price increase of no more than 10 percent. The Shah chose to disregard their warnings, no doubt because he shared Toufanian's anger at the way the Ford administration handled arms sales.

The CIA saw in the Shah's stubborn refusal to cooperate evidence of a deeper structural problem in U.S.-Iran relations, perhaps even an intelligence failure. On October 14 the agency invited colleagues from the NSC, the departments of State, Treasury, and Defense, the Defense Intelligence Agency, the Army, Navy, Air Force, and the Joint Chiefs of Staff to a three-hour seminar to help it review the performance of Ambassador Helms and his staff in intelligence gathering. For many of the officials it was the first time they had had a chance to compare notes. Concerns quickly poured forth and from the most unlikely sources. The representative from the National Security Council complained that private defense contractors were doing end runs around the White House by setting up their own lines of communication to the palace. A Pentagon official appealed to the CIA to help the Defense Department learn more about Iran's military preparedness. One of Kissinger's own staffers asked if anyone knew anything about the royal succession. Those in the room realized they could not answer even the most basic questions about the Shah, conditions inside Iran, or the U.S.-Iran relationship. "Washington does not have a clear perception of the Shah's long-range objectives," concluded David Blee, the CIA's national intelligence officer for the Middle East and the official who summarized the discussion for his superiors.

> For example, why is he acquiring such a vast array of sophisticated military hardware? The Shah states that adequate defenses against Communist-equipped Iraq are precautionary, yet the placement of new bases suggests other interests. In 1985 when oil revenues from Iranian production have peaked, and his oil rich neighbors are just across the Gulf, what does the Shah intend to do with his accumulated weaponry? Will he still claim and demonstrate concern for the stability of the area? Or will he have destabilizing objectives?

Henry Kissinger had personalized relations with the Shah, hoarded information, and sidelined the Shah's critics in the White House. He dominated policy making to such an extent that virtually no one else in the U.S. government—including his own senior staff—had the vital information they needed to do their jobs. Some of the participants in the CIA forum expressed concern that the Shah was too removed from the realities of ordinary life in Iran. "In this regard, it is particularly important to know what subjects are withheld from the Shah and the degree to which reports to him are doctored by his subordinates," wrote Blee. "To what extent do such practices warp his perspective, isolate him, and imperil his regime?" Until now, Ambassador Helms had insisted that his diplomats avoid antagonizing the Shah by shunning contacts with Iranian opposition leaders. Seminar participants unanimously agreed that the time had come for Helms and his staff to enter into a dialogue with the Shah's domestic critics: "While it is a politically difficult and sensitive matter for Embassy officials to meet with identified opponents of the Shah, the Mission should have the widest possible range of contacts."

Five days later General George S. Brown, the chairman of the Joint Chiefs of Staff, publicly raised doubts about the Shah's ambitions and his loyalty as an American ally. "Gosh, the programs the Shah has coming, it just makes you wonder about whether he doesn't someday have visions of the Persian Empire," he told an Israeli interviewer in remarks that made headlines. "They don't call it the Persian Gulf for nothing." Secretary of Defense Donald Rumsfeld played down the general's "obviously inelegant phraseology" and pointedly refused to reprimand him. Several days later the Shah told Tehran's English-language newspaper *Kayhan International* that Brown's comments were "truly hilarious" and that Brown had passed on an apology and regrets.

The Defense Department was digesting the results of its own intelligence assessment on U.S.-Iran relations, this one in the form of a survey of arms sales undertaken by David Ronfeldt, an analyst at the RAND Corporation. Ronfeldt set himself the task of answering two very basic questions—questions that no one at CIA or State had so far thought to ask: How did we get here? Where do we go from here? The United States, Ronfeldt concluded, had stumbled into a strategic trap of its own making by surrendering its leverage over its ally. The superpower had created a "superclient" and to the point where Iran's Shah, not America's president, managed the terms of the relationship. U.S. officials had naively underestimated the Shah's policy of "aggressive nationalism" and his desire simultaneously to lure the United States into deeper engagement in Iran while moving Iran "still further away from an image of excessive dependence on the United States." The United States, having lost sight of its policy objectives, and having lost control of its programs, now found itself trapped in Iran.

Ronfeldt delivered a blistering critique of the Nixon Doctrine, which had set up the Shah and other Third World dictators as regional gladiators: "In recent years the U.S. Government is frequently accused of favoring, if not of imposing, dictatorial rule in client states. The presumption is that dictators are somehow more subservient to U.S. interests. However, in the case of Iran and probably other countries this view seems inaccurate." America's multibillion-dollar investment in Iran made the United States "a potential hostage" to the Shah's ambitions with the added risk that America could be drawn into a future war fought by the Shah on his terms.

The report severely criticized the approach taken by Kissinger's State Department, which encouraged and signed off on unrestricted arms sales to Tehran as a way of recycling Iranian petrodollars. Given what the Defense Department was now dealing with, "there is little evidence that State's policies have indeed protected, much less enhanced, U.S. influence and leverage." Iran was totally unprepared for life after the Shah and a successor regime could turn out to be virulently anti-American. The Shah had so far resisted American efforts to broaden his political legitimacy. Nor would he do so until such time as he experienced "a major failure of leadership. . . . The Shah has not yet experienced such a failure—yet the excessive ambition of his recent goals in acquisitions for the development of Iran may well result in notable disorganization and disarray."

The United States was deeply, incontrovertibly enmeshed in Iran in ways reminiscent of its early and disastrous involvement in Vietnam. Decisions taken years earlier by the Nixon administration meant that President Ford lacked the ability to exert pressure on the Shah to compromise on the oil prices that now threatened to ignite a debt bomb, bring down the banks, and topple allied governments in Europe. Nor was that all. There had always been the risk that oil prices, arms sales, and the CIA bases would become entangled. That happened now, with just two weeks to go before Election Day, when in late October the influential television news show *60 Minutes* broadcast an interview in which the Shah frankly admitted that SAVAK conducted surveillance operations on American soil against Iranian dissidents. The disclosures caused such widespread revulsion and alarm that Kissinger had no choice but to launch an investigation. Jack Anderson reported that he had suddenly come into possession of a cache of files revealing that the CIA had trained the Iranian secret police in the fine arts of forgery, wiretapping, illegal entry, and break-ins. Anderson also publicly announced the name of SAVAK's senior handler, a diplomat assigned to the Iranian mission to the United Nations.

Richard Helms's decision to step down as U.S. ambassador to Iran at the end of 1976 was made in the knowledge that the CIA review was about to expose his record of failure as envoy to Tehran. His tenure had been an unmitigated disaster, not only for the U.S. national interest, but also for the Shah, who never learned the extent of the growing opposition to his policies in Washington. The scandal involving SAVAK was symptomatic of a relationship that had increasingly come to be one-way. Helms was aware that he faced almost certain prosecution on a charge of perjury related to a lie he had told senators during his confirmation hearing in February 1973.

Watergate was about to claim its last victim. With his career and reputation in ruins, the ambassador called on Court Minister Alam on October 24 to inform him of his decision. Helms broke with protocol when he urged Alam to talk to the Shah. He said the Iranian government had to respond more forcefully to attacks from human rights groups. And he warned against raising oil prices again, saying it would worsen Iran's standing in the United States.

President Ford's formal request to the Shah to oppose an increase in oil prices in December could not have come at a worse time. On October 30, Ambassador Helms received an "eyes only for the ambassador" cable with the following instructions from Henry Kissinger: "At the earliest appropriate time, and in any event, no later than [close of business] Monday, November 1, please deliver the following personal message from President Ford to His Imperial Majesty, Mohammad Reza Pahlavi." Embedded in the cable was President Ford's personal appeal to the Shah not to increase oil prices. Election Day was November 2. In the last week of the campaign the president was barnstorming the country furiously, trying to erase Jimmy Carter's slender lead in the polls. The American people knew nothing of the behind-the-scenes drama preoccupying his foreign policy team.

The president's letter to the Shah was firm and direct. Ford pointed out that improvements in the world economy over the summer had led to a modest but discernible increase in demand for Iran's oil. Iran's oil production had climbed back above 6 million barrels a day. Ford was making the point that the White House no longer accepted the Shah's argument that Iran's economy needed an end-of-year bailout in the form of another big increase in oil prices. Instead, it was the United States that needed a bailout if it was to prevent a financial meltdown. "Many countries have in fact virtually reached the end of their ability to borrow," wrote the president. "Several important industrialized countries which are experiencing economic difficulties and the attendant danger of political instability would encounter still more severe economic problems if faced next year with a new oil price increase. . . . This would add major new strains to the international financial system and intense pressure on both industrialized and oil-producing nations to provide balance of payments support. Thus, the fragile and uneven nature of the global economic recovery requires that responsible nations avoid action which would endanger it." President Ford made it clear that from now on progress on arms sales would be contingent on cooperation with oil prices. He urged the Shah not to play into the hands of his critics: "I am sure you have been fully informed of the Administration's successful resistance to Congressional attempts to block the sale of F-16 aircraft and other military equipment to Iran. The struggle with certain segments of American opinion on this subject has not been won, however, and I fear that there will be further and perhaps greater pressures next year."

Helms took the letter to Niavaran Palace on Sunday, October 31, where he was received by the Shah in his study at 10:00 A.M. local time. It was a poignant encounter for both men. They had known each other and collaborated since 1957. Helms had been involved in the planning for Operation Ajax, which had restored the Pahlavis to power. He had been the Shah's back channel, enabler, interlocutor, and apologist for two decades. Now they faced each other as adversaries. The cable that Helms sent back to Kissinger made it clear that he had stood his ground with the Shah to the point of breaching imperial decorum and court protocol:

> After His Majesty has opportunity to study message, reply will be forthcoming. His Majesty and I held a rapid-fire debate for about 10 minutes on various facets of crude oil price increase issue. Please assure the President that whatever the outcome of the December OPEC meeting, I took pains to insure that His Majesty is fully aware of the American position, American views, and American reasons for not wanting to see another price increase in the near future.

Foreign ambassadors do not engage in "rapid-fire" debates with foreign chiefs of state, least of all with one whose titles included King of Kings, Light of the Aryans, and Shadow of God. Helms gave the Shah what in diplomatic terms was the equivalent of a dressing-down. The letter the Shah wrote in reply and dated November 1 reflected deep anger at the humiliation he received at the hands of a mere ambassador. Ambassador Zahedi held the letter in reserve until the outcome of the presidential election was known in Tehran. The Shah stood his ground at least in part because he believed—erroneously as it turned out—that the oil market had turned in his favor. In fact, much of the recent demand for Iran's oil could be attributed to short-term panic buying by oil consumers stockpiling in advance of the OPEC meeting.

On Tuesday, November 2, Jimmy Carter defeated Gerald Ford to win the White House. Richard Helms's resignation as ambassador to Iran was announced the same day. Kissinger had long since given up on Ford. The president's clumsy responses to foreign policy questions during the televised debates with Carter had exasperated his secretary of state. "Look, I don't give a good god damn—I think this campaign is lost," he groused to Brent Scowcroft two weeks before Election Day. Before the votes had even been cast, Kissinger placed a call to Senator Ted Kennedy to assure him of his support should the senator from Massachusetts make a run for the presidency in 1980.

"You were right about the pause," Kissinger tartly remarked to Alan Greenspan. "It's just too bad it happened to coincide with the presidential election."

THE SHAH'S LESSON IN LEVERAGE

The last thing Kissinger needed on the eve of the OPEC meeting was a showdown with the Shah over the nefarious activities of Iran's secret police. It was better that that particular stone was left unturned. On November 4, Kissinger, Harold Saunders, and Roy Atherton met to discuss the progress of their investigation into whether SAVAK had violated U.S. laws. Saunders reported that the FBI and CIA were of no help because they had "no formal liaison with SAVAK agents on American soil." Kissinger wanted the matter put quickly and firmly to rest. "I told Zahedi I hoped that none of this was true because we could never accept it," he said. Kissinger said he wanted an assurance from the Iranian ambassador that "there is no evidence that they are doing it [spying and perhaps committing sabotage] and that we would never tolerate it."

Ardeshir Zahedi delivered the Shah's letter of reply to President Ford's appeal on oil prices on November 5. He had been careful to await the outcome of the election result. Any doubts about the deep offense the Shah had taken to recent events were confirmed by the tone of his letter. The Shah began by pointing out that Iran had held the line on oil prices at Bali although it had not been in its economic interest to do so. He stressed the importance of energy diversification, price indexing, and conservation. Even though Great Britain, France, and Italy faced a critical situation with their balance of payments, the Shah told the president that "this certainly does not justify our committing suicide by paying for their failure or inability to put their house in order by succeeding in making the necessary adjustments in their economy through domestic measures." The Shah declared President Ford's effort to reduce America's dependence on foreign oil a failure and blamed price increases for American commodities for Iran's own financial troubles. Then the leader of Iran issued a threat:

> You are no doubt aware, Mr. President, of my deep concern for the need to maintain close cooperation between our countries. However, if there is any opposition in the Congress and in other circles to see Iran prosperous and militarily strong, there are other sources of supply to which we can turn for our life is not in their hands. If these circles are irresponsible then it is hopeless, but should they be responsible, they will certainly regret their attitude to my country. Nothing could provoke more reaction in us than this threatening tone from certain circles and their paternalistic attitude.

What the Shah left unsaid—presumably he felt he did not need to spell it out in black and white—was that he had agreed to forgo a price increase at Bali in May 1976 as part of a broader deal with the White House not to raise the price of oil until the presidential election was out of the way. Ford had lost the election anyway. As the Shah saw it, he had kept his end of the bargain. Now, more than ever, the Shah needed to raise government revenue to meet Iran's internal and external financial commitments. The Shah believed that he had stuck to the terms of a deal that the American president was about to renege on. He remained convinced that he had been a loyal friend to the United States and a firm defender of America's interests in the Persian Gulf.

The Shah now turned his attention to the SAVAK affair. The Iranian Foreign Ministry issued a carefully worded statement that warned of retaliatory action if the Ford administration tried to punish or expel Iranian intelligence personnel based in the United States. Helms sent Kissinger a cable on November 7 to emphasize that the Shah was deadly serious about his threat of reprisal. The Iranian leader wanted the White House to stop the investigation. "The statement serves notice," Helms wired Kissinger, "that any restraints imposed upon, or actions taken toward, Iranian representatives in the United States would be reciprocated here." This was an unmistakable reference to the activities of CIA employees working out of Embassy Tehran and in the secret listening posts strung along the northern border with the Soviet Union. The Shah was now using the bases for leverage with the Americans. He would not tolerate another humiliation or accept any more terms imposed by his so-called allies. The gladiator was fighting back and would take no more orders from Caesar.

At 9:55 on the morning of November 8, Henry Kissinger telephoned Roy Atherton, who did not know about Helms's cable. Atherton said he had already spoken with Zahedi once about the matter and the envoy had assured him that the Iranians had done nothing wrong and that everything could be settled quietly. "With the line we were taking [Zahedi] said he had no problem," said Atherton.

"I don't want to know his problem," snapped Kissinger. "I want his assurances."

"We agreed to get together early this week. I want to go over with him . . ."

"I want an assurance from the Iranians that it was not being done."

"He told me they would not do anything improper or illegal," said Atherton. "I wanted to go over with him what is proper and legal within our laws."

"You will do it today." Kissinger was not going to put up with Zahedi's word games. He and Atherton both knew what the stakes were. Their comments also suggest that they knew the truth of the matter, that SAVAK agents had indeed engaged in espionage and quite possibly committed acts of sabotage on American soil. The potential existed for an explosive political scandal. The investigation had to be shut down.

"The problem is that there are a lot of things under our law that he may not be aware of," Atherton offered by way of an explanation: "He may give us an assurance of things that he does not know that are illegal."

"By the end of the day you will have done it, G-D, Roy. I want it by the end of the day."

"I will do it."

"Just cut out those staff meetings and speeches."

"Alright, I will get him in today."

Zahedi and Atherton met the next day. One of the Americans at the meeting recalled that the Iranian envoy delivered a typically "virtuoso performance" in which he smoothly blamed Iranian exiles living in Los Angeles for stirring up trouble. They were the ones, he insisted, who engaged in "intimidation and harassment." It was obvious that both sides wanted the issue to go away—and fast.

"Ambassador Zahedi was quick to assure us that SAVAK had violated no laws—even before we explained what laws were at issue," said the State Department official. "We cannot say that we gave him a thorough briefing on relevant U.S. law, although we can say that he had been warned."

On November 10 the State Department issued a public announcement. Its "inquiry" had failed to turn up evidence confirming "any illegal or improper activity" by Iranian diplomats in the United States. As far as Kissinger was concerned the matter was closed.

Over the next forty-eight hours two important developments touching on the Middle East helped convince Saudi leaders that the Ford administration was serious in its commitment to brokering a regional peace settlement. The United States accepted the Syrian presence in Beirut and the city succumbed to foreign occupation. On November 11, the United Nations Security Council unanimously voted to condemn Israel's construction of settlements on occupied Arab land. It was the first time the United States had sided with Israel's critics in the Security Council and cast a vote censuring its policies.

THE WHOLE SYSTEM MAY CRACK

Alan Greenspan, the chairman of the Council of Economic Advisers, was anxiously "pacing the floor" of his suite at the Thunderbird Country Club in Palm Springs on November 12. Greenspan conceded to a visitor that the American economy was "tracking under our projections" and that the summer-long "pause" had lasted longer than he expected. He said the problem was "a lack of confidence by investors in long-range prospects for the economy." There were fears of another round of high inflation "based in part on the huge external debt being carried by a number of industrialized countries as a result of past oil-price increases." Wall Street was nervous. Banking legend Felix Rohatyn declared that the growing debt situation "could lead to disaster because the political structures aren't there to cope with it." "After a brief Indian Summer in which recovery trends seemed discernible, the outlook for the industrialized nations of the world now has turned to decline—and the worst pessimism since the 1930s," reported the *Los Angeles Times.* "On top of all this, the industrialized world is holding its breath to see whether its oil bill is going to be hiked by another 10% or 15% when the Organization of Petroleum Exporting Countries meets to fix its new price scales in Qatar in the Persian Gulf in mid-December."

In November 1976 San Francisco–based Bank of America was the world's largest bank. To reassure investors that the bank was not at risk five senior bank officials traveled to New York City to announce the adoption of a "Voluntary Disclosure Code." It had taken officials ten months to produce a twenty-six-page public relations brochure. As part of its new commitment to full disclosure, Bank of America announced that it would bring greater transparency to the shaky home mortgage sector by sharing with borrowers "the bank's appraisal of the value of property they offered as collateral." It would also make public its foreign currency trades. Curiously, the code had little or nothing to say about the issue that forced its adoption in the first place—risky lending practices to foreign governments. Only groups and individuals deemed by bank officials to have "a legitimate need" to know would be eligible to receive *that* sort of information.

The situation in Western Europe deteriorated further. In the aftermath of the oil shock Richard Nixon and Henry Kissinger had drawn the historical analogy of the 1930s. They had no faith in the future of democracy in Southern Europe and were convinced that weak governments in Rome, Lisbon, and Madrid were ripe for subversion. Two years later their views had gained widespread currency. "I have never seen Europe so confused, so uncertain, and so pessimistic," said an American analyst. "Everybody sees things turning down again and this time nobody has any idea of how to get out of it." An economist with the OECD, the Organisation for Economic Co-operation and Development, concurred: "The real worry now is that another round of recession could provoke a real political and social crisis for some of our democracies." Nixon's fear of a leftist Popular Front–style government taking office in France seemed on the verge of coming to pass when Prime Minister Raymond Barre's austerity budget faltered. Unemployment in France had rocketed by 300,000 in just two months and now surpassed the one million mark. A poll conducted by the French magazine *L'Expansion* showed that three out of four businessmen regarded a Socialist-Communist victory in the 1978 general election to be a foregone conclusion. Capital began leaving France for safe havens. "Some observers believe the situation is beginning to resemble what happened in Italy two years ago, leading to the dramatic fall in the lira's value," reported *The Washington Post*. "There is a feeling quite suddenly which we have never experienced before, at least not since the war, that economic events are out of our hands, beyond our control—that whatever policies governments adopt they can no longer really cope or control the economic influences which are working against us" said one French government official. "France scares the hell out of me," a Ford administration official admitted to *The Wall Street Journal*.

In Rome, the government approved an austerity budget that called for deep spending cuts; its passage required the cooperation of Enrico Berlinguer's Communist Party. Italy's external debt had ballooned from $7 billion to $17 billion in just three years and for the last eight months of 1976 the cost of the country's fuel imports had soared by 45 percent above the corresponding period last year. "What will it take to convince the Western world that the OPEC problem is not, in fact, manageable?" asked an Italian economist. "A mass moratorium on debt payments by the poor countries?

Something has to be done to meet the problem. So much of it traces right back to oil." Another 10 percent price hike would throw the carefully crafted Italian austerity program off-balance by $700 million. A 15 percent price increase would mean a revised balance-of-payments deficit of $1 billion.

Prime Minister Mario Soares held on in Lisbon as rumors swirled that extremists within the Portuguese military were plotting a right-wing coup. The Spanish government also held its ground in the face of severe challenges from the left and right of Spanish politics. A nationwide strike led by trade unions was followed several days later by a huge rally in downtown Madrid to mark the one-year anniversary of the death of dictator Francisco Franco.

The alarm spread to North America on November 15 when voters in the French-speaking Canadian province of Quebec awarded a majority of seats in the national assembly to the separatist Parti Québécois led by René Lévesque. Here too the lingering effects of the oil shock had come into play. Unemployment in Quebec was 8.5 percent, well above the national average of 7.1 percent, and was forecast to hit 9.1 percent in 1977. Lévesque had made the province's high unemployment and low economic growth a centerpiece of his campaign. Canada's weak economy was blamed for fueling provincial populism and for taking the country to the brink of dissolution. "Discontent over inflation and unemployment is shaking governments in Britain and Italy, fomenting rising left-wing sentiment in France, and rekindling separatist dreams in Canada," reported *Time*. It noted that "the quiet optimism" of the spring had given way to "galloping global jitters. . . . The shock that could turn sluggishness into recession could come from another big hike in oil prices by the Organization of Petroleum Exporting Countries, which has scheduled a price meeting in Qatar for December 15."

WE SHOULD NOT OVERTHROW THIS GOVERNMENT

The White House moved into high gear. By now there should have been no doubt in anyone's mind that the Ford administration had decided to break OPEC in whichever way it could. Kissinger's argument that Middle East petrodollars could be recycled to benefit the domestic U.S. economy had been exposed as a fallacy. Higher oil prices had not moved the American economy away from its dependence on foreign oil. Higher prices had not increased Western security in the Persian Gulf, strengthened the region's conservative pro-American monarchies, or enhanced America's strategic objectives. Instead, high oil prices had brought the economies of the Western industrialized world to the brink of disaster and overheated the economy of Iran. "It seems to have taken the defeat of the Ford administration, the near-bankruptcy of Italy and England, the seemingly unsolvable dislocations of international trade and payments—with no end in sight—to jolt US policy makers from their theory that OPEC's price rises would somehow pay off for the United States," observed the *Los Angeles Times*. One of President Ford's economic advisers put it this way: "How can you run a rational international system when equilibrium means a $40 billion deficit for the whole world against three oil producers with a population less than New York's?"

On November 18, three days after the disastrous electoral result in Quebec, Kissinger informed Ford that he had spoken to the Iranian and Saudi ambassadors about the grave danger of imposing higher fuel bills on Western democracies. "I called in the Saudi and Iranian Ambassadors," said Kissinger. "The Saudi was sympathetic but the Iranian was belligerent. We have weighed in with our European allies." He thought they had done enough. "I think a public mission would be counterproductive," he said. "So do the two Ambassadors and our own Ambassadors. [Germany's Helmut] Schmidt has already said he could absorb 15 percent. The Saudis said they might have to accept 5 percent."

Ambassador Zahedi had a very different recollection of his meeting with Kissinger. He said Kissinger gave every appearance of being embarrassed at having to raise oil prices for discussion. "He was shy," said Zahedi. "He knew we would not budge. Maybe in his heart he thought we were right. He did not even talk seriously. It was in his office. We walked into his office." Kissinger did not make an outright request to the ambassador about the Doha conference but dangled instead the promise of a meeting with President-elect Carter if Zahedi could persuade the Shah to reverse course and support a price freeze. Then Zahedi understood Kissinger to say something that gave the ambassador pause. Kissinger, Zahedi recalled, indicated that he would not be handing over certain of his Iran files to Carter's White House transition team. Instead, Kissinger said he was having them sent to Nelson Rockefeller's estate at Pocantico Hills in New York for safekeeping. "He was not willing to give the records to the Carter administration," said Zahedi. He was now in the uncomfortable position of believing that information possibly vital to the future of U.S.-Iran relations was being deliberately withheld from officials with whom he would now be working. Zahedi did not know what the files Kissinger was referring to contained—or why the American secretary of state wanted to hold them back from the incoming administration. The first the public knew of Kissinger's decision to store his papers on the Rockefeller estate came over the Christmas holiday break when the State Department admitted that the secretary's telephone transcripts, which had been trucked to Pocantico, would now be granted along with other official documents to the Library of Congress, there to remain under his control for at least twenty-five years. Kissinger acted to head off a threatened lawsuit by a group of reporters who had learned of the stash. However, Zahedi's recollection of his conversation with Kissinger raises the possibility that other papers, in addition to the telcons, were also sent to Pocantico. If the papers are in existence, their location remains a mystery. Dr. Kissinger did not reply to the author's request for an interview.

Kissinger did not lead the effort to resolve the worsening financial crisis nor was he at the president's side during the final confrontations with Saudi and Iranian envoys. Was Kissinger disassociating himself from a strategy that he believed would end in disaster? Washing his hands of a potential debacle? Or had Ford shut him out of the process? Kissinger certainly understood that Bill Simon and Sheikh Yamani now held all the cards. President Ford, desperate for a way out of this crisis and faced with the Shah's refusal to cooperate, had no choice at this late stage but to throw in his lot with the Saudis.

The Nixon-Kissinger policy of delegating power and arms to Iran to patrol the Persian Gulf, defend West Asia, and safeguard the oil fields of Saudi Arabia had been torn apart by its own irreconcilable contradictions. King Khalid of Saudi Arabia was on the verge of replacing the Shah as master of OPEC and Iran as America's indispensable partner in the region. Kissinger knew what that meant but even now failed to grasp the full dimensions of the financial hurricane moving in from offshore. The day after the election Kissinger had met with Ed Yeo, Under Secretary for Monetary Affairs at Treasury. Yeo had just flown back from West Germany after meeting with German officials to try to put together a rescue package for Great Britain. A transcript of their conversation confirms that Kissinger had not devoted much if any attention to Britain's worsening financial situation. Yeo relayed German chancellor Schmidt's view that it was imperative they keep Prime Minister Callaghan in power. "He has a terrible view of Margaret Thatcher," reported Yeo. "He says that she is a bitch, she is tough, she lacks scope and cannot lead." Callaghan's own cabinet "is all trying to hang him.

He is terribly concerned about the instability of sterling. . . . There is terrific intrigue in the cabinet. They are chopping each other to pieces." Kissinger was puzzled by the scale of the crisis.

"You know I didn't realize before how staggeringly high the British interest rates are," he confessed. "Why can't the British have our system?" When Yeo began to explain, Kissinger asked him to slow down. "Remember, I am just using you as my economic tutor," he interjected. "Give me the idiot lecture." Later, the secretary of state plaintively asked, "What happened to bring Britain to this place?"

Ford and Kissinger reconvened on November 23. The president appeared agitated. "After you left the meeting on Friday, we discussed oil prices," he said. "Then on Saturday Arthur Burns told me he was very worried about the impact of a price increase. He thought a delegation should go there [to Doha], headed by me or the Vice President. I told him I would talk to the Vice President. The Vice President mentioned the oil deal with the Shah."

"We can't get it now," said Henry. He was referring to Frank Zarb's ill-fated negotiations with Hushang Ansary to buy oil from Iran under the table. Cutting a deal was no longer in the Shah's best interests. "There is no shortage [of oil] now. We could have gotten it last summer. It would be humiliating for you to go. You would have come back with no price increase if you were not to be humiliated. I feel the same way though less so about the Vice President's going. If you really feel strongly, he could go. If you feel you need it—but the Europeans aren't doing much, and you have no clout. I just don't think it is the thing to do. You could call in the Ambassadors."

"Let's set that up for early next week," said the president. He was now focused on this, his last and greatest crisis as American president. "I want to be well-prepared, with the facts on the economics, political support, etc."

Kissinger had some bad news for Ford. When it came to oil prices, the administration had no leverage left with Tehran. "On the economics, you have a tough agreement with the Shah," he explained. "He will show how you jacked military prices up 80 percent over the past few years. The best is the political argument—that you will have to blast them for an increase and that they shouldn't put themselves in a bad light when they need our help in the Middle East. Burns is irresponsible making a suggestion like that."

"He is concerned about the world financial impact," said Brent Scowcroft in a rare moment of public disagreement with his mentor. Tensions in the White House were running high. How had they let things get so out of hand—to the point where the United States was faced with a choice between Italy and Iran? Here was the true cost of eight years of secret deals and blank checks: the possible collapse of the U.S. banking system, the peaceful Communist takeover of NATO allies, and a devastating recession in the industrialized nations.

"I agree with that, just not his prescription for dealing with it," said Kissinger. "Maybe we could get it postponed. I would call in the Saudi first. Zahedi, of course, is such a fool. What he will report will bear no relation to what you tell him."

Later in the day President Ford placed a telephone call to the West German chancellor, Helmut Schmidt, who had narrowly won his own re-election campaign. The two leaders worked well together and Schmidt was genuinely sorry to see Ford leaving office. Ford told Schmidt that he had been on the phone to Prime Minister Callaghan, who warned that if the IMF imposed too stringent conditions on its loan, the resulting spending cuts "could touch off massive strikes and bring down the pound as well as his government." Schmidt wanted the British prime minister to make tough cuts in spending without placing his own political future at risk. "It is in the economic interest that we impose strong conditions on the British," he told Ford. "We should not go so far as to overthrow this government. There is no one else to take the reins and there may be a period of disorder which could affect us all deeply."

Ford told Schmidt he was "very worried" about oil prices. The chancellor concurred and pledged his support to White House efforts to restrain the big producers.

I HAVE FOUGHT HARD FOR SAUDI ARABIA

Ambassador Ali Alireza was ushered into the Oval Office at 9:58 A.M. on Monday, November 29, 1976. The White House was monitoring events in the South Pacific, where a few hours earlier Australia had devalued its currency and New Zealand's government suspended foreign exchange trading. Officials still weren't sure if they were watching the first signs of a global financial panic. The president met the ambassador alone. The White House did not want to draw attention to the meeting or encourage media enquiries.

"I am gravely concerned about the world economic situation and the possible impact of an increase in oil prices," said President Ford. "I am deeply worried about the economic situation both in the more industrial states and in the less developed countries, which are very vulnerable. In

Portugal we have been working hard to get a moderate government operating and eliminate Communist influence. A deterioration in this economic situation could reverse the progress we have made. In Italy also there are grave economic problems, which if the present government can't solve, it will undoubtedly bring Communists into the government. Great Britain is now trying to negotiate an IMF loan to stabilize its currency." He mentioned the situation Down Under. "I have fought hard for Saudi Arabia and supported the closest of relations between us," President Ford reminded his guest. "I have [fought] against irresponsible actions on the boycott of the part of the Congress. I will continue to do so because our aims and our objectives are identical. I will continue to do so even after I leave office. But it is difficult when the American people see a price increase which does such damage around the world. I want to help, but when my economists tell me of the jeopardy a price increase could put the world economy recovery in, I want to work with you to deal with this problem."

Ambassador Alireza did not need to mention the Shah when he responded that when it came to oil prices "the problem is political not economic. We will do everything we can without breaking OPEC. But if you could bring pressure to bear on other members it would be helpful. If through your good office you can persuade other producers."

Ford expressed his appreciation for Saudi Arabia's willingness to extend financial assistance to Italy and Great Britain. He was appreciative, he said, of Saudi Arabia's "responsible leadership in Lebanon."

Ambassador Alireza picked up on this point. "I hope you can restrain the neighbor to the south," he said in an allusion to Israel. "Without Syrian troops in the area, the guerrillas will have a free hand." The Saudi was apparently responding to a statement issued the day before by Prime Minister Rabin of Israel when he declared that the possibility of a Syrian military presence on his country's border with southern Lebanon was "intolerable."

The president said the White House was aware of the situation: "We are working with the Israelis on that point and I am hopeful that the Lebanese situation can be resolved."

I THINK THE SHAH HAS THE MESSAGE

Kissinger was back in the Oval Office on Friday, December 3. He had just returned from Mexico City, where he had escorted Rosalynn Carter, the wife of the president-elect, to the inauguration of President José López Portillo. "She was actually quite nice," Kissinger told Ford. "I got the im-

pression that he has been telling her how to stand, what to say, which side
to present to the camera, until she is stiff as a board. But believe me, she
knows nothing. Her whole world is rural Georgia. You can't believe the
things she asked me." Gerald Ford, who knew better than most the full
weight of the awesome responsibility now thrust on the Carters, expressed
sympathy for them: "Actually, in that regard I feel a little sorry for them."

The White House was still absorbing the latest bad news on the economic front. The number of jobless Americans had climbed back up to
8.1 percent. Alan Greenspan admitted that the U.S. economy had weakened
beyond his earlier optimistic predictions. He reported "a higher degree of
caution" from both consumers and the business sector. Then the country's
two biggest steel companies announced plans to hike their prices by 6 percent for 1977. Oil producers were big customers of the U.S. steel industry.
They argued that they were now justified in their decision to raise their
own prices to offset this latest new import expense from the West. President Ford and his advisers called on the steel companies to reverse their
decision, arguing that it jeopardized the entire economy. It was hard to ask
Middle Eastern oil producers not to raise the prices of their commodities
when U.S. industry was doing just that. Kissinger told the president he had
spoken again with the Saudi ambassador: "He said you were very impressive but the steel price increase was killing them."

"I raised hell with my people about that," replied Ford. "It is outrageous.
Should I get Zahedi in?"

"I think so, just so we keep the record straight," said Kissinger. He told
·the president he had some good news: "I think the Shah has the message.
He is talking 10 percent now, so I would guess it will be 7–8 percent." Kissinger's enthusiasm was misplaced. The president and his economic advisers had made it very clear that they wanted *no* price increase for 1977. And
once again Kissinger had misinterpreted the Shah's intentions. The Shah
had been clear that he would not, indeed *could* not, settle for anything less
than a 15 percent price increase.

"Okay, let's get him in," said the president, "but it gripes me when our
people pull the rug out from under me."

Chapter Twelve

OIL WAR

"Bankruptcy is worse than defeat."

—The Shah, 1977

"Our great diplomacy with the Saudis is what did it."

—Henry Kissinger, 1977

I WANT TO HAVE NO CONFRONTATION

The looming showdown over oil prices was a harsh reminder that despite the best efforts of the Nixon and Ford administrations to promote fuel efficiency and encourage energy conservation, the American economy was more exposed than ever to the whims of Middle Eastern oil producers. Forty percent of America's oil needs was now being met by foreign suppliers, which represented a 4 percent increase in crude imports over the past three years. Nixon's cherished Project Independence had long since been abandoned. "The brave conservation measures of late 1973 and early 1974 have been replaced by a so-what spirit," reported *Time*. "Chicago's Commonwealth Edison Co. has no qualms about urging viewers of its TV commercials to leave house lights on when they are on a trip because 'a darkened house is an invitation to burglars.' The small, fuel-saving cars that motorists snapped up in 1974 are now the very models gathering dust in dealer showrooms." White House officials had another big problem on their hands. Secretary of State Kissinger's original objective had been to break OPEC without hurting Iran's economy, which was highly vulnerable to sudden fluctuations in the petroleum market. The collapse of the Zarb-Ansary talks meant there was still no mechanism in place to shield Iran's primary revenue stream from sudden market turbulence.

President Ford welcomed Ambassador Ardeshir Zahedi of Iran into the Oval Office at 10:00 A.M. on December 7, 1976. Zahedi had been summoned from New York, where he had spent the previous day with Nelson and David Rockefeller. By unhappy coincidence for both the president and the ambassador it was also Pearl Harbor Day. The president was joined by National Security Adviser Brent Scowcroft and chief economic adviser Alan Greenspan. Greenspan's presence was an indication of the severity of the deepening financial crisis in Europe and on Wall Street. Ford began by offering his warm regards to the Shah and assuring the ambassador of his "great personal regard and affection for him. I hope that in the future years the close relations we have between our two countries will continue." Ford wasted no time in getting to the heart of the matter: "But I want to talk about an issue which troubles me—the Doha meeting and a possible oil price increase. I have read the Shah's letter very carefully. I both agree and disagree with it. I agree with him wholeheartedly with his points on conservation. . . . I do disagree with him on the issue of oil price and its relation to industrial prices. These are honest differences between friends."

Ford talked about "the impact that an increase will have" and told the ambassador that there was no room for compromise because "there is unanimity among my advisers that the world economic health is not good. Any increase in the price of oil would have a serious impact on the world financial structure. . . . I am a strong supporter of the Shah. I think he has done great things for his country and is a strong force for moderation and stability in the Middle East." This was true. In his second televised debate with Governor Carter the president had defended the Shah when the Democrat stated his opposition to the sale of F-14 fighter jets and warships to Iran "before their delivery was completed to the United States' armed forces." Ford had replied by praising Iran as "a good ally." Now Ford reminded Zahedi that bilateral relations extended to areas other than defense. "But we have to look at it in a broader perspective now and I think an increase would have a serious impact on the world economic structure," he said.

Zahedi said it was too late. "I don't want to take your time, but two years ago when prices were going up I talked to Secretary Kissinger and Secretary Simon and would have gone to the area right then and would have helped," he told Ford, who was presumably startled at this disclosure. "But the past is the past." He reminded Ford of the Shah's futile offers to sell to the United States surplus quantities of Iranian oil at a generous discount. The president's letter to the Shah on the eve of the presidential election had been a mistake. Zahedi upbraided the president: "Had I known of your letter to His Imperial Majesty, I would have urged that it be held earlier or not at all. The timing was not good." The Shah wanted the president to know that "we do understand the problem, and we have been thinking of only a 10 percent increase. . . . There will be an increase. What would be moderate?"

"The only way we can reassure the world economy is to have no increase."

"That is not possible."

"I am telling you the facts," the president insisted. "Any increase would jeopardize the economy and no increase would be a shot in the arm. The next best would be a delay. Is that possible?"

"Now, it is impossible," replied Zahedi. He knew, as the Americans should also have known, that Iran's economy was in trouble again. In October the Shah had grudgingly conceded for the first time that government expenditures exceeded receipts. "Instead of carte blanche expenditure, the government was told to economize in all areas, finish the projects now underway, and leave the rest of the Fifth Plan objectives for the Sixth Plan," wrote top officials of the Plan and Budget Organization. Prime Minister Amir Hoveyda dutifully launched a high-profile anticorruption campaign and studied ways to eliminate waste. But oil money was the foundation of the economy. Oil money bonded the throne to its stakeholders, the military, middle class, big industry, farmers, and merchants. Even as the government called for economization the popular press kept up a drumbeat of new big spending initiatives that promised better days. The headlines in Tehran's English-language *Kayhan International* newspaper in December 1976 told the story: "New Loans for House Purchasing Workers"; "New Plan Will Double Third Party Coverage"; "Nothing Should Be Kept from People—Empress"; "Government Loan Payment to Be Studied"; "Jobs for Returnees"; "Iran Is 'Shopping Around for Arms'"; "Master Plans Under Way for 90 Towns." For the Shah to be denied his oil money now would be to expose him as an emperor with no clothes.

Ambassador Zahedi disclosed Kissinger's request from earlier in the year not to raise oil prices until the election was over: "If it were done early in the fall—when Secretary Kissinger and I were joking about it—if you had asked for March, it would have been easy. But Secretary Kissinger said wait until after the election. I know how you spoke up for Iran and the Shah is deeply grateful. I don't believe any of the OPEC countries would agree to a delay because it would look like they were forced to."

"That's why I asked you to come in quietly," said the president. "I want to have no confrontation, and that is why this meeting is private."

Greenspan interjected. Zahedi didn't seem to be getting the point or the president's sense of urgency. The White House was facing a possible collapse of the banking system. Greenspan took the discussion back to December 1973 and the Shah's doubling of oil prices in Tehran. "I think it is a fact that the world has not yet adjusted to the earlier increase," said Greenspan. He explained that the lending flexibility of three years earlier "has vanished," and "the international financial structure is now stretched thin." The economies of the industrialized countries were paused because the "huge increase in debts" had shaken the confidence of the markets, government, and business.

President Ford then moved on to the critical situation facing allied governments and economies throughout Southern Europe. "The situation in several countries is very serious. Take Italy. They are having serious economic problems but at the bottom it is political. If the government can't cope there will be Communists in the government. In France, the situation is potentially serious, with strong Communist forces." Governments in Portugal and Spain were hanging on by a thread. "Any increase adds to the danger of a financial crisis, to failure in some governments, even to the danger of military crisis."

Ardeshir Zahedi was unmoved by their appeals. "I think there is no doubt there will be an increase, especially after the steel price increase in this country," he said. "Many newspapers are now speculating there will be a 7–15 percent increase. We would not accept a big increase. There will be an increase, but we are concerned about the security situation in Europe. We know more than most how important Europe is and the dangers of being isolated. That is why we are giving bilateral help to the Europeans." Zahedi's next comment may have given Ford and Greenspan reason for pause: "Unless people get a shock, they won't realize we have to switch from oil." What did the ambassador mean? Was the Shah planning a repeat of the catastrophic price increase three years earlier? Zahedi predicted the Shah would settle for a 10 percent price increase. Or maybe 15 percent. Although he did not know what the final outcome would be, Zahedi assured the president, "we would fight anything over 15 percent. Less than 10 percent, I honestly don't know, but I honestly don't think so. The Shah said I could promise you he would be moderate and very moderate."

On December 9, the State Department declared that no oil price increase for 1977 was justified "and any oil price increase could have damaging consequences on the world's economy." Also on December 9, Italy repaid a $486 million loan to Britain so that the British government could repay the first installment on its $5.9 billion standing credit. The British met their deadline but Italy was left with less than $2 billion in foreign exchange reserves. The finances of the Western industrialized world were beginning to resemble a giant Ponzi scheme.

SHEIKH YAMANI'S CHRISTMAS BOX

During his trip to Mexico City to attend the inauguration of President López Portillo, Henry Kissinger had quietly received an envoy sent by King Juan Carlos of Spain. Manuel del Prado, chairman of the board of Iberia, Spain's national airline, warned Kissinger that the king was worried about the possibility of right-wing revolt by disaffected army officers. Pro-Franco elements in the army had not reconciled themselves to the new Spain. "Our problem is the Army," confided del Prado. "It would probably revolt if we legalized the Communist Party." The king wanted to pave the way for the eventual legalization of the Communist Party while at the same time ruling out immediate Communist participation in a coalition government. In the past few days Communist Party leader Santiago Carrillo Solares, banished from his homeland since the civil war, had illegally slipped into Spain to hold a press conference. Franco loyalists had reacted angrily to what they saw as a dangerous provocation by the left.

Spain inched its way through December. The great crisis for the government and for democracy came on the eleventh day when masked gunmen kidnapped Antonio María de Oriol y Urquijo, president of the Council of State, the fourth most powerful man in the kingdom. Basque terrorists claimed responsibility for the brazen daylight raid in downtown Madrid that struck at the heart of the Spanish state. Agitators on the right used this episode to argue that the government had lost control. Prime Minister Adolfo Suárez was now less confident of winning an overwhelming yes vote in the December 15 referendum. Several days later, riot police battled hundreds of leftist demonstrators in the center of Madrid. The leaders of Spain's opposition parties received death threats from unidentified fanatics and were placed under armed guard. Spanish police meanwhile mounted a desperate search for the kidnapped Council of State president.

While Spain seethed, Portugal's fever broke on December 13. Voters gave the country's minority Socialist Party government "a qualified vote of confidence" and averted a crisis. Democracy in Portugal was safe for now.

The next day, December 14, OPEC oil ministers arrived in Doha. Sheikh Zaki Yamani told reporters that Saudi Arabia favored a six-month price freeze. Even a 5 percent price increase would be a mistake because the economic recovery among Western consumer nations "is not as strong as we hoped it would be." Simultaneously in Washington, Ambassador Alireza had a 4:51 meeting with President Ford and National Security Adviser Scowcroft. The ambassador handed Ford a letter from King Khalid pledging "to reach a reasonable and acceptable minimum increase" in the price of crude oil. Khalid wrote that he had taken note of President-elect Carter's pledge to oppose "any legislation against the boycott of Israel, and that he will use leverage on Israel to prevent it from committing any act of aggression against the Arabs in Southern Lebanon. Undoubtedly, this was a good initiative on his part, and we would like to wish him every success during his presidency for the good of his country and the world at large."

The president expressed his thanks to Ambassador Alireza: "I deeply appreciate the position your country is taking to moderate and hold down prices."

"Since our last meeting I received a call from Jidda that we hope to keep it a maximum of 10 percent, and are hoping for 6 to 7 percent," the ambassador explained. "But with the attitude of the oil companies, a 5 percent increase is built in." When Ford asked if it was possible to postpone the increase until March 1977, Alireza replied that the idea had no support within the cartel.

The attention of the world's media was focused on the conference hall in Doha's Gulf Hotel. With the exception of the United Arab Emirates, Yamani's call for a price freeze was not taken seriously by his eleven colleagues. "We are used to such statements," sneered the Libyan delegate. "This is a game that he always plays," the Iraqi minister assured reporters. It was nothing more than a "maneuver" because "all want to raise the price, even Yamani." Still, Yamani formally presented his proposal for a six-month prize freeze. When he was rebuffed, he led the Saudi delegation in a walkout. Yamani drove to the airport and flew back to Riyadh to consult with Crown Prince Fahd about their next move. While he was away the rest of the cartel, with the exception of the minister from UAE, voted in favor of raising the price of oil in two stages. The first stage, to take effect January 1, would see prices go up 10 percent to $12.70 a barrel. The second stage, to take effect July 1, would raise the price of oil another 5 percent, taking it to $13.30 a barrel. If enforced, OPEC's first phase 10 percent increase would add $3.5 billion to the U.S. fuel bill for 1977 and 2 cents a gallon to the price of gasoline.

Dozens of journalists awaited Yamani's return from Saudi Arabia with his instructions. "Any sign of white-robed movement at the far end of the Gulf Hotel's huge lobby had a gaggle of reporters and an efflorescence of cameramen on their feet in an instant," reported one eyewitness. Word that Yamani had reached an elevator set off a stampede of reporters, and "so many tried to cram into the lift that it jammed between floors. Muffled banging reached the desperate crowd of wordsmiths waiting below. An Italian reporter shrieked at the guards, 'Help them, they are dying of suf-focation!'" The correspondent for *Newsweek* was mobbed by reporters who mistook him for the oil minister from Ecuador. Hotel management tried to restore order by expelling the journalists from the building for the afternoon. During a security check they discovered a group of American reporters hiding out in the bowling alley. "Late night dramas, rumors, camaraderie, the chance to make up almost anything and call it informed speculation . . . this show had everything," gushed one reporter. "It even had a good story."

Back in London, the British government unveiled tough new auster-ity measures to cut public spending ahead of a meeting of the IMF board to consider Prime Minister Callaghan's urgent request for an emergency bailout. Cuts of $1.69 billion in 1977 and $2.51 billion for the following year provoked angry scenes in the House of Commons. From the right, the Conservatives led by Margaret Thatcher went on the offensive over the government's "incompetent management of the economy during three wasted years at Treasury." The ruling Labour government's own left wing denounced fiscal austerity as "essentially Tory policies which originated with the bankers. This is a bankers' strategy." For his part, U.S. treasury secretary Simon declared himself satisfied with the "excellent" efforts of the Callaghan government to stabilize Great Britain's finances and impose fiscal discipline.

Yamani returned to Doha after an absence of eight hours. He issued no formal statement and retired to his suite. The tension continued to build. The next morning the oil minister emerged to make the announcement the White House had been waiting for: Saudi Arabia would not abide by the majority decision to raise the price of crude exports by 15 percent in 1977. Saudi Arabia would instead unleash its petropower and attempt the most radical intervention in the market ever by an oil producer. Saudi exports of crude oil would rise in price by 5 percent on January 1 instead of the 10 percent offered by Iran and the price hawks. Saudi Arabia would also try to flood the market by lifting the ceiling on its domestic oil production from 8.5 million barrels a day to 11.8 million. In December 1976, Saudi Arabia and its ally United Arab Emirates were responsible for producing approximately 10 million barrels a day of OPEC's combined 30 million barrels. Their act of rebellion threatened to dislocate not only the market but also the economies of OPEC member states that were heavily dependent on ensuring that prices stayed high. Yamani's announcement at Doha offered price relief to consumers even as it threatened to run the hawks from the market and drive their economies to the wall.

The great oil war of 1977 was underway. Yamani was making it clear—to the Shah, to OPEC, and to the world—that the Saudis, the world's biggest producer and exporter of petroleum, were finally taking charge of their destiny and becoming masters of their own house. "Is it fair for all OPEC to get together to decide the price of Saudi crude?" the oil minister asked reporters. "Is it fair for others to decide against our will?" And with that Yamani stalked out of the Gulf Hotel, not even bothering to attend the closing session.

Iran had the most to lose from a two-tier, flooded oil market. The giant petrostate stood to lose billions of dollars in revenue from oil exports. "Heavy crudes are the focus of the Opec struggle, because Saudi Arabia's extra production is largely of heavier crude, which also makes up a big share of Iran's total amount," reported *The Economist*. Throttling Iran's revenue stream meant fewer funds available to lavish on schools, housing, health, forestry, public works, food subsidies, and military equipment. In his usual indomitable style, the Shah had already earmarked or spent billions of dollars that he would now never see. The Americans and the Saudis had finally called his bluff. For diplomatic reasons the Iranian leader dared not publicly attack King Khalid or other members of the Saudi royal family. But Zaki Yamani made for a convenient foil and the Iranian state media swung into action. "The third world and all progressive nations everywhere are angry and detest Yamani for having sold the real interests of his country and of OPEC to imperialism," declared the editors of *Rastakhiz*, the newspaper representing Iran's single political party. Television stations and radio networks derided Yamani as a "puppet," the "saboteur who knifed OPEC from behind." "If one has to create a museum of traitors, Zaki Yamani will gain a special rank among those traitors to their own country, nation, king and fellow OPEC members," declared *Ayandegan* newspaper. The widely read *Kayhan* told its readers that Yamani had "triggered an oil war between Saudi Arabia and OPEC" and it accused American oil companies of profiteering from a two-tier market to the tune of $4 billion.

The Economist cleverly described the outcome at Doha as Sheikh Yamani's "Christmas box" to the outgoing Ford administration, the incoming Carter administration, banks on Wall Street, and cash-strapped Great Britain and Southern Europe. Here was the price relief so desperately sought by Treasury Secretary Simon since the summer of 1974. While it was the case that the world's fuel bill would still rise by another $10 billion in 1977, it helped enormously that the powerhouse economies of the United States and Japan would be spared the worst of the financial burden. The United States still produced 60 percent of its domestic fuel needs and relied on Saudi Arabia for much of the remainder, while the Saudis supplied Japan with 37.4 percent of its petroleum imports. Member states of the European Community were not quite so fortunate—their collective fuel bill was set to rise by an estimated $4 billion. However, the Europeans would also benefit from something consumers hadn't seen in quite some time: a buyer's market. In Great Britain, the government estimated that the consumer price index would go up by only half a percent.

Saudi Arabia's radical intervention in the market provoked intense speculation about what Saudi leaders wanted or hoped to achieve. Yamani offered three justifications. He explained to West Germany's *Der Spiegel* that the Saudis acted to prevent a Communist takeover of Western Europe. "We are extremely worried about the economic situation of the West, worried about the possibility of a new recession, worried about the situation in Britain, Italy, even in France and some other nations," he said. "And we do not want another regime coming to power in France or Italy." When Yamani was asked if he was referring to Communists, he answered, "Yes. The situation in Spain is not so healthy either and the same applies to Portugal. If the economic recovery does not take place it will not only have political significance for Saudi Arabia, it will hit Saudi Arabia economically."

Yamani made it clear that future Saudi cooperation on oil pricing and production would be linked to the future of the Middle East peace process. "We expect the West, especially the United States, to appreciate what we did." Oil prices and issues of war and peace in the Middle East were now directly connected, a troubling prospect that "has raised all sorts of possibilities for future American diplomacy," reported *The New York Times*, even as it "carries with it the possibility of tragic misunderstandings if the anticipated moves by the Carter administration next year fail to produce results."

One month later, Yamani reiterated that "there is a strong link between oil and politics which existed way back in the past and will exist way out into the future."

There was no doubt that the Saudis also acted with ruthless dispatch because they feared Iran and the predatory intentions of the Shah. A flooded oil market would disrupt the supply of petrodollars the Shah relied on to acquire military equipment and nuclear technology from the West. Oil industry analysts described the Saudi maneuvering as part of "a well-conceived framework that will direct the oil as precisely as possible for maximum impact," by which they meant it would retard Iran's ability to spend money freely. Columnists Evans and Novak reported with great confidence that Crown Prince Fahd had acted because he saw the urgent need "to slow down neighboring Iran's rapid economic and military development."

Henry Kissinger had feared the day when Saudi Arabia would use its oil power as leverage to influence U.S. foreign policy toward Israel and Iran. Saudi Arabia provided the United States with 25 percent of its imported petroleum and had $40 billion invested in the domestic American economy. This was in stark contrast to Iran, which by December 1976 provided the United States with only 5 percent of its imported oil. The Saudis enjoyed enough clout "to affect US interest rates and the strength of the dollar on foreign exchange markets in the unlikely event they should choose to do so."

"We are reaching the point where we are more dependent upon them than they are on us," conceded a U.S. diplomat in the aftermath of Yamani's oil coup. "No matter what good friends they are, that is an unhealthy position for us." Yet his was the minority view at a time when U.S. officials were confident they could manage Saudi petropower to the American strategic advantage. Some administration officials and diplomats made no effort to hide their pleasure at seeing the Shah receive his comeuppance.

"Yamani went into the OPEC meeting intending to stick it to Iran," chortled an American observer in Doha. "We'll show the Shah who is boss of OPEC, is what he was thinking." The alliance forged between Treasury Secretary Simon and Sheikh Yamani at Simon's Virginia estate two and a half years before had borne fruit. Saudi Arabia now replaced Iran in U.S. affections as its closest ally in the Persian Gulf. Articles began appearing in American newspapers lauding the courage of the Saudi royal family in words previously reserved for the Pahlavis of Iran. Yamani was hailed as the "Talleyrand of the Oil World." "Saudi Arabia Comes of Age" declared the

Los Angeles Times. "Saudis' Influence Is Growing" announced *The New York Times.* An American with "deep roots" in Saudi Arabia was quoted saying that Saudi Arabia was "the best goddamn base we have ever had."

Wall Street welcomed the news that the economy had escaped a double-digit increase in the price of oil. The Shah of Iran had taken a bullet for them—next time banks and lenders might not be so lucky. Paul Volcker, president of the Federal Reserve Bank of New York, warned the financial community of the dangers of complacency. Risky lending practices had taken the American banking system and international financial networks to the cliff's edge. Volcker called for a more cautious approach to banking practices and foreign lending when he urged "closer monitoring of their operations by the Federal Reserve and other regulatory bodies." He proposed establishing a "financial safety net" to help countries staggered by high fuel costs avoid defaulting on their debt repayments. "Unsustainable tensions are building up," he said. No one wanted to see another global financial crisis triggered by Wall Street.

President Ford expressed his gratitude and relief in a letter to King Khalid. "While I continue to fear that even a modest increase may lead to unfortunate setbacks among developed and developing economies, your own example of restraint was most commendable and, I am sure, very difficult under the circumstances," wrote the president. "I regret that most of the other OPEC nations were not motivated by the same shared sense of concern for the health of the world economy upon which we all depend. . . .

President Ford's national security team cheered two victories on the same day. King Khalid's decision to break OPEC and stand up to the Shah coincided with a triumphant poll result in Spain. King Juan Carlos's national referendum to approve free elections and introduce political reforms passed by the overwhelming margin of 94.2 percent in favor. The worst case scenarios envisioned by White House officials had not eventuated. The world economy remained fragile, but the banks held, and the prospect of a catastrophic wave of defaults triggered by another round of high fuel costs receded. Great Britain, Italy, and Portugal earned a precious few months to stabilize their economies. Savoring these triumphs, Gerald Ford publicly attacked the majority vote within OPEC for a 15 percent price increase as "irresponsible and shortsighted" actions by leaders who ignored "the destructive consequences of their action." His comments were chiefly directed at the Shah, who had led the charge for a higher price. Treasury Secretary Simon insisted that OPEC's 15 percent increase was unenforceable because the Saudis would simply steal their market share.

There was further good news on January 3 when the IMF approved a $3.9 billion loan to Great Britain on condition that the Callaghan government implement the strict austerity measures announced a month earlier. The "performance clauses" in the IMF contract marked the final humiliation for the once proud island nation that only thirty years before had ruled an empire stretching from Singapore to Aden. Several days later a consortium of ten industrialized nations stepped in for a second time to defend the value of the pound sterling by putting together a $3 billion standby credit.

Henry Kissinger thought he knew who deserved accolades for saving the West in the final hours of the Ford presidency. On the morning of Tuesday, January 4, 1977, the secretary of state and President Ford were in the Oval Office. "We should also get credit for what happened to the OPEC prices," declared Kissinger. "I have said all along the Saudis were the key. Only they can raise production to make it stick. Our great diplomacy with the Saudis is what did it." President Ford kept his own counsel and said nothing. Kissinger's remark suggested that he did not understand what he was taking credit for. The White House had calculated the potential damage to Western economies from a 15 percent price increase. Did U.S. officials undertake a similar risk analysis to measure the impact on the Iranian economy if oil did *not* rise in price by 15 percent? The surprising answer is yes. The National Security Council *did* try to assess the possible damage to Iran's economy. But officials erred when they underestimated the severity of the economic problems in Iran and the financial pressures on the Shah. Working in crisis conditions and apparently in the greatest of secrecy, analysts assumed that Iran's economy had rebounded from the recessionary conditions of 1975. They did not understand that if the Saudi oil coup was successful then as *The Economist* noted, "[oil] producers that lie farthest from their markets, and those with the highest proportion of relatively undesirable heavy crude, will be the worst sufferers. Iran—now badly in need of cash—fits both these categories."

Ambassador Richard Helms had one last piece of business to attend to before he flew home to face prosecution and trial. The SAVAK scandal refused to go away. On Sunday, December 26, Court Minister Alam attended the ambassador's farewell luncheon and was surprised to see him weep. Helms's tears may have had something to do with the mess he was leaving behind and the fact that he was flying home, his reputation shredded, to face indictment and possible imprisonment. The following day, in one of his last official acts as U.S. envoy, the ambassador forwarded Kissinger a message from the Shah reassuring the White House that "SAVAK is not authorized to conduct activities counter to U.S. law." Helms made it clear that he wanted the matter dropped. He warned Kissinger against getting into "an inflammatory, public brouhaha over possibly ill-advised intelligence activity" by the Iranians on American soil. "As you know," he reminded Kissinger, "we are very beholden here in the intelligence area and therefore correspondingly vulnerable." He flew out later that day, apparently pessimistic about the Shah's future for staying in power. "By the time I left Tehran it was becoming clear that Iran was headed for serious trouble," he wrote in his memoir.

In early January, Embassy Tehran sent Kissinger a message using a special double-encrypted code on its "Roger Channel," which was indecipherable even to the CIA. The Shah wanted the White House to know that if the Justice Department took action against SAVAK personnel in the United States he "would not be able to overlook the presence of 70 of your people who are carrying out activities contrary to Iranian law," or of "others whom we do not know about officially." On the eve of the handover of power to President-elect Jimmy Carter America's "special relationship" with Iran had devolved into blackmail, intimidation, and threats against U.S. government personnel and CIA operatives.

The scandal over Richard Hallock also resurfaced to cause new complications. On January 2, 1977, *The Washington Post* published a front-page exposé by Bob Woodward revealing intimate details about the Ibex spy program. Someone had leaked to the *Post* portions of transcripts of the Shah's private conversations with Hallock, who as Secretary of Defense Schlesinger's personal liaison had been entitled to one-on-one meetings with the king at the palace. According to Hallock's notes, in 1976 the Shah had accused Pentagon officials of involvement in "malfeasance" and "crude deceptions" in the sale of expensive radar technology to Iran. The Shah had railed that "the chicanery of Pentagon officials and their military civilian representatives here was intolerable. Patience was unavoidable until the election, but not necessarily longer than that. . . . [His Majesty's] disenchantment with American officials, Rumsfeld in particular, was virtually complete."

Six days after Woodward's article appeared, General Toufanian fired off an anguished two-page letter to Rumsfeld denying the Shah had made the comments attributed to him and at the same time requesting that "your government determine if the documents mentioned exist, and if so, their origin and present location." He expressed alarm that "sensitive security information, safeguarded by our two governments," had been leaked. He reminded Rumsfeld that "it was the U.S. Department of Defense that first introduced Mr. Richard Hallock to the Government of Iran and strongly endorsed his activities and functions in writing to His Imperial Majesty." Iran had since terminated Hallock's contract and "we can assume no responsibility for any activity he engaged in which was not specifically authorized by this government during his period of employment."

Rumsfeld's crisp letter of response to the general was all of five sentences. He did not deny that the transcripts existed, nor did he offer to help recover or secure them. In fact, Rumsfeld did not mention them at all, nor did he mention Hallock. The secretary of defense merely expressed satisfaction with the state of U.S.-Iran defense relations and delivered what may have been intended as his final insult: "This relationship has been nurtured by the frank and candid exchange of views."

During the presidential campaign Carter had attacked Simon's handling of the economy. Democrats argued that Simon's harsh deflationary policies impeded economic recovery and imposed unnecessary hardships on working families. "I don't know anybody in the Ford administration that Jimmy detests as much as he does Simon," confided an insider. Eliot Janeway, a prominent economist and syndicated columnist, and a vociferous critic of the Shah, reached out to Carter's transition team to set up a meeting between the two men. He wanted to make sure that the new president-elect was personally briefed on the outgoing administration's problems with the Shah and OPEC. Janeway later wrote that although he did not attend Simon's briefing with Carter, the outgoing Treasury secretary assured him "President Carter asked me all the right questions."

WE'RE BROKE

On January 1, 1977, Mohammad Reza Shah held a long audience with Court Minister Alam and accused the Saudis of betrayal. "We must give them the thrashing they deserve." The next day was worse. Alam was greeted with the shattering news that Iran faced financial ruin. "We're broke," admitted the Shah. "Everything seems doomed to grind to a standstill, and meanwhile many of the programs we had planned must be postponed." He expected oil exports to fall by as much as 30 percent. When Alam tried to offer reassurance, the Shah railed against Yamani and the Saudis. "It's going to be tough," the Shah admitted. A few days earlier, during an interview with the newspaper *Kayhan*, the Shah had foolishly lashed out at his own people, blaming them for Iran's financial crisis and implying they needed to tighten their belts. Iran had become "a paradise of indolence and sloth." It was time for everyone to roll up their sleeves. "If we do not revise [our policies] we shall not survive," he said. The King of Kings declared that he would "lead this nation into the great civilization, by force if necessary." Anyone who disagreed with him should pack their bags: "We shall take them by the tail and throw them out—like mice."

Iran waited for the Saudi deluge. "The question now is whether Yamani will flood the market with oil," the Shah grimly conceded in an interview with *BusinessWeek*. "If he does this, for a little while it may force us to decrease our production. And if this happens it will affect our economic plans, our military plans, our military buildup, and especially our foreign aid program. . . . I am worried somewhat about internal developments. If we do not have the amounts of money we thought we would have, it will slow down a bit. But the economy is overheated, and this will cool a bit." When Yamani boasted that the Saudis were prepared to boost Saudi oil production by 50 percent, taking it as high as 14 million barrels a day, the Shah went on French television to denounce "an act of aggression." He told William Schmidt of *Newsweek* magazine that Yamani was "[Washington's] colonial appointee to pump all the oil of Saudi Arabia" and bitterly compared the Saudi oil minister to Judas Iscariot. "We shall suffer a great deal if it continues this way," he said. "But we are not going to give way or give up. . . . And if we are driven out of the market . . . this will affect our whole policy."

Schmidt asked the Shah what he thought of Yamani's argument that a 15 percent rise in the price of oil "might weaken some West European countries and make a Communist takeover more likely. What's your answer to that?"

"I am just laughing," the Shah snorted.

"You don't take seriously, the potential of Communist take-overs?"

"That is very possible, but not because of the 5 percent increase of Sheikh Yamani instead of 10."

"But isn't there a level at which oil price increases would play havoc with Western economies?" asked Schmidt.

"This is not the real point," replied the Shah. "It is that your societies are not well run. You have no government and no leadership. I am not talking about America because it is a world of its own. I am talking about the Europeans."

Iran's income from petroleum made up 85 percent of foreign exchange receipts. In the run-up to Doha oil companies had rushed to stockpile crude supplies, fearing another big price increase after New Year's. They were reluctant to take sides in the oil war and were especially wary of antagonizing Iran because the Shah made it clear he would never again do business with customers who canceled their existing purchase orders. For now, the oil companies preferred to deplete their existing inventories and hold back on placing new orders. Companies not already locked into deals with Iran rushed to sign up with the Saudis. The result of the confusion in the market was that in the first nine days of 1977 Iranian oil production plunged 38 percent over the previous month, the equivalent of 2 million barrels a day, as new orders dried up. In just five days the National Iranian Oil Company reported that twenty-five new customers had reduced their Iranian oil purchases from 1.2 million barrels a day to 693,000 barrels a day. Income from oil for the month of January dropped to $460 million from the previous year's $672 million. By one estimate the country was losing $20 million a day. The price gap between Saudi and Iranian heavy crudes was now 7 percent, more than enough enticement for Iran's wavering customers to take their business elsewhere. Big drops in Iranian oil production had happened before. The difference this time was that production in January 1977 was lower than even a year earlier when Iran's output had all but collapsed in the face of falling consumer demand in the West. Other oil producers such as Kuwait also experienced a sharp decline in orders and production. But little Kuwait had not banked its entire fortune on a crash industrialization program of the sort that left Iran permanently slaked for fresh infusions of petrodollars.

Starved of the oil revenues it had long feasted on, Iran's economy teetered on a precipice. "Iran needs a quick agreement to end Opec's two-tier oil pricing," reported *The Times* of London. "Many Opec members have suffered a substantial loss of oil exports since oil prices rose on January 1. None is feeling the financial effects as acutely as Iran." Iran's central bank estimated that total income from oil for the year would fall to $19.5 billion from $22 billion. The Fifth Plan, ending in March 1978, would be short by between $10 billion and $12 billion. On January 11, Iran's government abruptly tore up its financial estimates, imposed a spending freeze, and canceled a loan intended to help bail out Britain's shattered economy. Tehran was forced instead to accept a $500 million loan of its own, one hastily cobbled together by a consortium of American and European banks led by David Rockefeller's Chase Manhattan. Even the armed forces were not spared retrenchment. The start of construction at the massive naval base at Chabahar on the Persian Gulf was postponed. General Dynamics, the manufacturer of the F-16, was asked if it would accept payment in oil for the $3.8 billion worth of aircraft already under order.

The Shah's inner circle was in a panic. Arriving in London on Friday, January 7, Finance Minister Hushang Ansary confided to Ambassador to the Court of St. James Parviz Radji that "he had forewarned everyone about the untenability of our stance at Doha, and predicts the next six months will be particularly difficult economically in Iran." Parviz Mina, a director with the National Iranian Oil Company, also flew in to London. "Normally a quiet, reserved and soft-spoken man, I now see him in a state of agitation over the outcome of the recent OPEC meeting in Doha," the ambassador wrote in his journal. Mina explained to Radji that Iran would bear the brunt of the price collapse. "So all the reduction will be Iran's," he said. "And yet the situation is being presented to the Iranian public as a great victory. Goodness knows what will happen when the bills start rolling in for payment."

Court Minister Alam took to his bed for two weeks with a high temperature. The cancer that would soon kill him was sapping his strength. As he pondered his fate and the future of the Pahlavi dynasty, Alam summoned the nerve to write a letter to the Shah warning him that dangerous days lay ahead for monarchy. "We have squandered every cent we had only to find ourselves checkmated by a single move from Saudi Arabia," he wrote. "Your Majesty, we are now in dire financial peril and must tighten our belts if we are to survive." He urged the Shah to restore public confidence in the government and jail corrupt officials.

In late January, at the Shah's insistence, Alam departed Tehran to receive medical treatment in Paris. He had already been bedridden for three weeks. "We have been thwarted over oil prices and the prospect for our future relations with the USA is bleak indeed," he wrote from his sickbed. Prime Minister Hoveyda visited him in Paris and confided that there was "an atmosphere of unease" in Iran but he could not put his finger on the cause.

February brought a respite and hope that Iran's economy might be able to ride out the storm. The Shah let it be known through General Toufanian that he would fight the Saudis. "Bankruptcy is worse than defeat," he said, and ordered the military to reduce expenditures. However, bitterly cold winter weather in the United States and Western Europe led to a surge in demand for Iran's heavy-grade fuel oil. In the United States, demand on some days exceeded 20 million barrels. Iran's position was also helped by high winds that buffeted the Persian Gulf and prevented tankers from taking on oil at Saudi Arabia's Ras Tanura terminal. Ras Tanura was a marvel of the oil industry and a potent symbol of Saudi petropower. On a single day in early February 1977, "18 ships are taking on oil, and seven more, anchored further offshore, are waiting for clearance to move to berths . . . a tanker is in and out with its load in 45 hours." If Ras Tanura had a vulnerability it was lack of storage capacity. It could maintain only a four-day stockpile. That meant even minor interruptions to supply led to loading delays. Thanks to the stormy weather conditions that held down the flow of Saudi oil into the system, Iran's oil production rebounded 30 percent in February over the previous month to reach 5.5 million barrels of oil a day. When North American and European economies revived in the spring, as they were widely expected to, demand for Middle East oil would rise in line with factory orders and industrial activity. "If they [the countries that opted for a 10% increase] can survive the initial drop in output, there should be a strong increase in demand in the second half that may even absorb any future increases in Saudi production," reported one Western oil company official.

The roller-coaster ride continued when March and April brought the Shah and Iran's oil industry back down to earth. Saudi Arabia's drive to open the spigots and ramp up oil production finally took hold, even as warmer spring weather in the United States and Europe led to a sharp fall in oil consumption. Saudi crude exports soared to 9.3 million barrels a day in March, an increase of 540,000 barrels over February, with the country's total oil production topping out at 9.7 million barrels a day. Iran, rapidly losing its market share, faced a fiscal blowout. The Shah's Fifth Plan, the symbol of Iran's "Big Push" and the empire's engine for growth, was finally rendered "inoperable" and its financial estimates set aside altogether. In April, Iran's oil production fell 16 percent, a sharp drop of 864,000 barrels a day. "Since oil had been expected to underwrite 78 per cent of the revised Plan, the impact of such fluctuations in international demand was dramatic," wrote Robert Graham, the correspondent for the *Financial Times*. "Iran had returned to the unstable conditions of the 1950s when the size of its oil revenue had never been certain."

The struggle between Saudi Arabia and the rest of the cartel exposed the depth of hostility in the Arab world toward the Saudi royal family and revealed alarming fissures at the heart of the Saudi state. King Khalid was bitterly denounced from Beirut by Yasser Arafat's Palestine Liberation Organization for selling out OPEC and the Arab world's oil power to the

United States and Israel. Saudi Arabia's oil industry was centered in its Eastern Province, a region with a large and restless Shi'a population that harbored long-standing grievances against the ruling Saud dynasty. In the spring of 1977 there were reports of unrest among Aramco oil workers unhappy at implementing the directive to flood the market. Saudi oil fields and facilities were also struck by a series of mysterious blazes that knocked out pipelines and processing plants.

These troubling incidents did not pass unremarked in Tehran. On Thursday, May 12, Court Minister Alam was in an audience with the Shah when the phone rang. "Clearly it was to report an enormous fire at an oil field somewhere," wrote Alam. "I was alarmed and, contrary to my usual discretion, asked HIM for details. 'Oh, it's nothing disastrous,' he replied. 'It's in Saudi Arabia. Why else do you suppose I sit here so relaxed.'" The fire at the Abqaiq pipeline and pumping station complex run by Aramco knocked out more than half the kingdom's total oil production. "The sky was black over the Abqaiq oilfield, 40 miles south of the Aramco headquarters here, as the remaining oil in the pipes and overflow dikes was allowed to burn itself off," reported *The Washington Post*. One man was killed and thirteen injured in an inferno that took four days to bring under control and cost Saudi Arabia $100 million in lost revenue. The incident also marked a serious if temporary setback in Saudi efforts to flood the market and hold down oil prices. The Western media accepted assurances from Aramco and the Saudi government that the fires were the result of mechanical or human failure. Local reports suggested otherwise, hinting that Shi'a saboteurs had blown up oil facilities in an attempt to panic the royal family and disrupt Saudi oil production. A few weeks later, Saudi authorities broke up a coup attempt by thirteen Saudi air force pilots with plans to bomb the royal palaces, seize power, and declare an "Arabian republic."

In Iran in the spring of 1977 there were classic signs of structural breakdown and dislocation with shortages of electricity, telephone service, water, gas, and basic foodstuffs. Guests checking into the Intercontinental Hotel in Tehran were supplied with flashlights as a precaution against rolling power blackouts that lasted up to half a day. "Tehran's streets are so packed with automobiles that the traffic jams entail a serious waste of time," remarked a visitor to the capital in April. "A few months ago, the country ran out of eggs," reported *Los Angeles Times* correspondent Joe Alex Morris. "An emergency call went out, and eggs were flown in from Eastern Europe. Then there were too many eggs." Morris recounted what happened next: "Desperate, the government asked the American embassy how quickly a powdered egg factory could be set up. Discouraged at the response, it shipped the eggs back to Europe, by air of course, to be made into powdered eggs and shipped back. An expensive way to satisfy a growing public demand for eggs."

The Iranian government was making progress on at least one front in the battle to restore order to the national economy. Cargo was moving again at Khorramshahr, the port hobbled by shortages of labor and equipment, and which was now open twenty-four hours a day, seven days a week. Temporary jetties were rushed into construction at a cost of $32 million to speed up the unloading and loading of cargo and oil. But was it all too late? "Iran in the past three years has made itself a kind of test case for an extreme hypothesis of development economics—the strategy of the 'big push,' which was fashionable in the early days of development studies," *The Times* of London reported in early 1977 of the Shah's belated effort to bring the Iranian economy back under control. "The economy careened towards total chaos, and there were dangerous symptoms of social unrest. . . . Economic growth is certainly desirable, but it should be accompanied by progress toward a more humane and tolerant society. Otherwise the tensions that it generates must sooner or later erupt in violent form and carry away the regime that presided over it."

The Iranian government revised its budget forecast for 1977 down from $22 billion to $19.5 billion. It anticipated crude exports would drop from 5.4 million barrels a day to 4.6 million barrels of oil a day. "And even though this year's oil revenues actually may exceed last year's," reported *The Wall Street Journal*, "the total for the five-year development plan ending on March 30, 1978, probably will fall short by $10 billion to $12 billion from the originally forecast $102 billion." The shortfall would only get worse if demand for oil dropped in the second half of 1977. "The current five-year estimate for petroleum revenues . . . thus underscores one of the flaws of the original development plan: It lacked flexibility to adjust to a lag in money inflows. Moreover, the rapid economic growth has been accompanied by rapid inflation, recently calculated at a 15.5 percent annual rate." This was no surprise to the Shah's Plan and Budget Organization, which three years earlier had explicitly warned the palace against locking Iran into a fixed-term spending plan based on oil prices staying high. "The drop in oil exports indicates that the Government is now confronted with fluctuating income from this course," was how the government minister responsible for the PBO, Abdul Majid Majidi, delicately put it.

That spring Queen Farah visited Paris. For some time Drs. Flandrin,

Bernard, and Milliez had wanted to brief the queen on her husband's condition. They were alarmed by a recent incident in which the Shah's valet had noticed the Shah's deliberately mislabeled chlorambucil container was empty and replaced the medication with the harmless drug whose name was written on the label. The mix-up had caused severe health complications, enlarging the Shah's spleen and affecting his blood count. The French doctors viewed Farah's cooperation as essential to avoid future medical mishaps. The Shah disagreed and refused their request to meet with his wife. After months of debating the ethics of the issue, Bernard and Flandrin decided to go ahead anyway. Without informing the Shah they arranged through an intermediary to meet the queen in private while she was in Paris. The meeting took place in the greatest of secrecy.

"Fearing a foreseeable deterioration of the disease, we wanted his wife to be informed, so that she could be morally and psychologically prepared for what would inevitably happen one day," recalled Professor Georges Flandrin. "And so we had a very difficult message to give her, and what is more, it had to be done with absolute secrecy and, if I may be so bold, behind the backs of the patient, his secret service, our families, and our friends, not to mention our enemies and anyone else who would be naturally curious." Together with Professor Abbas Safavian, Alam's doctor, they broke the crushing news to the Shah's wife that they had been secretly treating her husband for cancer for three years.

The Pahlavi court's excruciating kabuki ritual continued. Queen Farah achieved the tricky task of persuading her husband to allow her to sit in on his next medical checkup with the doctors, though he still knew nothing about her secret briefing in Paris. Relations between husband and wife were such that even now the illness was not discussed openly between them. The doctors used the word "cancer" when they spoke to her but referred to "lymphoma" or "Waldenström's disease" when they talked to the Shah. The queen did not feel it was her place to raise the subject with him either. She asked the doctors to be frank with him but they held back. She later concluded that her husband most likely understood his fate. She recalled a comment he made to French president Válery Giscard d'Estaing when Giscard called on the royal family at St. Moritz in 1975. "When the French president expressed his surprise at the speed of growth in Iran, my husband confided to him without any explanation, 'My problem is that I haven't enough time. I won't be remaining in power for long. I intend leaving in seven or eight years. I will be over sixty. I would prefer to leave earlier, but my son is still too young. I will wait until he is ready, but I want the essentials to be in place before he takes over. He will have difficulties in the beginning. It's up to me to bring about the transformation of Iran. I am determined to do it.'" The Shah's doctors also gradually accepted that their patient understood that he was living under a death sentence. "I am only asking you to help me maintain my health for two years, enough time for the Crown Prince to have finished his year in the US and spend another in Tehran," he told them in the summer of 1977.

THAT MOMENT I WAS SHAKING

On May 12, the same day a fire shut down Saudi Arabia's Abqaiq pipeline and pumping station complex, Secretary of State Cyrus Vance arrived in Tehran to attend a ministerial meeting of CENTO member states.

Cyrus Vance was the first high-ranking member of the new administration to meet with the Shah. He had a general awareness of the strained relations between the Ford White House and the Iranians but knew no specifics. He wanted to know where things stood. On January 17, 1977, just three days before Jimmy Carter's inauguration, Vance had taken a helicopter down to Charleston, West Virginia, to attend the swearing-in of Jay Rockefeller, Nelson's and David's nephew, as governor of West Virginia. Also in attendance that day was Iranian ambassador Ardeshir Zahedi. When Vance learned of Zahedi's presence he asked him to join him for the flight back to Washington. The pilot took a detour so the two men could have more time together. Vance arranged for a follow-up meeting at the State Department between the ambassador and an aide. "Everything they asked, I answered," he said. When Vance asked Zahedi what he thought was the biggest impediment to better relations he said he gave a one-word answer: "Oil. It was oil."

Yet in order to ask the right questions, Carter's foreign policy advisers needed to have detailed information at their fingertips. Zahedi said he did not volunteer information on topics such as Iran's internal political situation because "It was the duty of the host country to show their records [to Carter's transition team], not for me to show our records to them." He had in mind the files he believed Henry Kissinger had moved to Nelson Rockefeller's estate at Pocantico Hills.

President Carter's ambassador-designate, William Sullivan, was not in Tehran when Secretary Vance arrived there in May. He was in Washington preparing to testify before Congress at his confirmation hearing. During the six-month lag between the departure of Helms and the arrival of Sullivan, Iran's internal situation had taken a turn for the worse. Not since the early 1950s had the Pahlavi throne been so isolated abroad and vulnerable at home. The Shah had dynamited his long-standing ties to Washington's conservative Republican political establishment but without building bridges to the Democrats. He had managed to alienate or antagonize the Israelis over the Kurds, Great Britain and the European Community over high oil prices, and the Soviet Union and Arab states over the Ibex electronic eavesdropping project and Iran's rapid military buildup.

The Shah feared a return to the days of Kennedy and Johnson when arms sales were linked to progress on political and economic reforms. He decided to preempt the new administration in Washington by announcing a raft of measures designed to improve the Pahlavi regime's image in Western capitals. The Shah knew that Cyrus Vance had served as President Kennedy's secretary of the army and that Sullivan was a career diplomat who had just spent four years managing another of Nixon's troublesome gladiators, President Ferdinand Marcos of the Philippines. The Shah gave permission to the International Committee of the Red Cross to visit Iranian jails and meet with detainees to investigate their conditions and treatment. An estimated three hundred to four hundred political prisoners were released back into society. Iranians were encouraged to bring any complaints and grievances they had to the attention of the governing Resurgence Party, which in turn would forward them to the attention of the government. This was how Iran's one-party state was supposed to work in theory as a conduit to manage the flow of public expression. It did not work that way. Embittered Iranians overflowed town hall meetings to denounce official corruption and "demand more schools, roads and social benefits and to criticize the Government for not providing them fast enough." Students, intellectuals, and opposition politicians saw the Shah's staged opening as a convenient cover for them to call for an end to dictatorship and a return to constitutional rule and parliamentary democracy. The Shah's government had achieved the stupendous feat of mobilizing its severest critics.

The Shah was perplexed by the high priority Jimmy Carter placed on morality and human rights in foreign policy and national security policy. The new president announced a sweeping review of the way the United States sold military equipment and nuclear technology to its allies. Alam assured him that Washington "will never abandon us," and opined that Carter's talk on human rights was a public relations gimmick.

The Shah's skittishness about American intentions—and his bitterness toward the Saudis—revealed itself in an interview with *Newsweek* when he indirectly accused Carter of moral hypocrisy and showing favoritism toward the compliant Saudis. "If you Americans are going to be so moral, you must apply a single standard to the whole world," he complained.

> How about Saudi Arabia which, from the lack of American comment, would appear to be a paradise of human rights? If I have a few thousand Communist people in prison so that others can live in a free society, it is magnified and talked about endlessly. But do you ever talk about the hundreds of thousands who were murdered in Cambodia? . . . I cannot believe that the U.S. would be so shortsighted as to cut off arms sales to my country. That would create a widening breach between you and the primary force for stability in this area. . . . If America refuses to sell us arms, if you say that only you and the Russians are entitled to have major armaments, you will be treating us like slaves.

President Carter and his top officials were aware of the Shah's insecurities and went to great lengths to offer him reassurance. Yet Carter and his foreign policy advisers appeared to have been working in something of an information vacuum. There is no indication that Kissinger briefed his successors on the byzantine deals he had negotiated. There was no paper trail to document the swaps and trades worked out between officials in the White House and Niavaran Palace. Carter and his staff were only now beginning to comprehend the scale of their Persian inheritance. On the question of arms sales, one official used an apt comparison to hint at the scale of the commitments already in the pipeline and that could not be reneged on without provoking a reaction from the Shah: "The problem we're faced with is how do you turn a 500,000-ton supertanker around?"

"It was quite apparent in Washington that the shah was apprehensive about the new Carter administration," recalled Gary Sick, the Iran desk officer on the National Security Council. "It was also evident that the United States had no visible strategic alternative to a close relationship with Iran. Policy bridges had been burned years before. Consequently, the Carter administration devoted considerable efforts during its first year to reassure the shah that there was no intent to alter the basic nature of the relationship."

William Sullivan, a man who did not suffer fools gladly, expressed ambivalence about taking up the post of American ambassador. When he asked the secretary of state why he was being sent to Tehran, Vance replied that the president wanted a professional in the role of ambassador. The Shah would benefit from having someone who could speak frankly with him. Sullivan's background was ideal because he had "considerable experience in dealing with authoritarian governments and with leaders who were forceful personalities." Sullivan was not convinced. By his own estimation he was "innocent of any detailed knowledge of Iran. . . . I had never lived in the Islamic world and knew little about its culture or ethos." He had been holding out for Mexico City. Vance told him that an understanding of Iranian politics, history, and culture was "considered secondary qualifications for this post." Sullivan needn't have felt bad. He was inheriting a diplomatic mission whose political counselor, George Lambrakis, "didn't want to be there," an economics counselor who had never served in the Middle East, and a new CIA station chief who spoke no Farsi but had presumably picked up a great deal of Japanese during a thirteen-year posting to Tokyo. "The Embassy's disarray," recalled a former U.S. diplomat, "made it very easy for the Iranians to play them off against one another."

In advance of his trip to Iran, Vance received a briefing paper on U.S.-Iran relations from his deputy, Roy Atherton, who had served Kissinger in the same capacity. Atherton's memo revealed the scale of the American investment in Iran since Nixon's visit in May 1972. U.S. exports of civilian goods to Iran now averaged $3 billion a year, with $1.5 billion in American capital investment tied up in Iran. Fifty American universities had established links with Iranian counterparts or with the Iranian government. Approximately thirty thousand Iranian students were enrolled at American colleges in the United States, while tens of thousands of American nationals resided in Iran. The irony, as Atherton saw it, was that the very success of the Nixon Doctrine in strengthening Iran had led to a backlash in the United States against Washington's Persian project. "There is wide concern in this country, reflected in the media, public and Congress, that Iran is needlessly overarmed and that the 30,000 Americans there will produce dangerous frictions in our relationship or would be hostages in the event of a conflict," Atherton cautioned Vance. "The Shah is broadly viewed as arrogant, imperial and dictatorial, which he is, but this is a caricature which overlooks his extraordinary intelligence, energy and singleminded dedication to his country's rebirth and modernization. Regardless of their distortions these perceptions now somewhat limit our flexibility in dealing with Iran." Iran's single-minded pursuit of high oil prices was "the principal nettle" in U.S.-Iran relations. Atherton advised the secretary of state not to badger the Shah about human rights because it could lead to "serious friction."

It was the view of the experts at the State Department that although the Shah was not loved or perhaps even particularly liked by his subjects, "the vast bulk of the Iranian people support his policies, at least passively, and there are no serious contenders for power." Iranian terrorist groups were "small, well armed and disciplined" and received support from Libya and also from Palestinian and European terrorist groups. But the terrorists did not enjoy the support of the Iranian people and "except for the remote possibility of a successful assassination, are not an immediate threat to the Shah." The Shah's campaign of self-criticism through the Resurgence Party was a step in the right direction because it encouraged "popular political participation, particularly at the local levels," thus drawing the lightning away from the Shah. Atherton identified two potential weak spots, of which the first was that the Shah's "failure so far to develop political institutions could cause instability at the time of transition from his authoritarian rule." The second weak spot was Iran's economy, which was beset with shortages of skilled labor, transportation bottlenecks, and was highly vulnerable to sudden fluctuations in the oil market. "A major (and unexpected) reduction in crude oil production and export, however, would be a crippling setback; the economy, for at least two more decades, will be highly-dependent on this one resource," he wrote. Atherton had identified the major structural weakness in the Pahlavi state: the Shah's "oily legs." That made his description of U.S. objectives toward oil prices and OPEC all the more surreal.

> At issue is whether Saudi Arabia can bring sufficient pressure on the sales of its Gulf neighbors, particularly Iran, to re-establish the Saudi veto over OPEC price decisions. High world demand and bottlenecks in Saudi Arabia have spared the higher priced producers from feeling any pressure thus far and they are likely to remain in a stronger position for several months before bargaining strength begins to shift in favor of the Saudis toward the end of the year. Our interest in moderating the OPEC price path is served by a continuation of the Saudi policy until they have demonstrated a convincing potential to flood the market to the detriment of the key upper tier producers.

U.S. officials understood that a sudden fall in Iranian oil receipts threatened the Shah's rule. Yet their decision to support Saudi efforts to flood

the market had *guaranteed* that Iran would see a sharp decline in its petroleum exports, presumably with harmful effects for the Iranian economy.
The course of action American officials pursued would help bring about
the outcome they feared the most. As late as May 1977, despite mounting
evidence to the contrary, the State Department still confidently believed
that Iran had been spared "feeling any pressure thus far" in its oil war with
Saudi Arabia. It was the Shah, said Atherton, who held the upper hand in
the struggle for mastery of the oil market. How much pressure did U.S. officials think Iran could withstand from a two-tier flooded oil market before
its economy sustained serious or perhaps even irreversible structural damage? No one knew because no one had thought to ask.

In Tehran, Secretary of State Vance personally offered the Shah Washington's continued support while gently reminding him that times had
changed and that he needed to change with them. Vance did not deliver
a human rights lecture to the Shah, nor did he link arms sales to progress
on human rights. "No such linkage has been discussed," Vance said at the
conclusion of their two-and-a-half-hour meeting. The new administration
wanted to make it clear that concerns over human rights would not stand
in the way of close bilateral relations and cooperation on security matters.
When Vance did raise the sensitive subject of human rights it was to the
CENTO ministerial meeting and he placed it in the context of their own
national self-interest rather than high-minded notions of individual morality. "Each country's growth, prosperity and stability sooner or later depend
upon its ability to meet the aspirations of its people for human rights,"
he told the gathering. Improving the lives of their people would actually
strengthen their legitimacy at home. For his part, the Shah was pleased
with how the talks went and reassured by Vance's knowledge of the Middle
East.

A macabre tradition had developed in which red-carpet visits to Iran by
U.S. officials were accompanied by grisly acts of terrorism. Sure enough,
several hours before the American party landed two gunmen were killed
during a pitched two-hour battle in the heart of downtown Tehran, not
far from the American embassy compound. Ten days later, U.S. diplomat
John Stempel met with Yoram Shani, the first secretary of Israel's unofficial embassy in the capital, at Xanadu restaurant in Tehran. The Israelis
enjoyed close ties with SAVAK and from time to time Shani made low-key
trips into the Iranian countryside disguised as an Australian tourist. Several weeks earlier Shani had alerted Stempel to a bloody episode in which
SAVAK agents had stormed the wrong house, killing its occupants just as

the real terrorists emerged from the building next door. Shani described these casualties as "unnecessary civilian deaths." In the latest incident, the Iranian government had labeled the gunmen "Islamic Marxists." But Shani told Stempel that the Israelis did not see it that way. It believed the men to be "fanatical right-wing Moslems." The two-hour gun battle had occurred outside the offices of the Jewish Immigration Agency in Tehran, and Shani implied that the attackers had at one point fought their way inside the complex before being cut down in a hail of gunfire. Stempel was also told that just two days earlier seven members of the security forces had been killed trying to clear terrorists from two safe houses in the capital.

On Sunday, May 29, Court Minister Alam had an audience at the palace. The Shah made the pointed observation that during a recent tour of South Tehran he had seen thousands of veiled women. This came as an unpleasant surprise to the man who more than any other had granted Iranian women their legal, civil, and political rights. In 1977 37 percent of university-level students were female and half of all applicants to medical schools were women. There were female members of parliament and elected to local councils. Women benefited from equal pay and equal opportunity legislation. Married women were legally entitled to seek a divorce, and single women could obtain an abortion without prior permission from a male family member. The government's minister of state for women's affairs, Mahnaz Afkhami, explained to a *New York Times* reporter that Iranian women were undergoing a "spiritual revival." She herself had recently visited holy cities in Saudi Arabia and Iraq. "I found it in myself," she said. "There seems to be a need for religion, as if we have moved too fast in a direction that is not native to us." It was a revival "against emptiness" but should not be perceived as a backlash against the king's political and economic reform.

In June, Queen Farah flew to the United States to undertake a series of official engagements in Aspen, Los Angeles, New York, and Washington and, more important, to ingratiate herself with the Carters. The meeting at the White House did not go well. The new president's effusive Southern charm grated on the queen's sensitivities. "I had just left Aspen where the talk was about such things as the meaning of development, unified approach, balance between political and economic change, justice and the like," she later told her husband's biographer. "The first thing President Carter told me was, 'You look more beautiful in person than in your pictures.' I am sure he meant that as a compliment. But I found it insulting."

Farah's summer sojourn was troubling for another reason. At every stop the Iranian party was hounded by hundreds and sometimes thousands of jeering demonstrators holding signs that read: "Down with the Shah!," "No More Arms for the Fascist Shah," "U.S. Advisers Out of Iran." During the queen's speech at a luncheon in Manhattan attended by the governor and city dignitaries a young blond woman suddenly leaped to her feet and shrieked, "That's a lie!" It was on this trip that she noticed for the first time that young protesters were holding up pictures of a stern-looking bearded cleric. "And so I asked the name of the mullah who was idolized by our young demonstrators and whose defiant look meant nothing to me." The queen learned that he was Ayatollah Ruhollah Khomeini, the hard-line cleric who had led the 1963 revolt against her husband's White Revolution reforms. "It struck me as unusual," she said. "I had always thought of students as young, idealistic, liberal, progressive individuals seeking freedom. Why would a student in America demonstrate for Khomeini and carry his picture as an emblem of his belief?"

Ambassador Ardeshir Zahedi spent 1977 outside Iran, preferring to focus on his official duties rather than deal with the increasingly political atmosphere at court where those closest to the throne intensified their jockeying for position. He heard the murmurings of unrest back home and forwarded the most detailed complaints and warnings to the palace. Zahedi had also become aware of new rumors circulating about the Shah's health. He took these in his stride. He had spent long enough in the Shah's company, particularly on the long foreign trips, to suspect that the king had a weak immune system. The Shah frequently caught cold, and on occasion he had experienced reactions to foodstuffs like strawberries and meat. The Shah was famously allergic to Iranian caviar. Early in the Carter administration, Zahedi had been called to attend a meeting with retired Admiral Stansfield Turner, the new director of central intelligence. Turner told Zahedi: "We have actually studied the Shah's position. And there is nothing wrong with him. The only thing is, he is looking rather tired." Zahedi told Turner that the Shah took a single Valium capsule before bed to help him sleep. Perhaps the Valium was to blame for the king's haggard appearance? At Turner's request Zahedi talked to the Shah and the Shah agreed to stop taking his nightly Valium.

Yet an incident that occurred during the queen's trip to Aspen made Ambassador Zahedi wonder if something else was going on. He received a request from the palace to send American cancer specialists to Tehran to treat Queen Mother Taj al-Malouk, who had been diagnosed with brain cancer. After the doctors returned from Tehran, Zahedi thanked them by inviting them to dine at the embassy. The mood at the table was lighthearted until one of the doctors casually mentioned an audience he had had with the Shah. "You know, I have heard the Shah," said the doctor to the ambassador. "He is very intelligent. But I never knew he knows so much about medicine. The questions he was asking, it was as though he was a doctor of cancer." It suddenly dawned on Zahedi that there might be another patient back at the palace—the *real* patient. "That moment I was shaking," he recalled. He immediately telephoned the Shah and demanded to know what was going on. Was His Majesty ill? Had the doctors been sent to Tehran as part of an elaborate ruse? The Shah put Zahedi's mind at ease. No, he replied, it was nothing serious, only a touch of gout. He even recycled a joke of Alam's whose moral was that gout sufferers enjoyed longer lives. The Shah's deception worked. For now, at least, his ambassador's suspicions were allayed.

PLEASE GOD THAT WE MAY BE SPARED THIS

In the summer of 1977 Iran's industrial production slumped 50 percent and inflation was running between 30 and 40 percent. Oil production fell an average of 390,633 barrels a day in June and daily crude exports by 923,594 barrels. The numbers for July were even worse. Iran produced 4,713,767 barrels a day but exported only 4,180,896 barrels a day. What made these figures exceptional was that apart from several days in the spring when Saudi Arabia's oil production briefly topped 11 million barrels a day, Saudi leaders had still not fully opened the throttle. They were aware of their growing isolation in the Arab world, sensitive to the prospect of more domestic unrest, and no doubt feeling the "extraordinary pressure" being brought to bear on them by Iran. By now enough Saudi crude had been pumped into the system to prevent the Shah's first-phase 10 percent price hike from taking effect. Spare capacity was returning to the market just as oil from the Alaskan pipeline and the North Sea fields were set to come on line. Saudi Arabia had proven its point. Iran and the other OPEC hardliners "no longer take us for granted," said Yamani.

The Saudis and the Iranians were both looking for a way out of the Oil War. On June 29, OPEC released a statement in Vienna announcing that the two protagonists had settled their differences. Iran agreed to forgo its second stage 5 percent increase set to take effect on July 1. Saudi Arabia and UAE agreed they would lift the price of their crude exports by 5 percent to bring them into line with the rest of the cartel. OPEC also agreed to freeze prices for all of 1978. The decision by the majority of the cartel not to implement the July 1 price hike saved Western consumers $2 billion. Speaking in Riyadh on the same day, Crown Prince Fahd also assured President Carter that the West need not fear a second oil embargo. "We will not cut the flow of oil to America or to anyone," he said.

The Shah had no choice but to settle. He was a beaten man and he knew it. Even at this late stage only thirteen of Saudi Aramco's thirty-five oil fields were in production. "So there is a lot of room for expansion," noted *The Economist*. Iran's waterlogged economy risked being swept away in the deluge. *Petroleum Intelligence Weekly* described the saturated oil market as "sloppy," especially in heavy crudes, and observed that "there seems little hope of a rebound in prices before the fourth quarter." *BusinessWeek* described the United States and Western Europe as "awash with oil. . . . With storage tanks all over Europe brimful and 40 cargoes of crude oil reportedly floating aboard tankers with nowhere to go, the companies believe market forces now dictate much lower production levels." There was so much surplus crude in the system that refiners began dumping oil "at less than cost" and Middle East oil producers slashed their prices by 20 cents per barrel. "At present time, there is a glut in the market," conceded Oil Minister Jamshid Amuzegar of Iran. Indeed, so much oil had been pumped into the system that the market remained in a slump for the rest of 1977. By December even Saudi Arabia was forced to cut its daily production to 8.3 million barrels, a move that prompted *The Wall Street Journal* to report that "the Persian Gulf kingdom is singlehandedly trying to dry up the oil glut" it had created earlier in the year.

Industry observers were unanimous that Saudi Arabia had won the war and driven Iran from the market. The Vienna compromise, said *BusinessWeek*, marked "a clear-cut Saudi victory," even though in the first few weeks of the battle "it looked as if the Saudis had bitten off more than they could chew." The fire at Abqaiq and cold winter in Europe and the United States had offered price relief to the Iranians. But these turned out to be temporary aberrations. Saudi Arabia's oil production was "once again hovering around 10 million bbl a day as the world oil market goes into a seasonal slump." If Iran had insisted on implementing its threatened 5 percent second-stage price hike on July 1, "the Saudis could indeed have swamped the market and driven prices down." The Saudis were pleased with the Carter administration's progress in forging a Middle East peace deal. Besides, high oil prices encouraged energy conservation in the United States, something the Saudis were keen to discourage: "If the West weaned itself from OPEC oil, the Saudis might end up with a lot of oil that nobody wants."

A thick blanket of brown grime and suffocating heat unfurled itself over Tehran and brought fresh hardships to the people of Iran. Low rainfall and lengthy delays in dam construction placed strains on the electrical grid that led to frequent power outages. "These blackouts have caused widespread inconvenience and, above all, economic losses," reported the *New York Times* correspondent. "Government officials must walk up seven and eight stories to their offices. Tourists get caught in elevators. Office workers swelter in 100-degree-plus temperatures without air conditioning." In London, Ambassador Radji learned from a visitor recently returned from Tehran that "the blackouts have proved a colossal embarrassment to the regime and have provided an outlet for everyone's pent-up and long-smoldering discontent. The situation has laid indecently bare the Government's repeated assurances that increased military expenditures would not be at the cost of improvements in people's living standards."

From the religious stronghold of Qum, senior Ayatollah Khonsari telephoned Court Minister Alam to inform him that water and power supplies had been cut. Even Alam's neighborhood was not spared, and he purchased a generator to keep the telephones in his house working. He feared the situation was getting out of hand. "It terrifies me that one day everything will simply cave in around us. Please God that we may be spared this." Alam described the government's empty response as "like a scene from some incredible farce."

The government urged shopkeepers to close their doors at 8:00 P.M. and factory owners to release their workers for early summer holidays. Conditions were especially deplorable in the restive southern suburbs, where "cuts sometimes last 8 to 10 hours a day." The burden of the dysfunction was falling on the poorest Tehranis. Those who ventured onto the streets of south Tehran in the summer of 1977 were struck by the sullen atmosphere and the large numbers of young men standing around waiting for something to do. Many had come from the countryside to find work or seek a better life for their families. But the economic slowdown halted new building construction and led to high job losses. Former U.S. diplomat Bill Lehfeldt, by now working in the private sector and a frequent visitor to Tehran, scoffed at the efforts of the Iranian government to minimize the problem. "There was more under- and unemployment than you could shake a stick at," he remembered. "I realize they had to manufacture numbers for things, but if you went down into South Tehran in 1977 on a warm summer's day, you wondered why the place didn't blow up earlier. People were flocking to the town from the countryside, from the small villages all over the country, hoping to get in on the gravy train and crammed into impossible living quarters in South Tehran, by and large. And all looking for jobs."

It was around this time that General Hassan Pakravan and his wife, Fatemeh, took a road trip to Kashan and Natanz. It was Pakravan who had intervened to save Khomeini's life in 1963. Two years later the Shah had replaced him as head of SAVAK with General Ne'matollah Nasiri, an odious character who showed a great deal more flair for his real estate investments than he did watching the Shah's back. Since then, Pakravan had served as the Shah's ambassador to Pakistan and then France before accepting a high post as court adviser. On their way to Kashan the Pakravans drove through south Tehran, a part of the capital they hadn't seen in many years. "I couldn't believe my eyes!" Mrs. Pakravan later recounted. "I just couldn't believe my eyes—the conditions in which people lived! It was incredible! Some of them lived in pens, completely patched up with pieces of nylon on them. The open-air canals were heaped with dirt and garbage. The water was black and smelly. You could not imagine what it was [like]. You cannot visualize it."

When General Pakravan returned to Tehran he sought an audience with the Shah because, his wife later recalled, he was "terribly worried" by what he had seen. The general described to the king the appalling conditions in south Tehran. "If you're not going to do something immediately from a human point of view, do it for your own safety, because this is a powder keg. Two million people living like that—your capital city is going to explode and we'll all be swept away by the explosion." The next day Pakravan showed photographs of what he had seen to the queen. After that the Shah began to receive Pakravan on a regular basis. These were apparently distressing encounters for both men. One day Pakravan returned home and told his wife, "Whenever I see the Shah I have the sense impression he is like a drowning man who sees me as some safety to which to cling." Mrs. Pakravan said of those last days of life on the volcano: "It was too late, too late, too late."

The conditions for a general uprising were in place. In the summer of 1977 a small but growing number of wealthy Iranians and longtime foreign residents quietly put their affairs in order, emptied their bank accounts, and sent family members out of the country on extended "vacations." James Saghi, a businessman who "saw the writing on the wall," sold his house at a profit, and moved to California's Napa Valley. Others who got out early were American passport holders Bill Shashua, Tehran's Peugeot dealer, who confided to a friend that "everything was going to fall apart," and Lloyd Bertman, who had lived in Iran since the early 1950s. Bertman shared with a friend his strong personal sense that "there are things that are happening that make me uncomfortable, so I'm going to leave." These individuals were perceptive and knew Iran well enough to see what was coming.

WE'VE SURRENDERED TO THE SAUDIS

On Thursday, August 4, the Shah telephoned Court Minister Alam in Paris to ask for his resignation. Two days later, Amir Abbas Hoveyda resigned as prime minister. The Shah appointed Oil Minister Jamshid Amuzegar as Iran's new prime minister and elevated Hoveyda to Alam's old post as court minister.

Alam was puzzled by both appointments. Hoveyda's premiership had ended in failure and Amuzegar had never demonstrated a capacity to lead, let alone inspire. Amuzegar announced sweeping cuts to government spending and imposed harsh austerity measures that led to even higher job losses among poor, unskilled, and semiskilled Iranians. In his first few weeks in office the new prime minister fired 1,700 people from the Finance Ministry and announced his intention to break the back of the Plan and Budget Organization, which he inexplicably blamed for the economic mess. "The PBO had become a super-ministry," he said in an interview with Joe Alex Morris of the *Los Angeles Times*. "I've asked the PBO to drop all responsibilities for implementation of projects. We're cutting down other employees and putting them in other ministries where they won't be sitting around as stumbling blocks." Morris reminded his readers that three years earlier the PBO had warned "of the dangers of all-out development, and most of its predictions have come true. The report was ignored at the time." Amuzegar's course correction was "a gamble, a race against time, with built-in contradictions that are bound to sharpen the conflicts within the society as time goes on." It was doubtful the new government could meet the rising expectations of Iran's swollen, sullen urban underclass. Amuzegar's final words as the interview drew to a close were not reassuring. "Wish me luck," he said. Luck was in short supply in Iran in the late 1970s. Amuzegar lost his job a year later and eventually fled to exile. Morris, a fifty-one-year-old father of two, took a sniper's bullet to the heart in Tehran on February 9, 1979, the day the Iranian monarchy was finally overthrown.

The end of empire was at hand. "In the past few months we've backed down on oil prices," wrote Alam in one of his final diary entries. "We've surrendered to the Saudis, which means in effect to Carter. Oil prices are to remain frozen until the end of next year. . . . These diaries must come to an end. There is nothing left for me to write now that I'm cut out of my meetings with HIM."

In early April 1978 Alam wrote a final letter to the Shah. "He suggested that if the crisis were allowed to fester, revolution would be unavoidable," wrote his biographer. "The situation, he said, was far more serious than the Mossadeq crisis of 1953." Alam's death eight days later on April 13 spared him the collapse he fully anticipated. The notebooks he had quietly kept since 1968 were removed from Iran and deposited for safekeeping in Switzerland. Alam instructed his wife not to publish them "until such time as the Pahlavi dynasty no longer ruled Iran."

THE LAST HURRAH

"We never took him seriously."

—Richard Helms

Five months earlier, on November 15, 1977, the Pahlavis traveled to Washington for a state visit that officials on both sides had hoped would reinvigorate U.S.-Iran relations and ease recent strains over oil prices, arms sales, nuclear power, and human rights.

Iranian officials saw the Shah's twelfth trip to Washington and especially the official welcoming ceremony on the grounds of the White House as an ideal opportunity to stage a "spontaneous" televised show of support for the beleaguered crown. Ambassador Zahedi recalled that he expressed doubts about the wisdom of the plan but was overruled by the palace. More than one thousand Iranian expatriates traveled to the capital from Chicago and Los Angeles. SAVAK picked up the tab, which included free round-trip airfare, hotel accommodations, and $150 per person. The Iranians also arranged for 422 of 464 Iranian officers enrolled in military training programs at Lackland Air Force Base in Texas to fly to Washington so the royalist crowd would be stacked with boisterous young men. Student protesters opposed to the Shah also mobilized in record numbers and headed for the capital. The U.S. Park Police was responsible for providing security at the event. On the eve of the Shah's arrival, *The Washington Post* reported "some of the most intense preparations for street demonstrations seen here since the days of the Vietnam antiwar movement." The FBI and the State Department both warned the police to prepare for a potential clash. The bureau passed along what it considered solid intelligence that Iranian students were buying large quantities of oil that could be used to manufacture Molotov cocktails. "We updated [police agencies] on Iranian student activity," said a State Department official. "Our basic conclusion? We were going to have trouble. . . . Our security people were very concerned."

The Park Police and Interior Department later denied that the information they received had been that specific. "Iranian student demonstrators in the past . . . had been orderly and peaceful," said Major James Lindsay, the commanding officer, "and with no evidence of impending trouble, a decision was made to have only a small-low-key police presence at the Ellipse." He was apparently unaware of an August 1967 incident in which student protesters had violently clashed with police in an attempt to disrupt President Johnson's welcoming ceremony for the Shah. Lindsay took the view that young hotheads in the crowd might react more aggressively to an intrusive police presence. On the day of the state welcome he deployed only 151 police officers—including two dozen on horseback—to patrol the Ellipse, where the rival Iranian factions had been told they could set up their pickets. Riot police armed with gas masks, shields, and truncheons were held in reserve, well away from the crowds, stationed in buses several blocks from the White House grounds.

The Pahlavis flew into Virginia on November 14 and spent the night in Colonial Williamsburg. Ambassador Sullivan was intrigued to see so many young protesters holding up Khomeini's portrait. He knew who he was. "Although I appreciated the role that Ayatollah Khomeini had played in the struggle between the shah and Shi'a clergy, this was the first time I had seen his name and portrait invoked in the struggle by the Iranian students against the shah's regime," he recalled later. Like the queen, Sullivan was perplexed that a man with a feudal outlook could command any following outside religious circles. The following morning the Shah and his party flew to Washington, where they landed on the Mall in two helicopters, then drove on to the White House. Sullivan noticed that the two groups of protesters, now numbering in the thousands, "were separated only by light, collapsible fencing erected in a narrow space of not more than twenty yards. A mere scatting of park police moved in that twenty-yard stretch of no man's land."

The trouble began as soon as the Carters and the Pahlavis walked to the dais for the national anthems and speeches. The students used the twenty-one-gun salute as the signal to launch their assault on the royalists. From his vantage point, Ambassador Sullivan watched as "a sudden surge of activity erupted on the ellipse." Screams, cries, and insults filled the air as masked protesters armed with clubs, plastic shields, bike helmets, and pickets stormed the bleachers where Pahlavi loyalists sat. Others raided the building site of the now ironically named "Pageant for Peace," an annual holiday tradition on the Ellipse, and made off with nail-studded planks with which to club their victims. "Children and elderly persons appeared stunned and frightened," reported the *Washington Post* correspondent at the scene. Hundreds of people stampeded toward 17th Street to escape the melee. "It's terrible, terrible," sobbed a young woman who fled the scene. A fusillade of sticks and bottles rained down on the police, who fell back in disarray, then regrouped and fired tear gas. Sirens filled the air and there were wild scenes in the streets around the White House. A pickup truck was driven through police lines. Trash cans were set ablaze. Office workers who tried to pass through Lafayette Square were jostled and harassed by Iranian students. Other students armed with sticks attacked a car on H Street whose driver they suspected was a SAVAK agent. A convoy of ambulances rushed to evacuate more than 120 injured people, three with serious head injuries, to local area hospitals where emergency room personnel treated the wounded in different rooms "to keep them from fighting each other."

On the White House lawn stunned dignitaries and reporters watched armed snipers with binoculars move into position on the executive mansion's rooftop. Down below, the two first couples were engulfed in a cloud of tear gas, choking back tears and wiping their eyes with handkerchiefs. Television viewers in Iran and elsewhere watched the astonishing spectacle of their king being tear-gassed on the American president's front lawn. "We then went into the reception rooms," said Queen Farah, who had long feared exactly this sort of breakdown in security, and who immediately suspected sinister motives on the part of her husband's critics in the administration. "President Carter and his wife begged us to forget the incident—they were truly embarrassed—but I thought to myself that in Richard Nixon's time the demonstrators would never have been allowed to come so close to us. Didn't permissiveness show a desire on the part of the new administration to embarrass us?"

The violence outside the White House was not isolated. There was a near-simultaneous rising by two thousand student protesters at Aryamehr University in Tehran demanding an end to dictatorship and support for human rights. Riot police arrested fifty students and injured forty in the ensuing clashes. That night rampaging students set ablaze six banks and two car dealerships. The next day saw a bigger confrontation when ten thousand protesters and five hundred riot police fought running battles through the streets of downtown Tehran. Perhaps it was appropriate, given everything that had happened the past nine years, that the fuse of revolution had been lit on the White House lawn.

Mohammad Reza Shah, the second and last Pahlavi king, died in exile in Egypt on July 27, 1980. Today Queen Farah is a vocal critic of Iran's Islamic Republic and continues to speak out in support of women's rights. Their eldest son, Reza Pahlavi, is also a prominent opponent of the current regime in Tehran. The couple's youngest child, Princess Leila, died of a drug overdose in 2001, and her brother, Prince Alireza, committed suicide in 2011.

The Shah's former son-in-law, foreign minister, and ambassador to Washington, Ardeshir Zahedi, lives in exile in Switzerland and is writing his memoirs. In the early 1980s Richard and Pat Nixon visited Zahedi at his home in Montreux. Their traveling companion, former treasury secretary Bill Simon, stayed behind on the French side of the border. Zahedi made it clear that the Shah's nemesis would never be welcome in his house. He continues to speak out about events in Iran and the Middle East.

Ahmed Zaki al-Yamani was sacked as Saudi Arabia's oil minister in 1986 after a series of disputes with King Fahd, who ascended the throne after the death of his brother King Khalid in 1982. Yamani left the kingdom and went on to found the Center for Global Energy Resources in London in 1990.

Douglas MacArthur II, who survived an assassination attempt in Iran in 1970, died in 1997, aged eighty-eight.

Joseph Farland, Richard Nixon's luckless ambassador to Iran during election year 1972, died in 2007 at the age of ninety-two.

Former President Richard Nixon attended the Shah's state funeral in Egypt in 1980.

Richard Hallock, the Pentagon's Grey Ghost, amassed a fortune through his companies Intrec and Quaestor before his death in 1999. The Richard R. Hallock Foundation is a donor to the National Infantry Museum, supports student scholarship programs, and funds a student college lecture series. In May 2010 the foundation announced a $2 million grant to Columbus State University to create a military history professorship, the Col. Richard R. Hallock Distinguished University Chair in Military History. "In his long, subsequent career at the Pentagon, [Colonel Hallock] was renowned for pursuing the interests of America's soldiers, sometimes in the teeth of vigorous bureaucratic opposition," read the press release announcing the gift. "Upon leaving active service in 1967, Col. Hallock became an adviser to Defense Secretary James Schlesinger and consulted on political-military affairs, particularly in the Middle East."

James Schlesinger, who served as secretary of defense from 1973 to 1975, also served as the first secretary of energy in President Carter's cabinet from 1977 to 1979. Schlesinger went on to become an influential policy adviser to presidents and to the Pentagon. In the private sector he served as chairman of the board of trustees of MITRE Corporation. Most recently, Schlesinger conducted a review of how the United States handles its arsenal of tactical nuclear weapons.

Treasury Secretary William E. Simon returned to the private sector but remained active in Republican Party politics. He is today widely regarded as one of the most influential conservatives of the late twentieth century and one of the driving forces behind the "Reagan Revolution" of the 1980s. As treasurer and then president of the United States Olympic Committee, Simon presided over the 1984 summer games in Los Angeles. He founded a merchant bank, William E. Simon & Sons, sat on corporate boards at Halliburton, Xerox, and Citibank, served as president of the Richard Nixon Presidential Archives Foundation, for twenty years as president of the Olin Foundation, and in addition served as trustee for the Heritage Foundation and Hoover Institution. The business school at the University of Rochester is named after him. Simon was implicated in the Iran-contra scandal when his name appeared as an officer on the board of an entity called the Nicaraguan Freedom Fund, a not-for-profit group established with seed money to provide "humanitarian" support for the contra rebels fighting to overthrow the government of Nicaragua. Simon, who remained a favorite of the Saudis, died on June 3, 2000, at age seventy-two.

Henry Kissinger left government service and successfully fashioned himself as a senior statesman. In 1982, he founded Kissinger Associates, an international business consultancy firm, hiring former National Security Adviser Brent Scowcroft and appointing his old rival Bill Simon to the board of directors. Over the past two decades Kissinger's younger hires have risen to places of prominence in the Washington firmament. Perhaps the most well known are Timothy Geithner, secretary of the treasury in the administration of Barack Obama, and the official tasked with leading the American response to the worldwide financial crisis and recession that began in 2007, and J. Paul Bremer, President George W. Bush's hapless administrator in Iraq following the 2003 invasion and occupation of that country. Kissinger unsuccessfully fought to prevent the release of the telephone transcripts cited in this book.

In the second volume of his three-volume memoirs, *Years of Upheaval* (1982), Kissinger denied that the Shah was granted a blank check to buy unrestricted amounts of military equipment from the Nixon administration: "This is disingenuous; there was no blank check." He claimed that Nixon's 1972 pledge to the Shah on arms sales had solely to do with the F-14 and F-15 fighter aircraft, making no mention of Nelson Rockefeller's involvement in the original decision. Consider the following curious passage from *Years of Upheaval*:

> In any event, only one ignorant of our governmental processes or eager to score debating points could argue that this single directive by Nixon survived Watergate and his resignation and drove all the decisions of the two subsequent administrations—during which 90 percent of the major arms sales were in fact made. I doubt that Presidents Ford and Carter were even aware of the directive—as I had forgotten it—when they approved later arms purchases that were incomparably larger than those approved under Nixon.

Former U.S. ambassador to Iran Richard Helms died in 2002 at the age of eighty-nine. In November 1985 he participated in a seminar held at the Foreign Service Institute to consider the lessons of the U.S. experience in Iran. According to author James Bill, who attended the event and took notes, Helms had this to say about one of the worst strategic setbacks in American history: "Is it necessary that the United States win every battle . . . that the U.S. run the world? I don't think so. At times things are going to go sour. Let's not go around biting our nails about it."

A colleague once asked Helms what he and Kissinger had really thought about the Shah. Helms replied with contempt: "We never took him seriously."

ACKNOWLEDGMENTS

From the very beginning, Professor Gary Sick of Columbia University gave generously of his time, offering wise counsel and encouraging me to persist in my efforts. Gary helped me work through analytical problems and decipher some of the most puzzling transcripts and the questions they posed. Ahmad Ashraf, managing editor of the *Encyclopaedia Iranica*, introduced me to the diaries of Court Minister Asadollah Alam and provided me with an Iranian perspective. He directed me to sources, made introductions, and helped guide my inquiry. Ahmad and Gary both reviewed the manuscript and provided feedback for which I am deeply appreciative. They have been mentors in the truest sense of the word. Suffice to say, any errors contained in this book are mine and my responsibility.

I owe a special debt of gratitude to former government officials and retired diplomats who agreed to meet with me to help interpret documents, share insights, and offer reminiscences. They too are still trying to understand the origins and fallout from the 1979 Iranian Revolution. In the United States, former Ford administration officials General Brent Scowcroft, James Schlesinger, and Frank Zarb offered invaluable insights into oil policy during the crisis days of the mid-1970s. Diplomats Henry Precht, Bill Lehfeldt, and Charlie Naas, now retired, helped provide a diplomatic perspective of events, shared stories, and helped decipher declassified documents. Defense strategist Edward Luttwak talked to me about U.S. power projection in a time when America was perceived to be weak at home and abroad. Former Iranian foreign minister and ambassador Ardeshir Zahedi opened his home in Montreux, Switzerland, and spent two days answering my questions, offering his own perspective, and talking about the personalities and events of that earlier era. Former Secretary of Defense Donald Rumsfeld and former Chairman of the Federal Reserve Alan Greenspan declined my requests for interviews. I did not receive responses from the office of former Secretary of State Henry Kissinger or from Iranian economist Jahangir Amuzegar.

On the sole question of the Shah's cancer diagnosis, I approached the office of Queen Farah seeking clarification. I would like to thank Mr. Kambiz Atabai, the queen's chief of staff, for forwarding my request, and I especially thank H.M. Queen Farah for considering and responding to my questions.

General Brent Scowcroft's collection of papers deposited at the Gerald R. Ford Presidential Library in Ann Arbor, Michigan, is one of the most important troves of documents available to American foreign policy scholars. Thank you to Geir Gunderson and his colleagues at the library for fulfilling so many research requests, and also to Nancy Mirshah for locating the wonderful photographs from President Ford's administration. Thanks also to Pamela Eisenberg at the Richard Nixon Library in Yorba Linda, California, for locating pictures from the Nixon administration.

Scholars who study U.S.-Iran relations during the Cold War invariably turn to the collection of documents housed at the National Security Archive at George Washington University. The National Security Archive provides an unparalleled service to historians through its collection of documents "Iran: The Making of US Policy, 1977–80," as well as through the Kissinger telephone transcripts.

The papers of former Secretary of the Treasury William E. Simon are open to scholars at Lafayette College's Skillman Library. Although I was unable to visit the library, the library staff, and especially Diane Wyndham Shaw, located documents and mailed them to me.

I am grateful to Professor Gholam Reza Afkhami and the Foundation for Iranian Studies in Maryland for making available the foundation's invaluable collection of oral history interviews conducted with former high-ranking U.S. officials and diplomats. The holdings of FIS offer a unique historical record and I am appreciative to Professor Afkhami and his staff for their efforts and assistance during the course of my research.

My contacts at Associated Press Images, which provided many of the photographs in *The Oil Kings*, were Paata Stanley and Dawn Cohen.

Had it not been for the editors of the *Middle East Journal* my research would never have been published at all. I am appreciative to John Calcrese and his colleagues at *MEJ* and for the outstanding work they do. Tehran-based *Los Angeles Times* correspondent Borzou Daragahi first brought the 2008 *MEJ* article to mainstream public attention. I would like to thank Borzou, my friend and classmate from Columbia University's Graduate School of Journalism, for the interest he has shown in my work.

Halfway through my research I returned to my country of birth, New Zealand, to enroll in the Ph.D. history program at Victoria University in Wellington. My dissertation supervisors, Dr. Dolores Janiewski and Dr. Rob Rabel, understood that a unique opportunity presented itself when Simon & Schuster expressed interest in a book, and it was with their agreement I relocated to Greece for a year to write the manuscript. I would like to thank them for their advice and support, and also Victoria's administrative and library staff for their support and contributions in helping to make this book happen. I completed my undergraduate degree at Victoria twenty years ago, so returning for a Ph.D. was like completing the circle.

I would like to thank the librarians at the Wellington Public Library and also the staff at the Parliamentary Library of New Zealand for their patience with my many research requests.

I would be remiss if I did not say a special thank-you to Dr. Mark Sherwood and the fine staff at Wellington Public Hospital for the superb surgical and aftercare procedures that got me back on my feet. I continued my physical rehabilitation in Greece at Maggie Michailidou's wonderful Ergofit Gym in Athens, where Giota Koutsoukou and Nikos Vavoulas provided training and friendship.

It is a brave soul who takes under her wing an unknown writer with virtually no track record of published work. I am one of the luckiest writers around to have as my agent Sandra Dijkstra. Sandy's enthusiasm for my work and her attention to detail have been a source of inspiration and motivation. To Sandy and her wonderful staff at the Sandra Dijkstra Literary Agency—Natalie, Elisabeth, Elise, and Andrea—thank you for everything you have done and continue to do.

At Simon & Schuster, I had the great fortune to have Bob Bender as my editor. I am grateful to Bob for taking a chance on a first-time writer and guiding me through the process. For me this has been a thoroughly enjoyable and straightforward collaboration and one that I hope will be the first of many—at no point did writing *The Oil Kings* feel like work. A special thank-you to Associate Editor Johanna Li, who helped me bring the elements of the book together.

Writing a first book is in many ways a joint project made possible by friends and family. To those generous friends who gave me a bed for the night, took me out to dinner, called, e-mailed, and checked in, and who have been so enthusiastic, this book is also for you.

Finally, my parents moved heaven and earth to help me achieve my dream of writing a work of history and it is to my family, for their tremendous support, that this book is dedicated. I hope it makes up for the long absences.

NOTES

INTRODUCTION

PAGE

1   *"Why should I plant a tree"*: Abolqasem Ferdowsi, translated by Dick Davis, *Shahnameh: The Persian Book of Kings* (New York: Penguin, 2006), 252.

1   *flew to Riyadh:* "Cheney Meets Saudi King for Talks," *New York Times*, November 26, 2006.

1   *one fifth of the world's proven oil reserves:* The U.S. Energy Information Administration makes country analysis briefs available on its Web site. The one on Saudi Arabia can be accessed at http://www.eia.doe.gov/emeu/cabs/Saudi_Arabia/pdf.pdf.

1   *largest producer within OPEC:* Ibid. Saudi Arabia was the world's "largest producer and exporter of total petroleum liquids" in 2010. The kingdom has the world's largest crude oil production capacity. The latest statistics on world oil production and consumption can be found on the Web site for the U.S. Energy Information Administration at http://www.eia.doe.gov. Another good source of information is the CIA *World Factbook* at https://www.cia.gov/library/publications/the-world-factbook. "In 2009," reports US EIA, "Saudi Arabia exported an average of 1 million barrels of oil a day to the United States, accounting for 9 percent of US petroleum imports."

1   *"to find common ground":* Sheryl Gay Stolberg and Jim Rutenberg, "Rumsfeld Resigns as Defense Secretary After Big Election Gains for Democrats," *New York Times*, November 9, 2006.

1   *"since America came into Iraq uninvited":* Nawaf Obaid, "Stepping into Iraq; Saudi Arabia Will Protect Sunnis if the U.S. Leaves," *Washington Post*, November 29, 2006.

2   *"Iran's profits from oil rose last year":* Nazila Fathi, "Iranian's Plans for Economy Spur Widespread Concern," *New York Times*, May 1, 2006.

2   *King Midas complex:* "The legendary King Midas was the first Middle Eastern

ruler to cherish the belief that untold mineral wealth would enable him to realize all his dreams and ambitions," wrote historian Nikki Keddie in "The Midas Touch: Black Gold, Economics and Politics in Iran Today," *Iranian Studies* 10, no. 4 (Autumn 1977): 243. "But just because all he touched turned into gold, he soon discovered he could no longer eat. . . . Oil income is clearly not an evil in itself, but large oil income often tempts governments into over-ambitious capital-intensive urban-centered projects that bring on a host of difficulties."

2 *"Critics said that his plans"*: Nazila Fathi, "Iranian's Plans for Economy Spur Widespread Concern," *New York Times*, May 1, 2006.

3 *80 percent of income from exports*: https://www.cia.gov/library/publications/the -world-factbook/geos/ir.html.

3 *"A member of the Saudi royal family"*: Hassan M. Fattah, "Bickering Saudis Struggle for an Answer to Iran's Rising Influence in the Middle East," *New York Times*, December 22, 2006.

4 *"massive Saudi intervention"*: Nawaf Obaid, "Stepping into Iraq; Saudi Arabia Will Protect Sunnis if the U.S. Leaves," *Washington Post*, November 29, 2006.

5 *severing its ties*: "Saudi Arabia Fires Security Consultant for Iraq Remarks," *Washington Post*, December 7, 2006.

5 *"[Obaid] is widely expected to return"*: Hassan M. Fattah, "Bickering Saudis Struggle for an Answer to Iran's Rising Influence in the Middle East," *New York Times*, December 22, 2006.

5 *"The Saudi government disavowed"*: Helene Cooper, "Saudis Say They Might Back Sunnis if U.S. Leaves Iraq," *New York Times*, December 13, 2006.

5 *not falling below $42 a barrel*: According to *The New York Times*: "The Saudi government does not disclose what oil price it uses when it builds its budget, but analysts at Samba Financial Group, a bank in Saudi Arabia, say they be-lieve the price is $42 a barrel for 2007, with oil production at about 9 million barrels a day. With oil averaging $66 a barrel last year, the kingdom recorded a budget surplus of nearly $71 billion, Samba said, five times more than in 2005." See Jad Mouawad, "Saudi Officials Seek to Temper the Price of Oil," *New York Times*, January 28, 2007.

5 *surpass $80 a barrel*: Jad Mouawad, "Oil Prices Continue to Rise, with a Close Above $78," *New York Times*, August 1, 2007.

5 *rocketed to $98*: Jad Mouawad, "Oil Price Drops Sharply as Global Agency Sees Demand Falling," *New York Times*, November 14, 2007.

5 *President Bush personally appealed to King Abdullah*: Steven Lee Myers, "Bush Prods Saudi Arabia on Oil Prices," *New York Times*, January 16, 2008.

5 *250,000 barrels a day*: Jad Mouawad, "As U.S. Economy Lags, Oil Nations Rethink Cuts," *New York Times*, March 3, 2008.

5 *to 9.7 million barrels*: Jad Mouawad, "Saudis Vow to Ignore OPEC Decision to Cut Production," *New York Times*, September 11, 2008.

5   *$118 in May:* Jad Mouawad, "Oil Price Rise Fails to Open Tap," *New York Times*, April 29, 2008.

6   *$147.27 in July:* William J. Broad, "Experts Point to Deceptions in Iran's Military Display," *New York Times*, July 12, 2008.

6   *$107 a barrel:* Jad Mouawad, "As Oil Prices Fall, OPEC Faces a Balancing Act," *New York Times*, September 5, 2008.

6   *not fall below $90:* As reported in *The New York Times*: "The drop in prices has already created problems for oil producers. Iran and Venezuela both need oil prices at $95 a barrel to balance their national budgets, Russia needs $70 and Saudi Arabia needs $55 a barrel, according to Deutsche Bank estimates." Jad Mouawad, "Oil Prices Slip Below $70 a barrel," *New York Times*, October 17, 2008.

6   *$43 a barrel:* Jad Mouawad, "OPEC Plans Further Output Cut," *New York Times*, December 17, 2008.

6   *$33 in January 2009:* Clifford Krauss, "No Change in Oil Goal, Cartel Is Watchful," *New York Times*, December 22, 2009.

6   *"While much scholarly focus":* Andrew Scott Cooper, "Showdown at Doha: The Secret Oil Deal That Helped Sink the Shah of Iran," *The Middle East Journal* 62, no. 4 (Autumn 2008).

8   *"that rarest of leaders":* Henry A. Kissinger, *White House Years* (Boston: Little, Brown, 1979), 1261.

9   *"readers who seek understanding":* William Shawcross, "Through History with Henry A. Kissinger," *Harper's* 258, no. 1548 (May 1979): 39.

11 *imports almost two thirds of its oil:* According to *Politifacts*, in 2009 the percentage of U.S. oil imports was 62 percent. See http://www.politifact.com/truth-o-meter/statements/2010/jun/07/john-kerry/kerry-says-us-imports-more-oil-now-911. "Imported oil accounts for about two-thirds of U.S. consumption," reports the CIA *World Factbook*: https://www.cia.gov/library/publications/the-world-factbook/geos/us.html.

11 *"I am saddened that it is politically inconvenient":* Alan Greenspan, *The Age of Turbulence* (New York: Penguin, 2007), 463.

CHAPTER ONE: A KIND OF SUPER MAN

PAGE

15 *"If someone wraps a lion cub in silk":* Abolqasem Ferdowsi, translated by Dick Davis, *Shahnameh: The Persian Book of Kings* (New York: Penguin, 2006), 263.

17 *Your Majesty, you're like the radiant sun:* Ibid., 328.

17 *"I like him, I like him and I like the country":* Conversation Among President Nixon, Ambassador Douglas MacArthur II, and General Alexander Haig, Washington, April 8, 1971, 3:56–4:21 P.M. Monica Belmonte, Editor; Edward C. Keefer, General Editor, *Foreign Relations of the United States, 1969–1976*, Vol. E-4, Documents on Iran and Iraq, 1969–1972 (Washington: United States Government Printing Office), Office of the Historian, Bureau of Public Affairs.

18   *Standing erect in elevator shoes:* The Shah had a well-known preoccupation
      with his height. According to his biographer, Marvin Zonis, who interviewed
      the Shah, the monarch was "known to wear elevator shoes and shoes with
      relatively high heels. One can also look in vain for a picture of the Shah
      standing side by side with Empress Farah, for that would show all too clearly
      that she was taller than he." Marvin Zonis, *Majestic Failure: The Fall of the Shah*
      (Chicago: University of Chicago Press, 1991), 14.

18   "*I pointed out that it will provide*": Asadollah Alam, *The Shah and I: The
      Confidential Diary of Iran's Royal Court, 1969–77* (New York: St. Martin's,
      1991), 48.

18   "*The Shah is clearly the most important person in Iran*": National Security Coun-
      cil Files, VIP Visits, Visit of the Shah of Iran, October 21–23, 1969 (1 of 2),
      Box 920, National Archives, College Park, MD.

18   *a stunning blue and maroon Persian rug:* Julie and David Eisenhower's rug is
      listed along with other gifts presented to the Nixon family and collated as
      a part of the Watergate political corruption investigation in the late 1970s.
      List of Foreign Head of State Gifts Presented to President and Mrs. Nixon
      by H.I.M. Mohammad Reza Pahlavi, Shahanshah of Iran; by H.I.H. The
      Princess Ashraf; by H.I.M. The Empress Farah; and by H.E. Ardeshir Za-
      hedi, February 2, 1978, Eric Hooglund, project editor, *Iran: The Making of
      U.S. Policy, 1977–80*, National Security Archive (Alexandria, VA: Chadwyck-
      Healey, 1990), Document Reference No. 01316.

19   "*stole the show*": Alam, 49.

19   *two thirds of the world's known petroleum reserves:* Warren Unna, "Guam Policy
      Near Test in Gulf," *Washington Post*, February 16, 1970.

19   *one third of the petroleum used by the free world:* Daniel Yergin, *The Prize: The
      Epic Quest for Oil, Money, and Power* (New York: Simon & Schuster, 1991),
      566.

19   *89 percent of oil used by the U.S. military:* Memorandum from the President's
      Assistant for National Security Affairs (Kissinger) to President Nixon, Wash-
      ington, October 22, 1970, *FRUS 1969–76*, Vol. E-4.

19   *$1.5 billion in revenue:* Ibid.

19   *employed twelve thousand American expatriates:* Ibid.

19   "*assigned an area from Malaysia to South Africa*": Arthur Veysey, "Soviets Eye
      Rich Persian Gulf as British Withdraw," *Chicago Tribune*, June 6, 1971.

19   *Fifty-five percent of NATO Europe's oil:* Ibid.

19   *90 percent of Japan's petroleum supplies:* Ibid.

19   *25 million barrels of oil:* Bernard Gwertzman, "It Was like Coming Home
      Again," *New York Times*, July 29, 1973.

20   *twenty-one miles wide at its narrowest point:* The United States Department of
      Energy hosts a Web site that includes profiles and statistics for the world's
      transportation "choke points": www.eia.doe.gov/cabs.

20   *"interrupted by a few mines":* Arnaud de Borchgrave, "Colossus of the Oil Lanes," *Newsweek,* May 21, 1973, 15.

20   *"The Gulf is one big gasoline bomb":* Arthur Vesey, "Soviets Eye Rich Persian Gulf as British Withdraw," *Chicago Tribune,* June 6, 1971.

20   *During a stopover on the island of Guam he described his vision:* Robert B. Semple Jr., "Nixon Plans Cut in Military Role for U.S. in Asia," *New York Times,* July 26, 1969. Nixon's remarks in Guam on July 25, 1969, were not included in a set speech. Instead, he spoke to reporters accompanying him to Vietnam, as the official State Department historian later noted, "[The president's] remarks were on a background basis, for attribution but not direct quotation." See Louis J. Smith and David H. Herschler, eds., and David S. Patterson, general ed., *Foreign Relations of the United States, 1969–76,* Vol. 1: *Foundations of Foreign Policy, 1969–72* (Washington, D.C.: U.S. Government Printing Office, 2003), 91. Nixon later claimed that his comments had been taken out of context: "The Nixon Doctrine was interpreted by some as signaling a new policy that would lead to total American withdrawal from Asia and from other parts of the world as well. . . . The Nixon Doctrine was not a formula for getting *out* of Asia, but one that provided the only sound basis for America's staying *in* and continuing to play a responsible role in helping the non-Communist nations and neutrals as well as our Asian allies to defend their independence." Richard Nixon, *RN: The Memoirs of Richard Nixon* (New York: Grosset & Dunlap, 1978), 395.

20   *"The U.S. is no longer in a position":* Warren Unna, "Guam Policy Near Test in Gulf," *Washington Post,* February 16, 1970.

20   *"dealing with the Vietnam drawdown":* Author interview with Dr. James Schlesinger, June 5, 2009.

21   *"His goal was to make Iran":* FISOHA interview with Armin Meyer, by William Burr, Foundation for Iranian Studies, Washington, D.C., March 29, 1985, 1–19.

22   *Operation Ajax:* Almost sixty years later, the 1953 coup remains a subject of intense debate among Iranian and Western scholars. Questions remain about the extent of the CIA's role in the affair. Exiled Iranian scholars have challenged the conventional interpretation of events, arguing instead that the "coup" was actually a nationalist uprising by Iranians in support of the throne. For a straightforward account of the events of 1953, see Mark J. Gasiorowski, "Coup D'etat of 1332 S/1953," *Encyclopaedia Iranica* Web site, December 15, 1993, www.iranicaonline.org. See also the collection of academic essays in Mark J. Gasiorowski and Malcolm Byrne, *Mohammad Mossadegh and the 1953 Coup in Iran* (Syracuse: Syracuse University Press, 2004). The view that the CIA was the instrumental player is advanced by Stephen Kinzer in his best-selling book *All the Shah's Men: An American Coup and the Roots of Middle East Terror* (Hoboken: John Wiley & Sons, 2003). Biographies

of the major Iranian participants in the 1953 coup can be found on the *Encyclopaedia Iranica* Web site at www.iranicaonline.org, and also in Abbas Milani's two-volume *Eminent Persians: The Men and Women Who Made Modern Iran, 1941–1979* (Syracuse: Syracuse University Press, 2008). Opposing views of the crisis are found in Gholam Reza Afkhami, *The Life and Times of the Shah* (Berkeley: University of California Press, 2009), and Darioush Bayandor, *Iran and the CIA: The Fall of Mossadegh Revisited* (London: Palgrave Macmillan, 2010). Two authors have recently written a book that places the 1953 coup alongside other twentieth-century Western interventions in the Middle East, focusing on the personalities of the coup makers, in this case the CIA's Kermit Roosevelt. See Karl E. Meyer and Shareen Blair Brysac, *Kingmakers: The Invention of the Modern Middle East* (New York: W. W. Norton, 2008).

22   *"I just know that he would have been":* FISOHA interview with Richard Helms, by William Burr, Foundation for Iranian Studies, Washington, D.C., July 10 and 24, 1985, 1–2.

22   *"I think it was agreed":* Ibid., 1–3.

22   *Helms followed events:* Ibid.

22   *"rather important" role:* Ibid., 1–4.

22   *"intimately involved in the planning":* Ibid., 1–1.

23   *"The CIA felt they had sort of a proprietary interest":* FISOHA interview with Douglas MacArthur II, by William Burr, Foundation for Iranian Studies, Washington, D.C., May 29, 1985, 1–53.

23   *the two code names it assigned the Shah:* Andrew Borowice, "Shah Cracks Political Whip," *Washington Post*, August 11, 1975.

23   *"I just think it is going to be a miracle":* James A. Bill, *The Eagle and the Lion: The Tragedy of American-Iranian Relations* (New Haven: Yale University Press, 1988), 136.

23   *"they are dead":* Ibid.

23   *less than 23 percent and often up to one third:* During the 1950s the figure was as high as 35 percent. Robert Graham, *Iran: The Illusion of Power*; rev. ed. (London: Croom Helm, 1979), 170.

23   *"The basis of the Twitchell Doctrine":* FISOHA interview with Armin Meyer, by William Burr, Foundation for Iranian Studies, Washington, D.C., March 29, 1985, 1–23.

24   *"maintained our relationship":* Ibid., 1–31.

24   *"The Iranians were forced to go through":* Ibid., 1–28.

24   *"a little annoyed":* Ibid., 1–29.

24   *the most lucrative 100,000 square miles:* Amin Saikal, *The Rise and Fall of the Shah: Iran from Autocracy to Religious Rule* (Princeton: Princeton University Press, 1980), 48.

24   *economic aid would not resume:* "Nixon Ties Aid to Iran to Settlement on Oil," *New York Times*, December 13, 1953.

24   *"the oil assets belonged, in principle, to Iran"*: Yergin, 476.

24   *"oily legs"*: The term "oily legs" was coined by Jahangir Amuzegar, whose brother, Jamshid, was appointed prime minister of Iran in August 1977. Jahangir Amuzegar, *The Dynamics of the Iranian Revolution: The Pahlavis' Triumph and Tragedy* (Albany: State University of New York Press, 1991), Part 4, Chapter 11, 171.

24   *"oil revenues are the foundation"*: A concise and thorough explanation of the role oil revenues played in propping up the Pahlavi state can be found in Marvin Zonis, *The Political Elite of Iran* (Princeton: Princeton University Press, 1971), 322–25.

25   *topped the billion-dollar mark:* Ibid., 323.

25   *"public revenues will permit us"*: Ibid., 324.

25   *"His Majesty must see to it"*: Ibid.

25   *"The British advise me"*: Alam, 173.

25   *the prodding of the Eisenhower administration:* For detailed accounts of how Iran's oil consortium was established, see Chapter 23 of Yergin, 475–78; Chapter 2 of Saikal, 48–51; and Chapter 9 of Afkhami, 187–207.

25   *"light and sweet"*: For a straightforward explanation of how the oil markets work—there are several markets—and to learn more about the different gradations of crude oil, see the BBC Web site at http://news.bbc.co.uk/2/hi/904748.stm. "Crude oil comes in many varieties and qualities, depending on its specific gravity and sulphur content which depend on where it has been pumped from," notes the BBC. " 'Sweet' crude is defined as having a sulphur content of less than 0.5%. Oil containing more than 0.5% sulphur is said to be 'sour.' "

26   *"any drop in production"*: Saikal, 50. Saikal notes that the agreement "was kept secret from the public and the Iranian government until 1974."

26   *"bail out King Faisal's defense budget"*: Alam, 220.

26   *In 1971 he hosted a luncheon:* Ibid.

26   *"ripe for subversive activities"*: Telegram 16 from the US Delegation to the 2,500 Centenary Celebrations in Shiraz, Iran, to the Department of State, October 15, 1971, 2010Z, *FRUS 1969–76*, Vol. E-4.

26   *"serious trouble"*: Ibid.

26   *"a militarily strong Iran could safeguard"*: Ibid.

26   *"It is not likely"*: Stephen D. Krasner, "The Great Oil Sheikdown," *Foreign Policy* 13 (Winter 1973–74): 133.

27   *when investment becomes self-renewing:* Dana Adams Schmidt, "Iran's Prosperity Thrives like a Bubbling Oasis," *New York Times*, December 9, 1968.

27   *"getting steeper all the time"*: Ibid.

27   *"The growth of the gross national product"*: Ibid.

27   *Ardeshir Zahedi:* To learn more about Ardeshir Zahedi, see the first of two volumes of his planned four-volume set of memoirs: Ardeshir Zahedi, *The*

Memoirs of Ardeshir Zahedi, Vol. 1: *From Childhood to the End of My Father's Premiership* (Bethesda, MD: Ibex, 2006), and Ardeshir Zahedi, *The Memoirs of Ardeshir Zahedi*, Vol. 2: *Love and Marriage, Ambassador to Washington and London* (Bethesda, MD: Ibex, 2010). See also Pari Abasalti, ed. *Ardeshir Zahedi: Untold Secrets* (Los Angeles: Rah-e-Zendegi, 2002). Abbas Milani also has a profile of Zahedi in *Eminent Persians*, 327–40.

28   *"It was Zahedi and Shahnaz"*: Milani, *Eminent Persians*, 334.

28   *kicking him under the table*: Author interview with Ardeshir Zahedi, September 14–15, 2010.

28   *"Don't create a problem, Ardeshir"*: Ibid.

28   *"a great man"*: Ibid.

28   *One evening in early 1967*: Ibid.

29   *"And I got kind of mad"*: Ibid.

29   *"long hours"*: Exchange of Toasts Between the President and His Imperial Majesty Mohammad Reza Shah Pahlavi, Shahanshah of Iran, State Dining Room, National Security Council Files, VIP Visits, Visit of the Shah of Iran, October 21–23, 1969 (1 of 2), Box 920, National Archives, College Park, MD.

29   *"We talked about security"*: Author interview with Ardeshir Zahedi, September 14–15, 2010.

29   *"In my judgement, the Nixon Doctrine"*: FISOHA interview with Armin Meyer, by William Burr, Foundation for Iranian Studies, Washington, D.C., March 29, 1985, 1–21/22.

30   *"their system has worked for them"*: *Foreign Relations of the United States, 1969–76, Volume I, Foundations of Foreign Policy, 1969–72*, 6. Nixon followed up the Bohemian Grove speech with an article in *Foreign Affairs*. See Richard M. Nixon, "Asia After Viet Nam," *Foreign Affairs* 46, no. 1 (October 1967): 113–25.

30   *Later on in the White House*: Author interview with Dr. James Schlesinger, June 5, 2009.

30   *"You've been a good friend"*: Author interview with Ardeshir Zahedi, September 14–15, 2010.

30   *Nixon had few if any true friends*: In 1970 Nixon told his cousin, the writer Jessamyn West, "I haven't a friend in the world." Anthony Summers, *The Arrogance of Power: The Secret World of Richard Nixon* (New York: Penguin, 2000), 105.

30   *"If I take a liking to someone"*: The Shah was a stickler for court protocol and social rank. Like Nixon, he did not cultivate friendships. James O. Jackson, "Shah: Dedicated, Dominant, Distrustful," *Chicago Tribune*, January 8, 1978.

30   *"one of those myths"*: FISOHA interview with Richard Helms, by William Burr, Foundation for Iranian Studies, Washington, D.C., July 10 and 24, 1985, 2–60.

30   *Visitors to the Nixons' homes*: List of Foreign Head of State Gifts Presented to

President and Mrs. Nixon by H.I.M. Mohammad Reza Pahlavi, Shahanshah of Iran; by H.I.H. The Princess Ashraf; By H.I.M. The Empress Farah; and By H.E. Ardeshir Zahedi, February 2, 1978, Eric Hooglund, project editor, *Iran: The Making of U.S. Policy, 1977–80*, National Security Archive (Alexandria, VA: Chadwyck-Healey, 1990), Document Reference No. 01316.

31   *"The President has a strong feeling":* Telcon, Kissinger-Sisco, 8:00 A.M., September 18, 1970, National Security Archive.

31   *"a strong leader":* Memorandum of Conversation, Washington, April 1, 1969, 10:00 A.M., *FRUS 1969–77*, Vol. E-4.

31   *"more venturesome":* Memorandum of Conversation, Washington, April 1, 1969, *FRUS 1969–77*, Vol. E-4.

32   *one million barrels of oil a day:* Henry A. Kissinger, *Years of Upheaval* (Boston: Little, Brown, 1982), 857. Curiously, Kissinger's notes from his meeting with the Shah in April 1969 do not include this detail.

32   *officials recommended a $100 million extension:* Record of National Security Council Interdepartmental Group for Near East and South Asia Meeting, Washington, April 3, 1969, *FRUS 1969–77*, Vol. E-4.

32   *"although Iran's economic progress":* Ibid.

32   *"The general issue since this [arms sales] program":* Memorandum from the President's Assistant for National Security Affairs (Kissinger) to President Nixon, Washington, April 29, 1969, *FRUS 1969–77*, Vol. E-4.

33   *The Shah had also been warned:* Alam, 39.

33   *"Briefed HIM on recent developments":* Ibid.

33   *"a traumatic event in my memory":* Farah Pahlavi, *An Enduring Love: My Life with Shah* (New York: Miramax, 2004), 119.

34   *"A few years later I refused to accompany my husband":* Ibid.

34   *Among the 105 guests:* To read the list of guests who attended the October 1969 state visit, see Marie Smith, "Formal Era Back with the Shah," *Washington Post*, October 22, 1969.

34   *the president and the Shah lavished praise on each other:* To read a transcript of the state toasts, see Exchange of Toasts Between the President and His Imperial Majesty Mohammad Reza Shah Pahlavi, Shahanshah of Iran, State Dining Room, National Security Council Files, VIP Visits, Visit of the Shah of Iran, October 21–23, 1969 (1 of 2), Box 920, National Archives, College Park, MD.

34   *a five-year, $11 billion economic development plan:* Thomas F. Brady, "Iran and Western Companies Clash over Oil," *New York Times*, March 9, 1968.

34   *20 percent a year:* Ibid.

34   *"a giant poker game":* Ibid.

34   *bankrolled Kurdish guerrillas:* See Alam, 39, 41.

35   *daily intelligence briefs from the CIA:* Nixon harbored an antipathy toward the CIA in general. CIA director Richard Helms first became aware that Nixon

was not reading his President's Daily Brief even before Inauguration Day in January 1969. Helms wrote in his memoir that he was never sure "how often Nixon even glanced at his PDB." Richard Helms with William Hood, *A Look over My Shoulder: A Life in the Central Intelligence Agency* (New York: Ballantine, 2003), 377–79.

35   *"impossible fags"*: Henry Kissinger's biographer, Walter Isaacson, described how when Nixon met with the NSC staff "for the first and last time" in March 1969 he commiserated with them for having to deal with those "impossible fags" at the State Department. Walter Isaacson, *Kissinger: A Biography* (New York: Simon & Schuster, 2005), 197.

35   *a history of correcting the Pentagon's top brass:* "He was familiar with everything going on in the world," Ambassador Armin Meyer recalled of the Shah. "He could tell you the price of rice in Mazanderan [province] as over the price in the Philippines. In military things he was smarter than most of our Pentagon people." FISOHA interview with Armin Meyer, by William Burr, Foundation for Iranian Studies, Washington, D.C., March 29, 1985, 1–18.

35   *Nixon squirmed to avoid personal confrontations:* Kissinger recalled that Nixon displayed "an extraordinary nervousness" when he first met the president-elect on November 25, 1969. "His manner was almost diffident; his movements were slightly vague, and unrelated to what he was saying, as if two different impulses were behind speech and gesture." Henry A. Kissinger, *White House Years* (Boston: Little, Brown, 1979), 11. Kissinger's biographer Walter Isaacson related in great detail Nixon's propensity for sequestering himself in a White House hideaway with a notepad for hours at a time. Kissinger concluded that Nixon "dreaded meeting new people or conveying a disappointing decision to someone's face." Isaacson, 145.

35   *"The Shah is in dead earnest":* Telegram 4054 from the Embassay in Iran to the Department of State, October 6, 1969, 1230Z, *FRUS 1969–76*, Vol. E-4.

35   *"nudge oil companies":* Ibid.

35   *sold on the idea by Herbert Brownell:* Memorandum for the President Through John Ehrlichman from Clark Mollenhoff, "Potential Problem Area in Connection with the Visit of the Shah of Iran," October 17, 1969, *FRUS 1969–76*, Vol. E-4.

35   *"and Iran would use the proceeds":* Ibid.

35   *"there have been some scandals":* Ibid.

36   *his schedule for October 18:* Telegram 04195 from the Embassy in Iran to the Department of State, October 14, 1969, 1000Z, National Security Council Files, VIP Visits, Visit of the Shah of Iran, October 21–23, 1969 (1 of 2), Box 920, National Archives, College Park, MD.

36   *giving in to the Shah's demands:* Intelligence Note No. 743 from Deputy Director George C. Denney Jr., of the Bureau of Intelligence and Research to Secretary of State Rogers, Washington, October 17, 1969, *FRUS 1969–76*, Vol. E-4.

36 *"deepening the involvement"*: Memorandum from Harold Saunders of the National Security Council Staff to the President's Assistant for National Security Affairs (Kissinger), Washington, October 20, 1969, *FRUS 1969 76*, Vol. E-4.

36 *American personnel be deployed:* Intelligence Note No. 295 from the director of the Bureau of Intelligence and Research (Hughes) to Secretary of State Rogers, Washington, April 22, 1969, *FRUS 1969–76*, Vol. E-4.

37 *"concerned about the implications"*: Memorandum from Harold Saunders of the National Security Staff to the President's Assistant for National Security Affairs (Kissinger), Washington, October 20, 1969, *FRUS 1969–76*, Vol. E-4.

37 *"What is the use of friendship"*: Telegram 116791 from the Department of State to the Embassy of Iran, July 15, 1969, 2048Z, *FRUS 1969–76*, Vol. E-4.

37 *"Although we have suggested that the President"*: Memorandum from Harold Saunders of the National Security Council Staff to the President's Assistant for National Security Affairs (Kissinger), Washington, October 20, 1969, *FRUS 1969–76*, Vol. E-4.

37 *"is a persistent bargainer"*: Memorandum from the President's Assistant for National Security Affairs (Kissinger) to President Nixon, Washington, October 21, 1969, *FRUS 1969–76*, Vol. E-4.

37 *a private meeting that lasted an hour and forty minutes:* President Richard Nixon's Daily Diary, Tuesday, October 21, 1969, http://nixon.archives.gov/virtuallibrary/documents/dailydiary.php.

37 *"excellent understanding of Iran"*: Memorandum of Conversation, Washington, October 22, 1969, 10:00 A.M., *FRUS 1969–76*, Vol. E-4.

37 *to boost Iran's income from oil:* Ibid.

38 *"an overkill capability"*: Ibid.

38 *"the problem of strengthening"*: FISOHA interview with Douglas MacArthur II, by William Burr, Foundation for Iranian Studies, Washington, D.C., May 29, 1985, 1–18.

38 *"didn't completely promise"*: Telcon, Kissinger-Laird, 2:30 P.M., October 23, 1969, National Security Archive.

39 *"a way will be found"*: Memorandum from the Executive Secretary of State (Eliot) to the President's Assistant for National Security Affairs (Kissinger), Washington, December 1, 1969, *FRUS 1969–76*, Vol. E-4.

39 *"Predictably, the Shah will be sharply disappointed"*: Ibid.

39 *"As there is no written record"*: Ibid.

39 *"There are, as you know"*: Letter from President Nixon to the Shah of Iran, Washington, February 23, 1970, *FRUS 1969–76*, Vol. E-4.

39 *"we should have no"*: Telegram 1247 from the Ambassador in Iran to the Assistant Secretary of State for Near East and South Asian Affairs (Sisco), April 1, 1970, 1430Z, *FRUS 1969–76*, Vol. E-4.

39 *"The Shah continues to play hard":* Memorandum from the President's Assistant for National Security Affairs (Kissinger) to President Nixon, Washington, May 13, 1970, *FRUS 1969–76*, Vol. E-4.

39 *"would have trouble digesting":* Memorandum of Conversation, Washington, April 14, 1970, *FRUS 1969–76*, Vol. E-4.

40 *"threatened areas":* Ibid.

40 *"should the need arise":* Ibid.

40 *"There is little question":* Letter from Secretary of Defense Laird to Secretary of State Rogers, Washington, October 27, 1970, *FRUS 1969–76*, Vol. E-4.

40 *"the unique nature of Tehran's special relationship":* Letter from Deputy Secretary of Defense (Packard) to the Under Secretary of State (Richardson), Washington, April 14, 1970, *FRUS 1969–76*, Vol. E-4.

40 *a long breakfast with CIA director:* Memorandum for the Record, Washington, October 22, 1969, *FRUS 1969–76*, Vol. E-4.

40 *for the first time in 1957:* Richard Helms, *A Look over My Shoulder,* 417.

41 *"He agreed that he would sponsor it":* FISOHA interview with Richard Helms, by William Burr, Foundation for Iranian Studies, Washington, D.C., July 10, 24, 1985, 1–11.

41 *A second base:* In retirement Helms confirmed the existence of two CIA stations in Iran during this period. Ibid., 1–10.

41 *indirect personal connection:* Ibid., 1–1.

41 *"The Shah nodded his head":* Memorandum for the Record, Washington, October 22, 1969, *FRUS 1969–76*, Vol. E-4.

41 *"on grounds of cost, lack of urgency":* Memorandum from Harold Saunders of the National Security Council Staff to the President's Assistant for National Security Affairs (Kissinger), Washington, April 16, 1970, *FRUS 1969–76*, Vol. E-4.

41 *"vital to our national security":* Memorandum from the Office of the Director of the Central Intelligence Agency to the Honorable Henry A. Kissinger, Assistant to the President for National Security Affairs, included in Memorandum for the President from Henry A. Kissinger, April 16, 1970, *FRUS 1969–76*, Vol. E-4.

41 *"island of stability":* Memorandum from the President's Assistant for National Security Affairs (Kissinger) to President Nixon, Washington, April 16, 1970, *FRUS 1969–76*, Vol. E-4.

42 *One month later, at 3:00 P.M.:* "The President's Schedule," *New York Times,* May 14, 1970, and "For the Record," *New York Times,* May 15, 1970. This meeting was brought up by Ambassador Zahedi in our interview of September 14–15, 2010, when he recalled his encounter with Nixon after a meeting of CENTO ambassadors. Nixon's schedule confirms that the only time he met with CENTO ambassadors in the Oval Office in the 1969–72 period was on May 14, 1970.

42   *"Tell the Shah"*: Author interview with Ardeshir Zahedi, September 14–15, 2010.

42   *"he was not suggesting"*: Memorandum of Conversation, Washington, April 8, 1971, *FRUS 1969–76*, Vol. E-4.

43   *lobbied Kissinger to kill off a study*: Memorandum from the Director of the Central Intelligence Agency (Helms) to the President's Assistant for National Security Affairs (Kissinger), September 2, 1970, *FRUS 1969–76*, Vol. E-4.

43   *"exotic equipment"*: Memorandum from [name not declassified] of the Near East and South Asia Division of the Directorate of Plans, Central Intelligence, to the Deputy Director's Executive Assistant [name not declassified], August 10, 1970, *FRUS 1969–76*, Vol. E-4.

43   *"We don't know just how keenly"*: Central Intelligence Agency Office of National Estimates, "Nothing Succeeds like a Successful Shah," October 8, 1971, National Security Archive.

44   *At 3:56 on the afternoon of April 8, 1971:* All notes from the Nixon-MacArthur conversation are attributed to Conversation Among President Nixon, Ambassador Douglas MacArthur II, and General Alexander Haig, Washington, April 8, 1971, 3:56–4:21 P.M.," *FRUS 1969–76*, Vol. E-4. This citation also covers all subsequent remarks made by Nixon, MacArthur, and Haig during their April 8, 1971, conversation in the White House.

45   *"scared stiff"*: FISOHA interview with William Lehfeldt, by William Burr, Foundation for Iranian Studies, Washington, D.C., April 29, 1987, February 9 and April 19, 1988, 1–9.

45   *"These boys opened fire"*: FISOHA interview with Douglas MacArthur II, by William Burr, Foundation for Iranian Studies, Washington, D.C., May 29, 1985, 1–32.

45   *"I am particularly anxious that this matter"*: Telegram 5142, from the Embassy in Iran to the Department of State, December 1, 1970, 0955Z, *FRUS 1969–76*, Vol. E-4. Ambassador MacArthur provided a vivid description of the attempted assassination or kidnapping in 1985. See his FISOHA interview, by William Burr, Foundation for Iranian Studies, Washington, D.C., May 29, 1985, 1–32 and 33.

46   *The ambassador was haunted by a remark:* Ibid., 1–23.

47   *"Both our countries"*: "Israeli Mission Flourishes in Iran," *Washington Post*, June 8, 1969.

47   *5 Takht-e Jamshid Avenue:* Ibid.

47   *sixty thousand Iranian Jews:* Ibid.

47   *$40 million worth of Iranian oil:* Ibid.

47   *Yet Tehran's newest supermarket:* John K. Cooley, "Israeli Mission Functions 'Diplomatically' in Iran," *Christian Science Monitor*, May 9, 1970.

47   *film distribution companies:* Ibid.

47   *El Al, flew two regularly scheduled flights:* Ibid.

47   *dig deep water wells in Qazvin:* Ibid.

48   *The U.S. Embassy cabled Washington:* Telegram 668, from the Embassy in Tehran to the Department of State, February 24, 1970, 140Z, *(FRUS) 1969–76,* Vol. E-4.

48   *thirty thousand soccer fans:* Ibid.

48   *the Shah's 1963 White Revolution:* For fuller discussion of the White Revolution, its origins, the reforms, and their impact on Iranian society and the Pahlavi dynasty, the following books are helpful: Afkhami, Chapter 10, 208–37; Ali M. Ansari, *Modern Iran Since 1921: The Pahlavis and After* (London: Longman, 2003), Chapter 6, 147–65; Said Amir Arjomand, *The Turban for the Crown: The Islamic Revolution in Iran* (New York: Oxford University Press, 1986), Chapter 3, 71–74; Nikki R. Keddie, *Roots of Revolution: An Interpretive History of Modern Iran* (New Haven: Yale University Press, 1981), Chapter 7, 160–82; and A. Saikal, Chapter 3, 71–96.

49   *"a numb and dispirited snake and lice who float in their own dirt":* Baqer Moin, *Khomeini: Life of the Ayatollah* (London: I. B. Tauris, 1999), 89.

49   *"O Mr. Shah, dear Mr. Shah":* Ibid., 104.

49   *it was Alam who issued the order for troops:* The June 1963 crackdown is a subject of lively debate among Iranian scholars with some suggesting the Shah was in charge. Most believe that Alam stiffened the Shah's backbone when he offered to take responsibility if the bloodshed led to even more unrest. "Who else but Your Majesty had the courage to support me," Alam asked the Shah on January 22, 1973. "Nobody," answered the Shah. Alam, 279–80. See also Afkhami, 235–36, and Milani, *Eminent Persians,* Vol. 1, 51–52.

49   *General Hassan Pakravan:* To learn more about General Pakravan's life, see his biography in Milani, *Eminent Persians,* 474–82.

49   *"a man of great culture":* Farah Pahlavi, *An Enduring Love,* 131.

CHAPTER TWO: GUARDIAN OF THE GULF
PAGE

51   *"Iran will get all available sophisticated weapons":* Telegram 4575, Major General Williamson to Under Secretary of Defense Kenneth Rush, June 5, 1972, National Security Archive.

51   *"Now is time to cash in credit with Iranians":* Telegram 192358, from the Department of State to the Embassy in Iran, October 20, 1972, 2246Z, *FRUS 1969–76,* Vol. E-4.

51   *Shell blasts and the crackle of rifle fire:* The following newspaper articles describe in detail the Iranian takeover of the three islands: John K. Cooley, "As Britain Exits, Iran Commandeers Head of Persian Gulf," *Christian Science Monitor,* December 2, 1971; William Dullforce, "Iran Seizes 3 Strategic Gulf Islands," *Washington Post,* December 1, 1971; "Iranian Troops Occupy Three

Strategic Islands in Persian Gulf, and a Sheikdom Protests," *New York Times*, December 1, 1971.

51   *"I will wipe my ass"*: Author interview with Ardeshir Zahedi, September 14–15, 2010.

52   *expelled sixty thousand Iranian nationals*: "Thousands of Iranians Are Expelled from Iraq," *New York Times*, January 1, 1972.

52   *"close to $1 billion"*: John K. Cooley, "Iraqi-Iranian Relations Nearing Crisis," *Christian Science Monitor*, January 8, 1972.

52   *"We will not use our fist"*: Ibid.

52   *35 cents to $2.15*: Amin Saikal, *The Rise and Fall of the Shah: Iran from Autocracy to Religious Rule* (Princeton: Princeton University Press, 1980), 116. Saikal's Chapter 4, "The Emergence of Iran as an Oil Power," 97–131 is essential reading to gain an understanding of the Shah's oil policies and Iran's emergence as a Middle East petropower.

52   *"Am I hearing the big voice of a superpower?"*: Asadollah Alam, *The Shah and I: The Confidential Diary of Iran's Royal Court, 1969–1977* (New York: St. Martin's, 1991), 192.

52   *"Finally Iran was able to rely on oil"*: Robert Graham, *The Illusion of Power*, rev. ed. (London: Croom Helm, 1979), 36.

52   *The Shah boasted to Alam*: Alam, 197.

53   *roads, tourist facilities, public health clinics*: The Iranian government failed to capitalize on the influx of foreign press by encouraging reporters to focus on the magnificence of the tent city to the detriment of more practical achievements such as road construction, health, and education. For a thorough account of the planning that went into the Persepolis celebrations from the Iranian perspective, see Gholam Reza Afkhami, *The Life and Times of the Shah* (Berkeley: University of California Press, 2009), Chapter 18, 404–15.

53   *Zahedi wrote a strongly worded letter*: Abbas Milani, *Eminent Persians: The Men and Women Who Made Modern Iran, 1941–1979* (Syracuse: Syracuse University Press, 2008), Vol. 1, 330.

53   *"plebeian looking gentleman"*: Alam, 98.

53   *Carnival Cruise atmosphere*: The Persepolis celebrations—dubbed "The Party of Parties"—attracted worldwide interest and were broadcast live on the American television network NBC. A photo essay appeared in the October 30, 1971, edition of *Paris Match*, "La Fête Des Fêtes," 50–63. Reporter Sally Quinn, who attended Persepolis, wrote colorful and shrewdly perceptive articles for *The Washington Post* describing in often humorous detail the leaders' tent encampment in the desert. Quinn's interview with Empress Farah, who took the lead in planning Persepolis, is particularly insightful: Sally Quinn, "It Isn't Easy Being the Empress of Iran," *Washington Post*, October 8, 1971. Alam's diary does not mention the actual festivities. As someone who was

consumed with the event planning he abandoned his diary writing for the year due to pressures of work. For a defense of the Persepolis celebrations, see Afkhami, Chapter 18, 404–22.

53 *"the Shah's revenge":* As described by Sally Quinn in "The Party's Over," *Washington Post*, October 16, 1971.

53 *"acquired nearly $750 million":* Memorandum for Dr. Brzezinski, The White House, from Anthony Lake, National Security Council, "Attachment: One-Volume Compilation of Summaries of Documents Relating to the US-Iranian Relationship, 1941–79, January 29, 1980." The memorandum is included in the National Security Archive's collection of diplomatic documents, Eric Hooglund, project editor, National Security Archive, *Iran: The Making of U.S. Policy, 1977–80* (Alexandria, VA: Chadwyck-Healey, 1990). See Chapter 2 "Military/Security Issues," Document Reference No. 03558, 9.

53 *"had fallen to a six-year low":* Office of Economic Research and Coordinated Within the Directorate of Intelligence, "Intelligence Memorandum: Some Revenue Implications of the 14 February Oil Settlement with the Persian Gulf States," The Central Intelligence Agency (March 1971), *FRUS 1969–76*, Vol. E-4.

54 *more than 10 percent of GNP:* Office of National Estimates, "Memorandum: Nothing Succeeds like a Successful Shah," The Central Intelligence Agency (8 October 1971), National Security Archive, Document Reference No. IR00757.

54 *"not have enough money to pay":* Ibid.

54 *"the Shah of Iran is counting upon you":* Rogers's memorandum of December 2, 1971, is included with a cover letter sent by Kissinger to the president on December 28: Memorandum from the President's Assistant for National Security Affairs (Kissinger) to President Nixon, Washington, December 28, 1971, *FRUS 1969–76*, Vol. E-4.

55 *"the bitch":* Nixon's feelings toward Mrs. Gandhi were no secret in the White House. Walter Isaacson, *Kissinger: A Biography* (New York: Simon & Schuster, 2005), 373.

55 *It was Nixon's belief that Mrs. Gandhi had deceived him:* Telcon, Kissinger-Nixon, 11:15 P.M., September 18, 1973, National Security Archive.

55 *"I was treating her as a leader":* Ibid.

55 *Kissinger egged on the president:* Telcon, Nixon-Kissinger, December 4, 1971, National Security Archive.

55 *"Because we are sympathetic to anything":* Telcon, Afshar-Kissinger, December 4, 1971, National Security Archive.

55 *"another thing we have done":* Telcon, Nixon-Kissinger, December 4, 1971, National Security Archive.

56 *Kissinger briefed Ambassador Huang Hua:* For a detailed account of who attended the talks and what was discussed, see Memorandum of Conversa-

tion, Friday, December 10, 1971, 6:05 P.M.–7:55 P.M., New York City, East Side, National Security Archive.

57 *to monitor Kissinger's back-channel communications:* Walter Isaacson described the methods used by Laird at Defense and the Joint Chiefs of Staff at the Pentagon to spy on Kissinger in his biography of the national security adviser. See Chapter 18, "Winter of the Long Knives," and in particular the section "Yeoman Radford's Spy Ring, December 1971," 380–85.

57 *"Henry was very Machiavellian":* Ibid., 198.

57 *"He worked his technique marvelously":* Author interview with Dr. James Schlesinger, June 5, 2009.

58 *young Radford was a social friend of . . . Jack Anderson:* The Radford-Anderson relationship is detailed in Isaacson, 383.

58 *"with considerable feeling tinged with bitterness":* Telegram 77, from the Embassy in Tehran to Secretary of State Rogers and Assistant Secretary for Near Eastern and South Asian Affairs (Sisco), January 5, 1972, 1235Z, *FRUS 1969–76,* Vol. E-4.

58 *"replied stonily that he had visited us":* Ibid.

58 *"While I had my doubts previously":* Memorandum from the President's Assistant for National Security Affairs (Kissinger) to President Nixon, Washington, December 28, 1971, *FRUS 1969–76,* Vol. E-4.

58 *at 4:04 P.M., local Tehran time:* See the president's daily schedule for a minute-by-minute breakdown of his overnight stay in Tehran at http://nixon.archives .gov/virtuallibrary/documents/dailydiary.php.

58 *"absorb and return the affection":* Robert B. Semple, "Nixon Welcomed Warmly by Iranians," *New York Times,* May 31, 1972.

58 *"Tens of thousands of ordinary citizens":* Ibid.

58 *"the most jubilant overseas welcome":* Courtney R. Sheldon, "Iranian Cheers Warm Nixon," *Christian Science Monitor,* May 31, 1972.

59 *"that the streets were not nearly so well-lined":* Alam, 222.

59 *The Shah had asked his court minister:* According to Alam's diary, the Shah "then went on to say that he would like to meet Nixon in private on the first day of his stay. Only Kissinger should be allowed to attend a second meeting." Alam, 212.

59 *The Shah fretted:* During a trip to Iran by West Germany's chancellor, Willy Brandt, the Shah warned him "that one effect of East-West détente in Europe would be to allow the Soviets to increase pressure on the Middle East." Ibid., 211.

59 *two of the thirteen men convicted and executed:* The International Commission of Jurists, *The Review* 8 (June 1972), National Security Archive Document Reference No. IR0074.

59 *gunned down on his own doorstep:* "Chief of Iran Military Court Dies of Assassins' Bullets," *New York Times,* April 12, 1971.

59   *The Shah's nephew:* An account of the attempted kidnapping of Prince Shahrem, the son of the Shah's twin sister, Princess Ashraf, appeared in a feature article on the Shah's rule and record in office: Jonathan C. Randel, "The Shah's Iran: Arms Debts and Repression Are the Price of Progress," *Washington Post*, October 10, 1971.

60   *bombers struck American landmarks:* No mention of the bombings appeared in the American press. Embassy Tehran filed its own description of the attacks to Secretary of State Rogers. Telegram 331, from the Embassy in Iran to the Department of State, January 17, 1972, 1950Z, *FRUS 1969–76*, Vol. E-4.

60   *bombs ripped through a pro-government political rally:* The rally had been carefully staged by the regime to counter complaints about human rights abuses in Iran. It turned out to be one more embarrassment for the Shah. Telegram 1218, from the Embassy in Iran to the Department of State, February 29, 1972, 1410Z, *FRUS 1969–76*, Vol. E-4.

60   *"criticism and dissatisfaction with the United States":* Airgram A-56, from the Embassy in Iran to the Department of State, February 22, 1971, *FRUS 1969–76*, Vol. E-4.

60   *"The past year or so has seen":* Office of National Estimates, "Memorandum: Nothing Succeeds like a Successful Shah," Central Intelligence Agency (8 October 1971), National Security Archive, Document Reference No. IR00757.

60   *"The manner in which the Shah projects his royal will":* Ibid.

60   *"Financial difficulties arising from overspending":* Ibid.

60   *"His demise will usher in change":* Ibid.

60   *"producing increasing internal dislocations":* Memorandum from the President's Assistant for National Security Affairs (Kissinger) to President Nixon, Washington, May 18, 1972, *FRUS 1969–76*, Vol. E-4.

60   *"voiced concern":* Ibid.

60   *a wish list of five big-ticket items:* Memorandum from the Deputy Secretary of Defense (Rush) to the President's Assistant for National Security Affairs (Kissinger), Washington, May 18, 1972, *FRUS 1969–76*, Vol. E-4.

61   *The Defense Department recommended "in principle":* Ibid.

61   *Kissinger drafted a memorandum:* Memorandum from the President's Assistant for National Security Affairs (Kissinger) to President Nixon, Washington, May 18, 1972, *FRUS 1969–76*, Vol. E-4.

61   *"Precise and frank talk about":* Memorandum from the President's Assistant for National Security Affairs (Kissinger) to President Nixon, Washington, October 21, 1969, *FRUS 1969–76*, Vol. E-4.

61   *Within ten minutes of their arrival:* See the president's daily schedule for a minute-by-minute breakdown of his overnight stay in Tehran at http://nixon.archives.gov/virtuallibrary/documents/dailydiary.php.

61   *no other American or Iranian officials were present:* FIOSHA interview with Har-

old Saunders, by William Burr, Foundation for Iranian Studies, Washington, D.C., February 12 and 27, April 8 and May 1, 1987, 2–55.

61 *Their first session involved:* As an example of how little we actually know about what transpired in Nixon's private talks with the Shah, there are three widely varying time frames for their first session on the late afternoon of May 30, 1972. Alam in his diary says the president and the Shah met for one and a half hours. See Alam, 222. The president's daily schedule allotted him an hour and forty-five minutes, from 5:30 P.M. until 7:14. See http://nixon.archives. gov/virtuallibrary/documents/dailydiary.php. Kissinger's notes say that the three men met from 5:35 P.M. until 6:35. See Memorandum of Conversation, Tehran, May 30, 1972, 5:35 P.M. to 6:35 P.M., *FRUS 1969–76*, Vol. E-4. Kissinger's notes have been proven to be unreliable. The president's schedule was prepared in advance and probably did not reflect a late start or early end to the talks, let alone a runover in time. Because Alam was on the scene and watching events like a hawk, then jotting them down in his diary, his version is the most reliable.

61 *The Shah said he hoped:* Memorandum of Conversation, Tehran, May 30, 1972, 5:35 P.M. to 6:35 P.M., *FRUS 1969–76*, Vol. E-4.

62 *Prime Minister Hoveyda took Kissinger out clubbing:* Alam was of the opinion that Hoveyda wanted to pump Kissinger for details of his talks with the Shah. See Alam, 222–23. A photograph of Nadina Parsa dancing for Kissinger was published in the next day's *Washington Post. The New York Times* also mentioned the incident. See Robert B. Semple Jr., "Bomb Rocks Site in Iran Just Before Visit by Nixon," *New York Times,* June 1, 1972, and Carroll Kilpatrick, "Nixon's Departure from Iran Marred by Terrorist Explosions," *Washington Post,* June 1, 1972.

62 *sat in Kissinger's lap:* Carroll Kilpatrick, "Nixon's Departure from Iran Marred By Terrorist Explosions," *Washington Post,* June 1, 1972.

62 *when he spotted Kissinger skulking:* Alam, 223.

62 *But the Shah had instructed Alam:* Ibid., 212.

62 *"In connection with the schedule":* Memorandum from the President's Assistant for National Security Affairs (Kissinger) to President Nixon, Washington, May 18, 1972, *FRUS 1969–76*, Vol. E-4.

62 *"fondness for martinis":* For a vivid description of Nixon's drinking habits, see Isaacson, 145–46.

62 *"the only time [the president] drank a lot":* Ibid., 262–63.

62 *The president's imbibing:* Ibid., 145–46.

62 *"obscenities," "my drunken friend," etc.:* Ibid., 145.

63 *the first bombs went off:* Carroll Kilpatrick, "Nixon's Departure from Iran Marred by Terrorist Explosions," *Washington Post,* June 1, 1972.

63 *attracting the attention of Alam:* Alam, 223.

63 *"Oh, it's nothing very serious":* Ibid., 230.

63   *a loud roar shook the area behind them:* For an account of the terrorist attacks, see Robert B. Semple Jr., "Bomb Rocks Site in Iran Just Before Visit by Nixon," *New York Times*, June 1, 1972; Carroll Kilpatrick, "Nixon's Departure from Iran Marred by Terrorist Explosions," *Washington Post*, June 1, 1972; and "Tomb in Iran Bombed Before Visit by Nixon," *Los Angeles Times*, June 1, 1972.

63   *the illiterate, ambitious, and strong-willed Reza Khan:* For further reading on Reza Shah and the origins of the Pahlavi dynasty, including the reforms of the 1920s and 1930s, see Ervand Abrahamian, *A History of Modern Iran* (Cambridge: Cambridge University Press, 2008), Chapter 3, 63–96; Afkhami, Chapters 1, 2, 3–41; Ali M. Ansari, *Modern Iran Since 1921: The Pahlavis and After* (London: Longman, 2003), Chapters 2, 3, 20–74; Said Amir Arjomand, *The Turban for the Crown: The Islamic Revolution in Iran* (New York: Oxford University Press, 1986), Chapter 3, 59–68; and Sandra Mackey, *The Iranians: Persia, Islam and the Soul of a Nation* (New York: Plume, 1998), Chapter 6, 157–86.

64   *"every advantage, yet they couldn't":* Alam, 223.

64   *Alam urged the Shah not to let terrorists:* Ibid.

64   *"any of the reported incidents":* "Tomb in Iran Bombed Before Visit by Nixon," *Los Angeles Times*, June 1, 1972.

64   *"I'm going to withdraw the statement":* Carroll Kilpatrick, "Nixon's Departure from Iran Marred by Terrorist Explosions," *Washington Post*, June 1, 1972.

64   *the leaders held a final round of talks:* Alam's diary, Nixon's schedule, and Kissinger's notes all agree on one thing: the second session of formal talks on Wednesday, May 31, lasted an hour and a half, beginning at 10:30 A.M. and concluding at noon.

65   *"with a discussion of terrorism":* Memorandum of Conversation, Tehran, May 31, 1972, 10:30 A.M. to 12:00 P.M., *FRUS 1969–76*, Vol. E-4.

65   *an intimate luncheon for twenty-one:* The guest list for the Nixons' luncheon at Saadabad Palace on May 31, 1972, is attached to the president's daily schedule at http://nixon.archives.gov/virtuallibrary/documents/dailydiary.php.

65   *"he'd like to see the culprits executed":* Alam, 224.

65   *five young Iranians accused of subversive activities:* The Washington Post reported the executions "last week for a string of alleged terrorist acts, bringing the total of such executions to 38 in the past 16 months." Carroll Kilpatrick, "Nixon's Departure from Iran Marred by Terrorist Explosions," *Washington Post*, June 1, 1972.

65   *Iran's dreaded secret police:* For an overview of SAVAK's functions in the 1970s and its management under General Ne'matollah Nasiri, see Afkhami, Chapter 17, 381–403; Graham, 67–71; and Milani, *Eminent Persians*, 468–73.

65   *"the Kremlin may be a palace":* Asadollah Alam recalled Nixon's remarks in his

diary. See Alam, 224. No reporters were in the room. However, the White House press secretary gave at least one American reporter a general overview of the president's comments—minus the comment about his wish to have American citizens executed. Nixon's remarks about his stay in the Soviet Union were softened to read: "While the Kremlin is a great palace, to be there for eight days is a long time." Carroll Kilpatrick, "Nixon's Departure from Iran Marred by Terrorist Explosions," *Washington Post*, June 1, 1972.

66 *recalled his surprise:* Alam, 224.

66 *students ran out and hurled rocks:* American reporters and U.S. and Iranian officials were witness to the assault on the presidential convoy as it drove to the airport. See Alam, 225, and Carroll Kilpatrick, "Nixon's Departure from Iran Marred by Terrorist Explosions," *Washington Post*, June 1, 1972.

66 *"ensure that Nixon and his entourage":* Alam, 221.

66 *"agreed to sell U.S. nuclear power plants":* "The Growing U.S. Involvement in Iran," The United States Department of Defense, January 22, 1975, National Security Archive, Document Reference No. IR00927. There is no doubt that Nixon, Kissinger, and the Shah discussed the possibility of Iran attaining nuclear technology and fuels at their Tehran meeting in 1972. This was alluded to in a January 1975 report prepared by the U.S. Department of Defense on the American presence in Iran. The authors of the report made one factual inaccuracy: they mistakenly placed Nixon in Tehran in 1974 instead of 1972. They then cited Secretary Kissinger's November 1974 visit to Iran as the occasion for further consultations and the signing of a joint communiqué on cooperation in the field of nuclear energy. See "The Growing U.S. Involvement In Iran," The United States Department of Defense, January 22, 1975, National Security Archive. The Shah believed Iran had to obtain nuclear power to sustain its economy once its oil reserves ran out in the first decades of the twenty-first century. The issue of nuclear power would also be discussed during the Shah's July 1973 state visit to Washington.

66 *"Iran will get all available sophisticated weapons":* Telegram 4575, Major General Williamson to Under Secretary of Defense Kenneth Rush, June 5, 1972, National Security Archive.

66 *twenty thousand:* William J. Coughlin, "Egypt Ousts Russ Advisers, Experts," *Los Angeles Times*, July 19, 1972.

66 *"operational positions in Iranian units":* Memorandum from Harold Saunders of the National Security Council to the President's Assistant for National Security Affairs (Kissinger), Washington, August 2, 1972, *FRUS 1969–76*, Vol. E-4.

67 *asked Kissinger for guidance:* Ibid.

67 *Farland had helped facilitate:* In the first volume of his memoirs, *White House Years*, Kissinger wrote of Farland: "We were fortunate that our Ambassador

in Pakistan at that moment was a man outside the regular Foreign Service Establishment." For more details on Farland's role as China intermediary, see Henry A. Kissinger, *White House Years* (Boston: Little, Brown, 1979), 722–23.

67 *Farland was a former agent:* Farland's status as a former FBI agent was reported in his obituary in *The New York Times*. Dennis Hevesi, "Joseph Farland, 92, Envoy Who Helped in Kissinger Ruse," *New York Times*, February 1, 2007. Farland was ambassador to the Dominican Republic in 1960. Opponents who wanted to overthrow the nation's dictator, Rafael Trujillo, approached the ambassador at a cocktail party to ask him for sniper rifles. Farland personally relayed their request to the CIA upon his recall in May 1960. Trujillo was assassinated a year later, on May 30, 1961, reportedly with weapons supplied by the CIA. *Washington Post* columnist Jack Anderson frankly described Farland as a CIA agent. Thomas Powers, *The Man Who Kept the Secrets: Richard Helms and the CIA* (New York: Alfred A. Knopf, 1979), 167.

67 *"this is one of those cases":* Kissinger's reply to Embassy Tehran was made on August 31, 1972. But the archival reference is included as a bundle with the actual request, which dates from August 2. Memorandum from Harold Saunders of the National Security Council to the President's Assistant for National Security Affairs (Kissinger), Washington, August 2, 1972, *FRUS 1969–76*, Vol. E-4.

67 *Kissinger on June 15, 1972, informed:* Memorandum from the President's Assistant for National Security Affairs (Kissinger) to Secretary of State Rogers and Secretary of Defense Laird, Washington, June 15, 1972, *FRUS 1969–76*, Vol. E-4.

67 *"WOW!":* Ibid.

67 *Nixon sent John Connally:* Kissinger's aide Harold Saunders briefed Nixon on Connally's talks with the Shah on July 12, 1972. Memorandum from Harold Saunders of the National Security Council to President Nixon, Washington, July 12, 1972, *FRUS 1969–76*, Vol. E-4.

67 *preferred successor:* In his memoir Nixon wrote of John Connally's decision to leave the White House during the Watergate scandal: "I tried to talk him into staying, but my heart was not in it; I could not ask a man I liked and respected—and who I hoped would succeed me in the White House in 1976—to tie himself to my troubles." Richard Nixon, *RN: The Memoirs of Richard Nixon* (New York: Grosset & Dunlap, 1978), 908. Walter Isaacson wrote that Nixon angled for a way to appoint Connally, his "golden boy," to the post of secretary of state in 1973. See Isaacson, 502.

67 *the 40 Committee:* Also described as the "interagency group in charge of reviewing covert activities" in Isaacson, 258.

67 *presented with a single piece of paper:* U.S. House Select Committee on Intelligence, *CIA: The Pike Report* (Nottingham: Spokesman, 1977), 196. Details of the Kurdish operation were investigated by the U.S. House Select Com-

mittee on Intelligence led by Congressman Otis Pike. The Pike Report and its findings on covert operations and abuses by the CIA during the Cold War were leaked to the *Village Voice* newspaper in February 1976. It was published in book form in 1977 in Great Britain.

68   *"encouraging separatist aspirations":* Ibid., 211.

68   *"Furthermore, the road is open-ended":* Ibid.

68   *"negative views were not presented more forcefully":* Ibid., 212.

68   *"has hesitated to push US armament sales":* Memorandum from Harold Saunders of the National Security Staff to the President's Assistant for National Security Affairs (Kissinger), Washington, July 14, 1972, *FRUS 1969–76*, Vol. E-4.

68   *"counseled accordingly":* Ibid.

68   *"And what about Kissinger?":* Alam, 232.

68   *"should leave decisions on what to buy":* Memorandum from Harold Saunders of the National Security Staff to the President's Assistant for National Security Affairs (Kissinger), Washington, July 14, 1972, *FRUS 1969–76*, Vol. E-4.

68   *"The decision to let the Shah buy":* FISOHA interview with Harold Saunders, by William Burr, Foundation for Iranian Studies, Washington, D.C., February 12 and 27, April 8 and May 1, 1987, 2–56.

69   *and approved the sale:* Alam, 230.

69   *a crisply worded presidential directive:* Memorandum from the President's Assistant for National Security Affairs (Kissinger) to Secretary of State Rogers and Secretary of Defense Laird, Washington, July 25, 1972, *FRUS 1969–76*, Vol. E-4.

69   *"pretty much gives us carte blanche":* Letter from Jack C. Miklos to The Honorable L. Douglas Heck, Minister-Counselor at the American Embassy, Tehran, Iran, July 26, 1972, Eric Hooglund, project editor, *Iran: The Making of U.S. Policy, 1977–80*, National Security Archive (Alexandria, VA: Chadwyck-Healey, 1990), Document Reference No. 00784.

70   *John Ehrlichman was reassuring the president's personal lawyer:* Kalmbach met with Ehrlichman on July 26 and demanded an assurance that what he was about to do—raise hush money—was legal "and that this is something that is proper that I should go forward with." Ehrlichman replied, "Herb, this is proper. It's for those fellows [the Watergate defendants] and their attorneys' fees and their families. Herb, you are to go forward with this." J. Anthony Lukas, *Nightmare: The Underside of the Nixon Years* (Athens: Ohio University Press, 1999), 253.

70   *During a six-hour aerial inspection:* Alam, 233.

70   *"Turning to the practicalities of the election":* Ibid.

70   *Governor Nelson Rockefeller of New York placed a telephone call:* Telcon, Kissinger-Rockefeller, 2:58 P.M., July 28, 1972, National Security Archive.

71   *At 1:45 P.M. Kissinger phoned Rockefeller:* Telcon, Kissinger-Rockefeller, 1:45 P.M., July 29, 1972, National Security Archive.

71   "[The Shah] had no control": Author interview with Dr. James Schlesinger, June 5, 2009.

72   to relay Nixon's response: Alam, 233.

72   to cough up a million dollars: Anthony Summers, The Arrogance of Power: The Secret World of Richard Nixon (New York: Penguin, 2000), 396.

72   totaling $2 billion: Pranay Gupte, "Lobbyists in Iran Paid by Grumman," New York Times, December 13, 1975.

72   fiscal year 1972–73 came to $2.8 billion: Hossein Razavi and Firouz Vakil, The Political Environment of Economic Planning in Iran, 1971–83: From Monarchy to Islamic Republic (Boulder: Westview, 1984), 63.

73   a secret $10 million Nixon presidential campaign fund: Bernard Gwertzman, "GAO Report Asks Justice Inquiry into GOP Funds; Says 'Apparent Violations' Were Committed by Nixon Re-election Committee," New York Times, August 27, 1972.

73   Nixon's "Mexican laundry": "The Mexican Laundry and the Presidency," Washington Post, September 15, 1972.

73   four cashier's checks worth $89,000: Ibid.

73   it was the president's "wish": Marjorie Hunter, "CIA Memo Said to Quote Haldeman on Nixon 'Wish' to Halt FBI Fund Study; Denial by Ex-Aide," New York Times, May 22, 1973.

73   Anderson was close to Watergate burglar Frank Sturgis: Agis Salpukas, "Suspect in Raid on Democrats Drew $89,000 from Bank, Hearing Is Told," New York Times, June 24, 1972.

73   "the Shah had routed hundreds of thousands of dollars": Jack Anderson, "Shah Link to Nixon Campaign Hinted," Washington Post, June 10, 1974. Ferdinand Marcos, the dictator of the Philippines, was also suspected of making illegal donations to the Nixon campaign in 1972. Summers, 396.

73   "the Shah had transferred more than $1 million": Ibid.

73   the Nixon campaign discouraged donations: Summers, 396–97.

73   "It's all very mysterious": Jack Anderson, "Shah Link to Nixon Campaign Hinted," Washington Post, June 10, 1974.

73   Later, in 1974, Anderson gleefully recalled: Ibid.

73   "Our inquiries, including overseas calls": Ibid.

74   CIA Director Helms . . . inviting Anderson to lunch: "CIA Files Show 16 Agents Spied on Jack Anderson in One Day," Los Angeles Times, May 5, 1977.

74   Operation Mudhen: Ibid.

74   He asked Rogers to sue: Author interview with Ardeshir Zahedi, September 14–15, 2010.

74   "The President's preoccupation": Arthur F. Burns Handwritten Journals, Journal II (Blue Notebook), Gerald R. Ford Library, November 5, 1971, 135.

74   A telephone transcript from February 1972: Telcon, Kissinger-Flanagan, 12:35 P.M., February 7, 1972, National Security Archive.

75   *"My lips are sealed"*: Author interview with Henry Precht, June 4, 2009.

75   *Ambassador Farland received a notice from the White House:* Telegram 192358, from the Department of State to the Embassy in Iran, October 20, 1972, 2246Z, *FRUS 1969–76*, Vol. E-4.

75   *"I wanted to punch Kissinger in the mouth"*: Isaacson, 453.

75   *"You don't understand"*: Stanley Karnow, *Vietnam: A History* (New York: Penguin, 1997), 663.

75   *Operation Enhance Plus:* Ibid.

76   *"entire Iranian air force"*: Telegram 192358, from the Department of State to the Embassy in Iran, October 20, 1972, 2246Z, *FRUS 1969–76*, Vol. E-4.

76   *"Now is time to cash in credit"*: Ibid.

76   *"accelerated delivery of military equipment"*: Telegram 6317, from the Embassy in Iran to the Department of State, October 21, 1972, 1520Z, *FRUS 1969–76*, Vol. E-4.

76   *"We believe that peace is at hand"*: Isaacson, 459.

76   *an additional sixteen aircraft:* Telegram 196855, from the Department of State to the Embassy in Iran, October 30, 1972, 2115Z, *FRUS 1969–76*, Vol. E-4.

77   *left behind a piece of paper:* Telegram 6520, from the Embassy in Iran to the Department of State, October 31, 1972, 1345Z, *FRUS 1969–76*, Vol. E-4.

77   *"we will have to offer"*: Ibid.

77   *The Shah was incensed:* Telegram 6611, from the Embassy in Iran to the Department of State, November 4, 1972, 1405Z, *FRUS 1969–76*, Vol. E-4.

77   *"atmosphere and spirit of goodwill:* Telegram 6611, from the Embassy in Iran to the Department of State, November 4, 1972, 1405Z, *FRUS 1969–76*, Vol. E-4.

77   *He dismissed as bogus:* Telegram 210666, from the Department of State to the Embassy in Iran, November 18, 1972, 1948Z, *FRUS 1969–76*, Vol. E-4.

78   *"several sales previously consummated"*: Ibid.

CHAPTER THREE: MARITAL VOWS

PAGE

79   *"We welcome you here"*: "Nixon and Shah Exchange Praise, Confer in Oval Office," *New York Times*, July 25, 1973.

79   *"Nixon has the audacity to tell me"*: Asadollah Alam, *The Shah and I: The Confidential Diary of Iran's Royal Court, 1969–1977* (New York: St. Martin's, 1991), 277.

79   *American oil imports from Saudi Arabia:* "Saudi Arabia Supplying More U.S. Oil," *New York Times*, November 11, 1972.

80   *"the swing producer for the entire world"*: Daniel Yergin, *The Prize: The Epic Quest for Oil, Money, and Power* (New York: Simon & Schuster, 1991), 594.

80   *21 percent of global oil production:* Ibid.

80   *"Oil isn't a weapon"*: Rachel Bronson, *Thicker than Oil: America's Uneasy Partnership with Saudi Arabia* (Oxford: Oxford University Press, 2006), 112.

80   *"My main worry was"*: Geoffrey Robinson, *Yamani: The Inside Story* (London: Simon & Schuster, 1988), 203.

80   *"Fuel policy emanates from everywhere"*: "America's Energy Crisis," *Newsweek*, January 27, 1973, 39.

80   *"Here we were"*: Arthur F. Burns Handwritten Journals, Journal I (Green Notebook), Gerald R. Ford Library, May 26, 1971, 141.

81   *"a field Kissinger knew nothing about"*: Walter Isaacson, *Kissinger: A Biography* (New York: Simon & Schuster, 2005), 428.

81   *"Peterson, that's just a minor economic consideration"*: Ibid.

81   *"I did not really want to make Henry secretary of state"*: Ibid., 502.

81   *"I had not been involved in the negotiation"*: Henry A. Kissinger, *Years of Upheaval* (Boston: Little, Brown, 1982), 867.

81   *On August 2, 1972, Connally phoned Kissinger:* Telcon, Connally-Kissinger, 12:32 P.M., August 2, 1972, National Security Archive.

82   *"I've sort of lost track"*: Telcon, Jamieson-Kissinger, 9:05 A.M., August 5, 1972, National Security Archive.

82   *"were using us"*: Telcon, Connally-Kissinger, 1:40 P.M., August 5, 1972, National Security Archives.

83   *"the companies would become instruments of nations"*: Kissinger, *Years of Upheaval*, 868.

83   *"if they get into a confrontation with us"*: Telcon, Connally-Kissinger, 1:40 P.M., August 5, 1972, National Security Archive.

83   *"during a change of administration"*: Richard Helms with William Hood, *A Look over My Shoulder: A Life in the Central Intelligence Agency* (New York: Ballantine, 2003), 410.

83   *"The President rose from a small sofa"*: Ibid., 411.

84   *"new blood"*: Ibid.

84   *"Get rid of the clowns"*: Ibid., 410.

84   *blamed former spy chief Allen Dulles:* Ibid., 382.

84   *"The explanations for [Nixon's] attitudes"*: Ibid.

84   *sanctioned lawbreaking:* J. Anthony Lukas, *Nightmare: The Underside of the Nixon Years* (Athens: Ohio University Press, 1999), 29.

84   *lying to the public and his own employees:* Ibid.

84   *"Nixon and Helms have so much on each other"*: Stanley I. Kutler, *The Wars of Watergate: The Last Crisis of Richard Nixon* (New York: W. W. Norton, 1992), 201.

84   *"surprised at the Agency policy"*: Richard Helms, 411.

84   *"a good butcher"*: Kutler, *The Wars of Watergate*, 100.

84   *"Suddenly, as if it were a totally new idea"*: Cynthia Helms, *An Ambassador's Wife in Iran* (New York: Dodd, Mead, 1981), 2.

85   *"floored by the prospect"*: Richard Helms, 411.

85   *"I'm not sure how the Russians might interpret"*: Ibid.

85   *"That's a good point"*: Ibid., 412.

85   *"Iran is in an area":* Cynthia Helms, 2.

85   *"Dick and I talked for long hours":* Ibid., 3.

85   *"He feels more positively about it":* Thomas Powers, *The Man Who Kept the Secrets: Richard Helms and the CIA* (New York: Alfred A. Knopf, 1979), 311.

86   *Haldeman and Ehrlichman gossiped:* Isaacson, 466.

86   *"He's been under care":* Ibid.

86   *Kissinger confronted Helms:* Richard Helms, 412.

86   *"I was silent for a moment":* Ibid.

86   *"Henry bristled a bit":* Ibid.

86   *Their conversation on the evening of November 28, 1972:* Telcon, Kissinger-Haldeman, 7:30 P.M., November 28, 1972, National Security Archive.

87   *"we understand word has gone out":* Telegram 7749, from the Embassy in Iran to the Department of State, December 27, 1972, 1318Z, Monica Belmonte, Editor; Edward C. Keefer, General Editor, *Foreign Relations of the United States, 1969–1976*, Vol. E-4, Documents on Iran and Iraq, 1969–1972, Washington: United States Government Printing Office, Office of the Historian, Bureau of Public Affairs.

87   *"was literally in tears of grief":* Alam, 264.

87   *"for 15 minutes of your time today":* Telcon, Farland-Kissinger, 10:55 (no A.M. or P.M. given), December 23, 1972, National Security Archive.

87   *"you're the best intelligence professional I know":* Telcon, Helms-Kissinger, 11:30 A.M., December 15, 1972, National Security Archive.

87   *a call came through to inform him:* Richard Helms, 412.

88   *Helms's biographer Thomas Power:* Thomas Power, *The Man Who Kept the Secrets: Richard Helms and the CIA* (New York: Alfred A. Knopf, 1979), 310.

88   *the oil tanker* Overseas Aleutian: "Soviet Oil on the Way to East Coast; Amount Still Small, but It's a Big 'First'; Stocks Down from '72," *Christian Science Monitor,* January 9, 1973.

88   *Texaco, the company that serviced:* Robert J. Samuelson, "3 Airlines' Flights Disrupted by Shortage of Fuel in N.Y.," *Washington Post,* January 10, 1973.

88   *Natural gas supplies were cut off:* Thomas O'Toole, "Lack of Fuel Is Crippling Middle West; 6 Midwest States Hurt by Shortages of Fuel," *Washington Post,* January 6, 1973.

88   *The Denver school system shut down:* Ibid.

88   *an eternal flame dedicated to war veterans:* "Eternal Flame Put Out due to Gas Shortage," *Hartford Courant,* January 11, 1973.

88   *In Sioux City:* Thomas O'Toole, "Lack of Fuel Is Crippling Middle West; 6 Midwest States Hurt by Shortages of Fuel," *Washington Post,* January 6, 1973.

89   *postponed resumption of classes:* "Oil-Rich Texas University Caught in Fuel Shortage," *Wall Street Journal,* January 11, 1973.

89   *Mississippi's chicken broiler industry:* Gene Smith, "Northeast Is Bracing Itself for Possible Energy Crisis," *New York Times,* January 15, 1973.

89   *barges were requisitioned:* Ibid.

89   *"If anyone still needs evidence":* "Nation Without Power," *New York Times*, January 21, 1973.

89   *"We've had a happy era of low costs":* "America's Energy Crisis," *Newsweek*, January 22, 1973, 38.

89   *250,000 tons of U.S. wheat:* "Soviet Oil on the Way to East Coast; Amount Still Small, but It's a Big 'First'; Stocks Down from '72," *Christian Science Monitor,* January 9, 1973.

90   *"the nation's total energy resources":* "America's Energy Crisis," *Newsweek*, January 22, 1973, 39.

90   *oil production peaked at 11.3 million barrels per day:* Yergin, 567.

90   *2.2 million barrels of oil per day in 1967 to 6.2 million barrels per day in 1973:* Ibid., 567, 591.

90   *19 percent of domestic consumption in 1967 to 35 percent:* Ibid. For more news analysis from the period on U.S. oil imports, see Ray Vicker, "Fight over Fuel; Oil Crisis Points Up Huge Western Reliance on Producing Nation," *Wall Street Journal*, February 4, 1972, and, Edward Cowan, "Oil Imports Climbing with No End in Sight; Upward Trend to U.S. Affluence and Fuel Needs Oil Imports Are Continuing to Climb," *New York Times*, May 22, 1973.

90   *70 percent of the world's proven oil reserves:* Marvin Howe, "In Middle East, Oil Pays the Way," *New York Times*, January 21, 1972.

90   *the United States imported 28 million barrels of oil:* David Ottaway, "Saudi Threat to Cut Oil Flow Million Barrels Daily Reported," *Los Angeles Times*, September 5, 1973.

90   *"Like it or not, during the next decade":* Lawrence Mosher, "Arab Oil Policy Means a Crisis for US," *Chicago Tribune*, September 16, 1973.

90   *"3 million barrels per day of excess capacity":* Yergin, 586.

91   *"in light of our long friendship":* Alam, 277.

91   *"I say to hell":* Ibid.

91   *would not have their contracts renewed:* "Iran Tells Oil Consortium Pact Will Not Be Renewed," *New York Times*, January 24, 1973.

92   *a new five-year $32.5 billion economic development plan:* "Iran Tells Oil Firms to Sharply Increase Production or Leave When Pacts Expire," *Wall Street Journal*, January 24, 1973.

92   *Iranian arms orders exploded from $500 million:* Memorandum for Dr. Brzezinski, The White House, from Anthony Lake, National Security Council, "Attachment: One-Volume Compilation of Summaries of Documents Relating to the US-Iranian Relationship, 1941–79, January 29, 1980," Eric Hooglund, project editor, *Iran: The Making of U.S. Policy, 1977–80*, National Security Archive (Alexandria, VA: Chadwyck-Healey, 1990).

92   *Richard Helms saw President Nixon:* Memorandum of Conversation, 2/14/73,

folder "Nixon, Ambassador Helms," Box 1, National Security Adviser, Gerald R. Ford Library.

93   *"I want you not just to think of your CIA background"*: Ibid.

93   *"As a matter of fact"*: FISOHA interview with Richard Helms, by William Burr, Foundation for Iranian Studies, Washington, D.C., July 10 and 24, 1985, 2–63.

94   *"What happened to our understanding"*: Richard Helms, 412.

94   *"our policymakers"*: Bernard Gwertzman, "Fulbright Warns of a War over Oil," *New York Times*, May 22, 1973.

95   *a secret visit to Tehran:* Alam, 287.

95   *"I found the Shah very relaxed"*: Memorandum of Conversation, 9:50–10:40 A.M., Saturday, May 12, 1973, Dr. Kissinger's Office in the White House, National Security Archive.

95   *"should be out of here in a few years"*: Bernard Weinraub, "U.S. Quietly Sending Servicemen to Iran," *New York Times*, May 2, 1973.

96   *five hundred American soldiers, sailors, and Marines:* Ibid.

96   *"He wants the latest stuff"*: Ibid.

96   *On the morning of June 2:* "U.S. Officer Shot Dead by Iran Gunmen," *Washington Post*, June 3, 1973.

96   *"As he passed a* kucheh*"*: Cynthia Helms, 33.

96   *The Helmses had arrived in Tehran:* The date was April 5, 1973. "Helms Assumes Post as Iran Ambassador," *Los Angeles Times*, April 6, 1973.

97   *"It was like coming home again"*: Bernard Gwertzman, "It Was like Coming Home Again," *New York Times*, July 29, 1973.

97   *"Aren't you annoyed that the Americans"*: Ibid.

97   *"Why else has Helms been sent here?"*: James Bill, *The Eagle and the Lion: The Tragedy of American-Iranian Relations* (New Haven: Yale University Press, 1988), 213.

97   *"May God save America!"*: Arthur F. Burns Handwritten Journals, Journal I (Green Notebook), Gerald R. Ford Library, April 22, 1973, 181.

97   *"evidently was the first foreign visitor"*: "Nixon and Shah Exchange Praise, Confer in Oval Office," *New York Times*, July 25, 1973.

97   *"probably come down to the office"*: Telcon, Kissinger-The President, 11:25 A.M., July 18, 1973, National Security Archive.

98   *"all those beautiful broads"*: Isaacson, 364.

98   *comparable to a moral vice:* In his book on Henry Kissinger, Walter Isaacson recorded several choice scenes in which Nixon expressed displeasure at news reports of Kissinger on the Hollywood social circuit. "He's making a fool of himself," Nixon told Haldeman on one occasion. "Grown men know better. Henry has got to stop this. Do something. Do something." Ibid.

98   *asked his daughter Julie:* Telcon, Eisenhower-Kissinger, 7:45 P.M., July 10, 1973, National Security Archive.

98   *"Nixon's Secret Agent"*: "Nixon's Secret Agent," *Time*, Vol. 99, No. 6, Feb. 7, 1972.

98   *"Danny, what I'm calling you about"*: Telcon, Kaye-Kissinger, 7:55 P.M., July 10, 1973, National Security Archive.

99   *"great admiration"*: Farah, Shahbanou of Iran, trans. Felice Harcourt, *My Thousand and One Days* (London: W. H. Allen, 1978), 120.

99   *enjoyed the company of continental blondes*: William Shawcross, *The Shah's Last Ride: The Fate of An Ally* (New York: Simon & Schuster, 1988), 339–41. Shawcross interviewed one of Madame Claude's girls, Ange, who provided a vivid depiction of her time as the Shah's favorite paramour.

99   *"pimps"*: Gholam Reza Afkhami, *The Life and Times of the Shah* (Berkeley: University of California Press, 2009), 51.

99   *"born courtier"*: Ibid.

100   *"The encounters did not always conclude"*: Ibid., 53.

100   *"Farah knew about her husband's adventures"*: Ibid.

100   *a nineteen-year-old*: Shawcross, 96.

100   *exercise his rights as a Muslim husband*: Afkhami, 53–54.

100   *"They have spread the rumor"*: Habib Ladjevardi, ed., *Memoirs of Fatemeh Pakravan*, Harvard Iranian Oral History Project (Cambridge: Center for Middle Eastern Studies, Harvard University, 1998), 97–98.

100   *One report claimed that she fled to Europe*: Shawcross, 96. Shawcross wrote that the queen's flight to Europe was in 1972. Alam's diaries now confirm that the Gilda affair unfolded in the summer of 1973.

101   *"sun-drenched red-carpeted platform"*: "Nixon and Shah Exchange Praise, Confer in Oval Office," *New York Times*, July 25, 1973.

101   *"We welcome you here"*: Ibid.

101   *two hundred protesters across the street*: Murrey Marder, "Shah Arrives to Bid for Bombers," *Washington Post*, July 25, 1973.

101   *a two-hour tête-à-tête*: All comments from this first session of talks are quoted directly from Memorandum of Conversation, Meeting with His Imperial Majesty Mohammad Reza Shah Pahlavi, Shahanshah of Iran on Tuesday, the 24th of July at 10:43 A.M.–12:35 P.M., in the Oval Office, National Security Archive.

101   *blocked by Kissinger from sitting*: Author interview with Ardeshir Zahedi, September 14–15, 2010.

101   *control the official transcript*: "He wanted to write it in his own way," recalled Zahedi. This explains the gaps in the historical record noted by historians curious to learn more about Nixon's promises to the Shah on arms sales, oil prices, and nuclear energy. Ibid.

101   *yawned his way through the meeting*: Ibid.

102   *the second round of talks*: All comments from this session of talks are quoted directly from Memorandum of Conversation, Meeting with His Imperial

Majesty Mohammad Reza Shah Pahlavi, Shahanshah of Iran on Tuesday, the 24th of July, 5:00–6:40 P.M., the Shah's Reception Room at the Blair House, National Security Archive.

106 *"a renewal of vows"*: FISOHA interview with James Schlesinger, by William Burr, Foundation for Iranian Studies, Washington, D.C., May 15 and June 27, 1986, 1–20.

106 *He sang "Tea for Two"*: Donnie Radcliffe and Dorothy McCardle, "Chateaubriand and Tony Martin," *Washington Post*, July 25, 1973.

106 *"unusual friendliness to reporters"*: Ibid.

106 *"a strapless tube of sequins"*: Linda Charlton, "The Shah and Empress of Iran Are Feted at a White House State Dinner," *New York Times*, July 25, 1973.

106 *"I can't understand what it's all about, can you?"* Donnie Radcliffe and Dorothy McCardle, "Chateaubriand and Tony Martin," *Washington Post*, July 25, 1973.

106 *"and rejected comparison"*: Dana Adams Schmidt, "Shah Proclaims Iran Newest 'Big Power,' " *Christian Science Monitor*, July 27, 1973.

106 *given him everything he asked for*: Alam, 308.

CHAPTER FOUR: CONTINGENCIES

PAGE

107 *"It's America's inaction"*: Asadollah Alam, *The Shah and I: The Confidential Diary of Iran's Royal Court, 1969–1977* (New York: St. Martin's, 1991), 326.

107 *"Can't we overthrow one of the sheikhs"*: Memorandum of Conversation, 11/29/73, folder "Kissinger, Schlesinger, Colby, Moorer," Box 2, National Security Adviser, Gerald R. Ford Library.

107 *the largest desert warfare training exercises*: "Reservists Join Regulars in Marine Corps Exercise," *Washington Post*, August 20, 1973.

107 *"Officially, no parallels are drawn"*: David DeVoss, "The Marines Battle for Argos," *Time*, August 27, 1973, 29.

107 *"Although most troops were lectured"*: Ibid.

108 *"They told us not to say anything political"*: Ibid.

108 *"The Pentagon has a computer plan"*: Ibid.

108 *"the entire war, all its battles"*: Ibid.

108 *"I can give you my opinion"*: Ibid.

108 *They retreated to their tents with crates of beer*: "Reservists Join Regulars in Marine Corps Exercise," *Washington Post*, August 20, 1973.

108 *Men fainted in the heat*: Ibid.

108 *writing an article on skiing in Europe*: David DeVoss, "The Marines Battle for Argos," *Time*, August 27, 1973, 29.

108 *"Our unit was supposed to be in a tank battle"*: Ibid.

108 *"Can you picture Hogan's Heroes"*: "Reservists Join Regulars in Marine Corps Exercise," *Washington Post*, August 20, 1973.

108   *"Goddamn!" screamed Dennis:* David DeVoss, "The Marines Battle for Argos," *Time*, August 27, 1973, 29.

108   *"Come on men!":* Ibid.

109   *30 percent of its oil:* Daniel Yergin, *The Prize: The Epic Quest for Oil, Money, and Power* (New York: Simon & Schuster, 1991), 578.

109   *2 million people:* "The Arab World: Oil, Power, Violence," *Time*, April 2, 1973, 19.

109   *daily exports of 2.3 million barrels of oil:* "Libya Takes More U.S. Oil Firms," *Washington Post*, September 2, 1973.

109   *expelled Libya's Italian community:* "The Arab World: Oil, Power, Violence," *Time*, April 2, 1973, 19.

109   *$200 million order:* Ibid., 18.

109   *"This Qaddafi is a real nut":* Memorandum of Conversation, 5/15/75, folder "Ford, Kissinger, Iranian Shah Mohammad Reza Pahlavi," Box 11, National Security Adviser, Gerald R. Ford Library.

109   *30 cents a barrel:* Yergin, 580.

109   *over rolls and a revolver:* This episode is recounted in ibid., 579.

109   *"commercial bargaining":* Henry A. Kissinger, *Years of Upheaval* (Boston: Little, Brown, 1982), 859.

110   *jumped 72 percent:* "The Arab World: Oil, Power, Violence," *Time*, April 2, 1973, 18.

110   *"did not as a general practice":* Kissinger, *Years of Upheaval*, 864.

110   *"Our hands-off policy":* Ibid., 865.

110   *"increasingly alarmed by the escalating demands":* Ibid., 870.

110   *"a quick word because I know":* Telcon, Clements-Kissinger, 10:14 A.M., May 15, 1973, National Security Archive.

110   *"with extreme urgency":* Yergin, 596.

110   *"because I don't think anyone":* Telcon, Clements-Kissinger, 10:14 A.M., May 15, 1973, National Security Archive.

111   *"I had in all the heads of the companies":* Telcon, Rush-Kissinger, 7:10 P.M., May 29, 1973, National Security Archive.

111   *"Henry wanted State":* Walter Isaacson, *Kissinger: A Biography* (New York: Simon & Schuster, 2005), 503.

112   *"Tell the president to go fuck himself":* Ibid.

112   *"for Nixon my appointment":* Kissinger, *Years of Upheaval*, 423.

112   *"in reducing Treasury's role":* Arthur F. Burns Handwritten Journals, Journal II (Blue Notebook), Gerald R. Ford Library, April 4, 1974, 200.

112   *"cause economic trouble for the French?":* Ibid., April 19, 220–21.

112   *"H. at times strikes me as a madman":* Ibid.

112   *the Libyan leader announced the expropriation:* Henry Tanner, "Libya Takes over All Oil Companies Operating There," *New York Times*, September 2, 1973.

112   *hiking their oil prices by 30 percent:* David Otttaway, "Saudi Threat to Cut

Oil Flow Million Barrels Daily Reported," *Los Angeles Times*, September 5, 1973.

112   *refuse payment in dollars:* Ibid.

112   *"restrict oil production increases":* Jim Hoagland, "Faisal Seen Backing Cairo by Using Oil to Press U.S.," *Washington Post*, September 2, 1973.

112   *8.5 million barrels to 20 million barrels:* Ibid.

112   *11 million barrels of oil per day:* Nicholas C. Proffitt, "An Arab Blend of Oil and Politics: Faisal's Threat," *Newsweek*, September 10, 1973, 15.

112   *require 24 million:* Ibid.

113   *from 1.6 billion tons in 1970 to 2.8 billion tons:* Juan de Onis, "Arabs' Emerging Oil Strategy," *New York Times*, September 4, 1973.

113   *an annual 6.9 percent:* Ibid.

113   *soared by 30 percent:* Ibid.

113   *"Faisal is no bluffer":* Nicholas C. Proffitt, "An Arab Blend of Oil and Politics: Faisal's Threat," *Newsweek*, September 10, 1973, 13.

113   *warnings provided to them:* For details of the warning provided to Nixon and Kissinger by King Hussein of Jordan, see Patrick Tyler, *A World of Trouble: The White House and the Middle East—From the Cold War to the War on Terror* (New York: Farrar, Straus & Giroux, 2009), 125. Soviet leader Leonid Brezhnev's warning is described in detail in the same book on pages 122–30. Nixon's account can be read in his memoir. See Richard Nixon, *RN: The Memoirs of Richard Nixon* (New York: Grosset & Dunlap, 1978), 885.

113   *"The result would be catastrophic for them":* Memorandum of Conversation Between Abba Eban, Israeli Minister of Foreign Affairs, and Dr. Henry Kissinger, Assistant to the President for National Security Affairs, Saturday, May 12, 1973, 9:50–10:40 A.M., National Security Archive.

113   *"Sadat is not bright":* Ibid.

114   *"told us in August, 1973":* "Aramco Aide Says Faisal Warned U.S. Last August of War," *New York Times*, February 22, 1974.

114   *"Logic requires":* Nicholas C. Proffitt, "An Arab Blend of Oil and Politics: Faisal's Threat," *Newsweek*, September 10, 1973, 12.

114   *"a more suitable political atmosphere":* Ibid.

115   *"keep the Persian Gulf":* Memorandum of Conversation, 9/5/73, folder "Kissinger, Schlesinger," Box 2, National Security Adviser, Gerald R. Ford Library.

115   *"Let's talk contingency plans":* Ibid. When the author asked Dr. Schlesinger to review the transcript and place it in context, he paused before giving a considered and measured response. He said he misspoke when he used the words "contingency plans" during his September 5, 1973, discussion with Kissinger. A contingency plan, he explained, would describe what the United States might do. It would have been more accurate for him to have said to Kissinger, "Let's talk *contingencies.*" That would have implied what the *Iranians* might do. Left unsaid was the reality that the Shah would never have invaded

and occupied Kuwait without receiving the permission of his American ally. Schlesinger was reluctant to provide details about the role the Shah was supposed to play in any U.S. decision to seize oil fields in Kuwait and Saudi Arabia. He did confirm that he had not been briefed by Kissinger on the meeting with the Shah in Blair House in July 1973 when Persian Gulf contingency planning was first raised. He left the impression that he believed at the time that he had inherited a contingency plan prepared by U.S. officials—not one developed in Tehran. Dr. Schlesinger offered his views in an interview with the author on June 5, 2009.

115 *"The Shah wants to know if the F-14 and F-15 mix"*: Memorandum of Conversation, 9/5/73, folder "Kissinger, Schlesinger," Box 2, National Security Adviser, Gerald R. Ford Library.

115 *"Oil without a market"*: Bernard Gwertzman, "A Mideast Pledge: President Is Seeking a Settlement to End Oil Threats by Arabs," *New York Times*, September 6, 1973.

116 *"Because of our relationship with Nixon"*: Author interview with Ardeshir Zahedi, September 14–15, 2010.

116 *"It was hardly market forces"*: Editorial, "Inflation, Oil and the Press Conference," *Washington Post*, September 9, 1973.

116 *"dangerous poppycock"*: Rowland Evans and Robert Novak, "Mr. Nixon's Empty Threat," *Washington Post*, September 10, 1973.

116 *news reports of the Marine exercises in the Mojave*: Jim Hoagland, "Arab Fear of Invasion Stirs Anger Toward U.S.," *Washington Post*, September 24, 1973.

116 *"to drop paratroopers"*: Henry Tanner, "U.S. Neutrality on Mideast Urged," *New York Times*, October 4, 1973.

116 *"Do they think in Washington"*: Jim Hoagland, "Arab Fear of Invasion Stirs Anger Toward U.S.," *Washington Post*, September 24, 1973.

116 *"Nixon gang"*: Ibid.

116 *"The backlash is definitely there"*: Ibid.

117 *"My God, doesn't he realize"*: Rowland Evans and Robert Novak, "Mr. Nixon's Empty Threat," *Washington Post*, September 10, 1973.

117 *"Because he was advised by a fool"*: Harry B. Ellis, "Saudis Becoming 'Bankers' to the World,' " *Christian Science Monitor*, October 10, 1973.

117 *"are no longer compatible"*: Clyde H. Farnsworth, "Oil Nations Will Ask Rise in Prices at Oct. 8 Parley," *New York Times*, September 17, 1973.

117 *The fourth Arab-Israeli war*: Robert MacFadden, "Arabs and Israelis Battle on Two Fronts; Egyptians Bridge Suez; Air Duels Intense," *New York Times*, October 7, 1973; "Black October: Old Enemies at War Again," *Time*, October 15, 1973, 6.

117 *"Tell him he's under an obligation"*: Alam, 326.

118 *a Mirage jet loaded with an atomic bomb*: as recalled in Tyler, 141.

118 *Early on the morning of October 10*: For a complete transcript of their conversa-

tion, see Kissinger-Schlesinger, 8:27 A.M., October 10, 1973, National Security Archive.

118   *to a dramatic and historic pause at 2:05 P.M.*: James M. Naughton, "Agnew Quits Vice Presidency and Admits Tax Evasion in '67; Nixon Consults on Successor," *New York Times*, October 11, 1973.

118   *"with barely trembling hands"*: Ibid.

118   *President Nixon nominated Gerald Ford:* John Herbers, "Gerald Ford Named by Nixon as the Successor to Agnew," *New York Times*, October 13, 1973.

119   *quit the talks:* Felix Kessler, "Persian Gulf Oil Producers, Western Firms Halt Talks; Concerns Mull OPEC Demands," *Wall Street Journal*, October 10, 1973.

119   *"would have exceptionally serious":* Clyde H. Farnsworth, "Talks Collapse on Oil Price Rise," *New York Times*, October 12, 1973.

119   *At 12:49 A.M. on Saturday, October 13:* For a complete transcript of their conversation, see Schlesinger-Kissinger, 12:49 A.M., October 13, 1973, National Security Archive.

120   *"As Israel began to fall apart":* Isaacson, 521.

120   *"The step is being taken":* John W. Finney, "U.S. Reported Ready to Replace Some Jet Fighters Lost in Israel," *New York Times*, October 14, 1973.

120   *Nixon's national security team:* For a full transcript of their meeting, see Memorandum of Conversation, Approximately 9:16 A.M.–11:00 A.M., Sunday, October 14, 1973, The Situation Room in the White House, National Security Archive.

122   *Saudi oil minister Zaki Yamani warned:* Edward Cowan, "A Saudi Threat on Oil Reported," *New York Times*, October 16, 1973.

122   *8.5 million barrels per day, with 600,000 of those bound for:* Ibid.

122   *"the policy we followed in 1958":* Dana Adams Schmidt, "Nixon Hints U.S. Intervention," *Christian Science Monitor*, October 16, 1973.

122   *monthly 5 percent cuts in production:* Richard Eder, "U.S. Chief Target: Reduction Is Smaller Than Expected—Effect Uncertain," *New York Times*, October 18, 1973.

123   *from $3.01 per barrel to $3.65:* "Rise in Oil Prices Seems a Record," *New York Times*, October 19, 1973.

123   *10 percent:* "Saudis Cut Oil Output by 10% to Put Pressure on U.S.," *New York Times*, October 19, 1973.

123   *from $4.90 to $8.92:* William D. Smith, "Cutoff in Oil to U.S. Ordered by Libya," *New York Times*, October 20, 1973.

123   *jumped by 70 percent to $5.11:* "Rise in Oil Prices Seems a Record," *New York Times*, October 19, 1973.

123   *"We are masters of our own commodity":* Yergin, 606.

123   *"Stunned and confused":* William D. Smith, "Cutoff in Oil to U.S. Ordered by Libya," *New York Times*, October 20, 1973.

123 *"what the producing countries appear to have done"*: Ibid.

123 *"at least one million barrels"*: Ibid.

123 *fired Watergate special prosecutor Archibald Cox:* Douglas E. Kneeland, "Nixon Discharges Cox for Defiance; Abolishes Watergate Task Force; Richardson and Ruckelshaus Out," *New York Times*, October 21, 1973.

124 *"not surprised"*: "Oil Flow to U.S. Halted by Saudis," *New York Times*, October 21, 1973.

124 *The next day, Kuwait, Qatar, Bahrain, and Dubai:* Richard Eder, "4 More Arab Governments Bar Oil Supplies for U.S.," *New York Times*, October 22, 1973.

124 *"as agitated and emotional as I had ever heard him"*: Kissinger, *Years of Upheaval*, 581.

124 *"those bastards"*: Tyler, 169.

124 *drunken stupor:* In *A World of Trouble*, Patrick Tyler writes: "By evening on October 24, Nixon, exhausted by the week's events, was drinking heavily. See Tyler, 67. Presidential historian Robert Dallek, noting Haig's and Kissinger's opinion that Nixon was "too distraught to participate in the preliminary discussion," raised the possibility that the president was not only inebriated but sedated during the crisis. See Robert Dallek, *Nixon and Kissinger: Partners in Power* (New York: HarperCollins, 2007), 530. Roger Morris, a Nixon aide, later quoted aides to Kissinger as saying Nixon was "upstairs drunk . . . slurring his words and barely roused when Haig and Kissinger tried to deal with him in the first moments of the crisis." See Anthony Summers, *The Arrogance of Power: The Secret World of Richard Nixon* (New York: Penguin, 2000), 460.

125 *Kissinger asked Haig if he should wake up the president: Dallek*, 530.

125 *"No I haven't"*: Ibid.

125 *"who was shuttling back and forth"*: Author interview with Dr. James Schlesinger, June 5, 2009.

125 *"Haig reported that the President was about and following events"*: Ibid.

125 *"stood down their forces"*: Ibid.

126 *"increases readiness without the determination"*: Kissinger, *Years of Upheaval*, 587–88.

126 *he told his colleagues that Nixon:* In *Years of Upheaval*, Kissinger alleges that he "did not know what conversations Haig had had with Nixon in the early hours of the morning." In fact, Kissinger knew very well the president was passed out upstairs in the Residence, and that he and Haig had engaged in an elaborate deception with their colleagues to hide the extent of Nixon's true condition. Kissinger, *Years of Upheaval*, 593.

126 *Kissinger turned to Admiral Thomas Moorer:* Author interview with Dr. James Schlesinger, June 5, 2009.

126 *To reinforce the message:* The additional steps are outlined in Kissinger, *Years of Upheaval*, 589.

126 *"to move at full speed"*: Ibid., 589.

126 *"sped to secret positions off the Soviet coast, prepared to launch"*: Summers, 460.

126 *"If we can't do what is right"*: Kissinger, *Years of Upheaval*, 589.

126 *"You and I were the only ones for it"*: Dallek, 530.

126 *"dreadfully anxious"*: Alam, 330.

126 *Kissinger telephoned Israeli ambassador Simcha Dinitz:* For a complete transcript of their conversation, see Kissinger-Dinitz, 9:38 A.M., October 26, 1973, National Security Archive.

127 *120,000 barrels of oil per day:* Drew Middleton, "U.S. Air Force and Navy Help on Saudis' Defenses," *New York Times*, November 18, 1973.

128 *a Soviet flotilla of ninety vessels:* Ibid.; Drew Middleton, "U.S. Navy Setback Giving Soviet an Edge in Mideast," *New York Times*, November 10, 1973.

128 *"Well, we only have one facility"*: Telcon, Schlesinger-Kissinger, 3:03 P.M., October 23, 1973, National Security Archive.

128 *"The Naval War College"*: As recounted in Jeffrey Robinson, *Yamani: The Inside Story* (London: Simon & Schuster, 1988), 101.

128 *the first shipment of Northrop F-5E jet fighters:* Drew Middleton, "U.S. Air Force and Navy Help on Saudis' Defenses," *New York Times*, November 18, 1973.

128 *thirty Phantom F-4 aircraft:* Ibid.

128 *"We are tracking down"*: Juan de Onis, "Saudi Arabia Is Tracking 'Every' Barrel of U.S. Oil," *New York Times*, November 6, 1973.

129 *met over breakfast on Saturday, November 3:* Memorandum of Conversation, 11/03/73, folder "Kissinger, Schlesinger, Colby, Moorer" Box 2, National Security Adviser, Gerald R. Ford Library.

129 *its native population:* Edward R. F. Sheehan, "Unradical Sheiks Who Shake the World," *New York Times Magazine*, March 24, 1974.

129 *"I was prepared to seize Abu Dhabi"*: Robinson, 102. Dr. Schlesinger told Jeffery Robinson, author of *Yamani*, that he had been prepared to order the invasion of Abu Dhabi. But he provided no information on the actual military planning that was involved. He confirmed to this author the validity of those attributed statements. He also confirmed that the invasion would have been an amphibious operation involving the Marines. Declassified transcripts of the Washington Special Action Group meetings in 1973 provide revealing new details and suggest that the plan came closer to activation than anyone outside the White House ever knew. Indeed, Schlesinger's remarks confirm that Marines were being moved into place in the last week of November and readied for action. In his interview with the author, Dr. Schlesinger confirmed that version of events.

129 *"Something small"*: Ibid.

129 *"Abu Dhabi would give us what we want"*: Memorandum of Conversation, 11/03/73, folder "Kissinger, Schlesinger, Colby, Moorer" Box 2, National Security Adviser, Gerald R. Ford Library.

130   *the Shah received formal notification:* Alam, 330.

131   *"allow any foreign power to establish":* Dev Muraka, "Growing U.S. Ties to Iran Irk Kremlin," *Christian Science Monitor,* June 5, 1975.

131   *"opined that the Watergate affair":* National Security Council Files, VIP Visits, Visit of the Shah of Iran, July 24–26, 1973 (1 of 2), Box 920, National Archives, College Park, MD.

131   *stopped receiving fortnightly reports:* Alam, 316.

131   *8.3 million barrels to 6.2 million barrels:* Juan de Onis, "Kissinger Fails to Sway Saudis from Oil Embargo," *New York Times,* November 10, 1973.

131   *"You can make Israel withdraw":* Memorandum of Conversation, 11/29/73, folder "Kissinger, Schlesinger, Colby, Moorer," Box 2, National Security Adviser, Gerald R. Ford Library.

132   *"for the time being":* Bernard Gwertzman, "U.S. Retaliation on Oil Rejected," *New York Times,* November 20, 1973.

132   *"countermeasures":* Marilyn Berger, "Arabs Warned by Kissinger on Oil Cutoff," *Washington Post,* November 22, 1973.

132   *"because your whole economy":* "Saudi Arabia Warns U.S. Against Oil Countermoves," *New York Times,* November 23, 1973.

132   *Kuwait laid land mines:* "Kuwait Threatens Oilfield Destruction Should U.S. Step In," *New York Times,* January 10, 1974.

132   *"the Arab character of Jerusalem":* "Faisal Interview," *Washington Post,* November 23, 1973.

132   *"They think we knocked off [King] Idris":* Memorandum of Conversation, 11/29/73, folder "Kissinger, Schlesinger, Colby, Moorer," Box 2, Gerald R. Ford Library.

132   *"a very interesting message from Saudi Arabia":* Telcon, Schlesinger-Kissinger, 10:15 A.M., November 28, 1973, National Security Archive.

133   *"is a friend of the United States":* Memorandum of Conversation, 11/29/73, "Kissinger, Schlesinger, Colby, Moorer," Box 2, National Security Adviser, Gerald R. Ford Library.

133   *Eighty-nine percent of the fuel:* Memorandum from the President's Assistant for National Security Affairs (Kissinger) to President Nixon, Washington, October 22, 1970, Monica Belmonte, editor; Edward C. Keefer, General Editor, *Foreign Relations of the United States, 1969–1976, Vol. E-4, Documents on Iran and Iraq, 1969–1972,* Washington: United States Government Printing Office, Office of the Historian, Bureau of Public Affairs, Vol. E-4.

134   *"Can't we overthrow one of the sheikhs":* Memorandum of Conversation, 11/29/73, "Kissinger, Schlesinger, Colby, Moorer," Box 2, Gerald R. Ford Library.

134   *"The energy crisis is like Watergate":* "A Time of Learning to Live with Less," *Time,* December 3, 1973, 35.

134   *"through the wind-blown Atlantic":* Ibid., 33.

134   *reduce private automobile use by 30 percent:* Ibid.

134   *impact of a 9.6 percent jump:* Ibid.

134   *18 percent reduction:* Ibid.

135   *"proprietor of a licensed house of prostitution":* Ibid., 35.

135   *"has found a way to retain heat":* Ibid.

135   *"Tell the people to turn off their electric blankets and cuddle":* Ibid.

135   *a woman was crushed to death:* Ibid., 46.

135   *gossip exchanged between two shoppers:* Ibid.

135   *"It's a mad final fling":* "The Beleaguered Islands," *Newsweek*, November 26, 1973, 38.

135   *shedding 133 points:* "A Time of Learning to Live with Less," *Time*, December 3, 1973, 34.

135   *prices of Cadillacs collapsed 25 percent:* Ibid., 35.

135   *closing sixteen assembly plants:* Ibid.

135   *10 percent reduction in oil consumption:* "Prospects for America," *Newsweek*, December 3, 1973, 40.

136   *"Oil is like bread":* "Shah Asks End of Oil Embargo," *Washington Post*, November 23, 1973.

136   *"In their hearts":* Author interview with Ardeshir Zahedi, September 14–15, 2010.

CHAPTER FIVE: OIL SHOCK
PAGE

137   *"If I was the President":* Telcon, Scowcroft-Kissinger, 9:35 A.M., January 30, 1974, National Security Archive.

137   *"To hell with Kissinger":* Asadollah Alam, *The Shah and I: The Confidential Diary of the Royal Court, 1969–1977* (New York: St. Martin's, 1991), 366.

137   *Fifteen miles outside Tehran:* The Army Day celebrations followed a highly scripted format each year. This account includes important details provided by Imperial Court Minister Asadollah Alam, and also by the American writer Richard T. Sale, who wrote about Army Day in the fourth of a series of highly critical articles on Iran that appeared in *The Washington Post* in 1977. Richard T. Sale, "Army Is the Keystone to the Shah's Power," *Washington Post*, May 11, 1977.

137   *"silver breastplates and helmets":* Ibid.

137   *a flyover of 150 Phantom jets:* Alam, 343.

138   *two secret auctions:* William D. Smith, "Price Quadruples for Iran Crude Oil," *New York Times*, December 12, 1973.

138   *less than 4 percent of Iran's:* Bernard Weinraub, "Iran Keeps Oil Flowing Despite Reported Pressure from Arabs," *New York Times*, December 18, 1973.

138   *43 percent of the petroleum consumed:* Bernard Weinraub, "Shah of Iran Urges Arabs to End Their Oil Embargo," *New York Times*, December 22, 1973.

138   *pulling their money from American banks:* Clyde H. Farnsworth, "Arabs Cut Funds at Banks of U.S.," *New York Times,* December 7, 1973.

138   *another 750,000 barrels:* Juan de Onis, "Arabs Set New Oil Cutbacks," *New York Times,* December 9, 1973.

138   *"dumbfounded"* and *"flabbergasted":* Bernard Weinraub, "Record Oil Prices in Iran Are Expected to Affect Arabs," *New York Times,* December 16, 1973.

138   *$17.40 per barrel:* William D. Smith, "Price Quadruples for Iran Crude Oil," *New York Times,* December 12, 1973.

138   *$1.5 billion in new government revenues:* Bernard Weinraub, "Record Oil Prices in Iran Are Expected to Affect Arabs," *New York Times,* December 16, 1973.

138   *"There are a lot of people groping":* Ibid.

138   *"The countries see how hungry":* Ibid.

138   *"wan and weary":* Bernard Weinraub, "Shah of Iran Urges Arabs to End Their Oil Embargo," *New York Times,* December 22, 1973.

139   *"until shale or gasification of coal becomes profitable":* Memorandum of Conversation, Meeting with His Imperial Majesty Mohammad Reza Shah Pahlavi, Shahanshah of Iran on Tuesday, the 24th of July at 10:43 A.M.–12:35 P.M., in the Oval Office, National Security Archive.

139   *"Of course it's going to rise":* Oriana Fallaci, "An Oriana Fallaci Interview: The Shah of Iran," *The New Republic,* December 1, 1973.

139   *from 5.8 million barrels per day:* Memo from the State Department to National Security Adviser, National Security Council Files, VIP Visits, Visit of the Shah of Iran, July 24–26, 1973 (1 of 2), Box 920, National Archives, College Park, MD.

139   *"You've increased the price of the wheat you sell us":* Oriana Fallaci, "An Oriana Fallaci Interview: The Shah of Iran," *The New Republic,* December 1, 1973.

140   *"explosive deficit in the balance of payments":* Hossein Razavi and Firouz Vakil, *The Political Environment of Economic Planning in Iran, 1971–1983: From Monarchy to Islamic Republic* (Boulder: Westview, 1984), 62.

140   *"Iranian purchases and orders":* Memo from the State Department to National Security Adviser, National Security Council Files, VIP Visits, Visit of the Shah of Iran, July 24–26, 1973 (1 of 2), Box 920, National Archives, College Park, MD.

141   *Major items on the Shah's shopping list:* The items are listed in the State Department's memo to Kissinger. Ibid.

141   *Moscow's new rapid mobility force:* Robert Graham, *Iran: The Illusion of Power,* rev. ed. (London: Croon Helm, 1979), 177. The Soviets' rapid mobility force had also been a top concern of White House officials when they declared their nuclear alert in October 1973 (see Chapter 4).

141   *"Although Iran's economic growth was averaging":* Michael Raoul-Duval Papers (Domestic Council; White House Intelligence Coordinating Group; White

House Operations Office), OPEC Objectives—FEA Study (1)-(2), Box 6, Prepared for Frank G. Zarb, Administrator, Federal Energy Administration, by International Energy Affairs, April 4, 1974, Gerald R. Ford Library.

141   *The $36 billion Fifth Plan:* Graham, 79.

141   *annual economic growth rate of 11.4 percent:* Razavi and Vakil, 70.

141   *"perilously close to absorptive capacity":* Ibid.

141   *The one third of the state budget:* Graham, 170.

142   *"The pressures for an increase":* Razavi and Vakil, 70.

142   *"anticipated inflows of financial resources":* Ibid., 68.

142   *"signaled that there was indeed an understanding":* Ibid.

142   *"that he thought there was a growing gap":* Memorandum for Dr. Henry A. Kissinger, Assistant to the President for National Security Affairs, from Mr. Kermit Roosevelt, April 26, 1972, "Meeting with the Shah of Iran," National Security Archive.

142   *plot to either kill or kidnap:* "12 Accused in Iran in Plot to Kill Shah," *New York Times,* October 3, 1973.

142   *"some sort of blood disorder":* Gholam Reza Afkhami, *The Life and Times of the Shah* (Berkeley: University of California Press, 2009), 548. According to Queen Farah, the symptoms of her husband's illness first appeared in the "autumn of 1973." See Farah Pahlavi, *An Enduring Love: My Life with the Shah* (New York: Miramax, 2004), 242.

144   *"listless; looked sad":* Arthur F. Burns Handwritten Journals, Journal II (Blue Notebook), Gerald R. Ford Library, December 6, 1973, 200–204.

144   *"not the slightest understanding":* Ibid.

144   *Helms left their meeting:* Alam, 350.

144   *"So we charged experts to study":* "A Talk with the Shah of Iran," *Time,* April 1, 1974, 41.

145   *The British ambassador later told Alam:* Alam, 348.

145   *"that he had assumed":* Walter Isaacson, *Kissinger: A Biography* (New York: Simon & Schuster, 2005), 563.

145   *"could not understand":* Telcon, Kissinger-Anderson, 3:10 P.M., June 5, 1975, National Security Archive.

145   *"use our influence for moderation":* Kissinger, *Years of Upheaval,* 885.

146   *"we are establishing the prices ourselves":* The U.S. embassy in Tehran obtained a summarized text of the Shah's remarks and forwarded them to Washington on January 23, 1974. "Department of State Airgram from American Embassy in Tehran, on Shah's Remarks to Delegates to Tehran OPEC Meeting, January 23, 1974," National Security Archive.

146   *double the price of a barrel of oil:* Bernard Weinraub, "Oil Price Doubled by Big Producers on Persian Gulf," *New York Times,* December 24, 1973.

146   *"The industrial world will have to realize":* Ibid.

146 *470 percent:* "Arab Oil Has Gone Up 470% in a Year," *New York Times*, December 30, 1973.

146 *$112 billion:* "Faisal and Oil: Driving Toward a New World Order," *Time*, January 6, 1975, 8.

146 *Iran quadrupled its oil revenues:* Ibid., 11.

146 *to climb to $98 billion:* Graham, 79.

147 *50 percent a year:* "Faisal and Oil: Driving Toward a New World Order," *Time*, January 6, 1975, 11.

147 *soared from $3.9 billion to $24 billion:* Ibid., 12.

147 *"Among other things, this means":* "Arab Oil Has Gone Up 470% in a Year," *New York Times*, December 30, 1973.

147 *France calculated:* "Energy: How High Is Up?", *Newsweek*, January 7, 1974, 22.

147 *Spain's $500 million trade surplus:* Joe Gandelman, "Madrid Loses Some of Its Glow," *Christian Science Monitor*, October 29, 1976.

147 *"In pushing up prices":* "The Shah Goes to the Brink," *The Economist*, December 29, 1973, 22.

147 *"The oil increase to us is $10 billion":* Memorandum of Conversation, December 28, 1973, "Kissinger, Schlesinger, Colby, Moorer," Box 3, National Security Adviser, Gerald R. Ford Library.

147 *"We had a policy in the Department of Defense":* Author interview with Dr. James Schlesinger, June 5, 2009.

148 *"Kissinger had nothing to contribute":* Arthur F. Burns Handwritten Journals, Journal II (Blue Notebook), Gerald R. Ford Library, January 8, 1974, 214.

148 *"The diplomatic response was to try":* FIOSHA interview with Richard Helms, by William Burr, Foundation for Iranian Studies, Washington, D.C., July 10 & 24, 1985, 1–37.

148 *"As I recall, His Imperial Majesty":* Alam, 350.

149 *"I was involved in delivering":* FIOSHA interview with Richard Helms, by William Burr, Foundation for Iranian Studies, Washington, D.C., July 10 & 24, 1985, 1–37.

149 *"idiot":* Alam wrote that on the eve of the Tehran conference the British ambassador read the morning's papers and realized that something was afoot. He wrote a letter for Alam to give to the Shah expressing concern "that OPEC is greatly to increase the posted price of Gulf crude." The ambassador wrote the note before the Shah held the press conference and before the final price was announced. Alam, 348. This exchange makes clear that the British ambassador did not know of the Shah's real intentions.

149 *"relations between the United States and the Saudis":* Author interview with Dr. James Schlesinger, June 5, 2009.

149 *a secretly recorded telephone conversation:* Telcon, Kissinger-Anderson, 3:10 P.M., June 5, 1975, National Security Archive.

150 *authorize an increase in Iranian oil production:* Dan Morgan, "Iran Asks Goods for Oil," *Washington Post,* January 18, 1974.

150 *"enable Iran":* Memo from the State Department to the National Security Adviser; National Security Council Files, VIP Visits, Visit of the Shah of Iran, July 24–26, 1973 (1 of 2), Box 920, National Archives, College Park, MD.

151 *"definitely using oil as a lever":* Dan Morgan, "Iran Asks Goods for Oil," *Washington Post,* January 18, 1974.

151 *The president had flown out to California:* "Energy: How High Is Up?," *Newsweek,* January 7, 1974, 18.

151 *"Look at Amin":* Memorandum of Conversation, 2/9/74, "Nixon, Kissinger, Shultz, Simon," Box 3, National Security Adviser, Gerald R. Ford Library.

151 *with fists and knives:* "Panic at the Pump," *Time,* January 14, 1974, 17.

151 *what looked like a hand grenade:* Ibid.

151 *"You are going to give me gas":* Ibid.

151 *gasoline trucks were hijacked:* Ibid., 18.

151 *Motorists in Hawaii:* "The Times They Are A-Changin'," *Newsweek,* February 18, 1974, 22.

152 *"and there have been scores of fist fights":* Ibid., 20.

152 *Truckers besieged the town of Streator:* Ibid., 21.

152 *"The key during that period":* Author interview with Frank Zarb, June 11, 2009.

152 *gas lines in the nation's capital:* "The Times They Are A-Changin'," *Newsweek,* February 18, 1974, 19.

152 *"I went into a line":* Telcon, Kissinger-Sisco, 9:20 A.M., February 18, 1974, National Security Archive.

152 *"If I was the President":* Telcon, Kissinger-Scowcroft, 9:35 A.M., January 30, 1974, National Security Archive.

152 *traffic deaths:* Memorandum of Conversations, 2/21/74, "Cabinet Meeting," Box 3, National Security Adviser, Gerald R. Ford Library.

153 *a man who "terrified" his staff:* Judy Bachrach, "William Simon, the Energetic Czar," *Washington Post,* January 13, 1974.

153 *"Clean off your desk":* Ibid.

153 *he contributed $15,000:* William E. Simon with John M. Caher, *A Time for Reflection: An Autobiography* (Washington, D.C.: Regnery, 2004), 54.

153 *"Albert Speer's position":* Ibid., 84.

153 *"A Fitzgerald Hero in Washington":* "The Whirlwind Confronts the Skeptics," *Time,* January 21, 1974, 22–27.

153 *He worked till ten o'clock each night:* Judy Bachrach, "William Simon, The Energetic Czar," *Washington Post,* January 13, 1974.

153 *half an hour a day at most:* Ibid.

153 *emptying buckets of cold water:* Benjamin Wallace-Wells, "Giuliani's Policy Professor," *Washington Post,* October 26, 2007.

153   *"fun, charming, enchanting and witty"*: Simon, 120.

153   *"NO! East Coast Establishment!"*: Ibid., 65.

153   *"I thought that Simon was a wipe-out"*: Telcon, Nixon-Kissinger, 7:00 P.M., January 23, 1974, National Security Archive.

154   *"He has himself locked in concrete"*: Telcon, Nixon-Kissinger, 5:35 P.M., February 5, 1974, National Security Archive.

154   *"in the presence of our ambassador"*: Telcon, Kissinger-Haig, 5:31 P.M., February 6, 1974, National Security Archive.

154   *Nixon held a thirty-five-minute meeting*: Memorandum of Conversation, 2/7/74, "Nixon, Ambassador al-Sowayel, Scowcroft," Box 3, National Security Adviser, Gerald R. Ford Library.

155   *"what ought to happen"*: Telcon, Nixon-Kissinger, 9:04 A.M., October 14, 1973, National Security Archive.

155   *American newspapers republished his interview*: Oriana Fallaci, "An Oriana Fallaci Interview: The Shah of Iran," *The New Republic*, December 1, 1973.

155   *"The sugar-coated image"*: "Shah of Iran: Visions, Wives." *Los Angeles Times*, January 7, 1974.

156   *"two or three times"*: Wolfgang Saxon, "Shah Finds No Cut in Oil Flow to the U.S.," *New York Times*, February 24, 1974.

156   *"created tremors in Washington"*: William D. Smith, "Oil Watchers Focus on the Shah of Iran," *New York Times*, March 7, 1974.

156   *he gashed his head*: Simon, 88.

156   *"in considerable pain and discomfort"*: Ibid., 89.

156   *"irresponsible and just plain ridiculous"*: "Denies Shah's Charge," *Chicago Tribune*, February 26, 1974.

156   *"Are you telling me the Shah of Iran"*: Simon, 89.

156   *"I'll say this Mr. Simon"*: Tim O'Brien, "Defends Nixon on Crisis 'End,' " *Washington Post*, February 27, 1974.

156   *twenty-four-hour Secret Service protection*: Simon, 93.

157   *"I remember the Secret Service"*: Ibid.

157   *"well-placed sources"*: "Simon May Have Hurt Chance for Promotion," *Chicago Tribune*, February 27, 1974.

157   *"consternation and anger"*: "Iran Considered Action Against U.S.," *Washington Post*, March 2, 1974.

157   *He apologized*: Alam, 361.

157   *"The Shah, in my opinion"*: Simon, 89.

157   *"We are going all out now on the Saudis"*: Telcon, Kissinger-Clements, 2:45 P.M., March 7, 1974, National Security Archive.

158   *"as you know, Mr. President"*: Telcon, Nixon-Kissinger, 5:50 P.M., March 11, 1974, National Security Archive.

158   *"Washington relies on Zaki Yamani"*: Alam, 359.

158 *The oil embargo was lifted:* Juan de Onis, "Most Arab Lands End Ban on Oil Shipments for U.S.; Saudis Plan Output Rise," *New York Times*, March 19, 1974.

158 *raising oil prices by a further 5 percent:* Juan de Onis, "Saudis Said to Have Issued Ultimatum to Prevent Oil-Price Increase at Parley," *New York Times*, March 20, 1974.

158 *8.3 million barrels a day:* William D. Smith, "Saudi Oil Output Up by Million Barrels," *New York Times*, March 26, 1974.

158 *11.2 million barrels a day:* Ibid.

158 *increase of 37 percent:* Ibid.

159 *Iraq's Saddam Hussein:* Daniel Yergin, *The Prize: The Epic Quest for Oil, Money, and Power* (New York: Simon & Schuster, 1991), 614.

159 *9 percent of the 55.8 million barrels of oil:* Ibid.

159 *"made even more severe":* Ibid.

159 *Kissinger hosted a top-level meeting:* The comments made during this meeting can be found in Secretary's Meeting with Oil Company Executives, Friday, March 29, 1974, 5:15 P.M., National Security Archive.

160 *"This reflects a sharp acceleration":* "Inflation Rises to 2-Digit Rate in 17 Countries," *Los Angeles Times*, April 12, 1974.

160 *Rates of inflation:* "Faisal and Oil: Driving Toward a New World Order," *Time*, January 6, 1975, 12.

160 *$10 billion fuel bill:* Ibid.

160 *rice harvests collapsed 40 percent:* Ibid.

162 *"The desire of Iran's leadership":* Michael Raoul-Duval Papers (Domestic Council; White House Intelligence Coordinating Group; White House Operations Office), OPEC Objectives—FEA Study (1)-(2), Box 6, Prepared for Frank G. Zarb, Administrator, Federal Energy Administration, by International Energy Affairs, April 4, 1974, Gerald R. Ford Library.

163 *"Iran is not a volcano":* Mohamed Heikal, *The Return of the Ayatollah: The Iranian Revolution from Mossadeq to Khomeini* (London: André Deutsch, 1981), 104.

163 *the Shah broke from his vacation:* Alam, 362.

163 *"In the 33rd year of an often uncertain reign":* "Oil, Grandeur and a Challenge to the West," *Time*, November 4, 1974, 28.

163 *"But I have so many aspirations":* Alam, 360.

163 *who asked him to send:* Ibid., 363.

164 *"I was told":* Email from Kambiz Atabai, office of Her Majesty Queen Farah Pahlavi, October 30, 2010, to the author.

164 *Dr. Fellinger later recalled:* Fellinger made his observations on the Shah's diagnosis to Dr. Amir Aslan Afshar, an aide to the king, after the revolution. Afshar recalled his discusion with Dr. Fellinger in an interview with Dr. Mostafa Alamouti in November 2003. The interview can be accessed online at www.iranvajahan.net.

164 *ending his association:* Author interview with Kambiz Atabai, November 2, 2010.

165 *"Had he gone":* Ibid.

165 *commented on his wan appearance:* Bernard Weinraub, "Shah of Iran Urges Arabs to End Their Oil Embargo," *New York Times,* December 22, 1973.

165 *Pompidou's quiet determination:* Alam, 361.

165 *"Pompidou is dying":* Memorandum of Conversation, 9/5/73, "Kissinger, Schlesinger, Wickham, Scowcroft," Box 2, National Security Adviser, Gerald R. Ford Library.

165 *"had an analysis made":* Memorandum of Conversation, Sir Alec Douglas-Home, Foreign and Commonwealth Secretary of Great Britain and Dr. Henry A. Kissinger, Secretary of State, Tuesday, February 26, 1974, 9:07 A.M.–10:45 A.M., National Security Archive.

165 *"two cars with flashing lights":* Farah Pahlavi, *An Enduring Love,* 244.

166 *Flandrin took note:* Ibid., 245.

166 *"as far as he was concerned":* Ibid., 247.

166 *They settled on a diagnosis:* Ibid.

166 *"We have to prepare":* Author interview with Kambiz Atabai, November 2, 2010.

166 *"The Shah is pushing":* Ibid.

166 *"To hell with Kissinger":* Alam, 366.

167 *Cabinda oil was low in sulfur:* Arthur Vecsey, "Perspective: Portugal Feeling Burden of Colonies," *Chicago Tribune,* May 1, 1974.

167 *Portugal's $400 million in income:* Ibid.

167 *$650 million annual cost:* Ibid.

167 *"Discontent over unchecked inflation":* "Portugal's Army Seizes Control and Proclaims Democratic Goal," *New York Times,* April 26, 1974.

168 *$200 million military base at Bandar Abbas:* Drew Middleton, "Shah of Iran Due in U.S. to Seek Weapons," *New York Times,* July 22, 1973.

168 *$600 million naval base at:* Ibid.

168 *secure an "option":* The word "option" was used by then Secretary of Defense Schlesinger to describe what he referred to as "conversations" between the Pentagon and Iranian officials over Chabahar: "I have no doubt that there were exploratory conversations on the part of naval officers with their Iranian counterparts regarding the availability of bases in the Indian Ocean during periods of emergency. Indeed, I vaguely recall those conversations. But that is quite different from a commitment as is implied here. A commitment by the United States to use certain facilities. Commitment is the wrong word. If they were seeking options on those facilities, that would have been quite appropriate. And indeed I expect that that indeed was the case." In fact, under the terms of the treaty signed between Iran and the Soviet Union in 1962, the Shah had promised Moscow he would never allow the construction of rocket-

launching sites by outsiders on Iranian soil. Schlesinger's use of the word "option" suggests that Tehran and Washington were looking for ways to avoid needlessly antagonizing the Soviet Union, which was always sensitive to base construction on its southern periphery. FISOHA interview with James Schlesinger, by William Burr, Foundation for Iranian Studies, Washington, D.C., May 15 and June 27, 1986, 2–53.

CHAPTER SIX: CRUEL SUMMER
PAGE

169 *"The financial markets"*: Memorandum of Conversation, 7/9/74, "Nixon, Simon, Scowcroft," Box 4, National Security Adviser, Gerald R. Ford Library.

169 *"I will have to meet and talk with the Shah"*: Memorandum of Conversation, 7/30/74, "Nixon, Simon, Rush, Scowcroft," Box 4, National Security Adviser, Gerald R. Ford Library.

169 the *"queen bee at the center of the hive"*: Ibid.

169 *"If you have money"*: Henry Mitchell, "Henry and the Prince and 1,400 Guests," *Washington Post*, June 8, 1974.

169 *sworn in almost a month earlier:* Bill Simon was confirmed by the Congress as the new treasury secretary on April 30, 1974, and sworn in on May 8. William E. Simon with John M. Caher, *A Time for Reflection: An Autobiography* (Washington, D.C.: Regnery, 2004), 104.

170 *5.7 million people living atop 132 billion barrels of crude oil:* "A Desert King Faces the Modern World," *Time*, January 6, 1975.

170 *"America runs on oil"*: Henry Mitchell, "Henry and the Prince and 1,400 Guests," *Washington Post*, June 8, 1974.

170 *"had been first in the swimming pool"*: "His Highness Prince Fahd had been the first in the swimming pool at an afternoon party, an utterly reliable source said—at this party every woman who went swimming got an Arabian dress." Henry Mitchell, "Henry and the Prince and 1,400 Guests," *Washington Post*, June 8, 1974.

170 *everyone ate from full plates:* "It was great, we ate out on the terrace and they ate it up. But we really filled their plate with more than they could handle." Telcon, Simon-Kissinger, 3:00 P.M., June 7, 1974, National Security Archive.

170 *turned down by David Rockefeller:* Arthur F. Burns Handwritten Journals, Journal II (Blue Notebook), Gerald R. Ford Library, 217–18.

170 *"grave shortcomings"*: Ibid.

171 *"What a mess!"*: Ibid.

171 *"Dependent on the West for military and diplomatic support"*: Henry A. Kissinger, *Years of Renewal* (New York: Touchstone, 1999), 672.

171 *"one minister of his training and capacities"*: Ibid., 673.

171 *"was, I think, a little hurt"*: Telcon, Simon-Kissinger, 10:45 A.M., June 21, 1974, National Security Archive.

172   *"[Bill Simon] and Henry had"*: Author interview with General Brent Scowcroft, April 6, 2010.

172   *"mesmerized"*: Ibid.

172   *"And whatever Yamani was"*: Ibid.

172   *"The two of them were always at loggerheads"*: Author interview with Frank Zarb, June 11, 2009.

172   *"With a two-by-four!"*: Ibid.

172   *In Yamani's telling of the story*: Yamani recounted the story to his biographer, Jeffrey Robinson, *Yamani: The Inside Story* (London: Simon & Schuster, 1988), 115–16.

173   *"We used to correspond quite regularly"*: Ibid., 206.

173   *His ambassador in Washington wisely talked him out of it*: Author interview with Ardeshir Zahedi, September 14–15, 2010.

173   *"By no means"*: Alam, 373.

173   *Alam assumed Nixon*: Ibid., 376.

173   *"There's more than meets the eye"*: Alam, 380.

174   *At 10:00 A.M. on July 9*: Memorandum of Conversation, 7/9/74, "Nixon, Simon, Scowcroft," Box 4, National Security Adviser, Gerald R. Ford Library.

174   *"He is getting a lot of mail"*: Arthur F. Burns Handwritten Journals, Journal II (Blue Notebook), Gerald R. Ford Library, April 21, 1974, 223.

174   *"began by expressing his skepticism"*: Ibid., June 24, 1974, 229.

174   *total $60 billion*: "Simon's Tough Tour," *Time*, July 29, 1974.

174   *King Faisal would hold $10 billion*: Ibid.

174   *"With Faisal, I have raised it privately"*: Memorandum of Conversation, 7/9/74, "Nixon, Simon, Scowcroft," Box 4, National Security Adviser, Gerald R. Ford Library.

176   *While in the French Riviera*: "Simon's Tough Tour," *Time*, July 29, 1974.

176   *"The Shah is a nut"*: "Simon to Skirt 'Nut' Meeting," *Chicago Tribune*, July 16, 1974.

176   *"Simon to Skirt 'Nut' Meeting"*: Ibid.

176   *"I am besieged by queries"*: Simon, 89.

176   *"taken out of context"*: Ibid.

176   *"Just exactly how do you call"*: Ibid.

176   *"was using the vernacular"*: James L. Rowe Jr., "Simon Calls Shah Quote 'Misleading,'" *Washington Post*, July 17, 1974.

176   *Kissinger telephoned Ambassador Ardeshir Zahedi*: Telcon, Kissinger-Zahedi, 4:23 P.M., July 15, 1974, National Security Archive.

177   *"I can remember it being rolled out one day"*: Eugene L. Meyer, "When the Iranians Bore Gifts: Remembering the Subtle Seduction of High US Officials by Zahedi," *Washington Post*, December 1, 1979.

177   *"He's certain they turned"*: Ibid.

177 *There had been a scene:* Author interview with Ardeshir Zahedi, September 14–15, 2010.

177 *Yamani hoped to break the Shah's lock:* Details of the oil auction were outlined in the following article by Juan de Onis, "Saudi Arabia and Iran in Oil-Price Stalemate," *New York Times,* September 10, 1974.

178 *"is speaking about lower oil prices":* Jack Anderson, "Shah of Iran Culprit in High Oil Prices," *Washington Post,* June 5, 1979.

178 *"My belief":* Ibid.

178 *the president was still asleep:* Simon, 111.

178 *he was told the president was in the Lincoln Sitting Room:* Ibid.

178 *"It was as if he could pull down a screen":* Ibid., 113.

179 *"The Arabs are acting like nouveaux riches":* Memorandum of Conversation, 7/30/74, "Nixon, Simon, Rush, Scowcroft," Box 4, National Security Adviser, Gerald R. Ford Library.

179 *The president clenched his fountain pen:* Jack Anderson, "Nixon Let Shah Drive Up Oil Prices," *Washington Post,* June 1, 1979.

179 *the first of four German banks to fail:* "Fears of Deep Recession Grow in Western Europe," *Washington Post,* August 30, 1974.

180 *predicted inflation of 20 percent in Britain:* Ibid.

180 *"In France there'll be a popular front":* Memorandum of Conversation, 2/9/74, "Nixon, Kissinger, Shultz, Simon," National Security Adviser, Gerald R. Ford Library.

180 *"We will have to aid Italy":* Memorandum of Conversation, 7/30/74, "Nixon, Simon, Rush, Scowcroft," Box 4, National Security Adviser, Gerald R. Ford Library.

181 *"the felon":* Arthur F. Burns Handwritten Journals, Journal II (Blue Notebook), Gerald R. Ford Library, December 6, 1973, 200–204.

181 *Everyone was lying to him:* "Nixon got very paranoid. . . . He thought at the end everyone was lying": Ronald Kessler, *In the President's Secret Service: Behind the Scenes with the Agents in the Line of Fire and the Presidents They Protect* (New York: Crown, 2009), 32.

181 *He was drinking every other night now:* Ibid.

181 *"[Treasury] would like to have a meeting":* Telcon, Kissinger-Ingersoll, 5:15 P.M., August 1, 1974, National Security Archive.

181 *had climbed from $2.8 billion:* Hossein Razavi and Firouz Vakil, *The Political Environment of Economic Planning in Iran, 1971–1983: From Monarchy to Islamic Republic* (Boulder: Westview, 1984), 63.

182 *revenues rocketed to $17.8 billion:* Ibid.

182 *"We have no real limit on money":* Lewis M. Simons, "Shah's Dreams Are Outpacing Iran's Economic Boom," *Washington Post,* May 26, 1974.

182 *$1 billion in oil receipts each month:* James Clarity, "Rich but Undeveloped, Iran Seeks More Power," *New York Times,* June 3, 1974.

182   *"For at least a dozen years"*: Ibid.

182   *"Inflation is running wild"*: Lewis M. Simons, "Shah's Dreams Are Outpacing Iran's Economic Boom," *Washington Post*, May 26, 1974.

182   *In the city of Mashhad:* James F. Clarity, "A 'Revolution' in Iran—Report on the Progress," *New York Times*, December 22, 1974.

182   *unable to feed their families:* Alam, 374.

182   *"standing on what appears to be the top of the world"*: Lewis M. Simons, "Shah's 'Phobia' Pushes Iran," *Washington Post*, May 27, 1974.

183   *movie stars Jeff Chandler and Sophia Loren:* Ibid.

183   *recorded the bizarre scene:* Alam, 387.

183   *approving the appointments and promotions:* Steven R. Ward, *Immortal: A Military History of Iran and Its Armed Forces* (Washington, D.C.: Georgetown University Press, 2009), 209.

183   *"His Imperial Majesty has an extraordinary ability"*: Lewis M. Simons, "Shah's Dreams Are Outpacing Iran's Economic Boom," *Washington Post*, May 26, 1974.

183   *"The primary topic in all our meetings"*: David Rockefeller, *Memoirs* (New York: Random House, 2003), 356.

183   *"increased dramatically"*: Ibid., 360.

183   *"we were never successful"*: Ibid., 361.

184   *"had told me that the Shah"*: Ibid., 359.

184   *"an arrogance that underlay"*: Ibid.

184   *"really feeling their oats"*: Ibid.

184   *"the embassy was certainly concerned"*: FISOHA interview with Richard Helms, by William Burr, Foundation for Iranian Studies, Washington, D.C., July 10 & 24, 1985, 1–42.

185   *"I not only make the decisions"*: Joseph Kraft, "What Restrains the Shah?," *Washington Post*, April 27, 1975.

185   *25.9 percent each year for the next five years:* Robert Graham, *Iran: The Illusion of Power,* rev. ed. (London: Croon Helm, 1979), 80.

185   *doubled from $35 billion to $69 billion:* Ibid., 78.

185   *"My head is spinning"*: Alam, 382.

185   *"was subject to the vagaries of world supply"*: Razavi and Vakil, 68.

185   *"At the end of the Ramsar meeting"*: Graham, 83.

186   *infatuation with Big Push economics:* Razavi and Vakil, 67.

186   *unveiled a $3 billion plan:* Eric Pace, "Teheran Planning One of the World's Largest Plazas," *New York Times*, September 1, 1975.

186   *a staff of five thousand:* Dee Wedemeyer, "Iran's Grand Library," *New York Times*, March 7, 1976.

186   *to rebuild the seven fluted columns of Xerxes:* Eric Pace, "Iran, Glorifying Her Past, Will Rebuild 7 Columns of Xerxes," *New York Times*, September 7, 1975.

186　*two supersonic Concorde airliners:* "Iranian Concorde Accords," *Wall Street Journal*, October 6, 1972.

186　*He signed a $6 billion trade deal with France:* "France in $6 Billion Iran Pacts; Premier Sees No Devaluations," *New York Times*, December 24, 1974.

186　*"I will sell you aspirins":* David Holden, "Shah of Shahs, Shah of Dreams," *New York Times Magazine*, May 26, 1974.

187　*At 10:00 A.M. on Saturday, August 3:* Memorandum of Conversation, 8/3/74, "Kissinger, Simon, Burns, Ingersoll, Enders," Box 4, Gerald R. Ford Library.

187　*"Falling prices would quickly bring the revenues":* Stephen D. Krasner, "The Great Oil Sheikdown," *Foreign Policy* 13 (Winter 1973–74): 131–32.

189　*total monetary reserves of $453 billion:* Leonard Silk, "Energy War Rumblings," *New York Times*, September 25, 1974.

189　*"the world banking system":* Ibid.

189　*"huge foreign debts":* Christopher C. Joyner, "The Petrodollar Phenomenon and Changing International Economic Relations," *World Affairs*, Vol. 138, No. 2 (Fall 1975), 152–76.

190　*"I would like to discuss the most important issue":* Simon, 114.

190　*"I expect to continue":* Ibid., 115.

190　*"seemed to hear nothing":* Ibid.

191　*"It's all over, Bill":* Ibid., 116.

191　*"Bill, what are you doing?":* Ibid.

191　*"walked past Ken and me":* Ibid., 117.

191　*"frozen in my spot":* Ibid.

191　*"The American people are too wise":* Ibid.

191　*Cynthia Helms, wrapped in a dressing gown:* Cynthia Helms, *An Ambassador's Wife in Iran* (New York: Dodd, Mead, 1981), 85.

191　*"It was a warm and starry night":* Ibid., 86.

192　*"For us, it was a dramatic and sobering moment":* Ibid.

192　*the then princely sum of $60,000:* Ibid., 11.

192　*Cynthia Helms likened the compound:* Ibid.

192　*a hybrid of contemporary American and Persian architecture:* William H. Sullivan, *Mission to Iran* (New York: W. W. Norton, 1981), 38.

192　*"We were charged a monthly rent":* Cynthia Helms, 11.

192　*"In inquiring why this was so":* Sullivan, 40.

192　*Shi'a Muslims cited cultural reasons:* Ibid.

193　*The warehouse was actually a basement:* FISOHA interview with Armin Meyer, by William Burr, Foundation for Iranian Studies, Washington, D.C., March 29, 1985, 1–44.

193　*took a close interest:* Richard Helms with William Hood, *A Look over My Shoulder: A Life in the Central Intelligence Agency* (New York: Ballantine, 2003), 421.

193　*Cynthia Helms came downstairs:* The account of the intruder at the embassy is found in Cynthia Helms, 52–54.

194   *galloping inflation of 18.7 percent:* Clyde H. Farnsworth, "Inflation in U.S. Worrying Europe," *New York Times,* September 5, 1974.

194   *800,000 unemployed:* "A Question of Stability—And Survival," *Time,* November 18, 1974, 17.

194   *a $2 billion loan:* Paul Hoffman, "Italian Reds Bid for Power Share," *New York Times,* September 2, 1974.

194   *Italy agreed to pay interest of 8 percent:* Ibid.

195   *buildings in the Portuguese capital Lisbon:* For an overview of voting patterns and electoral strength of support of Communist Party chapters in Western Europe, see "Western Europe's New Landscape," *Newsweek,* October 28, 1974, 10–13.

195   *Inflation was running at between 30 and 40 percent:* Bowen Northrup, "Living with Democracy: After Dictatorship, Portugal Finds Adjusting to Free Government Is Harder than Expected," *Wall Street Journal,* July 11, 1974.

195   *$2.8 billion trade deficit:* "New Greek Leaders Hope to Get Economy Back on Course 'Soon,' " *Wall Street Journal,* July 29, 1974.

195   *"perennial deficit in Greece's international payments account":* Ibid.

195   *Greek tourism revenues:* Charles Mohr, "Athens Expected to Move on Economic Problems," *New York Times,* July 27, 1974.

195   *"They want a new patron":* Steven V. Roberts, "Greek Minister Tours Western Europe," *New York Times,* September 6, 1974.

195   *"Nobody really wants them":* Ibid.

196   *"The increasing cost of oil":* Bernard Gwertzman, "Kissinger Sees Oil Crisis Periling Western Society," *New York Times,* September 27, 1974.

196   *"You have to look upon him":* Ibid.

CHAPTER SEVEN: SCREAMING EAGLE

PAGE

197   *Bring up a little lion cub:* Abolqasem Ferdowsi, translated by Dick Davis, *Shahnameh: The Persian Book of Kings* (New York: Penguin, 2006), 243.

199   *"I will tell the Shah":* Memorandum of Conversation, "Kissinger, Dinitz," Monday, December 23, 1974, 6:45–7:45 P.M., National Security Archive.

199   *"Pride comes before a fall":* Asadollah Alam, *The Shah and I: The Confidential Diary of Iran's Royal Court, 1969–1977* (New York: St. Martin's 1991), 391.

199   *"or face possible social unrest":* Harry B. Ellis, "Ford Told More Inflation May Spark Unrest; Narrows List for Key White House Posts," *Christian Science Monitor,* August 14, 1974.

199   *"My first priority":* Ibid.

199   *"Henry is a genius":* Walter Isaacson, *Kissinger: A Biography* (New York: Simon & Schuster, 2005), 601.

199   *"Ford has just got to realize":* Ibid.

200   *"I would take however long it required":* Ibid., 604.

200   *President Ford's first briefing on oil:* Memorandum of Conversation, 8/17/74, "Ford, Kissinger," Box 5, National Security Adviser, Gerald R. Ford Library.

201   *"Yes, and I think we all thought that":* Author interview with General Brent Scowcroft, April 6, 2010.

202   *"To some extent, arguments over oil prices":* Emphasis in the original document authored by Kissinger's aide Winston Lord. Briefing Memorandum for the Secretary of State from S/P Winston Lord, Department of State, "Strategies for the Oil Crisis and the Scenario for the September 28 Meeting," September 21, 1974, 6, Eric Hooglund, project editor, *Iran: The Making of U.S. Policy, 1977–80,* National Security Archive (Alexandria, VA: Chadwyck-Healey, 1990), Document Reference No. 00893.

202   *Iran's ambassador Ardeshir Zahedi was ushered into the Oval Office:* Memorandum of Conversation, 8/21/74, "Ford, Iranian Ambassador Ardeshir Zahedi," Box 5, National Security Adviser, Gerald R. Ford Library.

203   *Umar al-Saqqaf . . . stopped by the Oval Office eight days later:* Memorandum of Conversation, 8/29/74, "Ford, Kissinger, Saudi Arabian Foreign Minister Umar al-Saqqaf," Box 5, National Security Adviser, Gerald R. Ford Library.

204   *high-water mark of 1,051 points:* "Economic Ills: Any Prescription?," *Newsweek,* September 30, 1974, 32.

204   *collapsed a staggering 86 percent:* "Seeking Relief from a Massive Migraine," *Time,* September 9, 1974, 35.

204   *79 percent:* Ibid.

204   *"Investors have seemed frightened":* Ibid.

204   *Housing starts fell 38 percent:* Ibid., 39.

204   *taxpayer-funded bailout of $10 million a month:* Ibid.

204   *Massachusetts General Hospital stopped changing bed linen every day:* Ibid.

205   *rose by 5.6 percent:* Memorandum for the Vice President, July 3, 1975, U.S. Council of Economic Advisers, "Alan Greenspan—1975 (2)," Box 19, Gerald R. Ford Library.

205   *children living in poverty:* "Draft Copy of Report on Poverty in the United States," July 2, 1975, U.S. Department of Commerce, U.S. Council of Economic Advisers, "Alan Greenspan—1975 (2)," Box 19, Gerald R. Ford Library.

205   *real income declined 4 percent:* Memorandum for the Vice President, July 3, 1975, U.S. Council of Economic Advisers, "Alan Greenspan—1975 (2)," Box 19, Gerald R. Ford Library.

205   *46 percent of Americans told Gallup:* "Seeking Relief from a Massive Migraine," *Time,* September 9, 1974, 36.

205   *"the soaring cost of oil and fertilizer":* "Economic Ills: Any Prescription?," *Newsweek,* September 30, 1974, 38.

205   *"lost enough wheat":* Ibid., 39.

205   *child mortality in Tanzania:* Ibid., 38.

205 *207 percent annually in Chile:* Ibid., 31.

205 *the price of heating oil jumped 60 to 100 percent:* "Faisal and Oil: Driving Toward a New World Order," *Time*, January 6, 1975, 12.

205 *French president Válery Giscard d'Estaing:* Ibid.

205 *Electrical light displays were banned in Britain:* Ibid.

205 *the floodlights around the Acropolis:* Ibid.

205 *"making love to a corpse":* Peter R. Kann, "Land of No Peace: As Vietnamese Keep Losing Lives, US Loses Only Money," *Wall Street Journal*, September 13, 1974.

205 *"overwhelmed":* George McArthur, "A Crisis Swells Amid the Bustle," *Los Angeles Times*, June 3, 1974.

205 *$1.50 a gallon:* Ibid.

205 *vast oil deposits in the coastal waters off the Mekong Delta:* "South Vietnam: Land of High-Risk Opportunity," *Nation's Business*, March 1974, 26.

206 *"Please God, just let them bring in one well":* George McArthur, "A Crisis Swells Amid the Bustle," *Los Angeles Times*, June 3, 1974.

206 *"What happens in the economic realm":* Thomas E. Mullaney, "Scrutinizing Worldwide Ills," *New York Times*, September 8, 1974.

206 *$100 billion:* Ibid.

206 *$16 billion:* Ibid.

206 *"The quadrupling of the price":* Ibid.

206 *"a screaming eagle":* Leonard Silk, "Energy War Rumblings," *New York Times*, September 25, 1974.

206 *"The danger is clear":* Dennis Farney, "Ford Warns of Possible Retaliation if Oil Nations Threaten Economy," *Wall Street Journal*, September 24, 1974.

207 *"harsh and even threatening":* Ibid.

207 *"What has gone up by political decision":* Bernard Gwertzman, "Ford and Kissinger Warn Exorbitant Prices of Oil Imperil World's Economy," *New York Times*, September 24, 1974.

207 *"Yesterday's actions were a signal":* Marilyn Berger, "2 Objectives Seen in U.S. Moves on Oil," *Washington Post*, September 25, 1974.

207 *"economic catastrophe":* Rowland Evans and Robert Novak, "Economic Fears and Frustrations," *Washington Post*, September 28, 1974.

207 *"a drastic business decline":* Ibid.

208 *"on the brink of a terrifying collapse":* "How the City Was Saved," *The Economist*, January 5, 1974, 79–80.

208 *Franklin National:* "The Big Cash Crunch," *Newsweek*, September 30, 1974, 44.

208 *"in danger of succumbing":* Ibid.

208 *"skyrocketing escalation of energy costs":* Rowland Evans and Robert Novak, "Economic Fears and Frustrations," *Washington Post*, September 28, 1974.

208 *"America Warns the Arabs":* "U.S. Oil Warning Stirs Arab Anger," *Los Angeles Times*, September 25, 1974.

208 *"Ford Threatens to Seize"*: Ibid.

208 *"It is calling for cooperation"*: Ibid.

208 *"No one can dictate to us"*: "Shah Rejects Bid by Ford for Cut in Prices of Oil," *New York Times*, September 27, 1974.

209 *"Ford is an utter booby"*: Alam, 389.

209 *"Pride comes before a fall"*: Ibid., 391.

209 *He was much more preoccupied*: Ibid.

210 *"military understanding"*: "Shah Offers Plan for Indian Ocean," *New York Times*, September 29, 1974.

210 *"It was primarily used for university research"*: Maziar Baheri, "The Shah's Plan Was to Build Bombs," http://www.newstatesman.com, September 11, 2008.

210 *"I was resisting the efforts of American firms"*: Author interview with Dr. James Schlesinger, June 5, 2009.

211 *"Certainly, and sooner than is believed"*: Department of Defense, National Military Command Center, "Subject: Interview with the Shah," Message Center, June 24, 1974, National Security Archive.

211 *"I always suspected"*: Maziar Baheri, "The Shah's Plan Was to Build Bombs," http://www.newstatesman.com, September 11, 2008.

211 *"off the cuff"*: Department of Defense, National Military Command Center, "Subject: Shah's Alleged Statement on Nuclear Weapons," Message Center, June 25, 1974, National Security Archive.

211 *"At that time, reprocessing"*: William Burr, "A Brief History of U.S.-Iranian Nuclear Negotiations," *The Bulletin of the Atomic Scientists*, January/February 2009, Vol. 65, No. 1, p. 23.

211 *"If Iran were to seek a weapons capability"*: memorandum for Secretary of Defense, "Subject: Nuclear energy Cooperation With Iran (U)—Action Memorandum," June 22, 1974, National Security Archive.

211 *"I should make it meticulously clear"*: Michael Getler, "Long-Term Impact of Arms Sales to Persian Gulf Questioned," *Washington Post*, January 30, 1975.

211 *"By mid-1974, the shape and scope"*: Memorandum for Dr. Brzezinski, The White House, from Anthony Lake, National Security Council, "Attachment: One-Volume Compilation of Summaries of Documents Relating to the US-Iranian Relationship, 1941–79, January 29, 1980." The memorandum is included in the National Security Archive's collection of diplomatic documents, Eric Hoogland, project editor, *Iran: The Making of U.S. Policy, 1977–80*, National Security Archive (Alexandria, VA: Chadwyck-Healey, 1990). See Chapter 2, "Military/Security Issues," Document Reference No. 03558.

212 *"He was our baby, but now he has grown up"*: Jack Anderson, "Kissinger to Press Shah on Oil Costs," *Washington Post*, November 1, 1974.

212 *"The latest surge in oil revenues"*: Eric Hoogland, project editor, *Iran: The Making of U.S. Policy, 1977–80*, National Security Archive (Alexandria, VA: Chadwyck-Healey, 1990), Document Reference No. 00899.

212   *"The Shah's ambitious development program"*: Ibid., 2.

212   *"The cost of living in Iran"*: James F. Clarity, "Iran's Flood of Oil Money Aggravates Her Inflation," *New York Times*, October 7, 1974.

213   *a rash on his face*: Alam, 386.

213   *not responded to the French doctors' diagnosis*: Farah Pahlavi, *An Enduring Love: My Life with the Shah* (New York: Miramax, 2004), 251.

213   *"Medically, the patient was still in excellent shape"*: Farah Pahlavi, *An Enduring Love*, 252.

213   *"a very painful exercise"*: Alam, 388.

213   *$500 million project*: Seymour Hersh, "Iran Signs Rockwell Deal for Persian Gulf Spy Base," *New York Times*, June 1, 1975.

214   *According to one of the few published reports*: Seymour Hersh of *The New York Times* and Bob Woodward of *The Washington Post* provided the most detailed accounts of Ibex and the tensions it generated within the U.S. government and between the United States and Iran. Two articles by *Christian Science Monitor* reporters provide additional helpful insights. See Harry B. Ellis, "Behind 'Listening Post' Deal Closer U.S.-Iran Relations," *Christian Science Monitor*, June 5, 1975; Seymour Hersh, "Iran Signs Rockwell Deal for Persian Gulf Spy Base," *New York Times*, June 1, 1975; Dev Muraka, "Growing U.S. Ties to Iran Irk Kremlin," *Christian Science Monitor*, June 5, 1975; and Bob Woodward, "IBEX: Deadly Symbol of U.S. Arms Sales Problems," *Washington Post*, January 2, 1977.

214   *eleven ground monitoring posts*: Bob Woodward, "IBEX: Deadly Symbol of U.S. Arms Sales Problems," *Washington Post*, January 2, 1977.

214   *fifteen CIA employees*: Ibid.

214   *$50 million contract*: Seymour Hersh, "Iran Signs Rockwell Deal for Persian Gulf Spy Base," *New York Times*, June 1, 1975.

214   *the bidders were cautioned by the CIA*: Bob Woodward, "IBEX: Deadly Symbol of U.S. Arms Sales Problems," *Washington Post*, January 2, 1977.

214   *Rockwell hired Universal Aero Services Co. Ltd.*: Ibid.

214   *"the necessary marketing services"*: Ibid.

214   *On February 17, 1975*: Ibid.

214   *When he visited Andrews Air Force Base*: "Shah Visits Air Base and then Meets Schlesinger," *New York Times*, May 17, 1975.

214   *Toufanian, no stranger to intrigue*: For a comprehensive biography of General Toufanian's life, see Abbas Milani, *Eminent Persians: The Men and Women Who Made Modern Iran, 1941–79*, Vol. 1 (Syracuse: Syracuse University Press, 2008), 490–94.

215   *liable for the grand sum of $4,526,758*: Bob Woodward, "IBEX: Deadly Symbol of U.S. Arms Sales Problems," *Washington Post*, January 2, 1977.

215   *Chase Manhattan bank account in Geneva*: Ibid.

215   *the Ibex money trail*: As reported by Woodward, ibid. "It has become a standard

practice on 'covert' projects, such as Ibex, to hide or insulate some of the payments that go out to U.S. contractors," wrote Woodward. "This is done in the interests of secrecy. In the case of Ibex, letters of credit of more than $47 million were sent to Riggs [National Bank] by the Iranian government. Checks to contractors on the project were drawn following a series of complicated transactions involving the CIA and the Touche Ross Washington office." On one occasion, the Iranian government deposited a check for $5 million in Riggs National Bank in Washington "for payment on demand" by two men identified as CIA employees. A second time, former CIA employee Donald Patterson was paid a $55,000 commission to authorize payments of $1.1 million to the prominent auditing and accounting firm Touche Ross. His action in turn triggered "payments to U.S. defense contractors from another $47 million deposited at the Riggs bank by Iran." Touche Ross's contract included language that conveniently relieved the firm of "liability for any fraud, collusion, illegalities and malfeasance."

215   *shut out of Ibex:* Seymour Hersh, "Iran Signs Rockwell Deal for Persian Gulf Spy Base," *New York Times,* June 1, 1975.

215   *Office of Munitions:* Ibid.

215   *hire away former and:* Ibid.

215   *"amazed":* Ibid.

215   *"We can't say who the Shah's targets would be":* Ibid.

215   *front-page article:* Dev Muraka, "Growing U.S. Ties to Iran Irk Kremlin," *Christian Science Monitor,* June 5, 1975.

216   *"it will be built by Americans":* Ibid.

216   *climbed to 7.1 percent:* "The Economy: Trying to Turn It Around," *Time,* January 20, 1975.

216   *6.5 million unemployed:* "A World Out of Work," *Newsweek,* January 20, 1975.

216   *Ron and Jill Stuber:* The Stubers' story was reported in *The New York Times:* "U.S. Job Seekers Looking to Iran," *New York Times,* April 20, 1975.

216   *more than one hundred applications:* Ibid.

216   *"We are being flooded":* Ibid.

216   *seventeen thousand Americans were already living in Iran:* Director, Special Regional Studies, The Pentagon, "The Growing U.S. Involvement in Iran," January 22, 1975, National Security Archive.

216   *increase 20 percent a year:* Ibid.

216   *Sixty-eight percent of the incoming arrivals:* Ibid.

216   *"to provide advanced weapons systems":* Ibid.

216   *eighteen to thirty months:* Ibid.

217   *$6 billion in expenditure:* Ibid.

217   *eventually numbering fifty thousand:* Ibid.

217   *"Our ambition is to make as much of America":* Richard T. Sale, "The Shah's Americans," *Washington Post,* May 12, 1977.

217   *They worshipped at a Presbyterian church:* Director, Special Regional Studies, The Pentagon, "The Growing U.S. Involvement in Iran," January 22, 1975, National Security Archive.

217   *three exclusively American elementary and secondary schools:* Ibid.

217   *sixty school buses:* James A. Bill, *The Eagle and the Lion: The Tragedy of American-Iranian Relations* (New Haven: Yale University Press, 1988), 387.

217   *three football teams:* Ibid.

217   *the largest of its kind:* Ibid., 388.

217   *They preferred to buy their Coca-Cola:* Ibid.

217   *Georgetown University signed an $11 million contract:* "U.S. Job Seekers Looking to Iran," *New York Times*, April 20, 1975.

217   *George Washington University trained fifty-four Iranian army officers:* Ibid.

217   *Harvard accepted a $400,000 grant:* William Claiborne, "U.S. Colleges Help Plan Schools for Iran," *Washington Post*, April 9, 1975.

217   *New York's Columbia University accepted $361,000:* Ibid.

218   *"There are tons of dollars there":* Ibid.

218   *"We're spending so much money":* Alam, 524.

218   *Many of the government-to-government deals:* For a list of government-to-government contracts in 1974, see Director, Special Regional Studies, The Pentagon, "The Growing U.S. Involvement in Iran," January 22, 1975, National Security Archive, 12–13.

218   *U.S. defense contractors rushed to enter:* For a list of co-production contracts in 1974 see ibid., 21.

218   *"The major distributional change":* Ibid.

219   *"Many American families":* Ibid., 23.

219   *He liked to take his family:* William Lehfeldt's story of his family's drive into the countryside outside Kashan was included in an oral history interview. See FISOHA interview with William Lehfeldt, by William Burr, Foundation for Iranian Studies, Washington, D.C., April 29, 1987, February 9 and April 19, 1988, 3–139.

220   *The secretary of state assured the king:* Memorandum of Conversation, "King Faisal, Secretary Kissinger," Riyadh, October 13, 1974, National Security Archive.

220   *Kissinger was in Islamabad:* Memorandum of Conversation, "Bhutto, Kissinger," Prime Minister's Office, Islamabad, Pakistan, October 31, 1974, 1400–1530, National Security Archive.

223   *Kissinger was in Tehran:* Memorandum of Conversation, "Ansary, Kissinger," Saturday, November 2, 1974, 9:40 A.M.–10:35 A.M., Ministry of Economic Affairs and Finance, Tehran, Iran, Meeting of U.S.-Iran Joint Commission, National Security Archive. During the meeting Ansary recited a list of economic statistics to impress upon the Americans the great strides being made "under the dynamic leadership and initiative of His Imperial Majesty, the

Shahanshah." Iran expected "to pump $180 billion into the development of our country," and by 1983 Iran's gross national product would be $190 billion. Per capita income would reach $4,000 by that time. Industry would grow at a rate of 16–18 percent annually and agriculture by 7 percent. By 1983, "we hope we will produce one million cars a year, 3 million television sets a year, 3.2 million refrigerators a year . . . 400 million pairs of shoes, 15 million tons of steel and one million tons of aluminum." By 1983, every third Iranian household would have two cars and two telephones, and every family would have a television and refrigerator. The statistics were so fantastic as to be meaningless but that did not stop Kissinger from applauding the vision behind them, "Because you certainly think in big terms, and that is what the world needs right now."

223 *"Kissinger flew in this afternoon"*: Alam, 395.

224 *"hopeless old donkey"*: Ibid., 442.

224 *"that idiot Ford"*: Ibid., 440.

224 *"that Ford was so thick"*: Ibid., 486.

224 *"And one of the notions"*: Author interview with Brent Scowcroft, April 16, 2010.

225 *"the United States is now attempting"*: Murrey Marder, "Kissinger: Oil Price Cut Not Goal Now," *Washington Post*, November 3, 1974.

225 *"B-S," "F. Bull!"*: State Department Telegram, "Subj: Press Conference of Shah of Iran," November 2, 1974, National Security Archive.

225 *Kissinger was in the prime minister's residence*: Memorandum of Conversation, "Rabin, Peres, Kissinger," Thursday, November 7, 1974, 9:45–11:26 P.M., The Prime Minister's Residence, Jerusalem, National Security Archive.

227 Hawadess *published an interview*: Joseph Fitchett, "Shah Hints Policy Tilt to Arabs," *Washington Post*, December 13, 1974.

227 *"rushed to high officials"*: Rowland Evans and Robert Novak, "A Warning from the Shah," *Washington Post*, December 19, 1974.

227 *"is causing high-level consternation"*: Ibid.

228 *On Monday evening, December 23*: Memorandum of Conversation, "Kissinger, Dinitz," Monday, December 23, 1974, 6:45–7:45 P.M., The Secretary's Office, Department of State, National Security Archive.

228 *in December Kissinger and Zahedi agreed*: Telcon, "Kissinger-Zahedi," 8:48 A.M., December 10, 1974, National Security Archive.

CHAPTER EIGHT: POTOMAC SCHEHERAZADE
PAGE

229 *"You heard the Shah sold out the Kurds?"*: National Security Adviser: Kissinger Reports on USSR, China, and Middle East Discussions—Kissinger's Trip, Vol. I (2), Box 3, Gerald R. Ford Library.

229 *"Tehran continues to be"*: Memorandum of Conversation, The Secretary's Prin-

cipals and Regionals' Staff Meeting, July 7, 1975, 8:00 A.M., National Security Archive, 32–33.

229 *spot prices of $9.50 and $10 had been recorded:* Juan de Onis, "Arab Oil Exports Trail 1974's Pace," *New York Times,* March 1, 1975.

229 *from 30 million to 26 million barrels:* Ibid.

229 *$30 billion in spending commitments:* Harry B. Ellis, "Iran's Race to Modernize Before the Oil Runs Out," *Christian Science Monitor,* January 2, 1976.

229 *Iran was now running a giant deficit:* "Iranian Deficit Totals $4 Billion; Loans Asked," *Wall Street Journal,* July 28, 1975.

230 *"A sense of emergency engulfs Washington":* Harry B. Ellis, "Gloom Grips U.S. Economic Team," *Christian Science Monitor,* January 6, 1975.

230 *"other segments of the economy are collapsing":* Ibid.

230 *"the nation's output of goods and services declined":* "The Economy: Trying to Turn It Around," *Time,* January 20, 1975, 15.

230 *New car sales for December plummeted:* Ibid.

230 *Detroit automakers shed seventy thousand jobs:* "A World Out of Work," *Newsweek,* January 20, 1975, 34.

230 *"With few exceptions":* Ibid.

230 *"the base of our society":* U.S. Council of Economic Advisers, Box 19, "Greenspan, Alan—1975 (2), Memorandum for the Vice President, January 22, 1975, Gerald R. Ford Library.

231 *86 percent of Americans disapproved:* "The Economy: Trying to Turn It Around," *Time,* January 20, 1975, 15.

231 *"We are in trouble":* John Herbers, "Drastic Reversal," *New York Times,* January 14, 1975.

231 *an earnest conservative from Wyoming:* For a profile of Dick Cheney at this time, see Lou Cannon, "Stepping Out of Rumsfeld's Shadow," *Washington Post,* November 6, 1975.

231 *"They're like two peas in a pod":* Aldo Beckman, "Rumsfeld's Deputy O.K. with Ford," *Chicago Tribune,* July 21, 1975.

231 *"blitzkrieg":* Aldo Beckman, "Rise to Power Startling: Rumsfeld Puts 'Blitz' on White House," *Chicago Tribune,* March 23, 1975.

231 *"Mr. Rumsfeld has been accumulating power":* John Herbers, "Rumsfeld and Marsh Emerge as Key White House Powers," *New York Times,* January 12, 1975.

231 *"who his next Cabinet change might be":* Aldo Beckman, "Ford's Staff Chief: Don Rumsfeld Keeps Finding Room at the Top," *Chicago Tribune,* February 9, 1975.

231 *a man not known for his humility:* According to Kissinger: "Being junior to his colleagues did not crimp Enders's style, for humility was not one of his distinguishing characteristics": Henry Kissinger, *Years of Renewal* (New York: Simon & Schuster, 2000), 675.

232 *"That proposal set off the angriest debate"*: Rowland Evans and Robert Novak, "The Decisions at Vail," *Washington Post*, January 2, 1975.

232 *"would protect American domestic production"*: Memorandum of Conversation, Foreign Economic Policy, June 10, 1975, National Security Archive.

232 *President Ford was "irritated"*: Lou Cannon, "Simon Denies He Will Leave," *Washington Post*, January 17, 1975.

232 *"expected to leave the Cabinet soon"*: Ibid.

232 *"of a Wall Street bond trader"*: Joseph Kraft, "William Simon: On the Way Out?," *Washington Post*, January 14, 1975.

232 *rallied to provide Simon*: Lou Cannon, "Simon Denies He Will Leave," *Washington Post*, January 17, 1975.

232 *Arthur Burns also intervened*: Rowland Evans and Robert Novak, "The Campaign Against Simon," *Washington Post*, January 20, 1975.

233 *"I am the chief economic spokesman"*: Lou Cannon, "Simon Denies He Will Leave," *Washington Post*, January 17, 1975.

233 *"upsetting the established routine"*: FISOHA interview with James Schlesinger, by William Burr, Foundation for Iranian Studies, Washington, D.C., May 15 and June 27, 1986, 1–31.

233 *monetary reserves of $1.2 trillion*: Clifton Daniel, "Kissinger Remark on Force Sparks Wide Speculation," *New York Times*, January 7, 1975.

233 *"Let's try the low-cost option—war"*: Philip Shabecoff, "White House Declines to Add to Kissinger Remarks on Use of Force," *New York Times*, January 4, 1975.

233 *"a very dangerous course"*: Murrey Marder, "Kissinger: 'Use of Force' An Option," *Washington Post*, January 3, 1975. The *Post* article includes a full transcript of Kissinger's remarks to *BusinessWeek*.

233 Commentary *published a lengthy essay*: Robert W. Tucker, "Oil: The Issue of American Intervention," *Commentary*, Vol. 59, No. 1 (January 1975).

234 Harper's *published "Seizing Arab Oil"*: Miles Ignotus, "Seizing Arab Oil: The Case for U.S. Intervention: Why, How, Where," *Harper's* 250, no. 1498 (March 1975): 44–62.

234 *"Then there is Iran"*: Ibid., 60.

234 *"The Iranians could take Kuwait"*: Memorandum of Conversation, 9/5/73, folder "Kissinger, Schlesinger," Box 2, National Security Adviser, Gerald R. Ford Library.

234 *Department of Defense*: See Andrew Huggins, "Power and Peril: America's Supremacy and Its Limits," *Wall Street Journal*, February 4, 2004.

234 *developing contingency plans*: Andrew Marshall was appointed to the position of head of the Defense Department's Office of Net Assessment in 1973, the office responsible for developing military contingency plans, a post he has held ever since. He has been closely associated with the "neo-cons." Authorship of "Seizing Arab Oil" has been attributed over the years to Edward Luttwak,

a prominent defense consultant who in the mid-1970s worked for James Schlesinger. In an interview with the author in June 2009, he denied sole authorship of the article but confirmed that it was produced by Marshall's Office of Net Assessment, with which he was affiliated at the time. Luttwak has never denied "conveying" the article to *Harper's* editor Lewis Lapham for publication.

235   *"It has deeply shocked the upper echelons"*: John K. Cooley, "Who Wrote the Article: Oil Seizure Talk Irks U.S. Saudis," *Christian Science Monitor*, March 12, 1975.

235   *"Prince Fahd [of Saudi Arabia] asked me to convey"*: Memorandum of Conversation, 4/29/75, "Ford, Kissinger, Jordanian King Hussein," Box 11, National Security Adviser, Gerald R. Ford Library.

235   *"excessive" arms sales:* Michael Getler, "Arms Sales May Raise Oil Cost," *Washington Post*, April 28, 1974.

235   *"without national security studies"*: Michael Getler, "Long-Term Impact of Arms Sales to Persian Gulf Questioned," *Washington Post*, January 30, 1975.

236   *"has carried out a major National Security Council study"*: Ibid.

236   *"basically tactical"*: Ibid.

236   *"Also, at our instigation"*: Department of State Action Memorandum, To the Secretary, from Alfred A. Atherton, Jr., and Nelson F. Sievering, Jr., "Nuclear Energy Agreement for Cooperation with Iran," December 6, 1974, National Security Archive.

236   *half his nuclear power program:* Report of the NSSM 219 Working Group, Nuclear Cooperation Agreement with Iran, 1, National Security Archive.

236   *20 percent of a privately run:* Ibid.

236   *$1 billion in receipts:* Ibid.

237   *"obligated to place* all *its nuclear facilities"*: Emphasis in original. Department of State Action Memorandum, To the Secretary, from Alfred A. Atherton, Jr., and Nelson F. Sievering, Jr., "Nuclear Energy Agreement for Cooperation with Iran," December 6, 1974, National Security Archive.

237   *"could have serious"*: Report of the NSSM 219 Working Group, Nuclear Cooperation Agreement with Iran, National Security Archive.

237   *Shultz was ushered into the Oval Office:* For a transcript of the conversation, see Memorandum of Conversation, 2/7/75, "Ford, Kissinger, George Shultz," Box 9, National Security Adviser, Gerald R. Ford Library.

238   *"It was a tough issue"*: Author interview with Frank G. Zarb, June 11, 2009.

239   *described him as looking tanned:* Marilyn Berger, "Iran Oil Pledged to Israel," *Washington Post*, February 19, 1975.

239   *"Swiss police patrolled the airport"*: Ibid.

239   *"We have never boycotted anybody"*: Ibid.

240   *between $200 and $400 million:* Ibid.

240 *"The Iranian stuff is going well"*: Memorandum of Conversation, 3/4/75, "Ford, Kissinger," Box 4, National Security Adviser, Gerald R. Ford Library.

240 *"frightened of being assassinated"*: National Security Adviser: Kissinger Reports on USSR, China, and Middle East Discussions—Kissinger's Trip, Vol. I (2)," Box 3, Gerald R. Ford Library.

240 *"Why are all the flags up?"*: Ibid.

241 *four and a half hours*: Asadollah Alam, *The Shah and I: The Confidential Diary of Iran's Royal Court, 1969–1977* (New York: St. Martin's, 1991), 417.

241 *to allow Iranian Shi'a pilgrims*: FISOHA interview with Richard Helms by William Burr, Foundation for Iranian Studies, Washington, D.C., July 10 and 24, 1985, 1–34.

241 *the Kurds were losing ground*: Author interview with Ardeshir Zahedi, September 14–15, 2010.

241 *$16 million*: *The Pike Report* (Nottingham: Spokesman, 1977), 196.

241 *"acted in effect as a guarantor"*: Ibid.

241 *U.S. participation in the Kurdish operation*: Ibid.

242 *"[The Shah] has apparently used"*: Ibid., 214.

242 *"a uniquely useful tool"*: Ibid.

242 *The secretary of state insisted they continue*: Ibid., 197.

242 *"he trusted no other major power"*: Ibid., 212.

242 *"a gift of three rugs"*: Ibid.

242 *"As you are aware"*: Ibid., 213.

242 *"In the long run we believe Americans"*: For a full transcript of the Kissinger-Asad meeting, see National Security Adviser: Kissinger Reports on USSR, China, and Middle East Discussions—Kissinger's Trip, Vol. I (2), Box 3, Gerald R. Ford Library.

243 *a late working dinner with Prime Minister Yitzhak Rabin*: For a full transcript of the Kissinger-Rabin conversation, see Ibid.

244 *"There is confusion and dismay"*: *The Pike Report* (Nottingham: Spokesman, 1977), 215.

244 *"Is headquarters in touch with Kissinger's office"*: Ibid.

245 *"our hearts bleed"*: Ibid., 215–16.

245 *"No reply has been received"*: Ibid., 216.

245 *200,000 refugees*: Ibid., 217.

245 *"the United States Government refused to admit"*: Ibid.

245 *"It's like the wolf and the lamb"*: Memorandum of Conversation, 3/19/75, "Ford, Kissinger, Kuwaiti Ambassador Salem S. Al Sabah," Box 10, National Security Adviser, Gerald R. Ford Library.

246 *"People knew about Khomeini"*: FISOHA interview with Richard Helms by William Burr, Foundation for Iranian Studies, Washington, D.C., July 10 and 24, 1985, 1–34.

246   *As the king was greeting his guests:* The most vivid account of what happened that day comes from Yamani himself in an interview with biographer Jeffrey Robinson. Jeffrey Robinson, *Yamani: The Inside Story* (London: Simon & Schuster, 1988), 141–45.

246   *"mentally deranged":* Juan de Onis, "Saudis See Planning in the Assassination," *New York Times*, March 29, 1975.

247   *"An extraordinary conjunction of forces":* "Once Again, an Agonizing Reappraisal," *Time*, April 7, 1975.

247   *"Our Middle East policy":* Telcon, Kissinger-Fisher, 7:10 P.M., March 24, 1975, National Security Archive.

247   *"American foreign policy":* Joseph C. Harsch, "Kissinger and the Era of U.S. Pullback," *Christian Science Monitor*, March 28, 1975.

248   *Jackson wrote to Kissinger on March 22:* Rowland Evans and Robert Novak, "Kissinger and Jackson: The Feud Goes On," *Washington Post*, April 13, 1975.

248   *"Well, I think not, frankly":* Telcon, Kissinger-Javits, 2:20 P.M., May 8, 1975, National Security Archive.

248   *The ambassador was recalled from Tehran thirteen times:* Thomas Powers, *The Man Who Kept the Secrets* (New York: Alfred A. Knopf, 1979), 339.

248   *"In those days":* Richard Helms with William Hood, *A Look over My Shoulder: A Life in the Central Intelligence Agency* (New York: Ballantine, 2003), 436.

249   *"You sonofabitch!":* Powers, 339.

249   *an extensive briefing paper from his secretary of state:* Memorandum to President Ford from Secretary of State Henry Kissinger, "Strategy for Your Discussions with the Shah of Iran," May 13, 1975, Eric Hoogland, project editor, *Iran: The Making of U.S. Policy, 1977–80*, National Security Archive (Alexandria, VA: Chadwyck-Healey, 1990), Document Reference No. 00955.

250   *"Tell him you used more force than necessary":* For a transcript of the Ford-Kissinger conversation, see Memorandum of Conversation, 5/15/75, "Ford, Kissinger," Box 11, National Security Adviser, Gerald R. Ford Library.

251   *The Fords welcomed the Pahlavis:* Martha M. Hamilton, "President Greets Shah as 300 Picket in Park," *Washington Post*, May 16, 1975.

251   *Brent Scowcroft took notes:* Memorandum of Conversation, 5/15/75, "Ford, Kissinger, Iranian Shah Mohammad Reza Pahlavi," Box 11, National Security Adviser, Gerald R. Ford Library.

252   *"We picked her because the Shah":* Donnie Radcliffe and Jeanette Smyth, "Ford Dancing into the Night After Words of Praise from the Shah," *Washington Post*, May 16, 1975.

252   *"The Air Force String Players":* Cynthia Helms, *An Ambassador's Wife in Iran* (New York: Dodd, Mead, 1981), 184.

252   *"Shahbunny":* Sally Quinn, "Iranian Nights and Washington Daze," *Washington Post*, May 19, 1975.

252 *fixtures of the Washington establishment:* For a guest list of attendees to the Fords' state dinner for the Pahlavis, see *The Washington Post*, May 16, 1975, B1.

252 *The Shah was back in the Oval Office:* For a transcript of the conversation, see Memorandum of Conversation, 5/16/75, "Ford, Kissinger, Iranian Shah Mohammad Reza Pahlavi," Box 11, National Security Adviser, Gerald R. Ford Library.

253 *The Shah had spent the day at Andrews Air Force Base:* "Shah Visits Air Base and Then Meets Schlesinger," *New York Times*, May 17, 1975.

254 *"He posed for photographs":* Sally Quinn, "Iranian Nights and Washington Daze," *Washington Post*, May 19, 1975.

254 *It was the largest U.S. flag contributor:* L. William Seidman Economic Files (White House Economic Affairs Office), "Letter from O. Roy Chalk to President Ford," February 13, 1975, Airlines—Iranian Investment in Pan Am (1)-(4), Box 38, Gerald R. Ford Libary.

254 *"We have lost 30 to 35 percent":* Marilyn Berger, "New Oil Price Rise Expected by Shah," *Washington Post*, May 18, 1975.

254 *30–35 percent oil price increase:* "Iran Says Oil Prices Must Rise 30%–35% to Offset Inflation," *Wall Street Journal*, June 6, 1975.

254 *"America Bows Low as the Shah Pays a Visit":* Joseph Kraft, "America Bows Low as the Shah Pays a Visit," *Washington Post*, May 22, 1975.

255 *Each morning a car with an Iranian driver:* The most detailed account of the murders of Colonels Shaffer and Turner appeared in *The Washington Post*. See Andrew Borowiec, "U.S. Men Killed in Ambush," *Washington Post*, May 27, 1975.

255 *upward of two hundred:* Ibid.

255 *two government officials had been assassinated:* "Terrorist Violence, Triggered by Widespread Dissidence Among Young, Appears to Be Rising in Iran," *New York Times*, May 22, 1975.

255 *nine young detainees shot in Evin prison:* Andrew Borowiec, "U.S. Men Killed in Ambush," *Washington Post*, May 27, 1975.

255 *"A car blocked the path of their vehicle":* Ibid.

256 *the bombing of the American cultural center:* Andrew Borowiec, "Moslem Fundamentalists Fight Shah's Reforms," *Washington Post*, June 24, 1975.

256 *The attack on the colonels' car was in revenge:* Andrew Borowiec, "U.S. Men Killed in Ambush," *Washington Post*, May 27, 1975.

256 *"There was concern on my part":* FISOHA interview with Richard Helms, by William Burr, Foundation for Iranian Studies, Washington, D.C., July 10 and 24, 1985, 2–71.

256 *"I did away with the Peace Corps":* Ibid. For a discussion of the positive role played by the Peace Corps in Iran, see Bill, *The Eagle and the Lion*, 380.

256 *ten Americans managed 142 volunteers:* Director, Special Regional Studies, The

Pentagon, "The Growing U.S. Involvement in Iran," January 22, 1975, National Security Archive.

256 *fifty retired military personnel:* Memorandum for the President, "Subject: DOD Activities and Interests in Iran," The Secretary of Defense, May 17, 1975, National Security Archive.

256 *"strolled into the ancient Friday Mosque":* Bill, *The Eagle and the Lion,* 380. Sandra Mackey recounted the same incidents in her book. See Sandra Mackey, *The Iranians: Persia, Islam and the Soul of a Nation* (New York: Penguin, 1988), 252.

256 *"passed the time by drinking, fighting":* Eric Pace, "U.S. Influence on Iran: Gigantic and Diverse," *New York Times,* August 30, 1976.

257 *accosted by American men in the streets:* Bill, *The Eagle and the Lion,* 382.

257 *American defense contractors:* Author interview with Henry Precht, June 4, 2009.

257 *An Iranian taxi driver was shot:* Bill, *The Eagle and the Lion,* 380.

257 *"sand-niggers," "ragheads," and "stinkies":* Ibid., 381.

257 *"Americans are desecrating mosques":* Andrew Borowiec, "Moslem Fundamentalists Fight Shah's Reforms," *Washington Post,* June 24, 1975.

257 *"That's where Nixon and Kissinger went wrong":* FISOHA interview with Armin Meyer, by William Burr, Foundation for Iranian Studies, Washington, D.C., March 29, 1985, 1–50.

257 *"a disaster area":* Author interview with Dr. James Schlesinger, June 5, 2009.

257 *set up a hot line:* Ronald L. Soble, "Jobs Abroad: Can Promise Meet Reality?" *Los Angeles Times,* June 1, 1976.

257 *rampant drug use:* Ibid.

257 *offering its employees classes in Farsi:* Ibid.

257 *"Companies started sending workers to Iran too fast":* Ibid.

257 *The helicopter pilots employed by Bell:* "U.S. Arms Sales to Iran," *Middle East Research and Project Information* 51 (October 1976): 15–18.

258 *SAVAK informers:* Ibid.

258 *Ambassador Helms refused to meet with the pilots:* Ibid.

258 *"much the same as migrant workers":* Ibid.

258 *the driver of a U.S. embassy car:* Andrew Borowiec, "Shah Cracks Political Whip," *Washington Post,* August 11, 1975.

258 *"Well, in addition to Beirut":* Memorandum of Conversation, The Secretary's Principals' and Regionals' Staff Meeting, Monday, July 7, 1975, 8:00 A.M., National Security Archive, 32–33.

CHAPTER NINE: HENRY'S WARS
PAGE

259 *"Greenspan is terribly worried":* Memorandum of Conversation, 6/12/75, "Ford, Kissinger," Box 12, National Security Adviser, Gerald R. Ford Library.

259 *"The Shah is seeing French doctors"*: Author interview with Henry Precht, June 4, 2009.

260 *"all our economists"*: Memorandum of Conversation, 5/29/75, "Ford, Kissinger, FRG Chancellor Helmut Schmidt," Box 12, National Security Adviser, Gerald R. Ford Library.

261 *Schmidt and Ford met again:* Memorandum of Conversation, 7/27–28/75, "Ford, Kissinger, FRG Chancellor Helmut Schmidt, Foreign Minister Hans-Dietrich Genscher," Box 14, National Security Adviser, Gerald R. Ford Library.

261 *84.9 million barrels a day to 64.9 million barrels:* "Drastic Falls in Kuwait and Saudi Oil Output," *The Times* (London), May 20, 1975.

261 *slid 12 percent, to 5.4 million barrels:* "Iran Indicates It Will Press for Big Boost in Petroleum Price at Next OPEC Session," *Wall Street Journal*, September 9, 1975.

261 *17.7 percent:* John K. Cooley, "Budget Deficit Troubles Iran," *Christian Science Monitor,* July 31, 1975.

261 *8.1 million barrels a day:* "Iran Indicates It Will Press for Big Boost in Petroleum Price at Next OPEC Session," *Wall Street Journal*, September 9, 1975.

261 *27 percent in Kuwait and 41 percent in Libya:* Ibid.

262 *"economic path toward":* Hossein Razavi and Firouz Vakil, *The Political Environment of Economic Planning in Iran, 1971–1983: From Monarchy to Islamic Republic* (Boulder: Westview, 1984), 80.

262 *"By 1975 the economy was out of control":* Ibid., 83.

262 *on average 250 days:* Joe Alex Morris Jr., "Is It for Real: New Broom Stirs Lots of Dust in Iran," *Los Angeles Times*, October 7, 1977.

262 *a backlog of 800,000 tons of goods:* Harry B. Ellis, "Iran's Race to Modernize Before the Oil Runs Out," *Christian Science Monitor,* January 2, 1976.

262 *10 percent of the machinery:* Ibid.

262 *$2 billion in demurrage:* Joe Alex Morris Jr., "Is It for Real: New Broom Stirs Lots of Dust in Iran," *Los Angeles Times*, October 7, 1977.

262 *"eventually turned up in a warehouse":* Cynthia Helms, *An Ambassador's Wife in Iran* (New York: Dodd, Mead, 1981), 176.

262 *four thousand trucks:* Asadollah Alam, *The Shah and I: The Confidential Diary of Iran's Royal Court, 1969–1977* (New York: St. Martin's, 1991), 464.

262 *"The highways are choked":* "Confidential: Cable from Ambassador Helms to Department of State," August 4, 1975, National Security Archive.

262 *"The government had to scour":* Ibid.

262 *"During the summer of 1975":* Cynthia Helms, 173.

263 *A female World Bank employee:* Ibid., 172.

263 *Embassy Tehran conducted an evaluation:* "Confidential: Cable from Ambassador Helms to Department of State," August 4, 1975, National Security Archive.

264 *"history provides discouraging precedents":* Ibid.

264   *seminary students in Qum:* For a scholarly analysis of the 1975 unrest in Qum and its connection to the Islamic Revolution of 1978–79, see Charles Kurzman, "The Qum Protests and the Coming of the Iranian Revolution, 1975 and 1978," *Social Science* 27, no. 3 (Fall 2003): 287–325.

264   *"like a harlot":* Andrew Borowiec, "Moslem Fundamentalists Fight Shah's Reforms," *Washington Post*, June 24, 1975.

264   *halting spending:* "Drop in Oil Revenue Cited," *New York Times*, June 17, 1975.

264   *$10 billion shortfall in income:* Ibid.

264   *77 percent capacity:* Eric Pace, "Iran, Despite Her Oil Wealth, Is Borrowing on a Grand Scale," *New York Times*, August 15, 1975.

264   *Iranian banks were forced:* Ibid.

264   *"Our revenues have dwindled considerably":* Eric Pace, "Iran Is Exhorted to Develop Thrift," *New York Times*, May 28, 1975.

264   *The Shah's decision three months earlier:* To learn more about the Shah's decision to declare a one-party state in Iran in March 1975 and for more of his views on democracy and pluralism, the following references are helpful: Ervand Abrahamian, *A History of Modern Iran* (Cambridge: Cambridge University Press, 2008), Chapter 5, 149–54; Gholam Reza Afkhami, *The Life and Times of the Shah* (Berkeley: University of California Press, 2009), Chapter 19, 423–40; Ali M. Ansari, *Modern Iran Since 1921: The Pahlavis and After* (London: Longman, 2003), Chapter 7, 185–87; Abbas Milani, *The Persian Sphinx: Amir Abbas Hoveyda and the Riddle of the Iranian Revolution* (Washington, D.C.: Mage, 2004), Chapter 13, 274–80; and Amin Saikal, *The Rise and Fall of the Shah: Iran from Autocracy to Religious Rule* (Princeton: Princeton University Press, 1980), Chapter 8, 188–91.

265   *"there are vague signs":* Letter from the Embassy in Iran to the Country Director for Iran (Miklos), October 30, 1972, *Foreign Relations of the United States (FRUS) 1969–76*, Vol. E-4.

265   *the declaration of a one-party state:* "1-Party State Declared in Iran," *Washington Post*, March 3, 1975.

265   *"Press reports to the contrary":* Cable from Ambassador Helms to the Department of State, "The Iranian One-Party State," July 10, 1975, National Security Archive.

265   *"You knew the Shah before":* Memorandum of Conversation, "Kennedy, Kissinger," June 10, 1975, 5:30 P.M., Secretary's Office, National Security Archive.

267   *"just for your information":* Telcon, "Kissinger-Kraft," 10:43 A.M., February 21, 1975, National Security Archive.

267   *White House Economic Policy Board:* To learn more about how Ford's Economic Policy Board functioned, the following article is helpful: Philip Shabecoff, "President Ford's Economic Policy Machine," *New York Times*, July 20, 1975.

267 *attacked as "false"*: Harry B. Ellis, "Simon Challenges Shah on Oil Prices," *Christian Science Monitor*, May 27, 1975.

267 *"for political blackmail"*: Nick Thimmesch, "What Simon Says About the Shah of Iran," *Chicago Tribune*, June 5, 1975.

267 *"Secretary Simon is not bashful"*: Ibid.

268 *In the Oval Office on June 12*: Memorandum of Conversation, 6/12/75, "Ford, Kissinger," Box 12, National Security Adviser, Gerard R. Ford Library.

268 *"cannot understand why"*: Jack Anderson, "Whatever the Shah Wants?," *Washington Post*, June 22, 1975.

268 *"We definitely do not want"*: Memorandum of Conversation, "Kissinger, Zarb, Greenspan, Robinson, Gompert," June 23, 1975, 12:45–2:00 P.M., "Bilateral Oil Deal with Iran," National Security Archive.

270 *"additional supplies of oil"*: Alam, 427.

270 *"These aren't exactly"*: Ibid.

270 *"Behind the scenes"*: Jack Anderson and Les Whitten, "U.S. Aides Demolish the Shah's Arguments," *Washington Post*, June 27, 1975.

270 *"Jack Anderson called me last week"*: Telcon, "Kissinger-Simon," 3:18 P.M., June 27, 1975, National Security Archive.

270 *"They are small timers"*: Telcon, 5:45 P.M., August 13, 1975, "Kissinger-Robinson," National Security Archive.

270 *"There isn't a brain between the two of them"*: Telcon, August 15, 1975, "Kissinger, Robinson, Bremer," National Security Archive.

270 *"The Shah is a tough cookie"*: Memorandum of Conversation, June 23, 1975, 12:45–2:00 P.M., "Bilateral Oil Deal with Iran," National Security Archive.

271 *"They [the Israelis] want reimbursement"*: Memorandum of Conversation, 7/5/75, "Ford, Kissinger," Box 13, National Security Adviser, Gerald R. Ford Library.

271 *"CIA Finds Shah Insecure"*: Jack Anderson and Les Whitten, "CIA Study Finds Shah Insecure," *Washington Post*, July 11, 1975.

271 *"would not allow the column to be circulated"*: Jack Anderson, "The Shah's Connections," *Washington Post*, November 27, 1977.

272 *preventing his officials from reading CIA analyses*: Ibid.

272 *"I think you should just go ahead"*: Telcon, 12:30 P.M., July 14, 1975, "Kissinger, Zarb, Greenspan, Robinson, Scowcroft, Covey," National Security Archive.

273 *"Iran May Be Spending Beyond Means"*: Jack Anderson and Les Whitten, "Iran May Be Spending Beyond Means," *Washington Post*, July 31, 1975.

273 *President Ford received Prime Minister Takeo Miki*: Memorandum of Conversation, 8/6/75, "Ford, Kissinger, Miki," Box 14, National Security Adviser, Gerald R. Ford Library.

273 *73 percent of its oil*: Ibid.

274 *"Zarb and Greenspan are dragging their feet"*: Memorandum of Conversation,

8/7/75, "Ford, Kissinger," Box 14, National Security Adviser, Gerald R. Ford Library.

274 *"was paralyzed because of the hostility":* Author interview with General Brent Scowcroft, April 6, 2010.

274 *"very much disappointed":* Alam, 434.

275 *the Shah received a Saudi delegation:* Eric Hooglund, project editor, *Iran: The Making of U.S. Policy, 1977–80,* National Security Archive (Alexandria, VA: Chadwyck-Healey, 1990), Document Reference No. 00988.

275 *intended to replace him:* Linda Charlton, "U.S. Will Replace Envoy to Saudis in Big Shuffle," *New York Times,* August 21, 1975.

275 *"How was our Pro-consul there?":* Memorandum of Conversation, "Kennedy, Kissinger," June 10, 1975, 5:30 P.M., Secretary's Office, National Security Archive.

275 *"Although the Saudis":* Jack Anderson and Les Whitten, "U.S. Didn't Press Shah on Oil Prices," *Washington Post,* September 21, 1976.

275 *"the Shah of Iran for an armed invasion":* Jack Anderson and Les Whitten, "Saudis Suspect an Iran-U.S. Plot," *Washington Post,* September 17, 1976.

276 *"from what we know":* Eric Hooglund, project editor, *Iran: The Making of U.S. Policy, 1977–80,* National Security Archive (Alexandria, VA: Chadwyck-Healey, 1990), Document Reference No. 00988.

276 *declared before the Iranian parliament:* "Iran Indicates It Will Press for Big Boost in Petroleum Price at Next OPEC Session," *Wall Street Journal,* September 9, 1975.

276 *"I have read of some conversations":* Telcon, September 2, 1975, "Oil Price Increase and the Producer-Consumer Dialogue," National Security Archive.

277 *He wrote a "strictly personal" letter:* Jack Anderson and Les Whitten, "U.S. Didn't Press Shah on Oil Prices," *Washington Post,* September 21, 1976.

277 *six-page memo to the president:* Ibid.

277 *"could raise serious questions":* Alam, 438.

277 *"Have you seen the letter":* Ibid., 440.

278 *"I also appreciate very much":* Ibid., 438–39.

278 *"But why on earth":* Ibid., 442.

278 *10 percent increase in price:* "Oil-Price Boost of 10% Is Voted by OPEC Cartel," *Wall Street Journal,* September 29, 1975.

278 *"very happy":* "OPEC, Despite Pressure, Sticks Together," *New York Times,* September 29, 1975.

278 *"the walkout was also calculated":* Ibid.

278 *"can only be regarded by the Saudis":* Alam, 445.

279 *"Aide Denies Shah of Iran Is Ill":* Albin Krebs, "Aide Denies Shah Is Ill," *New York Times,* September 23, 1975.

279 *"The Shah is seeing French doctors":* Author interview with Henry Precht, June 4, 2009.

279   *he ruminated with at least one former colleague:* Author interview with General Brent Scowcroft, April 6, 2010.

279   *"I know that he lied to me about it":* FISOHA interview with Richard Helms, by William Burr, Foundation for Iranian Studies, Washington, D.C., July 10 and 24, 1985, 1–25.

281   *"We can anticipate":* Report of the NSSM 219 Working Group, Nuclear Co-operation Agreement with Iran, National Security Archive, 3.

281   *"potentially conflicting goals":* Memorandum for the Assistant to the President for National Security Affairs, Subject: Department of State Response to NSSM 219 (Nuclear Cooperation with Iran), April 18, 1975, National Security Archive, 1.

281   *"some are concerned":* Report of the NSSM 219 Working Group, Nuclear Cooperation Agreement with Iran, National Security Archive, 4.

281   *"fuel cycle capabilities":* Ibid., 4.

281   *"multinational plant":* Memorandum for the Assistant to the President for National Security Affairs, "Subject: Department of State Response to NSSM 19 (Nuclear Cooperation with Iran)," April 18, 1975, National Security Archive.

281   *"Iran has no dearth":* Telegram from Jack Miklos, Embassy Tehran, to the State Department, Washington, July 17, 1975, National Security Archive.

282   *"The Iranians recognize and resent":* Telegram from Ambassador Richard Helms, Embassy Tehran, to Joint Chiefs of Staff, Department of Defense, November 26, 1975, National Security Archive.

282   *"We recognize the importance":* Memorandum for the Assistant to the President for National Security Affairs, Subject: Nuclear Cooperation Agreement with Iran: NSSM 219 (C), The Secretary of Defense, April 25, 1975, National Security Archive.

282   *"I don't recall that I had any direct briefings":* FISOHA interview with James Schlesinger, by William Burr, Foundation for Iranian Studies, Washington, D.C., May 15 and June 27, 1986, 1–15.

283   *"I could not control it":* Ibid., 1–35.

283   *"I urged the Shah":* Ibid., 1–11.

283   *Schlesinger never learned about this directive:* Author interview with Dr. James Schlesinger, June 5, 2009.

283   *"is not correct or consistent":* Martin R. Hoffman Papers, "Memo for Mr. Schlesinger, June 19, 1975," Iran—Richard Hallock, 1974–76 (1)-(2), Gerald R. Ford Library.

284   *$20 million over five years:* Pranay Gupte, "Lobbyists in Iran Paid by Grumman," *New York Times,* December 13, 1975.

284   *"It was normal practice":* Ibid.

284   *Members of Congress demanded to know:* Ibid.

284   *second $200 million loan offered:* Ibid.

284   *an audit prepared by Northrop Corporation's accounting firm:* Ibid.

284 *$200 million in kickbacks:* Michael C. Jensen, "Bribes by Northrop of $450,000 for 2 Saudi Generals Reported," *New York Times,* June 5, 1975.

284 *Prominent among the "sales agents":* William H. Jones, "Northrop's Man in the Middle East," *Washington Post,* June 7, 1975.

284 *leveraged his background in intelligence:* David Binder, "Northrop Cites Undercover Role," *New York Times,* June 7, 1975.

284 *"running close to a billion dollars":* Ibid.

284 *"old personal friend":* Ibid.

284 *"The Shah could not have been more cordial personally":* Ibid.

284 *Roosevelt to ask the Shah to lobby:* Gaylord Shaw, "Senate Unit Tells of More Northrop Payoffs Abroad," *Los Angeles Times,* June 7, 1975.

285 *paid $2,697,067:* Martin R. Hoffman Papers, Directorate for Defense Information Press Division, "Query from Vern Guidry, *Washington Star,* May 28, 1976," Iran—Richard Hallock, 1974–76 (1)-(2), Gerald R. Ford Library.

285 *Hallock casually asked Schlesinger:* FISOHA interview with James Schlesinger, by William Burr, Foundation for Iranian Studies, Washington, D.C., May 15 and June 27, 1986, 1–42.

285 *"I simply told him it was totally unacceptable":* Ibid.

285 *Hallock's son had reportedly fallen ill:* Ibid., 1–43.

285 *"a multi-million dollar contract":* Barry Rubin, *Paved with Good Intention: The American Experience and Iran* (New York: Oxford University Press, 1980), 165.

285 *General Toufanian paid him a handsome cash settlement:* FISOHA interview with William Lehfeldt, by William Burr, Foundation for Iranian Studies, Washington, D.C., April 29, 1987, February 9 and April 19, 1988, 3–151. This charge was repeated to the author on background by a second former U.S. official who knew Hallock in Tehran.

285 *Thirty-five years later:* To this author, Dr. Schlesinger described Hallock's behavior with evident distaste as "kind of a total personal transformation. . . . He saw temptation and he could not resist it." Schlesinger added: "From what I gather [Hallock] did not give advice on cost-effective decisions but he may have given decisions on how to make cost-ineffective decisions. I kind of washed my hands of Dick when these issues about him surfaced. I must say that was a great personal disappointment. This was a fellow who was a good budgeteer, analyst, and suddenly if I want to believe what I hear was feathering his own nest." Author interview with Dr. James Schlesinger, June 5, 2009.

285 *"Spiro Agnew passed through":* Alam, 416.

285 *"was acquitted of any wrong-doing":* Alam., 469.

286 *"I have a paper on Iran and its problems":* Memorandum of Conversation, 9/2/75, "Ford, Schlesinger," Box 15, National Security Adviser, Gerald R. Ford Library.

286 *American population:* In his presentation to Ford, Schlesinger cites the number of Americans in Iran at 100,000. This number was too high. Schlesinger was

most likely referring to the total number of Americans in the Persian Gulf, not in Iran. Either that or Scowcroft, the note taker, misheard the original estimate and transcribed the wrong number.

286 *on October 10, Ford told Schlesinger:* Memorandum for Dr. Brzezinski, the White House, from Anthony Lake, National Security Council, "Attachment: One-Volume Compilation of Summaries of Documents Relating to the US-Iranian Relationship, 1941–79, January 29, 1980." See the National Security Archive's collection of diplomatic documents entitled Eric Hooglund, project editor, *Iran: The Making of U.S. Policy, 1977–80,* National Security Archive (Alexandria, VA: Chadwyck-Healey, 1990), Document 03555.

286 *$10 billion in U.S. weapons:* Memorandum for the President, "DOD Activities and Interests in Iran," May 19, 1975, National Security Archive. The archive had stamped a date of May 19, 1975, on the document, which may be a draft version of the one that went to the president's desk. But there is little doubt that this same document was the one that Schlesinger presented to President Ford on September 2, 1975.

286 *"the specter of severe management problems downstream":* Ibid.

286 *"Frankly, the U.S. itself":* Ibid.

287 *"Well, I had considerable concerns about it":* FISOHA interview with James Schlesinger, by William Burr, Foundation for Iranian Studies, Washington, D.C., May 15 and June 27, 1986, 1–11.

287 *[Alexis] de Tocqueville:* Alexis de Tocqueville, *The Ancien Régime and the Revolution* (New York: Penguin, 2008). Dr. Schlesinger confirmed his concerns in an interview with the author on June 5, 2009. As a student of history, Schlesinger was familiar with the writings of Tocqueville, the nineteenth-century French historian who had studied the origins of the French Revolution. He was also influenced by the work of Harvard historian Ernest May, whose seminal book, *Lessons of the Past,* was published in 1973. May used the examples of the American experience in World War II, the start of the Cold War, the Korean War, and escalation in Vietnam to warn policy makers that they "ordinarily use history badly." He cautioned officials in Washington not to assume that patterns of history were repeating themselves but to "free themselves from the analogies, parallels, or trend-readings which they might otherwise unthinkingly apply." Be imaginative, he urged, and be more discriminating. Avoid the history trap—avoid future Vietnams. Schlesinger took it to heart. Schlesinger did not raise Tocqueville when he met privately with the Shah in 1973 and then again in 1975 "because that was the kind of thing that is likely to have irritated him. And I felt the irritation unnecessary. But I stressed what was the substantive point about trained people. It did not—it affected his course of action somewhat, but not significantly, as we can see in retrospect."

288 *Zahedi informed the Shah:* Abbas Milani, *The Shah* (New York: Palgrave Macmillan, 2011), 331.

288 *"I hate to bring this up"*: Memorandum of Conversation, 10/2/75, "Ford, Kissinger," Box 15, National Security Adviser, Gerald R. Ford Library.

288 *known to history as the "Halloween Massacre"*: To learn more about the events of November 1975, the following newspaper and magazine articles provide a helpful context and a wealth of details: "Ford's Big Shuffle," *Newsweek*, November 17, 1975; "Ford's Costly Purge," *Time*, November 17, 1975; Lou Cannon, "Rumsfeld: Silent Architect," *Washington Post*, November 4, 1975; John W. Finney, "Ex-Pentagon Chief Met with President Sunday," *New York Times*, November 4, 1975; Leslie H. Gelb, "Ford Discharges Schlesinger and Colby and Asks Kissinger to Give Up His Security Post," *New York Times*, November 3, 1975; Nicholas M. Harrock, "General Graham Is Said to Have Quit as the Chief of Defense Intelligence," *New York Times*, November 4, 1975; and George C. Wilson, "Schlesinger-Kissinger Schism Deep," *Washington Post*, November 4, 1975.

289 *"shocked"*: Christopher Lydon, "Reagan Shocked at Schlesinger Ouster," *New York Times*, November 4, 1975.

289 *"The guy that cut me up"*: Telcon, 2:35 P.M., November 3, 1975, "Kissinger-Simon," National Security Archive.

289 *On December 22, Kissinger telephoned Robert Ellsworth:* Telcon, 5:20 P.M., December 22, 1975, "Kissinger-Ellsworth," National Security Archive.

CHAPTER TEN: THE SPIRIT OF '76

PAGE

291 *"I genuinely fear"*: Asadollah Alam, *The Shah and I: The Confidential Diary of Iran's Royal Court, 1969–1977* (New York: St. Martin's, 1991), 464.

291 *"The dilemma we are in"*: Memorandum of Conversation, 7/9/76, "Ford, Kissinger, Saudi Deputy Prime Minister Abdallah bin Abd al-Aziz-Saud," Box 20, National Security Adviser, Gerald R. Ford Library.

291 *"peaceful nuclear explosions"*: Department of Defense Cable 0508432, "Iranian Nuclear Policy," January 5, 1976, National Security Archive.

291 *Iran would not allow foreign governments:* Ibid.

292 *a hundred nuclear power plants:* Thomas O'Toole, "S. Africa Set to Sell Iran Uranium Ore," *Washington Post*, October 12, 1975.

292 *occupied territory of Namibia:* From Embassy Tehran, Department of State Airgram, Subject: The Atomic Energy Organization of Iran, April 15, 1976, National Security Archive, 15.

292 *"This story has been denied publicly"*: Ibid.

292 *"seeking foreign—including American"*: Telegram from Ambassador Richard Helms, Embassy Tehran, to Joint Chiefs of Staff, Department of Defense, November 26, 1975, National Security Archive.

292 *On January 12, a tetchy Henry Kissinger:* For a complete transcript of the Janu-

ary 12, 1976, meeting, see Secretary's Staff Meeting, Memorandum of Proceedings, January 12, 1976, 8:11 A.M., National Security Archive.

293 *another big price increase:* "Shah Threatens Oil Price Rise," *Washington Post,* January 18, 1976.

294 *Two days later:* Secretary's Staff Meeting, Memorandum of Proceedings, January 14, 1976, 8:00 A.M., National Security Archive.

294 *On January 19, Defense Secretary Rumsfeld hosted General Toufanian:* There are three independent sources to confirm the account of Rumsfeld's confrontation with General Toufanian. Their standoff occurred on January 19, 1976. On January 30, newspaper columnists Rowland Evans and Robert Novak devoted a column to it: Rowland Evans and Robert Novak, "The Troubles of the Arms Merchant," *Washington Post,* January 27, 1976. See also John W. Finney, "Iran May Reduce Arms Buying," *Washington Post,* February 4, 1976. A more detailed account of the quarrel was published in 1977 in a feature article in *The Washington Post*: Richard T. Sale, "Arms Quarrels Strain U.S.-Iran Ties," *Washington Post,* May 13, 1977.

294 *"uninformed . . . not his own man":* Ibid.

294 *"Yeah, but the price of your oil has tripled":* John W. Finney, "Iran May Reduce Arms Buying," *Washington Post,* February 4, 1976.

294 *Toufanian wrote a scathing assessment of Rumsfeld:* Bob Woodward, "IBEX: Deadly Symbol of U.S. Arms Sales Problems," *Washington Post,* January 2, 1977.

294 *"It's raw, it's awfully raw":* Richard T. Sale, "Arms Quarrels Strain U.S.-Iran Ties," *Washington Post,* May 13, 1977.

294 *"Attempting to bully Rumsfeld":* Rowland Evans and Robert Novak, "The Troubles of the Arms Merchant," *Washington Post,* January 27, 1976.

295 *"Nothing good would happen":* Bob Woodward, "IBEX: Deadly Symbol of U.S. Arms Sales Problems," *Washington Post,* January 2, 1977.

295 *"I genuinely fear . . .":* Alam, 464.

295 *"was stalling":* Cable 018839 from Deputy Secretary of State Sisco to Secretary Kissinger, "Oil Agreement with Iran," January 24, 1976, L. William Seidman Files (WH Economic Affairs Office), Scowcroft, Brent (White House National Security Adviser), (1)-(2), Gerald R. Ford Library.

295 *"The bastards have thrown down":* Alam, 459.

295 *plunged by 1.7 million barrels:* Ibid.

295 *$6 billion shortfall:* Ibid.

296 *reached an "understanding":* Cable 018839 from Deputy Secretary of State Sisco to Secretary Kissinger, "Oil Agreement with Iran," January 24, 1976, L. William Seidman Files (WH Economic Affairs Office), Scowcroft, Brent (White House National Security Adviser), (1)-(2), Gerald R. Ford Library.

296 *on January 30, Ansary telephoned Kissinger:* Telcon, "Kissinger-Ansary," 3:30 P.M., January 30, 1976, National Security Archive.

296 *436,000-strong armed forces:* Memorandum for the President, "DOD Activities and Interests in Iran," May 19, 1975, National Security Archive.

296 *"If you try to take an unfriendly attitude":* "U.S. Is Warned by the Shah Against Cutting Arms Flow," *New York Times,* March 15, 1976.

297 *Kissinger signed a presidential memo:* Memorandum from Henry A. Kissinger to the President, "Message for the Shah of Iran," February 11, 1976, National Security Adviser, Presidential Correspondence with Foreign Leaders, Box 2, Iran—The Shah (1)-(2), Gerald R. Ford Library.

298 *a breakfast meeting with Hushang Ansary:* Cable 037659 from Under Secretary Robinson to Secretary Kissinger, "Your Breakfast Meeting with Ansary, February 15, 1976," February 16, 1976, L. William Seidman Files (WH Economic Affairs Office), Scowcroft, Brent (White House National Security Adviser), (1)-(2), Gerald R. Ford Library.

298 *cable summary of the talks:* Ibid.

299 *"Are things moving satisfactorily":* Telcon, "Kissinger-Ansary," 4:48 P.M., April 2, 1976, National Security Archive.

299 *"Now the question was what did":* Author interview with General Brent Scowcroft, April 6, 2010.

300 *"mentally ill":* Telcon, "Kissinger-Zahedi," 10:55 A.M., June 1, 1976, National Security Archive.

300 *"What was it Simon said last year?":* Telcon, "Kissinger-Zahedi," 4:30 P.M., June 2, 1976, National Security Archive.

301 *He detested his Republican rival:* In the privacy of the Oval Office, Ford referred to "that son of a bitch Reagan" in Kissinger's presence. See Memorandum of Conversation, 8/30/76, "Ford, Kissinger," Box 20, National Security Adviser, Gerald R. Ford Library.

301 *"How did you make out with Ansary":* Memorandum of Conversation, 3/30/76, "Ford, Kissinger," Box 18, National Security Adviser, Gerald R. Ford Library.

302 *"I think it was probably":* Author interview with General Brent Scowcroft, April 6, 2010.

302 *helicopter to Nixon's oceanside retreat:* Author interview with Ardeshir Zahedi, September 14–15, 2010.

302 *"Let me talk to the Iranians":* Memorandum of Conversation, 3/30/76, "Ford-Kissinger," Box 18, National Security Adviser, Gerald R. Ford Library.

302 *"I have talked to the President":* Telcon, "Ansary-Kissinger," April 2, 1976, 4:48 P.M., National Security Archive.

302 *to buy one billion barrels of petroleum:* Memorandum for Brent Scowcroft from Robert Hormats, "Your Meeting with Secretary Kissinger and Frank Zarb, Saturday, March 13, 10:15 A.M.," L. William Seidman Files (WH Economic Affairs Office), Scowcroft, Brent (White House National Security Adviser), (1)-(2), Gerald R. Ford Library.

302 *"It is important that we move":* Ibid.

302   *to sell 300 million barrels:* Telcon, "Kissinger-Zarb," 12:29 P.M., August 3, 1976, National Security Archive.

302   *$3 discount per barrel:* Memorandum for Brent Scowcroft from Robert Hormats, "Your Meeting with Secretary Kissinger and Frank Zarb, Saturday, March 13, 10:15 A.M.," L. William Seidman Files (WH Economic Affairs Office), Scowcroft, Brent (White House National Security Adviser), (1)-(2), Gerald R. Ford Library.

302   *"Zarb's proposals would put him in a spot":* Telcon, "Kissinger-Ansary," 4:48 P.M., April 2, 1976, National Security Archive.

303   *"the artist had grasped Ford's native stupidity":* Alam, 486.

303   *an Iranian army tribunal:* "10 Iran Rebels Get Death for 8 Killings," *Los Angeles Times,* January 1, 1976.

303   *The dour public mood:* Eric Pace, "Troubled Iran Celebrates Reign of Shah's Father," *New York Times,* March 3, 1976.

303   *A rumor had taken hold:* Alam, 475.

303   *"Particularly on that day":* Farah Pahlavi, *An Enduring Love: My Life with the Shah* (New York: Miramax, 2004), 261.

303   *"traumatized by the conflicting winds":* Jane W. Jacqz, editor, "Opening Address by Her Imperial Majesty The Shahbanou of Iran," *Iran: Past, Present and Future* (New York: Aspen Institute/Persepolis Symposium, 1976), 9.

303   *"alarming":* Eric Pace, "Iranian Aides and Scholars Stress Urgency of Social Reforms," *New York Times,* October 10, 1975.

303   *"vulnerable to popular disaffection":* Ibid.

303   *"dangerous":* Eric Pace, "Tehran Projects Face Challenges," *New York Times,* June 6, 1976.

304   *"from poking his nose":* Alam, 472.

304   *swelling on her husband's upper lip:* Farah Pahlavi, *An Enduring Love,* 262.

304   *immersing her and their oldest son, Crown Prince Reza, in the art of statecraft:* Ibid.

304   *"Several times a week Reza and I":* Ibid.

304   *President Ford wrote a letter of congratulations:* Letter from President Ford to His Imperial Majesty Mohammad Reza Pahlavi, Shahanshah of Iran, March 19, 1976, Presidential Correspondence with Foreign Leaders, Box 2, "Iran— The Shah (1)-(2), National Security Adviser," Gerald R. Ford Library.

304   *the Shah's stricken reaction:* Cynthia Helms, *An Ambassador's Wife in Iran* (New York: Dodd, Mead, 1981), 83.

304   *"destroyed Persepolis":* Ibid.

304   *"the slowness of decision-making":* Alam, 477.

304   *"The steps leading":* Jehan Sadat, *A Woman of Egypt* (New York: Simon & Schuster, 1987). 342.

305   *"rather alarmed to see so many of the girls wearing the veil":* Alam, 483.

305   *"Charles Jourdan Incident":* The version of events described here was recalled by Fatemeh Pakravan, wife of General Hassan Pakravan, in an oral his-

tory interview for Harvard University: Habib Ladjevardi, editor, *Memoirs of Fatemeh Pakravan: Wife of General Hassan Pakravan: Army Officer, Chief of the State Intelligence and Security Organization, Cabinet Minister, and Diplomat*, Harvard Iranian Oral History Project VI, Iranian Oral History Project (Cambridge: Center for Middle Eastern Studies, Harvard University, 1998), 115–17.

306 *eighty-nine people in Tehran were killed:* Joe Alex Morris Jr., "Police Kill 2 Terrorists in Downtown Tehran," *Los Angeles Times*, May 13, 1977.

306 *four policemen and eleven terrorists were killed:* Eric Pace, "14 Reported Slain in Tehran Clash," *New York Times*, May 17, 1976, and, "Iran Violence Grows as Extremists Raided," *Christian Science Monitor*, May 21, 1976.

306 *"the entire movement":* Alam, 489.

306 *"Startrek to Iran, with Glitter":* William Brannigan, "Startrek to Iran, with Glitter," *Washington Post*, May 24, 1976, and "Suzy Says: Celebrities Inaugurate New York-Tehran Flight," *Hartford Courant*, May 19, 1976.

306 *"by all accounts the most refreshing":* William Brannigan, "Startrek to Iran, with Glitter," *Washington Post*, May 24, 1976.

307 *a smile to the face of Ambassador Helms:* Ibid.

307 *"They were wined, dined and entertained":* Jack Anderson and Eric Pace, "Iranian Aides and Scholars Stress Urgency of Social Reforms," *Washington Post*, October 10, 1975. Jack Anderson and Les Whitten, "Torture, Terror in Iran," *Washington Post*, May 29, 1976.

307 *The revered cleric's funeral:* Eric Pace, "A Mystery in Iran: Who Killed the Mullah?," *New York Times*, May 12, 1976.

307 *"Few regimes have been foolhardy":* Ervand Abrahamian, *A History of Modern Iran* (Cambridge: Cambridge University Press, 2008), 152.

307 *intrusive new measures:* Ibid.

308 *outright bribery in the form of $6 million in cash:* Seymour Hersh, "CIA Is Reported to Give Anti-Reds in Italy $6 Million," *New York Times*, January 7, 1976.

308 *the collapse of the lira:* Alvin Shuster, "Italy Is Showing Strain of Crisis," *New York Times*, January 22, 1976.

308 *$500 million—half its foreign currency reserves:* Alvin Shuster, "Italy Seeks Help to Bolster Lira," *New York Times*, January 23, 1976.

308 *$500 million loan:* Ibid.

308 *make emergency funds available:* Ibid.

308 *governed all major cities north of Rome:* Alvin Shuster, "Italy's Reds Build Power by Tactics of Moderation," *New York Times*, January 18, 1976.

308 *five of Italy's twenty regions:* Ibid.

308 *48 percent of the Italian population:* Ibid.

308 *"It has reached the point":* Ibid.

308 *"I find it hard to accept":* Memorandum of Conversation, "Kissinger, Cros-

land," Saturday, April 24, 1976, 9:15–10:50 A.M., Officer's Mess, Waddington RAF Base, Lincolnshire, UK, National Security Archive.

308 *double-digit levels of unemployment and inflation:* Jacque Leslie, "Violence in Spain Fed by Recession," *Los Angeles Times,* March 5, 1976.

308 *"We think that the political situation has improved":* Memorandum of Conversation, "Kissinger, Areilza," January 25, 1976, 9:45 A.M., Foreign Office Guest Villa, Madrid, Spain, National Security Archive.

309 *"We are now entering a period":* Memorandum of Conversation, "Kissinger, Soares," January 26, 1976, 3:30 P.M., The Department of State, National Security Archive.

309 *a roaring crowd of forty thousand:* Flora Lewis, "Italian Communist Chief, in Paris, Pessimistic on Election Result," *New York Times,* June 4, 1976.

309 *22 percent of Americans supported:* "22% in Poll Say U.S. Should Act if Italy Reds Win," *Los Angeles Times,* June 21, 1976.

309 *the Communists captured forty-nine new seats:* Alvin Shuster, "Christian Democrats Top Italian Vote but Red Gain Leaves Crisis Unresolved," *New York Times,* June 22, 1976; Alvin Shuster, "Communists Gain 49 Crucial Seats in Italy Contest," *New York Times,* June 23, 1976.

310 *Italy's neofascist far right:* Alvin Shuster, "Communists Gain 49 Crucial Seats in Italy Contest," *New York Times,* June 23, 1976.

310 *"The essential problem which we confronted":* Bernard Gwertzman, "Kissinger Voices Concern on Italy," *New York Times,* June 23, 1976.

310 *"Bill Simon is going to treat Italy":* Edwin L. Dale Jr., "IMF Loan Held Way to Aid Italy," *New York Times,* June 30, 1976.

310 *"Italy needs a democratic alternative":* Memorandum of Conversation, "Kissinger, Leber," July 1, 1976, 10:45 A.M., Secretary's Office, National Security Archive.

310 *elected a Communist to the powerful post of president:* Alvin Shuster, "Italy's Major Parties Give Reds a Key Legislative Post," *New York Times,* July 4, 1976.

310 *on July 10 he telephoned Henry Cabot Lodge:* Telcon, "Kissinger-Lodge," 12:05 P.M., July 10, 1976, National Security Archive.

310 *President Giovanni Leone asked:* Sara Gilbert, "Andreotti Named Premier in Italy," *Washington Post,* July 14, 1976.

311 *$11.51 per barrel:* Lewis W. Simons, "Oil Cartel Fails to Agree on Price Hike," *Washington Post,* May 29, 1976.

311 *15 percent price rise:* Ibid.

311 *something that Sheikh Yamani made clear was unacceptable:* Ibid.

311 *"In today's interdependent world":* Ibid.

311 *"in order to save":* Alam, 492.

311 *On June 1, Syrian armored divisions invaded Lebanon:* Henry Tanner, "Damascus Sends Troops and Tanks into Mid-Lebanon," *New York Times,* June 2, 1976.

312 *Melloy had been shot in the head and chest:* James M. Markham, "US Ambassa-

dor and Aide Kidnapped and Murdered in Beirut Combat Sector," *New York Times*, June 17, 1976.

312 *President Ford ordered the evacuation:* "US Bids Citizens Leave Lebanon," *New York Times*, June 19, 1976.

312 *incoming shells ripped through an airliner:* "Jetliner Blasted in Beirut Airport," *New York Times*, June 28, 1976.

312 *a dash for the Syrian border:* "Ford Orders Evacuation of Americans in Lebanon," *New York Times*, June 18, 1976.

312 *"the PLO might be so desperate":* Telcon, "Kissinger-Atherton," 6:40 P.M., July 12, 1976, National Security Archive.

312 *"the effective assistance":* Cable from President Ford to King Khalid, July 27, 1976, Presidential Correspondence with Foreign Leaders, King Khalid, Box 4, National Security Adviser, Gerald R. Ford Library.

312 *stomach pains, a skin rash, and headaches:* Alam, 489.

313 *"change of plan":* Ibid., 497.

313 *the basement of a building near Mehrabad airport:* "Iran Agents Kill 10 in Shootout," *Los Angeles Times*, June 30, 1976.

313 *Hamid Ashraf, the most wanted man in Iran:* Abbas Milani, *Eminent Persians: The Men and Women Who Made Modern Iran, 1941–1979* (Syracuse: Syracuse University Press, 2008), includes a chapter on the life of Hamid Ashraf, Vol. 1, 96–102.

313 *security forces ringed the neighborhood seven times:* Ibid.

313 *the number of jobless Americans:* Edward Cowan, "Jobless Rate Up to 7.5% for June from May's 7.3%," *New York Times*, July 3, 1976.

313 *Alan Greenspan, had gone before Congress:* Edwin L. Dale Jr., "Economy Will Outperform Forecast, Greenspan Says," *New York Times*, June 11, 1976.

314 *the steepest fall in consumer retail spending:* "Retail Sales Fell 1.2% Last Month to $52.64 Billion," *Wall Street Journal*, June 11, 1976.

314 *"Variations in the pace of economic activity":* Ibid.

314 *the June jobs report:* Edward Cowan, "Jobless Rate Up to 7.5% for June from May's 7.3%," *New York Times*, July 3, 1976.

314 *"Temporary pauses of this kind aren't uncommon":* "Burns Is Optimistic About the Economy, Calls Consumer-Outlay Lull Transitory," *Wall Street Journal*, July 1, 1976.

314 *"unsuitable entertainment":* Betty Ford with Chris Chase, *The Times of My Life* (New York: Harper & Row, 1978), 223.

314 *225 tall ships sailed up the Hudson River:* Richard F. Shepard, "Nation and Millions in City Joyously Hail Bicentennial," *New York Times*, July 5, 1976.

314 *"The Pentagon is incredible":* Memorandum of Conversation, "Kissinger, Helms, Atherton, Eilts, Pickering, Oakley," 8:00 A.M.–10:00 A.M., August 7, 1976, National Security Archive.

314   *a giant American flag lit up a mountainside:* As recounted in Sandra Mackey, *The Iranians: Persia, Islam and the Soul of a Nation* (New York: Penguin, 1998), 251.

314   *The next morning's:* New York Times *reported:* Clyde H. Farnsworth, "U.S. Banks' Bigger Role," *New York Times,* July 5, 1976.

315   *Wall Street was eager to establish a presence:* James M. Markham, "Spain's Foreign Debt Rise Is Worrying Businessmen," *New York Times,* December 1, 1976.

315   *"Concern has been expressed in Congress":* Clyde H. Farnsworth, "U.S. Banks' Bigger Role," *New York Times,* July 5, 1976.

315   *Some 40 percent of Bank of America's earnings:* Ibid.

315   *half of its outstanding loans:* Ibid.

315   *"some share of responsibility":* "IMF Aide Cites Banks' Role in Debt Problems of Developing Nations," *Wall Street Journal,* April 30, 1976.

315   *$250 billion at the end of 1975:* Ibid.

315   *40 percent of those totals:* Ibid.

316   *"disturbingly high levels":* Hobart Rowen, "Poor Nations' Borrowings Questions," *Washington Post,* June 17, 1976.

316   *"the ability of these countries":* Ibid.

316   *Peru, Indonesia, and Argentina:* Hobart Rowen, "Banks Questioned on Loan Policies," *Washington Post,* July 18, 1976.

316   *$15 billion and $17 billion in private bank loans:* Ibid.

316   *"in a greedy drive for profits":* Ibid.

316   *"How can presumably sophisticated bankers":* Ibid.

316   *In the first six months of 1976:* Edwin Dale Jr., "IMF Loans in 6 Months Top Any Previous Year's," *New York Times,* July 13, 1976.

316   *The biggest user of the fund was Great Britain:* Ibid.

316   *"possible collapse of the economy":* Michael Hatfield, "Healey Warning of 'Collapse of Economy,' " *The Times* (London), July 21, 1976.

317   *At 10:30 A.M. on Friday, July 9, 1976:* Memorandum of Conversation, 7/9/76, "Ford, Kissinger, Saudi Deputy Prime Minister Abdallah bin Abd al-Aziz-Saud," Box 20, National Security Adviser, Gerald R. Ford Library.

318   *2,500 Maverick air-to-surface missiles:* Leslie H. Gelb, "U.S. Ready to Sell Missiles to Saudis," *New York Times,* August 1, 1976.

318   *"the continuing build-up":* Ibid.

CHAPTER ELEVEN: ROYAL FLUSH

PAGE

319   *"Many countries have in fact":* Letter to His Imperial Majesty Mohammad Reza Pahlavi, Shahanshah of Iran. From President Gerald R. Ford, October 29, 1976, Box 2, Presidential Correspondence with Foreign Leaders: Iran—The Shah(z), Gerald R. Ford Library.

319 *"Nothing could provoke more reaction in us"*: Presidential Correspondence with Foreign Leaders, Iran—The Shah (2), "Letter from His Imperial Majesty the Shahanshah Aryamehr to President Gerald R. Ford," Box 2, National Security Adviser, Gerald R. Ford Library.

319 *released a damning report*: "U.S. Military Sales to Iran," A Staff Report to the Subcommittee on Foreign Assistance of the Committee on Foreign Relations, United States Senate, July 1976 (Washington, D.C.: U.S. Government Printing Office, 1976).

319 *"out of control"*: Leslie H. Gelb, "Study Finds Iran Dependent on U.S. in Using Weapons," *New York Times*, August 2, 1976.

319 *"without U.S. support on a day-to-day basis"*: Don Oberdorfer, "Uncontrolled Sale of Arms to Iran Traced to Nixon," *Washington Post*, August 2, 1976.

319 *"cynical and dangerous"*: Richard Bergholz, "President Defends Policies in Face of Carter Attack," *Los Angeles Times*, September 10, 1976.

319 *"It couldn't be a worse time"*: Memorandum of Conversation, 8/3/76, "Ford, Kissinger, Scowcroft," Box 20, National Security Adviser, Gerald R. Ford Library.

320 *"I am really mad"*: Memorandum of Conversation, 8/7/76, "Kissinger, Helms, Atherton, Eilts, Pickering, Oakley: Guidance for Ambassadors Eilts and Pickering," 8:00 A.M.–10:00 A.M., August 7, 1976, National Security Archive.

321 *"the most diligent statesman"*: Asadollah Alam, *The Shah and I: The Confidential Diary of Iran's Royal Court, 1969–1977* (New York: St. Martin's, 1991), 500.

321 *"a stupid, narrow-minded bunch"*: Ibid., 501.

321 *The Shah hosted the American delegation*: Thomas W. Lippmann, "Shah Denies Charge That Iran Buys Too Many Weapons," *Washington Post*, August 7, 1976.

321 *He had arranged a sightseeing trip*: Bernard Gwertzman, "Abroad with Kissinger, Some Exercises in Diplomacy," *New York Times*, August 12, 1976.

321 *a waste of his time*: Ibid.

321 *"The secretary appeared bored"*: Associated Press, "Kissinger's Diplomatic . . . If Queasy," *Chicago Tribune*, August 7, 1976.

321 *"looked away, paled"*: Bernard Gwertzman, "Abroad with Kissinger, Some Exercises in Diplomacy," *New York Times*, August 12, 1976.

321 *three hundred F-16s and two hundred F-18s*: "Iran Seeks 300 General Dynamics F16s, Near Double of What U.S. Agreed to Sell," *Wall Street Journal*, September 13, 1976.

322 *"Can the United States"*: Bernard Gwertzman, "Shah Cautions U.S. Against Arms Cut," *New York Times*, August 7, 1976.

322 *sell another $10 billion in military equipment*: Bernard Gwertzman, "Iranians Planning to Spend $10 Billion on U.S. Arms," *New York Times*, August 8, 1976.

322 *as an afterthought*: Author interview with Henry Precht, June 4, 2009.

322 *"on historical precedent"*: Henry A. Kissinger, *Years of Upheaval* (Boston: Little, Brown, 1982), 672.

322 *"idle musing"*: Ibid.

322 *"In Iran, I don't think we realize"*: Memorandum of Conversation, 8/13/76, "Ford, Kissinger," Box 20, National Security Adviser, Gerald R. Ford Library.

323 *Zarb returned to inform the president*: Author interview with Frank G. Zarb, June 11, 2009.

323 *"nit-picking Talmudic scholar"*: Ibid.

323 *Zahedi had grown close to Reagan*: Author interview with Ardeshir Zahedi, September 14–15, 2010.

323 *Zahedi had turned them down*: Ibid.

323 *stayed in the Reagans' hotel*: Ibid.

323 *"Ford was a nice, wonderful person"*: Ibid.

324 *"This is why Ford was maybe a little upset"*: Ibid.

324 *"Now that we have gotten rid of"*: Memorandum of Conversation, 8/30/76, "Ford, Kissinger," Box 20, National Security Adviser, Gerald R. Ford Library.

324 *a red Volkswagen veered sharply*: The most detailed account of the August 28, 1976, slayings of three American contractors in Tehran was offered by Ambassador Richard Helms to an associate who kept notes of their conversation. It was first reported by Bob Woodward. See Bob Woodward, "IBEX: Deadly Symbol of U.S. Arms Sales Problems," *Washington Post*, January 2, 1977.

325 *Cottrell had been shadowed*: Ibid.

325 *Cottrell was employed by Rockwell*: Paul B. Finney, "Letter from Tehran: Pomp, Progress, and Terrorism," *BusinessWeek*, November 22, 1976.

325 *"One of the pistols was stolen"*: Bob Woodward, "IBEX: Deadly Symbol of U.S. Arms Sales Problems," *Washington Post*, January 2, 1977. Former Secretary of Defense Schlesinger told the author that the theft was plausible and that it didn't surprise him. Author interview with Dr. James Schlesinger, June 5, 2009.

325 *tipped off by Israel's Mossad*: Alam, 503.

325 *"for this atrocity"*: Ibid.

325 *"stayed close to home"*: "Americans in Iran Wary After Killings," *Los Angeles Times*, August 30, 1976.

325 *170 frightened Americans*: William Branigan, "Frightened Americans Seek to Improve Security in Iran," *Washington Post*, August 31, 1976.

325 *registering at hotels under false names*: Paul B. Finney, "Letter from Tehran: Pomp, Progress, and Terrorism," *BusinessWeek*, November 22, 1976.

325 *twenty Chevrolets and limousines were outfitted*: Ibid.

325 *"sometimes had nightmares"*: Cynthia Helms, *An Ambassador's Wife in Iran* (New York: Dodd, Mead, 1981), 180.

326 *surrounded by sixteen*: Paul B. Finney, "Letter from Tehran: Pomp, Progress, and Terrorism," *BusinessWeek*, November 22, 1976.

326 *Ambassador Helms now asked his staff*: Author interview with Henry Precht, June 4, 2009.

326 *between 45,000 and fifty thousand Americans:* Ibid.

326 *Walter Mondale cited the deaths:* Robert Shogan, "Mondale Urges U.S. to Curb Arms Sales," *Los Angeles Times*, August 31, 1976.

326 *"The pattern is spurt and pause":* Philip Shabecoff, "Greenspan Finds Economic 'Pause,' " *New York Times*, August 31, 1976.

326 *"From an economist's standpoint":* Alan Greenspan, *The Age of Turbulence* (New York: Penguin, 2008), 75.

326 *7.9 percent:* Hobart Rowen and James L. Rowe Jr., "Jobless Rate Increases to 7.9 Per Cent," *Washington Post*, September 4, 1976.

327 *"Economists and analysts noted":* Leonard Silk, "Spending Shortfall: A Slowdown Reason?," *New York Times*, October 14, 1976.

327 *"the biggest budgetary gaffe":* Ibid.

327 *"in a state of chaos":* James L. Rowe Jr., "Handling a Longer Slowdown," *Washington Post*, November 14, 1976.

327 *"If the oil-producing countries":* Ibid.

327 *13.8 percent inflation:* Michael Keats, "Besieged British Economy Undergoes New Battering," *Washington Post*, September 23, 1976.

327 *1.5 million people out of work:* Ibid.

327 *"Things are going to get worse before they get better":* Ibid.

327 *12 percent:* Jim Hoagland, "France Freezes Prices," *Washington Post*, September 23, 1976.

327 *a three-month wage and price freeze:* Ibid.

327 *ceiling of $11 billion:* Ibid.

327 *The deal to sell thousands of new-generation smart missiles:* Leslie H. Gelb, "U.S. Ready to Sell Missiles to Saudi Arabia," *New York Times*, August 1, 1976.

328 *"The Saudis have been very helpful":* Memorandum of Conversation, 8/30/76, "Ford, Kissinger, Senators Case and Javits," Box 20, National Security Adviser, Gerald R. Ford Library.

328 *to deliver a letter from President Ford:* Telegram 6093 from the Embassy in Jidda to the Department of State, September 8, 1976, 1000Z, Box 205, L. William Seidman Files (WH Economic Affairs Office, Brent Scowcroft (White House National Security Adviser), (1)-(2), Gerald R. Ford Library.

328 *"will certainly not approve a price rise this year":* Ibid.

328 *"the main objective of the letter":* Memorandum for Brent Scowcroft from Robert Hormats and Robert B. Oakley, "Letter to King Khalid," Presidential Correspondence with Foreign Leaders, Saudi Arabia—King Khalid, Box 4, National Security Adviser, Gerald R. Ford Library.

329 *At 11:00 A.M. on Friday, September 17:* Memorandum of Conversation, "Ford, Saudi Arabian Foreign Minister Prince Saud bin Faisal Al-Saud," Box 21, National Security Adviser, Gerald R. Ford Library.

330 *at 3:00 P.M. on September 23:* "Strategy Paper for the President on December

Oil Price Decision," Box 5, OPEC—National Security Adviser, NSC International Economic Affairs Staff Files, Gerald R. Ford Library.

330 *1,000-point mark:* Richard L. Stout, "Stock Market Up, but Will It Sway the Voter?" *Christian Science Monitor,* September 23, 1976.

330 *of between 10 and 20 percent:* Bill Newkirk, "Oil Price Rise Dilemma," *Chicago Tribune,* October 11, 1976.

330 *Officials urged President Ford to write letters:* "Strategy Paper for the President on December Oil Price Decision," Box 5, OPEC—National Security Adviser, NSC International Economic Affairs Staff Files, Gerald R. Ford Library.

330 *Frank Zarb was assigned the task:* Ibid. Zarb confirmed that he traveled to Caracas to raise the issue of oil prices with Venezuelan officials in an interview with the author on June 11, 2009. He was reluctant to divulge what those discussions entailed.

331 *Kissinger was asked to meet:* Ibid.

331 *the U.S. Army Corps of Engineers:* "Strategy Paper for the President on December Oil Price Decision," Box 5, OPEC—National Security Adviser, NSC International Economic Affairs Staff Files, Gerald R. Ford Library.

331 *a record 293 million barrels:* Thomas O'Toole, "Oil Storage Tanks Brimming," *Washington Post,* October 30, 1976.

331 *more than three thousand advisers and guests:* Thomas E. Mullaney, "Bankers Seeking Answers at IMF," *New York Times,* October 5, 1976.

331 *$45 billion:* Leonard Silk, "The Problem of Enormous Buildup of International Debt," *New York Times,* November 11, 1976.

331 *$20 billion:* Ibid.

331 *$10 billion:* Ibid.

331 *"No one really knows":* Ibid.

332 *"to affect the credit worthiness":* Edwin L. Dale Jr., "Head of IMF Urges Halt to Borrowing to Cover Deficits," *New York Times,* October 4, 1976.

332 *"are approaching the limits":* Edwin L. Dale Jr., "Simon Says Nations Consuming Oil Face $50 Billion Deficit," *New York Times,* October 5, 1976.

332 *"We shall not waver!":* Labor Government in Britain Survives Parliament Challenge on Fiscal Policy," *Los Angeles Times,* October 12, 1976.

332 *$3.9 billion:* Peter T. Kilborn, "Britain to Ask IMF For $3.9 Billion Loan, Its Borrowing Limit," *New York Times,* September 30, 1976.

332 an *"economic policy so savage":* Hobart Rowen, "Pound Sinks to New Low," *Washington Post,* October 26, 1976.

332 *"Nobody wants to talk about it":* Ibid.

333 *"Of course, the economic situation is serious":* Memorandum of Conversation, "Kissinger, Forlani," September 30, 1976, National Security Archive.

333 *$300 million loan:* Ned Temko, "Portugal Seeks $300 Million in U.S. to Boost Reserves," *Washington Post,* November 4, 1976.

333   *Inflation was running to 30 percent:* Marvine Howe, "The Aftermath of Portugal's Revolution Is Expensive," *New York Times*, November 21, 1976.

333   *20 percent of the population:* Ibid.

333   *$4.3 billion oil bill:* Joe Gandelman, "Madrid Loses Some of Its Glow," *Christian Science Monitor,* October 29, 1976.

333   *ending television transmissions:* Ibid.

333   *62 miles per hour:* Ibid.

333   *"The energy crisis":* Ibid.

333   *a "hot autumn":* Stanley Meisner, "Observers See 'Hot Autumn' in Spain," *Los Angeles Times,* October 15, 1976.

333   *One third of Spain's outstanding foreign debt:* James M. Markham, "Spain's Foreign Debt Rise Is Worrying Businessmen," *New York Times,* December 1, 1976.

334   *"The growing foreign debt":* Ibid.

334   *"How much pressure has there been":* "The Western World Will Not Regret Our Progress March," *Kayhan Weekly International Edition* 9, no. 450 (December 18, 1976).

334   *"I cannot accept this as a crisis":* "Shahanshah: Iran Will Make It, Iranian-Style," *Kayhan Weekly International Edition* 9, no. 449 (December 11, 1976).

334   *"pure jealousy":* Ibid.

334   *no trouble absorbing a 15 percent rise:* "The Western World Will Not Regret Our Progress," *Kayhan Weekly International Edition* 9, no. 450 (December 18, 1976).

334   *"If you just decided to work a little more":* Ibid.

335   *An American visitor to Toufanian's office:* The visitor to Toufanian's office was *Washington Post* reporter William Brannigan, who wrote about their encounter. See William Brannigan, "Iran's Military, Oil Chiefs Split over Price Increase," *Washington Post,* December 9, 1976.

335   *a three-hour seminar:* Memorandum for Ambassador Edward S. Little, Chairman, Human Resources Committee, Central Intelligence Agency, from David H. Blee, National Intelligence Officer for the Middle East, "Subject: Reporting Assessment—Focus Iran," 4 November 1976. Eric Hooglund, project editor, *Iran: The Making of U.S. Policy, 1977–80,* National Security Archive (Alexandria, VA: Chadwyck-Healey, 1990).

336   *"Washington does not have a clear perception":* Ibid.

337   *"Gosh, the programs the Shah has coming":* Lee Lescaze, "General Brown Is in Hot Water Again," *Washington Post,* October 19, 1976.

337   *"obviously inelegant phraseology":* Ibid.

337   *"truly hilarious":* "Shah: Brown Has Apologized," *Washington Post,* October 26, 1976.

337   *a survey of arms sales undertaken by David Ronfeldt:* David Ronfeldt, Working Note: "U.S.-Iranian Arms Transfer Relationships: A Historical Analysis to

May 1972 (U)," Prepared for the Office of the Assistant Secretary of Defense (International Security Affairs), N-9586-ISA (Santa Monica: RAND Corp.: October 1976), Eric Hooglund, project editor, *Iran: The Making of U.S. Policy, 1977–80*, National Security Archive (Alexandria, VA: Chadwyck-Healey, 1990).

338   *the Shah frankly admitted:* Arthur Unger, "Mike Wallace Interview: Incisive Look at the Shah," *Christian Science Monitor,* October 21, 1976. A full transcript of the interview was published on page 22 of the October 22, 1976, edition of *The New York Times*: "The Shah on Israel, Corruption, Torture and . . ."

338   *Kissinger had no choice:* "U.S. Queries Iran on Snooping Here," *Washington Post,* October 29, 1976.

338   *Jack Anderson reported:* Jack Anderson, "Iran's SAVAK Copies CIA Dirty Tricks," *Hartford Courant,* October 29, 1976.

338   *SAVAK's senior handler:* Ibid. Anderson named the handler as Mansur Rafizadeh, an attaché at the Iranian mission to the United Nations.

339   *the ambassador called on Court Minister Alam:* Alam, 517.

339   *"eyes only for the ambassador":* Cable 267996, "Eyes Only for the Ambassador," October 30, 1976, Box 2, Presidential Correspondence with Foreign Leaders: Iran—The Shah (2), Gerald R. Ford Library.

339   *The president's letter to the Shah:* Letter to His Imperial Majesty Mohammad Reza Pahlavi, Shahanshah of Iran, from President Gerald R. Ford, October 29, 1976, Box 2, Presidential Correspondence with Foreign Leaders: Iran—The Shah (2), Gerald R. Ford Library.

339   *above 6 million barrels a day:* Joe Alex Morris Jr., "Oil Production Soars in Persian Gulf Area," *Los Angeles Times,* November 8, 1976.

340   *10:00 A.M. local time:* Cable 3109227, "For the Secretary from the Ambassador," October 31, 1976, Eric Hooglund, project editor, *Iran: The Making of U.S. Policy, 1977–80*, National Security Archive (Alexandria, VA: Chadwyck-Healey, 1990), Reference # 01117.

340   *"After His Majesty has opportunity":* Ibid.

340   *Richard Helms's resignation:* William Brannigan, "Helms Seen as Ready to Retire as U.S. Ambassador to Iran," *Washington Post,* November 2, 1976.

341   *"Look, I don't give a good god damn":* Memorandum of Conversation, "Kissinger, Scowcroft," 10:19 A.M., October 25, 1976, National Security Archive, 76.

341   *placed a call to Senator Ted Kennedy:* Memorandum of Conversation, "Kissinger-Kennedy," 2:50 P.M., October 22, 1976, National Security Archive.

341   *"You were right about the pause":* Greenspan, 76.

341   *"no formal liaison with SAVAK agents":* Memorandum of Conversation, "Kissinger, Atherton, Saunders, Murphy, Covey," 12:30 P.M., November 4, 1976, National Security Archive.

341 *"I told Zahedi I hoped"*: Ibid.

341 *Ardeshir Zahedi delivered the Shah's letter of reply:* Presidential Correspondence with Foreign Leaders, Iran—The Shah (2), "Letter from His Imperial Majesty the Shahanshah Aryamehr to President Gerald R. Ford," Box 2, National Security Adviser, Gerald R. Ford Library.

342 *The Iranian Foreign Ministry issued a carefully worded statement:* Jack Anderson, "Shah's Threats to Kissinger Revealed," *Washington Post,* July 31, 1979.

342 *"The statement serves notice"*: Ibid.

342 *Henry Kissinger telephoned Roy Atherton:* Telcon, "Kissinger-Atherton," 9:55 A.M., November 8, 1976, National Security Archive.

343 *Zahedi and Atherton met the next day:* Memorandum of Conversation, "Meeting with Ambassador Zahedi," November 9, 1976, Eric Hooglund, project editor, *Iran: The Making of U.S. Policy, 1977–80,* National Security Archive (Alexandria, VA: Chadwyck-Healey, 1990).

343 *"virtuoso performance"*: Ibid.

343 *"Ambassador Zahedi was quick to assure us"*: Ibid.

343 *"any illegal or improper activity"*: "No Improper Activities by Iran Envoys Found," *Hartford Courant,* November 11, 1976.

344 *Syrian presence in Beirut:* James F. Clarity, "Syrian Army Units Move into Beirut to Enforce Truce," *New York Times,* November 11, 1976.

344 *United Nations Security Council unanimously voted:* Peter Grose, "Vote by U.S. Against Israel at U.N. Linked to Effort for Mideast Talks," *New York Times,* November 12, 1976.

344 *"pacing the floor"*: Philip Shabecoff, "Greenspan Sees Recovery Slower than Ford Forecast," *New York Times,* November 13, 1976.

344 *"could lead to disaster"*: Hobart Rowen, "Other Nations' Debts May Plague U.S.," *Washington Post,* December 14, 1976.

344 *"After a brief Indian Summer"*: Don Cooke, "Portents of Gloom Seep into Forecasts on Global Economy," *Los Angeles Times,* November 21, 1976.

344 *Bank of America was the world's largest bank:* As described by *Time* magazine, "Away from Secrecy," *Time,* November 29, 1976, 40.

344 *"the bank's appraisal"*: Ibid.

345 *"a legitimate need"*: Ibid.

345 *"I have never seen Europe so confused"*: Don Cooke, "Portents of Gloom Seep into Forecasts on Global Economy," *Los Angeles Times,* November 21, 1976.

345 *"The real worry now"*: Ibid.

345 *300,000:* "Inflation Endangers Economy in France, Boosts Left's Hopes," *Washington Post,* November 13, 1976.

345 *the one million mark:* Richard F. Janssen, "France's Troubles Stir Washington Worries, Economic and Political," *Wall Street Journal,* December 8, 1976.

345 *three out of four businessmen:* "Inflation Endangers Economy in France, Boosts Left's Hopes," *Washington Post,* November 13, 1976.

345 *Capital began leaving France:* Ibid.

345 *"Some observers believe the situation":* Ibid.

345 *"There is a feeling quite suddenly":* Don Cooke, "Portents of Gloom Seep into Forecasts on Global Economy," *Los Angeles Times,* November 21, 1976.

345 *"France scares the hell out of me":* "France's Troubles Stir Washington Worries, Economic and Political," *Wall Street Journal,* December 8, 1976.

345 *the government approved an austerity budget:* Sari Gilbert, "Italians Pass Austerity Plan; Communist Abstention Is Key," *Washington Post,* November 13, 1976.

345 *$7 billion to $17 billion:* Takaski Oka, "Truffles and Joy Rides Jangle Italy's Finances," *Christian Science Monitor,* November 18, 1976.

345 *"What will it take":* Hobart Rowen, "Dealing with Italy's Economic Woes," *Washington Post,* December 2, 1976.

346 *$700 million:* Ibid.

346 *$1 billion:* Ibid.

346 *plotting a right-wing coup:* William Mathewon, "Portugal's Plight: Curing Economic Ills Is Crucial to Survival of Regime in Lisbon," *Wall Street Journal,* November 19, 1976.

346 *huge rally in downtown Madrid:* James M. Markham, "Franco Is Honored a Year After Death," *New York Times,* November 21, 1976.

346 *8.5 percent:* Robert S. Cameron, "Quebec Election May Have Major Impact, if Favored Separatist Party Gains Power," *Wall Street Journal,* November 15, 1976.

346 *national average of 7.1 percent:* Ibid.

346 *forecast to hit 9.1 percent:* Ibid.

346 *a centerpiece of his campaign:* "Separatists Win Staggering Victory In Quebec Election," *Los Angeles Times,* November 16, 1976.

346 *"Discontent over inflation":* "In the Shadow of a New Global Slump," *Time,* November 29, 1976, 33.

347 *"It seems to have taken the defeat":* Vivian H. Oppenheim, "OPEC Poised to Juggle Those Prices Again," *Los Angeles Times,* December 12, 1976.

347 *"How can you run":* Ibid. The official quoted was William Seidman, one of President Ford's top economic advisers.

347 *"I called in the Saudi and Iranian Ambassadors":* Memorandum of Conversation, "Ford, Kissinger," Box 21, National Security Adviser, Gerald R. Ford Library.

347 *Ambassador Zahedi had a very different recollection:* Author interview with Ardeshir Zahedi, September 14–15, 2010.

348 *The State Department admitted:* Associated Press, "Kissinger's Phone Transcripts Moved from Rockefeller Estate," *New York Times,* December 30, 1976.

348 *Kissinger had met with Ed Yeo:* Memorandum of Conversation, "Kissinger, Yeo, Sonnenfeldt, Rogers, Covey," 5:50 P.M., November 3, 1976, National Security Archive.

348 *"He has a terrible view of Margaret Thatcher"*: Ibid.

349 *"After you left the meeting on Friday"*: Memorandum of Conversation, "Ford, Kissinger, Scowcroft," Box 21, National Security Adviser, Gerald R. Ford Library.

350 *"could touch off massive strikes"*: Bernard D. Nossiter, "Britain Rejects Hard-Line Measures in Economic Crisis," *Washington Post*, December 4, 1976.

350 *"It is in the economic interest"*: Memorandum of Conversation, "Ford, Schmidt," November 23, 1976, Box 21, National Security Adviser, Gerald R. Ford Library.

350 *Australia had devalued its currency:* "Australia Devalues Currency by 17.5%," *New York Times*, November 29, 1976.

350 *New Zealand's government suspended foreign exchange trading:* Ibid.

350 *"I am gravely concerned"*: Memorandum of Conversation, "Ford, Saudi Ambassador Ali Alireza," November 29, 1976, Box 21, National Security Adviser, Gerald R. Ford Library.

351 *"intolerable"*: Flora Lewis, "Israeli Chief Insists That Only Lebanese Control Border Area," *New York Times*, November 29, 1976.

351 *Kissinger was back in the Oval Office:* Memorandum of Conversation, "Ford, Kissinger," December 3, 1976, Box 21, National Security Adviser, Gerald R. Ford Library.

352 *climbed back up to 8.1 percent:* "Jobless Rate Climbs to 8.1%, Wholesale Price Rise Is Level," *Wall Street Journal*, December 6, 1976.

352 *Alan Greenspan admitted:* Hobart Rowen, "Greenspan Says the Economy Is Weaker than Expected," *Washington Post*, December 3, 1976.

352 *"a higher degree of caution"*: Ibid.

352 *hike their prices by 6 percent:* Edward Cowan, "White House Criticizes Steel Price Rise," *New York Times*, December 3, 1976.

352 *"He said you were very impressive"*: Memorandum of Conversation, "Ford, Kissinger," December 3, 1976, Box 21, National Security Adviser, Gerald R. Ford Library.

CHAPTER TWELVE: OIL WAR

PAGE

353 *"Bankruptcy is worse than defeat"*: Eric Pace, "Iran Said to Review Arms Buying in U.S. Because of Oil Lag," *New York Times*, February 9, 1977.

353 *"Our great diplomacy"*: Memorandum of Conversation, "Ford, Kissinger," January 4, 1977, Box 21, National Security Adviser, Gerald R. Ford Library.

353 *Forty percent of America's oil needs:* "Fiddling Dangerously While the Fuel Burns," *Time*, December 20, 1976, 37.

353 *4 percent increase:* Ibid.

353 *"The brave conservation measures"*: Ibid.

354 *President Ford welcomed Ambassador Ardeshir Zahedi:* Memorandum of Conver-

sation, December 7, 1976, Box 21, "Ford, CEA Chairman Greenspan, Iranian Ambassador Ardeshir Zahedi," National Security Adviser, Gerald R. Ford Library.

354 *"before their delivery was completed"*: R. W. Apple Jr., "Carter Attacks, Ford Defends U.S. Foreign Stance in 2nd Debate," *New York Times,* October 7, 1976.

355 *"Instead of carte blanche expenditure"*: Hossein Razavi and Firouz Vakil, *The Political Environment of Economic Planning in Iran, 1971–1983: From Monarchy to Islamic Republic* (Boulder: Westview, 1984), 93.

355 *The headlines in Tehran's English-language* Kayhan International: See *Kayhan Weekly International Edition* 9, no. 448 (December 4, 1976), and *Kayhan Weekly International Edition* 9, no. 450 (December 18, 1976).

356 *"and any oil price increase"*: Don Oberdorfer, "U.S. Reiterates Its Opposition to OPEC Oil Price Increase," *Washington Post,* December 10, 1976.

357 *Italy repaid a $486 million loan:* "EEC Agrees to Pay Italy's British Debt," *New York Times,* November 3, 1976.

357 *"Our problem is the Army"*: Memorandum of Conversation, "Kissinger, del Prado," 10:20 A.M., December 2, 1976, National Security Archive.

357 *masked gunmen kidnapped:* James M. Markham, "Leading Spanish Aide Kidnapped in Madrid," *New York Times,* December 12, 1976.

357 *Prime Minister Adolfo Suárez was now less confident:* Joe Gandelman, "Referendum Puts Spanish Government on Defensive," *Christian Science Monitor,* December 13, 1976.

357 *battled hundreds of leftist demonstrators:* Miguel Acoca, "Leftists, Riot Police Clash at Madrid Demonstration," *Washington Post,* December 14, 1976.

357 *"a qualified vote of confidence"*: Marvine Howe, "Government Party Emerges as Winner in Portugal Voting," *New York Times,* December 14, 1976.

358 *a six-month price freeze:* Flora Lewis, "Saudi Arabia's Oil Minister Urges a 6-Month Price Freeze for OPEC," *New York Times,* December 15, 1976.

358 *"is not as strong"*: Ibid.

358 *a 4:51 meeting:* Memorandum of Conversation, "Ford, Saudi Ambassador Ali Alireza," December 14, 1976, National Security Adviser, Gerald R. Ford Library.

358 *"We are used to such statements"*: Joe Alex Morris Jr., "Oil Cartel Sharply Split over Issue of Price Hike," *Los Angeles Times,* December 16, 1976.

358 *"This is a game that he always plays"*: "The OPEC Supercartel in Splitsville," *Time,* December 27, 1976.

358 *"maneuver . . . all want to raise the price"*: "Saudi Minister Quits OPEC Talks," *Los Angeles Times,* December 16, 1976.

358 *prices go up 10 percent:* Roger Vielvoye, "Split in Opec Brings Two-Tier Oil Price Rises of 5% and 10%," *The Times* (London), December 17, 1976.

358 *$12.70 a barrel:* "Opec Eleven Charging Less than 10pc on Some Heavy Crudes," *The Times* (London), December 30, 1976.

358 *$13.30 a barrel:* Ibid.

359 *add $3.5 billion:* "Fiddling Dangerously While the Fuel Burns," *Time*, December 20, 1976, 37.

359 *2 cents a gallon:* Ibid.

359 *"Any sign of white-robed movement":* "Opec: The Inside Story of the Inside Story," *The Economist*, December 25, 1976, 78.

359 *"so many tried to cram into the lift":* Ibid.

359 *mistook him for the oil minister from Ecuador:* Ibid.

359 *hiding out in the bowling alley:* Ibid.

359 *"Late night dramas":* Ibid.

359 *Cuts of $1.69 billion in 1977 and $2.51 billion:* Peter Kilborn, "Britain Again Curbs Spending in Effort to Revive Economy," *New York Times*, December 16, 1976.

359 *"incompetent management of the economy":* Ibid.

359 *"essentially Tory policies":* Ibid.

359 *"excellent":* Ibid.

360 *8.5 million barrels a day:* "Sheikh Yamani's Christmas Box," *The Economist*, December 25, 1976, 78.

360 *10 million barrels a day . . . 30 million barrels:* "Saudi Arabia Pledges More Oil After Opec Price Split," *The Times* (London), December 18, 1976.

360 *"Is it fair for all OPEC":* "The OPEC Supercartel in Splitsville," *Time*, December 27, 1976, 49.

360 *"Heavy crudes are the focus":* "No First-Round Knock-out," *The Economist*, February 13, 1977.

360 *"The third world and all progressive nations":* Eric Pace, "Iran's News Media Assails Yamani," *New York Times*, December 21, 1976.

360 *"puppet":* "Iran Papers and Radio Call Saudi Traitor to Oil Cartel," *Los Angeles Times*, December 21, 1976.

360 *"saboteur who knifed OPEC from behind":* Ibid.

360 *"If one has to create a museum of traitors":* Ibid.

361 *$4 billion:* Ibid.

361 *"Christmas box":* "Sheikh Yamani's Christmas Box," *The Economist*, December 25, 1976, 78.

361 *$10 billion in 1977:* "The OPEC Supercartel in Splitsville," *Time*, December 27, 1976, 49.

361 *60 percent:* Ibid.

361 *37.4 percent:* Ibid.

361 *$4 billion:* Ibid.

361 *only half a percent:* "Saudi Arabia Pledges More Oil After Opec Price Split," *The Times* (London), December 18, 1976.

361 *"We are extremely worried":* "Saudis Kept Oil Down for Political Reasons," *The Times* (London), December 30, 1976.

361 *"We expect the West"*: Joe Alex Morris Jr., "Oil Price Rise Will Hold at 5%, Saudi Official Says," *Los Angeles Times*, December 18, 1976.

361 *"has raised all sorts of possibilities"*: Bernard Gwertzman, "Saudis Linking Oil to Price," *New York Times*, December 18, 1976.

362 *"there is a strong link"*: Flora Lewis, "Yamani Says Talks Loom on Ending Dual Oil Price," *New York Times*, January 28, 1977.

362 *"a well-conceived framework"*: Steven Rattner, "Saudis Picking New Oil Customers; Higher Output Seen Aimed at Iraq," *New York Times*, January 13, 1977.

362 *"to slow down neighboring Iran's"*: Rowland Evans and Robert Novak, "Oil Price Tensions," *Washington Post*, February 26, 1977.

362 *25 percent of its imported petroleum:* Jim Hoagland and J. P. Smith, " 'Coincidence of Objectives' Ties Saudis, U.S." *Washington Post*, December 20, 1977.

362 *$40 billion invested:* Ibid.

362 *5 percent of its imported oil:* Briefing Memorandum, April 30, 1977, "Your Meeting with the Shah, May 13, 1977," Eric Hooglund, project editor, *Iran: The Making of U.S. Policy, 1977–80*, National Security Archive (Alexandria, VA: Chadwyck-Healey, 1990), Briefing Book State, May 13, 1977, Document Reference No. IR01164.

362 *"to affect US interest rates"*: Jim Hoagland and J. P. Smith, " 'Coincidence of Objectives' Ties Saudis, U.S." *Washington Post*, December 20, 1977.

362 *"We are reaching the point"*: Ibid.

362 *"Yamani went into the OPEC meeting"*: "The Strain on OPEC," *Newsweek*, January 24, 1977, 47.

362 *"Talleyrand of the Oil World"*: Eric Pace, "Saudi Arabia's Sheik Yamani, Talleyrand of the Oil World," *New York Times*, January 30, 1977.

362 *"Saudi Arabia Comes of Age"*: Joe Alex Morris Jr., "Saudi Arabia Comes of Age in Arab Politics," *Los Angeles Times*, February 2, 1977.

363 *"Saudis' Influence Is Growing"*: Flora Lewis, "Saudis' Influence Is Growing," *New York Times*, January 30, 1977.

363 *"the best goddamn base we have ever had"*: Paul Martin, "Getting Stronger: 'The Best Base America Has Ever Had' in Saudi Arabia," *The Times* (London), February 21, 1977.

363 *"closer monitoring of their operations"*: Paul Lewis, "Paul Volcker Speaks Out," *New York Times*, December 19, 1976.

363 *"While I continue to fear"*: "Letter to King Khalid," December 29, 1976, Presidential Correspondence with Foreign Leaders, Saudi Arabia King Khalid, Box 4, National Security Adviser, Gerald R. Ford Library.

363 *94.2 percent in favor:* James M. Markham, "Madrid Rejoices over Poll Victory," *New York Times*, December 17, 1976.

363 *"irresponsible and shortsighted"*: "Mr. Ford Attacks 10pc Oil Price Rise as 'Irresponsible and Shortsighted,' " *The Times* (London), December 18, 1976.

363   *Treasury Secretary Simon insisted:* Ibid.

364   *$3.9 billion loan:* Hobart Rowen, "$3.9 Billion IMF Loan to Britain Is Approved, *Washington Post,* January 4, 1977.

364   *$3 billion standby credit:* Hobart Rowen, "Britain Receives $3 Bill Credit to Back Sterling," *Washington Post,* January 11, 1977.

364   *"We should also get credit":* Memorandum of Conversation, "Ford, Kissinger," Box 21, January 4, 1977, National Security Adviser, Gerald R. Ford Library.

364   *The National Security Council* did *try to assess:* Author interview with General Brent Scowcroft, April 6, 2010.

364   *underestimated the severity of the economic problems:* Ibid.

364   *"[oil] producers that lie farthest from their markets":* "The Saudis Are Serious," *The Economist,* January 1, 1977, 56.

364   *attended the ambassador's farewell luncheon:* Alam, 527.

365   *"SAVAK is not authorized":* Jack Anderson, "Shah's Threats to Kissinger Revealed," *Washington Post,* July 31, 1979.

365   *"an inflammatory, public brouhaha":* Ibid.

365   *He flew out later that day:* The *Los Angeles Times* reported that Helms returned to the United States from Iran on December 27, 1976. "Helms Leaves Last US Post," *Los Angeles Times,* December 27, 1976.

365   *"By the time I left Tehran":* Richard Helms, *A Look over My Shoulder: A Life in the Central Intelligence Agency* (New York: Ballantine, 2003), 421.

365   *"Roger Channel":* Jack Anderson, "Shah's Threats to Kissinger Revealed," *Washington Post,* July 31, 1979.

365   *"would not be able to overlook the presence":* Ibid.

365   *a front-page exposé:* Bob Woodward, "IBEX: Deadly Symbol of U.S. Arms Sales Problems," *Washington Post,* January 2, 1977.

365   *"your government determine":* Martin R. Hoffman Papers, Directorate for Defense Information Press Division, "Letter from General H. Toufanian, Vice Minister of War, to The Honorable Donald Rumsfeld, Secretary of Defense," January 8, 1977, Iran—Richard Hallock, 1974–76 (1)-(2), Gerald R. Ford Library.

366   *"This relationship has been nurtured":* Martin R. Hoffman Papers, Directorate for Defense Information Press Division, "Letter from The Honorable Donald Rumsfeld, Secretary of Defense, to General H. Toufanian, Vice Minister of War," January 19, 1977, Iran—Richard Hallock, 1974–76 (1)-(2), Gerald R. Ford Library.

366   *"I don't know anybody":* Eliot Janeway, "Carter Failed to Heed Warnings on Shah," *Chicago Tribune,* January 30, 1979.

366   *a meeting between the two men:* The Simon-Carter meeting is mentioned by Rowland Evans and Robert Novak, "Bush and Simon: Audiences with Carter," *Washington Post,* November 27, 1977.

366   *"President Carter asked me all the right questions":* Ibid.

366 *"We must give them"*: Alam, 535.

367 *"a paradise of indolence and sloth"*: David Hirst, "Shah Tells Iranians to Work," *Washington Post*, December 26, 1976.

367 *"The question now is whether Yamani"*: Ronald Taggiasco, "Tough Talk on Oil, Arms Investments," *BusinessWeek*, January 24, 1977, 36.

367 *14 million barrels a day*: "Yamani Says Saudis Can Raise Output of Oil by 50%," *New York Times*, January 15, 1977.

367 *"an act of aggression"*: J. P. Smith, "Saudis Failing to Meet Oil Production Promise," *Washington Post*, June 27, 1977.

367 *"[Washington's] colonial appointee"*: William E. Schmidt, "I'm Not Judas," *Newsweek*, January 24, 1977.

368 *85 percent of foreign exchange*: Nicholas Cumming-Bruce, "Shah Feels Pinch from Loss of Exports," *The Times* (London), February 18, 1977.

368 *plunged 38 percent*: "How the Opec Fight Will Be Won," *The Economist*, January 15, 1977.

368 *2 million barrels*: "Iran Reports Exports of Oil Decline 34.7%," *New York Times*, January 12, 1977.

368 *the National Iranian Oil Company reported*: "Iran Reports Decline of 10% in Oil Sales," *Los Angeles Times*, January 6, 1977.

368 *1.2 million barrels a day to 693,000 barrels a day*: Ibid.

368 *dropped to $460 million*: Parviz Raein, "Exports Drop Since Iranian Price Increase," *Washington Post*, January 12, 1977.

368 *$672 million*: Ibid.

368 *losing $20 million a day*: "Mystery Develops over Cheaper Crude from Saudi Arabia," *Wall Street Journal*, February 10, 1977.

368 *7 percent*: "How the Opec Fight Will Be Won," *The Economist*, January 15, 1977, 78.

368 *"Iran needs a quick agreement"*: Nicholas Cumming-Bruce, "Shah Feels Pinch from Loss of Exports," *The Times* (London), February 18, 1977.

368 *to $19.5 billion from $22 billion*: Ray Vicker, "Growing Pains: Despite Its Oil Money, Iran's Economy Suffers from Many Shortages," *Wall Street Journal*, April 11, 1977.

368 *between $10 billion and $12 billion*: Ibid.

368 *imposed a spending freeze*: Nicholas Cumming-Bruce, "Shah Feels Pinch from Loss of Exports," *The Times* (London), February 18, 1977.

368 *canceled a loan*: "Iran Plans Foreign Aid Cuts After Drop in Oil Revenues," *Los Angeles Times*, January 12, 1977.

368 *accept a $500 million loan*: "Iran's Cabinet Agrees on $500 Million Loan to Narrow Its Deficit," *Wall Street Journal*, January 17, 1977.

369 *massive naval base at Chabahar*: Eric Pace, "Iran Said to Review Arms Buying in U.S. Because of Oil Lag," *New York Times*, February 9, 1977.

369 *$3.8 billion worth of aircraft*: Ibid.

369   *"he had forewarned everyone"*: Parviz C. Radji, *In the Service of the Peacock Throne: The Diaries of the Shah's Last Ambassador to London* (London: Hamish Hamilton, 1983), 48.

369   *"Normally a quiet, reserved"*: Ibid., 49.

369   *"We have squandered every cent"*: Alam, 537.

369   *"We have been thwarted"*: Ibid., 538.

369   *Hoveyda visited him:* Ibid.

369   *"Bankruptcy is worse than defeat"*: Eric Pace, "Iran Said to Review Arms Buying in U.S. Because of Oil Lag," *New York Times*, February 9, 1977.

369   *20 million barrels:* James Tanner, "Fuel Feud: OPEC Oil-Price War Widens as the Cartel Watches US Demand," *Wall Street Journal*, April 20, 1977.

370   *"18 ships are taking on oil"*: Ray Vicker, "Push for Petroleum: Already Awash in Oil, Saudi Arabia Is Raising Its Rate of Production," *Wall Street Journal*, March 8, 1977.

370   *rebounded 30 percent:* "Iranian Oil Exports Rebounded with Rise of 30% Last Month," *Wall Street Journal*, March 3, 1977.

370   *5.5 million barrels of oil a day:* Ibid.

370   *"If they [the countries"*: "Unexpected Demand Frustrates the Saudi Oil Gamble," *The Economist*, February 21, 1977.

370   *soared to 9.3 million barrels:* James Tanner, "OPEC Oil-Price War Widens as the Cartel Watches US Demand," *Wall Street Journal*, April 20, 1977.

370   *increase of 540,000 barrels:* Ibid.

370   *topping out at 9.7 million barrels:* Ibid.

370   *rendered "inoperable"*: Jahangir Amuzegar, *The Dynamics of the Iranian Revolution: The Pahlavis' Triumph and Tragedy* (Abany: State University of New York Press, 1991), 180.

370   *production fell 16 percent:* Joe Alex Morris Jr., "Higher Price Cuts Iran Oil Output 16%," *Los Angeles Times*, May 16, 1977.

370   *"Since oil had been expected"*: Robert Graham, *Iran: The Illusion of Power*, rev. ed. (London: Croom Helm, 1979), 100.

370   *denounced from Beirut:* Mordechai Abir, *Saudi Arabia in the Oil Era: Regime and Elites, Conflict and Collaboration* (Boulder: Westview, 1988), 144.

371   *unrest among Aramco oil workers:* Ibid.

371   *when the phone rang:* Alam, 540.

371   *"The sky was black"*: Thomas Lippman, "Fire in Pipeline Still Restricting Saudi Oil Output," *Washington Post*, May 13, 1977.

371   *$100 million in lost revenue:* Abir, 144.

371   *Local reports suggested otherwise:* Ibid.

371   *declare an "Arabian republic"*: Ibid.

371   *supplied with flashlights:* Ray Vicker, "Growing Pains: Despite Its Oil Money, Iran's Economy Suffers Many Shortages," *Wall Street Journal*, April 11, 1977.

371   *"Tehran's streets are so packed"*: Ibid.

371 *"A few months ago":* Joe Alex Morris Jr., "Is It for Real: New Broom Stirs Lots of Dust in Iran," *Los Angeles Times,* October 7, 1977.

372 *Cargo was moving again:* Ray Vicker, "Growing Pains: Despite Its Oil Money, Iran's Economy Suffers Many Shortages," *Wall Street Journal,* April 11, 1977.

372 *cost of $32 million:* Ibid.

372 *"Iran in the past three years":* "Growing Pains in Iran," *The Times* (London), January 5, 1977.

372 *$22 billion to $19.5 billion:* Ray Vicker, "Growing Pains: Despite Its Oil Money, Iran's Economy Suffers from Many Shortages," *Wall Street Journal,* April 11, 1977.

372 *"And even though this year's":* Ibid.

372 *"The drop in oil exports":* Graham, 100.

373 *"Fearing a foreseeable deterioration":* Farah Pahlavi, *An Enduring Love: My Life with the Shah* (New York: Miramax, 2004), 264.

373 *used the word "cancer":* William Shawcross, *The Shah's Last Ride: The Fate of an Ally* (New York: Simon & Schuster, 1988), 237.

373 *"When the French president":* Farah Pahlavi, *An Enduring Love,* 266–67.

374 *"I am only asking you to help me":* Gholam Reza Afkhami, *The Life and Times of the Shah* (Berkeley: University of California Press, 2009), 549.

374 *When Vance learned of Zahedi's presence:* The encounter between Cyrus Vance and Ardeshir Zahedi at Jay Rockefeller's inaugural on January 17, 1977, was described to me by Zahedi in an interview conducted on September 15, 2010. For an account of the festivities in Charleston, see James Branscome, "Rockefellers: Political Outs, Ins," *Washington Post,* January 18, 1977.

374 *"Everything they asked, I answered":* Ibid. Author interview with Ardeshir Zahedi, September 14–15, 2010.

375 *three hundred to four hundred political prisoners:* Jay Ross, "Iran Puts Brakes on Development," *Los Angeles Times,* August 21, 1977.

375 *Iranians were encouraged to bring any complaints:* Marvine Howe, "Iranians Use Party to Voice Grievances," *New York Times,* July 10, 1977.

375 *"demand more schools":* Ibid.

376 *"If you Americans are going to be so moral":* "What Price Morality?," *Newsweek,* March 14, 1977.

376 *"The problem we're faced with":* Seymour Hersh, "Proposed Sales of Fighters to Iran Challenged Within Administration," *New York Times,* October 9, 1977.

376 *"It was quite apparent in Washington":* Gary Sick, *All Fall Down: America's Tragic Encounter with Iran* (New York: Random House, 1985), 22.

377 *"considerable experience in dealing with authoritarian governments:* William H. Sullivan, *Mission to Iran: The Last U.S. Ambassador* (New York: W. W. Norton, 1981), 16.

377 *"innocent of any detailed knowledge of Iran":* Ibid.

377 *"considered secondary qualifications":* Ibid.

377 *"didn't want to be there":* FISOHA interview with William Lehfeldt, by William Burr, Foundation for Iranian Studies, Washington, D.C., April 29, 1987, February 9 and April 19, 1988, 3–149.

377 *spoke no Farsi:* Ibid.

377 *"The Embassy's disarray":* Ibid., 3–153.

377 *Vance received a briefing paper:* Briefing Memorandum, April 30, 1977, "Your Meeting with the Shah, May 13, 1977," Secret, Eric Hooglund, project editor, *Iran: The Making of U.S. Policy, 1977–80,* National Security Archive (Alexandria, VA: Chadwyck-Healey, 1990), Briefing Book State, May 13, 1977, IRO1164.

379 *"No such linkage":* Joe Alex Morris Jr., "No Rights Link to Iran Arms Sale— Vance," *Los Angeles Times,* May 14, 1977.

379 *"Each country's growth":* Charles Mohr, "Vance, in Iran, Asserts Stability Depends on Rights," *New York Times,* May 15, 1977.

379 *a pitched two-hour battle:* Joe Alex Morris Jr., "Police Kill 2 Terrorists in Downtown Tehran," *Los Angeles Times,* May 13, 1977.

380 *"unnecessary civilian deaths":* Conversation with the First Secretary of the Israeli Mission, March 6, 1977, Eric Hooglund, project editor, *Iran: The Making of U.S. Policy, 1977–80,* National Security Archive (Alexandria, VA: Chadwyck-Healey, 1990), Document Reference No. IR01154.

380 *"Islamic Marxists":* Joe Alex Morris Jr., "Police Kill 2 Terrorists in Downtown Tehran," *Los Angeles Times,* May 13, 1977.

380 *"fanatical right-wing Moslems":* Conversation with the First Secretary of the Israeli Mission, May 23, 1972, Secret, Memorandum Tehran, Eric Hooglund, project editor, *Iran: The Making of U.S. Policy, 1977–80,* National Security Archive (Alexandria, VA: Chadwyck-Healey, 1990), Document Reference No. IR01176, 2. The account in the *Los Angeles Times* described the location of the attack as being near "a Jewish agency," which was assumed to be the Israeli trade mission in Iran.

380 *trying to clear terrorists from two safe houses:* Ibid.

380 *On Sunday, May 29:* Alam, 543.

380 *37 percent:* Marvine Howe, "Iranian Women Return to Veil in a Resurgence of Spirituality," *New York Times,* July 30, 1977.

380 *half of all applicants to medical schools:* Ibid.

380 *female members of parliament:* Ibid.

380 *elected to local councils:* Ibid.

380 *could obtain an abortion:* Ibid.

380 *"spiritual revival":* Ibid.

380 *ingratiate herself:* Alam, 550.

380 *"I had just left Aspen":* Afkhami, 449.

381 *"Down with the Shah!"* Judith Cummings, "Lunch for Empress Interrupted by Shout of 'Down with Shah,' " *New York Times,* July 8, 1977.

381 *"No More Arms for the Fascist Shah"*: Chris Woodyard and Richard C. Paddock, "Shah of Iran's Wife Honored; Protest Staged," *Los Angeles Times*, July 6, 1977.

381 *"U.S. Advisers Out of Iran"*: Ibid.

381 *"That's a lie!"*: Judith Cummings, "Lunch for Empress Interrupted by Shout of 'Down with Shah,' " *New York Times*, July 8, 1977.

381 *"And so I asked the name"*: Farah Pahlavi, *An Enduring Love*, 271.

381 *"It struck me as unusual"*: Afkhami, 449.

381 *Zahedi spent 1977 outside Iran*: Author interview with Ardeshir Zahedi, September 14–15, 2010. This paragraph is based on my interview with him.

382 *"You know, I have heard the Shah"*: Ibid.

382 *"That moment I was shaking"*: Ibid.

382 *slumped 50 percent*: Joe Alex Morris Jr., "Is It for Real? New Broom Stirs Lots of Dust in Iran," *Los Angeles Times*, October 7, 1977.

382 *30 and 40 percent*: Ibid.

382 *Oil production fell*: "Daily Iranian Crude Production and Exports Fell from June to July," *New York Times*, August 10, 1977.

382 *exported only 4,180,896 barrels*: Ibid.

382 *11 million barrels*: James Tanner, "OPEC's Plight: Cartel's Main Task Is to Prevent Price Drop; Saudi Output Is Key," *Wall Street Journal*, December 15, 1977.

382 *"extraordinary pressure"*: J. P. Smith, "Saudis Failing to Meet Oil Production Promise," *Washington Post*, June 27, 1977.

382 *"no longer take us for granted"*: James Tanner, "OPEC's Plight: Cartel's Main Task Is to Prevent Price Drop; Saudi Output Is Key," *Wall Street Journal*, December 15, 1977.

382 *OPEC released a statement in Vienna*: Steven Rattner, "9 in OPEC Drop Planned 5% Rise for Price of Oil," *New York Times*, June 30, 1977.

383 *$2 billion*: Ibid.

383 *"We will not cut the flow of oil"*: Ibid.

383 *thirteen of Saudi Aramco's thirty-five oil fields*: "Opec's Real Problems," *The Economist*, July 9, 1977.

383 *"So there is a lot of room for expansion"*: Ibid.

383 *"sloppy"*: "Glut Leads to Cuts in Opec Prices," *The Times* (London), July 25, 1977.

383 *"awash with oil"*: "The Oil Glut Shows OPEC's Production," *BusinessWeek*, August 22, 1977, 23.

383 *"at less than cost"*: "Glut Leads to Cuts in Opec Prices," *The Times* (London), July 25, 1977.

383 *20 cents per barrel*: Ibid.

383 *"At present time"*: James Tanner, "OPEC's Plight: Cartel's Main Task Is to Prevent Price Drop; Saudi Output Is Key," *Wall Street Journal*, December 15, 1977.

383   *8.3 million barrels:* Ibid.

383   *"the Persian Gulf kingdom":* Ibid.

383   *"a clear-cut Saudi victory":* "The Saudis Still Reign over OPEC," *BusinessWeek,* July 18, 1977, 19.

383   *"once again hovering":* Ibid.

384   *"If the West weaned itself":* Ibid.

384   *"These blackouts have caused":* Marvine Howe, "Iran Fights Power Shortage, Threat to Development," *New York Times,* July 11, 1977.

384   *"the blackouts have proved":* Radji, 93.

384   *water and power supplies:* Alam, 545.

384   *"like a scene from some incredible farce":* Ibid., 546.

384   *urged shopkeepers:* Marvine Howe, "Iran Fights Power Shortage, Threat to Development," *New York Times,* July 11, 1977.

384   *"cuts sometimes last 8 to 10 hours a day":* Ibid.

384   *"There was more under- and unemployment":* FISOHA interview with William Lehfeldt, by William Burr, Foundation for Iranian Studies, Washington, D.C., April 29, 1987, February 9 and April 19, 1988, 3–154.

385   *"I couldn't believe my eyes!":* Habib Ladjevardi, editor, Memoirs of Fatemeh Pakravan: Wife of General Hassan Pakravan: Army Officer, Chief of the State Intelligence and Security Organization, Cabinet Minister, and Diplomat, Harvard Iranian Oral History Project VI, Iranian Oral History Project (Cambridge: Center for Middle Eastern Studies, Harvard University, 1998), 120–22.

385   *"terribly worried":* Ibid.

385   *"If you're not going to do something":* Ibid.

385   *"Whenever I see the Shah":* Ibid.

386   *"saw the writing on the wall":* FISOHA interview with William Lehfeldt, by William Burr, Foundation for Iranian Studies, Washington, D.C., April 29, 1987, February 9 and April 19, 1988, 3–167.

386   *"everything was going to fall apart":* Ibid.

386   *"there are things that are happening":* Ibid., 3–168.

386   *fired 1,700 people from the Finance Ministry:* Joe Alex Morris Jr., "Is It for Real?: New Broom Stirs Lots of Dust in Iran," *Los Angeles Times,* October 7, 1977.

386   *"The PBO had become a super-ministry":* Ibid.

387   *a sniper's bullet to the heart:* Bill Billeter, "Joe Alex Morris Jr., *Times* Writer, Shot Dead in Iran," *Los Angeles Times,* February 10, 1979.

387   *"In the past few months":* Alam, 556.

387   *"He suggested that if the crisis":* Abbas Milani, *Eminent Persians: The Men and Women Who Made Modern Iran, 1941–1979,* Vol. 1 (Syracuse: Syracuse University Press, 2008), 44–45.

387   *deposited for safekeeping in Switzerland:* Alam, vii.

387   *"until such time":* Ibid.

EPILOGUE: THE LAST HURRAH

PAGE

388 *"We never took him seriously"*: Author interview, June 2009.

388 *Ambassador Zahedi recalled that he expressed doubts:* Author interview with Ardeshir Zahedi, September 14–15, 2010.

388 *More than one thousand Iranian expatriates:* Paul W. Valentine, "Shah of Iran's Friends, Foes Mobilize for His Visit," *Washington Post*, November 13, 1977.

388 *SAVAK picked up the tab:* Author interview with Ardeshir Zahedi, September 14–15, 2010. Also see Jim Hoagland, "Iran Embassy Role in '77 Marches Probed," *Washington Post*, February 9, 1979.

388 *$150 per person:* Paul W. Valentine, "Shah of Iran's Friends, Foes Mobilize for His Visit," *Washington Post*, November 13, 1977.

388 *422 of 464 Iranian officers:* Ibid.

388 *"some of the most intense preparations":* Ibid.

388 *warned the police:* Paul W. Valentine, "FBI Warned Park Police About Iranian Violence," *Washington Post*, November 29, 1977.

389 *manufacture Molotov cocktails:* Ibid.

389 *"We updated [police agencies]":* Ibid.

389 *denied that the information they received:* Ibid.

389 *President Johnson's welcoming ceremony:* "LBJ Calls Iran's Progress a Lesson 'Others Have to Learn,' " *Washington Post*, August 23, 1967.

389 *151 police officers:* Paul W. Valentine, "2 Iran Factions Clash; 24 Hurt at White House," *Washington Post*, November 16, 1977.

389 *two dozen on horseback:* Ibid.

389 *Riot police:* Ibid.

389 *"Although I appreciated the role":* William H. Sullivan, *Mission to Iran: The Last U.S. Ambassador* (New York: W. W. Norton, 1981), 126.

389 *"were separated only by light":* Ibid., 127.

389 *"a sudden surge of activity":* Ibid.

390 *Others raided the building site:* Linda Charlton, "Clashes and Tear Gas Mar Shah's Welcome in Capital," *New York Times*, November 16, 1977.

390 *"Children and elderly persons":* Paul W. Valentine, "2 Iran Factions Clash; 124 Hurt at White House," *Washington Post*, November 16, 1977.

390 *"It's terrible, terrible":* New York Times, November 16, 1977.

390 *A pickup truck was driven through police lines:* Washington Post, November 16, 1977.

390 *Office workers:* Ibid.

390 *120 injured people:* Ibid.

390 *"to keep them from fighting each other":* Ibid.

390 *armed snipers with binoculars:* Ibid.

390 *"We then went into the reception room":* Farah Pahlavi, *An Enduring Love: My Life with the Shah* (New York: Miramax, 2004), 270.

390   *two thousand student protesters:* William Brannigan, "Iranian Riot Police Clash with Students," *Washington Post*, November 17, 1977.

390   *ten thousand protesters:* Ibid.

391   *a $2 million grant to Columbus State University:* www.columbusstate.edu.

391   *"In his long, subsequent career at the Pentagon":* Ibid.

392   *He is today widely regarded:* See Simon's obituary in *The New York Times:* Richard W. Stevenson, "William E. Simon, Ex-Treasury Secretary and High Profile Investor, Is Dead at 72," *New York Times*, June 5, 2000.

392   *Nicaraguan Freedom Fund:* Thomas B. Edsall, "The Tower Commission Report; The Private War; Documents Seem to Link Lobbyists, Arms Supplies," *Washington Post*, February 27, 1987.

393   *"This is disingenuous":* Henry A. Kissinger, *Years of Upheaval* (Boston: Little, Brown, 1982), 669.

393   *"In any event, only one ignorant":* Ibid., 670.

393   *"Is it necessary that the United States win every battle":* James A. Bill, *The Eagle and the Lion: The Tragedy of American-Iranian Relations* (New Haven: Yale University Press, 1988), 356.

393   *"We never took him seriously":* The comment was recalled in an off-the-record portion of an interview the author conducted in June 2009.

BIBLIOGRAPHY

BOOKS

Aarts, Paul, and Gerd Nonneman, eds. *Saudi Arabia in the Balance: Political Economy, Society, Foreign Affairs.* London: Hurst, 2005.

Abasalti, Pari. *Ardeshir Zahedi: Untold Secrets.* Los Angeles: Rah-e-Zendegi, 2002.

Abir, Mordechai. *Saudi Arabia in the Oil Era: Regime and Elites, Conflict and Collaboration.* Boulder: Westview, 1988.

Abrahamian, Ervand. *A History of Modern Iran.* Cambridge: Cambridge University Press, 2008.

Afkhami, Gholam Reza. *The Life and Times of the Shah.* Berkeley: University of California Press, 2009.

Alam, Asadollah. *The Shah and I: The Confidential Diary of Iran's Royal Court, 1969–1977.* New York: St. Martin's, 1991.

Ambrose, Stephen E. *Eisenhower: Soldier and President.* New York: Simon & Schuster, 1990.

Amuzegar, Jahangir. *The Dynamics of the Iranian Revolution: The Pahlavis' Triumph and Tragedy.* Albany: State University of New York Press, 1991.

———. *Iran: An Economic Profile.* Washington, D.C.: The Middle East Institute, 1977.

———. *Managing the Oil Wealth: OPEC's Windfalls and Pitfalls.* London: I. B. Tauris, 2001.

Ansari, Ali M. *Modern Iran Since 1921: The Pahlavis and After.* London: Longman, 2003.

Arjomand, Said Amir. *The Turban for the Crown: The Islamic Revolution in Iran.* New York: Oxford University Press, 1986.

Avery, Peter, Gavin Hambly, and Charles Melville, eds. *The Cambridge History of Iran* (Seven Volumes). Cambridge: Cambridge University Press, 1991.

Axworthy, Michael. *Empire of the Mind: A History of Iran.* New York: Basic Books, 2008.

Bayandor, Darioush. *Iran and the CIA: The Fall of Mossadeq Revisited.* London: Palgrave Macmillan, 2010.

Bill, James A. *The Eagle and the Lion: The Tragedy of American-Iranian Relations.* New Haven: Yale University Press, 1988.

———. *George Ball: Behind the Scenes in U.S. Foreign Policy.* New Haven: Yale University Press, 1997.

Blanch, Lesley. *Farah: Shahbanou of Iran.* Tehran: Tajerzadeh, 1978.

Bronson, Rachel. *Thicker than Oil: America's Uneasy Partnership with Saudi Arabia.* Oxford: Oxford University Press, 2006.

Brzezinski, Zbigniew. *Power and Principle: Memoirs of the National Security Adviser, 1977–1981.* New York: Farrar, Straus & Giroux, 1983.

Bundy, William. *A Tangled Web: The Making of Foreign Policy in the Nixon Presidency.* London: I. B. Taurus, 1998.

Cannon, James. *Time and Chance: Gerald Ford's Appointment with History.* Ann Arbor: University of Michigan Press, 1994.

Carter, Jimmy. *Keeping Faith: Memoirs of a President.* New York: Bantam, 1982.

Catto Jr., Henry E. *Ambassadors at Sea: The High and Low Adventures of a Diplomat.* Austin: University of Texas Press, 1998.

Chubin, Shahram, and Sepehr Zabih. *The Foreign Relations of Iran: A Developing State in a Zone of Great-Power Conflict.* Berkeley: University of California Press, 1974.

Daalder, Ivo H., and I. M. Destler. *In the Shadow of the Oval Office: Profiles of the National Security Advisers and the Presidents They Served—From JFK to George W. Bush.* New York: Simon & Schuster, 2009.

Dallek, Robert. *Nixon and Kissinger: Partners in Power.* New York: HarperCollins, 2007.

Farmanfarmaian, Manucher, and Roxane Farmanfarmaian. *Blood and Oil: A Prince's Memoir of Iran, from the Shah to the Ayatollah.* New York: Random House, 2005.

Feldstein, Mark. *Poisoning the Press: Richard Nixon, and the Rise of Washington's Scandal Culture.* New York: Farrar, Straus & Giroux, 2010.

Ferdowsi, Abolqasem. Translated by Dick Davis. *Shahnameh: The Persian Book of Kings.* New York: Penguin, 2007.

Figes, Orlando. *A People's Tragedy: The Russian Revolution, 1891–1924.* London: Penguin, 1996.

Ford, Betty, with Chris Chase. *The Times of My Life.* New York: Harper & Row, 1978.

Ford, Gerald. *A Time to Heal: The Autobiography of Gerald R. Ford.* New York: Harper & Row, 1979.

Gaddis, John Lewis. *The Cold War.* London: Penguin, 2005.

Garza, Hedda. *The Watergate Investigation Index: Senate Select Committee Hearings and Reports on Presidential Campaign Activities.* Wilmington: Scholarly Resources, 1982.

Gasiorowski, Mark J., and Malcolm Byrne. *Mohammad Mossadeq and the 1953 Coup in Iran.* Syracuse: Syracuse University Press, 2004.

Graham, Robert. *Iran: The Illusion of Power.* rev. ed. London: Croom Helm, 1979.

Greene, John Robert. *Betty Ford: Candor and Courage in the White House.* Lawrence: University Press of Kansas, 2004.

Greenspan, Alan. *The Age of Turbulence.* New York: Penguin, 2008.

Greider, William. *Secrets of the Temple: How the Federal Reserve Runs the Country.* New York: Simon & Schuster, 1987.

Hartmann, Robert T. *Palace Politics: An Inside Account of the Ford Years.* New York: McGraw-Hill, 1980.

Heikal, Mohamed. *The Return of the Ayatollah.* London: André Deutsch, 1981.

Helms, Cynthia. *An Ambassador's Wife in Iran.* New York: Dodd, Mead, 1981.

Helms, Richard, with William Hood. *A Look over My Shoulder: A Life in the Central Intelligence Agency.* New York: Ballantine, 2003.

Hertog, Steffen. *Princes, Brokers and Bureaucrats: Oil and the State in Saudi Arabia.* Ithaca and London: Cornell University Press, 2010.

Holden, John, and Richard Johns. *The House of Saud: The Rise and Rule of the Most Powerful Dynasty in the Arab World.* New York: Holt, Rinehart & Winston, 1981.

Horne, Alistair. *Kissinger: 1973, the Crucial Year.* New York: Simon & Schuster, 2009.

House Select Committee on Intelligence. *CIA: The Pike Report.* London: Spokesman, 1977.

Hoveyda, Fereydoun. *The Fall of the Shah.* New York: Wyndham, 1979.

Huntington, Samuel P. *Political Order in Changing Societies.* New Haven: Yale University Press, 1968.

Isaacson, Walter. *Kissinger: A Biography.* New York: Simon & Schuster, 2005.

Jacqz, Jane W. *Iran: Past, Present and Future.* New York: Aspen Institute for Humanistic Studies, 1976.

Jones, Toby Craig. *Desert Kingdom: How Oil and Water Forged Modern Saudi Arabia.* Cambridge, Mass.: Harvard University Press, 2010.

Kapuscinski, Ryszard. *Shah of Shahs.* New York: Penguin, 1985.

Karl, Terry Lynn. *The Paradox of Plenty: Oil Booms and Petro-States.* Berkeley: University of California Press, 1997.

Karnow, Stanley. *Vietnam: A History.* New York: Penguin, 1984.

Keddie, Nikki. *Iran: Religion, Politics and Society.* London: Frank Cass, 1980.

———. *Modern Iran: Roots and Results of Revolution.* New Haven: Yale University Press, 2003.

———. *Roots of Revolution: An Interpretive History of Modern Iran.* New Haven: Yale University Press, 1981.

Keshavarzian, Arang. *Bazaar and State in Iran: The Politics of the Tehran Marketplace.* Cambridge: Cambridge University Press, 2007.

Kessler, Ronald. *In the President's Secret Service: Behind the Scenes with the Agents in the Line of Fire and the Presidents They Protect.* New York: Crown, 2009.

Kinzer, Stephen. *All the Shah's Men: An American Coup and the Roots of Middle East Terror.* Hoboken: John Wiley & Sons, 2003.

Kissinger, Henry A. *Diplomacy.* New York: Simon & Schuster, 1994.

———. *White House Years.* Boston: Little, Brown, 1979.

———. *Years of Renewal.* New York: Touchstone, 2000.

———. *Years of Upheaval.* Boston: Little, Brown, 1982.

Klare, Michael T. *Blood and Oil: The Dangers and Consequences of America's Growing Dependency on Imported Petroleum.* New York: Henry Holt, 2004.

———. *Resource Wars: A New Landscape of Global Conflict.* New York: Henry Holt, 2001.

Kurzman, Charles. *The Unthinkable Revolution in Iran.* Cambridge: Harvard University Press, 2005.

Kutler, Stanley I. *Abuse of Power: The New Nixon Tapes.* New York: Free Press, 1997.

———. *The Wars of Watergate: The Last Crisis of Richard Nixon.* New York: W. W. Norton, 1992.

Lacey, Robert. *Inside the Kingdom: Kings, Clerics, Modernists, Terrorists and the Struggle for Saudi Arabia.* New York: Penguin, 2009.

Lackner, Helen. *A House Built on Sand: A Political Economy of Saudi Arabia.* London: Ithaca Press, 1978.

Ladjevardi, Habib, ed. *Memoirs of Fatemeh Pakravan.* Iranian Oral History Project. Cambridge, Mass.: Center for Middle Eastern Studies, Harvard University, 1998.

LaFeber, Walter. *America, Russia and the Cold War, 1945–80.* Hoboken: John Wiley & Sons, 1980.

Laing, Margaret. *The Shah.* London: Sidgwick & Jackson, 1977.

Lenczowski, George, ed. *Iran Under the Pahlavis.* Stanford: Hoover Institution Press, 1978.

Lukas, J. Anthony. *Nightmare: The Underside of the Nixon Years.* Athens: Ohio University Press, 1999.

Luttwak, Edward N. *Strategy: The Logic of War and Peace.* Cambridge: The Belknap Press of Harvard University Press, 2003.

Mackey, Sandra. *The Iranians: Persia, Islam and the Soul of a Nation.* New York: Penguin, 1998.

Mann, James. *Rise of the Vulcans: The History of Bush's War Cabinet.* New York: Penguin, 2004.

May, Ernest R. *Lessons of the Past: The Use and Misuse of History in American Foreign Policy.* London: Oxford University Press, 1973.

Meyer, Karl E. and Shareen Blair Brysac. *Kingmakers: The Invention of the Modern Middle East.* New York: W. W. Norton, 2008.

Mieczkowski, Yanek. *Gerald Ford and the Challenges of the '70s.* Lexington: University Press of Kentucky, 2005.

Milani, Abbas. *Eminent Persians: The Men and Women Who Made Modern Iran, 1941–1979.* 2 vols. Syracuse: Syracuse University Press, 2008.

———. *The Persian Sphinx: Amir Abbas Hoveyda and the Riddle of the Iranian Revolution*. Washington, D.C.: Mage, 2004.

———. *The Shah*. New York: Palgrave Macmillan, 2011.

Milani, Mohsen M. *The Making of Iran's Islamic Revolution: From Monarchy to Republic*. Boulder: Westview, 1994.

Moin, Baqer. *Khomeini: Life of the Ayatollah*. London: I. B. Tauris, 1999.

Neustadt, Richard E., and Ernest R. May. *Thinking in Time: The Uses of History for Decision Makers*. New York: Free Press, 1986.

Nixon, Richard. *RN: The Memoirs of Richard Nixon*. New York: Grosset & Dunlap, 1978.

Noreng, Oystein. *Crude Power: Politics and the Oil Market*. London: I. B. Tauris, 2006.

Olmstead, Michael B. *History of the Persian Empire*. London: University of Chicago Press, 1948.

Oren, Michael B. *Power, Faith and Fantasy: America in the Middle East, 1776 to the Present*. New York: W. W. Norton, 2007.

Pahlavi, Ashraf. *Faces in a Mirror*. Englewood Cliffs: Prentice Hall, 1980.

Pahlavi, Farah. *An Enduring Love: My Life with the Shah*. New York: Miramax, 2004.

———. Translated by Felice Harcourt. *My Thousand and One Days: The Autobiography of Farah, Shahbanou of Iran*. London: W. H. Allen, 1978.

Pahlavi, Mohammad Reza. *Answer to History*. New York: Stein & Day, 1980.

Parsa, Misagh. *Social Origins of the Iranian Revolution*. Piscataway: Rutgers University Press, 1989.

Parsons, Anthony. *The Pride and the Fall: Iran 1974–79*. London: Jonathan Cape, 1984.

Patterson, James T. *Restless Giant: The United States from Watergate to Bush v. Gore*. Oxford: Oxford University Press, 2005.

Pollack, Kenneth M. *The Persian Puzzle: The Conflict Between Iran and America*. New York: Random House, 2004.

Potter, Lawrence G., *The Persian Gulf in History*. New York: Palgrave Macmillan, 2009.

Powers, Thomas. *The Man Who Kept the Secrets: Richard Helms and the CIA*. New York: Alfred A. Knopf, 1979.

Prados, John. *Safe for Democracy: The Secret Wars of the CIA*. Chicago: Ivan R. Dee, 2006.

———. *William Colby and the CIA: The Secret Wars of a Controversial Spymaster*. Lawrence: University Press of Kansas, 2009.

Radji, Parviz C. *In the Service of the Peacock Throne: The Diaries of the Shah's Last Ambassador to London*. London: Hamish Hamilton, 1983.

Rahema, Ali. *An Islamic Utopian: A Political Biography of Ali Shari'ati*. London: I. B. Tauris, 1998.

Ramazani, Rouhollah K. *Iran's Foreign Policy, 1941–73*. Charlottesville: University Press of Virginia, 1975.

Razavi, Hossein, and Firouz Vakil. *The Political Environment of Economic Planning in Iran, 1971–1983: From Monarchy to Islamic Republic*. Boulder: Westview, 1984.

Reich, Cary. *Rockefeller: The Life of Nelson Rockefeller, Worlds to Conquer, 1908–1958*. New York: Doubleday, 1996.

Robinson, Jeffrey. *Yamani: The Inside Story*. London: Simon & Schuster, 1988.

Rockefeller, David. *Memoirs*. New York: Random House, 2002.

Rosen, James. *The Strong Man: John Mitchell and the Secrets of Watergate*. New York: Doubleday, 2008.

Rothkopf, David J. *Running the World: The Inside Story of the National Security Council and the Architects of American Power*. New York: PublicAffairs, 2006.

Rubin, Barry. *Paved with Good Intentions: The American Experience and Iran*. New York: Oxford University Press, 1980.

Sadat, Jehan. *A Woman of Egypt*. New York: Simon & Schuster, 1987.

Saikal, Amin. *The Rise and Fall of the Shah: Iran from Autocracy to Religious Rule*. Princeton: Princeton University Press, 1980.

Schmitz, David F. *The United States and Right-Wing Dictatorships*. New York: Cambridge University Press, 2006.

Sciolino, Elaine. *Persian Mirrors: The Elusive Face of Iran*. New York: Free Press, 2000.

Shawcross, William. *The Shah's Last Ride: The Fate of an Ally*. New York: Simon & Schuster, 1988.

Shlaim, Avi. *Lion of Jordan: The Life of King Hussein in War and Peace*. London: Allen Lane, 2007.

Sick, Gary. *All Fall Down: America's Tragic Encounter with Iran*. New York: Random House, 1985.

Shalom, Stephen Roskamm. *Imperial Alibis: Rationalizing U.S. Intervention After the Cold War*. Boston: South End, 1993.

———. *October Surprise: America's Hostages in Iran and the Election of Ronald Reagan*. New York: Random House, 1992.

Simmons, Matthew R. *Twilight in the Desert: The Coming Saudi Oil Shock and the World Economy*. Hoboken: John Wiley & Sons, 2005.

Simon, William E., with John M. Caher. *A Time for Reflection: An Autobiography*. Washington, D.C.: Regnery, 2004.

Smith, Luise J., and David H. Herschuler, eds. and David S. Patterson, general ed. *Foreign Relations of the United States, 1969–1976*, Vol. I, *Foundations of Foreign Policy, 1969–1972*. Washington, D.C.: U.S. Government Printing Office, 2003.

Sullivan, William H. *Mission to Iran: The Last U.S. Ambassador*. New York: W. W. Norton, 1981.

Summers, Anthony. *The Arrogance of Power: The Secret World of Richard Nixon*. New York: Penguin, 2000.

Suri, Jeremi. *Henry Kissinger and the American Century.* Cambridge: The Belknap Press of Harvard University Press, 2007.

Tocqueville, Alexis de. *The Ancien Régime and the Revolution.* London: Penguin, 2008.

Tuchman, Barbara W. *The March of Folly: From Troy to Vietnam.* New York: Alfred A. Knopf, 1984.

Tyler, Patrick. *A World of Trouble: The White House and the Middle East—From the Cold War to the War on Terror.* New York: Farrar, Straus & Giroux, 2009.

Van Atta, Dale. *Melvin Laird in War, Peace, and Politics.* Madison: University of Wisconsin Press, 2008.

Ward, Steven R. *Immortal: A Military History of Iran and Its Armed Forces.* Washington, D.C.: Georgetown University Press, 2009.

Weiner, Tim. *Legacy of Ashes: The History of the CIA.* New York: Doubleday, 2007.

Werth, Barry. *31 Days: Gerald Ford, the Nixon Pardon, and a Government in Crisis.* New York: Random House, 2006.

Weston, Mark. *Prophets and Princes: Saudi Arabia from Muhammad to the Present.* Hoboken: John Wiley & Sons, 2008.

Woodward, Bob. *Maestro: Greenspan's Fed and the American Boom.* New York: Simon & Schuster, 2000.

———. *Shadow: Five Presidents and the Legacy of Watergate.* New York: Simon & Schuster, 1999.

Wright, Lawrence. *The Looming Tower: Al-Qaeda and the Road to 9/11.* New York: Alfred A. Knopf, 2007.

Yergin, Daniel. *The Prize: The Epic Quest for Oil, Money, and Power.* New York: Simon & Schuster, 1991.

Zahedi, Ardeshir. *The Memoirs of Ardeshir Zahedi.* Vol. 1: *From Childhood to the End of My Father's Premiership.* Bethesda, Md.: Ibex, 2006.

———. *The Memoirs of Ardeshir Zahedi:* Vol. 2 (1954–65): *Love and Marriage, Ambassador to Washington and London.* Bethesda, Md.: Ibex, 2010.

Zonis, Marvin. *Majestic Failure: The Fall of the Shah.* Chicago: University of Chicago Press: London, 1991.

———. *The Political Elite of Iran.* Princeton: Princeton University Press, 1971.

ARTICLES

Abrahamian, Ervand. "The Guerrilla Movement in Iran, 1963–77." *MERIP Reports,* No. 86, (March-April 1980).

———. "Iran in Revolution: The Opposition Forces." *MERIP Reports,* No. 75/76 (March-April 1979).

———. "Iran: The Political Challenge." *MERIP Reports,* No. 69 (July-August 1978).

———. "Iran: The Political Crisis Intensifies." *MERIP Reports,* No. 71 (October 1978).

———. "The 1953 Coup in Iran." *Science and Society* 65, no. 2 (Summer 2001).

Adelman, M. A. "Oil Fallacies." *Foreign Policy* 82 (Spring 1991).

―――. "Papers and Proceedings of the Eighty-sixth Annual Meeting of the American Economic Association." *The American Economic Review* 64, no. 2 (May 1974).

Akins, James E. "The Oil Crisis: This Time the Wolf Is Here." *Foreign Affairs* 51, no. 3 (April 1973).

Alvandi, Roham. "Muhammad Reza Pahlavi and the Bahrain Question, 1968–1970." *British Journal of Middle East Studies* 37, no. 2 (August 2010).

Amini, Parvin Merat. "A Single Party State in Iran, 1975–78: The Rastakhiz Party: The Final Attempt by the Shah to Consolidate His Political Base." *Middle Eastern Studies* 38, no. 1 (January 2002).

Ansari, Ali M. "The Myth of the White Revolution: Mohammad Reza Shah, 'Modernization,' and the Consolidation of Power." *Middle Eastern Studies* 37, no. 3 (July 2001).

Ashraf, Ahmad. "From the White Revolution to the Islamic Revolution," in *Iran After the Revolution: Crisis of an Islamic State*, S. Rahnema and S. Behdad, eds. London: I. B. Tauris, 1995.

―――. "Pahlavi—Mohammad Reza." In *Encyclopedia of the Modern Middle East* (New York: Macmillan, 2006).

Ashraf, Ahmad, and Ali Banuazizi. "The State, Classes and Modes of Mobilization in the Iranian Revolution," *State, Culture and Society* 1, no. 3, Spring 1985.

Brun, Thierry, and Dumont, Rene. "Iran: Imperial Pretensions and Agricultural Dependence." *MERIP Reports*, No. 71 (October 1978).

Caldwell, Dan. "The Legitimation of the Nixon-Kissinger Grand Design and Grand Strategy." *Diplomatic History* 33, no. 4 (September 2009).

Campbell, John C. "Oil Power in the Middle East." *Foreign Affairs* (October 1977).

Chubin, Shahram. "Iran's Strategic Predicament." *The Middle East Journal* 54, no. 1 (Winter 2000).

Cooper, Andrew Scott. "Showdown at Doha: The Secret Oil Deal That Helped Sink the Shah of Iran." *The Middle East Journal* 62, no. 4 (Autumn 2008).

Cottam, Richard W. "American Policy and the Iranian Crisis." *Iranian Studies* 13, no. 1/4 (1980).

―――. "The United States, Iran and the Cold War." *Iranian Studies* 3, no. 1 (Winter 1970).

Deese, David A. "Energy: Economics, Politics and Security." *International Security* 4, no. 3 (Winter 1979–80).

Dempster, Gregory M. "The Fiscal Background to the Russian Revolution." *European Review of Economic History* 10 (2006).

Dickey, Christopher. "The Oil Shield." *Foreign Policy* 85, no. 3 (May to June 2006).

Faghfoory, Mohammad H. "The Dynamics of the Iranian Revolution: The Pahlavis' Triumph and Tragedy." *The Middle East Journal* 47, no. 1 (Winter 1993).

―――. "Iran—Iranian Politics and Religious Modernism: The Liberation Movement of Iran Under the Shah and Khomeini." *The Middle East Journal* 45, no. 3 (Summer 1991).

Fatemi, Khosrow. "Leadership by Distrust: The Shah's Modus Operandi." *Middle East Journal* 36, no. 1 (Winter 1982).

Friedman, Thomas. "The First Law of Petropolis." *Foreign Policy* 154 (May-June 2006): 28–39.

Frings-Hessami, Khadiji. "Resistance to the Shah: Landowners and Ulama in Iran." *Middle Eastern Studies* 37, no. 3 (July 2001).

Furtig, Henner. "Conflict and Cooperation in the Persian Gulf: The Interregional Order and US Policy," *The Middle East Journal* 61, no. 4 (Autumn 2007).

Galvani, John, et al. "Saudi Arabia: Bulliah on America." *MERIP Reports*, No. 26 (March 1974).

Gately, Dermot. "A Ten-Year Retrospective: OPEC and the World Oil Market." *Journal of Economic Literature* 22, no. 3 (September 1984).

Goode, James. "Reforming Iran During the Kennedy Years." *Diplomatic History* 15, no. 1 (June 2007).

Halliday, Fred. "Iran: Trade Unions and the Working Class Opposition." *MERIP Reports*, No. 71 (October 1978).

Hayes, Stephen D. "Joint Economic Commissions as Instruments of U.S. Foreign Policy in the Middle East." *The Middle East Journal* 31, no. 1 (Winter 1977).

Healey, Denis. "Oil, Money and Recession." *Foreign Affairs* 58, no. 2 (Winter 1979).

Hoff, Joan. "A Revisionist View of Nixon's Foreign Policy." *Presidential Studies Quarterly* 26, no. 1 (Winter 1996).

Hoffman, Philip T., and Jean-Laurent Rosenthal. "New Work in French Economic History." *French Historical Studies* 23, no. 3 (Summer 2000).

Hudson, Michael C. "To Play the Hegemon: Fifty Years of U.S. Policy Toward the Middle East." *The Middle East Journal* 50, no. 3, Summer, 1996.

Issawi, Charles. "The 1973 Oil Crisis and After." *Journal of Post Keynesian Economics* 1, no. 2 (Winter 1978–79).

Joyner, Christopher C. "The Petrodollar Phenomenon and Changing International Economic Relations." *World Affairs* 138, no. 2 (Fall 1975).

Kazemi, Farhad. "Urban Migrants and the Revolution." *Iranian Studies* 13, no. 1/4, (1980).

Keddie, Nikki. "Iranian Revolutions in Comparative Perspective." *The American Historical Review* 88, no. 3 (June 1983).

———. "The Midas Touch: Black Gold, Economics and Politics in Iran Today." *Iranian Studies* 10, no. 4 (Autumn 1977).

Kibaroglu, Mustafa. "Good for the Shah, Banned for the Mullahs: The West and Iran's Quest for Nuclear Power." *The Middle East Journal* 60, no. 2 (Spring 2006).

Kimball, Jeffrey. "The Nixon Doctrine: A Saga of Misunderstanding." *Presidential Studies Quarterly* 36, no. 1 (March 2006).

Klare, Michael T. "Political Economy of U.S. Arms Sales." *Social Scientist* 4, no. 11 (June 1976).

Krasner, Stephen D. "The Great Oil Sheikdown." *Foreign Policy* 13 (Winter 1973–74).

Kurzman, Charles. "The Qum Protests and the Coming of the Iranian Revolution." *Social Science History* 27, no. 3 (Fall 2003).

Ladjevardi, Habib. "The Origins of U.S. Support for an Autocratic Iran." *International Journal of Middle East Studies* 15, no. 2 (May 1983).

Levy, Walter J. "Oil and the Decline of the West." *Foreign Affairs* (Summer 1980).

Licklider, Roy. "The Power of Oil: The Arab Oil Weapon and the Netherlands, the United Kingdom, Canada, Japan, and the United States." *International Studies Quarterly* 32, no. 2 (June 1988).

Little, Douglas. "Gideon's Band: America and the Middle East Since 1945." *Diplomatic History* 18, no. 4 (Fall 1994).

Litwak, Robert S. "Henry Kissinger's Ambiguous Legacy." *Diplomatic History* 18, no. 3 (Summer 1994).

Lytle, Mark. "Tragedy or Farce: America's Troubled Relations with Iran." *Diplomatic History* 13, no. 3 (July 1990).

Malnes, Raino. "OPEC and the Problem of Collective Action." *Journal of Peace Research* 20, no. 4 (December 1983).

McFarland, Stephen L. "A Peripheral View of the Origins of the Cold War: The Crises in Iran, 1941–47." *Diplomatic History* 4, no. 4 (October 1980).

Mejcher, Helmut. "King Faisal Ibn Abdul Aziz Al Saud in the Arena of World Politics: A Glimpse from Washington, 1950–1971." *British Journal of Middle Eastern Studies* 31, no. 1 (May 2004).

Moens, Alexander. "President Carter's Advisers and the Fall of the Shah." *Political Science Quarterly* 106, no. 2 (Summer 1991).

Moran, Theodore H. "Iranian Defense Expenditures and the Social Crisis." *International Security* 3, no. 3 (Winter 1978–79).

Nasr, Vali, and Ray Takeyh. "The Costs of Containing Iran; Washington's Misguided New Middle East Policy." *Foreign Affairs* 87, no. 1 (January-February 2008).

Nincic, Donna J. "From Sea-Lanes to Global Cities: The Policy Relevance of Political Geography." In *Being Useful: Policy Relevance and International Relations Theory*, ed. Miroslav Ninsic and Joseph Lepgold (Ann Arbor: University of Michigan Press, 2000).

Nordhaus, William D. "The 1974 Report of the President's Council of Economic Advisers: Energy in the Economic Report." *The American Economic Review* 64, no. 4 (September 1974).

Nye, Joseph S. "Energy Nightmares." *Foreign Policy* 40 (Autumn 1980).

Paine, Chris. "Iranian Nationalism and the Great Powers: 1872–1954." *MERIP Reports*, No. 37 (May 1975).

Penrose, Edith. "The Development of Crisis." *Daedalus* 104, no. 4 (Fall 1975).

Pollack, Gerald A. "The Economic Consequences of the Energy Crisis." *Foreign Affairs* (April 1974).

Quandt, William B. "Book Review—Majestic Failure: The Fall of the Shah by Marvin Zonis." *Political Science Quarterly* 107, no. 1 (Spring 1992).

Ravenal, Earl C. "The Nixon Doctrine and Our Asian Commitments." *Foreign Affairs* 49, 2 (January 1971).

Richards, Helmut. "America's Shah, Shahanshah's Iran." *MERIP Reports*, No. 40 (September 1975).

———. "Land Reform and Agribusiness in Iran." *MERIP Reports*, No. 43 (December 1975).

Ricks, Thomas. "U.S. Military Missions to Iran, 1943–78: The Political Economy of Military Assistance." *Iranian Studies* 12, no. 3/4 (Summer-Autumn, 1979).

Rostow, Dankwart A. "Who Won the Yom Kippur and Oil Wars?" *Foreign Policy* 17 (Winter 1974–75).

Samii, Abbas William. "The Shah's Lebanon Policy: The Role of SAVAK." *Middle Eastern Studies* 33, no. 1 (January 1997).

Sargent, Thomas J. "The Macroeconomic Causes and Consequences of the French Revolution." Federal Reserve Bank of Minneapolis (December 1991), www.minneapolisfed.org.

Scoville, James G. "The Labor Market in Prerevolutionary Iran." *Economic Development and Cultural Change* 34, no. 1 (October 1985).

Shihata, Ibrahim F. I. "Destination Embargo of Arab Oil: Its Legality Under International Law." *The American Journal of International Law* 68, no. 4 (October 1974).

Singer, S. Fred. "Limits to Arab Oil Power." *Foreign Policy* 30 (Spring 1978).

Smart, Ian. "Oil, the Super-Powers and the Middle East." *International Affairs* 53, no. 1 (January 1977).

Stathis, Stephen. "Nixon, Watergate and American Foreign Policy." *Presidential Studies Quarterly* 13, no. 1 (Winter 1983).

Stobaugh, Robert B. "The Oil Crisis: In Perspective." *Daedalus* 104, no. 4 (Fall 1975).

Stobaugh, Robert, and Daniel Yergin. "An Emergency Telescoped." *Foreign Affairs* 58, no. 3 (1979).

Stork, Joe. "Oil and the International Crisis." *MERIP Reports*, No. 32 (November 1974).

Summitt, April R. "For a White Revolution: John F. Kennedy and the Shah of Iran." *The Middle East Journal* 58, no. 4 (Autumn 2004).

White, Eugene Nelson. "The French Revolution and the Politics of Government Finance, 1770–1815." *The Journal of Economic History* 55, no. 2 (June 1995).

Zirinsky, Michael P. "Modern History and Politics—U.S. Foreign Policy and the Shah: Building a Client State in Iran." *The Middle East Journal* 46, no. 2 (Spring 1992).

INDEX